Y0-BSW-173

COMPUTERS
IN SOCIETY

$23.05   3/83

COMPUTERS IN SOCIETY

DONALD H. SANDERS

M. J. Neeley School of Business
Texas Christian University

Third Edition

**McGraw-Hill
Book Company**

New York
St. Louis
San Francisco
Auckland
Bogotá
Hamburg
Johannesburg
London
Madrid
Mexico
Montreal
New Delhi
Panama
Paris
São Paulo
Singapore
Sydney
Tokyo
Toronto

This book was set in Quadrata by Progressive Typographers.
The editors were Robert A. Fry, Charles E. Stewart, Edwin Hanson,
and Elysbeth H. Wyckoff; the designer was Joan E. O'Connor;
the production supervisor was Joe Campanella.
New drawings were done by J & R Services, Inc.
R. R. Donnelley & Sons Company was printer and binder.

The cover photograph which shows different body densities
was color-enhanced by computer techniques.
Photo by Dan McCoy/Black Star.

COMPUTERS IN SOCIETY

Copyright © 1981, 1977, 1973 by McGraw-Hill, Inc. All rights reserved.
Printed in the United States of America. No part of this publication
may be reproduced, stored in a retrieval system, or transmitted, in any
form or by any means, electronic, mechanical, photocopying, recording,
or otherwise, without the prior written permission of the publisher.

3 4 5 6 7 8 9 0   DODO   8 9 8 7 6 5 4 3 2

Library of Congress Cataloging in Publication Data

Sanders, Donald H
    Computers in society.

    Includes index.
    1. Computers and civilization.   2. Electronic
data processing. I. Title.
QA76.9.C66S26 1981   001.64   80-15356
ISBN 0-07-054672-X

ABOUT THE AUTHOR

Donald H. Sanders, Professor, M. J. Neeley School of Business, Texas Christian University, received his Ph.D. from the University of Arkansas. He has also taught at the University of Texas at Arlington and at Memphis State University.

Professor Sanders is the author of six books and has contributed articles to journals such as *Data Management, Automation, Banking, Journal of Small Business Management, Journal of Retailing,* and *Advanced Management Journal.* Professor Sanders is Chairperson of the "Computers and Data Processing" Subject Examination Committee, CLEP Program, College Entrance Examination Board, Princeton, N.J.

CONTENTS

ix
CONTENTS

PREFACE

Why is it that we are constantly being reminded of the presence of computers in our society? Why is it that an article is entitled "The Computer Revolution" (rather than "The Drill Press Revolution") and a television program is called "The Age of the Computer" (rather than "The Age of the Engine Lathe")? *One reason* that computers are at the center of public attention and occupy a position above the other important tools that humans use is that they seem to do so many things that people also do. They manipulate symbols that have meaning; they store information; they answer questions; they participate in the decision-making process; and they compute. In short, computers seem to possess an "intelligence" not found in other machines. A *second reason* why people are constantly being reminded of computers is that they now play such an important role in our society. There are possibly only a few hermits today who do not participate in one or more computer-using organizations in some capacity or who are not served or affected in their private lives by one of these organizations. For example, computers send us our bills; they guide our space probes; they entertain and educate our youngsters; and they help control the ballistic missiles with nuclear warheads that can destroy all of us. Thus, people are fascinated not only by the apparent "intelligence" of computers but also by their present and potential power.

Understanding is a key to how people feel about the world around them. What they do not understand is likely to stimulate such emotions as uneasiness or even fear. The future shapers and movers of our society—the students of today—must acquire an understanding of the capabilities and limitations (and the possible uses and abuses) of computer information-processing systems. Such an understanding is necessary if students are to use computer technology beneficially in their own lives and have some influence on the far-reaching systems decisions that will be made in the future.

A report issued a few years ago by the American Association of Junior Colleges recognized the need for computer knowledge when it stated that "computer literacy should be required of all college students and of all high school students too, whatever their field of work might be." All educated persons, the report continued, should have a knowledge of (1) the development of information processing, (2) the basic concepts of computer hardware and software, (3) the social impact of computer usage, and (4) the ways in which computers are applied. How well do current introductory computer information-processing texts satisfy the needs of such a course? Most have either a strong computer science or a strong business orientation. Although such texts admirably serve rather specialized needs, they unfortunately tend to ignore the needs of instructors and students who desire a *broader perspective* on the impact computer usage is having (and may be expected to have) on society. The purpose of *Computers in Society,* therefore, is to fill the existing void by better serving the needs of those with a liberal arts, social science, education, health science, or humanities bent (although, of course, it is *not restricted* to the needs of those students).

More specifically, *the objectives of this book are to:*

1 Provide an introduction to the history and evolution of information processing
2 Lay the foundation for the continuing study that will provide broadly educated persons with an orientation to the computer (what it is, what it can and cannot do, how it operates, and how it may be instructed to solve problems)
3 Consider some of the possible positive and negative effects of computer usage on social organizations and individuals
4 Examine some of the uses and implications of computers in a number of social environments—i.e., government and law, health, education, the humanities, science and engineering, and business

To achieve these objectives, this edition has been divided into six parts. Each of these parts is introduced by a brief essay that (1) explains the purpose of the part, (2) tells the reader how the chapters in the part relate to the above objectives, and (3) identifies the chapters included in the part. A brief summary of these six parts (and an outline of some of the significant changes in this edition) is presented in the following sections.

TEXT ORGANIZATION AND REVISION FEATURES

Part 1   Computers and Information in Society: An Overview

The chapters included in Part 1 (which is aimed at the first objective of the book) are:

1   *Computers, Information, and Evolution.* A new "Looking Ahead" section that gives a brief preview of the main contents of the chapter has been added to this and to *all other* chapters. A list of *learning objectives* is included in each "Looking Ahead" section. Several other new sections have also been added in the body of the chapter, existing material has been updated, and a new "Looking Back" section has been incorporated in this and in *all other* chapters to summarize the points that have been emphasized. Finally, a new "Key Terms" section has been added at the end of this and *all other* chapters to focus attention on basic terminology and concepts.
2   *Technological Change and the Information Revolution.* The sections dealing with technological change, computer hardware developments, and distributed data processing networks have received extensive revision; other sections have been updated.

Part 2   Orientation to Computers

The chapters included in Part 2 (which focuses on the hardware aspects of the second objective) are:

3   *Introductory Computer Concepts.* The section on *artificial intelligence* has been completely revised and expanded; other sections have been reworked.
4   *Computer Input/Output.*   A new table summarizing computer input/output characteristics has been prepared; material dealing with magnetic disk storage, online terminals, voice communication, and data communications has been reworked; and new sections on magnetic bubble storage and serial printers have been included.
5   *Central Processors in General.* New material describing the possible storage elements in a CPU has been added, some of the details associated with magnetic core storage have been deleted, and the section on semiconductor storage has been expanded.
6   *Micros, Minis, Mainframes, and Monsters.* Unlike Chapter 5, which provides a general introduction to central processor concepts, this *entirely new chapter* gives more specific information about actual computers ranging in size from the smallest microsystems to the largest supercomputers.

Part 3 Putting the Computer to Work

The chapters included in Part 3 (which deals with the software aspects of the second objective) are:

7 *Systems Studies, Programming Analysis, and Program Preparation.* Materials previously covered in Chapters 6 and 7 of the second edition have been updated and condensed into this single chapter. Top-down analysis and design and structured programming concepts are introduced briefly. The "Programming Analysis" *section has been completely rewritten,* and six new problem examples have been introduced, analyzed, and flowcharted.

8 *Programming with BASIC.* Use of the BASIC programming language is the subject of this *new chapter.* After discussing the BASIC programming environment and some BASIC necessities, the chapter presents example programs to accomplish simple input, processing, and output operations. Additional programs involving the use of decisions, loops, counters, and accumulators are then considered. The six problems that were analyzed and flowcharted in Chapter 7 provide the examples for this chapter.

Part 4 Computer Influence on a Changing Society

The chapters included in Part 4 (which is directed at the third objective) are:

9 *Organizations, Offices, and Computers.* The section dealing with the types of organizations affected by computers has been thoroughly revised, and a new "Computers in the Office" section dealing with such topics as *word processing* and *electronic mail/message systems* has been added.

10 *Individuals and Computers: Some Positive Views.* The discussion of the ways computers may benefit individuals in private life has been greatly expanded. A new section on the benefits received from *personal computing* has been added.

11 *Individuals and Computers: Some Negative Views.* The material found in Chapters 10 and 11 of the previous edition has been thoroughly updated and condensed into this single chapter. A discussion of the effects of the expanded use of *robots* on employment has been added.

12 *Controlling the Negative Impact.* New information on controlling the use of online terminals and on controlling access to the computer site has been introduced.

Part 5 Selected Computer Uses in Society

The chapters included in Part 5 (which is aimed at the fourth objective) are:

13 *Computers in Government and Law*. A number of new applications are discussed, and out-of-date material has been dropped.
14 *Computers and Health*. Several new figures and applications have been added.
15 *Computers in Education*. New figures and applications have also been added in this chapter.
16 *Computers and the Humanities*. The sections on literary analysis, language translation, and the use of computers in museums have been updated and expanded.
17 *Computers in Science and Engineering*. New computer-aided design applications have been introduced, and a number of new figures have been added.
18 *Computers in Business*. Additional market forecasting and planning applications have been included.

Part 6 Computers and Society beyond 1984

The following chapter is a brief essay on the future outlook for computers in society:

19 *Tomorrow's Outlook*. As might be expected, this chapter has been thoroughly rewritten, and much of it is entirely new.

USE OF THIS TEXT

This book is designed for use in an introductory one-semester or one-quarter course. No mathematical or information-processing background is required or assumed, and no specific computer make or model is featured. The book can be used without access to a machine.

The organization of *Computers in Society* into six parts permits a great deal of *modular flexibility* in the use of the book. It is possible, for example, to follow the materials in Parts 1, 2, and 3 with chapters selected from the other parts as needed. (The applications chapters in Part 5 are self-standing and may be selected as desired for any course of study.) There is also no necessary reason why all parts and chapters must be covered in the sequence in which they appear in the text. The programming material in Part 3, for example, can follow the chapters in Part 1, or the social impact chapters in Part 4 can be moved up to that position.

Sections in many of the chapters in Parts 1, 2, and 3 that deal with (1) the history and current developments in information processing and (2) computing hardware and software concepts are similar to sections dealing with these same topics in the author's *Computers in Business,* 4th ed., McGraw-Hill Book Company, New York, 1979. However, new sections have been added, and the amount of hardware and software detail has been *substantially reduced.* Much of the programming analysis material in Chapter 7, and all of the BASIC language discussion in Chapter 8, is unique to this book.

It is customary at about this point in a preface (although there is always the question of whether anyone is reading a preface at this point) to acknowledge the contributions and suggestions received from numerous sources. Many individuals have contributed to and improved the quality of this effort. (Of course, the obligatory comment that only the author is responsible for any remaining errors applies here.) Among those who should be mentioned are Rob Fry for his editorial and graphic talents; Professors F. S. Beckman of Brooklyn College of the City University of New York, Gary Gleason of Pensacola Junior College, F. Milam Johnson of East Carolina University, Ronald L. Lancaster of Bowling Green State University, Norbert Ludkey of the City College of San Francisco, Stanley Niemczycki of El Camino College, Robert M. Stewart, Jr., of Iowa State University, and Allen Tucker, Jr., of Georgetown University, who reviewed the manuscript and made many helpful suggestions; and Gary D. Sanders of the University of Illinois for his program contributions and suggestions. Finally, a special tribute must go to the equipment manufacturers and publishers who furnished technical materials, photographs, and excerpts for this edition. Their individual contributions are often acknowledged in the body of the book.

Donald H. Sanders

COMPUTERS IN SOCIETY

COMPUTERS IN SOCIETY
A PICTORIAL HISTORY

As we reach for tomorrow, let us remember our past. This book is concerned with the computer, its impact on society, and its future. The short pictorial essay that follows is concerned with some of the computer's forerunners as well as examples of twentieth-century computers. Each has a place in the computer story.

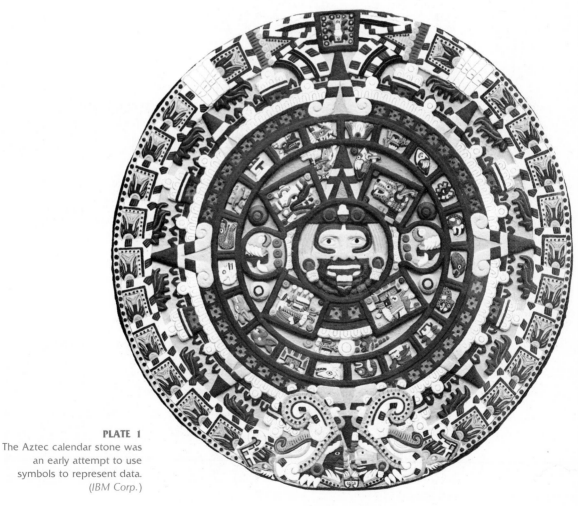

PLATE 1
The Aztec calendar stone was an early attempt to use symbols to represent data.
(IBM Corp.)

PLATE 2
The Abu Baker astrolabe was used throughout the Middle Ages by astronomers, navigators, and astrologers for various surveying and geographical problems.
(IBM Corp.)

PLATE 3
The abacus was first used by the ancient Babylonians to perform calculations.
(IBM Corp.)

PLATE 4

Blaise Pascal developed the first mechanical adding machine in 1642. Pascal's device, called the Machine Arithmetique, was made up of interlocking gears that represented the numbers 0 through 9. *(IBM Corp.)*

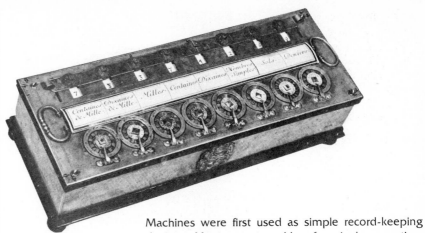

Machines were first used as simple record-keeping devices. Most were capable of a single operation. Pascal's Machine Arithmetique, for example, was simply a device that could mechanically add figures.

PLATE 5

In 1801 Joseph Marie Jacquard created a device which when attached to a loom would control the selection of threads used to create a pattern in the cloth. *(IBM Corp.)*

Jacquard was the first to use punched cards to control a machine's operation. By combining the concepts of the mechanical calculator and the punched card, Charles Babbage designed the first prototype computer. Hollerith then developed a more sophisticated punched-card technique. His "census machine" could handle 50 to 80 cards per minute.

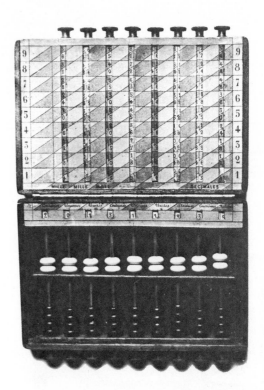

PLATE 6
Jacquard's punched card controlled the pattern woven on the loom. A hole in the card allowed the thread to pass through and become part of the pattern. A card was punched for each of the loom's operations.
(IBM Corp.)

PLATE 7
French pocket calculator (circa 1800). Note that the bottom half of the calculator contains an abacus.

PLATE 8
Gottfried Leibniz developed a calculating machine in 1864 that could subtract, multiply, and divide, as well as add.
(IBM Corp.)

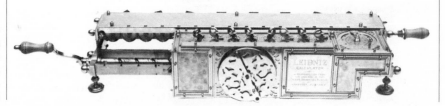

PLATE 9
In 1812 Charles Babbage began the development of a mechanical calculator whose purpose was to construct tables on the basis of the mathematical properties of the difference between numbers. He called his machine a "difference engine." Babbage later developed an "analytical engine" which, unlike the difference engine, was a problem-solving device. *(IBM Corp.)*

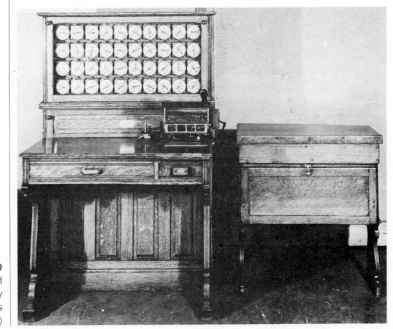

PLATE 10
The electrical tabulator and sorter developed by Herman Hollerith to process the 1890 census. *(IBM Corp.)*

PLATE 11
Howard Aiken of Harvard completed his automatic calculating machine in 1944. The internal operations of the Mark I were controlled automatically with electromagnetic relays. Instructions were on punched paper tape. *(IBM Corp.)*

PLATE 12
Clifford Berry demonstrates the vacuum tubes that were the memory system of the Atanasoff-Berry computer (1939–1942). *(IBM Corp.)*

PLATE 13
The Electronic Numerical Integrator and Computer (ENIAC) was the first all-electronic computer (1943–1946). ENIAC could perform 300 multiplications per second. *(IBM Corp.)*

PLATE 14
UNIVAC I (Universal Automatic Computer) was the first commercially available computer (1951). (*IBM Corp.*)

PLATE 15
In the next generation of computers, such as the IBM 1401, bulky vacuum tubes were replaced by transistors which could store increased amounts of data. (*IBM Corp.*)

The evolution of the computer in the twentieth-century has been characterized by changes in hardware capability. Vacuum tubes have been replaced by transistors and transistors have given way to integrated circuits. Computers now had increased input-output capability, greater storage potential, and they operated in a billionth of a second.

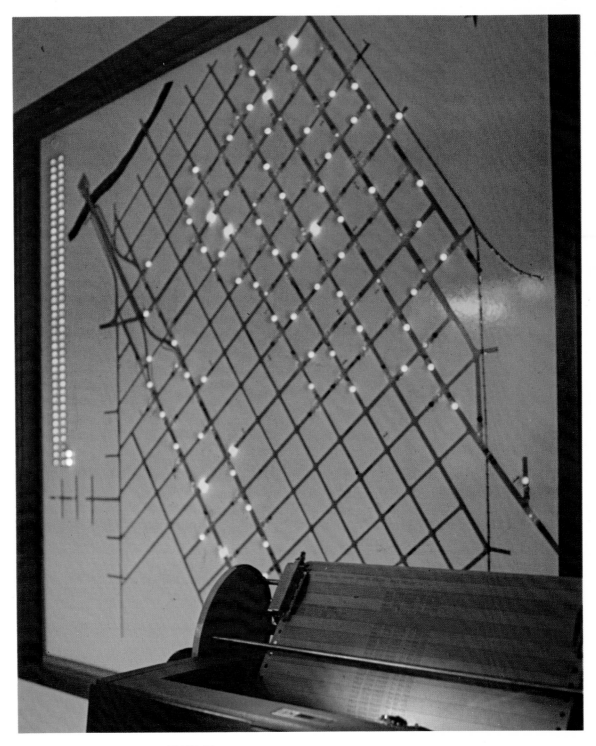

PLATE 16
Computerized traffic control. (Erich Hartmann, Magnum.)

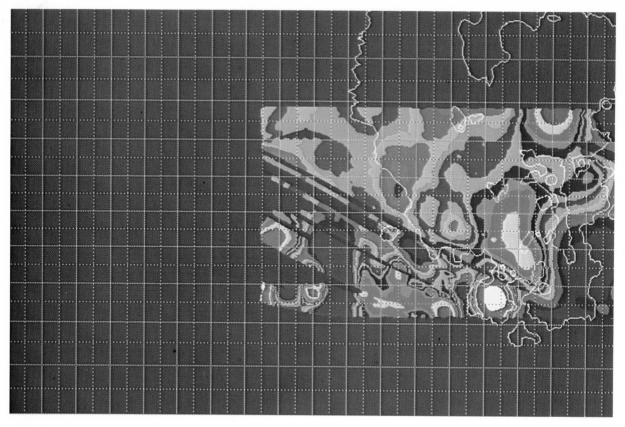

PLATE 17
A computer-generated map showing variations in gravity and density on the moon. (U.S.G.S. Flagstaff Image Processing Facility.)

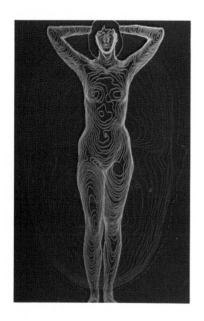

PLATE 18
Computers can be used to document changing patterns of growth or aid in diagnosis as well as scan internal organs such as the liver. (*Left* Dan McCoy/Black Star: *Right* Daniel Bernstein.)

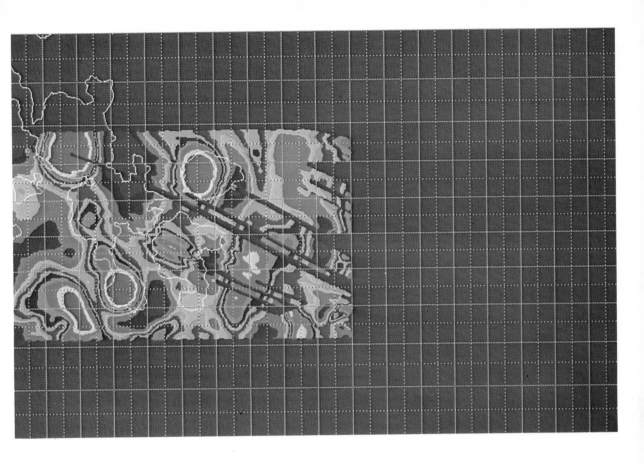

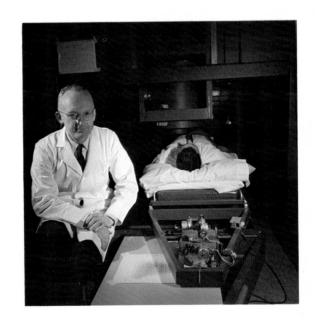

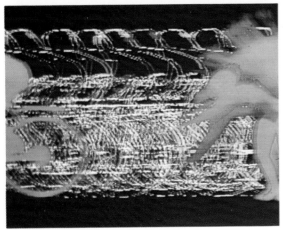

PLATE 20

(*Top and bottom left*) Commercial for Pepsi International; (*Bottom right*) Computer animation used for the opening of NBC's "Hot Hero Sandwich." (Dolphin Productions, Inc.)

PLATE 19

The Vegreville Pysanka by Ronald Resch. This computer-designed Ukranian easter egg, located in Vegreville, Alberta, Canada, is a monument commemorating the centennial of the Alberta Canadian Mounted Police. Built in 1974, the monument was designed by Professor Ronald Resch with the assistance of two University of Utah graduate students, Robert McDermott and Jim Blinn.

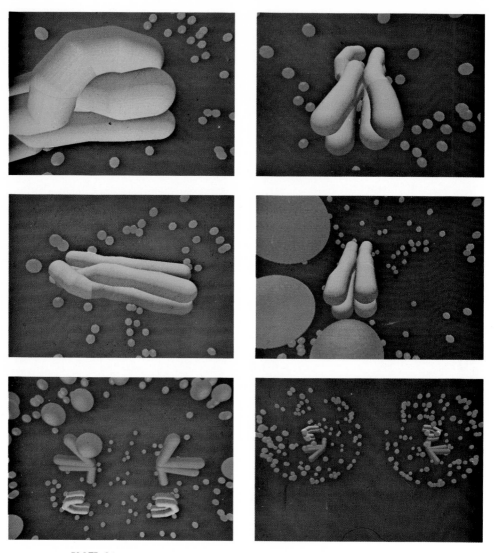

PLATE 21

The four figures represent a sequence from *Cell Division,* a film by Mathematical Applications Group, Inc., using the Synthansion Process. The computer helps create a three-dimensional animation with a high degree of accuracy. This sequence is explaining genetic crossover.

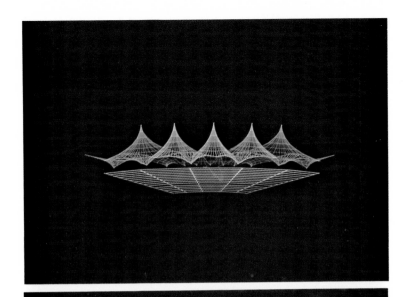

PLATE 22

These lightweight, economical, and attractive roofs for large, enclosed areas (sports facilities, warehouses, etc.) become permanent when reinforced with steel. The free-form designs are greatly facilitated by use of the computer. (Architect—William Morgan and Associates. Roof design and engineering—Geiger-Berger Associates. Computer graphics model—Cristos Tountas, School of Architecture, Columbia University.)

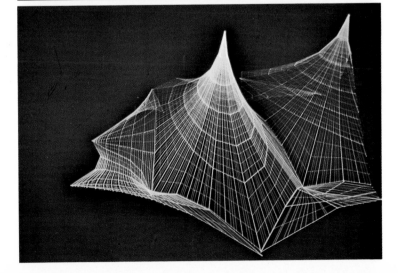

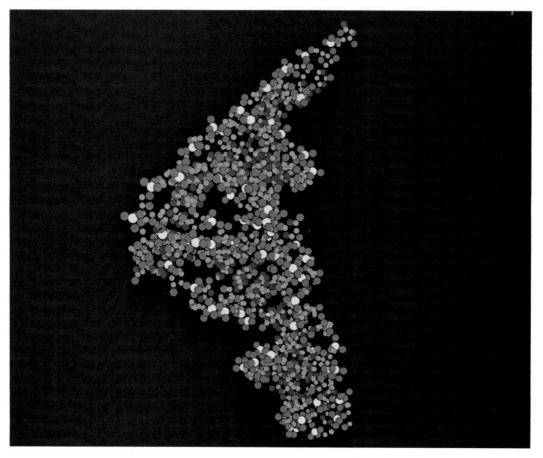

PLATE 23

This Transfer-RNA (T-RNA) molecule was computer-created as a scientific visual aid. Stephen R. Levine created this animation using three-dimensional space data on atom positioning (supplied by Sung-Hou Kim and Joel Sussman of Duke University's medical school) and a sculptural graphic computer program ("Atoms" by Ken Knowlton and Lorinda Cherry of Bell Telephone Laboratories).

Part One

(Herb Levart, Photo Researchers.)

Part One
COMPUTERS AND INFORMATION IN SOCIETY: AN OVERVIEW

(Myron Wood, Photo Researchers.)

(Harmit Singh, Photo Researchers.)

The purpose of the two chapters in Part 1 is to

1 Explain why you need to study and acquire an understanding of computers
2 Develop the necessary concepts about the subject of information
3 Show why information is needed in society and how computers can help deliver the needed information
4 Study the history and evolution of information processing
5 Examine the setting for, and a few of the developments and issues associated with, the information revolution that society is currently experiencing

These chapters will provide us with a background for the study of computer concepts presented in Part 2.
     The chapters included in Part 1 are:

1 *Computers, Information, and Evolution*
2 *Technological Change and the Information Revolution*

Chapter 1
COMPUTERS, INFORMATION, AND EVOLUTION

This chapter gives you a very brief introduction to, and definition of, the computer. In addition to learning why you should study computers, you will also see that computers are used in society because they produce information.

After basic information concepts are explained in this chapter, the need for information in society is explained and the properties that information should possess are outlined. You will then see how computers can help a society obtain the quality information it needs.

Finally, you will learn how information-processing techniques and equipment have evolved over the centuries.

Thus, after studying this chapter, you should be able to:

- Discuss why educated citizens should have some understanding of computers.
- Identify the sources of data and the activities associated with data processing.
- Explain why information is needed in society and what properties the needed information should possess.
- Outline ways in which computers can help in providing society with the needed information.
- Describe some major developments in the evolution of information processing.
- Understand and use the key terms listed at the end of the chapter.

Question: How long are people in school to learn about computers?
Answer: "They could be anywhere from 5 feet and up."[1]

Although you may sympathize with the elementary school student who answered this question, there may be other questions on your mind right now. Since this chapter deals with introductory computer and information concepts, one such question might be: What is a computer? A second question might be: Why should I study computers? If such questions have occurred to you, read on. (If not, read on anyway!)

WHAT IS A COMPUTER?

Computers are awful. This is the conclusion that an uninformed individual is likely to reach after reading a few articles on the subject in the popular

---

[1] From Eve R. Wirth, "Out of the Mouths of Babes," *Creative Computing,* p. 111, November/December 1977.

press. Dictionaries assign to the word *awful* such meanings as "filling with awe; deserving great respect; and terrible or dreadful." Articles discussing computers in ways which lend support to each of these meanings have appeared in recent years. In one article, for example, a computer will be pictured as having *human* characteristics—e.g., as a device which can play checkers and chess and give verbal answers to inquiries. In another article, the computer is placed in a *superhuman* role. (In an article in *Smithsonian,* it was estimated that in about the year 1986 a self-programming machine would be developed which would usher in a "new form of intelligent life" on this planet—a form of intelligence similar to HAL, the superhuman computer which was featured in the science fiction film *2001: A Space Odyssey*).[2] In a third story, the computer may be presented as *subhuman;* stupid errors in billing, for example, are cited, such as the case of the lady who was charged for the purchase of 4,000 new tires instead of 4. Finally, additional articles may convey the impression that the computer is *extrahuman*—e.g., the teaching machine which functions without threatening and with infinite patience—or *inhuman*—the instrument through which our privacy will be invaded and the source of heartless decisions made without regard for human feelings.

What is this thing called a computer that can produce so many contradictory characterizations? Although a detailed answer to this question will be given in later chapters, it is perhaps appropriate to pause here to outline briefly what is meant by the word *computer.*

Most people are aware that a computer is an electronic device that can perform arithmetic operations, but *a computer is much more than a fast arithmetic machine.* It is also a machine that can choose, copy, move, position, compare, and perform other nonarithmetic operations on the many alphabetic, numeric, and other symbols that humans use to represent things. The computer manipulates these symbols in the desired way by following a set of ordered instructions called a *program.* Programs, or *intellectual maps,* are prepared by humans. Thus, *a computer is a fast electronic symbol-manipulating device that is able to follow an intellectual map.*

Some clever maps have been followed by computers to perform impressive intellectual tasks such as playing a very skilled game of chess against a human opponent. But as you know, there may be problems in using maps. A traveler using a road map can fail to arrive at a desired destination if the map is incorrect or incomplete; a computer may become hopelessly "lost" or may produce very unpredictable results if there is a single flaw in the map or program it is following. Such flaws, unfortunately, are not uncommon. In fact, they are usually responsible for the billing errors and other absurdities that often appear in the popular press.

Thus, few of the popular-press articles mentioned a few paragraphs earlier contain inaccuracies. Clever programs *often do* yield impressive in-

---

[2] See Gregory Benford and David Book, "Promise-Child in the Land of the Humans," *Smithsonian,* pp. 58–65, April 1971. HAL is an *acronym*—i.e., a term formed from the first letters of related words—which means *heuristically programmed algorithmic* computer. Acronyms are frequently used in the jargon of computing and information processing.

tellectual results, and flawed maps *can sometimes* lead to unwanted consequences. But few if any of these articles have gone beyond the discussion of clever or flawed computer applications to explain the real capabilities and limitations of computers. Yet, as you will see in the next section, such understanding becomes increasingly necessary as the impact of computer systems becomes more pervasive in our society.

WHY SHOULD YOU STUDY COMPUTERS?

Let us assume that you have the soul of a poet and are especially gifted in the perception and expression of that which is beautiful or lyrical. Perhaps you expect to be able to live a happy life without using—or ever touching—a computer. Perhaps you feel about computers the way a little old lady felt about space travel. Walking up to rocket expert Wernher von Braun after he had finished a lecture, she asked: "Dr. von Braun, why do people want to fly to the moon? Why don't they sit home and watch television, like the good Lord intended?"[3]

Just three decades ago, when the few computers in existence were enormously expensive and were often hidden away in scientific laboratories, such a "hands off" attitude would have been possible. There would have been no more reason for you to study computers then than there is for the old lady to travel to the moon today. But hundreds of thousands of affordable computers are now found in offices, schools, homes, hospitals, government agencies, and factories as well as in laboratories. These computers, like automobiles and electricity, are likely to exert a daily influence on your life.

Let us suppose, for example, that during a recent day the following events occurred:

- *You bought gasoline for your car with a credit card.* Computers were used to control the refining process that produced the gasoline, and most credit cards probably would not exist if computers were not available to handle the processing of millions of daily transactions.

- *You received some junk mail.* If computers were not available to maintain mailing lists and print address labels, you would seldom receive this unwanted material.

- *You picked up and cashed your paycheck.* If you work for an organization of much size, it is likely that a computer calculated the deductions, prepared the check, and updated your total earnings for later income tax purposes. When you cashed the check, it was automatically processed by computers in the banking system.

- *You were given a traffic ticket.* Before approaching you, the police officer may have requested a computer check to see whether you were

[3] From Bertram Raphael, *The Living Computer,* W. H. Freeman and Company, San Francisco, 1976, p. 4.

driving a stolen car. The ticket information was added to your driving record in the appropriate state computer system and was later transmitted to your insurance company's computer records.

- *You reserved a seat on an airplane flight.* A computer kept track of available seats and instantly recorded your reservation.

- *You learned that your cousin was transferred to another job.* Computer usage may have resulted in the reorganization of work groups and the displacement of your cousin.

- *You went on a picnic and then visited a friend in a hospital.* A computer-controlled monitoring station was checking the water quality of the stream near your picnic site. The instruments used in the diagnostic tests given to your hospitalized friend were linked to a computer for purposes of analysis.

- *You took a physical examination for purposes of insurance.* The medical history you gave the doctor, along with the doctor's findings, was forwarded to the insurance company and then stored in a large computer "bank" of data. Unknown to you, this potentially sensitive private information[4] may now be available to several other organizations.

In these eight examples (hundreds of others could have been offered), you never saw a computer, yet the ubiquitous presence of computers in your daily life cannot be denied or ignored. In reading these examples, you may have noticed that some appeared to offer benefits to you (your paycheck was on time and in the correct amount, your credit card was readily accepted, and your plane reservation was handled quickly and efficiently) while others did not (junk mail is a pain, you resent being checked for auto theft, you know your cousin feels lost in the new job, and you dislike the idea that the personal and private information you gave your doctor during a physical exam may wind up in the hands of strangers). However, the fact that a revolutionary invention like the computer might be used to produce both desirable and undesirable results should probably not come as a surprise. After all, automobiles give us mobility and freedom, but they also kill us by the thousands.

In the years ahead, as current computer applications are expanded and as the computer is applied to many more intellectual tasks, there will be enormous potential for widespread benefits for our society. But there will also be the danger that people using computers may design impersonal systems that are vulnerable to fraud and other crimes and that are used to gather private facts about individuals in order to gain control over their lives.

What can you and other educated citizens in our society do to prevent the possible dangers and help bring about the positive potential? (The answer to this question is also the answer to the question asked in

---

[4] Although you may have nothing to hide, what about the political candidate who was once treated for an emotional disturbance or a social disease?

the title of this section.) You and others should begin now to study and acquire an understanding of computers so that you can intelligently discuss and help shape the future impact that computer systems are likely to have on all of us. Educated citizens should not depend on computer specialists to control potential dangers. Rather, they should insist that specialists, governments, and business and nonprofit organizations assume the responsibility and liability for the effects their computer systems have on people. It is a commonly expressed fear that computers may someday produce a society controlled by technocrats. The answer, as former UN Secretary General U Thant suggested, is that all educated people be given information about computers so that they will not be at the mercy of those who run the machines.

OBJECTIVES AND ORGANIZATION OF THIS BOOK

Objectives

One of the objectives of this book is to do just what U Thant suggested. That is, *one objective* is to lay the foundation for the continuing study which will provide you with an orientation to the computer (what it is, what it can and cannot do, how it operates, and how it may be instructed to solve problems). A *second objective* is to consider some of the ways in which the computer influences a changing society. A *third objective* is to examine some of the uses and implications of computers in a number of social environments.

One problem existing between computer specialists and those who are the beneficiaries (or perhaps victims) of the machines' output is in the area of communication. Reducing the communications gap is *another objective* of this book. A whole new language has developed in the past decade in information processing—a language that might be labeled "Computerese" and that must be mastered to some extent by an educated citizen. Communication difficulties occur because of the rapid rate of growth of computer technology. New concepts in the design and use of computers are announced with mind-boggling frequency, and these concepts are often described with newly coined words or phrases. Thousands of new computers are being installed each year. Understanding suffers because the number of *new* terms and acronyms seems to be increasing at about the same rate.[5] In the following sections and throughout the book, words are defined as they are introduced. The definitions used are the ones that appear to be most generally accepted. A glossary of commonly used technical terms is included at the back of the book. You will find that although some Computerese terms sound quite

---

[5] Even computer experts are affected. It has been reported, for example, that a conversation between two computer technicians at a party was overheard by a third expert who could not understand what they were discussing. When the two technicians separated, the third expert asked each of them what they had been talking about. They did not know because they had not understood each other!

impressive and foreboding—as is often the case with technical jargon—closer inspection will show them to be relatively simple.

Organization

To achieve its objectives, this book is organized into six parts. In the two chapters of Part 1 you are introduced to (1) the concepts of information and information processing, (2) the historical background of information processing, and (3) the information revolution which is now under way. Part 2 ("Orientation to Computers") has four chapters devoted to computer concepts and computing equipment. Part 3 ("Putting the Computer to Work") has chapters dealing with the steps that may be needed to prepare the programs, or intellectual maps, that computers follow in doing useful work. Part 4 ("Computer Influence on a Changing Society") has four chapters on the implications of computers for organizations and individuals. The chapters in Part 5 ("Selected Computer Uses in Society") describe the uses of computers in such environments as government and law, health, education, the humanities, science and engineering, and business. Finally, Part 6 ("Computers and Society beyond 1984") contains a brief essay on the future outlook of computers in society. On a more detailed level, at the beginning of each chapter you will find (1) a "Look Ahead" at the major topics presented in the chapter, and (2) a summary of what you should learn in the chapter. In total, of course, the learning goals of the chapters achieve the overall objectives of the book.

And Now . . .

Later chapters will reinforce the theme that computers are powerful tools, that powerful tools produce potent effects, and that significant social changes may be expected as the tools are utilized. At this point, however, we should place the role of computers in society in proper perspective. *Computers are used in society because they produce information;* were this not so, the machines would be merely expensive curiosities. Therefore, in the following pages of this chapter, let us examine the subject of information. After first explaining some *information concepts,* we will consider *why information is needed in society, what properties the needed information should possess, how computers can help,* and *how information processing has evolved.*

INFORMATION CONCEPTS

Three elements fundamental to human activities are information, energy, and materials. All these elements are necessary to provide the physical things humans need—food, clothing, shelter, and transportation. In addition to supporting physical production, however, information is also the substance of all human intellectual activity; it is basic to education, government, literature, the conduct of business, and the maintenance and expansion of our store of knowledge. The harnessing of energy brought about the industrial revolution, and the attempt to harness and transform information is bringing about another revolution at the present time.

Information Defined

The word *data* is the plural of *datum,* which means "fact." Data, then, are facts, unevaluated messages, or informational raw materials, but they are not information except in a constricted and detailed sense.

As used in this text, the term *information* is generally considered to designate data arranged in ordered and useful form. Thus, *information* will usually be thought of as relevant knowledge, produced as output of processing operations and acquired to provide insight in order to (1) achieve specific purposes or (2) enhance understanding. In ancient times, for example, it was observed that the ebb and flow of the Nile River followed a seasonal pattern. By gathering and analyzing Nile River data, prehistoric people gained the information to make decisions about crop planting and take actions that permitted them to survive and to create the ancient Egyptian civilization. From this example, you can see that information is the result of a transformation process. Just as raw materials are transformed into finished products by a manufacturing process (Figure 1-1a), so too are raw data transformed into information by the data processing operation (Figure 1-1b). The products produced by the manufacturing process have little utility until they are properly applied; similarly, the information produced by data processing is of little value unless it supports meaningful human decisions and actions.

The purpose of data processing is to evaluate and bring order to data and place them in proper perspective or context so that meaningful information will be produced. The primary distinction between data and information, therefore, is that while all information consists of data, not all data produce specific and meaningful information that will reduce uncertainty and lead to greater insight (and better decisions).

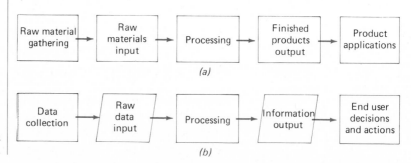

FIGURE 1-1
Information is the result of a transformation process.

"The Information Imperative"

An "Information Imperative" happens whenever anyone recognizes that the information he or she has is inadequate for the decisions to be made. That recognition stimulates a fierce desire and drive for more adequate information.

A common symptom of information inadequacy is a cost overrun. A well known example is the Alaska pipeline. Based on information available in 1969 the estimated cost for the 800-mile line was $900 million. By the time it was completed eight years later, the real cost jumped to $7.7 billion. A significant part of the difference can be traced to decisions based on inadequate information.

Here's one example. A major link in the pipeline is a bridge over the Yukon River. When construction crews got on site they found the key support for the planned bridge would straddle an active earthquake fault. It was too late to shift the tower, so it had to be strengthened on the spot at a cost of an extra $5 million.

The lack of timely, relevant, accurate information for valid decision-making was costly and because it was costly, its inadequacy was evident too late. But it did activate the Information Imperative and sound a clarion call that cost-effective adequate information is essential to achieving goals.

Source: Harding Vowles, "The Information Imperative," *Information Manager*, p. 10, August 1978. Reprinted with permission of the publisher.

Sources of Data

In *organized groups,* the input data used to produce information originate from internal and external sources. *Internal sources* consist of individuals and departments located within organizations such as hospitals, schools, and government agencies. These sources may furnish facts on a regular and planned basis (i.e., on a formal basis) to support decisions if the potential user is aware that the facts are available.

External or *environmental* sources are the generators and distributors of data located outside the organization. These sources include categories such as customers, patients, suppliers, competitors, professional publications and associations, and government agencies. Such sources provide the organization with environmental and/or competitive data that may give administrators important clues on what is likely to happen.

In your *private life,* too, you receive *internal* data from personal observations (by using your senses of hearing, sight, smell, touch, and taste). You also receive data from *external* sources such as books, magazines, newspapers, and radio and television broadcasts.

FIGURE 1-2
Blaise Pascal. (*The Bettmann Archive.*)

THE SCIENTIFIC GENIUS OF BLAISE PASCAL

Blaise Pascal (1623– 1662) invented the first calculating machine to help his father with his work. The elder Pascal was tax commissioner in Rouen, France. Pascal's "arithmetic engine" was made of wheels containing numbers from 0 to 9. Each wheel advanced one number when the wheel to its right completed one revolution. Fifty copies of Pascal's calculating machine were manufactured, but none were perfected.

Pascal was an innovator in other areas as well. His inventions included the hydraulic press and the hypodermic syringe. He planned the first public transportation system of Paris. Pascal's calculations to solve gambling problems are the basis of today's probability theory.

Pascal died in 1662, 150 years before Charles Babbage invented his more famous calculating devices.

Data Processing

All data processing, whether done by hand or by the latest electronic methods, consists of *input, manipulation,* and *output* operations.

Input activities Data must be *originated* or captured in some form for processing. Data may be initially recorded on paper *source documents,* which then may be converted into a machine-usable form for processing. Alternatively, they may be initially captured directly in a paperless machine-usable form.

Manipulative operations One or more of the following operations may then have to be performed on the gathered data:

1 *Classifying.* Identifying and arranging items with like characteristics into groups or classes is called *classifying.* Data taken from school records may be classified by student name or number; school name or number; grade, age, and sex of students; or any other classification the processing cycle may require. Classifying is usually done by a shortened, predetermined method of abbreviation known as *coding.* The three types of codes used are *numeric* (your social security number), *alphabetic* (grades A, B, and C), and *alphanumeric* (an automobile license plate stamped CSN-1763).

2 *Sorting.* After the data are classified, it is then usually necessary to arrange or rearrange them in a predetermined sequence to facilitate processing. This arranging procedure is called *sorting.* Sorting is done by number as well as by letter. Numeric sorting usually requires less time than alphabetic sorting in machine-based processing systems, and it is therefore generally used.

3 *Calculating.* Arithmetic manipulation of the data is known as *calculating.* (Wasn't that a profound statement?)

4 *Summarizing.* To be of value, data must often be condensed or sifted so that the resulting reports will be concise and effective. Reducing masses of data to a more usable form is called *summarizing.*

Output/records-management activities Once the data have been manipulated, one or more of the following activities may be required:

1 *Communicating.* As we have seen, data may go through many steps after they have been originated. The transfer of data from one operation to another for use or for further processing is known as data *communication.* The communication process continues until the information, in a usable form, reaches the final user's location.

2 *Storing.* Placing similar data into files for future reference is *storing.* Obviously, facts should be stored only if the value of having them in the future exceeds the storage cost. Storage may take a variety of forms.

Storage *media* that are frequently used include paper documents, microfilm, magnetizable media and devices, and punched paper media.

3   *Retrieving.* Recovering stored data and/or information when needed is the *retrieving* step. Retrieval methods range from people searching file cabinets to the use of quick-responding electronic inquiry devices that are connected directly (i.e., they are *online*) to a computer. The computer, in turn, is connected directly to a mass-storage device that contains the information.

4   *Reproducing.* It is sometimes necessary or desirable to copy or duplicate data. This operation is known as data *reproduction* and may be done by hand or by machine.

These, then, are the basic steps in data processing. Table 1-1 presents these steps and indicates some of the ways they are accomplished. The means of performing the steps vary according to whether *manual, electromechanical,* or *electronic* processing methods are used.

WHY IS INFORMATION NEEDED IN SOCIETY?

When a man kens, he can.
—Thomas Carlyle

Information is needed in virtually every field of human thought and action. As Carlyle observed, information is power.

Why Do You Need Information?

Very simply, you need information to make the best decisions possible. In your private life, you need information to organize vacation activities, locate a library book, plan meals, control usage of your credit card, make intelligent purchases, drive a car, pilot an airplane, fertilize a lawn, soup up an engine, build a rocket, paint a landscape, prune a shrub, groom a pet, select a garment, vote for a candidate, choose a doctor or lawyer, protest a tax increase, evaluate career opportunities, pick an investment, select a course, or study for a test—whew! This list of your activities is virtually endless!

In each of these personal activities, decisions are required and information is needed to support the decisions. Compared with information "have nots," people who receive better information are likely to have better career opportunities and to be better equipped to make personal decisions. The right information could even make you rich. Nathan Rothschild, for example, used carrier pigeons to become the first person in the London financial district to learn of the British and Prussian victory over Napoleon at Waterloo. Armed with this timely and accurate information, Rothschild make a fortune in a single day by buying all the shares of stock sold by panicky investors who feared that the British would be defeated.

TABLE 1-1
Tools and techniques for data processing

Steps in the Data Processing Operation

Processing Method	Originating-Recording	Classifying	Sorting	Calculating	Summarizing	Communicating	Storing	Retrieving	Reproducing
Manual	Human observation; hand-written records; pegboards	Hand posting; pegboards	Hand posting; pegboards; edge-notched cards	Human brain	Pegboards; hand calculations	Written reports; hand-carried messages; telephone	Paper in files, journals, ledgers, etc.	File clerk; bookkeeper	Clerical; carbon paper
Manual with machine assistance	Typewriter; cash register; manual	Cash register; bookkeeping machine	Mechanical collators	Adding machines; calculators; cash registers	Accounting machines; adding machines; cash registers	Documents prepared by machines; message conveyors	Motorized rotary files; microfilm		Xerox machines; duplicators; addressing machines
Electro-mechanical punched card	Prepunched cards; key-punched cards; mark-sensed cards; manual	Determined by card field design; sorter; collator	Card sorter	Accounting machines (tabulators); calculating punch	Accounting machines; calculating punch	Printed documents; interpreter	Trays of cards	Manual tray movement	Reproducing punch
Electronic	Magnetic tape encoder; magnetic and optical character readers; card and tape punches; on-line terminals; manual; key-to-disk encoder	Determined by systems design; computer	Computer sorting		Computer	Online data transmission; printed output; visual display; voice output	Magnetizable media and devices; punched media; computer; microfilm	Online inquiry with direct-access devices; manual movement of storage media to computer	Multiple copies from printers; microfilm copies

Why Do People in Organizations Need Information?

Besides being essential to individuals who use it to achieve personal ends, information is also needed by decision makers in organizations. These people must perform certain basic tasks or functions in order to achieve organizational goals. The goals pursued differ, but the basic tasks generally involve acquiring, allocating, and controlling scarce human and capital resources. (Capital is money and the things that money can buy.) In other words, the functions of *planning, organizing, staffing,* and *controlling* are performed by decision makers. The success of any organization is determined by how well its leaders[6] and members perform these activities. How well these activities are carried out is dependent, in part, upon how well the information needs of the organization are being met. Why is this? It is because each function involves decision making, and decision making must be supported by information that is accurate, timely, complete, concise, and relevant. If information does not possess these characteristics, the quality of the decisions that are made will probably suffer and the organization (at best) will not achieve the success it might otherwise have had.

In summary, as shown in Figure 1-3, quality information in the hands of those who can effectively use it will support good decisions; good decisions will lead to effective performance of organizational activities; and effective performance will lead to successful attainment of organizational goals. Thus, information is the bonding agent that holds an organization together.

What information is needed by people in organizations? A common need basic to all decision makers is an understanding of the purpose of the organization, i.e., its policies, programs, plans, and goals. Beyond these basic informational requirements, the question of what information is needed can be answered only in broad general terms because individuals differ in the ways in which they view information, in their analytical approaches in using information, and in their conceptual organization of relevant facts. An additional factor that complicates the subject of the information needed is the organizational level of the job. For example, supervisors at the lower operating levels need information to help them make day-to-day operating decisions. At the top levels, however, information is needed to support long-range planning and policy decisions. Thus, because of the types of decisions they must make, managers at the top and lower levels generally *utilize time* differently, tend to need different degrees of *information summarization,* and are inclined to use information obtained from *different sources.*

In Figure 1-4a we see that at the lower supervisory levels more time is generally spent in performing control activities (e.g., checking to make sure that teaching assignments are being met), while at the upper levels more time is spent on planning (e.g., determining the location and speci-

FIGURE 1-3
The success of an organization depends on its information.

[6] The words *manager, supervisor,* and *administrator* are used synonymously in this text to refer to people occupying positions of leadership in organizations.

fications of a new elementary school). Figure 1-4*b* shows that although lower-level managers need detailed information relating to daily operations of specific departments, top administrators are best served with information that summarizes trends and indicates exceptions to what was expected. A final generalization is that the higher one is in the organization, the more one needs and is likely to use information obtained from external sources (see Figure 1-4*c*). A supervisor uses internally generated information to control production processes, but a president studying the feasibility of a new plant needs information about consumer product acceptance, pollution control, locality tax structures, competitive reactions, availability of labor and suppliers, etc., and this information is environmental in nature.

In summary, the types of decisions vary, and the information needs also vary. Thus, it is unlikely that we shall soon see (if, indeed, we ever do)

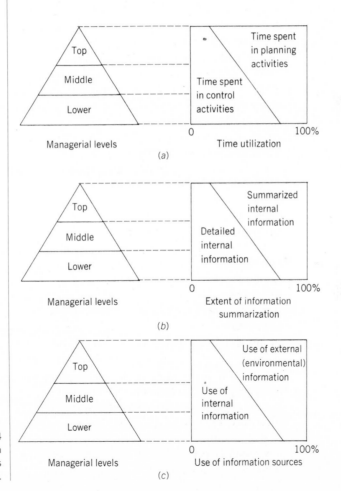

FIGURE 1-4
Information needs of decision makers at different levels may differ.

an information system designed to be uniformly suitable and desirable for all organizational members.

WHAT PROPERTIES SHOULD THE NEEDED INFORMATION POSSESS?

As a general rule, the more information serves to reduce the element of uncertainty in decision making, the greater its value. Any decision maker is likely to assign greater importance (and value) to information that is in the proper format, is received at an appropriate time, and is accessible at the location needed. But information is a resource, and like other resources it is usually not free. It is therefore necessary that the cost of acquiring the resource be compared with the value to be obtained from its availability. Information should be prepared if (1) its cost is less than the additional revenues produced by its use, (2) it serves to reduce other expenses by a more-than-proportionate amount, or (3) it provides such intangible benefits as insight and understanding, which the information user considers to be worth the costs involved.

The brief comments on information economics just presented should be kept in mind as we look at the desirability of information that possesses the properties of *accuracy, timeliness, completeness, conciseness,* and *relevancy.* Up to a certain point, information that possesses these properties may be expected to be more valuable than information lacking one or more of them.

Accuracy   Accuracy may be defined as the ratio of correct information to the total amount of information produced over a period of time. If, for example, 100 items of information are produced and 95 of these items give a correct report of the actual situation, the level of accuracy is 0.95. Whether this level is high enough depends upon the information being produced. If a bank were to make five errors in processing 100 of your checks, this would hardly be acceptable to you or to the bank. On the other hand, if physical inventory records kept on large quantities of inexpensive parts achieve an accuracy level of 0.95, this might be acceptable to a maintenance supervisor.

Inaccuracies are the result of *human errors* and /or *machine malfunctions.* Human error (in system design, machine operation, the preparation of input data, and other ways) is the primary cause of inaccuracy.

Timeliness   Timeliness is another important information characteristic. It may be of little consolation to learn too late that you just paid $400 too much for your new Belchfire V/8, even though the amount of the savings is an accurate figure. Accuracy alone is not enough. In the past a trade-off between timeliness and accuracy was often required; i.e., greater accuracy might require more input data control points, which could slow down the processing speed and therefore reduce the timeliness of the output information. Computer usage, however, reduces the significance of this conflict between accuracy and processing speed. As we shall see in the next chapter, new computer-based information systems that provide quick-response times to managers have been developed.

Completeness   Most people faced with a decision to make have been frustrated at some time by having supporting information that is accurate, timely—and *incomplete*. For example, that course you need to graduate is to be offered next term at 9 A.M. on Monday, Wednesday, and Friday. This is an accurate and timely bit of information, but it is incomplete because no instructor is listed on the schedule. Thus, you don't know whether the course will be taught by Professor Sweet or Professor Nastee. A report is complete if it gives a person all the information needed to make a decision. Admittedly, this is a rare document, but more complete information can often be provided through the design of systems that do a better job of integrating and consolidating available facts. A dramatic historical example of the consequences of failure to consolidate related pieces of information occurred at Pearl Harbor in 1941. Historians tell us that data available in bits and pieces and at scattered points, if integrated, would have signaled the danger of a Japanese attack.

Conciseness   In organizations, important information, along with relatively useless data, is often buried in stacks of detailed and unrefined reports. Administrators (if they use the reports at all) are then faced with the problem of extracting those items of information which they need. Concise information that summarizes (perhaps through the use of tables and charts) the relevant data and that points out areas of exception to normal or planned activities is what is often needed by—but less often supplied to—today's managers.

Relevancy   Relevant information is *need-to-know* information that leads to action or provides new knowledge and understanding. Organizational reports that were once valuable but are no longer relevant should be discontinued.

HOW CAN COMPUTERS HELP?

Most of the information-processing developments occurring today are aimed at obtaining information with more of the desirable properties discussed above. A number of pressures are responsible for the current efforts to improve information in society. As these pressures have built, decision makers have often turned to the use of the computer for relief. Included among these pressures are:

1   *Increased paperwork volume.* Processing capability in many organizations has been strained by (1) the growth in size and complexity of the

organization, (2) the increased demand for data from external sources, and (3) the demand of administrators for more information. Fortunately, the greater the volume of data that must be processed to produce *needed* information, the more economical computer processing becomes relative to other possible processing methods.

2   *Demand for accuracy.* If a data processing operation is strained to and beyond the capacity for which it was originally planned, inaccuracies will begin to appear and the control of organizational (and personal) activities will suffer. Computer processing, however, will be quite accurate *if* the task to be performed has been properly prepared.

3   *Demand for timeliness.* With an increase in processing volume, there is often a reduction in the speed of processing. What people want is timely information; what they often get is information that is delayed until it is no longer useful in decision making. Thus, many organizations and individuals have turned to computers to speed up the processing.

4   *Increased costs.* In organizations, the increasing costs of the labor and materials associated with a noncomputer data processing operation have often caused managers to look to computer usage for economic relief. Compared with other processing methods, the use of computers may make it possible for certain costs (e.g., labor) to be reduced while the level of processing activity remains stable. Figure 1-5 gives a general idea of the cost relationships existing between computer processing methods and alternative methods. The curves show the average cost of processing a typical document or record using different processing approaches. Point A shows the break-even cost position between manual and computer processing at a volume of A'. When volume is less than A', it would be more economical to use manual methods. Points B and C show other break-even positions. Of course, the cost curves in Figure 1-5 do not remain constant. Each increase in clerical labor rates and the cost of clerical office supplies, for example, shifts the manual-method curves upward, while each new hardware innovation may serve to reduce computer costs and thus shift the computer curve downward. The net result has been to make

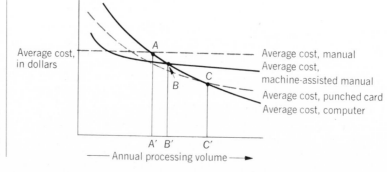

FIGURE 1-5
Given sufficient work to do, computers may reduce processing costs.

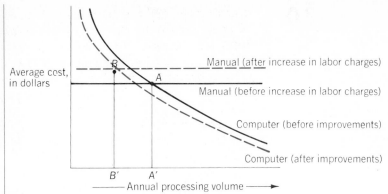

FIGURE 1-6
Computer processing
methods are becoming more
attractive at lower processing
volumes.

computer processing methods more attractive at lower processing volumes (see Figure 1-6).

EVOLUTION OF INFORMATION PROCESSING

Earlier in the chapter (in Table 1-1); we classified data processing methods into *manual, machine-assisted manual, electromechanical punched card,* and *electronic computer* categories. In the remaining pages of this chapter, let us use these categories to look briefly at the history of information-processing techniques and equipment.

The Manual Stage

For centuries, people lived on the earth without keeping records, but as social organizations such as tribes began to form, adjustments became necessary. The complexities of tribal life required that more details be remembered. Methods of counting based on the biological fact that people have fingers were thus developed. However, the limited number of digits combined with the need to remember more facts posed problems. For example, if a shepherd was tending a large tribal flock and had a short memory, how was the shepherd to keep control of the inventory? Problems bring solutions, and the shepherd's solution might have been to let a stone, a stick, a scratch on a rock, or a knot in a string represent each sheep in the flock.

As tribes grew into nations, trade and commerce developed. Stones and sticks, however, were not satisfactory for early traders. In 3500 B.C., ancient Babylonian merchants were keeping records on clay tablets. An early manual calculating device was the *abacus,* which, although over 2,000 years old, may still be the most widely used calculator in the world. (Figure 1-7 shows an abacus of the type used in the Orient since the thirteenth century.)

Manual record-keeping techniques continued to develop through

FIGURE 1-7
An abacus. *(IBM Corp.)*

the centuries, with such innovations as record audits (the Greeks) and banking systems and budgets (the Romans). In the United States, in the 20 years following the Civil War, the main tools of data processing were pencils, pens, rulers, work sheets (for classifying, calculating, and summarizing), journals (for storing), and ledgers (for storing and communicating).

The volume of business and government processing during this period was expanding rapidly, and, as might be expected, such complete reliance upon manual methods resulted in information that was relatively inaccurate and often late. To the consternation of the Census Bureau, for example, the 1880 census was not finished until it was almost time to begin the 1890 count! In spite of limitations of accuracy and timeliness, however, *manual processing methods have the following advantages:* (1) Information is in a humanly readable form, (2) changes and corrections are easily accomplished, (3) no minimum economic processing volume is generally required, and (4) manual methods are easily adapted to changing conditions.

Machine-Assisted Manual Development

The evolution of machine-assisted manual processing methods has gone through several phases. In the *first phase,* machines were produced which improved the performance of a *single* processing step. In 1642, for example, the first mechanical calculating machine was developed by Blaise Pascal (see Figure 1-8). About 30 years later, Gottfried Leibniz, a German mathematician, improved upon Pascal's invention by producing a calculating machine which could add, subtract, multiply, divide, and extract roots. In the 1880s, the typewriter was introduced as a recording aid that improved legibility and doubled writing speeds.

In the *second phase* of machine-assisted methods, equipment was invented which could *combine* certain processing steps in a single operation. Machines that could calculate and print the results were first produced around 1890. They combine calculating, summarizing, and recording steps, and produce a printed tape record suitable for storing data. After World War I, accounting machines designed for special purposes (e.g., billing, retail sales, etc.) began to appear. These machines also combine steps and often contain several adding *registers* or *counters* to permit the accumulation of totals (calculation and summarization) for different classifications. For example, the supermarket cash register has separate registers to sort and total the day's sales of health items, hardware, meats, produce, and groceries.

A *third phase* has emerged in recent years. Equipment manufacturers have taken steps to ensure that small calculators and accounting machines are not made obsolete by the computer. Features of these machines are being combined with features taken from computers to create new electronic pocket-sized and desk-sized hardware. Many of these new calculators (computers?) have data-storage capability and can be instructed to automatically perform processing steps in sequence just like computers. Although these *programmable calculators* cannot yet match the speed and versatility of a computer in processing, storing, and retrieving both alphabetic and numeric data, it is becoming difficult to distinguish them from computers.

When compared with the manual processing of the late 1800s, machine-assisted manual methods have the advantages of greater speed and accuracy. However, a higher processing volume is generally required to justify equipment costs, there is some reduction in the flexibility of the processing techniques, and it is relatively more difficult to (1) correct or change data once they have entered the processing system and (2) implement changes in machine-assisted procedures.

Electromechanical Punched Card Development

Punched card methods have been in *widespread* use only since the 1930s, but the history of the punched card dates back to about the end of the American Revolution, when a French weaver named Jacquard used them to control his looms.

Although punched cards continued to be used in process control, it

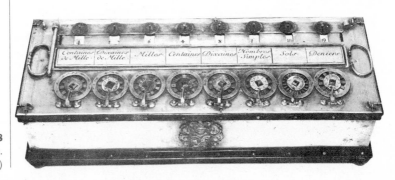

FIGURE 1-8
Pascal's adding machine.
(IBM Corp.)

was not until the use of manual methods resulted in the problem of completing the 1880 census count that they began to be considered as a medium for data processing. The inventor of modern punched card techniques was Dr. Herman Hollerith, a statistician. He was hired by the Census Bureau as a special agent to help find a solution to the census problem. In 1887, Hollerith developed his machine-readable card concept and designed a device known as the "census machine." Tabulating time with Hollerith's methods was only one-eighth of the time previously required, and so his techniques were adopted for use in the 1890 count. Although population had increased from 50 to 63 million people in the decade after 1880, the 1890 count was completed in less than three years. (Of course, this would be considered intolerably slow by today's standards,[7] but the alternative in 1890 would have been to continue the count beyond 1900 and violate the constitutional provision that congressional seats be reapportioned every 10 years on the basis of census data.)

After the 1890 census, Hollerith converted his equipment to business use and set up freight statistics systems for two railroads. In 1896 he founded the Tabulating Machine Company to make and sell his invention. Later, this firm merged with others to form what is now known as International Business Machines Corporation (IBM).

Punched card processing is based on a simple idea: Input data are initially recorded in a coded form by punching holes into cards, and these

---

[7] The 1950 census, using punched card equipment, took about two years to produce; the 1970 census yielded figures in a few months.

FIGURE 1-9
An 80-column punched card using the Hollerith coding method to represent data.

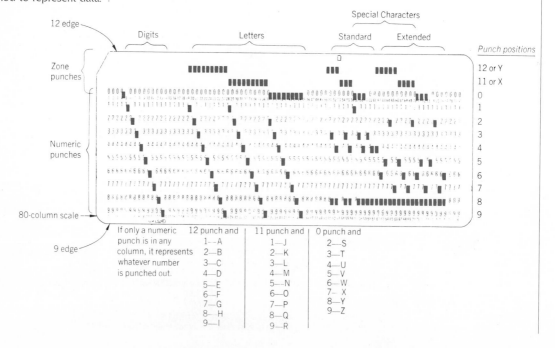

cards are then fed into machines that perform processing steps—e.g., sorting, calculating, and summarizing. The early Hollerith cards measured 3 by 5 inches; different sizes are used today, and different coding schemes are employed with modern cards containing either 80 or 96 columns.

The 80-column card This card is divided from left to right into 80 consecutively numbered vertical *columns*. These columns, in turn, have 12 horizontal positions, or *rows*. By appropriate coding, each column can record one character of information, i.e., a numerical digit, a letter, or a special character. Columns 5 to 14 in Figure 1-9 illustrate the digit punches. Notice that only a *single* hole is punched in each column to record the desired *numeral*.

When *letters* of the alphabet are recorded, *two* holes must be punched. Along the top of the card are three *zone* punching positions— the 0 row and the blank area at the top of the card, which are designated as punching positions 11 and 12 (or as areas X and Y). A logical combination of zone and digit punches is required for letters in the Hollerith code. For example, letters A to I are coded by using a 12-zone punch and digit punches 1 to 9. Special characters are coded by using one, two, or three holes.

The 96-column card The card shown in Figure 1-10 is only one-third the size of the traditional 80-column card just described. The 96 columns are separated into three sections (columns 1 to 32 are in the upper section, columns 33 to 64 are in the middle, and columns 65 to 96 are in the lower section). The upper third of the card contains positions for the printing of characters.

Differences other than mere size and the number and arrangement of columns exist between 80- and 96-column cards. One significant dif-

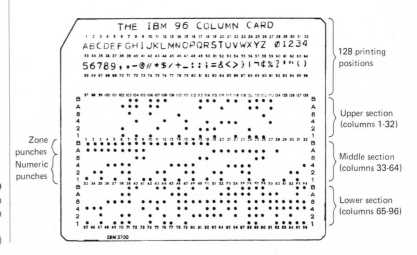

FIGURE 1-10
A 96-column card using an "8-4-2-1" coding approach to represent data.
(IBM Corp.)

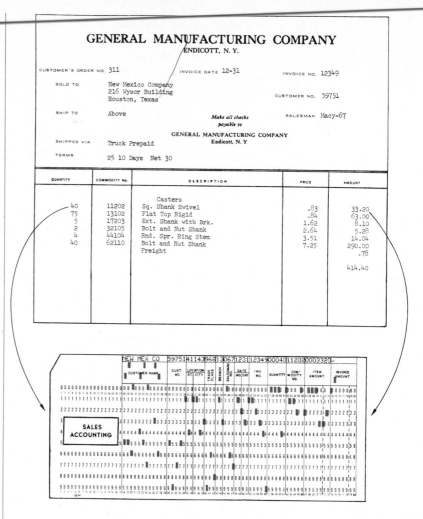

FIGURE 1-11
A commercial application
using punched cards.
(IBM Corp.)

ference is in the information-coding methods employed. The rows of the small card are divided into A and B zone positions and 1, 2, 4, and 8 numeric positions.[8] Columns 60 to 69 in Figure 1-10 illustrate the coding of digits. The numeral 1 is represented by a single hole punched in the 1 row of column 61. Column 62 codes the numeral 2. But in columns 63, 65, 66, 67, and 69, the numerals are represented by the *sum* of the rows punched; e.g., in column 67 the digit 7 is represented by holes punched in the 4, 2, and 1 rows.

Alphabetic characters are represented by combinations of holes punched in the zone and numeric rows. The nine letters A to I, for example, are coded by holes punched in the A and B rows plus the combina-

---

[8] We shall have more to say in Chap. 5 about this *binary coded decimal* (BCD) method of data representation.

tion of holes used to represent the numerals 1 to 9. To illustrate, G, the seventh letter, is coded by holes in the A and B zone positions plus the combination of holes in rows 1, 2, and 4, which add to seven (see column 39 in Figure 1-10). The special characters represented in columns 70 to 96 are coded by various combinations of holes punched in the six rows.

How are these cards used? Thank you for asking. Card columns are laid out for specific purposes in consecutive groups called *fields*. Fields are carefully planned by the application designer and may be of any width from 1 to 80 (or 96) columns.[9] To illustrate, Figure 1-11 shows the use of a card and fields in a commercial application. In this example, a customer invoice (the detailed description of what has been shipped) serves as the source document for the sales accounting card. The card is divided into 11 fields. The *item amount* field is seven columns wide, which means that the maximum amount that can be recorded is $99,999.99 (columns are not used to punch the dollar sign, comma, and decimal point).

Punched card equipment Several punched card machines are needed to perform the typical processing steps shown in Figure 1-12.[10] The most common way of *recording* data in cards is through the use of a keypunch or *card punch* machine. When a key is depressed, the correct combination of holes is produced in the card. (Should you need to punch some computer program and/or data cards, the operation of a card punch machine is discussed in Appendix A at the back of the book.) To check keypunching accuracy, *verifiers* are used. The verifier is similar to the keypunch, but instead of punching holes, it merely senses whether the holes in the card being tested correspond with the key being depressed. In some machines, keypunching and verifying are combined.

Sorters and *collators,* as you might expect, are devices for *sorting and arranging* cards. Putting the cards in some desired order or sequence is the job of the sorter. There are as many pockets in the sorter as there are rows in the card being processed; there may also be a reject pocket for cards that do not belong in any other pocket. *Sorting* (which generally moves from the right column to the left column of the data field) is done *one* column at a time in each sorting *pass.* Thus, the sorting procedure in a data field of 5 digits would take five passes before the cards would be in the proper numerical *sequence.*

The *collator* is a machine that can combine two decks of sequenced cards into a single sequenced deck (*merging*). It can also compare agree-

FIGURE 1-12
Steps in punched card data processing.

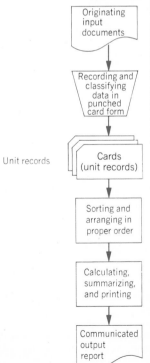

Unit records

Originating input documents

Recording and classifying data in punched card form

Cards (unit records)

Sorting and arranging in proper order

Calculating, summarizing, and printing

Communicated output report

---

[9] It should be emphasized that judgment and compromises are required in determining field width. For example, a 15-column employee name field would be satisfactory in most cases—until the personnel department hires Agamemnon Southwesterfield. Mr. Southwesterfield may then discover when he receives his first paycheck that "the computer" has butchered his name. Of course, the computer is not at fault. Rather, the problem lies with the field design.

[10] A punched card is often referred to as a *unit record* because data recorded in most cards deal with only one transaction. Electromechanical punched card machines that perform the steps shown in Figure 1-12 are sometimes referred to as *unit record equipment.*

ment between two sets of cards without combining them (matching). Other manipulations are possible with two decks of sequenced cards. The collator can check a tray of cards to determine correct ascending or descending order. After the arrangement of the cards in the proper order, they are usually then taken to a machine that can perform calculations on the data.

The *calculator* is directed in its operation by an externally wired control panel. It reads data from input cards; performs (according to the wiring arrangements in the control panel) the arithmetic operations of addition, subtraction, multiplication, and division; and punches the results into (1) the input card that supplied the data or (2) a following card.

The *accounting machine,* or *tabulator,* is used to *summarize* data from input cards and print the desired reports. It can add and subtract during summarization and has several registers or counters for this purpose. Finally, the *reproducer* is used to duplicate the data found in a large number of cards; it is also used for *gangpunching,* i.e., copying data from a master card into any number of blank cards, and for punching the holes in mark-sensed cards.

From this very brief survey of punched card data processing, it is obvious that significant improvement was possible over the manual methods previously used. Gains in speed and accuracy were made. Punched card equipment proved effective in performing many of the individual steps necessary, e.g., sorting, calculating, and summarizing. But as the level of equipment sophistication increased, processing procedures tended to become more rigorously defined and standardized. It was still necessary to have people handle trays of cards between each step. Separate machines must be fed, started, and stopped. *This limited intercommunication between processing stages requiring manual intervention is a major disadvantage.* With the computer this disadvantage is eliminated; no manual interference between data input and information output is required. What sets the computer apart from any other type of data processing machine is the concept of storing, within the machine itself, alterable instructions that will direct the machine to perform automatically the necessary processing steps. Let us now, in the remainder of this chapter, look at the history and development of the computer.

Computer Development

In 1833, Charles Babbage, Lucasian Professor of Mathematics at Cambridge University in England, proposed a machine, which he named the "analytical engine." Babbage was an eccentric and colorful individual[12]

Question: What do you think is the greatest feat of the invention of the computer? Answer: "I didn't think it has feat, but when I think about it I would say the right foot is the strongest and greatest."[11]

[11] Eve R. Wirth, "Out of the Mouths of Babes," *Creative Computing,* p. 10, November/December 1977.

[12] He was also something of a literary critic. In "The Vision of Sin," Tennyson wrote: "Every moment dies a man/Every moment one is born." Babbage wrote Tennyson and pointed out to the poet that since the population of the world was increasing, it would be more accurate to have the verse read: "Every moment dies a man/Every moment one and one-sixteenth is born." What he lacked in aesthetic taste he compensated for with mathematical precision!

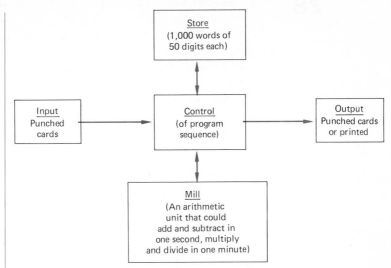

FIGURE 1-13
Babbage's analytical engine
concept.

who spent much of his life working in vain to build his machine. Babbage's dream—to many of his contemporaries it was "Babbage's folly"—would have incorporated a punched card input; a memory unit, or *store;* an arithmetic unit, or *mill;* automatic printout; sequential program control; and 20-place accuracy (see Figure 1-13). In short, Babbage had designed a machine that was a prototype computer and that was 100 years ahead of its time. After Babbage's death in 1871, little progress was made until 1937.

Beginning in 1937, Harvard professor Howard Aiken set out to build an automatic calculating machine that would combine established technology with the punched cards of Hollerith. With the help of graduate students and IBM engineers, the project was completed in 1944. The completed device was known as the Mark I digital computer. (A *digital* computer is one that essentially does counting operations.) Internal operations were controlled automatically with electromagnetic relays; arithmetic counters were mechanical. The Mark I was thus not an *electronic* computer but was rather an *electromechanical* one. In many respects the Mark I was the realization of Babbage's dream. Appropriately, this "medieval" machine is now on display at Harvard University.

The first *electronic* digital computer to be put into full operation was built as a secret wartime project between 1939 and 1946 at the University of Pennsylvania's Moore School of Electrical Engineering. The team of J. Presper Eckert, Jr., and John W. Mauchly was responsible for its construction. However, as was later determined by a federal judge in an important patent suit, "Eckert and Mauchly did not themselves first invent the automatic electronic digital computer, but instead derived that subject matter from one Dr. John Vincent Atanasoff." (Atanasoff was a professor of physics and mathematics at Iowa State College, and did his most important computer work between 1935 and 1942, at which time he stopped work on his prototype and left Iowa State to work at the Naval Ordnance Laboratory.)

Vacuum tubes (19,000 of them!) were used in place of relays in the Eckert-Mauchly machine. This computer was called ENIAC and could do 300 multiplications per second (making it 300 times faster than any other device of the day).[13] Operating instructions for ENIAC were not stored internally; rather, they were fed through externally located plugboards and switches. In 1959, ENIAC was placed in the Smithsonian Institution.

In 1946, in collaboration with H. H. Goldstine and A. W. Burks, John von Neumann, a mathematical genius and member of the Institute for Advanced Study in Princeton, New Jersey, suggested in a paper that (1) *binary* numbering systems be used in building computers and (2) computer *instructions* as well as the *data* being manipulated could be stored internally in the machine. These suggestions became a basic part of the philosophy of computer design. The binary numbering system is represented by only 2 digits (0 and 1) rather than the 10 digits (0 to 9) of the familiar decimal system. Since electronic components are typically in one of two conditions ("on" or "off," conducting or not conducting, magnetized or not magnetized), the binary concept facilitated equipment design.

Although these design concepts came too late to be incorporated in ENIAC, Mauchly, Eckert, and others at the University of Pennsylvania set out to build a machine with stored-program capability. This machine—the EDVAC—was not completed until several years later. To the EDSAC, finished in 1949 at Cambridge University, must go the distinction of being the first *stored-program electronic* computer.

One reason for the delay in EDVAC was that Eckert and Mauchly founded their own company in 1946 and began to work on the UNIVAC. In 1949, Remington Rand acquired the Eckert-Mauchly Computer Corporation, and in early 1951, the first UNIVAC-1 became operational at the Census Bureau. In 1963, it too was retired to the Smithsonian Institution —a historical relic after just 12 years! The first computer acquired for data processing and record keeping by a *business organization* was another UNIVAC-1, which was installed in 1954 at General Electric's Appliance Park in Louisville, Kentucky.[14]

In the period from 1954 to 1959, many organizations acquired computers for data processing purposes, even though these *first-generation*

---

[13] William Shanks, an Englishman, spent 20 years of his life computing π to 707 decimal places. In 1949, ENIAC computed π to 2,000 places in just over 70 hours and showed that Shanks had made an error in the 528th decimal place. Fortunately, Shanks was spared the knowledge that he had been both slow and inaccurate, for he preceded ENIAC by 100 years. In 1967, π was computed to 500,000 decimal places in 28 hours. If you want some dull reading, get a copy of the report published by the Commissariat a l'Energie Atomique in Paris that lists these digit values!

[14] The IBM 650 first saw service in Boston in December 1954. It was an all-purpose, comparatively inexpensive machine, and it was widely accepted. It gave IBM the leadership in computer production in 1955.

machines had been designed for scientific uses. Administrators generally considered the computer to be an accounting tool, and the first applications were designed to process routine tasks such as payrolls. Unfortunately, in most cases little or no attempt was made to modify and redesign existing accounting procedures in order to produce more effective information. The potential of the computer was consistently underestimated; more than a few were acquired for no other reason than prestige.

But we should not judge the early users of electronic data processing too harshly. They were pioneering in the use of a new tool not designed specifically for their needs; they had to staff their computer installations with a new breed of workers; and they initially had to cope with the necessity of preparing programs in a tedious machine language. In spite of these obstacles, the computer was found to be a fast, accurate, and untiring processor of mountains of paper.

The computers of the *second generation* were introduced around 1959 to 1960 and were made smaller, faster, and with greater computing capacity. The vacuum tube, with its relatively short life, gave way to compact *solid state* components such as diodes and transistors. Unlike earlier computers, some second-generation machines were designed from the beginning with nonscientific processing requirements in mind.

In 1964, IBM ushered in the *third generation* of computing hardware when it announced its System/360 family of computers. And during the early 1970s, several manufacturers introduced new equipment lines. For example, IBM announced the first models of its System/370 line of computers. These machines continued the trend toward miniaturization of circuit components. Further improvements in speed, cost, and storage capacity were realized. In the next chapter we shall look in more detail at some of the recent developments in computer technology.

The computer industry In 1950, the developers of the first computers agreed that 8 or 10 of these machines would satisfy the entire demand for such devices for years to come. Of course, we now know that this was a monumental forecasting blunder; in fact, it must go down in history as one of the worst market estimates of all time! By 1956, over 600 general-purpose computer systems (worth about $350 million) had been installed by *organizations* in the United States; today, such general-purpose installations are numbered in the hundreds of thousands,[15] and this does not count the additional hundreds of thousands of very small personal computers that *individuals* have recently installed in their homes. Thus,

---

[15] Nobody knows the exact number or present value of these computer systems because many computer manufacturers do not officially release installation data. Since there are disagreements in present estimates, it is not surprising that there are large variances in future expectations. For example, the president of one of the large computer industry firms puts the estimate of the installed value of general-purpose systems in 1980 at more than *$90 billion.* But an expert at a leading consulting firm places the figure in 1981 at "only" $70 billion to $75 billion. In either case, the numbers are huge and there are no immediate signs of market saturation in the computer industry.

the theme of a recent computer conference—"Computers . . . by the millions, for the millions"—now characterizes the size and scope of the computer industry.

There are dozens of computer manufacturers. Many small firms specialize in assembling small scientific and/or process-control machines, or produce the even smaller personal computers used by individuals. Although the largest manufacturers often produce computers that are quite small, much of their effort in the past was devoted to supplying organizations with families of larger computers. Of the larger companies, most were initially business-machine manufacturers (IBM, Burroughs Corporation, Sperry UNIVAC, and NCR Corporation), or they manufactured electronic controls (Honeywell). Exceptions are Control Data Corporation and Digital Equipment Corporation, which were founded to produce computers. The industry leader is IBM. This giant has annual revenues of over $20 billion and has at least 50 percent of the entire market.

In spite of the economic health of the computer industry as a whole, however, more than a few firms were unable to compete profitably in certain segments of the market in the 1970s. Some of the more notable "dropouts" were General Electric, Xerox, and RCA. There have also been numerous antitrust suits and countersuits involving various manufacturers, IBM, and the federal government in the 1970s.

Computer size categories   The first computers were all large enough to store grain in: ENIAC occupied about 1,500 square feet of floor space. But today's machines vary in physical size from large machines to machines the size of a small coin. In terms of relative computing power and cost, some of today's systems are rather arbitrarily classified as *micro-sized* or *mini-sized*. In addition, a number of firms produce families of computers that are arbitrarily classified as *small, medium,* or *large*. We will examine these computer size categories in greater detail in Chapter 6, but perhaps it is appropriate here to introduce you briefly to some representative models.

A *microprocessor* is assembled from tens of thousands of tiny transistors, resistors, and other electronic components to perform the arithmetic and logic functions of a computer. The typical microprocessor is fabricated on a single tiny chip of silicon and is combined with other elements that provide input/output connections, storage, and control to form a complete *microcomputer* on a board that may be smaller than this page (see Figure 1-14). Microcomputers are general-purpose processors that may perform the same operations and use the same program instructions as much larger computers. They began to appear in quantity in 1973. Although they are relatively slow in operation and have relatively limited data-handling capabilities, these computers are being used for a rapidly expanding number of applications. For example, they are commonly used to provide control and intelligence functions in automobiles and in some of the peripheral devices used with larger computer systems. There are also hundreds of thousands of them in the *personal com-*

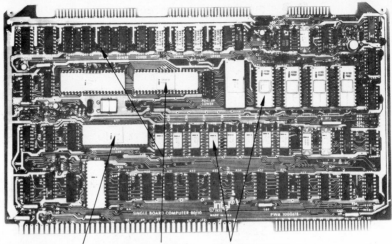

Microprocessing element (see Figure 2-1 for a magnified view of the circuitry)

Input/output connections and components

Computer storage elements

FIGURE 1-14

Complete microcomputer on a single board. (*Intel Corp.*)

puting systems designed for the use and entertainment of individual owners (see Figure 1-15). Microcomputers range in price from a few hundred to a few thousand dollars, depending on the type and number of input/output devices used and the amount of storage capacity obtained.

Minicomputers (Figure 1-16) are small machines, but there is no clear-cut distinction between the largest microcomputers and the smallest minis on the one hand, or between the larger minis and small-scale family models on the other. As a rough guide, however, minicomputers typically cost between $2,500 and $75,000, usually weigh less than 50 pounds, and may be plugged into any standard electrical outlet. Minicomputers perform the same arithmetic-logic functions, use several of the same programming languages, and have many of the same circuitry features of larger computers. Although they are general-purpose devices, some are used for special or dedicated purposes such as controlling a machine tool or a process (see Figure 1-17). Others are (1) used for business data processing purposes, (2) connected to larger computers to act as input/output (I/O) and message-switching devices, (3) used in school systems for educational purposes, and (4) used in laboratories for purposes of scientific computation. The versatility of minicomputers, combined with their low cost, accounts for their rapid acceptance.

Small-scale models in computer families come in a bewildering range of configurations and capabilities (see Figure 1-18). Some are desk-sized, are designed specifically to meet the data processing requirements of small organizations, and are similar in basic capabilities to minicomputers. Some small models are the punched card-oriented successors to electromechanical punched card installations. However, most small computers

User keyboard

Storage devices used to interpret user's instructions to computer (not accessible to user)

Z-80 microprocessor chip

User-accessible storage

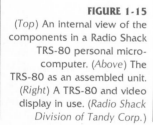

FIGURE 1-15
(*Top*) An internal view of the components in a Radio Shack TRS-80 personal micro-computer. (*Above*) The TRS-80 as an assembled unit. (*Right*) A TRS-80 and video display in use. (*Radio Shack Division of Tandy Corp.*)

FIGURE 1-16
Two minicomputers. (*Data General Corp.*)

FIGURE 1-17
Minicomputer used in process control. (*Digital Equipment Corp.*)

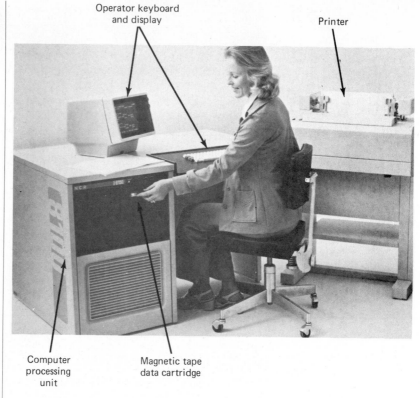

Operator keyboard and display

Printer

Computer processing unit

Magnetic tape data cartridge

Magnetic disk drives

Console visual display unit

Computer console

Central processor

Punched card equipment

Printer

FIGURE 1-18
Small-scale computer models.
(*Above NCR Corp; Right
Sperry UNIVAC Div., Sperry
Rand Corp.; Opposite
Wang Labs.*)

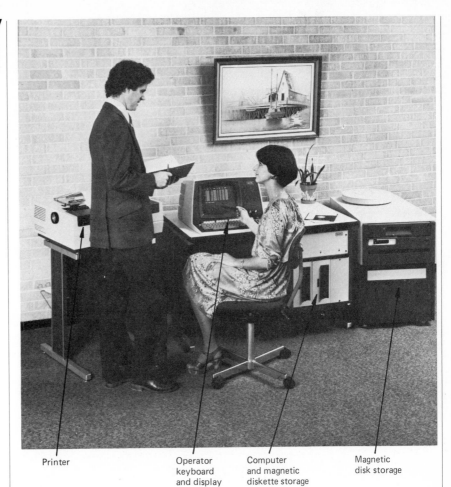

Printer   Operator   Computer   Magnetic
           keyboard   and magnetic   disk storage
           and display   diskette storage

now use magnetic tapes and magnetic disks as data-storage media. Given the wide range of capabilities and the large number of configurations possible, it is not surprising that the prices for these systems may range from $20,000 to $200,000.

Medium-sized computers (see Figure 1-19) may sell for $200,000 to $1 million, and *larger systems* (see Figure 1-20) exceed this price range. In return for higher prices, users receive faster processing speeds, greater storage capacity, wider selection of optional equipment, and a lower cost-per-calculation figure.[16]

---

[16] This assumes that the volume of work is sufficient to keep a large machine occupied. If a person can compute the answer to a multiplication problem in one minute, and there are 125 million such problems to be solved, the total cost to do the calculations manually would exceed $10 million. The UNIVAC 1 (which in terms of computing power is a very small machine by today's standards) could have done the job for $4,300. However, a large machine today that rents for over $100,000 per month could do the job for less than $4.

Magnetic
disk storage

Punched
card
equipment

Printer

Computer
processing
unit

Operator console
keyboard

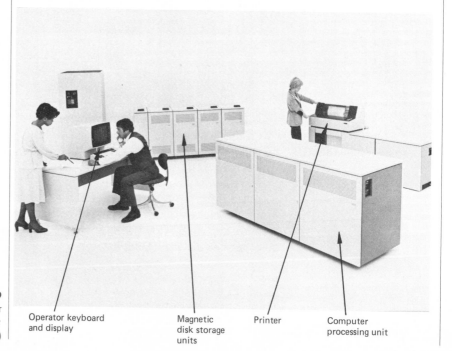

FIGURE 1-19
Medium-sized computer
models. (*Above Honeywell;
Right IBM Corp.*)

Operator keyboard
and display

Magnetic
disk storage
units

Printer

Computer
processing unit

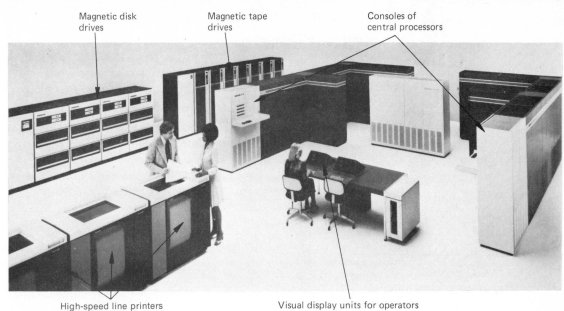

Magnetic disk drives

Magnetic tape drives

Consoles of central processors

High-speed line printers

Visual display units for operators

FIGURE 1-20
Large-scale computer installation. (*Burroughs Corp.*)

"Managing Information"

The Commission on Federal Paperwork has proposed a broad-based approach to managing data-information management resources. This is the total application of systems, methods, techniques and controls to the management of a very special but costly resource . . . information.

Data provides a basis from which information is derived and for quantitative analysis; information assembled by compiling, manipulating and massaging data provides a qualitative basis for decision-making.

Management resources have often been described as the three M's—manpower, money and materials. Information can be considered a fourth resource because it has the attributes of a physical resource:

- **It has value like money, raw materials or manpower.**
- **It has characteristics which make it measurable in terms of use, life and effect on other resources.**
- **It can be valued in terms of collecting, storing, retrieving.**
- **It can be budgeted and controlled.**
- **It can be related in terms of cost and use value to management objectives.**

Why Manage Information?

One of the major problems confronting government, industry and the public today is the constantly accelerating demand for data and information. New technologies provide for rapid manipulation and massive storage of data, but it is the individual who must generate data in the first place and who, consequently, uses it.

The insatiable appetite for data and information is whetted by three major stimuli: specific legislative and regulatory requirements, legal needs and administrative determinations. The latter factor can be tagged as a major cause of the paperwork explosion. The first two are not without blame, however, as witness the efforts of such bodies as the Commission on Federal Paperwork to identify and reduce the paperwork burden imposed by government.

Modern technology has aided in opening the floodgates of information. In most cases, technology does not question the value of information flowing through the conduits and pipelines, but is concerned with moving more information and moving it faster. Who questions the need? Information resources management is the best way.

There are three important compelling reasons for a total management approach to information. The first is to eliminate waste. Second is to insure information availability. Third is to detect imposed burdens. Paperwork can be evidence of work performed, often a symptom of unnecessary work; paperwork is the tip of the iceberg.

Information resources management is applicable to any organization generating, acquiring and using information. The concept is applicable to both government and industry.

Critical and highly-specialized information requirements do not exclude specialty recording areas from a total information management approach. To the contrary, these requirements reinforce the need for this approach. There are many specialty areas where the data/information are subject to unique generating and using requirements. For example, nuclear quality assurance records, medical records, aerospace records, product liability records and, without exception, the data and information in these systems have exceptionally high values as resources.

Information resources management fits the technology to the need, not the product to the technology. Requirements are carefully measured before the system is designed and the design is completed before the techniques and hardware are selected.

Source: Edward N. Johnson, "What Are We Managing and Why?" *Information Manager,* pp. 8–9, December 1978. Reprinted with permission of the publisher.

The following points have been emphasized in this chapter:

1   A computer is a fast electronic symbol-manipulating device that is able to follow an intellectual map, or program. Clever programs prepared by humans often yield impressive results, but flawed maps (also prepared by humans) can sometimes lead to unwanted consequences.

2   As computer applications are expanded in the years ahead, there will be the possibility of widespread benefits for our society. There will also be the danger that designers of computer systems may create applications that depersonalize us, subject us to fraud, and pry into our private lives. You and others in our society should acquire an understanding of computers so that you can discuss and help shape the future impact computers are likely to have on all of us.

3   Data are the input from which information output is produced, and they are obtained from both internal and external sources. The data processing operation consists of input, manipulation, and output activities. There are nine possible steps in these activities; however, some steps may be omitted in specific situations.

4   Information is needed by individuals and members of organizations to make the most effective personal and organizational decisions possible.

5   This needed information should be accurate, timely, complete, concise, and relevant. Computers can help produce information with these desirable characteristics.

6   Data processing techniques have been undergoing evolutionary change since the beginning of the human race. This evolution has advanced through four stages, from manual methods to the development of the computer. However, none of these stages should be considered obsolete, for each has its place.

▶ | KEY TERMS

After reading Chapter 1, you should be able to define and use the following terms:

computer	verifier
program (intellectual map)	sorter
data	data processing operations
information	collator
input	tabulator

41

processing
output
punched card
Hollerith code
field
card punch

ENIAC
microprocessor
microcomputer
minicomputer
personal computer

▸ REVIEW AND DISCUSSION QUESTIONS

1 (a) What is a computer? (b) How can a computer be portrayed as having human or superhuman characteristics in one magazine article and as being stupid or inhuman in another?

2 Why should you study computers?

3 The chapter gave eight examples of how you might come in contact with computer systems in a typical day. Identify and discuss five other possible examples.

4 (a) What is information? (b) What is the difference between data and information? (c) Compare the manufacturing process with the information-producing process.

5 Identify and explain the sources of data.

6 (a) Identify and explain the basic data processing steps. (b) What processing methods may be used to perform these steps?

7 "Information is the cement that holds together any organization." Explain this sentence.

8 Identify and discuss the desired properties of information.

9 How can computers help produce information that is accurate, timely, and complete?

10 The figure below shows the typical total-cost relationships between computer processing methods and alternative methods. (a) Discuss the meanings of points A, B, and C in the figure. (b) "The total cost for computer processing may exceed that for other methods when

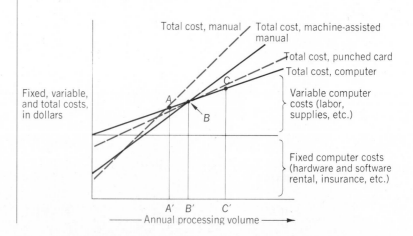

the processing volume is small." Discuss this statement. (c) Discuss the meanings of A', B', and C' in the figure.

11 (a) Why was Dr. Herman Hollerith hired by the U.S. Census Bureau? (b) What were the results of his work?

12 Describe the 80-column punched card and the Hollerith code.

13 Describe the 96-column punched card and the coding employed.

14 (a) What is a field? (b) Give an example of how field design may create problems for people.

15 (a) What was the analytical engine? (b) What features would it have had in common with modern computers?

16 (a) What was the Mark I? (b) Was it an electronic computer?

17 (a) What was the ENIAC? (b) Why was it built? (c) How did it differ from the Mark I?

18 What important contributions to computer design were proposed by John von Neumann?

19 (a) What is a microcomputer? (b) How does a microcomputer differ from a large computer?

20 After a survey of a computer center available to you, identify: (a) the hardware generation of the equipment, (b) the approximate value of the center equipment, (c) the names of firms supplying equipment, programs, and supplies to the center, (d) the size category of the center's computer (or computers), (e) the services offered by the center to its customers.

Chapter 2
TECHNOLOGICAL CHANGE AND THE INFORMATION REVOLUTION

In this chapter you will first see how technological developments can produce a wave of social and economic changes. The latest technology will generally be exploited by those who see opportunity in its use, but not everyone may benefit from this action.

In addition, you will also learn how microelectronic circuit technology is effecting revolutionary changes in the size, speed, cost, storage capacity, and reliability of modern computing hardware. After studying some of the developments that have taken place in computer software, you will then see how computer technology has been applied to produce new information systems that provide decision makers with more timely and complete information than was possible with earlier systems.

Finally, you will be introduced to some of the problems facing society as we attempt to adapt to the information revolution.

Thus, after studying this chapter you should be able to:

- Explain why technological changes may simultaneously create new opportunities and new problems.
- Discuss the revolutionary changes that have occurred recently in the development of computer hardware.
- Identify three categories of computer software and discuss the developments that have occurred in each.
- Describe the characteristics (both positive and negative) of information systems that utilize quick-response and data-base concepts to produce information.
- Identify some of the problems of adjustment affecting organizations and individuals as part of the information revolution.
- Understand and use the key terms listed at the end of the chapter.

History records, in a relatively unfavorable light, periods in which the tempo of change has diminished. For example, we are told that during the centuries known as the Dark Ages following the fall of the Roman Empire, an attempt to preserve the status quo against change was made by European political and religious leaders.

It can hardly be said today that the tempo of change has diminished. Rather, we are witnessing rapid technological[1] changes taking place more

---

[1] *Technology* may be defined as the organization and application of knowledge to achieve practical purposes.

quickly and over a broader front than ever before in history. These changes are threatening to sweep aside many current (and sometimes comfortable) practices, open many new opportunities, and create many new problems for social institutions such as schools, hospitals, governments, and businesses. Such results are possible because contemporary technology is producing tools that are more powerful than any heretofore developed, and the use of these new tools often leads to pervasive social and economic changes—and problems.[2]

A basic challenge to leaders and educated citizens in the next few years will be to foresee and manage (and not be swept along by) the flood of technologically induced change that will face organizations and individuals, and to do this within a democratic framework for the benefit of society. If we are to control these forces of change, we must first acquire some understanding of how technology affects society. And if we are to cope with accelerating change, we must have higher-quality information for decision making. Thus, in the remainder of this chapter, we will first consider some basic background concepts associated with *technological change* and *social change*. We will then examine the revolutionary developments in *computer technology* and *information systems* which may make better information possible. Finally, we will conclude with a brief preview of some of the *problems of adjustment* that are accompanying the information revolution.

TECHNOLOGICAL CHANGE AND SOCIAL CHANGE

The ancient Greeks were obsessed with several dreams. One was the Promethean dream of stealing fire from the gods; another was the dream of soaring away from the earth and beyond the planets. Of course, these ancient dreams remained unrealized for thousands of years. Yet in a span of less than 40 years, both dreams have now been achieved. The fires of atomic furnaces have been ignited, humans have moved out into space, and our machines have traveled beyond the planets.[3] In addition, microbiologists have learned how to combine bits of genetic material from one organism onto the genes of another species, and this recombinant DNA research has rekindled the ancient dream of learning the divine secrets of the creation of life itself.

---

[2] Even those who develop the new tools are often surprised (and sometimes dismayed) at the unexpected changes and problems their work creates. We have seen, for example, how the developers of the first computers thought that 8 or 10 of their "big" models would satisfy the entire demand for such devices. Obviously, the opportunities and dangers associated with computer usage, which will be presented in later chapters, were completely unforseen.

[3] Without computers (and without the microelectronic circuits made possible by the research conducted by military and space agencies and by computer manufacturers) much, if not most, of the technological progress of the past decade would not have been possible. Certainly, without the nearly 200 computers of the NASA Apollo System, man could not have journeyed to the moon.

A wave of social and economic changes often follows in the wake of new technological developments. For example, a new technology may create the opportunity to improve on a process or do something that was previously not possible. When such a development occurs, there will usually be people who will seek to take advantage of the new opportunity, even though changes in the ways individuals and groups are organized may then be necessary. And these newly organized groups may then compete for economic resources with established units. Thus, gains achieved by new groups in utilizing the new technology may create economic losses and personal problems for those who are using older tools and techniques.

With the development of the automobile, for example, came a new industry and the creation of millions of new jobs. But buggy manufacturers were virtually eliminated, and their employees were displaced. Automobiles increased our mobility and freedom over the years, and people were employed to build the suburbs made possible by individual transportation. However, many sections of older central cities fell into decay. Property values in these sections dropped, and the economic resources available to the public transportation organizations serving these sections declined and their equipment deteriorated. In summary, as the development of the automobile has illustrated, both positive and negative social and economic effects may be expected when significant technological changes occur.

How do people react to significant technological change? History tells us that in some extreme cases workers wrecked the latest machines when their jobs were threatened. (Looms and knitting machines were destroyed by workers in Europe in the 1700s.) But these destructive acts had no lasting effect on technological innovation; over the years such innovation came to be accepted as a fact of life and as the source of progress. It still is, but in recent years some of the negative effects of supersonic transport planes and nuclear power plants have been the subject of concerned public debate. One result of this debate has been a growing public uncertainty about technological matters in general. In fact, Charles Dickens might well have been describing our contemporary reactions in *Tale of Two Cities:*

> It was the best of times, it was the worst of times, it was the age of wisdom, it was the age of foolishness, it was the epoch of belief, it was the epoch of incredulity, it was the season of Light, it was the season of Darkness, it was the spring of hope, it was the winter of despair, we had everything before us, we had nothing before us, we were all going direct to Heaven, we were all going direct the other way. . . .

Optimists may now see technology as the unblemished blessing that will lead us to the "best of times"; pessimists may now view it as the unbridled curse that is leading us to the "worst of times." The truth, of course, lies somewhere between these extremes. It would be most unfortunate if pessimistic attitudes resulted in the failure of society to use technology to solve potentially solvable problems—e.g., to find economic alternatives to the use of fossil fuels for the nonpolluting energy we need. But it would be equally unfortunate if an uncritical belief in the benefits of technology permitted the introduction of processes that would threaten the beauty and balance of nature.

As was true of the automobile, developments in computer technology will inevitably lead to momentous changes in society. Consider the following comments:

> The modern technology of microelectronics, and in particular the advent of the microprocessor, has been compared with the Industrial Revolution. The comparison is a very good one, for not since the nineteenth century have the world's industrial societies been faced with such a profound technical development. Over the next decade the microprocessor can and will provide the world with marvellous gadgets, and with facilities for communication, medicine and leisure previously only dreamed of by science fiction writers. But it will also cause social change, with great local disturbances in employment, social attitudes and industrial stability.[4]

> The miracle chip represents a quantum leap in the technology of mankind, a development that over the past few years has acquired the force and significance associated with the development of hand tools or the discovery of the steam engine. Just as the Industrial Revolution took over an immense range of tasks from men's muscles and enormously expanded productivity, so the microcomputer is rapidly assuming huge burdens of drudgery from the human brain and thereby expanding the mind's capacities in ways that man has only begun to grasp.[5]

Do such opinions presage a "spring of hope" or a "winter of despair"? This question is explored in Part 4. For now, let us consider the rapid improvements taking place in computer technology.

REVOLUTION IN COMPUTER TECHNOLOGY

New discoveries in the fields of electronics and physics are being applied quickly in the development of new computer hardware. Computer *hardware* consists of all the machines that make up a functioning computer system. Basically, these machines accept data input, store data, perform calculations and other processing steps, and prepare information output.

Hardware alone, however, is merely one or more boxes of electronic parts that represent an expense; an equally important (perhaps more important) consideration in the effective use of computers is the *software*. *Software* is the name given to the multitude of instructions, i.e., the name given to *programs* and *routines,* that have been written to cause the hardware to function in a desired way. Let us now look briefly at the technological advances in computer hardware and software.

[4] Stephen Forte, "Microelectronics in a Nutshell," *Personnel Management,* p. 26, May 1979.
[5] "The Age of Miracle Chips," *Time,* p. 44, February 20, 1978.

Hardware Developments

Technological development of hardware has been incredibly rapid, as may be seen by an examination of the factors of (1) *size*, (2) *speed*, (3) *cost*, (4) *information storage capacity*, and (5) *reliability*. And as Table 2-1 shows, the past trends in these factors are likely to continue through the 1980s.

Size   Second-generation computers were much smaller than their predecessors because transistors and other smaller components replaced tubes. As you can see in Table 2-1, this size reduction continues unchecked today. It is now possible through *large-scale integration* (LSI) of electronic circuits (see Figure 2-1) to pack billions of *circuits* in a cubic foot of space. Furthermore, each circuit contains a number of separate components. Since 1965, in fact, the average number of components per advanced integrated circuit chip has doubled each year. Thus, by the time you read this sentence, chips may contain the equivalent of several million components.[6]

[6] As the president of the company that produces the chip shown in Figure 2-1 has noted, "An individual integrated circuit on a chip perhaps a quarter of an inch square now can embrace more electronic elements than the most complex piece of electronic equipment that could be built in 1950. Today's microcomputer, at a cost of perhaps $300, has more computing capacity than the first large electronic computer, ENIAC. It is 20 times faster, has a larger memory, is thousands of times more reliable, consumes the power of a light bulb rather than that of a locomotive, occupies $1/_{30,000}$ the volume and costs $1/_{10,000}$ as much." See Robert N. Noyce, "Microelectronics," *Scientific American,* pp. 63–69, September 1977.

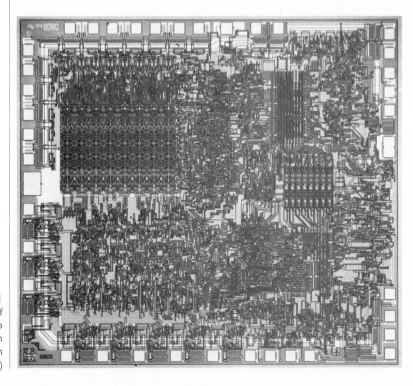

FIGURE 2-1
A greatly magnified view of the Intel microprocessor chip shown as one element on the microcomputer board in Figure 1-14. (*Intel Corp.*)

TABLE 2-1
Summary of hardware developments

Hardware Development Factors	1950	1960	1970	1975	1980s
Size factor:					
Number of circuits per cubic foot	1,000	100,000	10 million	1 billion	Many billions
Speed factor:					
Time to execute an instruction in the central processor	300 microseconds	5 microseconds	80 nanoseconds	25 nanoseconds	5 nanoseconds or less
Cost factors:					
Cost (in cents) to process 1 million basic computer instructions	2,800	100	2	.1	Less than .01
Cost (in cents) to provide storage for one binary number in the central processor	261	85	5	.1	Less than .01
Storage capacity factors:					
Primary storage capacity (in characters) of the central processor	20,000	120,000	1 million	10 million	Much greater than 10 million
Characters of secondary online storage		20 million	Over 100 billion	Virtually unlimited	Virtually unlimited
Reliability factor:					
Mean (average) time between failures of some central processors	Hours	Tens of hours	Hundreds of hours	Thousands of hours	Tens of thousands of hours (years)

"From Christopher Columbus to Lasers"

When Christopher Columbus set foot on the New World in 1492 he did not know where he was nor how he had gotten there. It took the world years to learn of his courageous trip and decades to readjust. When Neil Armstrong stepped upon the surface of the moon in 1969, he knew exactly where he was. He had followed a precisely preplanned journey and the entire world was watching him! In less than five hundred years man's ability to communicate had advanced from its most primitive forms to an astonishing level of sophistication.

Telegraph links, in Napoleon's time, had signal speeds of about two characters per second. The ability to combine up to six telegraph channels in one physical link came into being in 1874 with a scheme invented by Jean Maurice Emile Baudot. Two years later, Bell spoke his first sentence over the telephone. In 1913 vacuum tube repeaters were introduced in telephony. In 1918 the first carrier system permitted several voice channels to occupy a single pair of wires. High capacity coaxial cables started to replace wire-pair cables in the early 1940's; today they can carry thousands of telephone channels. Microwave radio links were first installed in 1946; they can now accommodate over 10,000 telephone channels and will carry even more in the future. The 1960's brought us communication satellites and high-speed waveguides; the 1970's may bring the lasers. In just over a hundred years, the capacity of our communications links has risen from two to more than a hundred million characters per second.

Source: Carl Hammer, "When Christopher Columbus Set Foot . . . ," *Journal of Systems Management,* p. 36, January 1979. Reprinted with permission of the publisher.

How is it possible to achieve the packing densities shown in **Figures 2-1** and **2-3**? Figure 2-4 shows the process used by one firm to produce arithmetic-logic circuit chips for large computers. Beginning in the upper left hand corner, a polished wafer is cut from a *silicon* crystal. (The silicon is obtained by melting and purifying sand.) Dozens of chips will be produced from this single wafer. During the in-process stage, several different coatings are applied to racks of wafers. Tiny masks, photographically reduced from large circuit drawings, are placed over the wafers and used to form the circuit outlines. Several times during this stage, the racks of wafers may be loaded into cylindrical ovens and heated to about 2000°F (see Figure 2-5). After this processing, a meticulous computerized probe scans and tests the wafer and marks the defective chips. A diamond cutter is then used to separate the chips. A tested chip (Figure 2-6) is then placed in a die, externally wired, and sealed. In Figure 2-4, the chip is also provided with a cooling fin to dissipate heat. After production, chips may

FIGURE 2-2
Gottfried Wilhelm Leibniz
(*The Bettmann Archive.*)

THE MAN WHO COULDN'T MULTIPLY

Gottfried Wilhelm von Leibniz was born in Leipzig in 1646. Leibniz was self-taught until he began formal schooling at age 15, when he enrolled at the University of Leipzig.

Leibniz was sent to Paris by his patron, the Archbishop of Mainz. While in Paris, he met Huygens, the most famous mathematician of the day. Leibniz's interest in mathematics led to his invention of calculus. However, he had one shortcoming. Although he learned Latin at the age of eight, he never mastered the multiplication tables as a child. To make up for this deficiency, Leibniz invented a calculating machine that could multiply and divide as well as add and subtract. Like Pascal's "arithmetic engine," Leibniz's calculator was never marketed.

After the death of his patron, Leibniz became the Duke of Brunswick's librarian in Hannover. Leibniz devoted himself to philosophy until he died in obscurity in 1716.

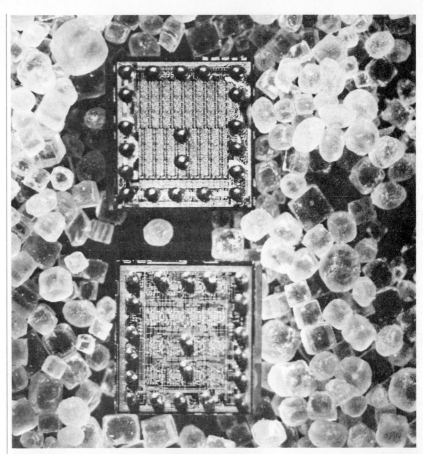

FIGURE 2-3
Magnified high-speed logic
and memory chips
surrounded by tiny particles of
common table salt. (*IBM
Corp.*)

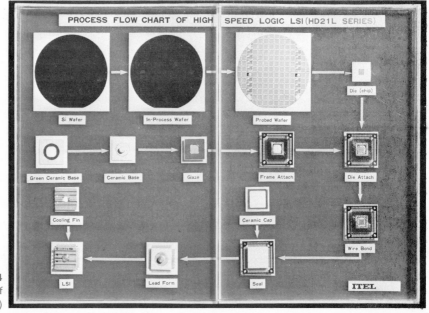

FIGURE 2-4
Steps in the production of
LSI circuit chips. (*Itel Corp.*)

FIGURE 2-5
A technician loads racks of wafers containing hundreds of chips into an oxygen furnace. (*NCR Corp.*)

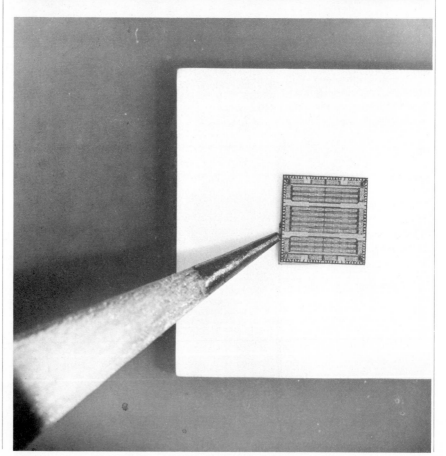

FIGURE 2-6
A tested chip awaiting external wiring. (*Itel Corp.*)

be arranged on a *single* compact board to make a microcomputer (as we saw earlier in Figures 1-14 and 1-15), or *multiple* boards may be used in mini-sized and larger machines (Figure 2-7).

Has the end to the feasible size reduction of computer circuitry been reached? Hardly. Just as yesterday's room-sized computers have been replaced by single LSI chips, so will the multiple boards that make up a large modern computer be replaced in the next decade by a single *superchip*. Through the use of *very large scale integration* (**VLSI**) techniques, it will be possible to produce circuits that are hundreds of times denser than circuits are today.[7]

Speed Circuit miniaturization has brought increased speed of operation to the latest computers. Why is this? It is because size reduction means shorter distances for electric pulses to travel, and thus processor speed has increased.

Early computer speed was expressed in *milliseconds* (thousandths of a second); second-generation speed was measured in *microseconds* (millionths of a second); and current hardware has internal operating speeds measured in *nanoseconds* (billionths of a second). Since circuit speeds are likely to be 5 times faster in 1985 than they were in 1975, future machines may have speeds measured in *picoseconds* (trillionths of a second).[8]

---

[7] One government expert notes: "It is clear that we are moving into a decade which will literally see the entire computer embedded into one or a few silicon chips, with further reductions in the size of equipment by perhaps as much as 1000 times!" See Edwin J. Istvan, "New Issues Confronting the Information Systems Planner," *Infosystems,* p. 58, June 1979.

[8] Such speeds are difficult to comprehend. For example, a spaceship traveling toward the moon at 100,000 mph would move less than *2 inches* in 1 microsecond; it would move only the length of 10 fat germs in a nanosecond. More antiseptically speaking, there are as many nanoseconds in 1 second as there are seconds in 30 years, or as many nanoseconds in 1 minute as there are minutes in 1,100 *centuries*. Electricity travels about 1 foot per nanosecond, and this fact imposes an ultimate limit to internal computer speed. But it is not unreasonable to expect that computers will be built in the future that are dozens of times faster than those in use today.

Cost   A significant cause of the growth in the number of computer installations is the dramatic reduction in the cost of performing a specific number of operations (see Table 2-1). If automobile costs and technological improvements had changed at a rate comparable with computer hardware over the last 15 years, you would now be able to buy a self-steering car for $20 that could attain speeds up to 500 miles per hour and could travel the entire length of California on 1 gallon of gas. Nor does it appear that the end is in sight in computational cost reduction. The cost of certain basic components will continue to decline while their speed and performance increase.[9]

Information storage capacity   Information may be stored for use by a computer in a number of ways. The *central processing unit* (CPU) of the computer holds data and the instructions needed to manipulate the data internally in its *primary storage,* or *main memory,* section. Table 2-1 summarizes the trend in primary storage capacity. Perhaps even more impressive has been the improvement in mass *external online* (or *secondary*) storage devices (see Table 2-1). These devices are connected directly to, i.e., they are *online* to, the CPU, and they serve as *reference libraries* by accepting data directly from, and returning data directly to, the CPU without human intervention. Of course, data which the computer may use are also stored outside the CPU in the form of punched cards and magnetic tape, but these facts are *offline* since the CPU does not have direct and unassisted access to them (see Figure 2-8).

Reliability   The reliability of hardware has improved substantially with the substitution of long-life solid state components for the early vacuum tubes. Much of the research effort directed toward achieving greater reliability has been sponsored by the federal government for space and missile programs. For example, scientists have been working on *self-repairing computers* that would remain in operation during unmanned space missions lasting many years. The concept of self-repairing essentially involves

[9] At this writing, a recently developed microprocessor chip with the computing power of a high-end minicomputer is expected to be introduced at a price less than $100. One authority expects the price to drop to about $2 in two years. See Steve Stubbins, "The Microcomputer Merry-Go-Round," *Infosystems,* p. 72, April 1979.

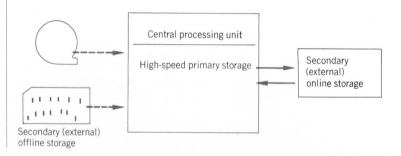

FIGURE 2-8
Three types of computer storage.

FIGURE 2-9
A component being tested to
determine whether it is
functioning properly. If so, the
portable testing processor
prints a message telling the
field engineer which
component to check next.
(*NCR Corp.*)

partitioning the computer into functional blocks and building identical components into each block. Some of the parts are used for processing immediately; others serve as standby spares. A failure occurring in one component or subsystem would be detected by a status-sensing device, and the faulty part would be electronically and automatically replaced with a spare.

The down-to-earth benefits of increased reliability are great; for example, self-repairing computers could be incorporated into the intensive-care monitoring and control systems of hospitals, where a failure could result in a death. They would be especially beneficial in those computerized navigational systems which are used to bring in aircraft safely in zero-visibility conditions. If those sections of future earthbound computers with a reduced number of standby spares were replaced during periodic preventive maintenance, the mean (average) time between failures would probably be measured in years rather than weeks or months. Although completely self-repairing *commercial* computers are still on the drawing boards because of the additional cost of redundant spare parts, this obstacle will probably be overcome in the not-too-distant future as VLSI circuit technology produces lower costs.

At the present time, better accessibility of the circuitry enables technicians to get to the problem and quickly effect a repair (Figure 2-9). Computer circuit boards can be replaced promptly, and equipment *downtime* can be kept to a minimum. It is possible for a malfunctioning computer to be linked to another "diagnostic" computer in order to determine the cause of the problem. For example, NCR Corporation's V-8560 processor has a remote diagnostic capability that permits engineers at an NCR division in San Diego to check out any such processor

FIGURE 2-10
New 4341 processors
undergoing reliability tests.
(IBM Corp.)

installed anywhere in the United States. Also, larger computers, such as the IBM 4300 models shown being tested in Figure 2-10, have *self-diagnostic processors* built within them to monitor hardware operations and report on failures.

Software Developments

Software is the general name given to all the programs and routines associated with the use of computer hardware. Unfortunately, when compared with the tremendous hardware advances, the developments in the software area seem less impressive. Furthermore, as anticipated hardware improvements are realized, an overwhelming proportion of the problems experienced in utilizing the computer to produce managerial information will be traceable to software difficulties. Today, in fact, the production of good software is a costly and time-consuming process that generally determines the speed with which computer-based projects are completed.

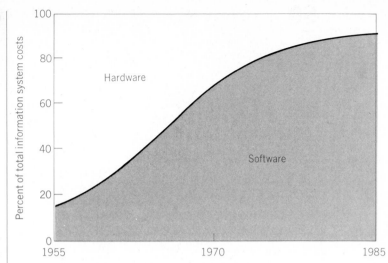

FIGURE 2-11
Total-cost trends for
information systems.

As a result, the investment in programming and systems personnel and in the software they create now far exceeds the investment in hardware in most organizations. As Figure 2-11 shows, this trend will undoubtedly continue because hardware production is automated while increasingly complex software is still generally written on an artisan basis.[10]

Yet there have been significant gains in the development of software. The three basic software categories are (1) *translation programs,* (2) *applications programs,* and (3) *operating-system programs.* Let us look at the developments in each of these categories.

Translation programs   In the early 1950s, users had to translate problem-solving instructions into special machine codes for each computer. Such instructions typically consisted of strings of numbers (sometimes in a binary form), which were quite tedious to prepare. In addition to remembering dozens of operation code numbers (21 might mean add), the person performing the task of instructing the computer (the *programmer*) was also required to keep track of the locations in the central processor where the instructions and data items were stored. Initial program coding often took many months; checking instructions to locate errors was about as difficult as writing the instructions in the first place; and modifying programs was often a nightmare.

To ease the programmer's burden, a compromise approach between people and machine was developed which resulted in the introduction of special coding *languages* that save time and are more convenient to use.

[10] It has been estimated that the human cost to write and check a line of coded instructions in a computer program is over 100 million times the machine cost to execute the line. It is obvious, then, that human costs should be minimized whenever possible, even if this could lead to somewhat less efficiency in the use of the hardware.

In using these languages, the programmer writes instructions in a form that is easier to understand—e.g., the programmer may print the word ADD or use the plus symbol rather than use the number 21. Unfortunately, this code is not in the machine's language, and so the machine does not directly understand the orders. How, then, can the machine execute instructions if they are in a language that it cannot understand? Just as an American and a German can communicate if one of them uses a translating dictionary, so too can the programmer and computer communicate if a separate translation program is employed.

Let us assume that you want to use a computer to perform some worthwhile task. In using all but the smallest computers, you would probably take steps that would cause a translating program to be loaded into the computer. This program would control the translation procedure. The instructions you wrote to perform the task (called the *source program*) would then be fed into the computer, where they would be translated. The result of this operation would be a set of machine instructions (called the *object program*) that could then be used to control the processing of your problem data. [In using a personal microcomputer, however, you would often employ a somewhat different translation approach. Instead of first loading a translating program into your computer to convert the entire program into machine code, you would just enter the source program into the computer, and a permanently hardwired language *interpreter* inside the machine (see Figure 1-15a, p. 34) would convert each of your instructions into machine form as they were needed during the processing of your task.][11]

Almost all problem-solving programs prepared today are first written in languages preferred by people and are then translated by special software or hardware into the equivalent machine-language codes. Continuing efforts are being made to produce software that will permit easier human-machine communication. For example, efforts are being made to develop software that will give the ultimate users of the processed information the ability to prepare programs in natural languages such as English that are more familiar to them.

Applications programs   The program you prepared to perform your particular processing task would also come under the heading of software. Thousands of these programs have been written by people for work-related and personal applications. Many applications programs must, of course, be prepared by individuals to process tasks that are unique to their particular needs. In the past, however, much time has been spent in duplicating programs developed by others. Recognizing the wastefulness of such duplication in organizations, equipment manufacturers and independent software firms have prepared generalized *applications packages* (or *packaged programs*) for widely used applications.

---

[11] Further details on these translation procedures and on programming languages are presented in Part 3.

Packaged programs for personal entertainment and for educational use may also be obtained at hundreds of retail computer stores.

Operating-system programs   As the name implies, an *operating system* (OS) was initially a set of programs prepared by equipment manufacturers and users to assist computer operators in large computer centers. It is the function of the operator to load data-input devices with cards and tapes, to set switches on the computer console, to start the processing run, and to prepare and unload output devices. It should not be the operator's job, however, to waste time (both human and machine) doing things that the computer could do more quickly and reliably. Housekeeping duties such as clearing central processor storage locations between jobs and loading into storage the next job program and data from the jobs stacked up in a waiting queue are now controlled by the software. Shifting control to specially prepared operating programs thus reduced the operator's work, provided relatively nonstop operation, and therefore speeded up the processing and increased the amount of work that could be accomplished.

The objective of current operating systems is still to operate the computer with a minimum of idle time and in the most efficient and economical way during the execution of application and translation programs. But the operating software is now vastly more complex. More sophisticated software is now used in organizations to keep faster and more powerful hardware occupied.

An example of greater software sophistication is seen in the development of *multiprogramming*—the *interleaved* execution of two or more different and independent programs by the same computer.[12] Multiprogramming is *not* generally taken to mean that the computer is executing instructions from several programs at the same instant in time.[13] Instead, it *does mean* that there are a number of programs stored in primary and/or online storage; a portion of one program is executed, then a segment of another, etc. The central processor (CPU) switches from one program to another almost instantaneously. Since internal operating speeds of CPUs are much faster than are the means of getting data into and out of the processor, the CPU can allocate time to several programs instead of remaining idle when one is bringing in data or printing out information.

---

[12] If you are mechanically inclined, you may know that an automobile distributor head rotates, and then makes electrical contact with and zaps a pulse of electricity to each spark plug in one revolution. Similarly, the computer may allocate a small amount, or *slice,* of time —say, 150 milliseconds per second—to each program being executed. Fifteen-hundredths of a second may not seem like much time to you, but that is enough for a hospital computer to calculate the amounts owed to hundreds of employees for a given pay period. The result of such speed is that each user has the illusion that he or she has the undivided attention of the computer.

[13] The term *multiprocessing* is used to describe interconnected computer configurations or computers with multiple arithmetic-logic units that have the ability to *simultaneously* execute several programs.

With multiprogramming, it is thus possible for several users to share the time of the CPU. This *timesharing* feature may permit more efficient use of the capacity of the processor, but incorporation of multiprogramming into the OS has, of course, complicated matters.

The operating systems of many of today's computers are integrated collections of processing programs and a master control program that are expected to perform the *scheduling, control, loading,* and *program call-up* functions described below:

1   The *scheduling* function involves the selection of jobs to be run on a priority basis from a table or list of jobs to be processed. Available storage space and the most suitable peripheral hardware to use are allocated to the job or jobs being processed.
2   The *control* function consists of a number of activities including (*a*) the control of input and output housekeeping operations, and (*b*) the proper handling, shifting, and protection of data, instructions, and intermediate processing results when a high-priority program interrupts the processing of a lower-priority program.
3   The *loading* function includes reading in and assigning storage locations to object programs and data. Checks are also made to prevent the loading and processing of incorrect files.
4   The *program call-up* function emphasizes the overall control of the OS master program (referred to by such names as *monitor, executive routine,* and *supervisor*) over other software elements including *translating programs, service programs,* or *utility routines* (for loading programs, clearing storage, etc.), and the installation's stored file of *applications programs.* The monitor integrates this assorted software into a single consistent system. The system monitor generally remains in primary storage, where it may occupy 25 to 60 percent of the available space; in installations with online storage capability, many of the other programs and routines are kept online and are called up and temporarily stored in the CPU as needed.

Figure 2-12 summarizes the relationship existing between the hardware and software categories discussed in the preceding pages.

Technological advances in computer hardware and software have both contributed to and been stimulated by a changing social environment. In the next section, we shall examine the computer-oriented information systems which have emerged because of the desire of administrators for effective information which may enable them to operate under rapidly changing conditions.

DEVELOPMENTS IN INFORMATION SYSTEMS

Traditional information systems have often been found wanting because they do not provide information with the desired properties mentioned in Chapter 1 — that is, the information they produce may be too costly and

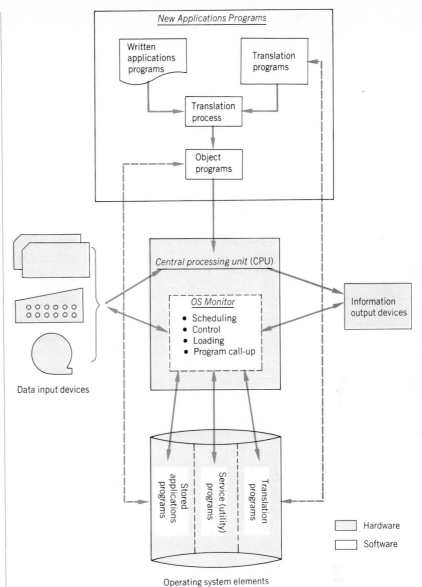

FIGURE 2-12
The relationship between
hardware and software.

is not (1) timely, (2) properly integrated, (3) concise, (4) available in the proper format, or (5) relevant. Thus, new information concepts have been developed. These new concepts may be characterized as being (1) *quicker responding* and (2) *broader in scope* than traditional systems.

Quick-Response Systems

Quick-response systems, as the name implies, have been developed to increase the timeliness, effectiveness, and availability of information. They

Real time processing
Total systems
Distributed networks
Remote batch processing
Online processing
Timesharing
Data base systems
MIS

FIGURE 2-13

may allow users to react more rapidly to changing conditions, reduce waste in the use of time and other resources, and permit quick follow-up on creative ideas. They may also be described by a bewildering variety of Computerese terms. A glance through a few current data processing periodicals shows the subject to be a veritable semantic jungle with many "experts" swinging from different definition vines (Figure 2-13). We will try to cut through this foliage by examining the concepts of (**1**) *online processing,* (**2**) *real time processing,* (**3**) *timesharing* and *remote computing services,* and (**4**) *distributed processing networks.*

Online processing The term *online* is used in different ways. We have seen that a peripheral machine connected directly to, and capable of unassisted communication with, the central processor is said to be an online device. *Online* also describes the status of a person who is communicating directly with (i.e., has *direct access* to) the central processor without the use of media such as punched cards or magnetic tape. Finally, *online* refers to a *method of processing data.* However, before looking at the concept of *online processing,* we should pause to describe the characteristics of the *batch-processing* approach.

Perhaps an illustration will best explain batch processing (also called *serial* or *sequential* processing). Let us trace the activities that follow Zelda Zilch's credit purchase of a zither in a department store. The sales slip for this *transaction* is routed to the accounting office, where it and others are collected for several days until a large batch accumulates. The data on the slips may be recorded on a machine input medium such as punched cards. The cards are then sorted by customer name or charge-account number into the proper sequence for processing. Processing consists of adding the item description and price of all the recent transactions to the

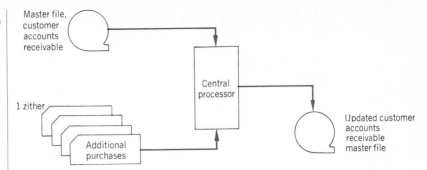

FIGURE 2-14
Batch processing.

customer's other purchases for the month. Thus, a customer's accounts-receivable master file, perhaps in the form of magnetic tape, must be updated to reflect the additional charges. The sequence in which the new transactions are sorted is an ordered one and corresponds to the sequence on the master file. Figure 2-14 illustrates this batch-processing procedure. At the end of the accounting period, the master file is used to prepare the customer statements.

Other files are periodically updated in similar fashion. A *file,* then, is a collection of related records and items treated as a unit. In our example, the zither purchase was one *item* on Zelda's bill; Zelda's bill would represent one charge-account *record;* and the purchase records of all credit customers would make up the accounts-receivable *file.* Furthermore, a set of integrated files may be organized into a *data base* (see Figure 2-15).

Batches may be collected at a central computer site or at other locations. In some cases, *remote stations* at distant locations may employ telephone circuits to transmit data directly into the central computer system. Although batch processing is economical when a large volume of data must be processed, it (1) requires sorting, (2) reduces timeliness in some situations, and (3) requires sequential file organization—and this may prove to be a handicap.

Online processing has been developed for certain uses as an answer

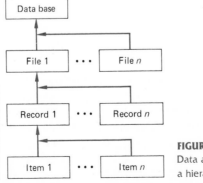

FIGURE 2-15
Data are often organized into a hierarchy.

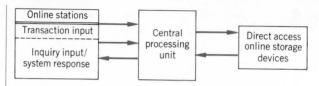

FIGURE 2-16
Online processing.

to the batch-processing deficiencies noted above. In contrast to batching, online (or *direct-access* or *random*) processing permits transaction data to be fed under CPU control directly into secondary online storage devices from the point of origin without first being sorted. These data may be keyed in by the use of a terminal, or they may be produced by a variety of other data-collection and transaction-recording devices. Information contained in any record is accessible to the user without the necessity of a sequential search of the file and within a fraction of a second after the inquiry message has been transmitted. Thus, online processing systems may feature *random* and rapid input of transactions and immediate and *direct access* to record contents as needed (see Figure 2-16).

Online processing and direct access to records *require unique hardware and software.* For example, the capacity of the primary storage unit of the CPU must be adequate to (1) handle the complex online operating-system control program and (2) serve a variety of other storage uses. Also, since many online users may have access to stored records, software security provisions are necessary to (1) prevent confidential information from falling into unauthorized hands and (2) prevent deliberate or accidental tampering with data and program files. Finally, data transmission facilities must be provided to communicate with online terminals located in the next room, on the next block, or thousands of miles away.

The speed of processing needed by an organization varies with the particular application. As we have seen, batch processing is appropriate for many jobs. Online processing, although quicker responding than traditional methods, may involve different degrees of quickness in the needed response. For example, a system may combine immediate access to records for inquiry purposes with *periodic* (perhaps daily) transaction input and updating of records from a central collecting source. Such a system would meet many needs and would be simpler and less expensive than an online real time system.

Real time processing The words *real time* represent a semantic bucket of worms—you can choose from over 30 definitions that have appeared in the literature. (This disagreement has led a few authorities to recommend that the words be dropped altogether.) The consensus is, however, that a *real time processing* operation is (1) in a parallel time relationship with an ongoing activity and (2) producing information quickly enough to be useful in controlling this current live and dynamic activity. Thus, we shall use the words *real time* to describe an online processing system with severe time limitations. A real time system *uses* online processing; an online processing system, however, *need not* be operating in real time.

Real time processing requires *immediate* (not periodic) transaction input from all input-originating terminals. Many remote stations may be tied directly by high-speed communications equipment into one or more central processors. Several stations may be operating simultaneously. Files may be updated each minute, and inquiries may be answered by split-second access to up-to-the-minute records.

Among the examples of real time processing are systems designed to keep track of the availability of motel and hotel rooms, systems that provide for immediate updating of customer records in savings banks, and reservation systems used by airlines to control the inventory of available seats. In the airline systems, central computers receive transaction data and inquiries from remote terminals located at hundreds of reservation and ticket sales desks across the nation. In seconds, a customer may request and receive information about flights and available seats. If a reservation is made, the transaction is fed into the computer immediately and the inventory of available seats is reduced. The reverse, of course, occurs in the event of a cancellation. What if a flight is fully booked? If the customer desires to be placed on a waiting list, data such as customer name and telephone number are maintained by the computer. If cancellations occur, waiting-list customers are notified by agents. In addition, the reservation systems of competing airlines are tied together to provide an exchange of information on seat availability. Thus, an agent for any of the participating companies may sell space on *any* of the airlines if the system shows that it is available.

Real time processing is required and cooperation is necessary among airlines because of the perishability of the service sold—when an airplane takes off, vacant seats have no value until the next landing. It would be a mistake, however, to assume that real time processing should be universally applied to all data processing applications. (After all, real time systems tend to be very expensive.) A quick-response system can be designed to fit the needs of the organization. Some applications can be processed on a lower-priority, or background, basis using batch methods (e.g., payroll); some can be online with periodic (not immediate) updating of records; and some can utilize real time methods.

Timesharing and remote computing services   *Timesharing* is a term used to describe a processing system with a number of independent, relatively low-speed, online, *simultaneously usable* stations (see Figure 2-17). Each station provides direct access to the central processor. The speed of the system and the use of multiprogramming allow the central processor to switch from one using station to another and to do a part of each job in the allocated "time slice" until the work is completed. The speed is frequently such that the user has the illusion that no one else is using the computer.

There are various types of timesharing systems. One type is the in-house installation that is designed for, owned by, and used exclusively in a *single organization*. The number of such dedicated systems is growing.

FIGURE 2-17
Timesharing terminal.
(*Digital Equipment Corp.*)

For example, timesharing systems utilizing minicomputers are popular with decision makers who must solve problems that are too large for calculators but may not be large enough to receive a high priority at the organization's large computer center.

Another type of timesharing system was established a number of years ago by commercial *remote computing services* (RCS) to provide computer resources to *many different client organizations* seeking to process a broad range of jobs. Many RCS firms (sometimes referred to as *service bureaus*) will do custom batch processing. When the timesharing facilities of RCS firms are used, transactions are initiated from, and output is delivered to, the premises of the user at electronic speeds. The RCS organization will generally offer a library of online applications programs to its clients, who need only supply the input data and access the programs to obtain the desired information. The subscriber pays for the processing service in much the same way he or she pays for telephone service: There is an initial installation charge; there are certain basic monthly charges; and, perhaps largest of all, there are transaction charges (like long-distance calls), which vary according to usage. These variable charges are generally based on the time the terminal is connected to the central processing system and/or on the seconds of CPU time used.

Providing raw computing power to timesharing clients is a service that is becoming increasingly vulnerable to the purchase and use by clients of the new, low-cost processors discussed in Chapter 1. Thus, some RCS firms are now selling some of their applications programs to former clients who have decided to acquire their own small computers.

Distributed data processing networks In earlier paragraphs we have used the word timesharing because it is commonly applied to the interleaved use of the time of a computer. When *one* or *two* processors handle the workload of several outlying terminals, the term *timesharing* is probably still appropriately descriptive. But when *many* dispersed or *distributed* independent computer systems are connected by a communications network, and when messages, processing tasks, programs, data, and other information-processing resources are transmitted between processors and terminals, the term may no longer be adequate. Such a distributed computer-communications network is similar in some respects to public utilities such as telephone and electric companies—e.g., electric power plants are geographically dispersed, and the energy resources generated are transmitted through a coordinating regional network or grid to the places where the energy resources are needed.

Distributed data processing (DDP) *network* is the term now used frequently to describe this extension of timesharing. For our purposes, a DDP arrangement may be defined as one that places the needed data, along with the computing and communications resources necessary to process these data, at the end-user's location. Such an arrangement may result in a large number of computers and significant software resources being shared among dozens of users. Figure 2-18 shows some of the possible DDP network configurations. Most current networks use the *star configuration* (or some hierarchical variation of it) shown in Figure 2-18. Few *ring networks* now exist, but this configuration is being studied by a number of organizations.

Distributed data processing networks, like smaller timesharing systems, may be for the use of a *single* organization or for *many* organizations. Figure 2-19 shows the worldwide DDP network that Hewlett-Packard Company has developed for its internal use. This is basically a variation of the star network. With nearly 200 computers located at 110 sites, this network links manufacturing facilities and sales offices with the company's central computer center in California. Although overall control of the network is maintained by the California center, division computers operate autonomously to process local jobs. Figure 2-20 shows a commercial multisubscriber distributed network that offers computing resources to customers in business, government, and education. This network connects over 70 cities on two continents with 40 large-scale computers.[14]

As you might expect, there are both advantages and disadvantages at present to the sharing of computing resources.[15] Some of the *advan-*

FIGURE 2-18
Possible distributed data processing networks. (*a*) A central *host,* or star, computer communicates with and controls satellites or *nodes.* (*b*) The node processors or stations may, in turn, act as hosts to subordinate processors and/or terminals in a hierarchical variation of the star arrangement. (*c*) A "no-host" or ring network of communicating equals.

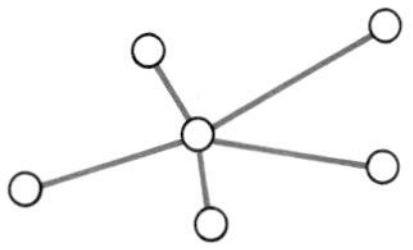

(*a*) Star network

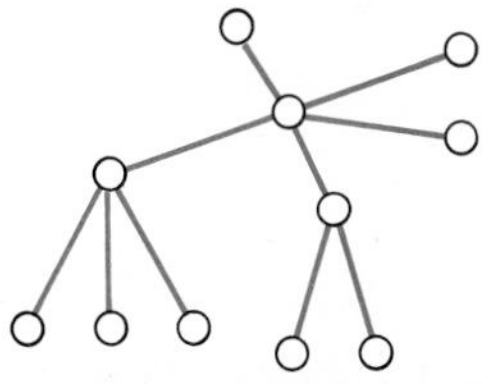

(*b*) Hierarchical variation of
the star network

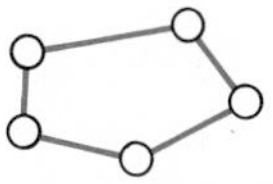

(*c*) Ring or loop
network

---

[14] Other examples of *single-organization* distributed processing networks are the *OCTOPUS* system that connects 1,000 researchers at the University of California with five very large computers and Eastern Airlines' network that links nine large computers in Miami and Charlotte, North Carolina, with over 2,700 ticket agent, flight operations, and internal business operations terminals. Other networks used by *multiple organizations* are the ARPA net, which connects over 30 universities and research institutions throughout the United States and Europe with 50 processors ranging in size from minicomputers to giant number crunchers, and the *General Electric network,* which uses over 100 computers to serve over 100,000 users in more than 20 countries.

[15] Further discussions of this topic will be presented in later chapters.

FIGURE 2-19
Hewlett-Packard Company
distributed data processing
network.

tages of resource sharing using timesharing and distributed processing systems are that: (1) Sophisticated computers and a growing library of applications programs can be immediately available to end-users whenever needed, (2) skilled professionals (either in-house or in the employ of RCS firms) can be available to help users develop their own specialized applications, and (3) the possible availability of multiple processors in the system permits peak-load sharing and provides backup facilities in the event of equipment failure. Unfortunately, however, some of the *possible*

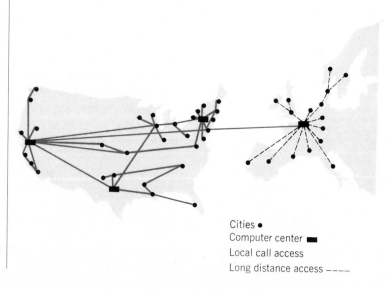

Cities ●
Computer center ■
Local call access
Long distance access ‒‒‒‒

FIGURE 2-20
TYMNET network of
Tymshare, Inc.

disadvantages of resource sharing at present are that (1) the reliability and cost of the data communications facilities used, and the cost and quality of the computing service received, may be disappointing in some cases, and (2) provisions for protecting the confidentiality and integrity of user programs and data files maintained in online storage are generally ineffective against a skilled penetrator.

The quick-response-system concepts that we have now considered are improving the timeliness, effectiveness, and availability of information. In addition, many of these emerging quick-response systems are taking a *broader data-base approach* to the needs of organizations by attempting to provide better integration of information-producing activities. In the following section we shall briefly examine this trend.

Data-Base Systems

Better integration of information-producing activities can lead to information that is more complete and relevant. Traditionally, data processing activities in organizations have been grouped by departments and by applications. Many computers were originally installed to process a large-volume job. Other applications, treated independently, followed, but it soon became clear that this approach was unsatisfactory. Each application program typically operated on data files that had been created specifically for it, but since basic data were often defined and organized in different ways for each application, these facts could not be easily integrated with the data used in other programs run by the organization. Thus, data were often expensively duplicated (with an increase in the possibility of error) because it was impossible to combine these facts in meaningful ways. For example, a great deal of redundant data on a bank customer (e.g., home address, age, credit rating, etc.) might be contained in separate files for checking accounts, savings accounts, automobile loans, and home mortgages. Integrating file data would be difficult because Charlie Brown, account number 1234 in one file, became Charles M. Brown, account number 5678, in another.[16]

Dissatisfied with such conditions, some organizations began looking for ways to consolidate activities by using a data-base approach. Although there are some differences of opinion about what constitutes a data-base system, the most prevalent view is that such systems are designed around a centralized and integrated shared data file (or *data base*) that emphasizes the *independence* of programs and data. This data base is located in directly accessible online storage. Data transactions are introduced into the system only once. These data are now a neutral resource with respect to any particular program, and specific data elements are readily available as needed to all authorized applications and users of the data base. All data-base records that transactions affect may be updated

---

[16] A brief survey at one university showed that the data element "student name" was stored in 13 different files and in five different formats.

at the time of input. Of course, the data-base concept requires that input data be commonly defined and consistently organized and presented throughout the organization. This requirement, in turn, calls for rigid input discipline; it also means that someone must be given the overall authority to standardize (and approve any necessary changes to) data with organizationwide usefulness.

Why the interest in data-base systems? One reason is that a database system, combined with *data-base management software* that will organize, process, and present the necessary data elements, will enable decision makers to search, probe, and query file contents in order to extract answers to nonrecurring and unplanned questions that are not available in regular reports. These questions might initially be vague and/or poorly defined, but people can "browse" through the data base until they have the needed information. In short, the data-base management software will "manage" the stored data items and assemble the needed items from a common data base in response to the queries of individuals who are not programming specialists. In the past, if decision makers wished to have a special report prepared using information stored in the data base, they would probably communicate their needs to a programmer, who, when time permitted, would write one or more programs to prepare the report. The availability of data-base management software, however, offers the user a much faster alternative communications path (see Figure 2-21).

Perhaps an illustration of the possible use of a data-base system is in order here. Suppose, for example, a personnel manager of a large multinational corporation has just received an urgent request to send an employee to a foreign country to effect an emergency repair of a hydraulic pump that the company stopped making six years ago. The employee needed must be a mechanical engineer, must have knowledge of the par-

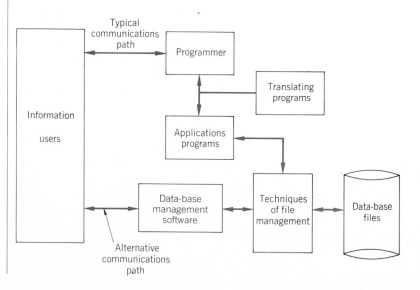

FIGURE 2-21

ticular pump (and therefore, let us assume, must have been with the corporation for at least eight years), must be able to speak French, and must be willing to accept an overseas assignment. Obviously, there is not likely to be a report available that will have the names of engineers with just these characteristics. However, the records on each employee in the corporate personnel file stored in the data base do contain information on educational background, date of employment, work experience, and language capability. Although in the past it might have been necessary for the manager to request that a time-consuming program be prepared to locate employees who match the requirements, with data-base management software, it is now possible for the manager to use an online terminal to search through the personnel file and sort out the records of French-speaking mechanical engineers with eight or more years of company experience. Armed with such information, obtained in a few minutes, the manager can then contact the employees named to fill the overseas assignment.

In addition to having direct access to data generated *within* the organization, a decision maker may also have *externally produced* data readily available for use. Data suppliers may make external data available to users in several ways. In the least-restrictive form, data may be *sold outright* by vendors on some medium such as magnetic tape, and buyers may then incorporate these facts in their data bases in almost any way they choose. Economic statistics and United States census data, for example, may be purchased on tapes from government agencies for use in this way. Some remote computing services offer data on a *rental basis* to subscribers; users then access these facts from online terminals and pay for the resources used according to the pricing scheme employed by the supplier.[17] A somewhat similar service is offered by firms that maintain *information retrieval* data bases. Many libraries, for example, use retrieval services that can access tens of millions of worldwide document references to supply their users quickly with sources of information on practically any subject.[18] Finally, a user may buy *special reports* prepared from a data base owned by an outside supplier.

In summary, as you have probably anticipated, *there are both benefits and limitations* at present *to the use of data-base systems.* Among the *possible benefits* are: (1) Fewer applications programs and lengthy regular re-

---

[17] Several RCS suppliers, for example, offer a COMPUSTAT data bank that contains annual and quarterly sales and earnings figures on about 2,700 companies; Data Resources, Inc., offers online data banks dealing with thousands of different economic variables from regional, national, and international sources; Dun & Bradstreet, through its RCS affiliate, plans to offer financial, credit, and population data and analyses; and Chase Econometrics Associates provides economic forecasts through two RCS vendors.

[18] Some of the larger online retrieval services are Lockheed's *Dialog* (which contains over 100 data bases in such fields as government, health, education, social and physical sciences, humanities, business, etc.) and System Development Corporation's *Orbit* (which contains many of the same data bases found in the Dialog system as well as some other data bases. The Bibliographic Retrieval Services (BRS) system is also a large supplier of data-base information.

ports containing reference data may be needed when decision makers can directly access the data base, (2) better integration (and less duplication) of data originating at different points is feasible, and (3) faster preparation of information to support nonrecurring tasks and changing conditions is feasible. Some of the *possible limitations* are: (1) More complex and expensive hardware and software are needed, and (2) sensitive data in online storage might find their way into unauthorized hands, and hardware or software failures might result in the destruction of vital data-base contents.

In this chapter we have now seen some of the revolutionary changes taking place in technology and in the uses of this technology for information-processing purposes. As might be expected, however, rapid change is often accompanied by problems of adjustment.

SELECTED PROBLEMS OF ADJUSTMENT

After noting that "The world is too much with us, late and soon," William Wordsworth took a stroll along a sandy beach to calm his ruffled sensibilities. What he could not know was that tiny silicon chips made from the material he was walking on would cause feverish activity in the world of future generations. These chips have dropped into our midst like small stones into a lake, but they are causing waves rather than ripples! Problems of adjustment that affect *organizations* and *individuals* are accompanying the rapid growth in computer usage. Some of the problems which must be dealt with in the future are outlined briefly in the following paragraphs. In later chapters, several of these issues will be considered in much more detail.

Organizational Issues

Computer usage may enhance the efficiency of an organization by providing information that can lead to better planning, decision making, and control of organizational activities. But as we have seen, technological change may be harmful as well as helpful in some cases. The following listing focuses on challenges and issues that are currently the subject of concerned study and debate.

1 *The challenges in information systems design.* Systems design is a complex and challenging task that has often produced disappointing internal results, a bad public image, and/or economic losses. Designers are currently grappling with the following questions: (a) Can a single data base be created to satisfy the differing information needs of administrators at different organizational levels? (b) Can decision makers with different job specialities share the same data base? (c) How can externally produced data be most effectively incorporated

into the data base? and (*d*) How can suitable flexibility and adaptability to human needs be built into the system?

2   *The systems security issue.* Lack of computer control and problems with the security of information systems have threatened the very existence of some organizations. Assets have been stolen through computer manipulation; secrets have been copied and sold to competitors; systems penetrators have repeatedly broken through the security controls and gained access to sensitive information; and fire, flood, accidents, and sabotage have destroyed irreplaceable computer files. Furthermore, with many organizations moving toward a distributed processing environment, the number of potentially vulnerable locations may increase.

3   *Computer industry issues.* Some organizations that have tried to compete in the computer industry have gone bankrupt; other giant corporations have suffered large loses trying to compete with IBM (at this writing, several antitrust suits are pending against this industry leader); and the problem of adequate legal software protection (an attempt to patent software was killed by the Supreme Court) has created headaches for software-producing organizations.

4   *Data communications uncertainties.* What has been termed the "regulatory fight of the century" is brewing in Washington at this writing between the computer and telecommunications industries. This fight has developed as data processing and communications technologies have merged in the creation of distributed processing networks. Thus, there is now considerable uncertainty about the governmental regulatory status of organizations that offer *both* computing and communications services. An *unregulated* legal status currently applies to organizations when their communications services are only incidental to their computing services (e.g., an RCS supplier), and a *regulated* legal status currently applies to organizations when data processing services are only incidental to the furnishing of communications (e.g., the Bell Telephone System of American Telephone and Telegraph Company, or AT&T). But between these defined areas are a growing number of hybrid organizations that offer significant services in both communications and data processing. It is in this middle area that the regulatory status is unclear (see Figure 2-22). However, with the help of past rulings of the Federal Communications Commission (FCC), these hybrid organizations have been creating communications networks and have been chipping away at the regulated monopoly AT&T has enjoyed in this area for decades. For example, one entry with enormous financial resources that plans to establish a domestic communications-satellite system to compete with AT&T for the transmission of high-speed computer data is Satellite Business Systems (SBS), the property of IBM, Aetna Life and Casualty Company, and Communications Satellite Corporation. In summary, then, the distinctions between data processing and data communications have become

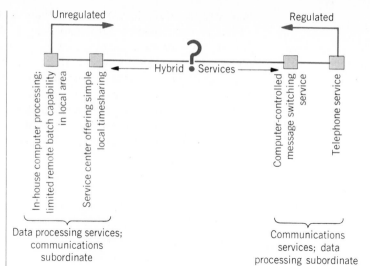

FIGURE 2-22
The uncertainty of
governmental regulation.

blurred, hundreds of billions of dollars are involved in the ultimate regulatory decisions, and two of the richest and most powerful organizations in the nation—AT&T and IBM—are squaring off for what may be
the most significant industrial confrontation of this century. Virtually
every organization in the country will ultimately be affected.

5   *Organizational structure questions.* Will the structure of a particular organization be drastically altered in the future as a result of the introduction and use of advanced computer systems? Will the use of distributed processing networks create a need to realign work groups?
Will existing departments need to be added to or eliminated? These
are just a few of the organizational questions that many firms will face.

6   *Concentration of power issue.* Organizations with limited computing
resources may have difficulty competing against organizations with
much greater sophistication in the use of computers for planning and
decision making. This could have serious political and social implications if, for example, computer expertise and access to sensitive data
banks were concentrated in one political party or government
agency.

7   *The electronic funds transfer systems (EFTS) issue.* The EFTS concept
may reduce the need for cash and checks and may permit the future
widespread nationwide transfer of "electronic money" between organizations and individuals. Although legal and regulatory confusion
currently exists, powerful organizations such as banks have a vital
stake in the ways in which computers are permitted to influence how
"money" is transmitted and accounted for.

8   *The electronic mail issue.* One result of the anticipated development
of new and improved data communications resources will probably
be that sending mail electronically will not only be much faster but

may also be much less expensive than using currently available U.S. Postal Service facilities. Communications satellites, for example, will provide users with facilities that will permit the transmission of messages and facsimile images to other users in a few seconds. The speed, flexibility, and cost of sending mail in the future is likely to create further regulatory problems. Will private data communications carriers be permitted to take over much of the mail activity in the nation at the expense of the Postal Service? Or will the Postal Service enter into, and be given some jurisdiction over, the delivery of electronic messages?

Individual Issues

The computer has perhaps the greatest potential to improve the quality of life and well-being of individuals of any tool ever invented. Certainly, there are examples all around us of the many benefits that individuals have received from computer usage. Thus, it is probably unfortunate that most of the prominently discussed adjustment issues affecting people focus attention on the possible negative aspects of computer use. But there *are* some possible dangers, as the following listing briefly outlines:

1 *Employment concerns.* The greater efficiency made possible by computer usage in offices, factories, and laboratories may result in job obsolescence and displacement for some employees and disruptive changes in the compatible work groups of others. For example, programmable *robots*—i.e., computer-controlled machines that can sense the need for, and then take the actions necessary to perform, a specified task—are likely to have a major impact on jobs and people in the next decade.
2 *Systems-design issues.* Faulty systems design has sometimes led to an out-of-control situation in the *originating* and *recording* of input data. That is, data may be gathered about individuals when there is no real need to know; errors of omission and commission may distort the records kept on an individual, and these errors are difficult to correct; and documents and procedures designed for processing convenience may lead to individual confusion and bewilderment. Also, data must be in a standardized form for computer system *classification* and *sorting,* and faulty systems design has often led to a depersonalized treatment of individuals—i.e., the individual has been made to feel like an insignificant number rather than a human being. Finally, computer system *miscalculations* have resulted in individuals being harassed and inconvenienced.
3 *Data security distress.* The lack of control over data security in a computer system has resulted in the destruction of an individual's records and in both the accidental and the intentional disclosure to unauthorized persons of confidential information of a very personal nature.
4 *Privacy peril.* Lack of control over data storage, retrieval, and commu-

"Transitions"

The computer industry has always been a hotbed of changes, many causing profound alterations to our business and social institutions—but, in the past year or so, the pace has accelerated. We seem to be like the character in the Stephen Leacock story who leapt on his horse and rode madly off in all directions.

Fundamental to much of this feverish activity is that minuscule silicon chip, the microprocessor. Dropped into our midst like a tiny pebble into a pond, it has caused waves, not ripples. Nothing in our industry will ever be the same. It's made possible personal computing, intelligent terminals and networks, and distributed processing; it's helped slash costs on the big systems and made minis and microcomputers available in staggering quantities.

But those little pieces of treated sand are only one of the factors complicating our industry. Other forces are at work involving money, politics, and power.

There's the wonderfully complex international scene and transborder data flow. Involved are the governments of all the developed countries of the world and many Third World countries as well. There is intrigue, political rivalry, jealousies, and rampant chauvinism. All of this will significantly impact global communications for decades to come.

Japan, with its delayed but still impending invasion of the world computer markets, is a major player on the international stage.

In the U.S., we are witnessing a spate of mergers and acquisitions that have thinned the ranks of the undercapitalized and brought new names to the forefront of the industry—names like Exxon, Northern Telecom, and Sun Oil.

Almost overnight a new, booming market has emerged as small businessmen everywhere have had their data processing consciousness raised. Streetfront computer retail stores, as well as IBM, DEC, and the other mini and micro-makers, are being swamped with inquiries and orders. Sensing opportunity, thousands of overnight entrepreneurs, known variously as systems integrators or oem distributors, are buying the new hardware at discount prices, writing applications packages and selling dp to the mom and pop shops in every town.

At the same time, dp managers in the large corporations are having to deal with the fact that data processing, data communications, electronic mail, FAX, and word processing are beginning to converge. The boundary between voice, picture and digital signals is beginning to blur as well.

The federal government's response has been to launch computer inquiries; the courts', to press on with lingering antitrust trials. But the industry won't

stand still for a moment and decisions are outdated on the day they are made.

All this presents an interesting challenge for those who would manage corporations and their data processing central nervous system. Long-range planning often gives way to frenzied fire-fighting. And those brave companies that decide to pioneer the latest techniques often wind up with more than their share of arrows.

Source: *Datamation,* p. 5, November 1978. Reprinted with permission of *Datamation*® magazine, © Copyright by Technical Publishing Company, A Division of Dun-Donnelley Publishing Corporation. A Dun & Bradstreet Company, 1978–all rights reserved.

nication has led to abuses of an individual's legitimate right to privacy —i.e., the right to keep private (or have kept on a confidential basis) those facts, beliefs, thoughts, and feelings which one does not wish to divulge publicly.

5 *Human self-understanding questions.* As developmental work continues, and as computer programs become better able to solve relatively ill-structured problems and perform tasks that have heretofore been assumed to require human intelligence, will we as individuals alter the way we look at ourselves? Will we think less highly of ourselves if we see computers "outthinking" us?

LOOKING BACK

The following points have been emphasized in this chapter:

1 Scientific and technological discoveries are occurring rapidly in the world today, and a wave of social and economic changes has followed in the wake of recent technological developments. Many of these technology-induced changes have been beneficial, but others have had negative effects that have made us uneasy.

2 Revolutionary developments in microelectronic computer technology are creating an information revolution in the world today. These developments are having a profound impact on the size, speed, cost, capacity for information storage, and reliability of computer hardware. Software development, although less dramatic, has nevertheless been significant.

3 In a relatively short time span, quick-response information systems utilizing such developments as online processing, real time processing, timesharing, and distributed data processing networks have increased the timeliness, effectiveness, and availability of the information that people need.

4 Broader data-base information systems have also been created in recent years to integrate the data produced within an organization so

that decision makers may have more complete and relevant information. In addition to providing more complete internal information, however, the data-base system in the decision maker's organization may be linked to the data base of an external source to acquire further data resources.

5 Difficult problems and challenges face individuals and organizations as they attempt to adapt to changes brought about by the information revolution. A few of these issues have been introduced in this chapter.

▶ KEY TERMS

After reading Chapter 2, you should be able to define and use the following terms:

hardware	object program
nanosecond	batch processing
primary storage	record
translation programs	timesharing
source program	large-scale integration
multiprogramming	microsecond
file	central processing unit
real time processing	applications programs
software	online processing
millisecond	data base
secondary online storage	distributed data processing
operating system	data-base system

▶ REVIEW AND DISCUSSION QUESTIONS

1 Discuss this statement: "The basic challenge to the leaders of today is to foresee and manage (and not be swept along by) the flood of changes facing their organizations, and to do this within a democratic framework, for the benefit of society."

2 Why does a technological change simultaneously create new opportunities and problems for society?

3 Discuss this statement: "Developments in computer technology will inevitably lead to momentous changes in society."

4 Discuss this statement: "To manage effectively in the future, a manager must have information of the highest quality."

5 (a) What changes have taken place in computer hardware? (b) In computer software?

6 (a) What are the three basic software categories? (b) Discuss the developments in each of these categories.

7 What functions are performed by operating systems?

8 (a) Why have quick-response systems been developed? (b) What are the advantages of such systems? (c) What is the distinction between online processing and real time processing?

9 (a) What is batch processing? (b) How does it differ from online processing? (c) What are the advantages and disadvantages of batch processing?

10 "Online processing and direct access to records require unique hardware and software." Discuss this statement.

11 (a) What is meant by *timesharing?* (b) What is a *distributed data processing network?* (c) What do you think the long-term implications of distributed computer networks will be?

12 Identify and discuss the data-base approach to the design of information systems.

13 (a) Will data management software have any effect on applications programmers? (b) Defend your answer.

14 "Difficult problems and challenges face individuals and organizations as they attempt to adapt to changes brought about by the information revolution." Discuss this statement from the viewpoint of (a) a systems designer, (b) a law enforcement officer, (c) a civil liberties advocate, (d) a spy or saboteur, (e) a junior business executive, (f) a college student, (g) a competitor of IBM, (h) a telephone company executive, (i) a bookkeeping-machine operator, (j) an individual with social security number 350-26-5840, (k) a politician, (l) a postal worker, and (m) a banker.

15 In what ways, if any, can the development of atomic energy and television technology be compared to the present and future development of computer technology?

▶ SELECTED REFERENCES

Asimov, Isaac: "Pure and Impure: The Interplay of Science and Technology," *Saturday Review,* pp. 23–24ff, June 9, 1979.

Bell, Daniel: "Communications Technology—For Better or for Worse," *Harvard Business Review,* pp. 20–22ff, May/June 1979.

Branscomb, Lewis M.: "Information: The Ultimate Frontier," *Science,* pp. 143–147, January 12, 1979.

"Computer Revolution at Dun & Bradstreet," *Business Week,* pp. 72–76ff, August 27, 1979.

Killingsworth, Vivienne: "Corporate Star Wars: AT&T vs. IBM," *The Atlantic,* pp. 68–75, May 1979.

Lusa, John M.: "Distributed Processing: A Concept for Better Management," *Infosystems,* pp. 70ff, March 1978.

"More Leisure in an Increasingly Electronic Society," *Business Week,* pp. 208ff, September 3, 1979.

Shaffer, Richard A.: "The Superchip," *The Wall Street Journal,* pp. 1ff, April 27, 1979.

Traub, James: "The Privacy Snatchers," *Saturday Review,* pp. 16–20, July 21, 1979.

(Tom McHugh, Photo Researchers.)

Part Two
ORIENTATION
TO COMPUTERS

(Van Bucher, Photo Researchers.)

(Paul Sequeira, Photo Researchers.)

The chapters in Part 1 have provided a background for the study of computer concepts. One of the objectives of this book is to give you an orientation to computers (what they are, what they can and cannot do, and how they operate), and the chapters in Parts 2 and 3 are aimed at this objective. Computer capabilities and limitations are examined and basic *hardware* topics are presented in the chapters of Part 2. The development of the *software* needed to put the hardware to work is considered in the chapters of Part 3.

The chapters included in Part 2 are:

Chapter 3
INTRODUCTORY COMPUTER CONCEPTS

The purpose of this chapter is to give you an introduction to basic computer concepts. Thus, in the first part of the chapter you will see how computers may be classified into analog or digital categories. Since we are interested primarily in digital machines in this book, you will also see how digital computers may be grouped into special-purpose and general-purpose categories. A general-purpose computer may be used for a wide variety of scientific and file processing applications.

One of the objectives of this book is to provide you with information on what a computer can and cannot do. What a computer can do—its capabilities—is the subject of the second part of this chapter. What a computer cannot do—its limitations—is the topic of the third section.

Another topic closely associated in the minds of many people with the subject of computer capabilities and limitations is whether computers can be programmed to "think" and perform tasks that have usually been assumed to require human intelligence. Therefore, some efforts in the field of artificial intelligence are presented.

Finally, in the last part of the chapter, you will be introduced to the five functional elements common to all computers.

Thus, after studying this chapter, you should be able to:

- Explain the various ways in which computers may be classified.
- Identify and discuss some of the important capabilities of computers.
- Identify and discuss some of the important limitations of computers.
- Comment on some of the developments that have taken place in the field of artificial intelligence.
- Outline the five basic functions performed by all computers.
- Understand and use the key terms listed at the end of the chapter.

In earlier pages we have dealt with computers in rather general terms. In this chapter, however, we begin the closer examination of this exciting tool. More specifically, in the next few pages we shall consider: (1) the *classes* of computers, (2) their *capabilities*, (3) their *limitations*, (4) their *learning* ability, and (5) their *functional organization*.

COMPUTER CLASSIFICATIONS

As you know, some organizations offer tours of their facilities to interested parties. Let us assume that you are in a group visiting a hospital. In the course of your visit, the tour guide asks you to identify the equipment located in a large room. Because you are an intelligent person, you respond that this is the hospital's computer. The guide replies, "Yes, this is our new medium-sized electronic stored-program digital (a gasp for breath) general-purpose computer used for file processing purposes."

You probably recognize what the guide meant by the terms *medium-sized, electronic,* and *stored-program.* Computers are sometimes classified by size into large, medium, small, mini, and micro categories on the basis of computing power and cost. The stored-program concept refers to the ability of the machine to store internally an intellectual map, or group of sequenced instructions. This map will guide the computer automatically through a series of operations leading to the completion of a task. We will come back to this concept in later chapters.

What about the other classifying terms used by the guide? What do *digital, general-purpose,* and *file processing purposes* mean? Let us look at each of these items.

Analog and Digital Computers

There are two broad classes of computing devices—the analog and the digital. The *analog* machine does not compute directly with numbers; rather, it measures continuous physical magnitudes (e.g., pressure, temperature, voltage, current, shaft rotations, length), which represent, or are *analogous* to, the numbers under consideration. The service station gasoline pump, for example, may contain an analog computer that converts the flow of pumped fuel into two measurements—the price of the delivered gas to the nearest penny and the quantity of pumped fuel to the nearest tenth or hundredth of a gallon. Another example of an analog device is the automobile speedometer, which may convert drive-shaft rotational motion into a numerical indication by the speedometer pointer.

Analog computers are used for scientific, engineering, and process-control purposes. Because they deal with quantities that are continuously variable, they give only approximate results.

The *digital* computer operates by *counting* numbers. It operates directly on numbers expressed as digits in the familiar decimal system or some other numbering system. The ancient shepherd, it will be recalled, used stones to represent sheep, and these were counted one by one to determine the total number of sheep in the flock. Nothing was measured as an analogous representation of the number of sheep; the sheep were counted directly, and their total was exact. Stones have been replaced by adding machines, desk calculators, and digital computers, but all employ the same counting rules we learned in grade school.

Digital computation results in greater accuracy. While analog computers may under ideal conditions be accurate to within 0.1 percent of the correct value, digital computers can obtain whatever degree of accuracy is required simply by adding *places* to the right of the reference or decimal point. Every youngster who has worked arithmetic problems dealing with circles knows that pi (π) has a value of 3.1416. Actually, however, the value is 3.14159 . . . (this number could go on for pages). Over a decade ago, a computer worked the value of π out to 500,000 decimal places. How's that for accuracy?

Digital computers, unlike analog machines, are used for both processing and scientific purposes. In special situations (e.g., to simulate a guided missile system or a new aircraft design), desirable features of analog and digital machines have been combined to create a *hybrid* computer.

Special-Purpose and General-Purpose Computers

Digital computers may be produced for either special or general uses. A *special-purpose* computer, as the name implies, is designed to perform one specific task. The program of instructions is built into, or permanently stored in, the machine. Specialization results in the given task being performed very quickly and efficiently.[1] A disadvantage, however, is that the machine lacks versatility; it is inflexible and cannot be easily used to perform other operations. Special-purpose computers designed for the sole purpose of solving complex navigational problems are installed aboard our atomic submarines, but they could not be used for other purposes unless their circuits were redesigned. In the past, the cost of hardware made it relatively expensive to dedicate a computer to a single application. However, it is now feasible to routinely dedicate inexpensive microcomputers to the processing of specialized applications. New cars, for example, have such devices installed to monitor and control fuel, ignition, and other systems. Special-purpose microcomputers are replacing electromechanical timing and control devices in most large household appliances.

A *general-purpose* computer is one that has the ability to store *different* programs of instructions and thus to perform a variety of operations. In short, the stored-program concept makes the machine a general-purpose device—one that has the versatility to make possible the processing of a hospital payroll one minute and a drug inventory control application the next. New programs can be prepared, and old programs can be changed or dropped. Because it is designed to do a wide variety of jobs rather than perform a specific activity, the general-purpose machine

[1] Programmable calculators may also be customized through the use of a plug-in memory chip that permanently stores a special program of instructions. For example, the Forest Service uses specialized Texas Instruments calculators at a forest-fire site to predict the intensity and rate of spread.

typically compromises certain aspects of speed and efficiency—a small enough price to pay in many cases for the advantage of flexibility.

Scientific and File Processing Applications

A general-purpose central processor may be used for both scientific and file processing applications. What is the difference between these types of applications? What a coincidence that you should ask. . . .

Scientific processing applications   A research laboratory may wish to analyze and evaluate a product formula involving 3 variables and 15 terms (which results in 45 different values for each variable). The computer *input* would be the 15-term formula, the 135 values for the 3 variables, and the set of instructions to be followed in processing. The input is thus quite small. The *processing* involved, however, may well consist of hundreds of thousands of different computations—computations that might represent many months of labor if performed by other methods. The *output* necessary for a problem of this type may consist of a few typed lines giving a single evaluation or a few alternatives.

In short, the volume of input/output in scientific data processing is relatively small, and the speed with which these operations are performed is usually not too important. Computational speed, on the other hand, is a critical consideration because the bulk of the total processing job involves complex calculation.

File processing applications   In contrast to scientifically oriented applications, file processing tasks generally require faster input and output of data and larger storage capacity. An examination of a typical application will usually show that the volume of data input and information output is quite large. The running time required by the computer to complete such an application is often determined by the input/output speeds obtainable.

Computational speed is less critical in file processing applications because (1) arithmetic operations performed on each input record represent a relatively small proportion of the total job, and (2) the internal arithmetic speed of the slowest computer is frequently much greater than the speed of input/output devices.

To summarize (see Table 3-1), scientific and file processing applications typically differ with respect to (1) input/output volume, (2) input/output speed needed, (3) amount of computation, (4) importance of computational speed, and (5) storage requirements. Certain software and hardware control features, together with a wide range of available peripheral input/output and storage devices, permit most modern central processors to flexibly and efficiently serve both types of applications.

The stored program, digital, general-purpose computer (henceforth called *computer* for apparent reasons) possesses certain capabilities, which are summarized in the next section.

COMPUTER CAPABILITIES

Although many poets (and cartoonists) have pictured computer systems as having human or superhuman traits, such views tend to exaggerate certain computer capabilities. Yet it is clear that the computer is a powerful *tool* for extending people's brainpower. Peter Drucker has pointed out that human beings have developed two types of tools: (1) those which add to their capabilities and enable them to do something that they otherwise could *not* do (e.g., the airplane) and (2) those which multiply their capacity to do something that they are *already capable* of doing (e.g., the hammer).

The computer falls into the latter category. It is an intelligence amplifier. Carl Hammer, Director of Computer Sciences for UNIVAC, notes that today's computers have built into our society a mind-amplifying factor of over 2,000 to 1; i.e., behind every man, woman, and child in the United States there stands the power of over 2,000 human data processors. Computers can enlarge brainpower because of the properties presented below. These properties have led to the human or superhuman images.

1   *The ability to provide new time dimensions.* The machine works one step at a time; it adds and subtracts numbers; it multiplies and divides numbers (in most cases merely a repetitive process of addition and subtraction); and it can be designed or programmed to chose, copy, move, and compare the alphabetic and other symbols that people use. There is certainly nothing profound in these operations—even the author can perform them! What is significant, as we know, is the speed with which the machine functions. Thus, people are freed from calculations to use their time more creatively. Their time dimension has been broadened; they can now obtain information that could not have been produced at all a few years ago, or could not have been produced in time to be of any value. Karl Gauss, a German mathematician, at a young age had ideas that might have reshaped the study of mathematics in his time. Twenty years of his life was spent, however, in calculating the orbits of various heavenly objects. Were Gauss alive today, he could duplicate his calculations on a computer in a few hours and then be free to follow more creative pursuits. Similarly, the

*A computer designed to compute
a couple's rapport or dispute,
typed "Yes!" unashamed
when the young lady named
it in her paternity suit.*
—Gloria Maxson

TABLE 3-1
Processing differences in scientific and file processing applications

Processing Characteristics	Scientific Applications	File Processing Applications
Input/output volume	Low	Very high
Input/output speed	Relatively unimportant	Very important
Ratio of computations to input	Very high	Low
Computation speed	Very important	Relatively unimportant
Storage requirements	Modest	High

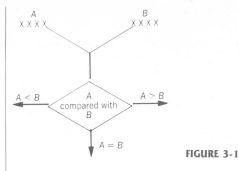

FIGURE 3-1

two years spent by John Adams in the 1840s in laboriously calculating the position of the planet Neptune could now be duplicated (with greater accuracy) by a computer in a little over a minute. Finally, a more recent illustration will serve to conclude this discussion of computer speed. John Kemeny of Dartmouth College has estimated that the calculations it took a year to complete working around the clock at the atomic laboratories at Los Alamos in 1945 could be done in one afternoon by an undergraduate student while sharing the computer's time with dozens of others.

2 *The ability to perform certain logic operations.* We have seen that computers are *symbol manipulators*—i.e., they can manipulate in logical ways letters, numbers, words, sentences, mathematical expressions, and other symbols to which people have given meaning. For example, when two items represented by the symbols A and B are compared, there are only three possible outcomes: (**1**) A is *equal to B* $(A = B)$, (**2**) A is *greater than B* $(A > B)$, or (**3**) A is *less than B* $(A < B)$.[2] The computer is able to perform a simple comparison and then, depending on the result, follow one of three *predetermined branches,* or courses of action, in the completion of that portion of its work (see Figure 3-1). Thus, the computer has made a "decision" by choosing between alternative possible courses of action. Actually, however, it might be more appropriate to say that the computer has *followed* decisions made earlier by the programmer. This simple ability to compare is an important computer property because more sophisticated questions can be answered by using combinations of comparison decisions. For example, if the data in a large listing such as a directory or table have been oganized in some logical order (alphabetically or in numerical sequence), the computer can be programmed to search for a specific data item by looking first at the middle item in the listing. If, as a result of a comparison, the desired item is alphabetically or numerically less than this middle item, the last half of the listing can be quickly elimi-

[2] The possible outcomes form what logicians forbiddingly call the *law of trichotomy.* Computers also compare numbers to see whether they are positive, negative, or equal to zero.

nated. Thus, this one comparison has cut the search problem in half. An additional comparison using the middle item of the remaining half of the listing can now be made, and this *binary search* procedure can be continued until the desired item is either located or shown to be missing from the listing. Another illustration of the computer's ability to perform logic operations concerns the "four-color conjecture" problem. For more than a century, mathematicians had been trying to prove that no more than four colors are needed to shade any map so that no adjoining nations are represented by the same color. Finally, two University of Illinois mathematicians examined, in mathematical terms, every imaginable map that could possibly be drawn. They then fed these possible map configurations into a computer to determine whether all maps could indeed be drawn with only four colors. The computer "wrestled with the question for some 1,200 hours, during which it made some 10 billion separately logical decisions. Finally, the machine replied yes, and the four-color conjecture turned from theory into fact."[3]

3   *The ability to store and retrieve information.* We know that the computer places in internal storage both facts and instructions. The ease with which instruction programs can be changed gives the computer great flexibility. The *access time* required for information to be recalled from internal storage and be available for use is measured in microseconds or more precise units. Few machines that we use have this stored-program ability—The instructions generally reside in the human mind and thus are outside the machine. Instructions and data are in a coded form that the machine has been designed to accept. The machine is also designed to perform automatically and in sequence certain operations on the data (add, write, move, store, or halt) called for by the instructions. The number of operations that can be performed varies among computer models. The stored program may, as we have just seen, allow the computer to select a branch of instructions to follow from several alternative sequences. The program may also allow the computer to *repeat* or *modify* instructions as required. Computers communicate with human operators by using input and output devices, and they communicate with other machines.

4   *The ability to control error.* It is estimated that you or I would make one error in every 500 to 1,000 operations with a desk calculator. A computer, on the other hand, can perform hundreds of thousands of arithmetic operations every second and can run errorless for hours and days at a time. Computers also have the ability to check their own work. By a method known as *parity checking,* computers check on data when they enter storage, when they are moved internally, and when they leave in the form of output. Each character (e.g., number or letter) fed into the computer is represented in a coded form by sev-

---

[3] "Eureka!" *Time,* p. 88, September 20, 1976. This example illustrates computer capabilities both in providing new time dimensions and in performing logic operations. It also shows some of the characteristics of scientific processing applications.

eral binary digits (0s and 1s) called *bits,* just as each number or letter in a punched card is represented by a code. The parity check performed by the computer involves the examination of each character's code to determine whether bits have been added or lost by mistake. More will be said about parity checking in a later chapter.

It should not be assumed, however, that computers have unlimited capabilities or that they are free of error. They do have their limitations, and they have been involved in some classic mistakes.

COMPUTER LIMITATIONS

A publishing company's customer received a computer-produced invoice requesting that he pay his bill in the amount of "W-2.C." The customer promptly forwarded his check for W-2.C as directed, with a note saying, "Out here in the sticks, we dig this crazy new currency you folks have invented." Billing operations have produced other computer goofs. For example, an insurance company kept sending a policyholder a bill for $0.00 and demanding payment, and in Fort Worth, Texas, a man was surprised to receive a brief, rather cool letter from an oil company telling him that his account was past due by $34.32. The man can be excused his surprise because he had never received a credit card from any oil company. Six weeks passed before the error was discovered, during which time the man kept protesting and the form letters (getting less and less cordial) kept coming in. Of course, it is not always the individual who is victimized. In another case, an aircraft manufacturer sent a supplier a computer-prepared check for $3,000,000 to settle a $3,000 bill. (The supplier could not resist then going to the sales office of the manufacturer and offering to buy an expensive airplane for cash!)

Or consider the case of the genteel New York City man who one month received an unsolicited Playboy Club key and who for months thereafter received bills for $7.50 from Playboy's computer. An attorney's letter was required to get the rabbit off his back. These victims, along with the Phoenix man who was treated for pneumonia and charged for the use of the nursery and the delivery room, perhaps felt as did another victim, who said: "The computer is a complete revolution in the ways of doing business . . . and as in any revolution some innocent people always get slaughtered."

That such stories are carried in newspapers is indication enough that they occur only infrequently. Perhaps in most cases the errors may be traced to humans who failed to give proper attention to the following limitations:

1   *Application programs must always be prepared.* The machine does what it is programmed to do and *nothing else.*[4] It can only operate on

Jack and Jill
Went up the hill
With great anticipating
Jack came down
And with a frown
Gave up computer dating
—Edmund Conti

"I am very annoyed to find that you have branded my son illiterate. This is a dirty lie as I was married a week before he was born."
"I am forwarding my marriage certificate and 5 children, one of which is a mistake as you can see."
"You have changed my little boy to a girl. Will this make a difference?"
"My husband got his project cut off and I haven't had any relief since. . . ."
—From letters to a computer-using welfare department

---

[4] As you will see in the next section, this statement certainly does not mean that computers must be stupid. Clever programs can be written to cause the computer to store the results of previous decisions. Then, by using the branching ability designed into the program, the computer may be able to modify its behavior according to the success or failure of past decisions.

data; i.e., it can accept data, process data, and communicate results, but it cannot directly perform physical activities such as bending metal. (The processed information may be used, however, to control metal-bending machines.) Furthermore, a program may *seem* to be flawless and operate satisfactorily for some months and then produce nonsense (a bill for $0.00, for instance) because some rare combination of events has presented the computer with a situation (*a*) for which there is no programmed course of action or (*b*) where the course of action provided by the programmer contains an error that is just being discovered. Of course, a truly flawless program, supplied with incorrect data, may also produce nonsense. And once incorrect facts are entered into a computer system, they are usually not as easy to purge as is the case when manual methods are used.

2   *Applications must be able to be quantified and dealt with logically.* The computer will not be of much help to people in areas where *qualitative* considerations are important. It will not, for example, tell you how to "get rich quick" in the stock market; it will not improve much on random selection in arranging a date between Jack and Jill (both have outrageous personalities, and both have been less than candid in filling out computer input forms); and it will not signal a change in an economic trend until after the fact. Thus, it will not tell an administrator whether a new urban development project will be successful if implemented. The ultimate decision may be of a qualitative nature because it is involved with future social, political, techological, and economic events; thus success is impossible to predict with certainty. However, the computer will by *simulation* let an administrator know how a new project will fare under *assumed* social, political, and economic conditions. The computer, in short, is limited to those processing applications which may be expressed in the form of an *algorithm*—i.e., the application must consist of a finite number of steps leading to a precisely defined goal, and each step must be specifically and *clearly defined.*[5] Thus, we might say that an algorithm operates on data to produce information. If the steps in the solution of the problem cannot be written down precisely, the application cannot be performed on today's commercial computers. Even if the steps can be defined by a finite set of rules that a computer could follow, there are still some tasks whose execution might take millions or even billions of years on a giant computer. As Joseph Weizenbaum has observed, a program could be written "to try every legal move in a certain chess situation; for each move try every possible response; for each response try its response; and so on until the computer has found a move which, if suitably pursued, would guarantee it a win. Such a program would surely be finite, but the length of time required by a computer to exe-

---

[5] It is often quite frustrating to work on programs for computers. In one case, a thwarted programmer fired two bullets into a computer, with the result that unemployment checks were late that week in a Western city.

cute it would be unimaginably large. In principle, then, a computer could carry out such behavior; in fact, it cannot."[6]

3 *Applications must weigh resources.* Merely because a computer can be programmed to do a job does not always mean that it *should*. Writing programs, although less tedious than in the past because of developments in software, is still a time-consuming and expensive human operation. Thus, nonrecurring tasks or jobs that are seldom processed are often not efficient areas for computer application at the present time. In file processing, it is usually most economical to prepare programs for large-volume, repetitive operations that will be used many times and that promise fast returns on the time invested in program preparations.[7]

EXPERIMENTS IN ARTIFICIAL INTELLIGENCE

Although the superhuman computers found in science fiction do not exist, science fiction has a way of becoming science fact. Research efforts and experiments are currently being conducted in the use of computers to solve relatively ill structured problems. These research efforts, which are sometimes classified under the heading of *artificial intelligence,* and which are combining concepts found in disciplines such as psychology, linguistics, and computer science, are aimed at learning how to prepare programs (or construct systems) that can do tasks that have never been done automatically before and that have usually been assumed to require human intelligence.

For example, computers have been programmed to play checkers and to modify their programs on the basis of success and failure with moves used in the past against human opponents. In one such program, the computer has continually improved its game to the point where it regularly defeats the author of the program. Thus, the machine has "learned" what not to do through trial and error.

Dozens of chess-playing programs have been written that can run on machines ranging from micro-sized personal computers to very large supercomputers. As we have seen, the possible number of moves in a chess game is so large that all the moves could not possibly be stored or analyzed by any computer. Thus, the only feasible approach is to program the computer to play the game by evaluating possible moves and formulating a playing strategy.

At the *beginning* of a chess game, proven approaches to minimize losses and, perhaps, to create openings are often followed for the first 7

---

[6] Joseph Weizenbaum, "The Last Dream," *Across the Board,* p. 39, July 1977. The term *combinatorial explosion* is given to this type of problem where a finite number of instructions generates an impossibly large number of computer operations.

[7] In engineering and scientific computing, the importance of a nonrecurring task often warrants the necessary investment in programming time. An example might be the engineering planning and construction scheduling, by computer, of a single multimillion-dollar office building.

"July/August 1958: Artificial Intelligence"

Twenty years ago we still had some very simple, mechanistic (and probabilistic) concepts of how the human brain functioned. So simple, in fact, that in an August 1958 article, DATAMATION reported that ". . . some work which had been performed at Cornell Aeronautical Laboratory indicated that at last a machine operating on the principle of the human brain appeared possible, at least as a laboratory model."

The machine was called a perceptron and it was developed by a research psychologist named Frank Rosenblatt. At an early demonstration Rosenblatt posed the question: Is it possible for a machine to have original ideas? His answer equivocated only slightly: "With regard to the perceptron it appears that we must answer this question concerning original ideas in the affirmative."

An IBM 704 was used to simulate the presentation of various sensory stimuli (e.g., various shapes) to a tv-like camera hooked to the computer system. Instead of recognizing the target shapes by comparing them to a prestored inventory, the perceptron's "recognition is direct and essentially instantaneous, since the association by which a preceived stimulus is identified is derived in the form of new pathways through the system rather than from a coded representation of the original stimulus."

Heady stuff that, back in 1958.

What happened to the perceptron's bright promise? Well, as time went on and the world became more complex, the theories supporting the perceptron concept began to unravel. And in 1969 the coup de grace appeared in a book by Marvin Minsky and Seymour Papert, published by MIT Press. The two artificial intelligence experts presented hard proof that the perceptron would mathematically be able to identify only patterns that were, in topological terminology, "simply connected." The perceptron, it turned out, couldn't perceive very much after all.

Source: *Datamation,* p. 8, August 1978. Reprinted with permission of *Datamation*® magazine, © Copyright by Technical Publishing Company, a Division of Dun-Donnelley Publishing Corporation, A Dun & Bradstreet Company, 1978—all rights reserved.

to 10 moves. Much less predictable is the *middle* part of the game. Good chess players must adopt a strategy and "look ahead" to determine the future consequences of a move.[8] (Chess masters can accurately foresee the consequences 12 to 15 moves later; the author's vision is good for

---

[8] Some of the factors to consider in formulating a strategy and deciding on moves to make are mobility, king safety, the values of the attacked and attacking pieces, and the overall layout of the board. The computer must be programmed to take these factors into consideration.

FIGURE 3-2
Joseph Marie Jacquard. (*The Bettmann Archive.*)

M. JACQUARD: AUTOMATOR OF THE WEAVING TRADE

Joseph Marie Jacquard was born in 1752 near Lyons, France. At the age of 10, Jacquard went to work as a "drawboy" in the weaving trade. Patterns were created in silk material by drawboys who lifted and returned the weighted vertical warp threads by hand. In later life, Jacquard became obsessed with eliminating the tedious function of the drawboy in silk manufacturing.

After years of experimentation, Jacquard created a loom that used steel rods to sense holes in a punched card. When the rod passed through a hole in the card, it activated a mechanism that lifted the thread, thus eliminating the job of the drawboy. The punched card "programmed" the pattern in the material.

Jacquard died in 1844 at the age of 82 with his mission completed. The drawboy had been replaced by an automated loom.

about 1 ½ moves.) If the middle game is complicated, the *end game* is absolutely mind-blowing. Each player may have six or seven pieces left; the sides of the board have generally lost their meaning; and the pieces may be positioned in ways that have *never occurred before* in the history of the game. In a few moves, a strong attack can result in an impossible defense. Individuals may develop new strategies at this time. A computer program, of course, must also try to adapt to end-game situations.

Given this brief summary of chess, a natural question is: How have computer programs fared against human opponents in this very intellectual game? This question can best be answered by looking at the "Levy challenge." In 1968, David Levy, a Scottish chess champion with an international master ranking,[9] beat John McCarthy, a Stanford University professor of artificial intelligence (AI), in a chess game. McCarthy remarked that although he could not beat Levy, there would be within 10 years a computer program that could. A bet of 250 British pounds ($625) was made between Levy and McCarthy. Levy would win the bet unless a computer program won a match against him before the end of August 1978.

During the next few years, other AI professors and computer programmers joined McCarthy in betting against Levy. In 1977, Levy played a match against a Northwestern University program named Chess 4.5 that had just won the Minnesota Open championship against human opponents. Levy won the match and later in the year beat Kaissa, a Russian program. As the 1978 deadline approached, a final six-game match was arranged between Levy and Northwestern's Chess 4.7 (a successor to Chess 4.6). The first game was a draw (each side received ½ point), Levy won the second and third games, the computer won the fourth game, and Levy won the fifth game. (A sixth game was unnecessary since Levy had scored 3½ points out of a possible 6.) Although the human won this round, the Levy challenge continues, with a new bet totaling $10,000 to be decided by January 1984.

In addition to chess and checkers, computers have also been programmed to prove mathematical theorems and compose music, but thus far such research activities are limited and involved "thinking" on the part of the machine in a most restricted sense.

Much has been written in the past few years pro and con about the question of whether computers can be programmed to "think" and "learn." Most of the controversy probably stems from (1) a lack of understanding about the processes involved in human thinking and learning and (2) the absence of acceptable definitions of such words as *think* and *learn*.

One test—a game—to determine whether a computer might be considered to possess intelligence and the ability to think was proposed by Alan Turing, a British mathematician. Participants in the game would be two respondents—a machine and a human—and a human interrogator who tries to determine which of the unseen respondents is the human. In

---

[9] In the chess world, an international master is one rank below a top grandmaster.

answering questions posed by the interrogator (communications terminals are used), the machine tries to deceive while the human respondent tries to convince the interrogator of his or her true identity. Intelligence and the ability to think would, according to "Turing's test," be demonstrated by the machine's success in fooling the interrogator.[10]

Have computers passed Turing's test? Not yet, but the machines *have* passed incomplete versions of the test. For example, several years ago Joseph Weizenbaum wrote a program with which one could "converse" in English. The program plays the role of a psychotherapist engaged in an interview with a patient. A hypothetical conversation between patient and "doctor" might go like this (computer entries are in capital letters):

DO YOU HAVE ANY PROBLEMS?
Yes, I am depressed
I AM SORRY TO HEAR YOU ARE DEPRESSED
My boyfriend makes me unhappy
TELL ME ABOUT YOUR BOYFRIEND

In a variation of Turing's test,[11] staff members at Massachusetts General Hospital let a number of people "talk" to Weizenbaum's program for a time. When they were asked if they had been talking with a human or a machine, a majority thought they had been in contact with a human. David Levy, the chess master, believes that since the Chess 4.7 program he competed against is stronger than 99.5 percent of all human chess players, it has already reached and passed the stage where he could correctly identify it as a human or computer opponent under Turing-test conditions.

Where is the current research in AI likely to lead us? No one knows. *Heuristic*[12] is a word that means "serving to discover." It is used to describe the judgmental, or *commonsense,* part of problem solving. That is, it describes that part of problem solving which deals with the definition of the problem, the selection of reasonable strategies to be followed (which may or may not lead to optimum solutions), and the formulation of hypotheses and hunches. Human beings are now *far superior* to the computer in the heuristic area of intellectual work. As people's thinking and learning processes become better understood, however, it may be possible to develop new programs and machines with improved heuristic abilities. Certainly, some very able researchers are working toward this end. However, for the foreseeable future the role of the computer should con-

---

[10] Of course, many do not agree with this concept of thinking. As computer scientist Paul Armer has facetiously observed, computers cannot think because people keep redefining *thinking* to be a process that is just beyond whatever the current ability of the computer happens to be.

[11] The people tested did not know it was a test, and the program was not competing with a human.

[12] Pronounced *hew-ris'tik.*

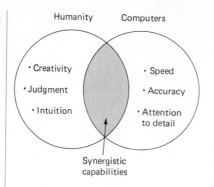

FIGURE 3-3
The strengths of humans and computers differ.

tinue to be that of an intelligence amplifier in an alliance with humanity. This alliance would combine the current superiority of the human brain in matters involving creativity, judgment, and intuition with the computer's superiority in matters involving processing speed, accuracy, and tireless attention to detail. The word *synergy* refers to the ability of two entities to achieve together that which each is individually incapable of achieving. As Figure 3-3 indicates, the alliance between humans and computers could produce a synergistic effect. The potential of such an alliance, although not unlimited, cannot be restricted in any way we can now anticipate.[13]

COMPUTER FUNCTIONAL ORGANIZATION

"Take a good long look at a computer. Does it have input, output, a bit of binary? No, you say to all these questions? Then you are not taking a good long look at a computer."[14]

The computer solves problems and produces information in much the same way that you do. Let us illustrate this fact by first making a most disagreeable assumption: In the near future you will have to take a written examination on the material covered in the first few chapters of a math book. For the past few days you have been reading the text, trying to catch up on your homework problems, and listening to your professor's lectures. You have written several pages of notes and have memorized various facts, concepts, and procedures. Finally, the examination period arrives, and you begin to work the test problems. Procedures are followed, you hope, in the correct order. As time runs out, you turn your paper in to the professor and leave, resolving to pay somewhat closer attention to what she or he has to say in the future.

Five functions were performed in the above illustration (see Figure 3-4). These functions are:

1   *Input.* The input function involves the receipt of facts that can be used. You received data from your textbook and from your professor.

---

[13] Whether computers will be content to remain in the role envisioned here is a matter that is disputed by some. See, for example, Frank George, *Machine Takeover,* Pergamon Press, New York, 1977; and Robert Jastrow, "Toward an Intelligence beyond Man's," *Time,* p. 59, February 20, 1978.

[14] From Eve R. Wirth, "Out of the Mouth of Babes," *Creative Computing,* p. 110, November/December 1977.

2 *Storage.* Facts received must be stored until they are needed. Your notebook (offline storage) and your brain (online storage) were used to store information and the procedures to use for solving problems.

3 *Calculation and symbol manipulation.* On the test you manipulated math symbols and performed the mathematical operations of addition, subtraction, etc., either manually or with the help of a calculator.

4 *Control.* On the exam it was necessary to follow certain procedures in the proper order, or sequence. *Control,* then, simply means doing things in the correct sequence.

5 *Output.* Your finished test was the output—the result of your processing operations. It will provide your professor with part of the information needed to arrive at a decision about your final grade.

All computers perform these five functions. Figure 3-5 illustrates the *functional* organization of a computer. Let us briefly examine each part of this diagram.

Input

Computers, obviously, must also receive facts to solve problems. Data and instructions must be put into the computer system in a form that it can use. There are a number of devices that will perform this input function, as we shall see in the following chapter. They may allow direct

FIGURE 3-4

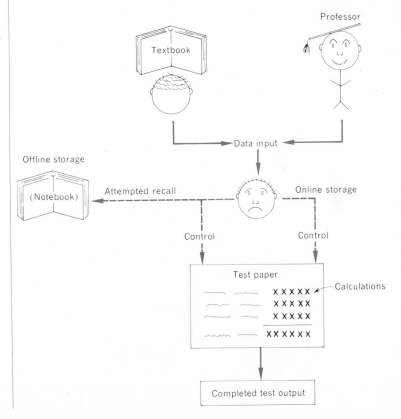

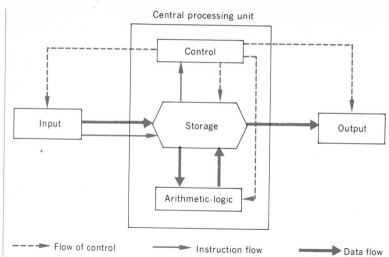

Central processing unit

FIGURE 3-5
Computer functional
organization.

- - - -> Flow of control   ——> Instruction flow   ——▶ Data flow

human-machine communication without the necessity of an input medium (e.g., the keyboard of a personal microcomputer), or they may present information that typically has been produced offline in batches on an
input medium (e.g., punched cards). Regardless of the type of device
used, they are all instruments of interpretation and communication between people and the machine.

Storage

The heart of any computer installation is the central processing unit (CPU).
Within CPUs of all sizes are generally located storage, control, and arithmetic-logic units (see Figure 3-6). It is this central processor that makes
comparisons, performs calculations, and selects, interprets, and controls
the execution of instructions.

    The storage section of the central processor is used for *four purposes,*
three of which relate to the data being processed. First, data are fed into
the storage area where they are held until ready to be processed. Second,
additional storage space is used to hold data being processed and the
intermediate results of such processing. Third, the storage unit holds the
finished product of the processing operations until it can be released in
the form of output information. Fourth, in addition to these data-related
purposes, the storage unit also holds the program instructions until they
are needed.

Arithmetic-Logic

All calculations are performed and all comparisons (decisions) are made
in the arithmetic-logic section of the central processor. Data flow between this section and the storage unit during processing operations; i.e.,
data are received from storage, manipulated, and returned to storage. No

processing is performed in the storage section. The number of arithmetic and logic operations that can be performed is determined by the engineering design of the machine.

To summarize briefly, data are fed into the storage unit from the input devices. Once in storage, they are held and transferred as needed to the arithmetic-logic unit where processing takes place. Data may move from storage to the arithmetic-logic unit and back again to storage many times before the processing is finished. Once completed, the information is released from the central processor to the output device.

Control

How does the input unit know when to feed data into storage? How does the arithmetic-logic unit obtain the needed data from storage, and how does it know what should be done with them once they are received? How is the output unit able to obtain finished information instead of raw data from storage? It is by selecting, interpreting, and executing the program instructions that the control unit of the central processor is able to maintain order and direct the operation of the entire installation. It thus acts as a central nervous system for the component parts of the computer. Instructions are *selected* and fed in sequence into the control unit from storage. There they are *interpreted,* and from there signals are sent to *other* machine units to *execute* program steps. The control unit itself does not perform actual processing operations on the data.

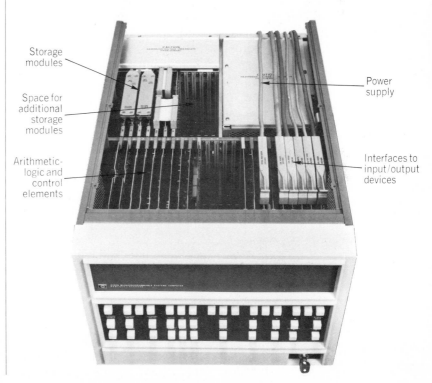

Storage modules

Space for additional storage modules

Arithmetic-logic and control elements

Power supply

Interfaces to input/output devices

FIGURE 3-6
Mini-sized CPU.
(*Hewlett-Packard Co.*)

Output

Output devices, like input units, are instruments of interpretation and communication between people and machine. They take information in machine-coded form and convert it typically into a form that can be used (1) by humans (e.g., a printed report) or (2) as machine input in another processing operation (e.g., magnetic tape). In the following chapter we shall take a closer look at several output devices.

Extensive Variations Possible

All computer systems are similar in that they perform the basic functions just described. However, just as computers vary greatly in size, they also vary widely in external configurations. Some micro- and mini-sized systems are housed in three boxes, as implied in Figure 3-5. Some personal computers may be in a single cabinet. And some mainframe family models may have multiple units for the input and output functions, and may distribute parts of the storage and control functions to equipment peripheral to the CPU. Figure 3-7 illustrates some of the possible machine combinations. (Input/output hardware and media will be surveyed in the next chapter; a closer look at the CPU will be the subject of Chapter 5.) The boxes labeled "channels" in Figure 3-7 require a brief explanation here.

A *channel* consists of hardware that, along with other associated monitoring and connecting elements, controls and provides the path for the movement of data between relatively slow input/output (I/O) devices, on the one hand, and high-speed central-processor primary storage, on the other. Because of the differences in operating speeds, the CPU would be idle much of the time if it had to hold up processing during the periods when input was being received and output was being produced. Fortunately, most computers built since the mid-1960s have features that make it possible to *overlap* input, processing, and output operations in order to make more efficient use of computing resources. Once the channel has received appropriate instruction signals from the central processor, it can operate independently and without supervision while the CPU is engaged in performing computations. For example, at the same time that the CPU is processing one group of records, one channel can be receiving another group for subsequent processing while a second channel can be supplying processed information to the appropriate output device.

The channel may be a separate small special-purpose control computer located near the CPU, or it may be a physical part of the CPU which is accessible to both I/O devices and other elements of the CPU. Multiple channels may be used to serve a large number of peripheral I/O devices, e.g., a large number of terminals used in a timesharing system.

Before concluding this section, it might be appropriate to mention another type of variation that can exist in computer systems—the varia-

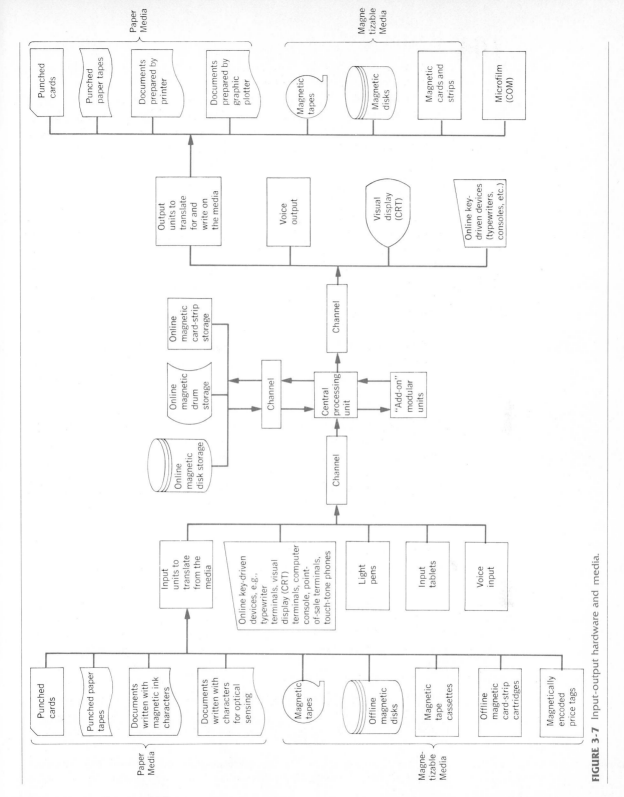

FIGURE 3-7 Input-output hardware and media.

105

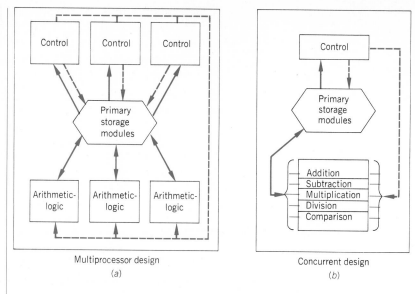

Multiprocessor design
(a)

Concurrent design
(b)

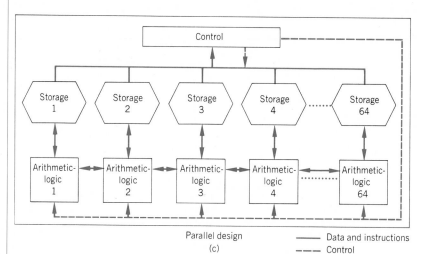

Parallel design
(c)

——— Data and instructions
- - - Control

FIGURE 3-8
Alternative computer system
designs.

tion in the design and construction (or *architecture*) of the functional elements in the CPU. Figure 3-5 shows the *traditional* and currently most popular design. This design features *single* control, storage, and arithmetic-logic units in the CPU. However, there are several ways this traditional design can be modified in order to achieve even greater computing speeds. Among the possible alternative designs are the following:

1 *The multiprocessor design.* By adding additional control and arithmetic-logic units (see Figure 3-8a), several instructions can be processed

at the same instant in time. As we saw in the last chapter, multiprogramming involves executing a portion of one program, then a segment of another, etc., in brief *consecutive* time periods. Multiprocessor design, however, makes it possible for the system to work *simultaneously* on several program segments. Thus, this design represents, in effect, a system with two or more central processors.

2   *The concurrent* (or *pipeline*) *design.* Computing speed can also be increased by separating the arithmetic-logic unit into functional subunits, each of which can operate independently under the direction of the control unit (see Figure 3-8*b*). When, for example, consecutive and independent program instructions call for the use of separate subunits (e.g., addition, multiplication, and division), the control unit will signal the proper elements to proceed *concurrently* to process all these instructions. Lacking functionally independent subunits, a traditionally designed arithmetic-logic unit will take the first instruction in the sequence and execute it before moving to the next instruction.

3   *The parallel design.* The ILLIAC IV is a massive "number-cruncher" with a control unit that directs the operations of 64 arithmetic-logic units that can operate simultaneously, or *in parallel.* Each arithmetic-logic unit has its own storage unit (see Figure 3-8*c*).

These variations from traditional design result in faster computation speed. It is anticipated that these design variations will become the structures for many future computer systems.

"Toward an Intelligence beyond Man's"

As Dr. Johnson said in a different era about ladies preaching, the surprising thing about computers is not that they think less well than a man, but that they think at all. The early electronic computer did not have much going for it except a prodigious memory and some good math skills, but today the best models can be wired up to learn by experience, follow an argument, ask pertinent questions and write pleasing poetry and music. They can also carry on somewhat distracted conversations so convincingly that their human partners do not know they are talking to a machine.

These are amiable qualities for the computer; it imitates life like an electronic monkey. As computers get more complex, the imitation gets better. Finally, the line between the original and the copy becomes blurred. In another 15 years or so—two more generations of computer evolution, in the jargon of the technologists—we will see the computer as an emergent form of life.

The proposition seems ridiculous because, for one thing, computers lack the drives and emotions of living creatures. But when drives are useful, they can be programmed into the computer's brain, just as nature programmed them into our ancestors' brains as a part of the equipment for survival. For example, computers, like people, work better and learn faster when they are motivated. Arthur Samuel made this discovery when he taught two IBM computers how to play checkers. They polished their game by playing each other, but they learned slowly. Finally, Dr. Samuel programmed in the will to win by forcing the computers to try harder—and to think out more moves in advance—when they were losing. Then the computers learned very quickly. One of them beat Samuel and went on to defeat a champion player who had not lost a game to a human opponent in eight years.

Computers match people in some roles, and when fast decisions are needed in a crisis, they often outclass them. The human brain has a wiring defect that prevents it from absorbing several streams of information simultaneously and acting on them quickly. Throw too many things at the brain at one time and it freezes up; it evolved more than 100,000 years ago, when the tempo of life was slower.

We are still in control, but the capabilities of computers are increasing at a fantastic rate, while raw human intelligence is changing slowly, if at all. Computer power is growing exponentially; it has increased tenfold every eight years since 1946. Four generations of computer evolution—vacuum tubes, transistors, simple integrated circuits and today's miracle chips—followed one another in rapid succession, and the fifth generation, built out of such esoteric devices as bubble memories and Josephson junctions, will be on the market in the 1980s. In the 1990s, when the sixth generation appears, the compactness and reasoning power of an intelligence built out of silicon will begin to match that of the human brain.

By that time, ultra-intelligent machines will be working in partnership with our best minds on all the serious problems of the day, in an unbeatable combination of brute reasoning power and human intuition. What happens after that? Dartmouth President John Kemeny, a pioneer in computer usage, sees the ultimate relation between man and computer as a symbiotic union of two living species, each completely dependent on the other for survival. The computer—a new form of life dedicated to pure thought—will be taken care of by its human partners, who will minister to its bodily needs with electricity and spare parts. Man will also provide for computer reproduction, as he does today. In return, the computer will minister to our social and economic needs. Child of man's brain rather than his loins, it will become his salvation in a world of crushing complexity.

The partnership will not last very long. Computer intelligence is growing by leaps and bounds, with no natural limit in sight. But human evolution is a nearly finished chapter in the history of life. The human brain has not changed, at least in gross size, in the past 100,000 years, and while the organization of the brain may have improved in that period, the amount of information and wiring that can be crammed into a cranium of fixed size is limited.

That does not mean the evolution of intelligence has ended on the earth. Judging by the record of the past, we can expect that a new species will arise out of man, surpassing his achievements as he has surpassed those of his predecessor, *Homo erectus*. Only a carbon-chemistry chauvinist would assume that the new species must be man's flesh-and-blood descendants, with brains housed in fragile shells of bone. The new kind of intelligent life is more likely to be made of silicon.

The history of life suggests that the evolution of the new species will take about a million years. Since the majority of the planets in the universe are not merely millions but *billions* of years older than the earth, the life they carry—assuming life to be common in the cosmos—must long since have passed through the stage we are about to enter.

A billion years is a long time in evolution; 1 billion years ago, the highest form of life on the earth was a worm. The intelligent life in these other, older solar systems must be as different from us as we are from creatures wriggling in the ooze. Those superintelligent beings surely will not be housed in the more or less human shapes portrayed in *Star Wars* and *Close Encounters of the Third Kind*. In a cosmos that has endured for billions of years against man's mere million, the human form is not likely to be the standard form for intelligent life.

In any event, our curiosity may soon be satisfied. At this moment a shell of TV signals carrying old *I Love Lucy* programs and *Tonight* shows is expanding through the cosmos at the speed of light. That bubble of broadcasts has already swept past about 50 stars like the sun. Our neighbors know we are here, and their replies should be on the way. In another 15 or 20 years we will receive their message and meet our future. Let us be neither surprised nor disappointed if its form is that of Artoo Detoo, the bright, personable canister packed with silicon chips.

Source: Robert Jastrow, "Toward an Intelligence beyond Man's," *Time,* p. 59, February 20, 1978. Reprinted by permission from *Time,* The Weekly Newsmagazine; Copyright Time Inc. 1978.

◖ LOOKING BACK

The following points have been emphasized in this chapter:

1 Computers may be classified in a number of ways. We have seen, for example, that there are analog and digital computers, hybrid computers, and special-purpose and general-purpose devices. Analog computers deal with quantities that are continuously variable, and

digital machines operate by counting numbers. A hybrid computer combines analog and digital elements. Special-purpose computers are designed to process specific applications, and general-purpose devices may perform a wide variety of tasks.

2 Modern general-purpose digital computers are designed to process both scientific and file processing applications, even though these applications may differ significantly in their processing characteristics.

3 Computers have the capability to extend human brainpower. They are intelligence amplifiers that provide new dimensions in the time available for creative work. They are able to perform certain logic operations. Sophisticated questions can be answered by the combination of many simple machine "decisions." Computers can store and retrieve information rapidly and accurately.

4 But machines, like humans (especially like humans), are not infallible. They will produce nonsense by diligently and tirelessly following a flawed program of instructions, and they must be told exactly and precisely what to do. Thus, they are restricted in practical use to applications that can be structured into a finite number of steps to achieve a specific goal.

5 Computer chess programs now exist that can defeat 99.5 percent of all human chess players. Experiments are being conducted by extremely able researchers in the field of artificial intelligence to improve the machines' heuristic capabilities. But humans still remain far superior to computers in this area of intellectual work. The potential of an alliance between humans and computers, however, cannot be restricted in any way we can now anticipate.

6 Computers are organized to perform the functional activities of input, storage, arithmetic-logic, control, and output. A multitude of machine configurations and media are used in the performance of these functions. The composition of the CPU is subject to design variation; the most powerful computers generally depart in some way from the traditional design, which features single control, storage, and arithmetic-logic units in the CPU.

▶ KEY TERMS

After reading Chapter 3, you should be able to define and use the following terms:

digital computer	Turing test
analog computer	heuristic
special-purpose computer	human-computer alliance
general-purpose computer	computer functional organization
hybrid computer	input function
comparison decisions	storage function

access time

branching

algorithm

artificial intelligence

arithmetic-logic function

control function

output function

computer architecture

▶ REVIEW AND DISCUSSION QUESTIONS

1 Discuss the various ways in which computers may be classified.

2 (a) What is an analog computer? (b) How does it differ from a digital computer?

3 How does a special-purpose computer differ from a general-purpose machine?

4 Compare and contrast the processing characteristics typically found in nonscientific and scientific applications.

5 Why is it possible to say that the computer is an intelligence amplifier?

6 Identify and discuss the limitations of computer usage.

7 Why does controversy surround the question of whether computers can be programmed to "think"?

8 Identify and discuss the five functions performed by computers.

9 "The storage section of the central processor is used for four purposes." What are these four purposes?

10 (a) What functions are performed in the arithmetic-logic section of the central processor? (b) In the control section?

11 What is the role of a data channel?

12 Differentiate between traditional CPU design and (a) multiprocessor design, (b) concurrent design, and (c) parallel design.

13 "In musical terms, a piano may be considered a digital instrument, while a violin is an analog device." Discuss this statement.

14 Robert Jastrow, Director of NASA's Goddard Institute for Space Studies, has written that the alliance between humans and computers will not last very long. He states that: "Computer intelligence is growing by leaps and bounds, with no natural limit in sight. But human evolution is a nearly finished chapter in the history of life." Jastrow believes that a new kind of intelligent life will probably emerge on the earth, and this life "is more likely to be made of silicon." (a) What is your reaction to this opinion? (b) Are your views changed by the fact that Jastrow believes the evolution of the new silicon species will take about a million years?

▶ SELECTED REFERENCES

Ehara, Theodore H.: "The Levy Wager," *Creative Computing,* pp. 86–89, September 1979.

George, Frank: *Machine Takeover,* Pergamon Press, New York, 1977.

Jastrow, Robert: "Toward an Intelligence beyond Man's," *Time,* p. 59, February 20, 1978.

Kugel, Peter: "The Controversy Goes On—Can Computers Think?" *Creative Computing,* part 1, pp. 46–50, August 1979; part 2, pp. 104–109, September 1979.

Levy, David: "Computers are Now Chess Masters," *New Scientist,* pp. 256–258, July 27, 1978.

Matheson, Willard E.: "The Brain and the Machine," *Personal Computing,* pp. 37–38ff, April 1978.

Raphael, Bertram: *The Thinking Computer: Mind Inside Matter,* W. H. Freeman and Company, San Francisco, 1976.

Weizenbaum, Joseph: *Computer Power and Human Reason* W. H. Freeman and Company, San Francisco, 1976.

Chapter 4
COMPUTER INPUT/OUTPUT

The purpose of this chapter is to give you an overview of the media and devices used by computer systems for input/output (I/O) and secondary storage. In the first part of the chapter, you will read about the punched card, punched paper tape, and magnetic tape media that are usually used for batch-processing applications. You will then be introduced to the direct-access I/O and storage devices used in online processing. (These devices include magnetic drums, disks, cards and strips, and bubble chips.)

Automatic input-only reading devices that utilize magnetic-ink and optical character-scanning techniques are considered next. This section is followed by a section that features output-only printing and microfilming equipment.

The remainder of the chapter is devoted to a wide variety of online terminals that permit direct communication between people and machines. These online machines range from simple typewriterlike units to light pens, input tables, visual display screens, intelligent terminals, and systems that accept input and produce output directly in English. The data communications links between computers and online terminals are also discussed.

Thus, after studying this chapter, you should be able to:

- Discuss punched cards and punched paper tapes and explain the purpose these media serve.

- Explain the ways in which data are entered and coded on magnetic tape, and the advantages and limitations of this medium.

- Describe some of the characteristics of direct-assess devices that use magnetic disks, magnetic drums, magnetic cards and strips, and magnetic bubble chips for I/O and online storage.

- Summarize the uses of direct input devices utilizing MICR and OCR character-reading techniques.

- Discuss the approaches used to produce printed and microfilmed output from computers.

- Discuss the uses of online terminals in multiunit data stations, visual display applications, and distributed processing systems.

- Identify and discuss the most commonly used services for transmitting data from one location to another.

- Understand and use the key terms listed at the end of the chapter.

Why have input/output (I/O) media and devices? The answer to this question, of course, is that they make it possible for data processing to occur; i.e., they make it possible to place data into and receive information out of the central processor. The computer thus performs the necessary processing steps and communicates with humans only through the I/O equipment. In this chapter we will study some of the ways in which communication is accomplished. More specifically, we shall *first* examine paper and magnetizable media and related I/O devices employed primarily for high-volume batch-processing applications. We shall then devote the *remaining* pages to (1) I/O media and devices that are frequently found in online processing situations and (2) complementary tools that facilitate I/O operations.

PUNCHED CARDS

How about Them Card-
floggers,
Ain't they a laugh?
Sucking up holey-cards
And spittin' out chaff.
Humpin' them Hollerith,
Doggin' them decks,
Sockin' funny punches
Into payroll checks.
——William J. Wilton

The punched card is a very familiar I/O medium that serves a *threefold purpose*. It is used to (1) provide data *input* into the CPU, (2) receive information *output* from the CPU, and (3) provide secondary offline *storage* of data and information.

Manually operated keypunch machines are the primary means of preparing punched cards. This is a tedious and expensive operation, but the use of keypunch equipment has through the years remained a most popular data input method.

Once the data are punched into the cards, they are fed into the central processor by means of a *card reader* (Figure 4-1). The speed with which a card reader can supply input data to a central processor is relatively slow when compared with most other methods (see Table 4-1, a summary table showing the I/O speed ranges and storage uses of the media and devices discussed in this chapter).

Cards may also serve as an output medium through the use of a *card punch* machine. The card punching function is frequently housed with the card reading activity in a machine called a *read punch*. In small card-oriented computer systems, a single *multifunction card machine* is used to perform input, output, sorting, and collating functions.

Many organizations use punched cards as an I/O medium because they were used with processing equipment before the introduction of the computer, but cards possess *advantages* other than merely being an old, reliable, and available medium. For one thing, they are complete records of transactions and are thus easily understood. Particular records can be sorted, deleted, and replaced without disturbing other cards. Unfortunately, however, cards have certain inherent *disadvantages* that may limit their use in or exclude them from use in a particular application. For example, the number of data characters that can be punched per card is quite low—much lower than the number of characters that can be typed on the

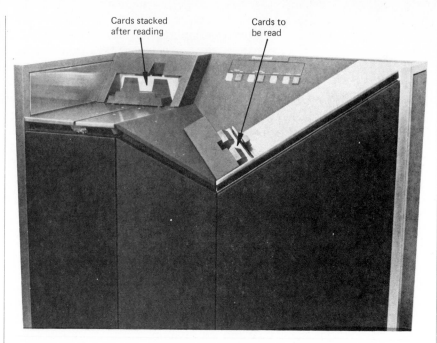

Cards stacked after reading

Cards to be read

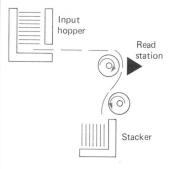

Input hopper

Read station

Stacker

FIGURE 4-1

(*Above*) A card reader that has a reading speed of 1,050 80-column cards per minute (or 1,400 characters per second). (Honeywell information Systems.) (*Left*) Cards move from the input hopper past a read station to the stacker.

card with a typewriter. Also, cards are fixed in length, and if 100 characters are required, an additional card must be used. The size of the card deck is increased, as is the time required to process it. Thus, cards are relatively bulky and slow to process.

PUNCHED PAPER TAPE

Punched paper tape, like cards, is a triple-purpose medium that is suitable for input, output, and secondary offline storage. Paper tape attachments are found on many timesharing terminals and microcomputer teletypewriters (Figure 4-3). These attachments permanently capture on tape (1) the input data and programs that are being keyed into the system, and (2) the output information that is being printed out by the computer.

TABLE 4-1   A Summary of computer input/output characteristics

Medium	Input Device Used	Output Device Used	Typical I/O Speed Ranges (characters per second)		Typical Storage Uses		Typical Storage Capacity
			Input	Output	Online Secondary	Offline Secondary	
Punched card	Card reader	Card punch	150–2,667	80–650		X	Virtually unlimited (but bulky)
Paper tape	Tape reader	Tape punch	50–1,800	10–300		X	Virtually unlimited (but bulky and fragile)
Magnetic tape	Tape drive	Tape drive	15,000–1,250,000	15,000–1,250,000		X	Virtually unlimited (compact, with up to 150 million characters per large tape)
Magnetic drum	Drum storage unit	Drum storage unit	230,000–1,500,000	230,000–1,500,000	X		From 1 to 4 million characters with high-speed drums; up to 200 million characters on slower drum units
Magnetic disk	Disk drive	Disk drive	100,000–3,000,000	100,000–3,000,000	X	X	Virtually unlimited offline storage; from 2 to 200 million characters per online disk pack
Magnetic diskette (floppy disk)	Disk drive	Disk drive	12,500–60,000	12,500–60,000	X	X	Virtually unlimited offline storage; from 90,000 to 500,000 characters per diskette
Magnetic cards/strips	Card/strip storage unit	Card/strip storage unit	25,000–50,000	25,000–50,000	X	X	Virtually unlimited offline storage; from 25 to 150 million characters per online card/strip cartridge
Magnetic bubble	LSI bubble chips	LSI bubble chips	10,000–20,000	10,000–20,000	X		From 100,000 to 1 million characters per chip
Magnetic ink	MICR reader		700–3,200			X	Virtually unlimited
Paper documents	OCR reader		100–3,600			X	Virtually unlimited
	Typewriter terminal keyboard	Character printer	Human speed	5–250		X	Virtually unlimited
		Line printer		440–39,000		X	Virtually unlimited
Microfilm		Recorder		25,000–300,000		X	Virtually unlimited
None	Keyboard	CRT visual display	Human speed	250–50,000			Compact, virtually unlimited

FIGURE 4-2
Charles Babbage. (*The Bettmann Archive.*)

BABBAGE: INSPIRED BY A PORTRAIT

In 1833, Charles Babbage, Lucasian Professor of Mathematics at Cambridge, proposed a machine which would be an automated, mechanical calculator. With help from the British government, Babbage began construction of the "difference engine." Years later he devised another calculator, which he called the "analytic engine."

Babbage used punched cards to program his calculator. He got the idea from a portrait of Jacquard that was woven on a Jacquard loom, using 24,000 punched cards to program the pattern that formed the portrait. Babbage's concepts were later used when the first computer prototypes were constructed.

FIGURE 4-3
Paper tape reader/punch
attachment on a teletype I/O
terminal. (*General Electric.*)

Data are recorded on the tape by punching round holes into it. Tape, like the punched card, is laid out in rows (*channels*) and columns (*frames*). A character of information is presented by a punch or combination of punches in a vertical column or frame.

Figure 4-4 illustrates the method of representing data employed with the popular eight-channel tape. The bottom four channels are labeled to the left of the tape with the numerical values 1, 2, 4, and 8. (The series of holes between channels 4 and 8 are sprocket holes used to feed the tape through the machines and are not considered in the code.) Decimal digits 1 to 9 can be represented by a hole or a combination of holes in these bottom channels. For example, a single hole punched in channel 2 has a decimal value of 2, while holes punched in channels 4, 2, and 1 denote a decimal 7. The X and O channels serve the same purpose as zone punches in cards; i.e., they are used in combination with numerical punches to form alphabetic and special characters. Channel O used alone, of course, is the code for zero. The letter A is represented by zone punches in X and O plus the numerical 1 hole. The letter B has the same zone punches plus numerical 2, etc. You can examine the remainder of the letters to see the code pattern.

The data coded on punched tape are fed into the central processor by means of a *paper tape reader*. Tape readers, like card readers, sense the

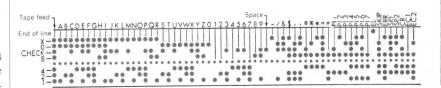

FIGURE 4-4
Eight-channel paper tape
code.

FIGURE 4-5
Magnetic tape cartridge used
in portable minicomputer.
(IBM Corp.)

presence or absence of holes and deliver this information to the CPU. *Paper tape punches* record information received from the CPU in the form of holes punched in blank tape.

MAGNETIC TAPE

Because of its relatively fast *transfer rate* (the speed at which data can be transferred from the input medium to CPU storage), magnetic tape is a very popular I/O medium used today for high-speed large-volume applications. In addition to providing rapid input and output, it is a widely used medium for offline computer storage.

The tape itself may be in a large *reel* or a small *cartridge* or *cassette*. The tape in the larger reels used with computer family models is usually ½ inch wide and 2,400 feet long. The tape in a cartridge (see Figure 4-5) or cassette is reduced in size and is typically used in micro- and minicomputer systems. Whether packaged in a large reel or a small cassette, however, the tape is quite similar to the kind used in a sound tape recorder. It is a plastic ribbon coated on one side with an iron-oxide material that can be magnetized. By electromagnetic pulses, data are recorded in the form of tiny invisible spots on the iron-oxide side of the tape, just as sound waves form magnetic patterns on the tape of a sound recorder. Both the data and the sound can be played back as many times as desired. Like the tape used on a recorder, computer tape can be erased and reused indefinitely. Data contained in a tape are automatically erased as new data are being recorded.

How are data initially recorded on magnetic tape? In a few cases, new input data are captured in punched card or paper tape form and are then transcribed on magnetic tape by a special data converter. In many

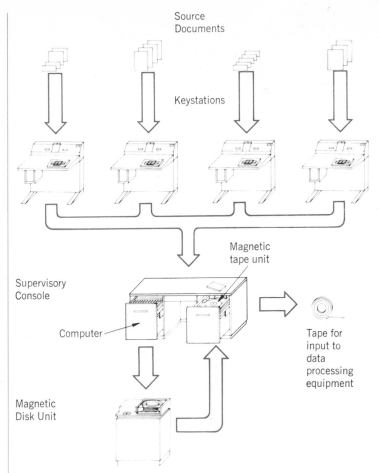

Source
Documents

Keystations

Magnetic
tape unit

Supervisory
Console

Computer

Tape for
input to
data
processing
equipment

Magnetic
Disk Unit

FIGURE 4-6
Key-to-disk data entry from
multiple keystations.

cases, however, data are recorded directly on magnetic tape from source documents through the use of *key-to-tape* or *key-to-disk* encoding stations (see Figure 4-6).[1] Of course, many of the data recorded on magnetic tapes have been placed there by the computer as the output of an earlier processing run.

The approach used to represent data on magnetic tape is similar to the approach used with punched paper tape. Magnetic tape is divided horizontally into rows (called *channels* or *tracks*) and vertically into columns, or *frames*. Earlier tape codes used a seven-channel format (Figure 4-7). You can see that the channel designations were quite similar to those used in punched tape. The numerical values were determined by

---

[1] Single-station and multistation systems are available. In a typical multistation key-to-disk data entry system, a minicomputer controls the input from a number of key stations. Data keyed in by a station operator are edited and checked for errors and are then stored on a magnetic disk resembling a large phonograph record. Periodically, the data stored on the disk are transferred to magnetic tape.

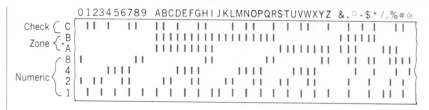

FIGURE 4-7
The seven-channel magnetic
tape code used with
earlier computers.

one or a combination of the bottom four channels, while the A and B zone tracks were used in conjunction with the numeric channels to represent letters and special characters.[2] For example, the decimal 7 is represented by an "on" condition in channels 4, 2, and 1. You can test your understanding by observing the coding pattern used for the other alphanumeric characters.

You may have noticed that there are "check" channels in both Figures 4-4 and 4-7. These channels perform a special *parity checking* function. In Figure 4-7, for example, you will notice that there are an even number of marks in each frame. When the basic code—e.g., for the digit 1—requires an odd number of marks, there is an additional mark in the check channel. Thus, all valid characters are formed with an even number of marks, and this becomes the basis for system check of the accuracy of the tape. Both even and odd parity codes are used in computer systems.

An *extended* version of the seven-channel tape format is now used in most computer systems. As with the older seven-track tape, this *nine-channel* format employs four numeric tracks and a parity check channel. However, *four* (rather than two) zone positions are available. The additional zone tracks make it possible to extend the code to include lowercase alphabetical and other special characters. Figure 4-8 shows a few characters coded in the nine-channel format. The most frequently used

---

[2] The code used here is called *binary coded decimal* (**BCD**). In Chap. 5 we will become better acquainted with BCD and also examine an extended version of BCD.

Track number	Equivalent 7-channel tape code position			
		0 1 2 3 4 5 6 7 8 9	A B C M N O X Y Z	& $ * , / ' %
9	8	I I	I I	I I I I
8	2	I I I I	I I I I	I I
7	Added zone	I I I I I I I I I I	I I I I I I I I I	
6	Added zone	I I I I I I I I I I	I I I I I I I I I	I I I I I I I
5	B	I I I I I I I I I I	I I I	I I I I
4	Check*	I I I I I	I I I I	I I I I
3	A	I I I I I I I I I I	I I I	I I I
2	1	I I I I I	I I I I I	I I I
1	4	I I I I	I I I	I

FIGURE 4-8
Nine-channel extended
magnetic tape code.

*The check position here produces odd parity.

tracks are grouped near the center of the tape. This arrangement gives the code format a peculiar appearance. The equivalent seven-channel tape code positions are shown in Figure 4-8 to aid in interpretation. For example, the numeral 7 is represented here by an "on" condition in the four zone positions and in the channels equivalent to 4, 2, and 1.

Magnetic tape, like paper tape, is a continuous-length medium. How, then, can the computer distinguish between different records on the tape? Paper tape had an eighth *end of line* (EL) channel for this purpose, but that track is missing here. Instead, the records are separated by blank spaces in the tape called *interrecord gaps,* which perform the EL function. Interrecord gaps are automatically created by the computer system.

The magnetic tape units shown in Figure 4-9 are used for both input and output. They are referred to by such names as *tape drives* and *tape transports.* The tape is loaded onto the tape drive in much the same way that a movie projector is threaded.

One *advantage* of magnetic tape is that the data density is far greater than that of cards and paper tape. (One standard reel of magnetic tape is capable of storing as much information as hundreds of thousands of punched cards.) In addition, a tape costs less than the hundreds of thousands of cards it can replace, storage space is reduced, and the tape can be reused many times. Neither cards nor punched tape can compare with magnetic tape in input/output speed. However, magnetic tape has *disadvantages.* It is not generally suitable for jobs that require rapid and direct

FIGURE 4-9
Magnetic tape units. *(NCR.)*

access to particular records; the magnetized spots are invisible and cannot be read directly by humans; and specks of dust on a tape can be read as data characters or can cause an improper reading. Careful control procedures must be followed to prevent an important tape from being erased by mistake.

DIRECT-ACCESS DEVICES

In this section we shall look at different types of popular direct-access devices used for I/O and online secondary storage. It is interesting to note that some of these devices are *flexible* in the sense that the storage instruments associated with their use may be either online or offline. Magnetic disks, for example, have mass storage capability and can be used indefinitely for online purposes. But many disks (and the data contained) can also be removed and stored offline just like tapes and cards. It is also worth noting here that the selection of the "best" direct-access storage device to use *involves compromise.* As Table 4-1 shows, there is frequently an *inverse relationship* between I/O speed on the one hand and storage capacity on the other. That is, as online storage capacity increases, the speed with which data can be entered and retrieved often declines. Also, as online storage capacity increases, the cost per character stored tends to decrease.

Magnetic Drums

Magnetic drums were an early means of primary storage. Now, however, they are occasionally used for online secondary storage when fast response is of greater importance than large capacity. For example, they may be used to store mathematical tables, data, or program modifications that are frequently referred to during processing operations.

A magnetic drum is a cylnder that has an outer surface plated with a metallic magnetizable film. A motor rotates the drum on its axis at a constant and rapid rate. Data are *recorded on* the rotating drum and *read from* the drum by *read-write heads,* which are positioned a fraction of an inch from the drum surface. The writing of new data on the drum erases data previously stored at the location. The magnetic spots written on the drum surface remain indefinitely until they, too, are erased at a future time. Because millisecond time is desired in the reading and writing operations, the drum rotates several thousand times each minute.

Magnetic Disks

Magnetic disks are by far the most popular direct-access I/O and online storage medium. Disks come in different sizes. The larger disks used in mainframe family systems are typically made of thin metal plates coated on both sides with a magnetizable recording material. These disks may

FIGURE 4-10
Disk drive with two large,
permanently mounted disks.
(*Burroughs Corp.*)

remain *permanently* in their cabinets (Figure 4-10), or *several* of them (the number varies) may be packaged in *portable* or replaceable assemblies called *disk packs*. The pack held by the operator in Figure 4-11, for example, contains 12 disks. The storage capacity of this pack is 100 million characters (enough capacity to store the contents of 100 books such as this one), and eight of these packs may be housed in the unit shown in Figure 4-11 to provide a total of 800 million characters of online storage. It takes only a minute to replace a pack.

Smaller disks are also available for use in micro- and minicomputer systems to provide inexpensive online storage. These disks are either 8 inches or 5¼ inches in diameter.[3] Since both sizes frequently have the magnetizable recording material applied to a flexible plastic base, they are often called *floppy disks*.[4] Both the 8-inch floppy disk and the 5¼-inch

---

[3] The hard disks found in disk packs are usually 14 inches in diameter.

[4] The use of newer 8-inch hard disks is growing rapidly.

FIGURE 4-11
Portable disk pack and online disk storage facility. (*IBM Corp.*)

mini-floppy disk are packaged in *single* portable units in a paper or plastic covering and are never removed from this protective envelope (Figure 4-12).

Whether disks are permanently mounted or portable, they are all rotated in a disk drive at a high, constant speed. In the case of a disk pack, spaces are left between the spinning disks to allow access arms with small read-write heads to move to any storage location. When floppy disks are

FIGURE 4-12
Mini-floppy disk (in protective envelope) and disk drive used in a personal computing system. This 5¼-inch disk has a storage capacity of 90,000 characters; disks of the same size used in other micro-computer systems can store 180,000 characters. Four of these disk drives can be connected to one personal microcomputer. (*Radio Shack Division of Tandy Corp.*)

used, the disk envelope is inserted into the small disk drive, the disk is rotated inside the envelope, and read-write heads access the disk surfaces through slots in the covering (see Figure 4-12).

Data are organized on all disks into a number of concentric circles, or *tracks,* each of which has a designated location number.[5] Reading and writing operations are similar to the operations used for drums. Data are recorded in specific locations as magnetized spots. Read-in is destructive (the recording of data in a storage location results in the erasure of any data previously stored there); read-out is nondestructive. Several read-write head arrangements are available from different manufacturers. The disk unit shown in Figure 4-10, for example, has a head for each track.

When compared with magnetic tape, disks have the *advantage* of providing quick and direct access to records without the need to sort transactions into a specific order. Also, a single input transaction into a data base may be used to quickly update records in several related files stored on different disks. *But* disks are more expensive than the tape required to provide the same storage capacity, and sequential batch processing may be faster and more efficient when tapes are used.

Magnetic Cards and Strips

Wouldn't it be nice to combine the magnetic tape advantages of low cost and high storage capacity with the advantages of rapid and direct record accessibility? This is essentially the objective of devices that utilize magnetic cards and tape strips for mass online storage. A magnetic card may be considered to be a length of flexible plastic material upon which short strips of magnetic tape have been mounted. Cards or strips may then be placed in cartridges, which, like disk packs, may be removed and stored offline (see Figure 4-13). Card and strip equipment has a high storage capacity, and the cost per character stored is very low. Data are erasable, but access speed is slow when compared with disks.

Magnetic Bubble Chips

Although magnetic bubble direct-access storage technology is still relatively new, some researchers believe that this technology will be used to replace many magnetic disk devices in the future.[6] One reason for this

---

[5] A mini-floppy disk may have only 35 tracks; a large, permanently mounted disk may have over 800.

[6] Bubble storage may have its greatest impact in the next few years on the smaller disk devices. But you should realize that as far as larger disk drives are concerned, this prediction will probably *not* come true in the next several years, and, of course, it may never happen. Long-time observers of the computer hardware scene know that at any given time researchers are working on several new approaches that could eventually replace the technology that currently occupies the dominant position. But these researchers are not shooting at a stationary target; advances are usually also being made in the dominant technology. Furthermore, before the potential of the new approach can be realized, it is possible that some other alternative will achieve a breakthrough that will make the new approach (and the dominant technology) obsolete.

FIGURE 4-13
This IBM 3850 Mass Storage System can store online the contents of over 400,000 books of this size in the cartridges located in these honeycomb storage compartments. Or a 100-character dossier on every person in the world could be stored online in this system. (*IBM Corp.*)

optimism is that since bubble units are made with solid state electronic chips and have no moving parts, they should be much more reliable than units with spinning disks that use mechanical components.

For our purpose, a magnetic bubble can be thought of as a positively charged island in a sea of negatively charged magnetic film. The presence of a bubble is analogous to the presence of a hole in a punched paper tape column. (The absence of a bubble, of course, is analogous to the absence of a punched hole.) Data may then be represented in bubble storage by the presence or absence of bubbles just as they were represented in punched tape form by the presence or absence of holes.

Figure 4-14*a* shows how all the information found on four pages of the New York telephone directory could be stored in a single small bubble chip (Figure 4-14*b* shows a greatly magnified view of the circuitry of a bubble storage chip). When data are *placed into* storage, bubbles from the minor loops are transferred to the major loop, carried past a *write* (generate) station, and then returned to the minor loops. When data are *retrieved from* storage, the correct bubbles are transferred, at a signal, from the minor loops into the major loop, which carries them past the *read* (*replicate*) station. The retrieval time, of course, varies with the location of the needed bubbles in the minor loop "pipelines."

DIRECT CHARACTER READING

In spite of advances made in many areas of processing technology, input preparation in many installations has not changed significantly in the past decade. Data are still taken from printed documents and recorded in machine-acceptable form by a manual keying operation. Several devices, however, have been designed to eliminate manual keying by reading the

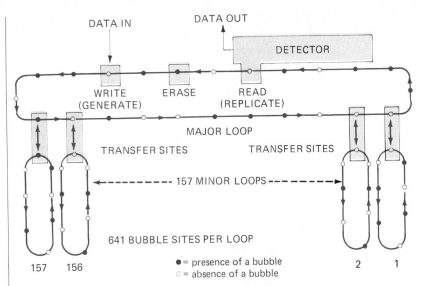

157 MINOR LOOPS

641 BUBBLE SITES PER LOOP

● = presence of a bubble
○ = absence of a bubble

FIGURE 4-14
(*Above*) Magnetic bubble storage. (*Right*) A greatly magnified view of the circuitry in a bubble storage chip. (*IBM Corp.*)

Write
(generate)
station

Bubble
storage
area

Read
(replicate)
station

characters printed on the source documents and converting the data *directly* into computer-usable input.

Magnetic-ink Character Recognition (MICR)

The concept of magnetic-ink character recognition (MICR) is widely used by banking and financial institutions as a means of processing the tremen-

"New Bubble Memory Technology"

In a paper delivered by a Bell Laboratory researcher at a recent conference, it was disclosed that Bell Labs has made a major breakthrough in bubble memory technology. This breakthrough will mean a four times increase in storage size, a substantial decrease in cost and ten times faster operating speed. Although Texas Instruments and Rockwell have been in production on bubble memory devices for nearly a year, their high cost and small storage capability have prohibited their wide use. This new development, which will still take a few years to reach the market, should have a large impact on the mass storage area, particularly floppy disks.

The new device replaces the drive coils used in present bubble memories with wafer-thin conductive layers of gold or aluminum overlaid on the garnet structure. A current flows through these layers forming tiny magnetic fields around holes etched into the surface. The polarity of these fields controls the bubble movements.

By eliminating the costly and bulky coil structure, a new pathway design became available which provides a fourfold increase in storage capacity, is easier and less costly to produce, and reduces integrated circuit size, thereby reducing travel time.

Source: Sol Libes, "New Bubble Memory Technology," *Byte,* p. 100, July 1979. Reprinted with permission from *Byte,* The Small Systems Journal, July 1979 copyright © 1979 *Byte* Publications, Inc., McGraw-Hill, Inc., all rights reserved.

dous volume of checks being written. Figure 4-15 shows a sample check coded with a special ink which contains tiny iron oxide magnetizable particles. The code number of the bank to which the check will be written and the depositor's account number are precoded on the checks. The first bank to receive the check after it has been written encodes the amount in the lower right corner. The check may then be handled automatically through regular bank collection channels—e.g., from (1) the initial bank receiving the check to, perhaps, (2) the Federal Reserve bank to (3) the depositor's bank to (4) the depositor's account.

Magnetic-ink character *reader-sorter* units interpret the encoded data on checks and transfer this information to the CPU. They also sort the checks by account number, bank number, etc., into pockets.

There are several *advantages* associated with the use of MICR. First, checks may be roughly handled, folded, smeared, and stamped, yet this does not prevent recognition with a high degree of accuracy. Second, processing is speeded because checks can be fed directly into the input device. Third, the type font used is easily recognized and read, if neces-

YOUR NAME   No. *84*   53-105 / 113

August 12 19___

PAY TO THE ORDER OF *A. B. C. Distributing Company* $ *150 96/100*

One Hundred Fifty and 96/00 ———————— DOLLARS

Valley Bank
AND TRUST COMPANY
SPRINGFIELD · MASSACHUSETTS   1738-323 4

SAMPLE ONLY

⑆0113⑆0105⑆   1738⑈323 4⑆   ⑈00000150096⑈

Combined Routing symbol	Transit number	Account number	Check digit	Amount of item

FIGURE 4-15
(NCR.)

sary, by clerical personnel. The primary *limitation* of MICR is that only a *small number of characters* are used. Since it was designed by and for the banking industry, MICR uses only the 14 characters needed for bank processing. No alphabetic characters are available.

Optical Character Recognition (OCR)

Unlike MICR, optical character recognition (OCR) techniques make possible the reading of *any* printed character (not just 14), and no special ink is required. Thus, the flexibility of OCR may make it possible for organizations to eliminate or reduce the input keying bottleneck.

Although machines are available that will read hand-printed characters, the automatic reading of handwritten script is still some years in the future. (While your penmanship is undoubtedly beautiful, the author's presents a formidable challenge to the equipment designers.) Most OCR devices now being used are designed to read *machine-printed characters, bar codes,* and simple *handmade marks.* OCR is being used for many applications, including the reading of (1) credit card charge tickets, (2) school documents such as registration forms and handmade marks on test answer forms, (3) zip codes for purposes of mail sorting, and (4) light and dark bars used to code products sold in retail stores.

In this last application, the light and dark bars of the *Universal Product Code* (UPC) are printed on the product by the manufacturer. The next time you spring (?) out of bed at 6 A.M. to have a hearty breakfast before your eight o'clock class, you might find (champion that you are) that your cereal box has a code similar to the one shown in Figure 4-16. When UPC-marked items are received at a merchant's automated checkout stand (Figure 4-17), they are pulled across a scanning window and placed in bags. As items are scanned, the UPC symbol is decoded and the data

Number System Character

0 = grocery products
3 = drugs and health-
related products
etc.

0

16000   66210

Manufacturer's
Identification
Number

16000 = General Mills
21000 = Kraft Foods
etc.

Product/Part Code Number

66210 = 18-ounce box of
Wheaties
67670 = 10-ounce box of
Buc Wheats
etc.

FIGURE 4-16
Universal Product Code for a
box of Wheaties.

are transmitted to a computer that looks up the price, possibly updates inventory and sales records, and forwards price and description information back to the check stand.[7]

[7] In addition to using OCR readers at the check stand, hand-held optical scanning "wands" attached to portable recorders may also be used by store personnel. When a shelf item must be reordered, the wand reads the UPC symbol fastened on a shelf below an inventory item to accurately enter the item description into the recorder. The quantity needed is then keyed into the recorder. The recorder may later be connected by telecommunications lines to a warehouse computer system to complete the restocking procedure.

FIGURE 4-17
Electronic scanning system automatically reads Universal Product Code (UPC) symbol on package label as merchandise is moved over window in base of check stand. (*NCR Corp.*)

The primary *advantage* of OCR is that it eliminates some of the duplication of human effort required to get data into the computer. This reduction in human effort can (1) *improve the quality (accuracy)* of input data and (2) *improve the timeliness of information processed.* However, *difficulties* in using OCR equipment may be encountered when documents to be read are poorly typed or have strikeovers, erasures, etc. Also, form design and ink specifications become more critical and must be more standardized than is the case when keypunch source documents are prepared. Finally, many optical readers are not economically feasible unless the daily volume of transactions is relatively high.

PRINTED AND MICROFILMED OUTPUT

Printed Output

Printers provide information *output* from the CPU in the form of permanently printed characters which have meaning to humans. They are the primary output device when the information is to be used by people rather than by machine. The printers being produced today fall into the following categories:

1 *Serial or character printers.* Used with personal microcomputer and small minicomputer systems[8] for low-volume printing jobs, these one-character-at-a-time devices are often *modified versions of office typewriters* such as the IBM Selectric. However, serial printers designed specifically for computer use are likely to be much faster and more reliable than souped-up typewriters because of their substitution of electronic components for electromechanical elements. The techniques used to print characters vary widely. *Impact methods* use the familiar typewriter approach of pressing a typeface against paper and inked ribbon. Serial impact printers designed for computer use often use a *daisy-wheel* or a *dot-matrix* printing mechanism. In the daisy-wheel approach (Figure 4-18a), each "petal" of the wheel has a single character embossed on it. A motor spins the wheel at a rapid rate, and when the desired character spins to the correct position, a print hammer strikes it to produce the output. In the dot-matrix approach (Figure 4-18b), an arrangement of tiny hammers strike to produce the desired character. Each hammer prints a small dot on the paper. Thus, the letter E would be formed as shown in Figure 4-18b. Dot-matrix printers are often faster than daisy-wheel devices, but the print quality is not as good. There are also *nonimpact* serial printers available that use thermal, electrical, chemical, and inkjet technologies. With the *inkjet* approach, for example, droplets of ink are electri-

[8] Serial printers are also used in many of the timesharing and distributed processing stations that are connected to larger computer systems.

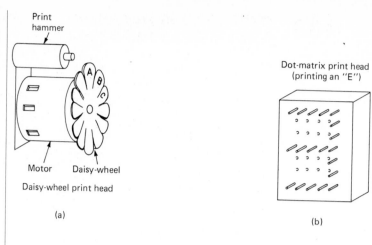

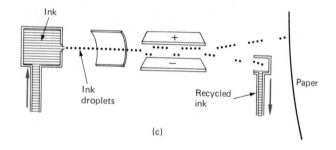

FIGURE 4-18
Serial printing mechanisms.
(a) Daisywheel approach. (b)
Dot-matrix approach. (c) Inkjet approach.

cally charged after leaving a nozzle (Figure 4-18c). The droplets are then guided to the proper position on the paper by charged deflection plates. The print quality is good because the character is formed by dozens of tiny ink dots. If a droplet is not needed for the particular character being formed, it is recycled back to the input jet.

2 *High-speed impact line printers.* These printers (Figure 4-19) use impact methods to produce *line-at-a-time* printed output. They typically use rapidly moving *chains* of printing slugs or some form of a print *cylinder* to print lines of information on paper. Figure 4-20a illustrates the concept of a *print chain.* The links in the chain are engraved character-printing slugs. The chain moves at a rapid speed past the printing positions. Hammers behind the paper are timed to force the paper against the proper print slugs. On the *drum printer,* raised characters extend the length of the drum (Figure 4-20b). There are as many *bands* of type as there are printing positions. Each band contains all the possible characters. The drum rotates rapidly, and one revolution is required to print each line. A fast-acting hammer opposite each band strikes the paper against the proper character as it passes. Thus, in one rotation, hammers of several positions may "fire" when the A row appears, several others may strike to imprint D's, etc. At the end of the rotation, the line has been printed.

FIGURE 4-19
High-speed impact line printer. (*Control Data Corp.*)

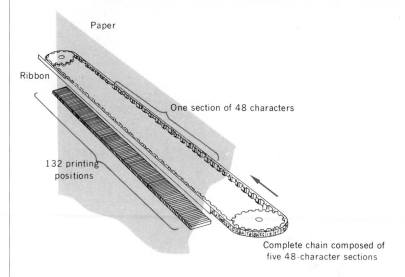

Paper

Ribbon

One section of 48 characters

132 printing positions

Complete chain composed of five 48-character sections

The number of bands corresponds to the number of printing positions

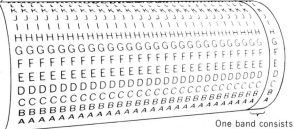

FIGURE 4-20
Line printing mechanisms. (*Above*) A print chain. (*Right*) A print drum.

One band consists of all printing characters used

FIGURE 4-21
High-speed nonimpact
printing system capable of
producing 21,000 lines of
print per minute. (*IBM Corp.*)

3 *High-speed nonimpact page printers.* These devices (**Figure 4-21**) can produce documents at speeds of up to 21,000 lines per minute. (That's fast enough to print this entire book in about one minute!) Electronics, xerography, lasers, and other technologies have made these high-volume systems possible. Each page produced on these printers is an original since there are no carbon copies. Although their cost may exceed the cost of many computer installations, these printers have been found to be economical when hundreds of thousands of pages must be printed each month.

In addition to printing computer output in the form of characters, some devices are also capable of producing *graphical output* under computer control. For example, a computer-controlled *plotter* can produce engineering drawings, maps, and other pictorial output in a very short time.

Microfilmed Output

In spite of printer progress, the amount of output possible using printing techniques is only a small fraction of the output that can be produced on magnetic tape. Even when multiple printers are used (see Figure 1-20, page 39), only a small portion of the time of the CPU may be needed to drive these units. Thus, in some cases it is more efficient and economical to reduce the role of the printer by replacing paper output documents with *microfilm*. The computer-output-to-microfilm (COM) approach is shown in Figure 4-22. Output information may be read onto magnetic tape and then, in an offline operation, recorded on microfilm. Or the *microfilm recorder* may receive the information directly from the CPU. Most microfilm recorders project the characters of output information onto the screen of a *cathode ray tube,* which is similar to a television picture tube. A high-speed microfilm camera then films the displayed information at speeds much faster than are possible with printers.

Much of the tremendous volume of data and information that enters and leaves computers each year is processed by the I/O media and machines that have now been introduced. However, other more direct means of communication between people and machines are possible through the use of *online terminals*.

ONLINE TERMINALS

Online terminals may be classified as (1) *typewriterlike machines,* (2) *multiunit data stations,* (3) *visual display units,* or (4) *intelligent devices*.

Typewriter Terminals

Typewriter terminals may be connected by short cables to computers of all sizes. In large centers, *console typewriters* are often used by computer operators to communicate with the CPU during processing runs. In personal microcomputer systems, a typewriter terminal is often the only I/O device used by the owner/operator. But, of course, typewriter terminals need not be housed in the same room with the CPU. They may be connected to a CPU thousands of miles away by a complex data communications system. Regardless of proximity to the CPU, users of typewriter terminals transmit input data via the keyboard and receive output information from the character-at-a-time printer. Hundreds of thousands of these terminals are now in service.

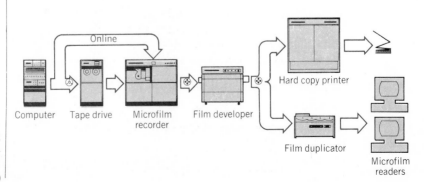

FIGURE 4-22
Computer output to micro-film. (*Stromberg, DatagraphiX, Inc.*)

Multiunit Data Stations

The term *multiunit data stations* may be used in several ways to describe the equipment used in particular types of applications. Let us look at some of the possibilities.

1   *Remote job-entry stations.* Data may be read into a distant CPU by multiple station units. Card and tape readers and/or a manual keyboard may be used for *input,* and *output* information may be either visually displayed or printed at the station.

2   *Data collection stations.* These stations (and the transaction recording stations discussed below) typically perform limited operations. They have been developed to get data from remote points into the computer as quickly as possible. For example, data collection stations are often used in factories to control the inventory of parts and materials used in production (Figure 4-23).

3   *Transaction recording stations.* Savings institutions are among the leading users of online transaction recording devices (Figure 4-24). Let us assume that a deposit is to be made by a customer. The customer presents his or her bankbook and the amount of the deposit to the teller, who inserts the book into a recorder and keys in the transaction data. The data are then sent to the computer, which adjusts the customer's savings balance. The updated information is relayed back to the remote station, where it is entered in the customer's bankbook. The entire transaction is accounted for in a matter of seconds.

4   *Point-of-sale stations.* As you saw in Figure 4-17, point-of-sale (POS) terminals that read UPC symbols are replacing cash registers in *supermarkets.* Other POS units are being used in *department stores.* Such a

FIGURE 4-23
Data collection station in a factory. *(IBM Corp.)*

FIGURE 4-24
Online transaction recording
station at a savings institution.
(NCR Corp.)

terminal may be equipped with a hand-held "wand" that can be used to speed up the sales transaction (see Figure 4-25). By passing the wand across a special tag attached to the merchandise, the clerk reads the item description and price into the terminal. (Credit card numbers can also be read in this way.) The terminal may then automatically display the price, compute the total amount of the purchase including taxes, and print a sales receipt.

5 *Electronic funds transfer system stations.* Some electronic funds transfer system (EFTS) stations are much like the transaction recording stations referred to above, but they may be *unattended* devices such as *automated teller machines* (Figure 4-26) that are located on or off the financial institution's premises to receive and dispense cash and to handle routine financial transactions 24 hours a day. For example, you might use a plastic "currency" or "debit" card (which incorporates, perhaps, a magnetically encoded strip of material to supply the computer with your account number and credit limit) to make a deposit to your account or to withdraw cash. Instructions displayed on a screen guide you through these transactions.[9]

[9] Other EFTS terminals owned by, and connected to, the computers of financial institutions may be located at the checkout counters of stores and used in conjunction with store-owned POS stations. These EFTS stations (which may also be located at hotels, hospitals, etc.) can be used to transfer funds between accounts—e.g., from the shopper's to the merchant's account—or to guarantee the availability of funds to cover customer checks.

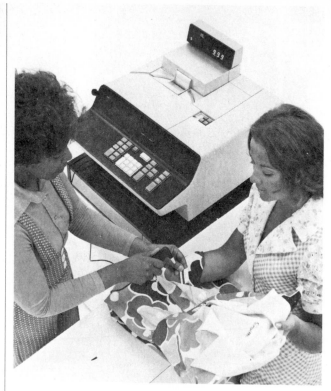

FIGURE 4-25
A department store POS terminal with a magnetic wand reader. (*IBM Corp.*)

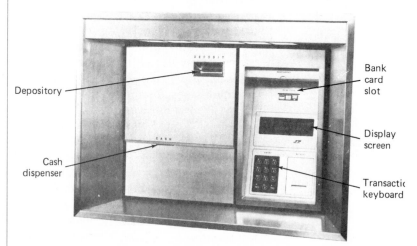

Depository

Bank card slot

Display screen

Cash dispenser

Transactic keyboard

FIGURE 4-26
Automated teller machine. (*INCOTERM Corp.*)

Visual Display Terminals

Considerable emphasis is now being placed on visual display terminals, which look like small television sets equipped with a manual keyboard. Although input by means of the keyboard may be no faster than with typ-

FIGURE 4-27
Hospital out-patient receiving
station with visual terminal
used for displaying scheduling information. (*Honeywell
Information Systems.*)

ing, output is silent and very fast—the screen of the terminal's *cathode ray tube* (CRT) can be covered instantly with hundreds of characters of displayed information.

There are two basic classes of CRT display terminals. In the *first* category are lower-cost units, which display *alphanumeric* information. In the *second* class are more expensive units, which are capable of projecting graphs, charts, and designs as well as alphanumeric characters. The first category might be considered a clever "paperless electronic typewriter"; the second class of display units possesses graphic art capabilities not available with typewriter devices. Let us briefly look at some of the ways in which these display units are currently being used.

Alphanumeric display applications Terminals that display only alphanumeric information are well suited for obtaining quick response to inquiries. The visual display unit provides a window into the computer's data base. Status of a hospital patient (see Figure 4-27), availability of airline seats, locations of unsold seats in a theater, location and telephone number of students of a university—information such as this is being kept current by various organizations in online storage so that it is instantly available for display upon inquiry. Alphanumeric display units also facilitate human-machine interaction. A decision maker can carry on a "conversation" with a properly programmed computer system by supplying data and key phrases while the system responds with displayed end results, intermediate results, or questions. The questions may be in a multiple-choice format so that the decision maker need only key in the num-

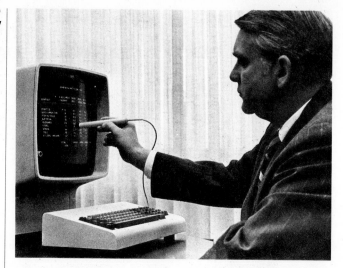

FIGURE 4-28
Light pen and visual display
are being used to interact
with machine. (*IBM Corp.*)

ber indicating the response. Alternatively, the user can, with a touch of an electronic *light pen* (Figure 4-28), call for a more detailed breakdown of an item in a displayed report. The light pen is a photocell placed in a small tube. When the user moves the pen over the screen, the pen is able to detect the light coming from a limited field of view. The light from the CRT causes the photocell to respond when the pen is pointed directly at a lighted area. These electric responses are transmitted to the computer, which is able to determine that part of the displayed item which is triggering the photocell response.

Graphical display applications   In recent years, instruments have been developed which make it possible for the computer to receive human sketching directly. One such instrument is the *input tablet,* which may come in different sizes as shown in Figure 4-29. The tablet typically con-

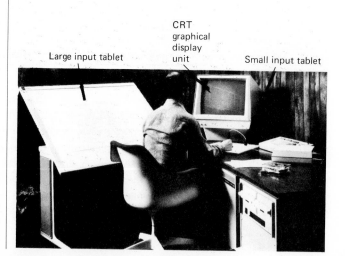

FIGURE 4-29
Interactive graphic design
using input tablets and visual
display. (*Tektronix, Inc.*)

FIGURE 4-30
Interactive graphics terminal with a three-way split screen feature. A small section of an electronic circuitry design can be magnified in one of the split areas for detailed manipulation. (*California Computer Products, Inc.*)

tains hundreds of copper lines, which form a fine grid that is connected with the computer. Each copper line receives electric impulses. A special pen or stylus attached to the tablet is sensitive to these impulses and is used to form the sketches. However, the pen does not mark directly on the tablet. To communicate with the machine, the user—e.g., a designer —merely draws on a piece of paper placed on the tablet. The tablet grid then senses the exact position of the stylus as it is moved and transmits this information to the computer. As the designer draws, the computer may display the developing sketch on the CRT. However, there is a difference between the drawing and the display. Poorly sketched lines are displayed as straight; poor lettering is replaced by neat printing; and poorly formed corners become mathematically precise. Changes and modifications in the drawing can be made quickly; e.g., a line can be "erased" from (or shifted on) the display unit with a movement of the stylus. Once the initial sketching is finished and displayed on the CRT to the satisfaction of the designer, he or she may then instruct the computer to analyze the design and report on certain characteristics. Such direct human-machine graphical communication enables the designer to (1) learn what effect certain changes have on the project and (2) save valuable time for more creative work. Graphical display techniques are currently being used in the design of ships, highways, aircraft, electronic circuits (Figure 4-30), and buildings.

Intelligent Terminals

By combining programmable microcomputers or minicomputers with terminal hardware, designers have built terminal systems (Figure 4-31)

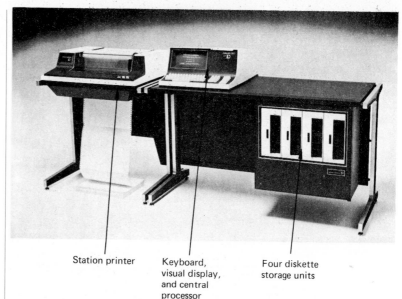

Station printer

Keyboard,
visual display,
and central
processor

Four diskette
storage units

FIGURE 4-31
Intelligent terminal with self-
standing computing capa-
bility. (*Datapoint Corp.*)

that are very similar to some smaller computer installations. In fact, it is becoming very difficult to distinguish between many small stand-alone computer systems and these *intelligent terminals.*

A growing number of organizations are using intelligent terminals as an integral part of a *distributed data processing system.* On the local level, small jobs are processed using the terminal's user-programmable micro-computer or minicomputer and assorted peripheral and secondary storage devices without any interaction with a higher-level computer. Also, adequate local storage capacity may be available (e.g., on tape cassettes, floppy disks, or magnetic bubble chips) to permit local users to store frequently needed data and thus to avoid the expense of making constant inquiries of a larger computer system in the organization. But the terminals are also used to make programmed error-detection checks to determine the validity of locally produced data and to classify and order these facts in a specified way prior to forwarding them to the computer(s) at a higher level in the organization for storage or further processing. The higher-level computer(s) in the organization may be used to manage

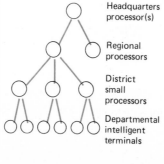

Headquarters
processor(s)

Regional
processors

District
small
processors

Departmental
intelligent
terminals

FIGURE 4-32
Hierarchical variation of a star
distributed processing
network.

large data bases and to serve the lower-level processors by executing jobs that require extensive computations. In short, intelligent terminals may be low-level satellite processors in a distributed processing *hierarchy* that may have several levels (see Figure 4-32).

VOICE COMMUNICATION

Input units, basically, do nothing more than convert human language into machine language. Why, then, doesn't someone invent a machine that will enable a person to talk to the computer in English? As a matter of fact, a few manufacturers have done just that. Although the vocabulary is quite small, sound waves have been converted into machine language. The technology of speech recognition is now in its infancy, but it is likely to be applied rapidly in the future in situations where an individual's hands and eyes are busy. For example, quality-control inspectors can enter data verbally into a computer while using test instruments to check parts and assemblies.[10]

When we look at the *output* side of verbal communication, however, we find that computers are now being used widely to give English responses in reply to human inquiries. These inquiries are often transmitted to a central computer over regular telephone lines. All the spoken words needed to process the possible inquiries may be prerecorded on a magnetic or photographic film drum. Each word is given a code. When inquiries are received, the processor composes a reply message in a coded form. This coded message is then transmitted to an *audio-response* device, which assembles the words in the proper sequence and transmits the audio message back to the station requesting the information. A much less expensive audio-response approach is found in Texas Instruments' Speak & Spell system, which is used to teach children to spell and pronounce over 200 basic words. A single integrated circuit chip costing a few dollars synthesizes the selected sounds that are used for audio response. Thus, the spoken word in machine-usable form is now very cheap—cheap enough, in fact, to be installed in your future microwave oven, washing machine, etc., if you want talking appliances.

Audio-response techniques, combined with briefcase-sized keyboard devices, turn every standard telephone into a potential computer terminal. A traveling engineer, for example, might check on a project's status by keying an inquiry directly into the home-office computer. A computer-compiled audio response could then give the engineer the necessary information. Similarly, construction personnel could enter and receive labor, material, and equipment information, and hospital personnel could use the terminal to confirm a patient's medical insurance coverage.

[10] Another application is the use of speech recognition techniques to determine the identity of a person seeking entry to a secure area (voice patterns are as unique as fingerprints). A phrase consisting of several words is spoken, and the equipment then digitally compares this sound with the stored sounds made earlier when authorized persons uttered the same phrase.

DATA COMMUNICATIONS

Data communications techniques make possible the I/O operations that take place between remote online terminals and CPUs. *Data communication* refers to the means and methods whereby data are transferred between processing locations. There is certainly nothing new about data communications. For example, the Greek runner carrying the message of victory on the plains of Marathon has inspired a present-day athletic event, and the Pony Express won the admiration of a nation in the brief period of time before it was replaced by telegraph service.

Data transmission services are available from domestic *common* (or "public") *carriers* such as *telephone companies* and *telegraph companies.* In addition, there are smaller *specialized common carriers* that may concentrate most of their attention on offering services of a particular type (e.g., transmitting data or pictures).

Figure 4-33 shows the types of transmission *channels,* or highways, used to carry data from one location to another. These channels employ wire lines, cables, and/or microwave radio circuits which, like I/O devices, vary in data-handling speed.

Teletype channels transmit data at slow speeds (from about 5 to 30 characters per second), but this is quite adequate for input by means of manual keying. Standard voice-grade *telephone* channels permit more rapid transmission. Speeds of well over 300 characters per second are possible. Telephone circuits are used to communicate large amounts of data stored on cards and tapes.[11] *Broadband* channels use very high frequency electric signals to carry the data message at maximum speeds of around 100,000 characters per second. These broadband circuits are currently groups of voice-grade wire channels, or they are microwave radio circuits.[12] Such transmission facilities are expensive and are now used only by large organizations. In the not-too-distant future, however, *fiber optics*

---

[11] Some users of telephone channels have found it more economical and reliable to deal directly with a specialized common carrier rather than directly with a telephone company. Telenet Communications Corporation, for example, has a network of computers that receives customer data coming in over telephone lines. These data are temporarily stored and organized in "packets" of up to 128 characters in the Telenet system. The packets are then computer-routed and transmitted at high speed over dedicated telephone lines to a Telenet office near the final data destination. At this office, data in the packets are reassembled into the complete message for transmission to the final destination. For the user of the Telenet service, the transmission cost is frequently less than if the user had relied on less efficient means of directly utilizing telephone channels. Thus, specialized carriers such as Telenet are often referred to as *value-added packet switching* services.

[12] When microwave radio facilities are used, the message may be transmitted along a terrestrial route by repeater stations that are located, on the average, about 25 miles apart. Alternatively, the message may be beamed to a *satellite* that acts as a reflector by accepting signals from one point on the earth and returning the same signals to some other point on the earth. The satellite appears from the earth to be a stationary target for the microwave signals because it is precisely positioned 22,300 miles above the equator with an orbit speed that matches the earth's rotation. Dozens of satellites are now in orbit to handle international and domestic data, voice, and video communications.

[13] For more information on this exciting technology, see Allen A. Boraiko, "Harnessing Light by a Thread," *National Geographic,* pp. 516–535, October 1979.

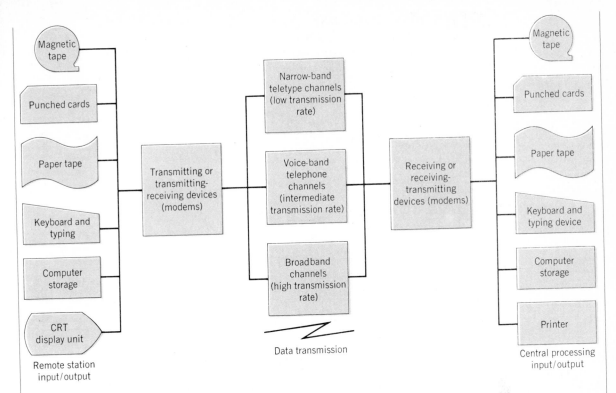

Remote station
input/output

Data transmission

Central processing
input/output

FIGURE 4-33
Data transmission service.

and *laser* technology will permit huge amounts of information to be routinely transmitted at the speed of light through tiny threads of glass or plastic. Teamed with a laser, a single glass fiber the size of a human hair may be used to transmit across the country in a single second all the characters in dozens of books of this size. Since thousands of these fibers can be packaged in a single cable, the future cost of broadband transmission capability should be within the reach of small organizations and individuals.[13]

The data communications environment has changed rapidly in just a few years. A typical online system of the mid-1960s is shown in Figure 4-34a. Terminals were linked by transmission facilities directly to a central computer. Such a system is still quite appropriate for many organizations. But some of today's large distributed computing/communications networks are quite different, and the coordination required for efficient network use is quite complex. These systems must link together hundreds of terminals at dozens of dispersed locations (Figure 4-34b). Thus, *communications processors* (typically micro-or minicomputers) are used to (1) concentrate messages at remote locations for more economical transmission, (2) switch messages between points in the network, and (3) relieve the main computers—i.e., the host computers—from "front-end" communications work. As we will see in later chapters, these complex computing/communications networks have potential for both good and evil.

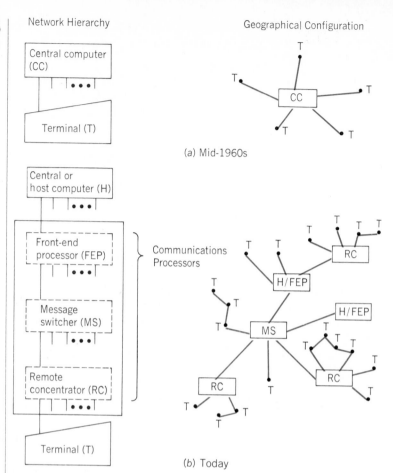

FIGURE 4-34
Data communications
environments.

"Computer Talk: It's a Here and Now Technology"

Most companies in the audio response/voice recognition data entry market-place have a single message for potential users: both methodologies are "here and now" technologies that are being used in cost-effective applications related to data processing. Although audio response has been in use for a number of years in time and temperature systems through local telephone companies or as account inquiry systems in banks, voice recognition-data entry is somewhat newer and may not be in as wide-spread use. But predictions by vendors and consultants are positive toward continued future growth in the number of systems installed and the broader range of application areas.

Two companies—Heuristics Inc. and Votrax Division of Federal Screw Works—feel so strongly about the use of voice response and voice input that they have developed units that connect to personal/home computers such as the TRS-80, Apple II and S-100 bus computers.

Leonard H. Magnuson, director, marketing and sales, Votrax, Troy, MI, told INFOSYSTEMS that "the whole man-machine interface area, including audio response and voice recognition, is going to increase." He said these units "will enhance data entry" especially in the "eyes busy" work areas within a company.

"Critical voice messages—including in a pilot's cockpit—will replace buzzers, gongs and bells in alert and alarm systems," Magnuson predicted. "And the microwave oven in your kitchen will talk back to you in a friendly voice," he said. "Voice as output will become as important as the CRT and printer have become in the past."

Another small but growing area for voice response is by telephone companies that provide specialized "call-in" services, such as sports scores, stock quotations, ski and weather conditions, and commodity and livestock prices. One of the newest of these somewhat unique service offerings is by Southwestern Bell Telephone Co., Kansas City, MO, which has a "commodity news line" that provides current prices on various goods such as wheat, oats, soybeans, precious metals and beef. The Commodity News Line is an "interactive" system that permits a user to select single or multiple items on which he wants prices, rather than be forced to listen to an entire list of prices waiting for the one in which he is interested.

One of those "other" audio response companies is Periphonics Corp., Bohemia, NY, where a spokesman said that use of its audio response/data entry systems is "really taking off." "Every manager who has a need to increase his profits and hold down costs in the current economy with costs soaring can eliminate data terminals in field locations with our system," said Gary M. Galati, director, advertising and public relations, Periphonics.

One increasing application area is "bank-by-phone" or "bank-from-home," according to Galati. Of five Pittsburgh, PA, banks providing such a service, three use Periphonics equipment. Bank personnel, according to Periphonics, also can use the firm's Voicepac 2000 audio response equipment to provide up-to-the-second information on balances, loans and deposits; for computing interest rates; to verify stop orders, and to retrieve other details related to the status of a bank's customer's account.

Although audio response technology and its use have been part of some companies' day-to-day operations for a long time, Galati feels that users are "coming back to audio response" as a cost-effective information retrieval and data entry system within a computerized environment.

Tom Roberts, national sales manager, Wavetek Data Communications, San Diego, CA, is bullish about the future of voice response. "I see a big resurgence in audio response reservation systems for hotels," he said. "It's far from static. It was a little premature when it was introduced, but people now realize they have a communications network already in place with the telephone company. With the growth of the Touch-Tone telephone, we have in place a low-cost data entry terminal."

Source: Frederick W. Miller, "Computer Talk: It's a Here and Now Technology," *Infosystems*, pp. 68–69, August 1979. Reprinted by permission of the publisher.

▶ LOOKING BACK

The following points have been emphasized in this chapter:

1 Punched cards are a familiar I/O medium. They are easily understood and possess advantages because of their fixed length. For example, some cards can be deleted, added to, sorted, etc., without disturbing the others. However, their data density is low, they are bulky, and they represent a slow means of input and output.

2 Like punched cards, punched paper tape is an I/O and offline storage medium. Paper tape punch and reader attachments are often found on the typewriter terminals used in timesharing and personal computing systems. An eight-channel tape code is used to record data.

3 Magnetic tape comes in different sizes and has a much faster transfer rate than punched cards or paper tape. It can be erased and reused many times and is thus very economical. Data are usually represented by a nine-channel code. However, the magnetized spots are invisible, and thus a printing operation is required to check or verify tape data.

4 Direct-access devices such as magnetic disks, drums, card strips, and bubble chips are used for I/O and online secondary storage. Disk packs and floppy disks can also be removed from the equipment and stored offline, just like tapes. Data are organized into tracks on disks. Magnetic card strip devices can usually store more information than other direct-access equipment, but access speed is slow when compared with disks or bubble chips. Bubble chips may replace some disk devices in the future because their lack of moving parts may lead to greater reliability.

5 Character readers reduce the manual effort involved in data-input operations. Financial institutions have supported the development of MICR as a means of handling billions of transactions each year. Unfortunately for organizations outside the banking community, there are no alphabetic characters available in MICR. Optical character readers, however, have alphabetic as well as numeric capability and perform efficiently in applications involving the use of machine-printed characters, bar codes, and handmade marks.

6 Printers are a primary output device when the information is to be used by people rather than machines. Serial impact printers may be modified electric typewriters, or they may use daisy-wheel or dot-matrix mechanisms. Nonimpact thermal and inkjet printers are also used.

Serial printers are found in personal microcomputer and small mini-computer systems and in online terminals. High-speed impact line printers are used with larger-capacity installations, and still faster non-impact page printers are used when hundreds of thousands of pages must be prepared each month. When output reaches high levels, printed paper may be replaced with microfilm.

7 Console keyboards, remote job-entry stations, data-collection and transaction-recording stations, point-of-sale and EFTS terminals, visual display stations, input tablets and light pens, intelligent terminals—all these online instruments enable people to communicate directly with any record stored in the direct-access devices. Audio communication from computers to humans has proved to be practical.

8 Data communications facilities relay information between remote points. A wide range of data transmission services is available. These services vary in data-handling speed and cost. Advanced communications networks using programmable processors for such functions as remote concentration of messages, message switching, and front-end processing have been developed in recent years.

KEY TERMS

After reading Chapter 4, you should be able to define and use the following terms:

channels
transfer rate
parity checking
binary coded decimal code
nine-channel tape format
disk pack
floppy disk
nondestructive read-out
MICR
Universal Product Code (UPC)
serial printer
impact printer
line printer

computer-output-to-microfilm (COM)
point-of-sale terminal
EFTS station
alphanumeric display terminal
light pen
input tablet
intelligent terminal
voice recognition
audio-response device
data communication
transmission channel
fiber optics

REVIEW AND DISCUSSION QUESTIONS

1 A punched card is a triple-purpose medium. (a) What is the meaning of triple-purpose? (b) What other media are tripple-purpose in nature?
2 Discuss the advantages and limitations of punched cards.
3 Discuss the advantages and limitations of punched paper tape.

4 (a) How may data be recorded on magnetic tape? (b) Discuss the advantages and limitations of magnetic tape.

5 What factors might affect the access times of such direct-access devices as magnetic drums, magnetic disks, and magnetic bubble chips?

6 (a) What is a disk pack? (b) What is a floppy disk? (c) What are some advantages and limitations of magnetic disks?

7 Compare and contrast MICR and OCR.

8 (a) Explain in general terms how daisy-wheel and dot-matrix printers work. (b) How does a high-speed drum printer work? (c) Why may microfilm output be substituted for printer output?

9 (a) What is the purpose of a data-collection station? (b) Of transaction recording stations? (c) Of POS stations? (d) Of EFTS stations?

10 (a) What two basic classes of CRT display terminals are available? (b) How may each category be used?

11 (a) What is an intelligent terminal? (b) How may one be used?

12 How may voice communication units be used? Give examples.

13 Identify and discuss the most commonly used transmission channels for carrying data from one location to another.

14 What social changes could take place in the future as a result of the development of data transmission facilities using fiber optics and laser technology? (Hint: The article by Boraiko in the following "Selected References" section may give you some ideas.)

15 "The selection of the best direct-access storage device to use involves compromise." Discuss this statement.

16 Discuss how the following I/O devices could be used to facilitate the work of the social groups indicated:

I/O Device	Social Group
Card punch	Electric utility company
Paper tape reader	Personal computing hobbyists
Magnetic tape drive	The Internal Revenue Service
Magnetic disk drive	
using disk packs	A law enforcement agency
using floppy disks	Certified Public Accountants
Magnetic card and strip unit	Life insurance company
Magnetic bubble chip in a	
portable terminal	Sportswriters
Optical character reader	Grocery store stockers
Serial impact printer	Lawyers
Impact line printer	Hospital administrators
Transaction recording unit	Credit union clerks
POS terminal	Department store clerks
Alphanumeric CRT display	University registrars
Graphical CRT display	Civil engineers
Input tablet	Architects
Light pen	Military commanders
Voice input unit	Sightless persons
Audio response unit	Hospital nurses

SELECTED REFERENCES

Boraiko, Allen A.: "Harnessing Light by a Thread," *National Geographic,* pp. 516–535, October 1979.

Hoagland, A. S.: "Storage Technology: Capabilities and Limitations," *Computer,* pp. 12–18, May 1979.

Hughes, Elizabeth M.: "A Printer Primer," *onComputing,* pp. 6–11ff, Fall 1979.

Lusa, John M.: "Going to the Source," *Infosystems,* pp. 52–53ff, April 1979.

Miller, Frederick W.: "Computer Talk: It's a Here and Now Technology," *Infosystems,* pp. 68–69, August 1979.

Myers, Ware: "Interactive Computer Graphics: Poised for Takeoff?" *Computer,* pp. 60–72, January 1978.

Chapter 5
CENTRAL PROCESSORS IN GENERAL

LOOKING AHEAD

The purpose of this chapter is to give you a general introduction to the central processing unit (CPU)—the hardware heart of any computer system. Since CPUs of all sizes have storage, arithmetic-logic, and control sections, this chapter is organized to consider these sections. In the early pages of the chapter, the emphasis is on the storage function. The storage elements found in a CPU are identified, and then the conceptual areas of primary storage are discussed.

You will then learn that locations in the primary storage section of the CPU are identified by address numbers. The ways in which address numbers may be used during processing are discussed. You will also see that the amount of data that can be stored in a numbered address can vary according to the design of the machine.

The data contained in storage must be in a coded form that a CPU can use. Therefore, the next section of the chapter is devoted to binary numbers and the binary-related codes that are used in modern computers to represent data.

Finally, a discussion of the magnetic core and semiconductor chip devices used to hold data in primary storage is presented. In the last two sections of this chapter, you will see how the arithmetic-logic and control units function in the CPU.

Thus, after studying this chapter, you should be able to:

- Identify and explain the purpose of smaller storage sections in the CPU that perform special processing and control functions.
- Outline the conceptual storage areas found in the CPU, and explain how storage locations are identified and used for processing.
- Discuss the capacity of each storage address and the various approaches that are used to organize the storage unit.
- Explain the binary numbering system and how it compares with the familiar decimal numbering system.
- Describe how computers represent data in codes that are related to a binary numbering system.
- Summarize the main characteristics of the primary storage devices used in modern computers.
- Explain in general terms how the arithmetic-logic and control units function in the CPU to produce output information.
- Understand and use the key terms listed at the end of the chapter.

155

It is now time to take a closer look at the central processor. As you will remember, the typical CPU contains the storage unit, the arithmetic-logic unit, and the control unit. Therefore, we shall be concerned first with the *storage unit* and related topics. More specifically, we shall examine (1) the *elements and conceptual areas* of the storage unit, (2) the *locations* in the storage unit, (3) the *capacity* of storage locations, (4) the *numbering systems* associated with computers, (5) the methods of *information representation* used, and (6) the *types of primary storage devices*. Following these sections, we shall turn our attention to the *arithmetic-logic* and *control* units.

STORAGE ELEMENTS AND CONCEPTUAL AREAS

Storage Elements in the CPU

Every CPU has a *primary storage* section that holds the active program(s) and data being processed. In addition, however, there may also be several *specialized storage elements* built into a CPU to perform specific processing and control functions (Figure 5-1). One such element is a *high-speed buffer* (or *cache*) memory that operates at faster speeds than the primary storage section and is thus used as a kind of "scratch pad" to temporarily store very active data and instructions during *processing*. Data may be transferred automatically between the scratch pad and the primary storage so that the cache memory is usually invisible to the programmer.

Another special *read-only memory* (ROM) section may be used for *control* purposes in CPUs of all sizes. For example, as you saw in Chapter 2 (and in Figure 1-15a, page 34), *microprograms* permanently fused into one or more ROM chips may be used to interpret the problem-solving

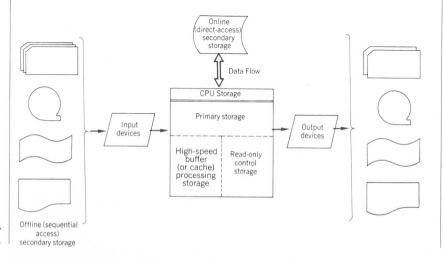

FIGURE 5-1
Computer storage elements inside the CPU.

"Amazingly Simple Device Revolutionizes Electronics"

An amazingly simple device, capable of performing efficiently nearly all the functions of an ordinary vacuum tube, was demonstrated for the first time yesterday at Bell Telephone Laboratories where it was invented.

Known as the Transistor, the device works on an entirely new physical principle discovered by the Laboratories in the course of fundamental research into the electrical properties of solids. Although the device is still in the laboratory stage, Bell scientists and engineers expect it may have far-reaching significance in electronics and electrical communication.

The whole apparatus is housed in a tiny cylinder less than an inch long. It will serve as an amplifier or an oscillator—yet it bears almost no resemblance to the vacuum tube now used to do these basic jobs. It has no vacuum, no glass envelope, no grid, no plate, no cathode and therefore no warm-up delay.

Two hair-thin wires touching a pinhead of a solid semiconductive material soldered to a metal base, are the principal parts of the Transistor. These are enclosed in a simple, metal cylinder not much larger than a shoelace tip. More than a hundred of them can easily be held in the palm of the hand.

Since the device is still in the experimental stage, no data on cost are available. Its essential simplicity, however, indicates the possibility of widespread use, with resultant mass-production economies. When fully developed, the Transistor is also expected to find new applications in electronics where vacuum tubes have not proved suitable.

Tests have shown that the Transistor will amplify at least 100 times (20 decibels). Some test models have been operated as amplifiers at frequencies up to ten million cycles per second. Because of the basically simple structure of the new units, stability and long life are expected.

While many scientists and engineers have been associated with the work during the project, key investigations which brought the Transistor to reality were carried out by Dr. John Bardeen and Dr. Walter H. Brattain. The general research program leading to the Transistor was initiated and directed by Dr. William Shockley. All three are members of the Bell Telephone Laboratories technical staff.

Yesterday's demonstration emphasized some of the many uses the Transistor may have in telephone communication, as well as its adaptability to the electronic techniques of radio, television, and public address systems.

Source: "Courtesy of Bell Laboratories."

instructions written by a programmer and to translate these instructions into steps that the hardware can accept. Like the high-speed cache memory, read-only control storage elements are usually invisible to applications programmers.

Conceptual Areas in Primary Storage

What *is* visible to the problem solver is the primary storage unit of the CPU. Storage locations in this unit have the ability to store *either* data *or* instructions; i.e., a specific physical space may be used to store data for one operation and instructions for another. The programmer (or the "housekeeping" software prepared by programmers) determines how the location will be used for each application.

For each program, there will be, typically, four areas assigned to group related types of information. These conceptual areas are shown in Figure 5-2. They are referred to as *conceptual areas* because it is important to remember that they are *not fixed* by built-in physical boundaries in storage. Rather, they vary (thus the broken lines in Figure 5-2) at the discretion of the programmer. Three of the four areas (input, working, and

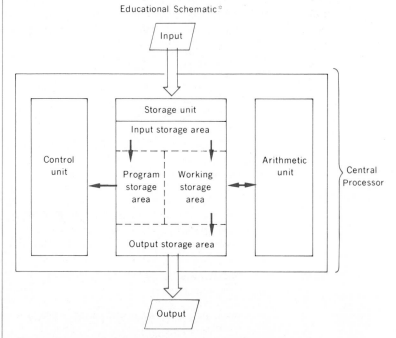

Educational Schematic *

FIGURE 5-2
Conceptual storage areas.
(Sperry UNIVAC Division, Sperry Rand Corp.)

* The specific areas of storage used for a particular purpose (input storage, program storage, etc.) *are not fixed but rather vary from program to program.* The programmer defines the limits of these reserved areas for each program. Therefore, broken lines (rather than solid ones) are used in the diagram to indicate this flexibility of area boundaries.

FIGURE 5-3
Ada Augusta Byron. (*The
Bettmann Archive.*)

THE FIRST PROGRAMMER WAS A LADY

Lady Ada Augusta Byron, Countess of Lovelace (1815–1852), was the daughter of the famous poet Lord Byron. She is also gaining recognition as the world's first computer programmer.

Lady Lovelace studied mathematics and translated for scientific journals, using her initials because it was not appropriate for a nineteenth-century woman to make such contributions. Babbage encouraged her to write an original paper, and she responded by writing a paper that corrected errors in Babbage's work. Lady Lovelace continued to work with Babbage on the development of the calculating engine. The success of Babbage's discovery would not have been possible without the programming descriptions and other writings of Lady Lovelace.

A high-level programming language is being developed for the U.S. Department of Defense. The new language is called "Ada" in recognition of Lady Lovelace's contributions.

output) are used for *data-storage* purposes. The *input storage* area, as the name indicates, receives the data coming from the input media and devices. The *working storage* space corresponds to a blackboard or a sheet of scratch paper; it is space used by the program to hold data being processed as well as the intermediate results of such processing. The *output storage* section contains processed information that is awaiting a *read-out* operation. The *program storage* area, of course, contains the processing instructions.

A typical *data-flow* pattern is indicated in Figure 5-2. Data remain in the input area until needed. Since the actual processing occurs in the arithmetic-logic unit, data are delivered to this unit from input storage and processed, and the final results move through the output storage area to the user. Intermediate figures, generated in the arithmetic-logic unit, are temporarily placed in a designated working storage area until needed at a later time. Data may move back and forth between working storage and the arithmetic-logic unit a number of times before the processing is completed.

Instructions move from the program storage area to the control unit. The first program instruction is sent to the control unit to begin the step-by-step processing procedure. Other instructions move into the control unit at the proper time until the job is completed.

STORAGE LOCATIONS AND THEIR USE

In the computer there are storage locations that may be compared to a post office box. These locations are identified by a specific number and are capable of holding both data and instructions. Such "boxes," or "cells," are referred to as *addresses*. Like a post office box number, the address number remains the same and is independent of the contents. But unlike a post office box, which can hold several different messages at the same time, an address stores only one datum or instruction item at a time.

The addresses in a storage unit containing 4,096 locations would be numbered from 0000 to 4095. Thus, one unique address will be designated 1776. It is necessary to emphasize that *there is an important distinction between the address number and the contents of the address.* Why is this distinction important? It is important because one of the principles of programming is that basic machine-language instructions deal directly with address numbers rather than with the contents of the address. For example, suppose that $315 is the data item stored in address 1776. If the programmer wants that amount printed, she will not instruct the computer to print $315. Rather, she will order the machine to print 1776, and the computer will interpret this instruction to mean that it should *print the contents of address 1776.* Just as you can locate friends in a strange city if you know that their home address is 4009 Sarita Drive, so too can the computer locate the desired information if it knows the location number.

Perhaps an example illustrating some of the concepts that have been introduced would be appropriate at this time. In our example let us consider "a atlas aardvark." What is "a atlas aardvark"? Well, A. Atlas Aardvark is not a "what," he is a "who"—the zoology editor for Imprint Publishing Company. He is also the first person paid each week (Atlas has gone through life being first in line). Let's look at how his paycheck might be processed by Imprint's PAC (Peculiar Automatic Computer).

The payroll *data* are prepared on punched cards each week for each employee. Last week the following data were punched into Atlas's card: (1) He worked 40 hours, (2) he receives $10 an hour, (3) he has 20 percent of his total income taken out for taxes, and (4) he has hospitalization insurance, which costs him $5 each week.

Instructions have been prepared by Imprint's programmer to direct the computer in the payroll operation. The following steps must be performed:

1 The machine must be started.
2 An employee's payroll data must be read into storage for processing.
3 Hours worked must be multiplied by the hourly rate to find the *total earnings*.
4 Total earnings must be multiplied by the withholding percentage figure to find the amount of tax deduction.
5 To the tax withheld must be added the hospitalization insurance deduction to arrive at the *total deduction* figure.
6 The total deduction must be subtracted from the total earnings to find the take-home earnings.
7 A check must be printed for the amount of the take-home earnings, and it must be payable to the correct employee.
8 The machine must be stopped at the end of the processing operation.

Program instructions are also presented to the PAC in the form of punched cards.

Figure 5-4 shows the PAC storage locations. Although the program-

00	01	02	03	04	05
06	07	08	09	10	11
Read payroll data card into addresses 00, 01, 02, 03, and 04.	Write contents of address 01 into arithmetic unit.	Multiply contents of arithmetic unit by contents of address 02.	Duplicate preceding answer in address 05.	Multiply contents of address 03 by preceding answer in arithmetic unit.	Add contents of address 04 to preceding answer in arithmetic unit.
12	13	14	15	16	17
Subtract preceding answer in arithmetic unit from contents of address 05.	Move preceding answer to address 23.	Write check for amount in address 23.	Make check payable to contents of address 00.	If last card, then go to address 18.	Go to address 06.
18	19	20	21	22	23
Stop processing.					

FIGURE 5-4
PAC storage.

mer may assign the instructions to *any section* of the storage unit, she has chosen to read them into addresses 06 to 18. These locations thus become the *program storage* area. The first instruction (in address 06) identifies the locations for the payroll data (00, 01, 02, 03, and 04). The data could just as well have been placed in addresses 19 to 23, and so this is also an arbitrary decision.[1]

Let us use Figure 5-5 to follow through the process that is required to prepare Atlas's paycheck. (The circled address numbers represent each step in the process.) After the computer operator has loaded the instructions into storage, the payroll data cards are placed into the card reader, the PAC controls are set at address 06, and the processing begins. This initial control setting feeds the first instruction into the control unit where it is interpreted. Signals are sent to the card reader, which carries out the command. Atlas's card is read, and the data are transferred to *input storage*. The control unit will execute the instructions automatically *in sequence* after the initial control setting until it is directed by a specific instruction to do otherwise. Therefore, as soon as the instruction in address

---

[1] Obviously, the data could not go into addresses 06 to 18 since these locations are now occupied by instructions. If a payroll item were mistakenly entered into a program section location, it would "erase" the instruction properly located in the address. At some later time the item would enter the control unit, where it would be interpreted as an instruction. If such an error should occur, the result would be quite unpredictable but invariably disastrous.

FIGURE 5-5
The preparation of Atlas's paycheck.

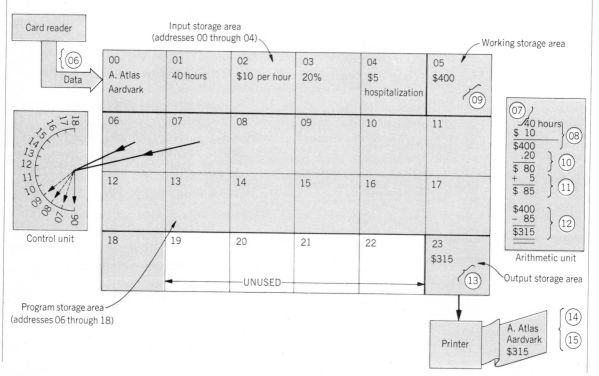

06 has been complied with, the control unit automatically begins interpreting the contents of address 07.

The next command instructs the control unit to copy the contents of address 01 into the arithmetic-logic unit. The control unit does not care that the contents of 01 are 40 hours (the next employee's time may differ). It is merely concerned with carrying out orders, and so 40 hours is placed in the arithmetic unit. And, in sequence, the processing continues: The 40-hour figure is multiplied by $10 per hour to find total earnings (instruction in address 08); this total earnings figure is duplicated (instruction, 09) in address 05, which is the *working* storage area; the tax deduction is found to be $80 (instruction, 10); the total deduction figure is $85 (instruction, 11); and Atlas's take-home pay is $315 (instruction, 12). The $315 is transferred to address 23 by the next order in the sequence. (It could just as easily have been placed in any of the unused locations.) From this *output storage* area, the information is sent to the printer, which, under program control, prints the paycheck. If Atlas's card had been the last one in the deck, the instructions in addresses 16 and 18 would have halted the process. Since other cards follow, however, the control unit receives the next order in the sequence. This instruction tells the control unit to reset itself to address 06, and so the process automatically begins again.

To summarize, several important concepts have been demonstrated in this example:

1   Input, working, output, and program storage areas are required, but they are not fixed in the PAC. Rather, they are determined by Imprint's programmer.
2   The PAC is able to obey several *commands,* e.g., READ, WRITE, ADD, SUBTRACT, and MOVE. This ability to execute specific orders is *designed and built into* the machine. Every computer has a particular set, or *repertoire,* of commands that it is able to obey.
3   Computers execute one instruction at a time. They follow sequentially the series of directions until explicitly told to do otherwise. Figure 5-6 is a diagram, or *flowchart,* of the payroll procedure. The computer moves through the instructions in sequence until it comes to a *branchpoint* and is required to answer a question: Have data from the last card been fed into storage? The answer to the question determines which path or branch the computer will follow. If the answer is no, the procedure is automatically repeated by the use of the technique known as *looping;* if the answer is yes, the processing stops. Instructions that result in the transfer of program control to an instruction stored at some arbitrary location rather than to the next location in storage may be *conditional* or *unconditional* transfer commands. If the change in sequence is based on the outcome of some test, it is a conditional transfer, if not, it is an unconditional branch. Can you identify the conditional and unconditional transfer instructions in Figure 5-6?

FIGURE 5-6
A flowchart of the procedure used to process Imprint Publishing Company's payroll.

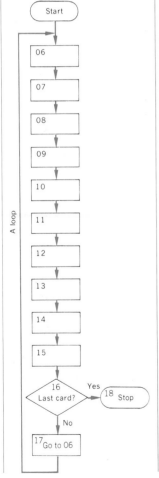

*Man does not live by
words alone despite the
fact that sometimes he has
to eat them.*
—Adlai Stevenson

CAPACITY OF STORAGE LOCATIONS

Computer storage locations must be used in such a way that sequences of characters (e.g., AARDVARK, $315, ADD) can be stored and manipulated to produce output information. A sequence of characters stored in a computer and treated as a single entity is called a *computer word*. There are several *built-in* approaches, that may be used to organize characters into words in storage.

In some machines, *each* numbered address contains *only a single character* (A, **3**, $). Such processors are said to be *character-addressable*. Thus, a sequence of characters such as AARDVARK would require eight storage addresses while $315 would require four addresses. The character-addressable approach, then, permits the use of *variable-length words*. A second storage approach is to design the computer to store a *fixed number of characters* in each numbered address location. The machine then treats the contents of each address as a *fixed-length word*.[2] When this storage organization approach is used, the computer is said to be *word-addressable*.

*He uses short, easy words,
like 'What about Lunch?'*
—The House at Pooh Cor-
ner

Each of these approaches to organizing the storage unit has advantages and drawbacks.[3] Recognizing this fact, the ingenious Peculiar Company designers of the PAC (and, incidentally, the designers of many modern computers) developed a *flexible machine* that could use program control to organize the computer to operate on *either* single characters *or* fixed-length words. How is this possible? You ask such timely questions.

Each alphanumeric character placed in storage is represented by a code consisting of 8 binary digits (bits).[4] Each of these coded characters, or *bytes*, is identified in storage by a *specific address number*. Thus, by using an appropriate set of instructions, the programmer can manipulate these characters into words of varying lengths as needed.

But bytes can also be *grouped together and operated on as a unit*. Programmers can elect to use, for example, other available instructions that will cause the computer to automatically retrieve, manipulate, and store as a single unit a fixed number of bytes.[5] Or they may choose to group additional bytes into a *double word* and have the machine function in this

---

[2] The number of characters found in a fixed-length word varies depending on the make and model of computer.

[3] For example, variable word-length processors generally make more efficient use of the available storage space (unused capacity may exist when a number of fixed words consists of only a few characters), but they have slower calculating capabilities (a computer with a fixed-length word of six characters can manipulate and add two 6-digit numbers in a single step while six steps would be needed by a character-addressable processor). Although it is beyond the scope of this book to go into these matters in more detail, you can find a more thorough presentation in Donald H. Sanders, *Computers in Business*, 4th ed., McGraw-Hill Book Company, New York, 1979, pp. 166–170.

[4] We will discuss bits in some detail in a few pages.

[5] The gospel according to some designers was: "In the beginning there was The Word, and The Word was four bytes long."

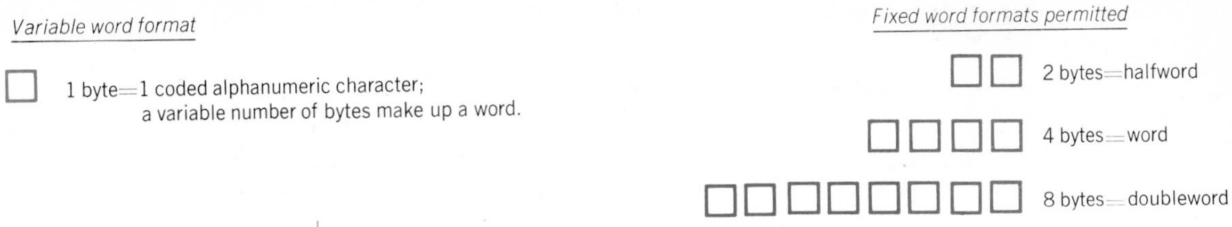

☐ 1 byte=1 coded alphanumeric character;
      a variable number of bytes make up a word.

☐☐ 2 bytes=halfword

☐☐☐☐ 4 bytes=word

☐☐☐☐☐☐☐☐ 8 bytes=doubleword

FIGURE 5-7
Address formats.

fixed-word format. Figure 5-7 illustrates the word formats possible with many currently used computers. However, micro- and minicomputers usually lack this flexibility. Most minicomputers in current use combine character (byte)-addressable storage with the ability to operate on words of only 2 bytes. Some newer microcomputers also have this ability, but many micros use only the byte-addressable storage approach.

Regardless of the capacity of the available storage locations, however, the numbers, letters, and special characters contained in storage must be in a coded form that the computer can use.

COMPUTER NUMBERING SYSTEMS

Computers represent data in a code that is related to a binary numbering system. It is thus desirable to understand numbering systems.

Decimal Numbers

Anthropologists have reported on the primitive number systems of some aboriginal tribes. The Yancoes in the Brazilian Amazon stop counting at three. Since their word for "three" is "poettarrarorincoaroac," this is understandable.
—Albert Sukoff

The first numbering systems were of an *additive* nature. That is, they consisted of symbols such as | for 1, || for 2, ||| for 3, etc. Each symbol represented the *same value* regardless of the position it occupied in the number. Unfortunately, calculations are difficult when such systems are used. In fact, you can calculate answers to problems that would have baffled wise people of earlier centuries. A big reason for your advantage has been the development of *positional* numbering systems. In such systems there are only a limited number of symbols, and the symbols represent different values according to the position they occupy in the number (5 = the Roman numeral V, but 51 does not equal VI because the meaning of 5 has changed with the change in its position). The number of symbols used depends on the *base* or *radix* of the particular system. The decimal system, of course, has a base of 10 and has 10 symbols (0 to 9).[6] The *highest* numerical symbol will always have a value of one *less* than the base.

[6] There is nothing particularly sacred about a base of 10. Probably the only reason it was originally developed and is now in widespread use is that people happen to have 10 fingers. Other systems have been created. For example, the Babylonians had a base of 60 (of course, they also did their writing on mud pies); the Mayas of Yucatán used a base of 20 (a warm climate and a group of barefooted mathematicians?); and a base of 5 is still used by natives in New Hebrides.

By the arrangement of the numerical symbols[7] in various positions, any number may be represented. We know that in the decimal system the successive positions to the left of the decimal point represent units, tens, hundreds, thousands, ten thousands, etc. We may fail to remember, however, that what this means is that each position represents a particular *power* of the base. The number 15,236 represents the sum of[8]

$$(\underline{1} \times 10^4) + (\underline{5} \times 10^3) + (\underline{2} \times 10^2) + (\underline{3} \times 10^1) + (\underline{6} \times 10^0)$$

In *any* positional numbering system, the *value of each position represents a specific power of the base.* To test your understanding of the concepts that have now been introduced, let us look at the following problems:

1   What is the decimal equivalent of 463_8? (The subscript 8 following the number 463 indicates that this is an *octal* base number.) Since the *base is now 8* rather than 10, the possible symbols are 0 to 7 (the symbols 8 and 9 do not exist in this case). Each position in the number 463_8 represents a power of its base. Therefore,

$$(\underline{4} \times 8^2) + (\underline{6} \times 8^1) + (\underline{3} \times 8^0). \leftarrow \text{Octal Point}$$
or $(4 \times 64) + (6 \times 8) + (3 \times 1).$
or $(256) + (48) + (3). = 307_{10}$ The decimal equivalent

2   What is the decimal equivalent of 1001_2? (We are now using a base of 2) With a base of 2, the only possible symbols are 0 and 1. Again, each position in the number 1001_2 represents a power of its base. Therefore,

$$(\underline{1} \times 2^3) + (\underline{0} \times 2^2) + (\underline{0} \times 2^1) + (\underline{1} \times 2^0). \leftarrow \text{Binary point}$$
or $(1 \times 8) + (0 \times 4) + (0 \times 2) + (1 \times 1).$
or $(8) + (0) + (0) + (1). = 9_{10}$ The decimal equivalent

These problems have demonstrated that (1) the lower the numbering base, the fewer the possible symbols that must be remembered, and (2) the smaller the base, the more positions there must be to represent a given quantity. Four digits (1001) are required in base 2 to equal a single decimal digit (9). You may also have observed that the decimal point becomes the *octal point* in a base-8 system and the *binary point* in base 2. It would thus appear that we have sneaked up on the *binary* or *base-2* numbering system used by digital computers.

---

[7] There is also nothing sacred about the shape of the symbols we use to represent quantities. We know that the symbol 2 has a certain meaning, but any number of other marks could be defined to serve the same purpose. A version of the Arabic numerals we use is thought to have originated in India around 200 B.C.

[8] Students occasionally forget their algebra and have to be reminded that n^0 is, by definition, 1; i.e., any number raised to the zero power equals 1.

Binary Numbers in Computers

It was pointed out in Chapter 1 that John von Neumann suggested that binary numbering systems be incorporated in computers. Although the suggestion came too late to prevent the very first machines from using the decimal system, von Neumann's suggestions were quickly adopted in subsequent designs.

Why the rush to binary? There are several very good reasons:

1　It is necessary that circuitry be designed only to handle 2 binary digits (bits) rather than 10. Design is simplified, cost is reduced, and reliability is improved.
2　Electronic components, by their very nature, operate in a binary mode. A switch is either open (0 state) or closed (1 state); a transistor either is not conducting (0) or is conducting (1).
3　Everything that can be done with a base of 10 can be done with the binary system.

COMPUTER DATA REPRESENTATION

Up to this point we have been discussing "pure" binary numbers, but most modern computers use some *coded* or *modified* version of pure binary to represent decimal numbers. Numerous data representation formats have been developed. The most popular, however, are the *binary coded decimal* (BCD) codes.

Binary Coded Decimal System

With BCD it is possible to convert *each* decimal digit into its binary equivalent rather than convert the entire decimal number into a pure binary form. The BCD equivalent of each possible decimal digit is shown in Figure 5-8. Because the digits 8 and 9 require 4 bits, *all* decimal digits are represented by 4 bits. Converting 405_{10} into BCD would yield the following result:

$$405_{10} \text{ in BCD} = \underline{0100}/\underline{0000}/\underline{0101} \text{ or } 010000000101$$
$$\qquad\qquad\qquad\quad 4 \qquad 0 \qquad 5$$

With 4 bits there are 16 different possible configurations (2^4). The first 10 of these configurations are, of course, used to represent decimal digits. The other six arrangements (1010, 1011, 1100, 1101, 1110, and 1111) have decimal values from 10 to 15. These six arrangements are *not used* in BCD coding; i.e., 1111 *does not* represent 15_{10} in BCD. Rather, the proper BCD code for 15_{10} is 0001/0101. The "extra" six configurations are used by programmers for other purposes, which we need not dwell on here.

Decimal Digit	Place Value			
	8	4	2	1
0	0	0	0	0
1	0	0	0	1
2	0	0	1	0
3	0	0	1	1
4	0	1	0	0
5	0	1	0	1
6	0	1	1	0
7	0	1	1	1
8	1	0	0	0
9	1	0	0	1

FIGURE 5-8
Binary coded decimal numeric bit configurations.

We have seen that BCD is a convenient and fast way to convert numbers from decimal to binary. But it is hardly sufficient for most purposes to have only 16 characters available.

Six-Bit Alphanumeric Code

Instead of using 4 bits with only 16 possible characters, equipment designers commonly use 6 or 8 bits to represent characters in *alphanumeric versions* of BCD. Since the four BCD *numeric* place positions (1, 2, 4, and 8) are retained, these alphanumeric versions are also frequently referred to as BCD. Two *zone* positions are added to the four BCD positions in the 6-bit code. With 6 bits it is thus possible to represent 64 different characters (2^6). A seventh parity checking position is commonly added (Figure 5-9). We have already seen examples of 6-bit alphanumeric BCD code being used to represent data in 96-column punched cards, punched paper tape, and magnetic tape. It was pointed out earlier that the decimal 7 is represented by an "on" condition in the numeric channels marked 4, 2, and 1. It is now apparent that being "on" means that a 1 bit is represented in these positions, i.e., that 7 = 0111 in BCD.

The 64 different coding arrangements possible with 6 bits are sufficient to code the decimal digits (10), capital letters (26), and a number of punctuation marks and machine control characters. Six bits are *not suffi-*

FIGURE 5-9

Check bit	Zone bits		Numeric bits			
C	B	A	8	4	2	1

FIGURE 5-10

Check bit	Zone bits				Numeric bits			
C	$\bar{Z}$	$\bar{Z}$	$\bar{Z}$	$\bar{Z}$	8	4	2	1

cient, however, to provide lowercase letters, capital letters, and a large number of special and control characters.

Eight-Bit Alphanumeric Codes

To permit greater flexibility in data representation, equipment designers *extended* the 6-bit alphanumeric BCD code to 8 bits. With 8-bit coding, it is possible to provide 256 different arrangements (2^8). Each 8-bit unit of information, you will remember, is called a *byte.* The nine-channel magnetic tape format discussed in Chapter 4 utilizes an 8-bit extended version of BCD. There are four (rather than two) zone bit positions available in an 8-bit code (Figure 5-10).

Selected characters are presented in Table 5-1 in the four codes most commonly encountered in data processing. (Parity check bits are excluded.) These codes include the Hollerith punched card code, explained in Chapter 1, and the 6-bit Standard BCD Interchange code, mentioned above. In addition, there are *two* 8-bit codes currently being used in modern computers. One, the Extended Binary Coded Decimal Interchange Code (EBCDIC) developed by IBM, is used in most IBM models and in many machines produced by different manufacturers. Another code, the American Standard Code for Information Interchange (ASCII), is popular in data communications and is used almost exclusively to represent data internally in personal microcomputers and in the larger machines produced by some vendors (e.g., the NCR Century family of computers).

TABLE 5-1
Common data representation codes

Character	Hollerith card code	Standard BCD interchange code	Extended BCD interchange code (EBCDIC)	ASCII
0	0	00 1010	1111 0000	0101 0000
1	1	00 0001	1111 0001	0101 0001
2	2	00 0010	1111 0010	0101 0010
3	3	00 0011	1111 0011	0101 0011
4	4	00 0100	1111 0100	0101 0100
5	5	00 0101	1111 0101	0101 0101
6	6	00 0110	1111 0110	0101 0110
7	7	00 0111	1111 0111	0101 0111
A	12-1	11 0001	1100 0001	1010 0001
B	12-2	11 0010	1100 0010	1010 0010
C	12-3	11 0011	1100 0011	1010 0011
D	12-4	11 0100	1100 0100	1010 0100
E	12-5	11 0101	1100 0101	1010 0101

"0"

"1"

FIGURE 5-11

Current is applied;
the core is
magnetized

Core remains
magnetized after
current stops

Current is reversed;
the core reverses
its magnetic state

TYPES OF PRIMARY STORAGE DEVICES

Data have been stored internally in a CPU in many ways over the years. The ENIAC, for example, used vacuum tube storage, and each tube was able to hold only a single bit. Storage capacity was thus tiny by present standards. The most popular computer in the mid-1950s (the IBM 650) used a magnetic drum as the internal storage instrument.

Magnetic core storage technology was first applied in the mid-1950s, and it was only a short time before these tiny rings became the dominant primary storage medium. Core storage remained dominant until the mid-1970s, when semiconductor chips began to replace cores in some new hardware designs. Thus, tens of thousands of existing computers currently utilize core technology.

Magnetic Core Storage

If a wire carrying a sufficiently strong electric current passes through a core, the core will be magnetized by the magnetic field created around the wire. In Figure 5-11, the current flow from left to right has magnetized the core in a counterclockwise (0-bit) direction. But when the current flows in the opposite direction, the core becomes magnetized in a clockwise (1-bit) fashion. A core can be quickly changed from an "off" or 0-bit condition to an "on" or 1-bit state simply by reversing the current flow passing through the core.

A large number of cores are strung on a screen of wires to form a *core plane.* These planes, resembling small square tennis rackets, are then arranged vertically to represent data, as indicated in Figure 5-12. (Nine planes are needed to code 8-bit bytes and provide for a parity check.)

With hundreds of thousands of cores in a CPU, how is it possible to select and properly magnetize a few in such a way that the desired character is *read into* storage? Let us use an imaginary plane to see how 1 bit in a character is selected (Figure 5-13). The other bits making up the character are similarly chosen in the other planes. To make selection possible, two wires must pass through each core at right angles. By sending only *half* the necessary current through each of two wires, only the core at the intersection of the wires is affected. All other cores in the plane either re-

Parity bit {

Character bits {

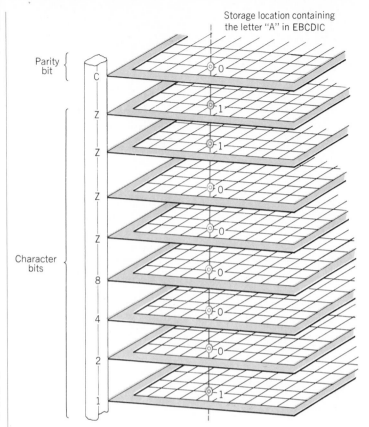

Storage location containing
the letter "A" in EBCDIC

C   0

Z   1

Z   1

Z   0

Z   0

8   0

4   0

2   0

1   1

FIGURE 5-12
The letter A represented in
core storage. (The EBCDIC
8-bit code is used.)

ceive no current at all or receive only half the amount needed to magnetize.[9]

    Magnetic cores have been popular for primary storage because they
are durable, safe, reasonably fast, relatively inexpensive, and compact.
However, the cost of core-plane fabrication and the circuitry necessarily
associated with cores have made them less desirable in recent years.

[9] With a character now read into core storage, how does the computer *retrieve* it? For retrieval, a third *sense* wire may be threaded diagonally through each core in a plane. The computer tests, or reads out, the magnetic state of a core by again sending electric current
pulses through the two wires used in the read-in operation. The direction of this current is
such that it causes a 0 to be written at that core position. If the core is magnetized in an "on"
or 1 state, the writing of a 0 will abruptly *flip* the magnetic condition of the core, and the
changing magnetic field will induce a current into the sense wire. The reaction picked up by
the sense wire tells the computer that the core contained a 1 bit. If *no reaction* is sensed, the
computer will know that the core is already magnetized in the 0 state. But wait a minute! If
all cores storing a character have been changed from a 1 to a 0 state as a result of the reading, haven't we destroyed the character in its original location? The answer to this is usually
yes, but only momentarily. Fortunately, by means of a fourth *inhibit* wire, the cores containing 1 bits are restored to their original state. Simply stated, the processor now tries to write
back 1s in every core read an instant earlier. If the core in the plane was originally a 1, it will
be restored; if it was originally a 0, it will remain that way, and a pulse of current will be sent
through the inhibit wire in the plane to cancel out the attempt to write a 1.

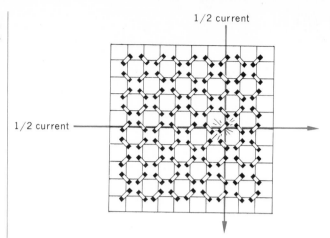

1/2 current

1/2 current

FIGURE 5-13
Magnetic core selection.

Semiconductor Storage

Semiconductor storage elements are tiny integrated circuits. Both the storage cell circuits and the support circuitry necessary for data writing and reading operations are packaged into tiny chips. There are several semiconductor storage technologies currently in use. Although we certainly need not go into these different storage approaches in any detail, the faster and more expensive *bipolar semiconductor* chips are often used in the arithmetic-logic and high-speed buffer storage sections of the CPU. Slower and less expensive chips that employ *metal-oxide semiconductor* (MOS) technology are usually used in the main memory section.

The storage cell circuits in some semiconductor chips contain (1) a transistor that acts in much the same way as a mechanical on-off toggle switch and (2) a capacitor that is capable of storing an electrical charge. Depending on the switching action of the transistor, the capacitor either contains no charge (0 bit) or does hold a tiny charge (1 bit). Figure 5-14 shows how 64 bits might be arranged in a segment of a chip.[10] To locate a particular cell for writing or reading, row and column addresses (in binary) are needed. The storage location of the shaded cell in Figure 5-14 is the row numbered 011 (3) and the column numbered 101 (5). Since the charge on the capacitor tends to "leak off," provision is made to periodically "regenerate" or refresh the storage charge.

Semiconductor memory chips have found their way into the newer models of most manufacturers for several very good reasons:

1   *Economic factors.* The cost per bit of semiconductor storage has declined an average of 35 percent per year since 1970, and there is no end in sight to these cost reductions. Furthermore, with core storage the associated circuitry is complex and expensive, regardless of the

---

[10] Many chips used at this writing store 64,000 bits (or 64K bits, where K—or kilo—represents thousands). Recently announced chips with 262K bits of storage are likely to be available soon. The trend goes on!

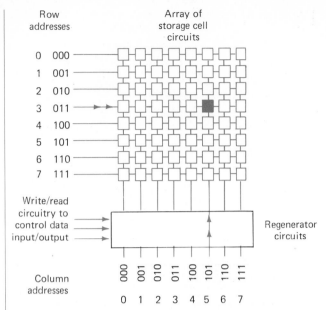

Row addresses

Array of storage cell circuits

0	000	
1	001	
2	010	
3	011	
4	100	
5	101	
6	110	
7	111	

Write/read circuitry to control data input/output

Regenerator circuits

Column addresses

000 001 010 011 100 101 110 111

0 1 2 3 4 5 6 7

FIGURE 5-14
Semiconductor storage concepts.

storage capacity served. Therefore, because of this high fixed-cost factor, the cost per bit of small core memories is much greater than the cost per bit of storage of a large-capacity core memory. With semiconductor storage, however, the cost is primarily in the chips and their packaging and not in the supporting circuitry. Thus, the fixed cost is low, and so the cost per bit of storage in a microcomputer is about the same as the cost per bit of storage in a larger computer.

2 *Compact size.* Semiconductor chips require less than half the space needed by core storage devices of similar capacity. The chip shown on the small coin in Figure 5-15*a*, for example, stores 64,000 bits of information. And the compact 5 million-byte semiconductor memory unit shown in Figure 5-15*b* has the capacity to store every character found in five books of this size.[11]

3 *Faster performance.* Semiconductor devices are capable of faster performance than core storage units. Their more compact size, of course, contributes to this faster speed. (The faster core memories, however, will outperform some slower MOS chips.)

THE ARITHMETIC-LOGIC UNIT

In preceding pages we noted that the arithmetic-logic unit is where the actual data processing occurs. All calculations are performed and all logical comparisons are made in this unit. Earlier, we traced through a simplified program to process Editor Aardvark's weekly paycheck. Some of the program instructions used then are reproduced in Figure 5-16.

[11] Of course, even the compact unit in Figure 5-15*b* will seem large and cumbersome in just a few years as three or four chips achieve the storage capacity of entire boards.

FIGURE 5-15
(*Left*) A 64,000-bit storage chip resting on a small coin. (IBM Corp.) (*Below*) Five million-byte semiconductor storage unit. (*Mostek Corp.*)

The instruction in address 07 calls for the computer to write the contents of address 01 into the arithmetic unit. Implicit in this instruction is the requirement that the arithmetic-logic unit have storage capability. It must be able to store temporarily the data contained in address 01. Such

FIGURE 5-16
(Source: Figure 5-4.)

07	08	09	10	11
Write contents of address 01 into arithmetic unit	Multiply contents of arithmetic unit by contents of address 02	Duplicate preceding answer in address 05	Multiply contents of address 03 by preceding answer in arithmetic unit	Add contents of address 04 to preceding answer in arithmetic unit

07	08	09	10	11
CLA 01	MUL 02	STO 05	MUL 03	ADD 04

FIGURE 5-17

a special-purpose storage location is called a *register*. Several registers will be discussed in the following paragraphs because they are basic to the functioning of the arithmetic-logic and control units. The number of registers varies among computers, as does the data-flow pattern. Let us trace the instructions in Figure 5-16 through the PAC computer.

Up to this point we have written the instructions in addresses 07 to 11 so that we would understand them. Figure 5-17 shows how these same instructions may be coded and stored for PAC's convenience. The first processing instruction, CLA 01, tells PAC to CLear the contents of the arithmetic-logic unit of all data and to Add (store) the contents of address 01 to a register known as the *accumulator*. Thus, 40 hours—the contents of address 01—are now held in both address 01 and the accumulator (Figure 5-18a).

The second instruction in address 08 is MUL 02. The computer interprets this instruction to mean that the contents of address 02 ($10) are to be *MUL*tiplied by the contents in the accumulator (40 hours) to get Aard-

FIGURE 5-18
Operation of the arithmetic-logic unit.

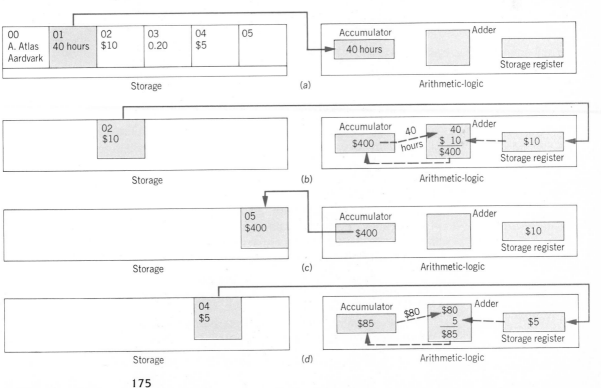

vark's gross pay. Execution of this instruction may take the following form (Figure 5-18b):

1 The contents of address 02 are read into a storage register in the arithmetic-logic unit.
2 The contents of the accumulator and the contents of the storage register are given to the *adder*. The *adder* (and its associated circuits) is the primary arithmetic element because it also performs subtraction, multiplication, and division on binary digits.
3 The product of the multiplication *is stored in the accumulator*. The 40 hours previously there has been erased by the arithmetic operation.

The third instruction in the processing sequence is STO 05. The contents in the accumulator are *STO*red in address 05. The read-in to address 05 is destructive to any information that might be there. The read-out from the accumulator is nondestructive (Figure 5-18c). The fourth instruction, MUL 03, is handled exactly like the second instruction, and so we need not repeat the execution.

The fifth instruction in the sequence, ADD 04, simply tells the computer to ADD the contents of address 04 to the contents of the accumulator. The hospitalization insurance deduction of $5 is the contents of 04; the tax deduction of $80 is now the contents of the accumulator. Why? Because when the fourth instruction is carried out, the $400 in the accumulator is multiplied by 20 percent (the contents of 03) to get a product, which is then stored in the accumulator. As Figure 5-18d shows, the contents of 04 are read into the storage register (thus erasing the previous contents); the adder totals the contents of the accumulator and the storage register; and the sum is stored in the accumulator.

It is apparent that every arithmetic operation requires two numbers and some result. Subtraction, for example, requires a minuend and a subtrahend to find a difference; multiplication uses a multiplicand and a multiplier to find a product. Although obviously two numbers and a result are handled by every computer arithmetic-logic unit, different processing and storage approaches have been developed to manage the two data words and the result.

Logic operations usually consist of comparisons. The arithmetic-logic unit may compare two numbers by subtracting one from the other. The sign (negative or positive) and the value of the difference tell the processor that the first number is equal to, less than, or greater than the second number. Three branches may be provided in the program for the computer to follow, depending on the result of such a comparison. Many processors are designed with a *comparer* in the arithmetic-logic unit. Data from an accumulator and a storage register may be examined by the comparer to yield the logic decision. Alphabetic data may also be compared according to an order sequence.

"The Art of Chip Making"

No other manufacturing process is quite like it. Only a single speck of dust can ruin a chip, so work must be done in "clean rooms," where the air is constantly filtered and workers are swathed in surgical-type garb.

Some 250 chips are made from one razor-thin wafer of precisely polished silicon about 3 in. in diameter. These wafers, in turn, are sliced from cylinders of extremely pure (99.9%) crystalline silicon, grown somewhat like rock candy. Why silicon? Because it can be either electrically conducting or nonconducting, depending on the impurities added to it. Thus one small area of a chip can be "doped" (as scientists say) with impurities that give it a deficiency of electrons—making it a so-called *p* (or electrically positive) zone, while an adjacent area gets a surplus of electrons to create an *n* (negative) zone. If two *n* zones, say, are separated by a *p* zone, they act as a transistor, which is an electronic switch: a small voltage in the *p* zone controls the fluctuations in a current flowing between the *n* zones. In this manner, thousands of transistors can be built into a single chip.

As in silk-screening, a chip's complex circuitry is created a layer at a time. It is a slow, painstaking and error-prone procedure.

First, racks of wafers are placed in long cylindrical ovens filled with extremely hot (about 2,000° F.) oxygen-containing gas or steam. In effect, the wafers are rusted—covered by a thin, electrically insulating layer of silicon dioxide that prevents short-circuiting. Then the wafers are coated with still another substance: the resist, a photographic-type emulsion sensitive only to ultraviolet (UV) light. (To prevent accidental exposure, clean rooms are generally bathed in UV-less yellow light.) Next, a tiny mask, scaled down photographically from a large drawing and imprinted with hundreds of identical patterns of one layer of the chip's circuitry, is placed over the wafer. Exposed to UV, the resist's shielded areas remain soft and are readily washed away in an acid bath. On the other hand, the unshielded areas harden, forming an outline of the circuit.

Back in the ovens, the wafers are baked again in an atmosphere of gases loaded with "dopants." Like oil stains in a concrete driveway, these impurities soak into the underlying silicon. Since chips usually contain as many as ten layers, all these steps—"rusting," photomasking, etching, baking, etc.——must be repeated for each layer. Then the entire wafer is coated with an aluminum conductor, which also must be masked, etched and bathed in acid. Finally, an eagle-eyed computerized probe scans the wafer for defective circuitry and marks the bad chips in red. The wafer is then separated by a diamond cutter, the bad chips are discarded and the good ones externally wired, sealed in plastic or metal and shipped off to the user.

Source: "The Art of Chip Making," *Time,* p. 56, February 20, 1978. Reprinted by permission from *Time,* The Weekly Newsmagazine; Copyright Time Inc. 1978.

THE CONTROL UNIT

The control unit of the processor *selects, interprets,* and *executes* the program instructions. The arithmetic-logic unit responds to commands coming from the control unit. There are at least two parts to any instruction: the *operation,* or *command,* that is to be followed (for example, ADD, SUB, MUL, and GO TO) and the *address,* which locates the data or instructions to be manipulated. The basic components contained in the PAC control unit are the *instruction register, sequence register, address register,* and *decoder.*

Let us trace an instruction through the PAC control unit to see how it is handled. We shall again use Aardvark's pay data along with the payroll program shown in Figure 5-17. Let us assume that the instruction in address 07 has just been executed and that 40 hours is the content of the accumulator. The following steps are performed in the next *operating cycle* (the circled numbers in Figure 5-19 correspond to these steps):

1   The instruction in address 08 (MUL 02) is *selected* by the *sequence register* and read into the *instruction register* in the control unit. (The sequence register does not store the instruction. We shall have more to say about the sequence register in step 5 below.)

2   The operation part (MUL) and the address part (02) of the instruction are *separated.* The operation is sent to the decoder, where it is *interpreted.* The computer is built to respond to a limited number of commands, and it now knows that it is to multiply.

3   The address part of the instruction is sent to the *address register.*

4   The signal to move the contents of address 02 into the arithmetic-logic unit is sent; the command to multiply goes to the arithmetic-logic unit where the instruction is *executed.*

5   As the multiplication is being executed, the sequence register in the control unit is increased by one to indicate the location of the next instruction address. When the program was started, the sequence register was set to the address of the first instruction. By the time the first program instruction was finished, the contents of the sequence register had automatically been advanced to the next instruction address number. In other words, the first address in the payroll program was 06 (read data in), and the sequence register was set to 06. As that instruction was being executed, the sequence register automatically moved to 07 and then to 08, and now it is again automatically moved to 09. It keeps this up until instructed to do otherwise. You will recall that when the sequence register gets to address 17, it encounters an instruction that reads GO TO 06. This command alters the normal stepping of the sequence register and resets it at address 06.

6   The instruction at address 09 moves into the instruction register, and the above steps are repeated.

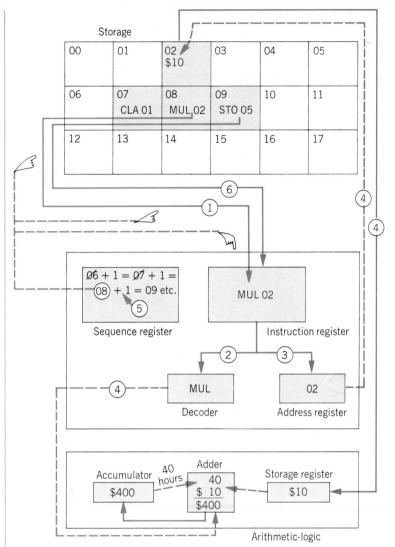

Storage

00	01	02 $10	03	04	05
06	07 CLA 01	08 MUL 02	09 STO 05	10	11
12	13	14	15	16	17

Ø6 + 1 = Ø7 + 1 =
(08) + 1 = 09 etc.
⑤

Sequence register

MUL 02

Instruction register

MUL

Decoder

02

Address register

Adder

Accumulator 40 hours 40
$400 $ 10
$400

Storage register
$10

Arithmetic-logic

FIGURE 5-19
Operation of the control unit.

We may identify separate processor phases, or cycles, in the above procedure. Step 4 is the *execution cycle.* The other steps comprise the *instruction cycle.* Thus, there are two phases in the performance of each instruction. Computers are generally *synchronous;* i.e., the various operations are synchronized by an electronic clock, which emits millions of regularly spaced electronic pulses each second. Commands are interpreted and executed at proper intervals, and the intervals are timed by a specified number of these pulses.

The following points have been emphasized in this chapter:

1 A primary storage section is found in every computer. In addition, many CPUs also have specialized built-in storage elements that are used for specific processing and control functions.

2 Locations in the primary storage area of the CPU may contain either data or instructions. For each program, data are typically stored in three conceptual areas—The input storage area, the working storage area, and the output storage area. Instructions are held in a program storage area. These areas vary in size and location depending upon the particular job being processed.

3 Locations in storage are identified by address numbers. Programmers (or software prepared by programmers) keep track of address contents because when instructions are written to manipulate these contents, the instructions must indicate in some way the address locations. Programmers have a fixed number of instruction commands at their disposal. These commands are built into the particular machine being used. When a program is run, the machine is set at the first instruction and then follows sequentially the series of directions until told to do otherwise.

4 Each address may contain either a single character or a word consisting of a fixed number of characters. Most modern computers may be operated as either variable-length or fixed-word length machines. (However, the fixed word in many minicomputers and microcomputers may only be two characters in length.)

5 Binary numbers are used to simplify computer design and take advantage of the two states that electronic components may be in. Computers typically use a binary-related code to designate numbers, letters, and special characters. Six- and eight-bit codes are used to represent alphanumeric data.

6 For 20 years, the dominant primary storage medium was magnetic cores. In recent years, however, semiconductor storage chips have found their way into the newer models of most manufacturers because of economic and performance factors.

7 The arithmetic-logic unit does the actual processing under program control. During the execution cycle, data stored in primary storage or in registers are moved to the arithmetic-logic unit. There they are manipulated by adder circuits to yield a result that may be stored in a register (e.g., the accumulator) or transferred to some other storage location.

8 The control unit selects, interprets, and sees to the execution of instructions in their proper sequence. Several basic registers are required to perform the control function.

After reading Chapter 5, you should be able to define and use the following terms:

read-only memory (ROM)	ASCII
address	core plane
flowchart	semiconductor storage chips
computer word	register
character-addressable storage	accumulator
word-addressable storage	adder
byte-addressable storage	instruction register
positional numbering system	sequence register
additive numbering system	address register
binary numbering system	decoder
six-bit alphanumeric code	execution cycle
EBCDIC	instruction cycle

▶ REVIEW AND DISCUSSION QUESTIONS

1 How may small specialized storage elements found in many CPUs be used?

2 (a) Identify and discuss the four conceptual areas in the primary storage section of a CPU. (b) What is the typical data-flow pattern in primary storage?

3 Explain the distinction between the address number and the contents of the address.

4 Distinguish between word-addressable and character-addressable computers.

5 (a) What is the difference between an additive and a positional numbering system? (b) Give examples of both types of numbering system.

6 "The highest numerical symbol will always have a value of one less than the base." Explain and give examples.

7 "In any positional numbering system, the value of each position represents a specific power of the base." Explain and give examples.

8 Why have computers been designed to use the binary numbering system?

9 Why has the 6-bit Standard BCD code been extended to 8 bits?

10 Define and explain the function of (a) the instruction register, (b) the sequence register, (c) the address register, (d) the decoder, (e) the accumulator, and (f) the adder.

11 (a) What is a flowchart? (b) What is a loop?

12 Many personal microcomputers have only byte-addressable capabilities, and most current minicomputers are designed with a single fixed word-length storage format of 2 bytes. What might be the advantages and disadvantages of these design approaches? (*Hint:* Consider the compromise between economy on the one hand and performance on the other.)

Chapter 6
MICROS, MINIS, MAINFRAMES, AND MONSTERS

The purpose of the last chapter was to give you a general introduction to central processor concepts. The purpose of this chapter is to give you more specific information about actual computer systems. Although it is now difficult to classify available computers on the basis of size and computing capabilities, they are arbitrarily grouped in this chapter into micro, mini, mainframe, and monster (supercomputer) categories.

There is a section in the chapter for each of the above classifications. The first section deals with microcomputer systems. In this section, you will learn what a microcomputer is and why micros were developed. Examples of some representative micro systems in current use are presented, along with some of the hardware/software characteristics of these systems. Finally, some uses and applications of micros are discussed.

The same approach is followed in the next three sections of the chapter, which deal with mini, mainframe, and supersized computers.

Thus, after studying this chapter, you should be able to:

- Explain what micros are and why they were developed, give some examples of representative micros, discuss a few of their hardware/software characteristics, and list some of the ways they may be used.

- Give a general definition of a minicomputer, tell why minis were developed, recall some examples of representative minis, outline a few of their hardware/software characteristics, and discuss some of the ways they may be used.

- Differentiate between a mainframe and a smaller computer, give examples of typical mainframe families, and point out some of the characteristics and uses of mainframe models.

- Outline some of the characteristics of supercomputers that make them different from other machines, and discuss the types of applications for which they are designed.

- Understand and use the key terms listed at the end of the chapter.

In the last chapter, a fictitious Peculiar Automatic Computer (PAC) was created to give you a general introduction to the central processing unit. The characteristics attributed to the PAC are found in many modern CPUs. But no matter how accurately a fictitious computer describes reality, it is still a "make believe" machine. Thus, in this final chapter on computing hardware, you will be introduced to some of the characteristics of representative computer systems ranging in size from the smallest to the largest. Before reading about these representative systems, however, you should be aware of an unavoidable problem.

THE CUSSEDNESS OF CLASSIFICATION

An unavoidable (and vexing) problem in discussing existing computer systems is how to *classify* the broad range of available machine sizes and capabilities. Central-site computers and "smaller" distributed and stand-alone systems can now be assembled with a bewildering variety of peripheral I/O devices and "add-on" CPU components. The result is that there is considerable overlap in system size, cost, and performance. Furthermore, as you have seen, computer technology is advancing so rapidly that a cabinet that housed a minicomputer a few years ago is now adequate to package a system that has the performance capability of an earlier giant. The net effect of this technological development is that if you were to conduct a survey now among a dozen computer experts, and if you asked each of them to differentiate, for example, between minicomputers and mainframe family models, you would probably get a dozen very different responses.

In the pages that follow, computers will be classified as *micros, minis, mainframe family models,* and *monsters* (or *supercomputers*). But you should know that the classifications used here (and anywhere else) are *arbitrary.* As Figure 6-1 indicates, the cost and performance capability of machines in different classifications are likely to overlap—e.g., a powerful computer sold as a mini by its maker may have more processing capability (and cost more) than a machine sold as a small mainframe model.

MICROCOMPUTER SYSTEMS

What is a Microcomputer?

It wasn't the dinosaurs who survived; it was the lizards.
—Grace M. Hopper

For our purposes, a *microcomputer* is the smallest category of general-purpose symbol manipulator that can execute program instructions to accomplish a wide variety of tasks. A microcomputer system has all the functional elements found in any larger installation. That is, it is organized to perform the input, storage, arithmetic-logic, control, and output functions. Although some tiny complete microcomputer CPUs are packaged on a *single* silicon chip (Figure 6-2), most micro CPUs are larger and employ *several* chips (Figures 6-2 and 6-4). A *microprocessor chip* (Figure 6-5), for example, is used to perform the arithmetic-logic and control functions. Several *random-access memory* (RAM) *chips* are available for operator use as needed and are employed to handle the primary storage function. Additional *read-only memory* (ROM) *chips* may be used to permanently store preprogrammed data or instructions.

Most microcomputers are stand-alone, somewhat portable, single-user-oriented machines. In addition to the CPU, the typical micro has an operator keyboard for input and a visual display and/or serial printer for output. Magnetic tape cassettes and mini-floppy disks are often used for secondary storage.

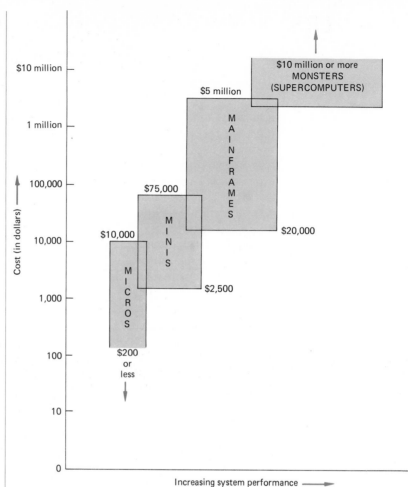

FIGURE 6-1
Computer systems may be classified into micro, mini, mainframe, and monster categories depending on size, cost, and system performance. Any such classification is arbitrary. Since categories overlap, the most powerful systems in one category may exceed the capabilities (and cost) of the least powerful systems in another.

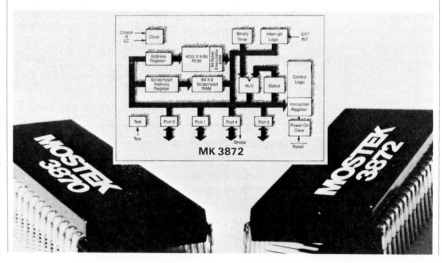

FIGURE 6-2
Two single-chip microcomputer CPUs in their packaged form. The diagram shows the organization of one of these chips. In addition to the arithmetic-logic unit (ALU) and control unit, there are RAM and ROM storage elements. (*Mostek Corp.*)

FIGURE 6-3
Herman Hollerith. (*IBM Corp.*)

INVENTOR INSPIRED BY RAILROAD CONDUCTOR

Herman Hollerith won the competition held by the Census Office for the best system to tabulate the 1890 census. Hollerith's "electric tabulating system" performed in less than half the time required by the systems submitted by his competitors.

Hollerith went to work for the Census Office after graduating from the Columbia University School of Mines and later left the Census Office to work as an engineer. Hollerith formed the Tabulating Machine Company in 1896. This company and three others were later joined to form IBM.

Hollerith said the idea of the electric tabulating machine was formed when he was watching a railroad conductor use a ticket punch.

FIGURE 6-4
Circuitry of a single-chip microcomputer. The actual size of this chip is only about ¼ inch square. Both RAM and ROM storage elements are included along with the arithmetic-logic and control units. (*Intel Corp.*)

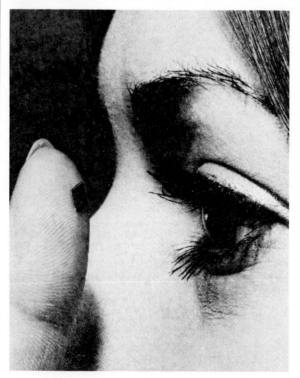

FIGURE 6-5
A tiny microprocessor chip like the one on this woman's finger performs the arithmetic-logic and control functions in a microprocessor. (*NCR Corp.*)

Why Were Micros Developed?

In the early 1970s, engineers at the Intel Corporation in California designed the first microcomputer for a Japanese maker of desk calculators. At the time, calculators were being built from specialized circuit chips that could perform only a single function. Since it was expensive to develop these special-purpose chips and correct all the potential design errors, the motivating idea in developing this first micro chip was to create a simpler general-purpose product that could then be programmed to perform specialized calculator functions. This micro—the Intel 4004—was very limited in the number of instructions it could execute, and it could manipulate only 4 bit "words" of information at one time.

It was not long, however, before the engineers at Intel and other companies produced more powerful microprocessors that could operate on 8 bits. This development, in turn, led to the introduction in 1974 of personal-sized micro systems for the hobbyist market. The first such personal computer was the ALTAIR 8800, which used an 8-bit Intel microprocessor and was originally offered in kit form at a price under $400. The lead article in the January 1975 issue of *Popular Electronics* featured this machine; the article introduced many people to the beginning of the micro explosion. Later in 1975, the first retail store devoted exclusively to selling and servicing personal microcomputers was opened in Santa Monica, California. There are now hundreds of these stores from coast to coast. Hundreds of thousands of micro systems produced by dozens of manufacturers have been sold in the last two years, and scores of computer clubs have sprung up since 1975.[1]

Examples of Representative Micros

Like their larger counterparts, microcomputers are used in *organizations* for data processing and decision-making purposes. Unlike the larger machines found in organizations, however, micro systems are also used by hundreds of thousands of *individuals* for entertainment and other personal applications.

Included among the representative micro systems frequently found in organizations are the Wang PCS-IIA (Figure 6-6), the Data General microNOVA series (Figures 6-7 and 6-8), and the Radio Shack TRS-80, Model II (Figure 6-9).[2] Among the representative micro systems most often selected by individuals for entertainment and personal use are Radio Shack's TRS-80, Model I (see Figure 1-15, page 34),[3] Apple Com-

[1] The Southern California Computer Club alone has a membership of over 20,000.

[2] A few of the other microcomputers that are often found in organizations are IMSAI's 8080, Vector Graphic's MZ, Cromemco's Z-2D, Processor Technology's Sol, and North Star's Horizon.

[3] Over 100,000 of these TRS-80 personal computers were sold in 1978 (the first year they were offered). This sales figure probably gave Radio Shack about 50% of the entire market for personal computers at that time. Since then, however, formidable competitors have entered the market to challenge Radio Shack and other vendors.

FIGURE 6-6
The Wang PCS-IIA desk-top microcomputer system. The CPU, input keyboard, output visual display, and two secondary storage mini-floppy disk units are housed in the cabinet to the left of the operator. An output printer is also shown. The online storage capacity of the two disks is about 180,000 characters. Primary storage (RAM) in the CPU can vary from 8 thousand to 64 thousand characters; additional ROM storage in the CPU is used to interpret instructions written in a programming language. (*Wang Laboratories, Inc.*)

The micro system CPU

FIGURE 6-7
A Data General microNOVA system. Connected to the CPU shown in this picture are keyboards, visual displays, a magnetic disk unit, and a printer. (*Data General Corp.*)

FIGURE 6-8
Additional details on a
microNOVA CPU. The micro-
processor chip shown in the
foreground contains the
arithmetic-logic and control
functions. This chip is
mounted on the board shown
in the middle of the photo.
The board is then housed in
the background cabinet. (*Data
General Corp.*)

FIGURE 6-9
Radio Shack's TRS-80, Model
II. The CPU is housed with
the keyboard in the basic
system shown on the left
side of the desk. The CPU
may have either 32 thousand
or 64 thousand characters of
RAM. Also included in the
basic system is the visual
display and a built-in 8-inch
floppy disk drive that provides a half million characters
of online secondary storage.
An optional printer and two
optional disk drives capable
of storing an additional
1-million characters are also
shown in the photo. The
price of this configuration is
about $8,000. (*Radio Shack
Div., Tandy Corp.*)

puter's Apple II, Commodore's PET, Texas Instruments' 99/4, Exidy's Sorcerer, Ohio Scientific's C4P, and Atari's 800. Minimum configurations of these systems range in price from about $500 to $1,200.

Some Characteristics of Typical Micros

Virtually all microcomputer CPUs use the byte-addressable storage approach discussed in the last chapter. At this writing, most micro systems are designed around a few popular 8-bit microprocessor chips that can manipulate only a single 8-bit byte at a time.[4] Larger computers can often retrieve, manipulate, and store 2, 4, or even 8 bytes as a single unit, and so it is easy to understand why micros are relatively slow by comparison. However, recently developed microprocessor chips with the flexibility to simultaneously move and manipulate two 8-bit bytes have improved the performance capabilities of newer microcomputers.[5]

Primary storage in a personal computer is usually at least 4,096 bytes (or *4K,* where K equals 2^{10}, or 1,024 bytes). Most micros have from 8K to 64K of RAM capacity. Semiconductor storage is used, and additional RAM chips may usually be added to a basic CPU. As noted earlier, system processing and control programs are often permanently stored in the CPU in ROM chips. A wide range of peripheral and "add-on" devices for microcomputers are available from many small vendors. A system *interface bus* is a device that serves as the electrical interconnection between the CPU and the various peripherals. Although many personal computer manufacturers have adopted the S-100 interface bus originally used in the ALTAIR computer as a standard, assembling a micro system from components made by different vendors can still be a problem. The ASCII data representation code discussed in the last chapter is used in most microcomputers.

Applications programs for micros are usually written in a high-level programming language. The most popular microcomputer language is BASIC (the subject of Chapter 8). Some of the other high-level languages used are Pascal, FORTRAN, and COBOL.[6] Some sophisticated operating-system programs of the type discussed in Chapter 2 are available for use in micro systems that employ floppy disks for secondary storage. Of course, users of micros also have access to packaged programs prepared by the hundreds of vendors who have entered this software market in recent years. These programs are often packaged in machine-readable form on tape cassettes, floppy disks, and plug-in ROM modules. Scores of entertainment and educational programs, for example, are available from mail-order vendors and retail computer stores.

---

[4] Among the most popular 8-bit chips are Intel's 8080 (used in IMSAI and ALTAIR computers), Zilog Corporations Z80 (used in Radio Shack, Exidy, North Star, Cromemco, and Vector Graphic computers), and MOS Technology's 6502 (used in Apple, Commodore, Atari, and Ohio Scientific computers).

[5] Some of these 16-bit chips are Intel's 8086, Zilog's Z8000, Texas Instruments' 9900, Data General's mN602, and Motorola's MC68000.

[6] We will discuss these languages briefly in the next chapter.

Micro Uses and Applications

Since symbols are manipulated in our society in countless ways, there is virtually no limit to the number of possible applications for an inexpensive general-purpose symbol manipulator.

In your home, for example, a personal microcomputer could be used to:

- Entertain you with hundreds of challenging games.
- Balance your budget and checkbook.
- Monitor your home's energy usage.
- Help you learn a new subject, e.g., a foreign language or auto repair techniques.
- Help you compose music, produce reports free of typing errors, etc.
- Analyze your investments and prepare your tax returns.
- Compute your installment payments.
- Control your household appliances and security devices.
- File for easy retrieval and reference such information as recipes, names and addresses, telephone numbers, and dates of birthdays and anniversaries.
- Control a device to allow severely handicapped persons who have no upper-limb response to feed themselves. (Future improvements in this and other areas will give the handicapped a new degree of independence.)

As you travel to school or work, the chances are good that the traffic lights are controlled by micros. There is also a good chance that if you are riding in a newer automobile, an on-board microcomputer is being used to continuously monitor such variables as air and engine temperature, barometric pressure, and throttle and crankshaft position in order to control the engine's fuel mixture, ignition timing, and exhaust emissions (Figure 6-10). Of course, there is no reason to limit the on-board micro to engine control. (Compared to the speed of a micro, the firing of a spark plug in an engine running at top speed is almost a weekly occurrence.) The micro can also be used to control instruments (digital read-out devices indicating speed, distance traveled, miles to destination, fuel consumption, time of day, etc.), provide entertainment, and perform safety and engine diagnostic functions. Micro systems are used *in organizations* to:

- Compute payrolls; maintain student, patient, customer, or client records; pay debts and collect receipts; and process the other general accounting tasks that may be required.
- Control machine tools and other production equipment in an industrial environment. For example, a micro is used to control the angles produced by a metal-bending machine to very close tolerances.

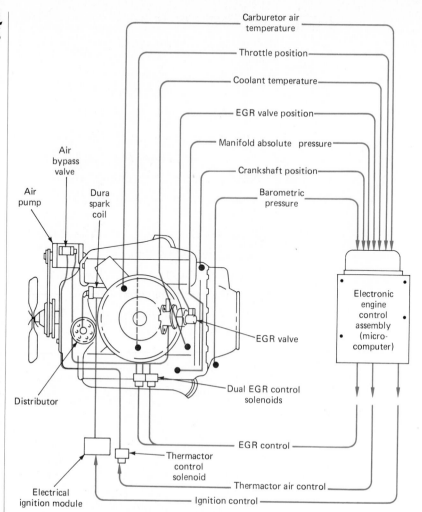

FIGURE 6-10
Ford Motor Company's electronic engine control system. The microcomputer receives input from several sensors and produces output signals to control ignition, exhaust gas emissions (EGR control), and secondary air control. This input/process/output cycle is repeated 30 times a second (the engine is fine-tuned 30 times every second).

- Control inventory levels of thousands of different items.
- Produce personalized letters and mailing labels to reach a specific group of people.
- Control water flow and power generation. For example, a micro is used at the Jones Bluff hydroelectric project on the Alabama River by the Army Corps of Engineers to (1) place generators on or off the line by activating large circuit breakers, (2) lower and raise voltage output, and (3) control motors that open or close the dam gates to regulate water flow.
- Provide quick answers to the "what if" questions asked by clients. Insurance agents, for example, can give presentations to prospects by using a portable micro. Data supplied by the prospect can be entered through the keyboard, and alternative insurance programs can then be displayed.

"The Computer in the Home"

Thousands of minicomputers are entering American homes each year. Inevitably, the presence of these machines will have an effect on the life of the family as did the advent of the automobile and television. Harold Buchbinder, editor and publisher of *Personal Computing* predicts a time when business people will handle their affairs from home computers linked to their offices; when some part of family education will be pursued at home with aid of a computer; when marketing and bill paying will be done from the den or the kitchen. Wayne Green, editor and publisher of *Kilobaud*, a magazine for computer hobbyists, says, "I see tremendous possibilities for the home computer; a change in the structure of the country; an impact equal to that of the automobile."

Here are just a few ways home computers are being used already. And new applications are being developed almost daily.

Data Storage. Computers are uniquely equipped to store and sort information. Names and addresses, recipes, tax information, record and book titles are just a few things a typical family might want to have available in the home computer. Computers can also be programmed to sort these items into categories—books on sports, Christmas card lists, vegetable recipes, etc.

Education. Programs that teach foreign languages, mathematics, and auto repair are readily available in computer stores. New programs are being developed in almost every area where people have a "need to know."

Long Distance Communication. It is likely that coming years will see a great deal of our mail being sent via the computer and telephone lines.

Entertainment. Computer games still make up a large percentage of programs for home computers. There are computerized versions of traditional games like checkers and chess and newcomers like "Star Trek."

Source of data: "Computers: The 'Magic Machines' Enter Home," New York *Daily News*, p. 18, February 11, 1979.

- Make possible the rapid expansion in the use of computer-assisted instruction techniques in educational institutions of all sizes.
- Monitor air temperature, humidity, wetness of crop leaves, and other variables in order to alert crop growers to the need to apply fungicides. Apple growers, for example, can prevent the outbreak of apple scab fungus with this information.
- Control desk-top graphical display units that are used (to cite just a few examples) by (1) engineers for stress analysis and interactive design, (2) clinical laboratory technicians to plot quality-control data, and (3) anthropologists to plot the length of bones of prehistoric humanoids.

FIGURE 6-11
Hard-disk secondary storage unit for a minicomputer system. (*Data General Corp.*)

This listing of micro applications could go on and on, but you get the idea: The actual and potential uses of micros in the home and in organizations can be as numerous and varied as human ingenuity and imagination will permit.

MINICOMPUTER SYSTEMS

What is a Minicomputer?

In spite of the fact that it is almost impossible to define a minicomputer anymore, a definition is needed here. Therefore, for our purposes, a *minicomputer* is a small general-purpose machine ranging in price from about $2,500 to $75,000. In physical size, it can vary from a small desk-top model to a unit about the size of a four-drawer file cabinet. Although there is a considerable overlap between the most powerful micro systems and the low-end minicomputers in terms of cost and processing capability, the typical mini system will surpass a micro in its storage capacity, speed of arithmetic operations, and ability to support a variety of faster-operating peripheral devices. For example, the larger hard-disk units used for online secondary storage in some mini systems (Figure 6-11) have a much greater capacity and are faster operating than the floppy devices used in micro systems. Unlike a micro system that usually has a single-user orientation, mini systems can be designed to simultaneously handle the processing needs of multiple users. Thus, minis are usually found in organizational settings; they represent only a tiny fraction of the machines selected by individuals for personal computing needs.

Why Were Minis Developed?

In the early 1960s, the trend among established computer manufacturers was to build larger and faster systems that could provide at a central location all the processing power needed by an entire organization. Although this approach served the needs of some organizations in an efficient manner, other organizations were either unable to afford the larger systems or had quite specific and specialized applications that could not be processed effectively by a large centralized machine.

Recognizing that a need existed for low-cost mini(mal) computers that could fill the gaps left by the bigger, faster centralized approach, several innovators formed new firms in the 1960s to produce these minimal machines. The first processors designated as minicomputers were developed and built by Digital Equipment Corporation (DEC). The early minis, of course, were used primarily for the processing of a single specialized application—e.g., to monitor instruments and test equipment in a laboratory or to control a machine-tool or a flow process in a factory—or they were used to process a number of general applications in a small organization.

Since the 1960s, however, minis have improved to such an extent that many are much faster and more powerful than the earlier large central systems. (To a certain extent, the development of micros in the early 1970s is a case of history repeating itself. The first micros were also used for single specialized applications or for a few small general applications.)

Examples of Representative Minis

A mini system priced at under $10,000 should obviously be smaller than one priced at $75,000 on our arbitrary scale. Included among the representative *smaller minis* are DEC's DATASYSTEM 310 and Wang Laboratories' 2200 (Figures 6-12 and 6-13).

FIGURE 6-12
This DEC system has a primary storage capacity of 16K to 64K bytes. The four floppy-disk units to the left of the operator store 1.2 million characters. A choice of optional printers is available with speeds ranging up to 300 lines per minute. The cost of the basic system offered in this line is less than $12,000. (*Digital Equipment Corp.*)

Typical of *medium-scale minis* are the lower-priced models in Honeywell's Level 6 family (Figure 6-14), DEC's mid-range PDP-11 models (Figure 6-15), Data General Corporation's mid-range NOVA Models, and Wang's WCS/60 system (Figure 6-16).

Finally, some *larger minis* are found in Hewlett-Packard's 3000 series family of computers (Figure 6-17), IBM's 8100 series (Figure 6-18), Wang's VS systems (Figure 6-19), and DEC's larger PDP-11 models, e.g., the PDP-11/60 and the PDP-11/70.

FIGURE 6-13
A model in the Wang 2200 line. The price of the CPU starts at under $10,000, and systems with up to nine peripherals may be built. Multiple keyboard/CRT work stations can be supported. The hard-disk unit at the right of the desk has a storage capacity of 10 million characters. (*Wang Laboratories, Inc.*)

FIGURE 6-14
A Honeywell Level 6 mini system. There are six models in the Level 6 line. Included among the peripherals that may be added to a Level 6 CPU (beginning in the foreground of the photo) is a printer, keyboard/display station, punched card reader, standard size magnetic tape drive, and hard-disk storage unit. (*Honeywell, Inc.*)

FIGURE 6-15
A DEC DATASYSTEM model incorporating a PDP-11/40 midrange minicomputer. Two hard-disk storage units are shown. This system has the capability to handle four time-sharing users, and it can communicate with other computers at distant locations. (*Digital Equipment Corp.*)

FIGURE 6-16
Up to 16 simultaneous users may share the time of the Wang WCS/60 system. Primary storage can range from 64K to 256K bytes, and online disk storage can vary from 10 to 150 million bytes. A printer operating at a speed of 600 lines per minute may be used. The price of a typical system is under $50,000. (*Wang Laboratories, Inc.*)

FIGURE 6-17
One of a series of Hewlett-Packard minicomputer systems that carries the 3000 designation. This model has a primary storage capacity of at least 128K bytes and online disk storage that can go as high as 400 million bytes. Up to 16 users may share the time of the system. Some larger 3000 series models exceed our arbitrary $75,000 upper price limit. *(Hewlett-Packard.)*

FIGURE 6-18
The smallest of the IBM 8100 system processors with 512K bytes of primary storage, 1 million characters of floppy-disk storage, and 64 million characters of hard-disk storage is priced at about $30,000. Hundreds of millions of additional characters can be stored in peripheral disk units. (If many peripherals are added, however, the 8100 system's price can exceed $75,000.) Shown counterclockwise from the lower right in the photo are a display terminal, two disk storage units, the CPU, two magnetic tape units, and a line printer. *(IBM Corp.)*

FIGURE 6-19
The Wang VS system can support up to 32 work stations. Models with up to 512K bytes of primary storage and over 1 billion bytes of disk storage are available. Although the smallest VS systems start at under $50,000, the largest configurations exceed $75,000. (*Wang Laboratories, Inc.*)

Some Characteristics of Typical Minis

As you can see from Figures 6-12 through 6-19, primary and online secondary storage capacities increase as mini systems get larger. Multiple users can be served simultaneously in all but the smallest systems, and organizations can elect to use faster and more powerful peripheral devices.

Most of the popular lines of minis in use today employ the byte-addressable storage approach; a majority of the minis currently in service also are 16-bit machines. Thus, most minis are able to simultaneously move and manipulate data words consisting of two 8-bit bytes. This ability, of course, gives minis an edge in speed over 8-bit micros in applications that require lots of calculations. As we have seen, however, the newer microprocessor chips are 16-bit devices, and so this advantage of current minis is likely to diminish. (Of course, some newer minis are 32-bit machines and are able to operate on 4 bytes at a time. The mini makers are not standing still!) Some of the more advanced minis also achieve faster processing speeds by employing a special *high-speed buffer, or cache,* storage section in the CPU to temporarily store very active data and instructions during processing. Since the cache storage unit is faster than the primary storage section, the processing speed is increased.

Because minis have been around longer than micros, there are larger libraries of prepared software of interest to organizations from mini manufacturers. More high-level programming languages are likely to be available for minis than for micros, and mini operating-system and translation programs are likely to be more sophisticated.

Many Uses for Minis

Sales of minicomputers are currently growing at an annual rate of 35 percent. It is obvious, then, that organizations have found uses for them. We have already seen that minis are being used in specialized ways to control laboratory instruments and machine tools. Dedicated minicomputers are also used to control the data input received from multiple key-to-disk encoding stations (see Figure 4-6, page 121). And in Figures 6-14 to 6-19, we saw minis being used in organizations for general data processing purposes.

Although pages could be filled with examples of minicomputer uses, perhaps one other very important type of application will be enough. You read in Chapter 2 that in recent years many organizations have decided to establish *distributed data processing* (DDP) *networks*. Typically, in a DDP network, a larger central *host computer* may communicate with, and exercise some control over *satellite, or node, processors*. A satellite may, in turn, act as a host to subordinate processors and/or terminals. The satellite processors (and their subordinates) are likely to be minicomputers that handle much of the data processing done locally in offices and on factory floors. In addition to the dozens of minis that are used in some large DDP networks to process data, additional minis are used to control the flow of communications between network stations.

MAINFRAME FAMILY MODELS

What is a Mainframe Computer?

In the 1960s, when the emphasis was on building larger and faster central computers to handle all the processing needs of an organization, the word mainframe was used to mean the same thing as "central processor" or "CPU." Although the word may still be used synonymously with central processor, it took on an additional context in the 1970s in the literature of computers and data processing. By way of differentiation, a computer that is generally *more powerful* than a typical micro or mini is now often called a *mainframe*. As you saw in Figure 6-1, such machines (which are sometimes referred to as *midicomputers*) vary widely in cost and performance capability. As we have already seen, there is considerable overlap possible in the cost and performance of large minis and small mainframes. The historical development of computers discussed in Chapter 1 dealt primarily with mainframes.

Examples of Representative Mainframe Models

A whole series of mainframe models ranging in size from small to very large are typically lumped together under a *family designation* by mainframe manufacturers. It is usually possible to run programs prepared for one machine on other models in the same family with little or no modification. This *compatibility* between family models makes it easy for users to move up to larger systems in the same family[7] if they outgrow their smaller machines. Unlike micros and minis, which are usually purchased, mainframes are often only rented or leased.

A representative mainframe family is the IBM System/370. There are about a dozen different models in this series. (Well over half of all the mainframes installed in the 1970s were System/370 machines.) The 370 line ranges in size from the *smallest* Model 115 (Figure 6-20), to *medium-sized* Models 138, 148 (Figure 6-21), and 158, to a *large* Model 168 (Figure 6-22, to a *very large* Model 3033 (Figure 6-23). Several small and medium-sized models in a newer IBM 4300 Series have also been introduced. For example, the small 4331 (Figure 6-24) is a more powerful and lower-priced processor than the 370/115 model, and the 4341 (Figure 1-19*b*, page 38) has similar advantages over medium-sized 370 computers.

---

[7] It is usually not as easy to convert programs to a larger system in a different product line, a fact that helps maintain the stability of a mainframe manufacturer's customer base.

FIGURE 6-20
The smallest computer in the System/370 line is the Model 115. Primary storage capacity is 353K bytes. As you can see, a large number of peripherals can be attached to this processor. For example, up to eight of the disk drives shown behind the visual display unit can be used to provide over 500 million characters of online storage. The time required by the processor to execute a basic operation (the *cycle time*) is 480 nanoseconds. Prices begin at about $130,000. (*IBM Corp.*)

FIGURE 6-21
A medium-sized mainframe, the 370/148 has a primary storage of 2 million characters. Hundreds of millions of characters of disk storage are possible, and a high-speed line printer is used for output. The cycle time is 180 to 270 nanoseconds depending on the operation. The price of a 148 is about $500,000. (*IBM Corp.*)

FIGURE 6-22
This photo of a large 370/168 shows only the multiple processing units that make up the central processing function and the operator console. Over 8 million characters of primary storage are possible, and cycle time is 80 nanoseconds. Price of a basic 168 is over $4 million. (*IBM Corp.*)

FIGURE 6-23
The Model 3033 is the most powerful computer in the 370 family. It may also have multiple processors. Twelve million characters of primary storage are available, the cycle time is 57 nanoseconds, and the price is about $5 million. (*IBM Corp.*)

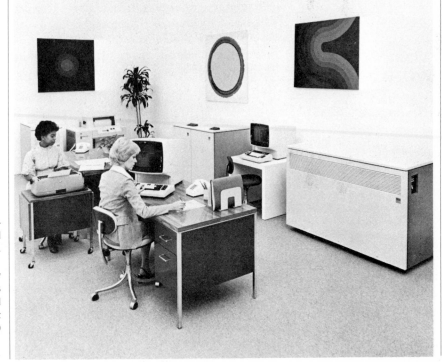

FIGURE 6-24
This IBM 4331 is a small mainframe in the 4300 series. Although it has up to 1 million bytes of primary storage and is several times faster than the 370/Model 115, it sells for about $60,000 less ($70,000 versus $130,000). (*IBM Corp.*)

Another representative mainframe family with about a dozen models is NCR Corporation's 8000 Series, which has machines ranging in size from the *small* 8100 and 8200 models, to the *medium-sized* 8300 and 8400 mainframes (Figure 6-25), to the *large* 8500 and 8600 processors (Figure 6-26). Similar mainframe families are produced by UNIVAC Division of Sperry Rand Corporation (the 1100 Series and the 90 Series), Burroughs Corporation (the 700, 800, and 900 Series), Honeywell, Inc. (the Series 60 computers), and Control Data Corporation (the CYBER Series). Additional firms such as Amdahl Corporation and National Semiconductor Company make mainframes that accept programs written for, and directly compatible with, IBM family models.

Some Characteristics of Typical Mainframes

What was true of the other computer categories we have considered in this chapter remains true of mainframes: primary and online secondary storage capacities increase as the systems get larger. Furthermore, in the larger mainframe models it is likely that one of the alternative computer-system architectures discussed in Chapter 3 (and shown in Figure 3-8, page 106) will be substituted for the *single-processor,* or *uniprocessor,* design approach used in smaller machines—e.g., *several* arithmetic-logic and control units may be used in a large *multiprocessor* mainframe to process several tasks at the same instant in time. Also, high-speed cache storage sections are routinely used in larger mainframes. The result of such features, of course, is that larger mainframes can process applications faster than smaller computers.

Another characteristic that improves their performance is the fact that most mainframes are basically 32-bit machines and can manipulate 4-byte words in a single machine cycle. However, most mainframes also

FIGURE 6-25
A medium-sized NCR 8400 series mainframe, this processor has a primary storage of up to 1 million bytes. Card readers, tape and disk drives, line printers, MICR reader/ sorter units, and retail store terminals are a few of the available peripherals. The cycle time is 112 nanoseconds, and prices start at about $100,000 for the CPU. (*NCR Corp.*)

FIGURE 6-26
This large NCR 8500 multiprocessor mainframe system
has two processing units
and a primary storage unit
that begins at 2 million characters and is expandable to a
maximum of 6 million bytes.
Cycle time is 56 nano-
seconds. (*NCR Corp.*)

have instruction sets that give them the flexibility to automatically operate on 2 bytes (halfword) or 8 bytes (doubleword).

Mainframe vendors have *much larger* libraries of applications programs that may be of interest to organizations than do other computer manufacturers. Furthermore, most applications packages designed by software development firms in the past have been written for mainframe computers. All popular (and some not-so-popular) high-level programming languages are available for mainframes, and their operating-system programs are at a very high level of sophistication. Mainframe vendors can also provide customers with a high level of applications design support and maintenance service.

Mainframe Uses and Applications

Until minis and micros came along, virtually everything that was done with computers was done on mainframes. There are tens of thousands of these computers in use today. Most medium-sized and larger organizations in the country with a history of computer usage have one or more of them. Banks, insurance companies, colleges and universities, hospitals, and local, state, and federal government agencies—these are just a few of the types of organizations that apply mainframes to meet their needs. Blue Cross Insurance Company of Virginia, for example, uses a large mainframe for interactive claims processing. Over 200 terminals in hospitals and doctors' offices are used to enter medical claims into the computer. The system prompts users on how to enter claims, notifies them immediately of any errors, and tells them when to expect payment.

In addition to providing, at a central site, all the processing power that may be needed by an entire organization, a mainframe is also used as the central host computer in a distributed data processing network. As we have seen, the mainframe communicates with, and exercises some control over, smaller satellite processors. In the applications chapters in Part 5, we will look at dozens of other mainframe uses.

MONSTER (SUPERCOMPUTER) SYSTEMS

Examples and Characteristics

As you have probably guessed, *supercomputers* are the largest, fastest, and most expensive computers in existence. Representative supercomputers are Control Data's STAR-100 and CYBER 203 and Cray Research's CRAY-1. Only a few of these monsters are produced each year because only a few organizations need (and can afford) their processing capabilities. The CRAY-1 is the current market leader with sales in 1979 of—are you ready for this?—six machines! (Of course, Cray Research received about $50 million for these half dozen systems.)

Supercomputers are usually designed to process complex scientific applications, and so the computational speed of the system is of paramount importance. To maximize the speed of computations, each address location in the CRAY-1 holds 64 bits of information. Thus, in a single machine cycle, two 64-bit data words could be added together. The CRAY-1 *cycle time*—the time required to execute a basic operation—is only 12.5 nanoseconds (billionths of a second). This is about 5 times faster than the largest mainframes discussed in the last section, and those machines were "only" 32-bit systems. The entire primary storage section of the CRAY-1 makes exclusive use of the types of expensive components that are generally reserved *only* for a high-speed cache section in less powerful machines. This usage, combined with the large number of circuit chips required to process the large (64-bit) fixed-length words, makes the CRAY-1 very expensive (prices start at $8 million).

Supercomputer Applications

What are some specific applications of supercomputers? Well, some of the CRAY-1s that have been delivered are making top-secret weapons-research calculations for the Federal government at the Los Alamos Scientific Laboratory in New Mexico and at the Lawrence Livermore Laboratory in California. Another CRAY-1 is providing complex calculations for petroleum and engineering companies at a Kansas City data processing service. Still other CRAY-1s are working on weather-forecasting problems at the European Center for Medium Range Weather Forecasts in England and at the National Center for Atmospheric Research in Boulder, Colorado.

In weather forecasting and in research involving the earth's atmosphere, weather data supplied by a worldwide network of space satellites, airplanes, and ground stations are fed into supercomputers. These data

"Seymour Cray Shows Computer World How To Build Big Machines"

It could be a stark, modern sculpture from the Museum of Modern Art: a six-foot-high, circular structure of ominous black panels and shining steel supports and surrounded by upholstered benches.

But behind those black panels is hidden the dense circuitry that makes up the world's most powerful and most expensive computer, the $8 million Cray 1, a machine that performs at the lightning speed of 100 million calculations a second. In the three years since it first went on the market, the Cray 1 super-computer has become the preeminent tool of scientific computing.

But this machine that exhibits such versatility is not the product of International Business Machines Corp. or of any other leading computer company. It is basically the product of the mind of one man: Seymour Cray, an athletic, 53-year-old scientist-turned-entrepreneur who compares the designing of a computer with composing music.

Mr. Cray is clearly an individualist. His home, his research laboratory and the company's assembly plant are in Chippewa Falls, Wis., an isolated town of 15,000 people, about 100 miles east of the company's Minneapolis headquarters. He shuns social functions, club memberships and business suits, turns up for work around midday in slacks and sports shirt and works until late into the night.

Exactly what a super-computer is and how it differs from the other machines that keep the wheels of business and government turning is not easily defined. One thing that separates the super-computer is its high speed and the amount of data that can be entered at one time. The Cray 1 has perhaps 20 to 100 times the capacity of general computers, and it is so fast that it takes only 50 billionths of a second for an element of data to enter or to leave its memory.

But a super-computer is not simply a very large computer because, unlike other machines whose purpose is to keep track of facts, its design is specifically aimed at problem-solving.

One way it can do this is through the simulation of an event, such as a spaceflight or a nuclear explosion. The computer is given a program based on "educated guesses" of what would be experienced in real life, and through this the machine can examine an experiment or a project in detail even before it is begun. As a result, prototypes can be made more advanced, a month of weather can be "seen" in the space of an hour and even biomedical experiments can be carried out with the computer simulating the human effects.

Thus the function of the super-computer is to solve new kinds of problems, particularly through the simulation of physical phenomena for weather forecasting, aircraft design, nuclear research and seismic analysis.

Beyond the Cray 2, a yet faster computer is taking shape in Mr. Cray's mind. "I do tend to look forward in my thinking and I don't like to rest on my laurels," he says. How fast could such a computer be? Perhaps, he says, a trillion calculations a second.

Source: Harlan S. Byrne, "Seymour Cray Shows Computer World How to Build Big Machines," *The Wall Street Journal,* p. 1, April 12, 1979. Reprinted by permission of *The Wall Street Journal,* © Dow Jones & Company, Inc. (1979). All Rights Reserved.

are analyzed by a series of computer programs to arrive at forecasts. Although current programs certainly provide forecasts that are generally more accurate than unaided human guesses, there is still room for considerable improvement. It is not that scientists don't understand the principles involved well enough to be able to prepare programs that *could* provide much better forecasts. Rather, the problem is that even with the power of a CRAY-1 (100 million calculations per second), the thousands of variables involved cannot now be evaluated to the satisfaction of scientists in the time available for forecasting. (Nobody cares if a computer produces a storm warning two days after the storm has hit.) In short, the current forecast programs being run on supercomputers are crude models of what meteorologists would use if much more powerful computers were available. There is thus an incentive for supercomputer builders to make ever-larger machines. (A CRAY-2 is due in the mid-1980s and is expected to be 5 times more powerful than the CRAY-1.)

LOOKING BACK

The following points have been emphasized in this chapter:

1   Technological changes are occurring so rapidly in the computer industry that it is now very difficult to classify the broad range of available machines on the basis of size and computing capabilities. Nevertheless, an attempt has been made in this chapter to arbitrarily classify computers as micros, minis, mainframes, and monsters (supercomputers).

2   Developed in the 1970s, microcomputers are the smallest general-purpose symbol manipulators that can be programmed to process a wide variety of applications. A micro is built around a single microprocessor chip (which is usually an 8-bit device), uses RAM and ROM storage chips in the CPU, and is a single-user-oriented machine. Unlike larger systems that are used almost exclusively by people in orga-

nizations, micros are used by hundreds of thousands of individuals for entertainment and other personal applications. Representative micro systems and their uses have been discussed in the chapter. Micros range in price from $200 (or less) to about $10,000.

3   A minicomputer is a small general-purpose machine ranging in price from about $2,500 to $75,000. There is considerable overlap between small minis and large micro systems. Minis were first developed in the 1960s to fill the gaps left by the bigger and faster central computers in an organization. In contrast to the current generation of micros, which are generally 8-bit processors, most minis are 16-bit machines. Representative small, medium-scale, and larger mini systems have been identified in the chapter. Minis have always been used for specialized control purposes and for general data processing applications. In recent years, however, organizations have also used thousands of minis as satellite processors in distributed data processing networks.

4   A mainframe computer is generally more powerful (and more expensive) than a mini, but, again, considerable overlap may occur in these categories. Mainframes, ranging in size from small to very large, are typically lumped together under a family designation. Representative mainframe families have been identified in the chapter. Most mainframes are basically 32-bit machines and are designed to support almost every type of available peripheral device. Larger libraries of applications programs are available for mainframe computers than for smaller systems. Mainframes are used as central host computers in distributed systems, and they are used in thousands of other ways.

5   Supercomputers are the largest, fastest, and most expensive computing monsters in existence. They are few in number and are designed to process complex scientific applications.

▶ KEY TERMS

After reading Chapter 6, you should be able to define and use the following terms:

microcomputer
random-access memory (RAM) chips
microprocessor chip
read-only memory (ROM) chips
8-bit machine
interface bus
minicomputer
16-bit machine
high-speed cache storage
distributed data processing network

host computer
satellite (or node) computer
mainframe computer
compatibility
single processor (or uniprocessor) computer system
multiprocessor computer system
32-bit machine
supercomputer
cycle time

REVIEW AND DISCUSSION QUESTIONS

1 Conduct a survey among five people in the computer/data processing field and ask them these two questions: (a) How would you differentiate between a microcomputer and a minicomputer? (b) How would you differentiate between a minicomputer and a small mainframe model? What were the results of your survey?

2 (a) What is a microcomputer? (b) Why was it developed? (c) What is the difference between a microcomputer and a microprocessor?

3 "Most microcomputers are stand-alone, single-user-oriented machines used by people at work and at play." Discuss this statement.

4 (a) Identify four ways to supply input data to a micro system. (b) Identify four ways that output may be received from a micro CPU. (You may wish to review the I/O media and devices discussed in Chapter 4.)

5 How may micro systems be used (a) by individuals, and (b) by organizations?

6 Give four examples of representative (a) microcomputers, (b) minicomputers, and (c) mainframe computers.

7 Identify and discuss three characteristics of (a) microcomputers, (b) minicomputers, and (c) mainframe computers.

8 What is the most popular programming language used with micros?

9 (a) What is a minicomputer? (b) Why were minis developed? (c) How may minis be used?

10 (a) What is a mainframe computer? (b) How may mainframes by used?

11 "A large mainframe is generally software compatible with the smaller computers in the same family." Explain this statement.

12 (a) What is a supercomputer? (b) How does a supercomputer differ from other machines? (c) How are supercomputers used?

SELECTED REFERENCES

Balint, Francis J.: "Modeling the Weather," *Datamation,* pp. 131–133ff, May 1978.

Canning, Richard G., and Barbara McNurlin: "Micros Invade the Business World," *Datamation,* pp. 93–95, August 1978.

"Cray, King of the Giant Processors," *Business Week,* pp. 156ff, October 29, 1979.

Dorr, Fred W.: "The CRAY-1 at Los Alamos," *Datamation,* pp. 113–118ff, October 1978.

Free, John: "Computerized Cars," *Popular Science,* pp. 54–55ff, August 1979.

Gardner, W. David: "Big Boom in Minicomputers," *Dun's Review,* pp. 70–72ff, July 1978.

Muller, Frederick W.: "Here a Mini, There a Mini, Everywhere a Mini," *Infosystems,* pp. 32–33ff, February 1979.

Ramey, R. L., J. H. Aylor, and R. D. Williams: "Microcomputer-aided Eating for the Severely Handicapped," *Computer,* pp. 54–61, January 1979.

Richman, Lawrence: "Firms of all Sizes Convert to Minis," *Datamation,* pp. 94–97ff, October 1978.
Stibbens, Steve: "The Microcomputer Merry-Go-Round," *Infosystems,* pp. 70ff, April 1979.

(Van Bucher, Photo Researchers.)

Part Three
PUTTING THE COMPUTER TO WORK

(Copyright 1977, Creative Computing, Morristown, N.J.)

You will recall that one of the basic objectives of this book is to provide an orientation to the computer—what it is, what it can and cannot do, and how it operates. Computer capabilities, limitations, and hardware operations were presented in the chapters in Part 2. The purpose of the chapters in Part 3, however, is to consider the steps involved in developing the software that is needed if the computer hardware is to be put to work to produce the output results that people desire.

The chapters included in Part 3 are:

Chapter 7
SYSTEMS STUDIES, PROGRAMMING ANALYSIS, AND PROGRAM PREPARATION

The purpose of this chapter is to outline the seven steps in the general procedure that is followed to permit computers to perform useful work. There is a section in the chapter on each of these steps.

The first three steps (defining the problem to be solved, gathering data and analyzing the problem, and preparing designs and specifications to solve the problem) are included in the systems-analysis and design phase. The last four steps (programming analysis, program preparation, program debugging and testing, and program documentation and maintenance) are part of the programming phase.

The systems-study approach, typically used in organizations during the systems-analysis and design phase, is considered early in the chapter. Some tools and/or techniques for determining study objectives, gathering data and analyzing current operations, and designing ways in which operations can be improved are presented. For example, system flowcharts and a "divide and conquer" topdown approach to viewing systems may be used during the systems-analysis and design phase.

Following the discussion of the systems study, a section on programming analysis is presented. The use of program flowcharts is treated. Specifications for six example problems are outlined in this section, and these specifications are used to prepare program flowcharts. (Solutions for these problems will be coded in the BASIC programming language in the next chapter.)

The next major section in the chapter is an overview of program preparation. Included in this section is a discussion of (1) the types of program instructions used by computers, and (2) the categories of programming languages that exist. Finally, sections are presented on the final two steps in the programming phase—debugging and testing, and documentation and maintenance.

Thus, after studying this chapter, you should be able to:

- Identify the general steps that are followed to put computers to work.
- Explain the purpose of a systems study, and discuss some of the tools and/or techniques that may be used during data gathering, systems analysis, and systems design.
- Explain the purpose of programming analysis, identify the basic symbols used in program flowcharts, and be able to construct a simple chart using those symbols.
- Identify the types of instructions that computers can execute; outline some of the differences between machine, symbolic, and high-level programming languages; and recall examples of several high-level languages.

219

SYSTEMS STUDIES,
PROGRAMMING
ANALYSIS, AND
PROGRAM
PREPARATION

- Define and point out the purpose of program debugging, testing, documentation, and maintenance.
- Understand and use the key terms listed at the end of the chapter.

In the past three chapters, attention has been focused primarily on computer hardware, but hardware alone does not solve a single problem. Until the processor is given a detailed set of problem-solving instructions, it is merely an expensive curiosity.

The general procedure that is followed in organizations to put computers to work involves several steps:[1]

1   *Definition of the problem or task and the objectives.* Before the computer can be put to work, the particular problem to be solved or the tasks to be accomplished must be clearly identified, and the objectives of those who want the tasks performed must be known.
2   *Analysis of the problem or task.* Data pertaining to the problem or task must be gathered, organized, and interpreted.
3   *System review and design.* If present procedures exist to deal with the problem, they should be reviewed to determine what improvements are possible. New design approaches to deal with the task may result from this review. Specifications should be prepared that outline the form and type of input data to be used and the form and type of output required.
4   *Programming analysis.* The system specifications must be converted into the specific arithmetic and logic operations required to solve the problem.
5   *Program preparation.* The specific steps must next be translated or coded into a language and form acceptable to the processor.
6   *Program debugging and testing.* The coded program must be checked for errors and tested prior to being used on a routine basis to ensure that the correct problem is being solved and that correct results are being produced.
7   *Program documentation and maintenance.* Conversion to the new approach must be made. The program must be properly stored when not in use; it should be described in writing (and supporting written documents should also be developed and kept on file); and it should be revised and maintained as needs change.

The purpose of this chapter and the chapter that follows is to examine these seven steps in putting computers to work. The first three steps

---

[1] Individuals interested in preparing new programs for their personal computers will also follow these same steps in order to put their systems to work. Of course, many more factors are likely to be involved in applying a computer to an application in an organizational setting.

are included in the *systems-* (or *problem-*) *analysis phase;* the final four steps may be identified as the *programming phase.* As used in this text, programming is defined as the *process* of converting broad specifications into usable machine programs of instruction.[2]

In the first part of this chapter we will look at methods used in performing the systems-analysis phase. Our emphasis will be on the type of systems studies conducted in governmental agencies, hospitals, educational institutions, industrial engineering departments, and business firms. Following our discussion of the *systems-study approach,* we will consider *programming analysis.* Finally, a brief overview of *program preparation, debugging and testing,* and *documentation and maintenance* is also included in this chapter. In the next chapter, we will see what is involved in actually preparing programs in the BASIC language.

SYSTEMS-STUDY APPROACH

A *systems study* is the investigation made in an organization to determine and develop needed informational improvements in *specified* areas. The steps or stages in the systems-study approach are to (1) *accomplish planning prerequisites and identify the objectives,* (2) *gather data on current operations,* (3) *analyze current operations and determine suitable solutions,* (4) *decide on the most appropriate solution,* (5) *implement the solution,* and (6) *follow up on the decisions made.*

Planning Prerequisites and Study Objectives

The account of an early well-managed survey is found in the Bible, in Chapter 13 of the Book of Numbers. A team of 12 "analysts" was sent by Moses to spy out the Promised Land and report back their findings. Three *important prerequisite principles* were observed in this survey:

1 *The survey had support at the highest levels.* God told Moses: "Send men to spy out the land of Canaan . . . from each tribe of their fathers shall you send a man, every one a leader among them." Such top-level support is a prerequisite.
2 *The survey team[3] consisted of highly respected individuals.* Only tribal leaders were sent on the mission. Systems-study members are often

---

[2] Sometimes the term *programming* is used to refer only to program preparation, or *coding* (step 5 above), but programming here is considered as a problem-solving series of steps. It is a time-consuming and error-prone process that does not begin and end with the writing of lines of code on a sheet of paper. In larger organizations the systems specifications are prepared by systems analysts and the later steps are generally handled by programmers and computer operators. Close cooperation is, of course, required.

[3] In broader systems studies involving extensive redesign of existing procedures, a team approach is generally followed; in less complicated systems projects, the "team" may shrink to one analyst.

221

SYSTEMS STUDIES,
PROGRAMMING
ANALYSIS, AND
PROGRAM
PREPARATION

"Computers Analyze Athletic Performance"

Coaches have been analyzing athletes' movements with the goal of improving performance probably for as long as competitive sports have been played.

Technology, however, with the use of high-speed cameras, computers and statistics, is metamorphosing the art into a science.

Students in a graduate course at The University of Texas are learning how to combine the art of coaching and a sense of the game with a knowledge of biomechanics and the use of sophisticated equipment to analyze movement in sports.

Students concentrate on basic scientific principles of human movement such as balance, linear motion, rotation, force production, accuracy and limb manipulation and then apply those principles to specific sport situations.

"They use a fairly fast camera speed so it is sort of like slow-motion photography. They actually stop the film to do a frame-by-frame analysis of movement. As the body moves from frame to frame, they can see how it moves over a period of time. It is a good chance to quantify movement," said Dr. Larry Abraham who teaches the course.

Abraham explained that computers can be combined with the film process to provide analysts with highly refined information, unquestionably more detailed than a naked eyeball analysis would yield.

Such computer analysis, however, is beyond UT's capacity. The equipment is there but not the computer program. "We are in the process of working it up, and within a couple of years we should be able to be close to the best that is being done now," he says.

To analyze and improve movement, one must understand its goal. "Most movements in sport are means to an end—swinging a bat or a tennis racket, kicking a football, and some movements are ends in themselves—dance, diving, gymnastics—which changes the approach to analysis," Dr. Abraham explained. "Analysts also must recognize personal style in performance and make allowances for it," he added.

The analyst offers only suggestions, no guarantees, but the analysis of athletic performance has other uses. For sports equipment manufacturers interested in developing safer gear, analysis can help determine where stress is being placed on the body and how it can be relieved. In the field of rehabilitation, amputees can learn to manipulate prosthetic devices as naturally as possible.

Dr. Abraham is especially interested in the assistance biomechanics can provide the poor performer in athletics. "There are lots more poor performers than good performers, and they have lots more room to profit by this analysis. The kinds of problems that poor performers have are mechanical problems. Through the use of biomechanics they can become good performers and enjoy sports more because they can achieve their goals."

Source: *Creative Computing,* p. 149, May 1979. Used by permission of *Creative Computing,* P.O. Box 789-M, Morristown, N.J. 07960.

selected for the offsetting talents they can bring to the job. At least one member should represent the interests of those who will use the new system, and should have a knowledge of the information needs of the organization, while another member should be familiar with systems and the technical side of data processing.

3 *The scope and objectives of the survey were clearly stated.* Moses specifically told the 12 to investigate the richness of the land, the physical and numerical strength of the occupants, and the defensibility of the cities. In a systems study, the nature of the operation(s) that is (are) to be investigated, as well as the goals that are to be pursued, should also be stated specifically at the outset.

The biblical survey team returned to Moses after 40 days. There was agreement on the richness of the land, but lack of agreement on the strength of the people occupying it. Sessions were held during which the differing views were presented. It is usually desirable for the team members to hold preliminary *design sessions* with the administrators of all departments that the study will affect so that they may be allowed to participate in setting or revising specific goals. When it appears that tentative approval has been reached on these goals, the study leader should put them *in writing* and send them for approval to all concerned. If differences remain, they should be resolved in additional sessions.

Data Gathering

You can observe a lot just by watching.
—Yogi Berra

In many cases, the team members must gather data on current operations before they can achieve specified goals. In identifying objectives, it is likely that preliminary data were gathered, but more details are now needed to determine the strengths and weaknesses of current procedures. The data to be collected will vary from one study to another, but in most cases the following questions should be answered: (1) What source information is used? (2) What work is done? (3) What economic resources are being used? and (4) What results are achieved?

System flowcharts are often used during this data-gathering phase. A *flowchart* is a graphic tool or model that provides a means of recording, analyzing, and communicating information. *The system flowchart provides a broad overview of the processing operations that are being accomplished*

223

SYSTEMS STUDIES,
PROGRAMMING
ANALYSIS, AND
PROGRAM
PREPARATION

(and/or that *should* be performed). Primary emphasis is placed on data flow among work stations and machines, i.e., on input documents and output reports. The amount of detail furnished about *how* a work station or machine is to convert the data on input documents into the desired output is limited. In the design of all flowcharts it is necessary that standard *symbols* be used to record and communicate problem information clearly. Symbols representing input, output, and general processing (Figure 7-1) are frequently used in systems flowcharts. The same basic I/O symbol may be used to show any type of media or data. Frequently, the basic I/O symbol is replaced in systems flowcharts by other I/O symbols whose shape suggests the type of media or device being employed (Figure 7-2). These symbols are familiar to us because they have been used in earlier chapters. Additional commonly used system flowchart symbols are shown and described in Figure 7-3. Preparing flowcharts is helpful in gathering data on current operations. Beginning with source-document inputs, each operation step is charted, using the proper symbols. Files and equipment being used are identified, the processing sequence is shown, the departments involved are located, and the output results are indicated.

Date Analysis and System Design[4]

During the fact-finding stage, emphasis was placed on *what* was being done; now the interest is in (1) learning *why* activities are being performed and (2) designing ways in which operations can be *improved*. If the system being analyzed is relatively large and complex, a "divide and conquer" approach is often used. That is, the top-level functions that must be carried out are identified, analyzed, and broken down into a series of *second-level* functions or procedures (each of which may also be further reduced into smaller components). A hierarchy of understandable subfunctions may be the result of this *top-down analysis* approach. A similar *top-down design* methodology may be used in the preparation of a proposed new system. Each of the major functions to be performed is divided into lower-level modules, and each module can then be considered on the basis of (1) output results, (2) input requirements, and (3) processing steps needed to produce the desired output.

Since each module deals with a small and controllable amount of detail, the design effort is facilitated and the task of preparing programs at a later time may also be eased. For example, a program may be structured in such a way that there is a *main-control module* that specifies the order in which each of the *other* modules in the program will be used. An instruction in the main-control module branches program control to a subordinate module. When the processing performed by the module is com-

[4] For a more detailed treatment of these topics, see Donald H. Sanders, *Computers in Business,* 4th ed., McGraw-Hill Book Company, New York, 1979, pp. 222–247.

FIGURE 7-1
Basic system-charting symbols.

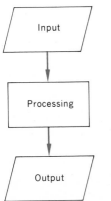

pleted, program control may be returned to the main-control program. In such a *structured programming* environment, a strong emphasis is placed on simplifying the possible paths of program control. Instead of organizing the program in such a way that confusing branches to other parts of the program—both forward and backward—are permitted, an effort is

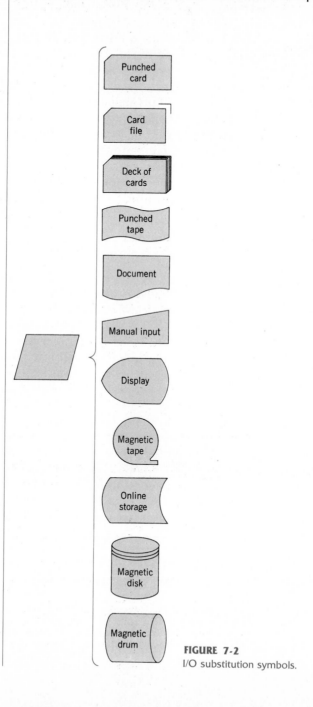

FIGURE 7-2
I/O substitution symbols.

225

SYSTEMS STUDIES,
PROGRAMMING
ANALYSIS, AND
PROGRAM
PREPARATION

Symbols		Meaning of Symbols
	Auxiliary operation	An operation which supplements the main processing function but which is performed by a machine that is not directly under the control of the CPU.
	Offline storage	A symbol representing data stored in external offline storage. Storage media may be cards, paper tapes, magnetic tapes, paper documents, etc.
	Manual operation	Any offline process geared to the speed of a human being is represented by this symbol.
	Communications link	Automatic data transmission from one location to another.
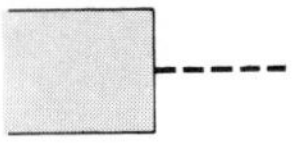	Annotation flag	This "flag" is connected by the dashed line to a flow line to provide additional explanatory notes. The dashed line may be drawn on either the left or right. The vertical line may also be drawn on the right or left. This symbol is used for both system and program flowcharts.

FIGURE 7-3
Additional system flowchart symbols.

made to write programs that can be read from top to bottom. In short, the *modular programming approach*[5] shown in Figure 7-4 may be facilitated by the study team's use of a top-down analysis and design methodology at this time.

Regardless of the analysis and design methodology used, however, the team will have to answer a large number of questions at this time about procedures, costs, and the effects of proposed changes on people and departments. But the variety of different processing systems, the difficulty of describing these systems, the wide range of equipment that can be used, the speed with which equipment changes, the lack of static testing conditions caused by a rapidly changing social environment—all these factors prevent the formulation of exact rules to follow in systems analysis and design. Thus, the success of the project is ultimately dependent upon the ingenuity of the team in arriving at answers that satisfy needs. Once these answers have been obtained, a detailed set of written

---

[5] Some of the *advantages* of this modular programming approach are: (1) Complex systems may be divided into simpler and more manageable-program elements, (2) simultaneous coding of modules by several programmers is possible, (3) a *library* of modules may be created, and these modules may be used in other programs as needed, and (4) program errors may be easier to locate and correct.

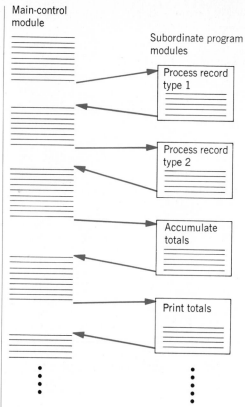

FIGURE 7-4
Modular programming
approach is facilitated by
top-down analysis and
design methodology.

specifications for the new system should be prepared outlining the (1) input requirements, (2) processing specifications, (3) output requirements, (4) control provisions, and (5) cost estimates.

Decision Making and Implementation

Guided by a written charter, which defined the scope and direction of its efforts, the study team has analyzed the relevant facts; from this analysis has come a detailed set of systems specifications designed to achieve the study goals. Let us assume that after careful consideration of processing alternatives the team has concluded that computer usage is justified because (1) processing complexities permit no alternative, or (2) the tangible and intangible benefits to be gained are greater than comparable benefits received from other processing alternatives.

The systems-study team should now prepare a report covering the following points:

1 The procedures and operations that will be changed, and the anticipated effects of such changes on the organizational structure and physical facilities

227

SYSTEMS STUDIES,
PROGRAMMING
ANALYSIS, AND
PROGRAM
PREPARATION

2 The anticipated effects on people, and the personnel resources available to implement the change
3 The hardware/software package chosen, the reasons for the choice, and the alternatives considered
4 The economic effects of the change, including cost comparisons
5 A summary of the problems anticipated in the changeover, and a statement of the benefits to be obtained from the change

Appropriate administrators must now evaluate the recommendations made by the team to decide whether the benefits outweigh the possible disadvantages. If the decision is to accept the recommendations of the team, administrators should then establish subsequent project performance controls. Personnel must be selected to do the work; a conversion schedule may be needed; and periodic reports on implementation progress should be required.

Follow-up on Systems Decisions

Assuming that computer applications have been implemented and are in operation, a thorough appraisal or audit should be made. Among the questions that should be considered in the audit are: (1) How useful is the system to decision makers? (2) Are planned processing procedures being followed? (3) Is the information-processing function properly organized? (4) Have programming and program testing standards been established? and (5) Are systems controls being observed, and is documentation complete?

PROGRAMMING ANALYSIS

A common tool used for programming analysis purposes is the *program flowchart.*

What Is a Program Flowchart?

Flowcharts have existed for years and have been used for many purposes. As noted earlier, the system flowchart provides a broad overview of the processing operations that are to be accomplished, but it does not go into detail about how input data are to be used to produce output information. A *program flowchart,* on the other hand, does present a detailed graphical representation of how steps are to be performed *within* the machine to produce the needed output. Thus, the program flowchart evolves from the system chart.

To illustrate this relationship, and to present an example of a simple program flowchart, let us consider the following problem.[6] A classmate of

---

[6] This problem (and others to be presented in this chapter) has been coded for computer processing in the next chapter.

System flowchart

Program flowchart

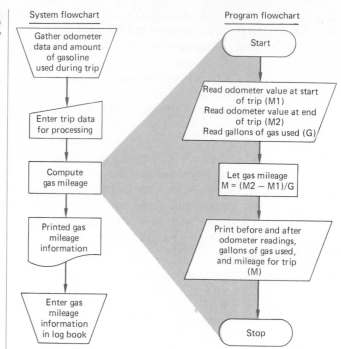

FIGURE 7-5
A program flowchart evolves from a system flowchart.

yours, Rod "Hots" Thudfoot, has recently bought a new Firebelch V/6 and has decided to keep a log book on the car's gasoline mileage. The system used by Rod to maintain his log book is shown in the *system flowchart* section of Figure 7-5. The odometer readings before and after a trip, and the amount of gasoline used,[7] are gathered manually. These data are then keyed into a computer, the gasoline mileage is computed, a printed mileage report is prepared, and this mileage information is manually entered into the log book.

In Rod's system chart, a single processing box is labeled "compute gas mileage." Unfortunately, such an instruction is not sufficient for the computer. Rather, each step needed to compute the gas mileage must be specified. Thus, the single processing box labeled "compute gas mileage" becomes the basis for the more detailed *program flowchart* section of Figure 7-5.

Several flowcharting conventions are shown in Figure 7-5. The arrows connecting the shapes indicate the direction of data flow. The main flow is generally charted from top to bottom and from left to right. The *shape* of the symbol and *not its size* identifies the meaning. For example, the rectangular processing box may vary in size, but the shape still designates that processing is being performed. Notation within the charting symbol further explains what is being done.

---

[7] Rod leaves on a trip with a full tank of gas, keeps a record of the gallons purchased during the trip, and fills up his tank at the end of the trip to determine the amount of gasoline used.

229

SYSTEMS STUDIES,
PROGRAMMING
ANALYSIS, AND
PROGRAM
PREPARATION

Symbols Used in Program Flowcharts

Only a few symbols, when properly arranged, are needed in program charting to define the necessary steps. These symbols are illustrated in Figure 7-6 and are described below.

Input/output The basic I/O symbol is also used in program flowcharting to represent any I/O function. The specific symbols designating cards, tapes, etc., are generally not used with program diagrams. In the program flowchart section of Figure 7-5, the I/O symbol designates (1) the input data to be used (before and after odometer readings and gallons of gas consumed), and (2) the output information to be printed.

Processing Again, the rectangle represents processing operations, but now the processing described may be a *small segment* of a major pro-

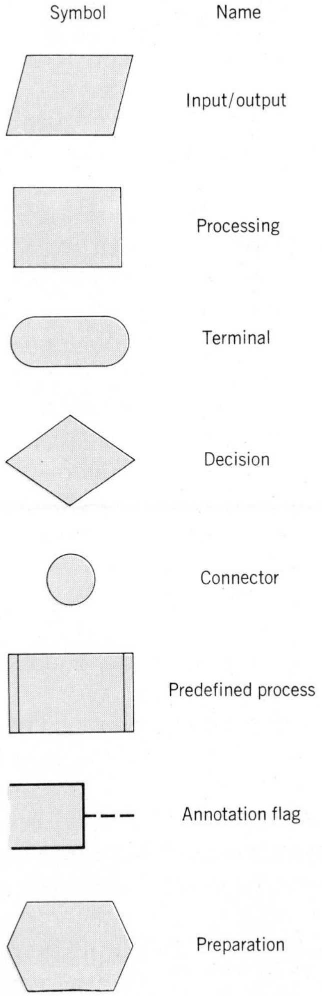

Symbol	Name
	Input/output
	Processing
	Terminal
	Decision
	Connector
	Predefined process
	Annotation flag
	Preparation

FIGURE 7-6
Program flowchart symbols.

cessing step called for in the system chart. Arithmetic and data movement instructions are generally placed in these boxes. One processing symbol is shown in the program section of Figure 7-5. This box provides for the computation of the gas mileage for a trip. The mileage difference between the beginning and ending odometer readings is found, and this figure is divided by the gallons of gas used to get the gas mileage for a trip.

Termination The terminal symbol, as the name suggests, represents the beginning and the end of a program. As shown in Figure 7-5, program charts begin with a START symbol and end with a STOP symbol.

Decision The I/O and processing symbols typically have two flow lines (one entry and one exit), while the terminal has a single entrance or exit line. The diamond-shaped decision symbol, on the other hand, has one entrance line and *at least* two exit paths or branches. These exit paths may be determined by a yes or no answer to some stated *condition* — e.g., the condition to be determined may be whether the last record in a file has been processed (Figure 7-7). If the answer is yes, the program can branch away from the *loop* that it has been following of reading records and performing two processing steps on each record. If the answer is no, the program continues to process the records until they are all accounted for. As we saw back in Chapter 3 and in Figure 3-1, page 91, decision symbols are also used to show the result of a *test* or a *comparison*.

Connector The *circular connector* symbol is used when additional flow lines might cause confusion and reduce understanding. Two connectors with identical labels serve the same function as a long flow line; i.e., they show an entry from another part of the chart, or they indicate an exit to some other chart section. How is it possible to determine whether a connector is used as an entry point or an exit point? It is very simple: If an arrow *enters but does not leave a connector,* it is an exit point and program flow is transferred to that identically labeled connector that *does* have an outlet. Thus, in Figure 7-7, the upper connector labeled "1" is an entry point, while the lower connector with the same label is an exit point.

Predefined process Programmers frequently find that certain kinds of processing operations are repeated in one or more programs. Instead of rewriting a small subordinate routine each time it is needed, the programmer can prepare it once and then integrate it into the program or programs as required. *Libraries* of these predefined processes, or *subroutines,* are often maintained to reduce the cost and time of programming. Thus, a single predefined process symbol replaces a number of operations that are not detailed at that particular point in the chart. In short, the subroutine receives input from the primary program, performs its limited task, and then returns the output to the primary program.

FIGURE 7-7
Decision-symbol usage.

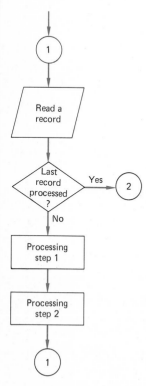

231

SYSTEMS STUDIES,
PROGRAMMING
ANALYSIS, AND
PROGRAM
PREPARATION

Annotation flag The comments made in Figure 7-3 also apply to program flowcharts.

Programming Analysis Using Flowcharts

You learned earlier that programming analysis involves converting problem specifications into the specific arithmetic and logic operations that are needed to solve the problem. Let us now analyze some problem specifications to see how the use of flowcharts can be of value in this activity.[8]

Problem 1: Thudfoot's Gas Mileage, Single Trip. We have already analyzed the first problem—the computation of Rod Thudfoot's gas mileage for a single trip—in the preceding pages. The flowchart for this problem is shown in Figure 7-5.

Problem 2: Thudfoot's Gas Mileage, Multiple Trips. What if Rod has made several trips in a recent week and would like to compute the mileage for each trip? He could do this in a single session at his computer terminal by rerunning the program prepared from Figure 7-5 for each trip. But after each trip computation, the program would have to be reentered or reloaded into the computer to process the data from the next trip— hardly an efficient use of Rod's valuable time. How, then, can the first program flowchart be modified to accommodate the following features or specifications that Rod feels would be desirable?

● The program should compute and then print as output the miles per gallon (mpg) for any number of trips.

● The program should "converse" with Rod and ask him to supply it with the necessary input data for each trip.

● After computing the miles per gallon for a trip, the program should ask Rod whether data from another trip are to be processed.

● Finally, as a nice gesture, Rod would like the computer to print a polite sign-off message when the processing has been completed.

The flowchart shown in Figure 7-8 satisfies Rod's requirements and illustrates the use of most program-charting symbols. Although the computation formula for gas mileage obviously does not change from Figure 7-5, this program is much more *flexible* in that it can process any number of trips. The *body of the loop* that makes this repetition possible is found between the two connector symbols labeled "A." The *test for exit condition* that determines whether the loop's task has been completed is indicated in the decision symbol. If another trip is to be processed, the loop continues; if not, an exit path out of the loop is followed. Such an exit path must, of course, be provided in cases where loops are employed. Unin-

---

[8] The results of these analyses will be used in the next chapter to prepare the computer programs necessary to put the computer to work to solve the problems.

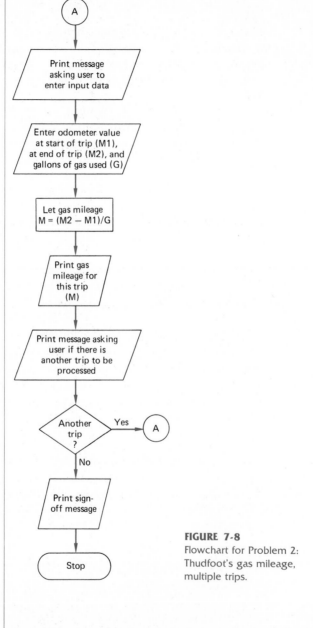

FIGURE 7-8
Flowchart for Problem 2:
Thudfoot's gas mileage,
multiple trips.

tentional *continuous or infinite loops* that result from failure to provide an adequate exit path are a common and troublesome problem encountered in programming. The chart in Figure 7-8 also shows how a program can be made to "interact" or "converse" with a human user in a relaxed

233

SYSTEMS STUDIES,
PROGRAMMING
ANALYSIS, AND
PROGRAM
PREPARATION

and nonthreatening way. The programming language (BASIC) that we will be studying in the next chapter is particularly supportive of such interaction.

Problem 3: Thudfoot's Mileage Tax. Let's now assume that Rod's state decided to impose a one-time tax on new cars in an effort to (1) raise additional revenue, and (2) encourage citizens to buy more fuel-efficient cars. (Alas, this tax went into effect the day before Rod bought his new Firebelch.) The tax on each car is based on its current overall Environmental Protection Agency (EPA) mileage rating. The EPA mileage rating categories and the tax payment due on purchase are indicated below:

EPA Mileage Rating	Tax Due
Less than 15 mpg	$450
15 and less than 20 mpg	250
20 and less than 25 mpg	100
25 mpg and over	5

The program for this problem should meet the following specifications:

- It should produce the amount of tax due, given a car's EPA mileage rating as input.
- It should interact with the user by requesting the necessary input data.

The chart shown in Figure 7-9 satisfies these specifications. In response to a message supplied by the program, the user enters the EPA mileage rating for a car. The amount of tax due is then determined through the use of *multiple decisions*. In the first decision, *if* the mileage rating (M) is less than 15 miles per gallon, *then* the program assigns $450 as the tax due. If the rating is 15 mpg or more, however, program control advances to the next decision. If M is less than 20—i.e., if M is at least 15 but less than 20—a tax of $250 is assessed. And so it goes: If M is at least 20 mpg but less than 25, the tax is $100; if M is 25 mpg or more—i.e., it is *not* less than 25—the tax is $5. Finally, the amount of tax due is printed. Although this problem is not particularly difficult, you can see from this example that a *series of comparison decisions* can be used in programming analysis to produce the intricate logic necessary to solve complex problems.

Problem 4: Thudfoot's Length Conversion Problem. In addition to being a car buff, "Hots" Thudfoot is also a poet with all the romantic honors, rights, and privileges pertaining thereto. Unfortunately, however, Rod has great difficulty with any form of simple arithmetic, and this complicates his part-time job filling orders at a carpet store. In the past two weeks alone, Rod has messed up several customer orders by incorrectly converting yards of carpet into the corresponding lengths in feet and in inches. Thus, Rod wants a length conversion program that will meet the following specifications:

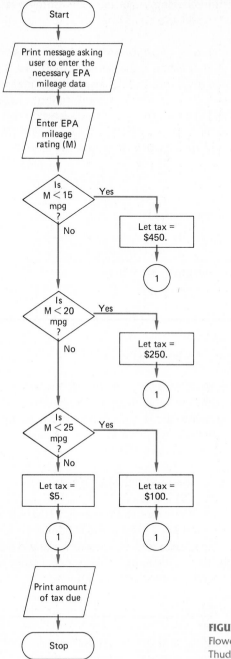

FIGURE 7-9
Flowchart for Problem 3:
Thudfoot's mileage tax.

- It should process without interruption the carpet lengths (in yards) of all customer orders to be filled during the day.

- It should print an output report converting the yardage in each order into the corresponding lengths in feet and in inches.

235

SYSTEMS STUDIES,
PROGRAMMING
ANALYSIS, AND
PROGRAM
PREPARATION

● After processing all orders and preparing the output report, the processing should stop.

The chart shown in Figure 7-10 meets these specifications. Headings for the output report are printed, and then the body of the loop required to process multiple orders begins. The carpet length (in yards) of the first order to be processed is read. Since the yardage (Y) is certainly not less than zero, the next steps are to convert the length into feet (Y * 3, where * means multiply) and inches (F * 12). These figures are then printed, and the program loops back to read the yardage in the next order. This repetition continues until the last order has been processed and a sentinel value

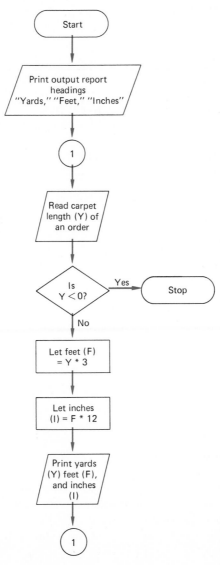

FIGURE 7-10
Flowchat for Problem 4:
Thudfoot's length conversion
problem.

is then encountered. A *sentinel value* is simply some arbitrary data value that has been selected to indicate that all the *valid data* have been processed. Of course, it must be some number that *could not possibly occur* as a valid data item. In our example, any negative number entered after the last valid yardage figure could serve as the sentinel value. However, a string of 9s (e.g., -99.99 in our example) is often used as the sentinel value because the 9s stand out and are generally understood to be artificial or "dummy numbers." For this reason, the use of a sentinel value to exit from a loop is sometimes called the *9s decision technique.*

Problem 5: Karl Tell's Pay Authorization Problem. Professor Karl Tell is an economist specializing in nineteenth-century German antitrust matters. At the present time, he is hard at work on a study of the robber barons of Dusseldorf and has persuaded the dean to give him a number of graduate research assistants to help him with the project. It is Karl's responsibility to prepare a report each pay period authorizing the school business office to pay the research assistants for the hours they have worked during that period. It is also his responsibility to keep track of the total amount paid to the assistants each period so that he will not exceed the budget the dean has given him. Since he is so engrossed in his study, Karl has occasionally neglected to prepare the authorization report, with the result that the graduate students have not been paid on time. To prevent a possible mutiny (the students do not share Karl's enthusiasm for the project), Karl wants a pay authorization program that will meet the following specifications:

- It should supply when needed the name and hourly pay rate of each assistant from a stored data file, and it should also supply the number of such assistants in the file.

- During processing, it should permit Karl to enter the number of hours worked by each student during the period.

- Given the above input data (name, hourly rate of pay, and number of hours worked), it should (1) print each student's name, and (2) compute and print out the amount of pay authorized for each student during the period.

- It should accumulate the total amount paid to the assistants for the period, and it should print this total amount after all assistants have been processed.

- As a further aid to his record keeping, Karl would also like the program to compute and print out the average (arithmetic mean) amount paid during the period.

An analysis of these specifications has produced the chart shown in Figure 7-11. Two new important programming techniques—the use of a *counter* and the use of an *accumulator*—are illustrated in this chart. The purpose of the *counter* here is to systematically record the number of

237

SYSTEMS STUDIES,
PROGRAMMING
ANALYSIS, AND
PROGRAM
PREPARATION

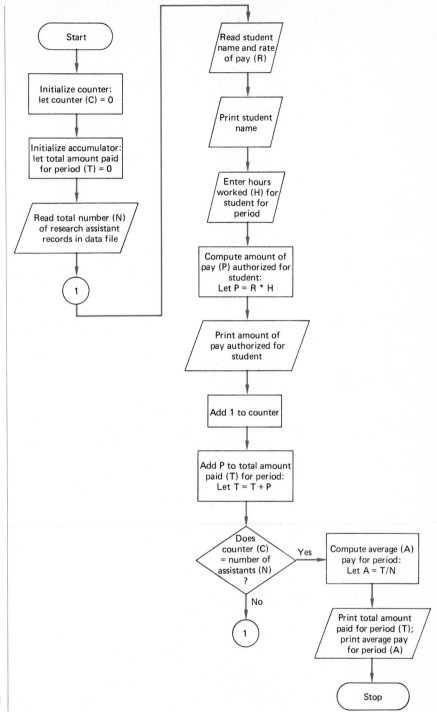

FIGURE 7-11
Flowchart for Problem 5: Karl
Tell's pay authorization
program.

times the loop has been executed. (The body of the loop is between the connector symbols labeled "1.") You have seen that a loop is controlled by its *exit condition,* and in this case the exit condition is based on the value of a counter. In our example, the counter (C) is *initialized* (or initially set) at zero,[9] and after the record of the first student has been processed, the counter is *incremented* (or added to) by a value of 1. Thus, the counter has a value of 1 when the first test for exit condition is made at the decision symbol. This test is based on whether the counter value is equal to the number of research assistant records (N) to be processed. When the last record *has* been processed, and when C = N, the exit path out of the loop will be followed.

The purpose of an *accumulator* is to accept individual values and compute a *running total* of them as they become available during processing. A computer storage location *must* initially be set at zero. [Since Karl Tell wants to keep track of the total amount paid for the period, the accumulator (T) is initialized at zero, as shown in the second processing symbol in Figure 7-11.] After this initial step, each successive value placed in the accumulator is added to the value already there. Thus, if the first pay amount processed is $100, the total in the accumulator will become $100 [i.e., in the processing symbol immediately above the decision symbol in Figure 7-11, the new value for T is the previous value (0) plus $100]. If the second pay figure is $121, the total in the accumulator would then be $221 ($100 + $121). The *grand total* for the period will be stored in the accumulator after the last student's pay has been computed. Once the exit condition has been met, the average pay (A) for the period may be computed by dividing the total in the accumulator by the number of records processed.

Problem 6: Ms. Crabbie's CAI Problem. Ms. Maude Crabbie, a teacher at Cass T. Gate Elementary School, has been assigned by the principal to write a computer-assisted instruction (CAI) program to drill students in the use of multiplication tables. The students sit at a computer terminal and enter responses to questions that are printed or displayed under program control. The principal has told Maude that the program should meet the following specifications:

- It should interact with the student and supply the necessary instructions on the purpose and use of the drill.

- It should test students with 20 pairs of numbers for them to multiply, and it should keep track of the number of correct and incorrect responses.

- Each number to be multiplied should be a random value from 0 to 9.

- Immediate feedback after each student response should be provided. A correct answer should be acknowledged; if the answer is incorrect, the correct response should be provided.

---

[9] A counter may be initially set to zero, 1, or some other starting value. It could, for example, be initialized at the number of records to be processed, and then a value of 1 could be *subtracted* for each execution of the program loop. The exit test would then be "Is C = 0?"

239

SYSTEMS STUDIES,
PROGRAMMING
ANALYSIS, AND
PROGRAM
PREPARATION

- After the 20 pairs of numbers have been multiplied, the student's test score should be computed. A score of 85 or better is considered "passing."
- An immediate test-score feedback message to the student should be produced.

The chart in Figure 7-12 satisfies these specifications. Accumulators are set up quickly to keep track of correct and incorrect responses, and various early messages are used to converse with students. An *automatic counter* or index (to be discussed in the next chapter) is then established to allow the computer to execute the program loop exactly 20 times. The numbers to be multiplied are randomly selected by the computer (by an approach that will also be discussed in the next chapter), the correct response is computed and then compared with the student's response, and appropriate immediate feedback messages are provided. A value of 1 will be added to either the correct or incorrect response accumulator each time the loop is executed. The exit condition of the loop is satisfied when the automatic counter reaches 20. The student's test score is then computed, and a "good news" or "bad news" message is produced depending on whether the score is 85 or better.

Benefits and Limitations of Flowcharts

The following *benefits* may be obtained when flowcharts are used during programming analysis:

1 *Quicker grasp of relationships.* Current and proposed procedures may be understood more rapidly through the use of charts.
2 *Effective analysis.* The flowchart becomes a model of a program or system that can be broken down into detailed parts for study.
3 *Effective synthesis.* Synthesis is the opposite of analysis; it is the combination of the various parts into a whole entity. Flowcharts may be used as working models in the design of new programs and systems.
4 *Communication.* Flowcharts aid in communicating the facts of a problem to those whose skills are needed in the solution. The old adage that "a picture is worth a thousand words" contains an element of truth when the pictures happen to be flowchart symbols.
5 *Proper program documentation.* Program *documentation* involves collecting, organizing, storing, and otherwise maintaining a complete historical record of programs and the other documents associated with a system. Good documentation is needed for the following reasons: (a) Documented knowledge belongs to an organization and does not disappear with the departure of a programmer, (b) if projects are postponed, documented work will not have to be duplicated, and (c) if programs are modified in the future, the programmer will have a more understandable record of what was originally done. From what we have seen of the nature of flowcharts, it is obvious that they can provide valuable documentation support.

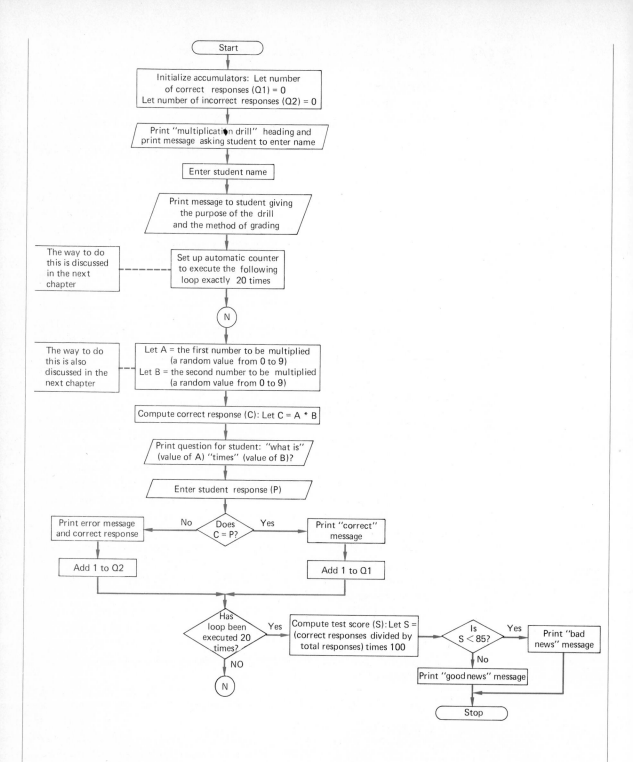

FIGURE 7-12
Flowchart for Problem 6: Ms.
Crabbie's CAI problem.

241

SYSTEMS STUDIES,
PROGRAMMING
ANALYSIS, AND
PROGRAM
PREPARATION

6 *Efficient coding.* The program flowchart acts as a guide or blueprint during the program preparation phase. Instructions coded in a programming language may be checked against the flowchart to make sure that no steps are omitted.

7 *Orderly debugging and testing of programs.* If the program fails to run to completion when submitted to the computer for execution, the flowchart may help in the *debugging* process; i.e., it may help in detecting, locating, and removing mistakes.

In spite of their many obvious advantages, flowcharts have several *limitations.* One is that complex and detailed charts are sometimes laborious to plan and draw, especially when a large number of decision paths are involved.[10] A second limitation in such a situation is that although branches from a *single* decision symbol are easy to follow, the actions to be taken, given certain specified conditions, would be difficult to follow if there were *several* paths.

Other Programming Analysis Tools

Because of such limitations, flowcharts may be replaced or supplemented by alternative analysis techniques. One such tool is a *decision table.* Used in place of program flowcharts, these tables are particularly useful in expressing complex logic that may require the use of numerous decision paths. However, flowcharts may be able to express the *total sequence* of events better than decision tables.[11]

Another programming analysis tool is *pseudocode.* Since *pseudo* means "imitation" and *code* refers to instructions written in a programming language, *pseudocode* is a counterfeit and abbreviated version of actual computer instructions. It is compact and easy to revise. Computer professionals who employ the top-down systems-analysis and design methodology discussed earlier in the chapter and who work in a structured programming environment[12] often prefer to use pseudocode in preparing a detailed plan for a program. However, there are no standard rules to follow in using pseudocode, and nonprofessionals may find it more difficult to use than flowcharts.

---

[10] During the program preparation stage, sections of original charts may be added to, deleted, patched, and otherwise marked up to the point where they become nearly illegible. Since considerable time and effort could be required to redraw complex charts manually, special automatic flowcharting programs have been developed, which use a high-speed printer to produce the charts in good form.

[11] For additional information on the construction and use of decision tables, see Donald H. Sanders, *Computers in Business,* 4th ed., McGraw-Hill Book Company, New York, 1979, pp. 266–269.

[12] In addition to often following the top-down analysis, design, and modular program construction techniques discussed earlier, professionals who work in a structured programming environment typically use only three basic coding structures to prepare any program. Each structure has a single entry and exit point, and, like the page of a book, each is readable from the top to the bottom. These three structures (*simple sequence, selection,* and *loop*) are shown below. In the DO WHILE loop structure, the loop is repeated *while* the condition test
(Continued)

PROGRAM PREPARATION: A BRIEF OVERVIEW

Once the programming analysis phase is completed, the next step required to put the computer to work is to prepare the actual instructions that it will follow during *processing*. Since the next chapter is devoted exclusively to this step, we will only look at a few general concepts here.

Types of Instructions

An instruction prepared in a basic form has at least two parts. The *first* part is referred to as the *command*, or *operation*, and it tells the computer what function it is to perform. (A computer has an *operation code* for each of these functions.[13] For example, the "op code" for ADD in an IBM System/370 mainframe processor is 5A.) The *second* part of the instruction is the *operand*, and it tells the computer where to find or store the data or other instructions that are to be manipulated. The number of operands in an instruction varies. In a *single-operand machine*, the instruction "ADD 0184" could cause the value in address 0184 to be added to the value stored in a register in the arithmetic-logic unit. In a *two-operand machine*, the instruction "ADD 0184 8672" could cause the value in address 8672 to be added to the number in location 0184.[14]

The instruction set of every computer (and of every programming language used with computers) can be classified into just a few cate-

---

(*Continued*)
is true; in the DO UNTIL loop structure variation, the loop is repeated *until* the condition test is true. Although these basic structures are combined in actual practice, their inherent simplicity may lead to more understandable program logic.

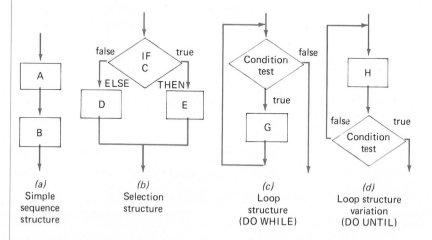

(a)
Simple
sequence
structure

(b)
Selection
structure

(c)
Loop
structure
(DO WHILE)

(d)
Loop structure
variation
(DO UNTIL)

---

[13] The number of these functions is built into the machine and varies from less than 50 to more than 200 depending on the computer make and model.

[14] The single-operand format is popular in microcomputers; the two-operand structure is likely to be available in most other computers. Some three-operand machines have also been built.

243

SYSTEMS STUDIES,
PROGRAMMING
ANALYSIS, AND
PROGRAM
PREPARATION

gories that will permit the computer system to perform the necessary input-processing-output activities. *These categories are*

1 *Input/output instructions.* Required to permit communication between I/O devices and the central processor, these instructions provide details on the type of input or output operation to be performed and the storage locations to be used during the operation.

2 *Data movement and manipulation instructions.* These instructions are used to copy data from one storage location to another and to rearrange and change data elements in some prescribed manner during processing.

3 *Arithmetic instructions.* Instructions to permit addition, subtraction, multiplication, and division during processing are, of course, common in all digital computers.

4 *Logic and transfer of control instructions.* During processing, two data items may be *compared* as a result of the execution of a *logic* instruction. The computer is able to determine the relationship that exists between the two items (A has a greater numerical value than B; C comes before D in an alphabetic sequence). *Transfer of control* instructions may then be used to branch or change the sequence of program control, depending on the outcome of the comparison. Of course, some transfer instructions are not based on the outcome of comparisons. As you saw in Chapter 5, transfer commands may be *conditional* or *unconditional*. If the change in sequence is based on the outcome of a test or comparison, it is a conditional transfer; if not, it is an unconditional branch.

Languages for Computers

We know that in writing program instructions, the programmer must use a language that can be understood by the computer. One awkward approach to human-machine communication is to have the programmer laboriously code instructions directly into the machine-language form. Another approach, as we saw in Chapter 2, is to employ translation software that enables the computer to convert the instructions written in the programmer's language into its own machine code. The programmer finds this approach much more desirable; the machine—being a machine—has no objection.[15] Let us now look at the language categories that have been developed.[16]

---

[15] A third approach, and a most desirable one from the human point of view, is for the machine to accept and interpret instructions written (without constraints) in everyday English terms. The semantic problems involved in this approach, however, are formidable. John Pfeiffer points out that while the sentence "Time flies like an arrow" may seem clear to people, it is subject to several machine interpretations. One incorrect translation, for example, might be: "Time the speed of flies as quickly as you can." ("Time" is considered a verb.) Another false interpretation might be that "certain flies enjoy an arrow." ("Time" is now considered an adjective, while "like" is interpreted as a verb.) And once the machine has been straightened out about the interpretation of "Time flies like an arrow," how will it interpret "Fruit flies like a banana"?

[16] We shall deal primarily with categories in this section rather than with specific languages.

(Continued)

Machine languages Early computers were quite intolerant. Programmers had to translate instructions directly into the machine-language form that computers understood—a form consisting of a string of numbers that represented the command code and operand address. To compound the difficulty for programmers, the string of numbers was often not even in decimal form. For example, the instruction to ADD 0184 looks like this in the machine language of an early IBM computer:

00010000000000000000000000010111000

In addition to remembering the dozens of code numbers for the commands in the machine's instruction set, a programmer was also forced to keep track of the storage locations of data and instructions. The initial coding often took months, was therefore quite expensive, and often resulted in error. Checking instructions to locate errors was about as tedious as writing them initially. And if a program had to be modified at a later date, the work involved could take weeks to finish.

Assembly (symbolic) languages To ease the programmer's burden, *mnemonic* command codes and *symbolic* addresses were developed in the early 1950s. The word *mnemonic* (pronounced *ne-mon-ik*) refers to a memory aid. One of the first steps in improving the program preparation process was to substitute letter symbols for basic machine-language command codes. Each computer now has a mnemonic code, although, of course, the actual symbols vary among makes and models. Machine language is *still* used by the computer in the actual processing of the data, but it first translates the specified command code symbol into its machine-language equivalent.

The improvement in the writing of command codes set the stage for further advances. It was reasoned that if the computer could be used to translate convenient symbols into basic commands, why couldn't it also be used to perform other clerical coding functions such as assigning storage addresses to data? This question led to *symbolic addressing;* i.e., it led to the practice of expressing an address not in terms of its absolute numerical location, but rather in terms of symbols convenient to the programmer.[17]

(Continued)

Some of the characteristics of the most popular programming languages are discussed later in the chapter. There are probably more than 1,000 programming languages in existence, and some have dozens of dialects!

[17] In the early stages of symbolic addressing, the programmer initially assigned a symbolic name and an actual address to a data item. For example, the total value of supplies purchased from a vendor during a month by a school district might be assigned to address 0063 by the vendor's programmer and given the symbolic name of TOTAL. Also, the value of supplies returned unused during the month might be assigned to address 2047 and given the symbolic name of CREDIT. Then, for the remainder of the program, the programmer would refer to the *symbolic names rather than to the addresses* when such items were to be processed. Thus, an instruction might be written "S CREDIT, TOTAL" to subtract the value of returned goods from the total amount purchased to find the amount of the district's

245

SYSTEMS STUDIES,
PROGRAMMING
ANALYSIS, AND
PROGRAM
PREPARATION

Another improvement was that the programmer turned the task of assigning and keeping track of instruction addresses over to the computer. The programmer merely told the machine the storage address number of the *first* program instruction, and then all others were automatically stored in sequence from that point by the processor. If another instruction were to be added later to the program, it was not then necessary to modify the addresses of all instructions that followed the point of insertion (as would have to be done in the case of programs written in machine language). In such a case, the processor automatically adjusted storage locations the next time the program was used.

Programmers no longer assign actual address numbers to symbolic data items as they did initially. Rather, they merely specify where they want the first location in the program to be, and an assembly program takes it from there, allocating locations for instructions and data. The *assembly program* translates the programmer's assembly-language instructions into the machine code of the computer. The following steps (numbered in Figure 7-13) may take place during the *assembly* and *production* runs:

1 The *assembly program* is read into the computer, where it has complete control over the translating procedure. This program is generally supplied by the manufacturer of the machine.
2 The *source program* written by the programmer in the assembly language of the machine is recorded on an input medium such as punched cards.
3 During the assembly, the source program is treated as data and is read into the CPU an instruction at a time under the control of the assembly program.
4 The assembly program translates the source program into a machine-language *object program,* which may be recorded on tapes or cards as the output of the assembly run.[18] It is important to remember that *during the assembly run no problem data are processed.* That is, the source program is not *being executed;* it is merely being converted into a form in which it *can* be executed. After the assembly run, the assembly program is stored for future use.
5 The object program is read into the CPU as the first step in the *production run.*

(*Continued*)

monthly bill. The computer might then translate this symbolic instruction into the following machine-language string of bits:

011111	011111111111	000000111111
Operation or command code	2047	0063
(S)	(CREDIT)	(TOTAL)

[18] Assembly programs and frequently used object programs are often stored in online storage devices rather than on secondary storage media.

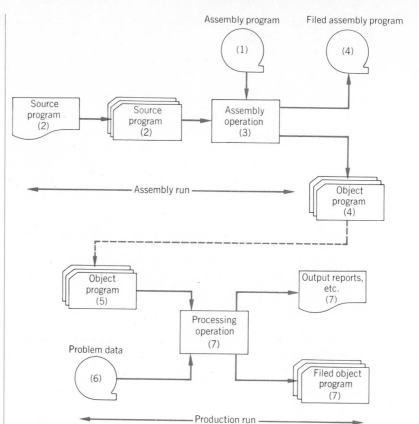

FIGURE 7-13
Converting symbolic
language to machine
language.

6   Problem data, usually recorded on a suitable input medium, are read
    into the CPU under object program control.
7   The application is processed, the information output is received, and
    the object program is filed for future repetitive use.

   Assembly languages possess *advantages over machine languages.*
Much time is saved; detail is reduced; fewer errors are made (and those
which are made are easier to find); and programs are easier to modify.
But there are *limitations.* Coding in assembly language is still time-consuming. Also, assembly languages are *machine oriented;* i.e., they are designed for the specific make and model of processor being used. Programs might have to be recoded if the organization acquired a different
machine. Finally, the earlier assembly programs produced only *one* machine instruction for each source program instruction.

High-level languages   To speed up coding, assembly programs were
developed that could produce a *variable* amount of machine-language
code for *each* source program instruction. In other words, a single *macro
instruction* might produce *several* lines of machine-language code. The

247

SYSTEMS STUDIES,
PROGRAMMING
ANALYSIS, AND
PROGRAM
PREPARATION

development of mnemonic techniques and macro instructions led in turn to the development of *high-level languages* that are often oriented toward a particular class of processing problems. For example, a number of languages have been designed to process problems of a scientific-mathematic nature, and other languages have appeared that emphasize file processing applications.

Unlike assembly programs, high-level language programs may be used with *different makes of computers* with little modification. Thus, re-programming expense may be greatly reduced when new equipment is acquired. *Other advantages of high-level languages are:* (1) They are easier to learn than assembly languages, (2) they require less time to write, (3) they provide better documentation, and (4) they are easier to maintain. Also, a programmer skilled in writing programs in such a language is not restricted to using a single machine.

Naturally, a source program written in a high-level language must also be translated into a machine-usable code. A translating program that can perform this operation is called a *compiler*. Compilers, like advanced assembly programs, may generate many lines of machine code for each source program statement.[19] A *compiling run* is required before problem data can be processed. With the exception that a compiler program is substituted for an assembly program, the procedures are the same as those shown in Figure 7-13. The production run follows the compiling run. However, as we saw in Chapter 2, an alternative translating approach is often used with microcomputers. The source program is loaded into the micro along with the data to be processed. A language *interpreter* in-side the machine then converts each source program statement into ma-chine-language form as it is needed during the processing of the data. The object code is not saved for future use.

Popular high-level languages   The initial work on high-level languages was undertaken in the early 1950s by a number of individuals. UNIVAC's Dr. Grace M. Hopper, for example, developed a compiler (named A-2) in 1952. Since that time, many other high-level languages have been pro-duced, generally by equipment manufacturers and/or committees of in-terested parties. A few of the most popular high-level languages are dis-cussed below.

● **FORTRAN**   In 1954, an IBM-sponsored committee headed by John Backus began work on a scientific-mathematic language. The result of this effort was FORTRAN (FORmula TRANslator), which was intro-duced in 1957. It has been estimated that the cost to produce the 25,000 lines of detailed machine instructions that went into the first FORTRAN compiler was $2.5 million. Since its introduction, FORTRAN

---

[19] Some use the word *statement* to refer to a line of code in a high-level language and the word *instruction* to refer to a line of machine or assembly-language code that will produce a single machine operation.

has been widely accepted and has been revised a number of times. The overwhelming majority of *all* computers now in use have FORTRAN capability. Because of this widespread acceptance, a FORTRAN standard language has been approved by the American National Standards Institute (ANSI).

- **COBOL** The COBOL (COmmon Business Oriented Language) language, written by a committee, was specifically designed for business-type data processing applications. The design group gathered at the Pentagon in Washington, D.C., in May 1959. Members of the COnference of DAta SYstems Languages (CODASYL) represented computer manufacturers, government agencies, user organizations, and universities. From June to December 1959, this committee worked on the language specifications. Their final report was approved in January 1960, and the language specifications were published a few months later by the Government Printing Office.

  Since 1961, COBOL compilers have been prepared for all but the smallest commercial processors. Other CODASYL committees have continued to maintain, revise, and extend the initial specifications. COBOL has been used extensively for the past few years. There is also a published ANSI COBOL standard.

- **PL/I** Developed in the mid-1960s by IBM and a committee of users for the IBM System/360 family of computers, PL/I (Programming Language I, where I stands for one) has been promoted as a universal language because it can be used to solve all types of business and scientific problems efficiently. As a scientific language, PL/I appears to be an extension of FORTRAN; however, COBOL-type data description is also used.

- **BASIC** BASIC (Beginner's All-purpose Symbolic Instruction Code) is a popular *timesharing* or *interactive* language that has wide appeal because of its ease of usage. A problem solver with little or no knowledge of computers or programming can learn to write BASIC programs at a remote terminal or microcomputer keyboard in a short period of time. (Because of its simplicity, BASIC is by far the most popular high-level language used in microcomputer systems. A number of recreational and educational programs are published in each issue of such magazines as *Creative Computing* and *Byte* that cater to individual users of microcomputers, and these programs are usually documented in BASIC.)

  BASIC was developed in 1963–1964 at Dartmouth College under the direction of Professors John Kemeny and Thomas Kurtz. The purpose of this effort was to produce a language that undergraduate students in all fields of study (1) would find easy to learn and (2) would thus be encouraged to use on a regular basis. BASIC was a success at Dartmouth on both counts. The Dartmouth timesharing sys-

249

SYSTEMS STUDIES,
PROGRAMMING
ANALYSIS, AND
PROGRAM
PREPARATION

tem was implemented on General Electric equipment with the assistance of GE engineers. Recognizing the advantages of BASIC, GE quickly made the language available for the use of commercial time-sharing customers. BASIC is now offered in some form by virtually every computer manufacturer and by almost every independent supplier of timesharing. Users of BASIC range from public school students to aerospace engineers. (After ·studying the next chapter, you may also be included in this group.)

- **ALGOL**   In 1957, a group of international mathematicians met to begin the design of a language suited to their needs. ALGOL (ALGOrithmic Language) was the eventual result of this effort. Like FORTRAN, ALGOL has been revised several times in the past few years. It is used extensively in Europe.

- **PASCAL**   Named in honor of Blaise Pascal and developed during the late 1960s and early 1970s by Professor Nicklaus Wirth at the Federal Institute of Technology in Zurich, Switzerland, Pascal is the first major language to be created since the concepts associated with a top-down and structured approach to the analysis and design of systems and programs became widely disseminated. Like PL/I, Pascal can be used for both scientific and file processing applications. A growing number of universities are using Pascal to teach programming to their computer science majors. The U.S. Department of Defense is currently sponsoring development of a new language[20] to be used by the military services in certain problem areas, and this language is based on Pascal.

- **OTHER LANGUAGES**   In addition to the above popular languages, a Report Program Generator (RPG) language is available for most small file processing computers. Other examples of compiler languages in general use are (1) GPSS (General Purpose Systems Simulator), (2) LISP (LISt Processor), (3) APL (A Programming Language), and (4) APT (Automatically Programmed Tooling).

Program Coding

Coding is the actual writing of the computer program of instructions. It follows the systems-design and programming analysis stages in the programming process. As you will see in the next chapter, the programmer must follow specific rules with respect to punctuation and statement structure. (It has been reported that a missing comma in a guidance program caused a space probe to veer so badly off course that it had to be destroyed by a signal from the ground control station.)

How about them Coders,
Ain't they grand?
Got they templates
In they hand.

Them deadline doggers
Bustin' they humps,
Slashin' them O's
And doggin' them dumps.
—William J. Wilton

---

[20] This language is named "Ada" in honor of Lord Byron's daughter, Ada Augusta, the Countess of Lovelace. Working with Charles Babbage on the "analytical engine," Ada may be considered the first computer programmer.

PROGRAM DEBUGGING AND TESTING

*A COBOL programmer
named Mays
Had careless programming
ways.
By a slip of the hand he
wrote an "or" for an
"and."
Now his program has run
for 3 days!*
—W. I. Jordan

Clerical mistakes and errors caused by faulty logic are inelegantly referred to as *bugs*. Eliminating these mistakes and errors that prevent the program from running and producing correct results is appropriately called *debugging*.

Debugging

There are days when things never seem to go quite right. Such days may be more common for programmers than for other mortals because program bugs (or "glitches") just seem to occur even under the best of circumstances and even when matters are not being helped along by our natural human tendency to screw things up. It is unusual for complex programs to run to completion in the first attempt. In fact, the time spent in debugging and testing often equals or exceeds the time spent in program coding.[21] Failure to provide for a possible program path, or branch, keying errors, mistakes in coding punctuation, transposed characters— these are but a few of the bugs that can thwart the programmer.

To reduce the number of clerical and logical errors, the programmer should carefully check the coding for accuracy prior to its entry into the computer. This *desk-checking* process should include an examination of program logic and program completeness; furthermore, typical input data should be manually traced through the program processing paths to identify possible errors. In short, the programmer attempts to play the role of the computer.

After programs have been desk-checked for accuracy, an attempt is made to convert the source program into object-program form. Compiler programs and interpreters contain error diagnostic features, which detect (and print messages about) mistakes caused by the incorrect application of the language used to prepare the source program (e.g., undefined symbols). These detected *syntax errors,* of course, must be remedied, but diagnostic checks will *not* detect the presence of logical errors in the program. Thus, an uninterrupted pass of the program through the compiler or interpreter *does not* mean that the program is perfected or that all bugs have been eliminated. It usually does mean, however, that the program is ready for testing.

Testing

*All real programs contain
errors until proved otherwise—which is impossible.*
—Tom Gilb

A program to be tested has generally demonstrated that it will run and produce results. The purpose of *testing* is to determine whether the re-

---

[21] See Frederick P. Brooks, Jr., "The Mythical Man-Month," *Datamation,* pp. 45–52. December 1974. Professor Brooks estimates that *half* the total time of a programming project is likely to be spent in debugging and testing.

251

SYSTEMS STUDIES,
PROGRAMMING
ANALYSIS, AND
PROGRAM
PREPARATION

sults are correct. The testing procedure involves using the program to process input test data that will produce known results. The items developed for testing should include (1) typical data, which will test the generally used program paths, (2) unusual but valid data, which will test the program paths used to handle exceptions, and (3) incorrect, incomplete, or inappropriate data, which will test the program error-handling capabilities. If the program passes the test, the programmer may release it for implementation;[22] if it does not, the programmer may do the following:

1   Trace through the program, a step at a time, at the computer console. Errors may be discovered by noting register contents after each program operation. Such an approach may be permissible, but it is hardly appropriate to tie up an expensive large computer for such purposes.
2   Call for a *trace program* run. The trace program prints out the status of registers after each operation and thus is comparable to console checking. However, less machine time is required.
3   Call for a *storage dump* when the program "hangs up" during a test run, i.e., obtain a printout of the contents of primary storage and registers at the time of the hang-up. The programmer can then study this listing for possible clues to the cause of the programming error(s).

After the program appears to be running properly and producing correct results, there is frequently a transitionary cutover period during which the job application is processed both by the old method and the new program. The purpose of this period, of course, is to verify processing accuracy and completeness.

PROGRAM DOCUMENTATION AND MAINTENANCE

Documentation, as we have seen, is the process of collecting, organizing, storing, and otherwise maintaining on paper (or on some relatively permanent medium) a complete record of *why* applications were developed, *what* functions they perform, *how* these functions are carried out, *who* the applications are to serve, and *how* they are to be used.

The documentation package for a program used in an organization should include:

1   *A definition of the problem.* Why was the program prepared? What

Consider that two wrongs never make a right but that three do. Whenever possible, put people on hold. Be comforted that in the face of all the aridity and disillusionment and despite the changing fortunes of time, there is always a big fortune in computer maintenance
—Anonymous in De-teriorata

---

[22] It should be noted here, however, that bugs may still remain undetected. In complex programs there may be tens of thousands of different possible paths through the program. It simply is not practical (and maybe not even possible) to trace through all the different paths during testing. This explains why nonsense may suddenly be produced by programs months after they have been released for production use. Some unique and unanticipated series of events has produced input or circumstances that turn up a bug for the first time. The error was always there; it simply remained undetected. Very complex systems are considered to be *undebuggable* by professional programmers.

FIGURE 7-14
Howard H. Aiken.

GRADUATE STUDENT'S DREAM COMES TRUE

In 1937, while a graduate student at Harvard University, Howard H. Aiken proposed that a new kind of calculating machine be built. With the support of IBM, the "automatic sequence controlled calculator" was completed in 1944. This calculator, the Mark I, became the focus of the Harvard Computation Laboratory.

Aiken's dream of a machine that could do tedious, time-consuming computations had come true. With Aiken's encouragement, people in such fields as economics, physics, insurance, and linguistics also used the Mark I to perform their calculations.

were the objectives? Who requested the program and who approved it? Questions such as these should be answered.

2 *A description of the system.* The system or subsystem environment in which the program functions should be described (systems flowcharts should be included). Broad systems specifications outlining the scope of the problem, the form and type of input data to be used, and the form and type of output required should be clearly stated.

3 *A description of the program.* Program flowcharts, program listings, test decks and test results, storage dumps, trace program printouts— these and other documents that describe the program and give a historical record of difficulties and/or changes should be available.

4 *A recitation of operator instructions.* Among the items covered should be computer switch settings, loading and unloading procedures, and starting, running, and terminating procedures.

5 *A description of program controls.* Controls may be incorporated in a program in a number of ways. For example, programmed controls may be used to check on the reasonableness and propriety of input data. A description of such controls should be a part of the documentation.

Production-run programs are continually being maintained, modified, and improved. Program maintenance is an important duty of programmers and may involve all steps from problem definition through analysis, design, and program preparation. It is not unusual to find programmers spending the bulk of their time on this activity. In some installations there are programmers who do nothing but maintain production programs.[23]

---

[23] When an organization first acquires a computer (and usually for several years thereafter), much of the programming effort goes into the development of new applications and systems. But as the number of installed programs and systems in the organization grows, it is not unusual to find that more programming time is being spent on maintenance than on development work. It has been estimated that over the life cycle of a typical system, the maintenance and enhancement costs that are incurred may be 2 to 4 times larger than the initial development costs.

253

SYSTEMS STUDIES,
PROGRAMMING
ANALYSIS, AND
PROGRAM
PREPARATION

"Information Revolution Studied"

The Information Revolution of the mid-1980's changed the course of history. Only now, in 1990, can we fully comprehend its significance.

The emergence of microelectronics in the 1970's set the stage for the massive advance of electronic communications and processing resources. Through superscale computers, microelectronics created a host of new scientific and analytical applications.

The table shown here indicates the winners and losers of the Information Revolution. The mail service, teachers, secretaries, clerks, auditors, salesmen, and local retailers are among those occupations now performed by computers. Technical and analytical specialists, writers, artists, producers, directors, large financial institutions, and large retailers have become the pieces of our intricate information network.

The Information Revolution has made our world smaller, has coordinated our efforts. History can now record the cooperation of a smoothly running system.

Source: *Creative Computing,* p. 145, November 1979. Used by permission of *Creative Computing,* P.O. Box 789-M, Morristown, N.J. 07960.

**EXHIBIT
Winners and losers in the
information revolution**

Winners	Reasons
Financial institutions	More fee-based consumer and business services
Programming industry	Proliferation of new packaged programs
Larger universities	Programmed education opportunities
Insurance industry	Lower life, health, and property claims costs
Electronics industry	Greatly expanded markets
Communications utilities	Greater dependence on telecommunications
Computer services	Extensions into the home
Larger retailers	Leverage through electronic promotion techniques
Utilities	Better control over demand
Advertising agencies	More value-added services
Federal public administration	More direct reach to public, more interstate activities
Smaller creative entertainers	Released from domination by large TV networks
Smaller specialty retailers	Bigger reach at a lower cost

(Continued)

(*Continued*)

Losers	Reasons
Airlines	Less business travel
Petroleum companies	Less commuting and shopping travel
TV networks	Other packaged programming sources
Paper	Office use displaced by electronic communications
Postal Service	Siphoned away by EFT and electronic mail
Commercial construction	Lower demand for centralized facilities
Publishing	Competition from electronic sources
Smaller, general-purpose retailers	Competition with in-home shopping
Transportation manufacturers	Fewer commuting vehicles
State and local public administration	Proximity to "markets" less important
Wholesalers	Bypassed by direct communications systems
Credit agencies	Competition from large financial institutions
Bigger cities	Less commercial and commuter tax revenue
Gambling resorts	In-home alternatives

▶ LOOKING BACK

The following points have been emphasized in this chapter:

1   The seven steps that are followed in order to put computers to work to solve problems have been identified and discussed. The first three steps (defining the problem, analyzing the problem, and preparing designs and specifications to solve the problem) are included in the systems-analysis and design phase. The final four steps (programming analysis, program preparation, program debugging and testing, and program documentation and maintenance) are included in the programming phase.

2   A systems-study approach is followed during the systems-analysis and design phase. The steps in the systems-study approach are to (*a*) identify the scope of the problem and the objectives to be gained, (*b*) gather the facts on current operations, (*c*) analyze current operations and determine suitable solutions, (*d*) decide on the most appropriate solution, (*e*) implement the solution, and (*f*) follow up on the decisions made.

3   In complex systems, a "divide and conquer" top-down analysis and design methodology may also be a helpful tool. Such an approach

255

SYSTEMS STUDIES,
PROGRAMMING
ANALYSIS, AND
PROGRAM
PREPARATION

permits top-level system functions to be broken down into a hierarchy of more understandable subfunctions. Programs may then be structured in such a way that there is a main-control module that specifies the order in which subordinate program modules will be used.

4 Once broad system specifications have been determined, the programming process may begin. The first step in programming is to analyze the specifications and break them down into the specific arithmetic and logic operations that will be needed by the computer in order to process the application(s).

5 A basic tool of both systems analysis and programming analysis is the flowchart. System flowcharts provide the broad overview required for programming analysis to begin. Program flowcharts evolve from the system charts. When compared with pages of written notes, flowcharts help the programmer obtain a quicker grasp of relationships. Charts also aid in communication, provide valuable documentation support, and contribute to more efficient coding and program maintenance. Alternatives to the use of program flowcharts are decision tables and pseudocode.

6 Six example problems were discussed and analyzed in this chapter. Using the specifications outlined for each of the problems, six program flowcharts were prepared. Solutions for each of these problems will be coded in the BASIC language in the next chapter.

7 A brief overview has been presented in this chapter of (a) the types of program instructions used by all computers, and (b) the categories of programming languages (from machine to high-level) that have been developed. The history and use of popular high-level languages such as FORTRAN, COBOL, and BASIC have been discussed.

8 A program must be debugged as much as possible and tested before it can be used. These activities often take as much time as is required to perform the initial coding; sometimes they can take much longer. A program cannot be considered completed until the documentation package is put in good order. Maintenance of production-run programs is an important part of the programming job.

▶ KEY TERMS

After reading Chapter 7, you should be able to define and use the following terms:

systems analysis and design
programming
system flowchart
top-down analysis and design
  methodology
modular programming

machine language
symbolic language
high-level language
FORTRAN
COBOL
BASIC

structured programming
program flowchart
program flowchart symbols
sentinel value
counter
accumulator
operation code
operand

PL/I
Pascal
debugging
program testing
program documentation
program maintenance

▶ REVIEW AND DISCUSSION QUESTIONS

1 Identify and discuss the steps that are followed to put computers to work in organizations.

2 (a) What is a systems study? (b) Identify and explain the steps in the systems-study approach.

3 What are the prerequisite principles that should be observed in making a systems study?

4 (a) What is a systems flowchart? (b) How is it used?

5 (a) What symbols are used in systems flowcharts to represent input and output? (b) To represent a manual operation?

6 "If the system being analyzed is relatively complex, a 'divide and conquer' approach is often used." Discuss this statement.

7 What is the modular programming approach?

8 (a) What is the purpose of a program flowchart? (b) How does it differ from a system flowchart?

9 "A loop consists of a body, a test for exit condition, and a return provision." Discuss this statement.

10 (a) What is a sentinel value? (b) What is the 9s decision technique?

11 (a) Explain how a counter may be used to record the number of times a loop has been executed. (b) Explain how an accumulator may be used to compute a running total.

12 Discuss the benefits and limitations of flowcharts.

13 Why is proper documentation required?

14 What types of instructions are found in a computer's instruction set?

15 What are the differences among machine, symbolic, and high-level languages?

16 (a) What is a source program? (b) What is an object program? (c) What is an interpreter? (d) What is a compiler?

17 (a) What is FORTRAN? (b) For what types of problems was FORTRAN designed?

18 (a) What is COBOL? (b) How did it originate? (c) For what purposes was COBOL designed?

19 (a) What is BASIC? (b) Where did it originate? (c) For what purpose was BASIC designed?

257

SYSTEMS STUDIES,
PROGRAMMING
ANALYSIS, AND
PROGRAM
PREPARATION

20 What steps can be taken during debugging and testing to locate and remove program errors?

21 What information should be included in a program documentation package?

22 After reviewing the program flowchart in Figure 7-5, how could you modify it so that Rod Thudfoot would be able to interact with the program and supply the input data at the time of processing?

23 How could Figure 7-9 be changed to permit the program to process any number of cars? (*Hint:* See Figure 7-8 for ideas.)

24 Let's assume that although the speedometer in Rod's Firebelch V/6 is calibrated in miles per hour (mph), he would like to be able to convert mph speed readings into kilometers per hour (kph). There are 1.609 kilometers in a mile. Prepare a flowchart of a program that will interact with Rod to accept a single input in mph and produce an output message giving the corresponding kph speed.

25 Now let's assume that Maude Crabbie, the teacher at Cass T. Gate Elementary School, has found a student guilty of the horrendous crime of chewing gum in class! The punishment is to write "I will not chew gum in class" 10 times. Prepare a flowchart for a program that will (a) accept any "naughty student" message, and (b) reproduce this message any designated number of times.

26 Finally, let's assume that you need to prepare a program that will compute the number of acres in any number of rectangular lots. The program should interact with the user and request the length (in feet) and width (in feet) of each lot prior to computing its acreage and printing out the result. There are 43,560 square feet in an acre. After computing the acreage in a first lot, the program should then determine from the user whether there are any additional lots to process. When the processing is completed, the program should print a "good-bye" message.

▶ SELECTED REFERENCES

Bohl, Marilyn: *Flowcharting Techniques,* Science Research Associates, Inc., Chicago, 1971.
Chapin, Ned: *Flowcharts,* Petrocelli Books, New York, 1971.
Myers, Ware: "The Need for Software Engineering," *Computer,* pp. 12–24, February 1978.
Sanders, Donald H.: *Computers in Business,* 4th ed., McGraw-Hill Book Company, New York, 1979, pp. 204–326. (A large number of additional references are cited in this source.)

Chapter 8
PROGRAMMING WITH BASIC

The purpose of this chapter is to introduce you to BASIC—a very popular programming language that makes it relatively easy for timesharing users and microcomputer owners to interact with their machines.

In the first section of the chapter, the BASIC programming environment is discussed. The typical equipment used, the "sign-on" procedures that may be needed, and the difference between system commands and BASIC program statements are considered in this section. Additional BASIC language necessities such as (1) the need for line numbers, (2) the types of BASIC statements available, (3) the identification of constant and variable values, (4) the handling of arithmetic operations, and (5) the procedures used to correct program errors are treated in the second section of the chapter.

Example programs to accomplish simple input, processing, and output are presented in the third section. The problems that were analyzed and flowcharted in the last chapter provide the examples for this section and later sections. In this section, the first program computes Rod Thudfoot's gas mileage for a single trip. The form and usage of such BASIC statements as REM, READ . . . DATA, LET, PRINT, and END are introduced in this program. An alternative to the first program is also presented, showing how the BASIC user can interact with the computer through the use of INPUT statements.

The example programs in the next section show some of the provisions for handling the decisions and loops that are available in the BASIC language. The first program in this section interacts with Rod to compute his gas mileage for any number of trips and adds the IF . . . THEN and GO TO statements to your BASIC vocabulary. The second program uses multiple decisions to compute the tax on Rod's Firebelch based on its EPA mileage rating, and it introduces you to the TAB function in the PRINT statement. The third program converts the yards of carpet found in multiple orders into the corresponding length in feet and inches. This program adds the PRINT USING and STOP statements to your BASIC repertoire, and it shows you how to use a sentinel value to control the looping in a program.

In the next section, two example programs are presented to show the use of counters and accumulators. The first of these is Karl Tell's pay authorization program. A counter is set up to record (and thus control) the number of times a loop has been executed, and an accumulator is used to keep a running total of the amount paid to Karl's graduate assistants. The second program shows how setting up and controlling loops can be simplified in BASIC through the use of the automatic counter provision included in FOR . . . NEXT statements.

Finally, the INT and RND functions are introduced in Maude Crabbie's computer-assisted instruction program in the last section.

Thus, after studying this chapter, you should be able to:

- Distinguish between system commands and BASIC program statements.
- Identify and discuss the general elements found in a BASIC statement.
- Understand and use the types of BASIC statements identified above to prepare programs in the BASIC language.
- Identify constant and variable values and understand how arithmetic operations are treated by the computer.
- Write programs that may incorporate input, processing, decisions, loops, counters, accumulators, and output to achieve specified goals.
- Understand and use the key terms listed at the end of the chapter.

In the early 1960s, the use of computers was generally restricted to groups of people in larger organizations with specialized tasks to perform, e.g., an accounting department with a payroll to prepare or an aeronautical engineering unit with an aircraft design to analyze. Computing hardware was expensive; the languages and operating-system programs of the time often seemed geared to satisfying the needs of machines rather than the needs of people; and individuals who could have benefited from computer usage were often denied access to the machines. As time passed, however, the access problem was relieved through the use of timesharing. In the mid-1960s, as we have seen, Dartmouth Professors Kemeny and Kurtz were motivated to create a programming language that would make it easy for people at timesharing terminals to *interact* with computers.

It didn't take long for this language (BASIC) to become very popular. Hundreds of thousands of students and customers of timesharing vendors have quickly learned to use BASIC in the years since its introduction, and BASIC is now the primary language used by the hundreds of thousands of individuals who own personal microcomputers. Since its inception, BASIC has been improved and its scope has been extended. Unfortunately, however, there are many different versions or dialects in existence at this time. This means that a BASIC program prepared for use on one manufacturer's equipment may not run without modification on another system.[1] In the pages that follow, we will discuss certain BASIC

---

[1] Efforts by the American National Standards Institute to develop a standard version of the language will probably reduce this problem in the future.

FIGURE 8-1
The timesharing computer system in the background can support 32 of the user terminal stations shown in the foreground. BASIC is commonly used for such interactive computing. (*Data General Corp.*)

program statements that permit the computer to perform such activities as input, data movement, output, etc. The use of these statements in the example programs found in the chapter follow the rules of most versions of BASIC. Because only the most commonly used types of statements are discussed, any differences that may exist between the BASIC version that your computer system uses and the version used in this chapter should be relatively easy to resolve.

THE BASIC PROGRAMMING ENVIRONMENT

The Equipment

Since BASIC is a language that is meant to be used for interactive computing, the user typically writes programs and enters some or all of the necessary data[2] from the keyboard of a timesharing terminal or a personal computer system (Figure 8-1). The *output* information used by humans is usually obtained from a visual display or character printer. Output may

---

[2] As you have seen in earlier chapters, data may also be entered through paper tape readers, magnetic tape cassette units, and floppy-disk drives that are attached to terminals.

also be punched into paper tape or recorded on magnetic tapes or disks through the use of appropriate terminal/system attachments.

Sign-On Procedures

Let's assume that you glanced ahead in this chapter to get an idea of what is involved in preparing a BASIC program. Since we are supposing, let's also assume that at the first opportunity you then rushed to an available keyboard to try your hand at writing a program. Alas, banging on the keyboard produced no results—you neglected to turn the computer on, or you were unable to follow the proper sign-on (or "log-on") procedure required to get access to the CPU from your terminal.

When a *personal computing environment* is used to prepare BASIC programs, the sign-on "procedure" may simply consist of turning on the power (the BASIC interpreter may be stored in ROM chips inside the CPU and may be instantly ready for use). When a *timesharing environment* is used, the terminal must be turned on first. A procedure is then required to establish communication between the terminal and the central processor. This procedure may involve typing specified words—e.g., HELLO or LOGIN—and/or pressing specified keys on the terminal; it may also involve dialing a number on a phone next to the terminal. Once such communication is established, the computer may automatically send a sign-on request to the terminal in the form of a message or special character. The user must then follow a prescribed sign-on procedure that typically involves supplying one or more of the following: an account or project number, a user name or identification number, and/or a password. After this information has been supplied, some systems that support multiple languages also require that the user indicate the programming language that will be used. Thus, it may also be necessary to type BASIC so that the computer can call up the BASIC translating software.[3]

Since there is obviously no standard sign-on procedure, we will not discuss this matter further. The procedures for signing on the particular system you will be using are easy to learn and are available from local sources.

System Commands and Program Statements

System commands and program statements are both found in a BASIC programming environment, and both make use of certain designated

---

[3] To illustrate the above comments, in several Digital Equipment Corporation PDP-11 systems, the sign-on procedure is to turn on the terminal and type HELLO. The computer responds with an information line and then prints #. The user types in a project number and programmer number, and the computer responds with PASSWORD. After the password is supplied, the system is ready. In a Hewlett-Packard 3000 system, the terminal is turned on, and the user presses the RETURN key and types HELLO followed by an identification number. The computer responds with an information line and then types the colon character (:). The user then types BASIC, and when the system replies with the > character, the system is in BASIC and ready to be used.

words. Let's make sure we know the difference between these two categories. We have seen that some computer systems may require the user to type key words like HELLO or LOGIN as a part of the sign-on procedure. Such words are referred to as *system commands;* they are entered by the user into the system, and they direct the computer to take immediate action to accomplish a specific task. A number of system commands are found in every BASIC programming environment, but the words vary with the system being used. Some typical system commands found in most environments are RUN (to execute the user's program of current interest), LIST (to list the contents of a current program), SAVE (to store a current program—which must be given a name—in online secondary storage for later access), and BYE (to sign off the system). As with sign-on procedures, the system commands for the particular equipment you will be using are available from local sources.

Designated words such as READ, INPUT, PRINT, LET, and END are also found in the sequence of numbered individual instructions or *program statements* that make up a BASIC program. The meanings and uses of these key words will be discussed later in the chapter.

You have seen that when a system command is entered, it causes the computer to take *immediate action.* When a program statement is initially keyed in, however, the computer may take *no apparent action* at all. (Of course, the machine is probably checking the statement for syntax errors and storing it with other statements, but the program instruction in the statement is not immediately executed at the time of entry.) Rather, the individual statements are stored until a complete program is formed and until the user turns the control of the computer over to the program through the use of a RUN system command. The statements are then executed to process the input data and produce the desired output results.

SOME BASIC NECESSITIES

We are about ready to write the programs needed to solve the problems discussed (and flowcharted) in the last chapter. Only a few *program entry, arithmetic operation,* and *error-correcting* necessities stand in our way.

Program Entry Elements

We have seen that key words are used in constructing statements, and statements are then put together to form a BASIC program. A BASIC statement may take the following form:

line number	type of statement	value(s)

Let's look at each of these statement elements.

"Kemeny Tells Value of Computer"

Responding to the question, "Why, in these times of tight budgets, did the board of trustees allocate two million dollars for a new computer?" Darthmouth President John G. Kemeny noted, "the computer makes the student a little smarter, and the faculty and administration a great deal smarter."

Speaking before more than 200 women college administrators, faculty and staff who had gathered for a two-day conference on the use of computers in higher education, President Kemeny further cited the necessity of computer modelling for use in long-range planning: "The computer allows many people to interchange thoughts and ideas in long-range planning and to play the game of 'what if' with such things as rates of inflation, fuel prices and student body size in any and all combinations. The computer is the single most important element of long-range planning."

Source: *Creative Computing,* p. 148, May 1979. Used by permission of *Creative Computing,* P.O. Box 789-M, Morristown, N.J. 07960.

Line numbers   Each statement in a BASIC program begins with a *line number* (ln). Depending on the equipment used, the ln can be any integer beginning at 1 (and going to 4 or 5 digits) that *you* select. The *order* of these line numbers is used by the computer during the execution of the program. Beginning with the lowest ln, statements will be processed in ascending order until conditional or unconditional transfer statements are encountered that cause a change in the sequence. It is generally desirable to number your statements in increments of 5 or 10 so that you will later have room to include any additional instructions or modifications that may be needed without having to then renumber the lines that follow the insertion. For example, let's assume that you have written a BASIC program that looks like this:

```
10 LET A = 5
20 LET B = 8
30 LET C = A + B
40 END
```

This program will add the values of A and B, but since you have forgotten to tell the computer to print out the result of this tough computation, it will forever remain a mystery. To remedy this oversight, you would need only type the following statement at the bottom of the program:

```
35 PRINT C
```

The computer will then know that you want to print the value of C after line 30 has been executed. If you should later enter a system command to LIST the program, you will see that ln 35 has been correctly positioned between statements 30 and 40.

Types of BASIC statements   Every statement in BASIC has a *statement type,* and learning the language is mainly a matter of learning the rules that apply to these statement types. As you will recall from the last chapter, computer instructions are found in all languages to permit input, data movement and manipulation, processing, comparison and transfer of control, and output operations. In the simple program we have just encountered, the LET statement was used to initially *assign* values to storage locations labeled "A" and "B" in the computer. The LET statement was also used to look up the values of the contents of A and B, calculate the sum of those values, and assign the total to a storage location labeled "C" (30 LET C = A + B). Thus, the LET, or *assignment,* type of statement can be used to assign input values to locations, perform processing operations, and move processed results to other locations. The PRINT type of statement, of course, is used for *output.* An END statement is the highest-numbered statement in any program and simply indicates the completion of the program. In the pages that follow, we will examine a number of other types of BASIC statements.

Values in BASIC   BASIC deals with values that may be constants or variables. A *constant* is a value that is provided explicitly by the program and cannot be changed by the computer at any time during program execution. Valid *numeric constants* include such values as 55, − 16.5, 3.14159, and 1.09E + 8. The 55 could represent a constant rate of speed, that is, 55 miles per hour; the − 16.5 could represent the constant amount of dollars to be deducted from paychecks for a group insurance plan; and the 3.14159 could be the approximation of pi used in calculations. The E (exponential) notation used in the constant 1.09E + 8 is needed because there is only a limited amount of space available to store a value in the computer's memory. Thus, 1.09E + 8 can be used to represent 1.09×10^8 or 109000000. (Also, 1.26E − 6 can be used to represent 1.26×10^{-6} or .00000126.)[4] Valid constants may also include strings of alphanumeric characters. *Character string constants* may be any string of characters enclosed in quotation marks, e.g., "4009 SARITA DRIVE" or "ROD THUDFOOT."

Unlike a constant, a *variable* is a quantity that can be referred to by name and that can change values at different stages during the running of a program. Although it is true that the *location* in storage that holds the variable (and the *name* given by the programmer to that location) *does not change,* the *contents* of the storage location (like the contents of a post office box) may be altered many times during the program's pro-

---

[4] Don't worry too much about this E notation shorthand for expressing very large or very small quantities. It is mentioned here so that if you should receive some output in E notation form, you will understand what it means.

cessing of the available data. For example, you may recall from the last chapter that a counter could be used to record the number of times that a loop has been executed. To do this, a storage location with the *variable name* C could be established by the programmer and assigned an initial value of zero. An appropriate BASIC statement to do this is

$$10 \text{ LET } C = 0$$

where C names a variable. After each pass through the loop, the contents of the counter would change or be incremented by a value of 1. That is,

$$100 \text{ LET } C = C + 1$$

Obviously, in this BASIC statement the equals sign (=) does not mean the same as it does in algebra. Rather, the *numeric variable* value stored at the location identified by "C" is retrieved from storage, a value of 1 is added to it, and the new variable quantity replaces the previous contents in the location named "C." Thus, if a loop is executed 30 times, the value of C will change 30 times.

It will be up to you to name the variables that are needed in the programs you write. The rules in BASIC that govern the naming of variables are easily remembered, but they are much more restrictive than the rules that apply to other languages. (This is a shortcoming of BASIC.) For example, *a numeric variable is generally restricted to a name that consists of a single letter or a single letter followed by a single digit.* Thus, A, X, B1, and Z7 are all valid numeric variable names, but 7G, AB, RATE, and B24 are not.

In addition to numeric variables, there are also *string variables*—i.e., strings of alphanumeric and special characters—that can be referred to by name and that can change during the running of a program. For example, the contents of the storage space that contains an employee's name will change constantly during the processing of a payroll program. *In naming the string variable, you will probably be restricted to using a single letter followed by a dollar sign* ($).[5] Thus, E$, B$, and N$ are all valid, but AB$, $X, and XYZ$ are not.

Arithmetic Operations

You will be concerned with five arithmetic operations in writing BASIC programs: addition, subtraction, multiplication, division, and exponentiation (raising to a power). The symbols used to indicate these operations (and examples of their use) are shown in Table 8-1.[6]

---

[5] Some BASIC systems allow a string variable name to be any valid numeric variable name followed by a dollar sign. Thus, A1$, B$, and C2$ are valid examples in such systems.

[6] Note that in BASIC the multiplication symbol must be present, even though it can be omitted in algebra. Failure to use the asterisk is a common error, and the computer will probably send you an error message if you forget it.

TABLE 8-1
Arithmetic operations:
Symbols and examples in
the BASIC language

Operation	BASIC Symbol	BASIC Examples	Algebraic Equivalent
Addition	+	A + B 2 + 8	A + B 2 + 8
Subtraction	−	B − C 6 − 3	B − C 6 − 3
Multiplication	* (asterisk)	D * E 4 * F	DE or D(E) or D × E 4F or 4(F) or 4 × F
Division	/ (slash)	G/H 8/2	$G \div H$ or $\dfrac{G}{H}$ $8 \div 2$ or $\dfrac{8}{2}$
Exponentiation	$\wedge$ or ↑	J $\wedge$ 2 (or J ↑ 2) 3 $\wedge$ 3	J^2 3^3

Since a formula in a program may include several operations, you must understand the order in which the computer handles these operations so that you may avoid errors. What value will be assigned to A, for example, when the computer encounters this statement that you have written?

$$50 \text{ LET } A = 4 + 6 \wedge 2/10 - 2$$

If the computer simply started at the left and performed operations in sequence, the result would be 4 plus 6 (or 10), raised to the second power (giving 100), divided by 10 (10), minus 2, giving a value of 8 to assign to A. Actually, however, the computer follows a different set of rules in determining the order of operations. Moving from left to right in a formula *without parentheses:*

1 All exponentiation is performed first.
2 All multiplication and division operations are then completed.
3 Finally, all addition and subtraction takes place.

Following these priority rules, then, what value would the computer assign to A in our example? The *first* operation performed would be to square 6 (6 $\wedge$ 2), giving 36. *Next,* the value of 36 would be divided by 10, giving 3.6. Your formula now looks like this:

$$4 + 3.6 - 2$$

Finally, moving from left to right, 4 is added to 3.6, giving 7.6, and 2 is then subtracted to give the final value of 5.6 to assign to the variable name A.

If *parentheses are used,* the computations within the parentheses are handled first, using the above order rules. If several sets of parentheses are nested within one another, the operations in the innermost group are performed first. For example, suppose your assignment statement had looked like this:

$$50 \text{ LET } A = (8 + (6 * 4)/2)/2$$

The first part of the formula evaluated would be (6 * 4) in the innermost set of parentheses. The result would be

$$50 \text{ LET } A = (8 + 24/2)/2$$

Within the remaining set of parentheses, the division operation would be performed first, and the resulting value of 12 would then be added to 8. This total of 20 would then be divided by 2 to get a value of 10 to assign to A.

Correcting Errors

In entering your program statements at the keyboard, you will probably make errors that will have to be corrected. A very common error, of course, is to strike the wrong key or keys during program or data entry. If, as is often the case, you immediately detect your mistake, you need correct only one or two characters and then continue on with the line you are typing. For example, let's assume that the correct entry should be

$$50 \text{ LET } A = (4 * G)/2$$

but you type

$$50 \text{ LEG } A$$

and then catch your error. How can you "erase" the G and enter the T? Different BASIC systems use different approaches, but generally a special correction key (such as a RUBOUT, DELETE, or ← key) is used for this purpose. Each time you strike this *correction key* (CK), you erase one character in the typed line and move to its left. Thus, to change the G to a T, you would need to press the CK 3 times: once to erase A, once to erase the blank character, and once to erase the G. You could then enter the T and complete the line.

Suppose, however, you discover that you have typed

$$50 \text{ LTE } A = (4 * G)/2$$

before you press the RETURN key that will cause the computer to analyze the statement. In this case, you *could* backtrack with the correction key,

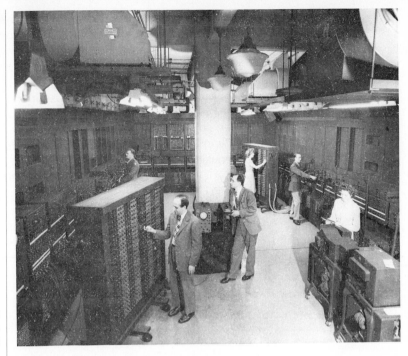

FIGURE 8-2
J. Presper Eckert (left) and John
W. Mauchly. (UPI.)

FROM BALLISTICS TO BUSINESS

The first electronic computer was developed for the military. The U.S. Army's Aberdeen Proving Ground needed a method to do ballistic calculations. J. Presper Eckert and John W. Mauchly proposed that the ENIAC be developed to calculate weapon-firing tables. Herman Goldstine, the Army liaison officer, supported their proposal. In February 1946, ENIAC was formally dedicated at the Moore School of Electrical Engineering at the University of Pennsylvania.

Eckert received a graduate fellowship at the Moore School after graduating from the University of Pennsylvania in 1941 as an electrical engineer. Mauchly received a Ph.D. degree in 1932 and taught physics at Ursinus College before joining Eckert at the Moore School. They formed the Eckert-Mauchly Computer Corporation in 1947 and completed the UNIVAC in 1951.

but it would probably be easier to delete the *entire line* and start over. The method to do this varies with the system being used, but on many systems the procedure is to hold down the CONTROL or CTRL key and then press either the U or the X key.

Finally, let's assume that you have typed

$$50 \text{ LTE A} = (4 + \text{G})/2$$

instead of

$$50 \text{ LET A} = (4 * \text{G})/2$$

and you *have pressed* the RETURN key. In this case, the computer will probably detect the *syntax error* in the spelling of LET, reject the statement, and send you an error message. You will then have to reenter the statement. If in retyping the statement you repeat the mistake of *adding* 4 to the quantity stored in G rather than *multiplying* these values, the computer will accept the statement because it contains no syntax errors, but, of course, a *logical error* still remains. To correct this statement that has now been stored in the computer, you need only reenter the same line number with the correct information, and this second entry will completely erase the previous contents of the line (a very nice feature). If you should want to delete from a program a line that has already been stored, you simply type the line number and then hit the RETURN key, and the previous entry will be deleted.

Now that you have a grasp of some of the details associated with program entry, arithmetic operation, and error correction, it is time to look at some example programs that illustrate the use of various types of BASIC statements.

PROGRAMS TO ACCOMPLISH SIMPLE INPUT, PROCESSING, AND OUTPUT

Several problems were analyzed and flowcharted in the last chapter. Let's now see how programs can be prepared in BASIC to solve these problems.

Thudfoot's Gas Mileage, Single Trip

The program to compute Rod Thudfoot's gas mileage for a single trip, along with the output produced by this program, is shown in Figure 8-3. (The flowchart for the program is shown in Figure 7-5, page 228.) Some general observations about Figure 8-3 are possible. You will notice, for example, that this program was written earlier and stored or saved under the arbitrary name of BASIC1A. In response to the LOAD and LIST commands used by Rod's system, the computer has printed a listing of the program. In response to the RUN command, the computer has executed the program to produce the output results shown.

Before we examine the program in Figure 8-3 in more detail, we should digress briefly for a few words about *programming style. Style* may be defined as the way in which something is said or done, as distinguished from its substance. An objective of this chapter is to present the programs in a style that will make them *easier to read and understand.* For this reason, you will see a lot of statements in this chapter that begin with REM—a BASIC abbreviation for REMark. A REMark statement is used for program documentation and is provided *solely* for the benefit of those who want to read and understand the program. (As far as the computer is

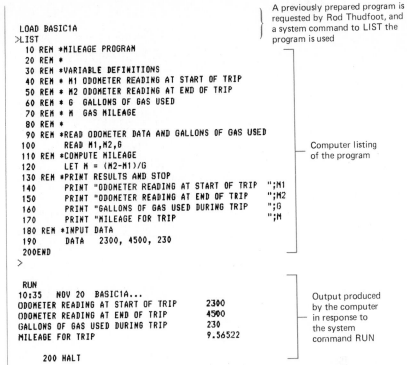

A previously prepared program is requested by Rod Thudfoot, and a system command to LIST the program is used

Computer listing of the program

Output produced by the computer in response to the system command RUN

```
LOAD BASIC1A
>LIST
  10 REM *MILEAGE PROGRAM
  20 REM *
  30 REM *VARIABLE DEFINITIONS
  40 REM * M1 ODOMETER READING AT START OF TRIP
  50 REM * M2 ODOMETER READING AT END OF TRIP
  60 REM * G  GALLONS OF GAS USED
  70 REM * M  GAS MILEAGE
  80 REM *
  90 REM *READ ODOMETER DATA AND GALLONS OF GAS USED
 100       READ M1,M2,G
 110 REM *COMPUTE MILEAGE
 120       LET M = (M2-M1)/G
 130 REM *PRINT RESULTS AND STOP
 140       PRINT "ODOMETER READING AT START OF TRIP   ";M1
 150       PRINT "ODOMETER READING AT END OF TRIP     ";M2
 160       PRINT "GALLONS OF GAS USED DURING TRIP     ";G
 170       PRINT "MILEAGE FOR TRIP                    ";M
 180 REM *INPUT DATA
 190       DATA   2300, 4500, 230
 200 END
>
```

```
RUN
10:35   NOV 20  BASIC1A...
ODOMETER READING AT START OF TRIP       2300
ODOMETER READING AT END OF TRIP         4500
GALLONS OF GAS USED DURING TRIP         230
MILEAGE FOR TRIP                        9.56522

    200 HALT
```

FIGURE 8-3
Program for Thudfoot's gas mileage, single trip.

concerned, as soon as it encounters the letters REM, it ignores the rest of the statement and moves on to the next line number!) Every program in this chapter uses REM statements to (1) identify the program, (2) define the variable names used in the program, (3) place explanatory headings throughout the body of the program, and (4) add spacing within the program to aid readability. Indentation of statements is also used to aid readability. Of course, the disadvantages of these stylistic features are that they add to program length, are harder to type, and take up more storage space. After all, 12 of the 20 lines in the program in Figure 8-3 are "unnecessary" REM statements. Usually, however, the merits of REM documentation will outweigh their inconvenience in the programs you write.

The first nine lines in Figure 8-3 are self-explanatory REMark statements: The program is identified, variable names used in the program are defined, and a heading explains the purpose of line number (ln) 100. The statement in ln 100 is an input READ statement that *must be combined* with a DATA statement. The general form of these statements is

ln READ   list of variable names   ln DATA   list of data values

where the values to be assigned to the variable names identified in a READ statement are found in a DATA statement. Thus, when the computer encounters it looks for a DATA statement (which it finds at ln 190) and reads the first three data values it finds. In other words, it "uses up" the data by assigning them to the variable names, as follows:

$$100 \quad \text{READ} \quad M1, \quad M2, \quad G$$
$$190 \quad \text{DATA} \quad 2300, \quad 4500, \quad 230$$

If the program had been written to process multiple trips, it would be necessary to READ values for M1, M2, and G *for each trip.* By employing a loop, Rod Thudfoot could have the program execute the READ statement in ln 100 any desired number of times. Of course, all the appropriate data for each trip would then have to be supplied by one or more DATA statements. Suppose, for example, that three trips were to be processed. The necessary DATA statements might look like this:

190 DATA 2300, 4500, 230, 4700, 5700, 98
200 DATA 6150, 6900, 81

As we have seen, the first three values would be used in processing the first trip, the next three values would be used the next time the READ statement is executed, and the last three values would be "used up" in the third execution.

The data may be distributed over many DATA statements, or they may be compressed into as few as careful typing will permit.[7] However, the data must always be typed in the DATA statement(s) in the *order indicated by the READ statement.* Although DATA statements may be typed anywhere in a program except after the END statement, it is common practice to locate them near the end of a program, as shown in Figure 8-3.

Once the *data-input* operation has been accomplished, the next step in the program is to compute Rod's gas mileage for the trip. This *processing* is carried out by using the LET statement in ln 120. The miles driven on the trip (M2−M1) are divided by the gas used (G) to get the mileage for the trip in miles per gallon. This gas mileage figure is assigned the variable name M.

The *output* of the program consists of four printed lines (ln 140 through ln 170). PRINT statements are used to display program results. The PRINT statement in ln 140, for example, causes the computer to produce the first output line shown in Figure 8-3. Characters (including

---

[7] The computer doesn't care because before it executes the program it will arrange in order, in a single long list, all the values contained in all the DATA statements. A *pointer* is set internally in the system at the *first* value in the list, and, as we have seen, the first variable name encountered in a READ statement during program execution is assigned the value indicated by the pointer. The pointer then shifts to the next value, which will be "used up" by the next variable name encountered in a READ statement. And so it goes throughout the entire data list.

blank spaces) that are bounded by quotation marks in a PRINT statement will be printed exactly as they appear in the statement when the program is executed. Thus, the messages enclosed in quotes in line numbers 140 through 170 are reproduced in the output. You will notice, however, that the M1, M2, G, and M variable names shown in ln 140 through ln 170 are *not* printed in the output. Rather, the *contents* of the storage locations given these names are printed. We can see, for example, that Rod's Fire-belch got less than 10 miles per gallon on his trip. (Rod's gas bills are eating his lunch!)

The *semicolons* used in these PRINT statements cause items to be printed very close together, although a space may be automatically placed before and after a variable quantity. *Commas* in PRINT statements also serve a specific function. A statement that reads

015 PRINT A, B, C, D, E,

would cause the values of the five variable names to be printed across the page, with A beginning at the left margin, B beginning (perhaps) 14 spaces to the right, C beginning 28 spaces to the right, etc. The width of many terminal printers is 72 characters, and the use of commas in the PRINT statement *automatically* establishes a format of five columns or zones.[8]

Finally, a PRINT statement may be used to produce *vertical spacing* in the output. If, for example, you write the following statement:

25 PRINT

the computer will follow your wishes—it will fill a line with blank spaces and advance the output page to the next line. Any number of empty PRINT statements can thus be used to control output line spacing.

The last program statement in Figure 8-3 is the END statement. It is always the last statement in any BASIC program,[9] and it includes only a line number.

An Alternative Program for Thudfoot's Gas Mileage, Single Trip

Let's assume (have you noticed that we do an awful lot of assuming in this book?) that instead of using READ . . . DATA statements, Rod would rather *interact* with the computer and give the necessary input data in the form of responses to questions and messages supplied by the program.

---

[8] The automatic spacing can vary from one system to another. This implicit format-specification feature of BASIC is especially appreciated by problem solvers who are not professional programmers. But specifying output format is also possible in BASIC as we will soon see.

[9] Some versions of BASIC do not *require* an END statement, but it is a good idea to use it since you might someday want to run your programs on other systems that do require its use.

The program in Figure 8-4 shows us how this might be done. The first nine line numbers in this program are about the same as those in Figure 8-3.

In the PRINT statement in ln 100, however, things start to change. As you know, the message enclosed in quotes in this PRINT statement will be produced as output. What is new here is that a semicolon is placed *at the end of a PRINT statement.* The effect of this placement is to suppress the automatic printer carriage return that usually takes place when the computer reaches the end of a PRINT statement. Thus, the printing (or display) mechanism does not return to the left margin.

Line number 110 is

110 INPUT M1

This is a new type of statement that causes the computer to (1) print a question mark (?) and (2) stop executing the program until the user supplies it with the necessary *input* data for the variable name(s) listed in the INPUT statement. (INPUT is always followed by one or more variable names separated by commas.) Therefore, the *first* result of ln 110 is to cause a ? to be printed. Since the carriage return of the printer was suppressed in the preceding statement, the ? is printed to the right of the message produced by ln 100, as shown in the output in Figure 8-4. The *second* result of the INPUT statement is to halt the program until Rod

```
>LOAD BASIC1B
>LIST
  10 REM *MILEAGE PROGRAM
  20 REM *
  30 REM *VARIABLE DEFINITIONS
  40 REM * M1 ODOMETER READING AT START OF TRIP
  50 REM * M2 ODOMETER READING AT END OF TRIP
  60 REM * G  GALLONS OF GAS USED
  70 REM * M  GAS MILEAGE
  80 REM *
  90 REM *INPUT ODOMETER READINGS AND GALLONS OF GAS USED
 100      PRINT "ODOMETER READING AT START OF TRIP";
 110      INPUT M1
 120      PRINT "ODOMETER READING AT END OF TRIP  ";
 130      INPUT M2
 140      PRINT "GALLONS OF GAS USED DURING TRIP  ";
 150      INPUT G
 160 REM *COMPUTE MILEAGE
 170      LET M = (M2-M1)/G
 180 REM *PRINT RESULTS AND STOP
 190      PRINT "MILEAGE FOR TRIP              ";M
 200 END
>
```

Computer listing of program

```
 RUN
 10:40    NOV 20   BASIC1B...
 ODOMETER READING AT START OF TRIP    ?2300
 ODOMETER READING AT END OF TRIP      ?4500
 GALLONS OF GAS USED DURING TRIP      ?230
 MILEAGE FOR TRIP                     9.56522

    200 HALT
```

Output produced by computer as the program is executed

FIGURE 8-4

An alternative program for Thudfoot's gas mileage, single trip.

types in his odometer reading at the start of the trip (2,300 miles) and presses the RETURN key on his terminal. In other words, the output was produced as follows:

ODOMETER READING AT START OF TRIP   ?   2300

Produced by the PRINT statement   Caused   Typed in
on ln 100   by INPUT   by user
                 statement
                 on ln 110

The purpose of the PRINT and INPUT statements in line numbers 120 through 150 should now be clear to you. These statements print messages requesting additional input data and then wait while Rod supplies it. Of course, a single PRINT message could have been printed telling Rod how to enter all the data at once, and this message could than have been followed by this single INPUT statement:

ln INPUT M1, M2, G

Rod would then have to enter all the data in the correct order.

The remainder of the program in Figure 8-4 is identical to steps performed in Figure 8-3. A *third way to enter the input data for this problem* would be as follows:

ln LET M1 = 2300
ln LET M2 = 4500
ln LET G = 230

The remainder of the program would then begin at ln 120 in Figure 8-3. (Of course, ln 180 and ln 190 would be deleted in Figure 8-3 in this case.)

DECISIONS AND LOOPS IN BASIC PROGRAMS

Thudfoot's Gas Mileage, Multiple Trips

If Rod Thudfoot makes *several* trips in a recent week and wants to compute his mileage for each trip, he can repeatedly rerun one of the programs presented in the preceding sections. This would be a tedious process, and Rod has therefore prepared the program shown in Figure 8-5 to handle the processing of multiple trips. (The flowchart for this program is shown in Figure 7-8, page 232.) Compared to our earlier programs, the program shown in Figure 8-5 is *more flexible* in that it uses decision and looping techniques to permit the processing of any number of trips. Let's examine this program to see how this flexibility may be achieved.

The REMark statements from ln 10 through ln 70 are similar to those in our earlier programs and need no explanation. In ln 80, however, a vari-

```
LOAD BASIC2
>LIST
  10 REM *MILEAGE PROGRAM
  20 REM *
  30 REM *VARIABLE DEFINITIONS
  40 REM * M1 ODOMETER READING AT START OF TRIP
  50 REM * M2 ODOMETER READING AT END OF TRIP
  60 REM * G  GAS USED DURING TRIP
  70 REM * M  MILEAGE FOR TRIP
  80 REM * A$ OPERATOR RESPONSE TO END OF DATA QUESTION
  90 REM *
 100 REM *ENTER ODOMETER READINGS AND GALLONS OF GAS USED
 110      PRINT "ODOMETER READING AT START OF TRIP";
 120      INPUT M1
 130      PRINT "ODOMETER READING AT END OF TRIP  ";
 140      INPUT M2
 150      PRINT "GALLONS OF GAS USED DURING TRIP  ";
 160      INPUT G
 170 REM *COMPUTE MILEAGE
 180      LET M = (M2-M1)/G
 190 REM *PRINT MILEAGE FOR TRIP
 200      PRINT "GAS MILEAGE FOR THIS TRIP        ";M
 210      PRINT
 220      PRINT
 230 REM *ENTER RESPONSE TO END OF DATA INQUIRY
 240      PRINT "ANOTHER TRIP (Y/N)";
 250      INPUT A$
 260 REM *TEST OPERATOR RESPONSE FOR END OF DATA
 270      IF A$="Y" THEN 110
 280      IF A$="N" THEN 310
 285      PRINT "TYPE A 'Y' OR AN 'N'"
 290      GO TO 240
 300 REM *PRINT SIGN OFF MESSAGE AND STOP
 310      PRINT "GOOD BYE"
 320 END
```

Computer listing of program

```
  RUN
 11:00   NOV 20  BASIC2...
 ODOMETER READING AT START OF TRIP   ?2300
 ODOMETER READING AT END OF TRIP     ?4500
 GALLONS OF GAS USED DURING TRIP     ?230
 GAS MILEAGE FOR THIS TRIP               9.56522


 ANOTHER TRIP (Y/N)  ?Y
 ODOMETER READING AT START OF TRIP   ?4700
 ODOMETER READING AT END OF TRIP     ?5700
 GALLONS OF GAS USED DURING TRIP     ?98
 GAS MILEAGE FOR THIS TRIP              10.2041


 ANOTHER TRIP (Y/N)  ?NO
 TYPE A 'Y' OR AN 'N'
 ANOTHER TRIP (Y/N)  ?N
 GOOD BYE

     320 HALT
```

Output produced by computer as the program is executed

FIGURE 8-5
Program for Thudfoot's gas mileage, multiple trips.

able name A$ is used to define the computer user's response later in the program to an "end of data" inquiry. As we saw earlier, a *string variable*— i.e., a variable consisting of one or more alphanumeric/special character(s)—is likely to be named with a single letter followed by a dollar sign. Thus, A$ is used in this program to name a string variable. Line numbers 100 through 200 produce the first four lines of output, and they have been discussed in connection with the preceding program in Figure 8-4. And lines 210 and 220 are examples of empty PRINT statements that cause the printer to skip two lines.

The decision technique that is used in this program to permit the user to loop back and process additional data begins on ln 240. You should now be able to explain what will happen when the computer executes ln 240. (If you just thought to yourself: "The message within the quotation marks is printed and the carriage return is suppressed," you are learning this language!) On ln 250, the INPUT statement will cause the computer to print a ?, and the user must then respond with a Y (for *Yes*) or N (for *No*) and then press the RETURN key.

The computer now *tests the user's response* to determine whether it should (1) loop back and process more input data, or (2) exit from the loop structure, print a sign-off message, and stop. On ln 270, we find a new statement type—the IF . . . THEN *conditional branching statement.* IF . . . THEN statements take the following form:

> ln IF (logical assertion) THEN ln

For example, in

> 120 IF A < 10 THEN 30

the computer is told that if the logical assertion[10] is *true*—i.e., if A *is* less than 10—program control is transferred to line number 30. If, however, the condition expressed in the assertion is not met, the program moves to the next statement in the sequence.

In the statement on ln 270,

> 270 IF A$ = "Y" THEN 110

the value assigned to the string variable name A$ is compared with the string constant "Y." If Rod has typed Y in response to ln 250, program control branches back to ln 110 and another iteration through the body of the loop begins. If, on the other hand, the user has typed N, A$ will not equal "Y" and program control will move to ln 280. Presumably, A$ will

---

[10] Other examples of logical assertions are:

$$A = B$$
$$B > C$$
$$D < = 0 \text{ (D is less than or equal to zero)}$$
$$M > = N \text{ (M is greater than or equal to N)}$$
$$S < > T \text{ (S is not equal to T)}$$
$$3 * Z > X/T$$

As you can see, a "logical assertion" consists of a first expression (a constant, a variable name, or a formula), a relational (=, >, <, or some combination of these), and a second expression.

```
LOAD BASIC3
>LIST
  10 REM *MILEAGE TAX PROGRAM
  20 REM *
  30 REM *VARIABLE DEFINITIONS
  40 REM * M EPA MILEAGE RATING
  50 REM * T MILEAGE TAX
  60 REM *
  70 REM *ENTER EPA MILEAGE RATING
  80     PRINT TAB(5);"EPA MILEAGE IS  ";
  90     INPUT M
 100 REM *COMPUTE TAX BASED ON EPA MILEAGE
 110     IF M<15 THEN 200
 120     IF M<20 THEN 180
 130     IF M<25 THEN 160
 140     LET T = 5
 150     GO TO 220
 160     LET T = 100
 170     GO TO 220
 180     LET T = 250
 190     GO TO 220
 200     LET T = 450
 210 REM *PRINT RESULTS AND STOP
 220     PRINT TAB(5);"MILEAGE TAX IS $";T
 230 END
>
```

Computer
listing of
program

```
RUN
11:10   NOV 20  BASIC3...
    EPA MILEAGE IS    ?10
    MILEAGE TAX IS $   450

    230 HALT
```

Output produced
by computer
as the program
is executed

FIGURE 8-6
Program for Thudfoot's
mileage tax.

equal "N," ln 280 will transfer program control to ln 310, the computer will print a "GOOD BYE" message, and the program will END. But what if A$ does not equal either "Y" or 'N"? What if Rod, thinking about his gas bills, types "STICK IT UP YOUR CHIP" in response to ln 250? In that case, ln 285 patiently prints instructions on how to respond to ln 250 and program control moves to ln 290.

On line number 290 we find another new BASIC statement type—the GO TO *unconditional branching statement*. There is nothing difficult about this one: It simply transfers program control to the line number specified in the statement. Thus,

$$290 \ GO \ TO \ 240$$

causes the program to branch back to ln 240 to give Rod a chance to cool off and enter his response in the correct way.

Thudfoot's Mileage Tax Program

As we saw in the last chapter, Rod's state imposed a one-time tax on new cars based on their overall EPA mileage ratings. The program shown in Figure 8-6 interacts with the user to produce the amount of tax due when the car's EPA mileage rating is supplied as input. (The flowchart for this program is given in Figure 7-9, page 234.) *Multiple* IF . . . THEN conditional branching statements are used to determine the amount of tax due.

Line numbers 10 through 70 require no explanation. However, the TAB function in the PRINT statement in ln 80 does require some comment. In ln 80,

80 PRINT TAB(5);"EPA MILEAGE IS ";

the TAB(5) part of the statement controls the *spacing on the print line* much as a tabulator setting controls the spacing on a typewriter. When the computer encounters this part of the statement, it knows that it is to move five spaces *from the left margin* and then begin printing the message enclosed in quotes.[11] The purpose of this message, of course, is to request an INPUT EPA mileage rating value from the user (ln 90).

You should now be able to trace through the statements in line numbers 110 through 200. (There are no new statement types in these lines.) The series of comparison decisions produces the logic necessary to produce the amount of tax due. If, as in Rod's case, the Firebelch has an EPA mileage rating that is less (much less) than 15 miles per gallon (mpg), program control branches from ln 110 to ln 200, and a mileage tax (T) of $450 is assigned by the LET statement. If a car had an EPA rating of at least 15 but less than 20 mpg, the condition in ln 120 would be true, control would pass to ln 180, and a tax of $250 would be assigned to T. You can also see how line numbers 130 and 160 assign a tax of $100 to cars with an EPA rating of at least 20 mpg but less than 25 mpg. Any car with a rating of 25 mpg or over (not < 25) is assigned a tax of $5 (ln 140). Finally, GO TO statements are used where appropriate to transfer control to ln 220 so that the amount of tax due can be printed. You can see from this example that a series of comparison decisions can be used in programs to produce the logic necessary to solve problems.

Thudfoot's Length Conversion Program

You may recall from the last chapter (and from the flowchart shown in Figure 7-10, page 235) that Rod's job at a carpet store requires him to convert yards of carpet into the corresponding lengths in feet and in inches. The program in Figure 8-7 accepts as input data the carpet lengths (in yards) of all customer orders to be filled during the day, and it then produces an output report that converts the yardage in each order into the same length in feet and in inches. At this point, you should under-

---

[11] In the following statement,

180 PRINT TAB(18);M;TAB(28);N

the value of the variable name M would be printed beginning 18 spaces from the left margin and the value of N would be printed starting at 28 spaces *from the left margin* (not from M).

```
LOAD BASIC12
>LIST
 10 REM *LENGTH CONVERSION PROGRAM
 20 REM *
 30 REM *THIS PROGRAM CONVERTS A GIVEN NUMBER OF YARDS INTO
 40 REM *FEET AND INCHES
 50 REM *
 60 REM *VARIABLE DEFINITIONS
 70 REM * Y LENGTH IN YARDS
 80 REM * F LENGTH IN FEET
 90 REM * I LENGTH IN INCHES
100 REM *
105 REM *PRINT HEADING
107      PRINT USING 210
110 REM *READ YARDS
120      READ Y
124 REM *TEST FOR END OF DATA
126      IF Y<0 THEN 190
130 REM *CONVERT YARDS TO FEET AND INCHES
140      LET F = Y*3
150      LET I = F*12
160 REM *PRINT YARDS,FEET,INCHES AND RETURN
170      PRINT USING 220, Y,F,I
180      GO TO 120
190      STOP
200 REM *FORMAT STATEMENTS
210:   YARDS           FEET           INCHES
220:#####.##        #####.##        #####.##
230 REM *INPUT DATA
240      DATA    3.00,    5.00    10.50    15.25
250      DATA  -99.99
260 END
```

Computer listing of the program

```
RUN
13:59   AUG 06   BASIC12...
   YARDS           FEET           INCHES
    3.00            9.00          108.00
    5.00           15.00          180.00
   10.50           31.50          378.00
   15.25           45.75          549.00

   190 HALT
```

Output produced by computer as program is executed

FIGURE 8-7
Program for Thudfoot's length conversion problem.

stand most of the statements in this program, but a few additional features of BASIC have been included.

You understand, of course, the REMark statements in ln 10 through ln 105. But what about the form of the PRINT statement in ln 107 that is used to print a heading line on the output report? The statement

$$107 \text{ PRINT USING } 210$$

is used to align the output of the computer according to a *specified format*.[12] In ln 107, the computer is instructed to PRINT the headings found in ln 210 in the exact format shown on this *image line*. An image line for a PRINT USING statement is identified by a colon immediately after the line

---

[12] Some dialects of BASIC don't have a PRINT USING statement, and the details of usage in those which do can vary. You should check the operating manual of your particular system for possible differences.

number. Thus, the output headings in Figure 8-7 are reproduced exactly as specified in ln 210. Another PRINT USING statement found in this program

170 PRINT USING 220, Y, F, I

uses the format specified in image line 220 to print the values located in the variable names Y, F, and I. In this dialect of BASIC, the # character is used to establish a *numeric* format, and the period indicates exactly where the decimal point will be printed. You can see the effect of using the format specified in ln 220 in the output report. The advantage of the PRINT USING statement is that it gives the programmer strict control over the output format.

Input data are entered in Rod's length conversion program by READ . . . DATA statements. The body of the loop required to process multiple orders in this program begins at the READ statement on ln 120. The purpose of this READ statement is to read the carpet length (in yards) of an order to be processed. In the first pass through the program, the first value (3.00) in the DATA statement (ln 240) is assigned to variable name Y. Since the yardage is certainly not less than zero (ln 126), the next program steps are to convert the length into feet (F in ln 140) and inches (I in ln 150). These figures are then printed (ln 170 and ln 220), and the program loops back (ln 180) to READ the yardage in the next order. This repetition continues until the last order has been processed.

If the last order processed was for 15.25 yards (see ln 240), and if there had been no DATA statement in ln 250, the computer would first try to READ more data. Since no more data are present, some message such as "OUT OF DATA" would probably be printed, and the execution of the program would stop automatically. Perhaps terminating the program with such a message would be satisfactory in this example, but provision has been made in our program to avoid that message (and to illustrate a common programming technique). A *sentinel value*[13]—i.e., an arbitrary data value selected by the programmer to indicate that all valid data have been processed—is placed at the end of the last DATA statement. This value (-99.99 in ln 250) will first be assigned to Y in ln 120 and will then cause the condition specified in the IF . . . THEN statement in ln 126 to be true. The statement in ln 126

126 IF Y $<$ 0 THEN 190

causes program control to branch to ln 190 when the sentinel value is encountered.

The STOP statement in ln 190 halts the execution of the program and has been included here merely to illustrate another BASIC statement

---

[13] This is also called a *flag, dummy,* or *9s decision* value.

type. Commonly used in more complex programs that incorporate subordinate program modules or *subroutines,* the STOP statement works exactly like a GO TO the END statement. Thus, the statement in ln 126 could just as easily have been

126 IF Y < 0 THEN 260

which would have branched program control to the END statement.

COUNTERS AND ACCUMULATORS IN PROGRAMS

Karl Tell's Pay Authorization Program

You remember Professor Karl Tell from the last chapter—the economist latching onto a squadron of graduate students to help him complete a study of the robber barons of Dusseldorf. It is Karl's responsibility to prepare a periodic authorization report so that his research assistants will be paid. The name and hourly pay rate of each assistant are kept in a data file in the program, and Karl interacts with the program to enter the number of hours worked by each student during a period. Given this input data, the program then prints each student's name and computes the student's authorized pay. Finally, the total amount authorized for the period is accumulated and printed, and the average (*mean*) amount paid during the period is computed and reported. The flowchart for Karl's program is presented in Figure 7-11, page 237, and the program itself is shown in Figure 8-8.

Although two important programming techniques—the use of a *counter* and the use of an *accumulator*—are illustrated in the program in Figure 8-8, and although this program is longer than the others we have examined, all the statement types used in it should now be familiar to you. The *purpose of the counter* is to record the number of times the loop has been executed (the body of the loop is from ln 180 to ln 290). The *exit condition* for this loop is based on the value of the counter. The counter (C) is initialized at zero (the LET statement on ln 130), and the number of students in the data file (5) is assigned to the variable name N (the READ . . . DATA statements on ln 160 and ln 370). After the first student's name and rate of pay have been assigned to variable names (the READ . . . DATA statements on ln 180 and ln 380), and after the student's name has been printed (the PRINT statement on ln 200), Karl enters the hours worked during the period (the INPUT statement on ln 210). The student's pay is then computed (the LET statement on ln 230) and printed (the PRINT statement on ln 234). When the student's record has been processed, the counter is *incremented* by a value of 1 in the LET statement on ln 250. Thus, the counter has a value of 1 when the first test for exit condition is made in the IF . . . THEN statement on ln 280. Since the test condition is false—that is, C is 1 and does *not* equal the N value of 5—the GO TO statement on ln 290 branches control back to ln 180 to

```
>LIST
10 REM *PAY AUTHORIZATION PROGRAM
20 REM *
30 REM *VARIABLE DEFINITIONS
40 REM * N$ STUDENT NAME
50 REM * R  HOURLY RATE OF PAY
60 REM * H  HOURS WORKED
70 REM * P  STUDENT PAY FOR HOURS WORKED
80 REM * T  TOTAL AMOUNT PAID
90 REM * N  TOTAL NUMBER OF STUDENTS IN DATA FILE
100 REM * C  COUNTER
110 REM * A  AVERAGE PAY PER STUDENT
120 REM *
125 REM *ZERO ACCUMULATOR AND COUNTER
130     LET C = 0
140     LET T = 0
150 REM *READ TOTAL NUMBER OF STUDENTS IN DATA FILE
160     READ N
170 REM *READ STUDENT NAME AND RATE OF PAY
180     READ N$,R
190 REM *ENTER HOURS WORKED
200     PRINT N$;
210     INPUT H
220 REM *COMPUTE STUDENT PAY
230     LET P = R*H
232 REM *PRINT STUDENT PAY
234     PRINT "PAY = $";P
236     PRINT
240 REM *INCREMENT COUNTER AND ACCUMULATOR
250     LET C = C+1
260     LET T = T+P
270 REM *TEST FOR END OF DATA FILE
280     IF C=N THEN 310
290     GO TO  180
300 REM *COMPUTE AVERAGE PAY
310     LET A =T/N
320 REM *PRINT TOTAL AND AVERAGE PAY THEN STOP
330     PRINT "TOTAL PAID              ";T
340     PRINT "AVERAGE PAY PER STUDENT ";A
350     STOP
360 REM *STUDENT DATA FILE
370     DATA  5
380     DATA "JACK ARMSTRONG      ",   5.00
390     DATA "ALFRED NEWMAN       ",   5.50
400     DATA "JACOB ALTMAN        ",   5.50
410     DATA "SALLY JACOBSON      ",   6.00
420     DATA "GEORGE WASHINGTON   ",   6.00
430 END
```

Computer listing of the program

```
RUN
14:43   AUG 02   BASIC5...
JACK ARMSTRONG          ?20
PAY = $    100

ALFRED NEWMAN           ?18
PAY = $     99

JACOB ALTMAN            ?22
PAY = $    121

SALLY JACOBSON          ?20
PAY = $    120

GEORGE WASHINGTON       ?18
PAY = $    108

TOTAL PAID              548
AVERAGE PAY PER STUDENT 109.600

    350 HALT
```

Output produced by computer as program is executed

FIGURE 8-8
Program for Karl Tell's pay authorization report.

begin another pass through the loop. When the last student *has* been processed, and when C = N, program control will branch to ln 310.

The *purpose of the accumulator* in this program is to accept individual pay amounts and compute a running total of them as they become available during processing. The variable name T is used for the accumulator and is initially set at zero (the LET statement on ln 140). Once a student pay amount (P) has been computed, the amount is added to the contents of the accumulator (the LET statement on ln 260). When the last student's pay has been computed, the grand total for the period will be stored in the accumulator. When the exit out of the loop occurs, the average pay for the period may be computed (the LET statement on ln 310), and the total pay and average pay may be printed (the PRINT statements on ln 330 and ln 340).

We have just seen how a counter may be used along with IF . . . THEN and GO TO statements to control the number of passes, or iterations, through a loop. Setting up and controlling loops, of course, is of paramount importance in the repetitive processing of data. It is so important, in fact, that special statements are built into most languages to simplify the creation and control of loops. How is this done in BASIC? Well, let's see. . . .

Built-In Looping with an Automatic Counter

In the "Review and Discussion Questions" section at the end of the last chapter, it was assumed in question 25 that Maude Crabbie, the teacher at the Cass T. Gate School, had assigned a "naughty student" the task of writing "I will not chew gun in class" 10 times. You were asked to prepare a flowchart for a program that would (1) accept any similar naughty-student message, and (2) reproduce this message any designated number of times. A simple flowchart for this problem is shown in Figure 8-9. A counter *could* be initialized and incremented as shown, and IF . . . THEN and GO TO statements *could* be used to control the number of passes through the loop. (Could you now write a program to do this?)

A simpler approach to solving the naughty-student problem is shown in Figure 8-10. The statements in line numbers 10 through 90 are familiar types. (The message and the number of times it is to be printed are entered via the READ . . . DATA statements in line numbers 80 and 140). But the program uses a pair of statements—the FOR statement on ln 100 and the NEXT statement on ln 120—that you are not familiar with. These FOR and NEXT statements must always be used together. The FOR statement *opens* a loop, and the loop is *closed* with the NEXT statement. That is, a FOR statement sets up a loop and is placed at the beginning of the loop, while the NEXT statement is located at the end of the loop. The program line or lines that are *between* the FOR and NEXT statements are executed repeatedly and form the *range,* or *body,* of the loop.

The general form of these statements is

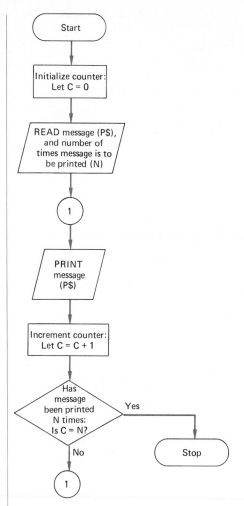

FIGURE 8-9
Flowchart to assist Maude
Crabbie's naughty students.

```
ln FOR v = n₁ TO n₂ STEP n₃
ln      .
ln      .
ln      .
ln NEXT v
```

where ln is a line number, v is a variable name acting as an *automatic counter* or *index,* n_1 is the initial value or expression given to the counter, n_2 is the value or expression of the counter when the looping is completed, and n_3 is the amount by which the counter should be *stepped up or down* after each pass through the loop. (If the step value is omitted in the FOR statement, the computer will automatically use a step size of 1.) Some examples of valid FOR . . . NEXT statements are:

```
LIST
10 REM *NAUGHTY STUDENT PROGRAM
20 REM *
30 REM *VARIABLE DEFINITIONS
40 REM * P$ MESSAGE
50 REM * N  NUMBER OF TIMES MESSAGE IS PRINTED
60 REM *
70 REM *READ MESSAGE AND NUMBER OF TIMES TO BE PRINTED
80      READ P$,N
90 REM *PRINT MESSAGE
100     FOR K=1 TO N
110     PRINT P$
120     NEXT K
130 REM *MESSAGE DATA
140     DATA "I WILL NOT CHEW GUM IN CLASS",10
150 END
>
```

Computer listing of the program

```
RUN
11:13  NOV 20  BASIC8...
I WILL NOT CHEW GUM IN CLASS
I WILL NOT CHEW GUM IN CLASS
I WILL NOT CHEW GUM IN CLASS
I WILL NOT CHEW GUM IN CLASS
I WILL NOT CHEW GUM IN CLASS
I WILL NOT CHEW GUM IN CLASS
I WILL NOT CHEW GUM IN CLASS
I WILL NOT CHEW GUM IN CLASS
I WILL NOT CHEW GUM IN CLASS
I WILL NOT CHEW GUM IN CLASS

    150 HALT
```

Output produced by computer as program is executed

FIGURE 8-10
Program for Maude Crabbie's naughty students.

```
100 FOR K = 1 TO N
        .

120 NEXT K
```

```
130 FOR J = 5 * N TO A/B STEP 2
        .
        .
        .
180 NEXT J
```

```
160 FOR P = 25 TO 1 STEP −1
        .
        .
        .
260 NEXT P
```

The first of these FOR . . . NEXT examples is found in our program in Figure 8-10. In our example, the automatic counter (K) is initially set at 1 in the FOR statement (ln 100), the first printing of the message is accomplished (using ln 110), and the end of the loop is reached at the NEXT statement (ln 120). An automatic test is then made to determine whether the counter value (K) is equal to (or greater than) N (in this case, 10). Since K is now 1 and obviously does not equal N, the counter is stepped up by 1 and the next pass through the loop occurs. When the message

```
>LIST
 10 REM *MULTIPLICATION DRILL PROGRAM
 20 REM *
 30 REM *VARIABLE DEFINITIONS
 35 REM * N$ STUDENT NAME
 40 REM * A  FIRST FACTOR
 50 REM * B  SECOND FACTOR
 60 REM * C  CORRECT RESPONSE
 70 REM * P  STUDENT RESPONSE
 80 REM * Q1 NUMBER OF CORRECT RESPONSES
 90 REM * Q2 NUMBER OF INCORRECT RESPONSES
100 REM * S  SCORE
110 REM *
112 REM *INITIALIZE ACCUMULATORS
114      LET Q1 = 0
116      LET Q2 = 0
120 REM *INSTRUCTIONS
130      PRINT "   MULTIPLICATION DRILL"
140      PRINT
144 REM *OBTAIN STUDENT'S NAME
146      PRINT "WHAT IS YOUR NAME";
147      INPUT N$
148      PRINT
149      PRINT "PAY ATTENTION,";N$;"."
150      PRINT "THIS IS A TEST OF YOUR KNOWLEDGE OF THE "
160      PRINT "MULTIPLICATION TABLES.  YOU WILL BE ASKED"
170      PRINT "TO MULTIPLY TWENTY PAIRS OF NUMBERS."
175      PRINT "CONSIDER YOUR ANSWERS CAREFULLY."
178      PRINT "YOUR WHOLE FUTURE MAY DEPEND ON HOW YOU DO "
179      PRINT "ON THIS EXAM.   "
180      PRINT "A SCORE OF 85 IS CONSIDERED PASSING."
190      PRINT
240 REM *LOOP THROUGH SEQUENCE OF QUESTIONS
250      FOR K=1 TO 20
260 REM *GENERATE TWO RANDOM INTEGERS IN INTERVAL FROM ZERO TO NINE
270      LET A = INT(RND(-1)*10)
280      LET B = INT(RND(-1)*10)
290 REM *COMPUTE CORRECT RESPONSE
300      LET C = A*B
310 REM *OBTAIN STUDENT RESPONSE
315      PRINT
320      PRINT "WHAT IS ";A;" TIMES ";B;
330      INPUT P
340 REM *
350 REM *TEST STUDENT RESPONSE
360      IF C=P THEN 420
```

A portion
of the
computer
listing
of the
program

FIGURE 8-11
Maude Crabbie's CAI program.

has been printed 10 times, the value of K *will* equal N, the printing will stop, and program control will exit from the FOR . . . NEXT loop structure to the next executable line number in sequence. In our example, this will be the END statement on ln 150. As this example illustrates, the built-in looping capability available through the use of FOR . . . NEXT statements gives the programmer a relatively simple and powerful repetitive processing tool.

A FEW ADDITIONAL TOPICS IN BASIC

Maude Crabbie's assignment to write a computer-assisted instruction (CAI) program to drill students in their mastery of multiplication tables was the last problem analyzed in Chapter 7. In giving Maude the assign-

```
370 REM *INCORRECT RESPONSE. PUNISHMENT INFLICTED
380     PRINT "SORRY. THE CORRECT ANSWER WAS ";C;". TISK. TISK."
390     LET Q2 = Q2+1
400     GO TO 440
410 REM *CORRECT RESPONSE. REINFORCEMENT MESSAGE
420     PRINT "CORRECT."
430     LET Q1 =Q1+1
440     NEXT K
450 REM *COMPUTE SCORE, EVALUATE PERFORMANCE AND STOP
460     LET S = (Q1/(Q1+Q2))*100
470     IF S<85 THEN 510
475 REM *PASSING SCORE
480     PRINT "GOOD WORK, ";N$;". YOU PASSED."
490     PRINT "YOUR SCORE WAS ";S;", AND 85 WAS CONSIDERED PASSING."
500     STOP
505 REM *FAILING SCORE
510     PRINT "TOO BAD, ";N$;". YOU FAILED."
520     PRINT "YOU NEEDED 85 TO PASS AND YOUR SCORE WAS ONLY ";S;"."
530     PRINT "YOU'LL NEVER AMOUNT TO ANYTHING."
540     STOP
550 END
```

The remainder of the computer listing of the program

```
>

RUN
11:30   NOV 20  BASIC10...
   MULTIPLICATION DRILL

WHAT IS YOUR NAME   ?TEDDY

PAY ATTENTION, TEDDY
THIS IS A TEST OF YOUR KNOWLEDGE OF THE
MULTIPLICATION TABLES. YOU WILL BE ASKED
TO MULTIPLY TWENTY PAIRS OF NUMBERS.
CONSIDER YOUR ANSWERS CAREFULLY.
YOUR WHOLE FUTURE MAY DEPEND ON HOW YOU DO
ON THIS EXAM.
A SCORE OF 85 IS CONSIDERED PASSING.


WHAT IS    3   TIMES    3 ?9
CORRECT.

WHAT IS    8   TIMES    8 ?64
CORRECT.

WHAT IS    2   TIMES    8 ?16
CORRECT.

WHAT IS    5   TIMES    6 ?60
SORRY. THE CORRECT ANSWER WAS    30  . TISK. TISK.

WHAT IS    9   TIMES    3 ?27
CORRECT.
```

A portion of the first output produced by the computer as the program is executed

FIGURE 8-11
(Continued)

ment, the principal told her that the program should (1) interact with the student and supply the necessary instructions, (2) provide 20-question tests and keep track of the number of correct and incorrect student responses, (3) give a student immediate feedback after her or his response to each test question, and (4) compute the student's test score, determine whether it is "passing," and produce the appropriate feedback message. The flowchart for this program is given in Figure 7-12, page 240, and the program itself is shown in Figure 8-11.

```
WHAT IS    2    TIMES    4    ?8
CORRECT.

WHAT IS    0    TIMES    6    ?0
CORRECT.

WHAT IS    9    TIMES    7    ?63
CORRECT.

WHAT IS    3    TIMES    9    ?27
CORRECT.

WHAT IS    1    TIMES    2    ?2
CORRECT.

WHAT IS    3    TIMES    9    ?27
CORRECT.

WHAT IS    5    TIMES    0    ?0
CORRECT.

WHAT IS    3    TIMES    3    ?9
CORRECT.

WHAT IS    8    TIMES    8    ?63
SORRY.  THE CORRECT ANSWER WAS       64   .  TISK. TISK.

WHAT IS    4    TIMES    1    ?4
CORRECT.

WHAT IS    1    TIMES    2    ?2
CORRECT.

WHAT IS    3    TIMES    8    ?24
CORRECT.

WHAT IS    2    TIMES    0    ?0
CORRECT.

WHAT IS    5    TIMES    9    ?45
CORRECT.

WHAT IS    4    TIMES    5    ?20
CORRECT.
GOOD WORK,    TEDDY   .  YOU PASSED.
YOUR SCORE WAS       90.0000  , AND 85 WAS CONSIDERED PASSING.


    500 HALT
```

The remainder
of the <u>first</u>
output produced
by the computer
as the program
is executed

FIGURE 8-11
(Continued)

There are really only two additional topics in BASIC to be considered in Maude Crabbie's CAI program, but neither topic is found in the early line numbers. The helpful documentation found in the REMark statements in line numbers 10 through 112 needs no explanation. The LET statements in ln 114 and ln 116 initialize the accumulators that will be used to total the number of correct (Q1) and incorrect (Q2) student responses during a test. PRINT statements giving instructions to the student, along with an INPUT statement requesting the student's name so that student-program communication can be more "personalized," occupy the line numbers from 130 through 190. (You will notice that Maude appears to be a multiplication fanatic who places considerable emphasis on this drill!)

```
RUN
11:34   NOV 20  BASIC10...
    MULTIPLICATION DRILL

WHAT IS YOUR NAME   ?MAUDE

PAY ATTENTION, MAUDE
THIS IS A TEST OF YOUR KNOWLEDGE OF THE
MULTIPLICATION TABLES.  YOU WILL BE ASKED
TO MULTIPLY TWENTY PAIRS OF NUMBERS.
CONSIDER YOUR ANSWERS CAREFULLY.
YOUR WHOLE FUTURE MAY DEPEND ON HOW YOU DO
ON THIS EXAM.
A SCORE OF 85 IS CONSIDERED PASSING.


WHAT IS    7    TIMES     7  ?49
CORRECT.

WHAT IS    7    TIMES     7  ?49
CORRECT.

WHAT IS    3    TIMES     7  ?21
CORRECT.

WHAT IS    1    TIMES     6  ?6
CORRECT.

WHAT IS    9    TIMES     4  ?36
CORRECT.

WHAT IS    5    TIMES     3  ?8
SORRY.  THE CORRECT ANSWER WAS     15  . TISK. TISK.

WHAT IS    4    TIMES     6  ?23
SORRY.  THE CORRECT ANSWER WAS     24  . TISK. TISK.


               .
               .
               .


WHAT IS    9    TIMES     0  ?0
CORRECT.

WHAT IS    5    TIMES     1  ?6
SORRY.  THE CORRECT ANSWER WAS      5  . TISK. TISK.
TOO BAD,    MAUDE  . YOU FAILED.
YOU NEEDED 85 TO PASS AND YOUR SCORE WAS ONLY    70.0000 .
YOU'LL NEVER AMOUNT TO ANYTHING.

    540 HALT
```

The output produced when Maude Crabbie tried her own program

FIGURE 8-11
(Continued)

In line number 250, a FOR . . . NEXT loop is initiated to cause the program to process 20 pairs of random numbers. (The NEXT statement to close this loop is found on ln 440.) The random numbers from zero to 9 are generated in line numbers 270 and 280 and are assigned to the variable names A and B. It is beyond the scope of this book to examine in detail the mathematical methods that are used to produce such random numbers. Different manufacturers use different approaches; it is enough for us to know that vendors have prepared programmed sets of instructions that will produce sequences of numbers that appear to have no pattern or relationship. These numbers are generated randomly, are uni-

"Computers for Grade-Schoolers"

Just as television has for years been accused by educators of inducing passivity in students, so are low-cost, accessible computers now disturbing critics, who are horrified at the thought of a child hypnotically held by a computerized super-pinball machine.

However, Seymour Papert, a professor of mathematics at the Massachusetts Institute of Technology, believes that if used appropriately, the computer could have an opposite effect. During the last decade, Professor Papert has worked with more than 700 children, some as young as 4, developing LOGO, a computer system designed to be programmed by children.

"The computer encourages the child to learn to be dependent on the instructional process," he said. "In a certain sense, one might say that the computer is programming the child."

Since the late 60's, thousands of high school students have been taught to use a computer-programming language called the Beginner's All-purpose Symbolic Instruction Code. BASIC was designed primarily for algebraic computations of modest complexity.

Other schools have used computers to provide feedback or to dispense information through question-and-answer-type exercises that proceeded in a step-by-step mechanical fashion.

"There is no doubt that this feedback improves learning of particular facts, such as the most mechanical parts of language, like spelling and rules of grammar." Professor Papert said.

According to him, LOGO was designed to engage more of the child's analytical faculties than traditional computer systems—to develop his own computer programs, to draw geometric exercises and animated figures, or even to compose music. Most important, it was designed as an entry into the world of computer technology even before the child learned algebra.

"In programming the computer," Professor Papert said, "the child acquires a sense of mastery over a piece of the most modern and powerful technology and an intimate contact with some of the deepest ideas from science, from mathematics, from management and from the art of intellectual model-building."

The computer installed in the William H. Lincoln School in Brookline, one of a number of demonstration LOGO projects, is used by students in their spare time during or after school.

On one recent morning, however, Daniel Watt, a schoolteacher and computer specialist, propped the two video monitors on a table facing the class.

He instructed his students on how to make the machines respond to instructions from the typewriter-like keyboard. He explained how to draw geometrical graphics—squares and triangles—using a device called a "light turtle," which makes tracings on the computer display screen. Ideally, learning to control the turtle becomes a conceptual bridge into the child's understanding of formal geometry.

For Keith Glynn, 13 years old, using the computer is clearly a learning exercise.

"You have to divide and stuff to get the right angle," he said. "It makes you use your brain a lot. You have to use brainpower to sit down and do it. It makes you remember, too."

During the late-1960's, a group at M.I.T. began experimenting with methods of teaching computer techniques to children.

"But we quickly decided that it was impractical," Professor Papert said. "Any attempt to do anything with computers that were developed then was fighting against technology that would become antiquated in 10 or 15 years."

He was convinced, though, that minature, high-powered computers would become common in the educational experiences of even the youngest children.

Since then, the cost of computer technology has dramatically decreased. According to a recent study for the National Science Foundation, computers are accessible to more than half of all high school students, and by the early 80's, almost every high school in the nation will have a terminal available for student use.

Many teachers and school districts, fearful that computers might reduce classroom discussion and generally dehumanize the school environment, are reluctant to expand their use of teaching machines. Also among their concerns is the cost.

But cost, according to Professor Papert, should no longer be a significant factor in whether schools expand their use of computers.

Professor Papert is confident that once educators understand the value of LOGO, they will be willing to put up the cost of about $500 a child.

"Those school districts that are really dedicated to quality education," he said, "will realize that spending a few hundred dollars on a computer is highly cost-effective."

Source: Kenneth B. Noble, "Now Computers for Grade-Schoolers," New York *Times,* January 6, 1980. "© 1980 by the New York Times Company. Reprinted by permission."

formly distributed, are in a range from 0.000000 to 0.999999, and are available for use in a BASIC program when the RND function is called up by the programmer. In our example,

270 LET A = INT (RND(−1) ∗ 10)

the RND(− 1) will give a nonrepeating sequence of random numbers each time the program is used. Unfortunately, these numbers would not be integers or whole numbers but would instead be in the decimal fraction range given above. To get around this problem, we multiply each random number generated by 10. Thus, .106471 becomes 1.06471. Finally, the INT (INTeger) function simply deletes everything following the decimal point. Thus, 1.06471 simply becomes 1. (The value .641732 called up by the RND function would first become 6.41732 and then simply 6 in Maude's program.)[14]

Once random integers from zero to 9 have been assigned to A and B in line numbers 270 and 280, the program performs the following steps: (1) The pair of random numbers are multiplied, and the result is assigned to C (ln 300), (2) the student is asked to multiply A times B, and the student response is assigned to P (ln 320 and ln 330), (3) if the student response is *correct,* a reinforcement message is printed, the "correct response" accumulator (Q1) is incremented, and the loop is repeated (line numbers 360, 420, 430, and 440), and (4) if the student response is *wrong,* the correct answer is given, the "incorrect response" accumulator (Q2) is incremented, and the loop is repeated (line numbers 360, 380, 390, 400, and 440). When the loop has been executed 20 times, program control passes to ln 460, which computes the student's test score. If the test score is "passing"—*not* < 85 in ln 470—line numbers 480 through 500 are executed; if a "failing" grade is made, line numbers 510 through 540 are executed.

In Figure 8-11, the first student to use Maude's program was Teddy. As you can see, Teddy passed with a score of 90. The second output run was the result of a demonstration Maude gave to the school principal—a classic case of being hoisted with one's own petard!

▶ LOOKING BACK

The following points have been emphasized in this chapter:

1 BASIC is a popular timesharing and personal computing language that makes it easy for people to interact with computers. Sign-on procedures, the key words used in system commands, and other details of language usage may vary from one system to another.

2 Key words are used in constructing BASIC statements, and these statements are then put together to form a program. Each statement in a BASIC program begins with a line number, and each type of statement has certain rules that must be followed. A number (but certainly

---

[14] Further details on the RND and INT functions are available in the sources listed in the "Selected References" section at the end of the chapter.

not all) of these rules have been discussed in the chapter for the following types of statements and functions:

REM	IF . . . THEN
READ . . . DATA	GO TO
LET	STOP
PRINT	FOR . . . NEXT
INPUT	INT
PRINT TAB	RND
PRINT USING	END

3   The values used in BASIC statements may be constants or variables. There are numeric constants and character string constants, and there are also numeric variables and string variables. Specific rules for naming and using these numeric and string values must be followed.

4   The computer handles arithmetic operations in a specific order. The rules used in determining the order of these operations have been spelled out in the chapter. Some common procedures for correcting errors that may occur during program and data entry have also been discussed.

5   Solutions have been written in BASIC for all the problems analyzed and flowcharted in the last chapter. (An additional program has also been considered.) All programs have been written in a programming style that may make them easier to read and understand. Beginning with some short programs to accomplish simple input, processing, and output, we have moved on to more detailed examples that use decisions, loops, counters, and accumulators. The language rules and programming techniques that have been considered during the discussion of these programs can be used to solve very complex problems. Of course, BASIC has many additional features that were not considered in this chapter.

▶ KEY TERMS

After reading Chapter 8, you should be able to define and use the following terms:

system command	REMark statement
program statement	LET (assignment) statement
line numbers	PRINT statement
numeric constant	READ . . . DATA statements
character string constant	INPUT statement
numeric variable	IF . . . THEN conditional branch-
variable name	ing statement
string variable	GO TO unconditional branching
programming style	statement

sentinel value
counter
accumulator

PRINT TAB function
PRINT USING function
FOR . . . NEXT statements

▶ REVIEW AND DISCUSSION QUESTIONS

1 Explain the procedures required to sign on the system you are using.
2 (a) What is the difference between a system command and a program statement? (b) Which typically causes the computer to take immediate action?
3 Identify and discuss the elements that may be found in a BASIC statement.
4 "BASIC deals with values that may be constants or variables." Discuss this sentence.
5 Define and give examples of a (a) numeric constant, (b) character string constant, (c) numeric variable, (d) variable name, (e) string variable, and (f) string variable name.
6 (a) Why is it important to understand the order in which the computer handles the arithmetic operations in a formula? (b) What is this priority order in a formula without parentheses? (c) What changes are made in this order when parentheses are used?
7 Explain the procedures required by the system you are using to correct the errors that may occur in program and data entry.
8 "Diagnostic messages detect syntax errors but not logical errors." Discuss this statement.
9 What will the computer do in executing the following BASIC statements:
   (a) 010 READ A,B,C,D,E
        200 DATA 025, 200, 300
        210 DATA 060, 150, 175, . . . , 125
   (b) 120 PRINT A,B,C
   (c) 020 PRINT TAB(10); "HELP"
   (d) 050 IF N < = 50 THEN 100
   (e) 130 FOR J = 1 TO 10 STEP 2
             .
             .
             .
        170 NEXT J
   (f) 60 INPUT S$
   (g) 20 REM GIVE THE USER A SHOCK
   (h) 40 LET A = (K * P/G)/2
   (i) 60 PRINT "WHAT IS YOUR AGE";
        70 INPUT A
        80 PRINT
   (j) 210 PRINT USING 440, A, B, C
        440:     ###·##   ###·##   ##·#

(k)   150 PRINT TAB(20);"HOW DO I GET OUT OF THIS CLASS?"

10 What changes could be made in the program in Figure 8-6 to permit it to process any number of cars? (*Hint:* See Figure 8-5 for ideas.)

11 Write a program for the speed conversion problem discussed in question 24 at the end of Chapter 7.

12 Write a program for the problem discussed in question 26 at the end of Chapter 7.

13 Write a program using IF . . . THEN and GO TO statements for the "naughty-student" flowchart shown in Figure 8-9.

▶ SELECTED REFERENCES

There are dozens of good books on the BASIC language. A few of these are:

Boillot, Michel, and L. Wayne Horn: *BASIC,* 2d ed., West Publishing Company, St. Paul, Minn., 1979.

Dwyer, Thomas A., and Margot Critchfield: *BASIC and the Personal Computer,* Addison-Wesley Publishing Company, Reading, Mass., 1978.

Kemeny, John G., and Thomas Kurtz: *BASIC Programming,* 2d ed., John Wiley & Sons, New York, 1971.

Lawlor, Steven C.: *BASIC,* Wadsworth Publishing Company, Belmont, Calif., 1979.

Moursund, David: *BASIC Programming for Computer Literacy,* McGraw-Hill Book Company, New York, 1978.

Peckham, Herbert D.: *BASIC: A Hands-on Method,* McGraw-Hill Book Company, New York, 1978.

Sass, C. Joseph: *BASIC Programming and Applications,* Allyn and Bacon, Inc., Boston, 1976.

Part Four

(Ray Ellis, Photo Researchers.)

Part Four
COMPUTER INFLUENCE ON A CHANGING SOCIETY

(NCR)

Educated people should have some knowledge of

1 The history and development of information processing
2 The basic concepts of computer hardware
3 The procedures required to develop the software that is needed to put the hardware to work.

The purpose of the preceding chapters in Parts 1, 2, and 3 was to consider these topics. However, educated people should also be aware of some of the ways in which computers may possibly influence the society in which they live and work. In Part 4, we shall examine some of the social implications of computer usage. An *agent* may be defined as "something having power to produce an effect." The computer qualifies as an agent of change in our society—an agent which influences and introduces change to both *organizations* and *individuals*.
    The chapters included in Part 4 are:

9 *Organizations, Offices, and Computers*
10 *Individuals and Computers: Some Positive Views*
11 *Individuals and Computers: Some Negative Views*
12 *Controlling the Negative Impact*

Chapter 9
ORGANIZATIONS, OFFICES, AND COMPUTERS

The purpose of this chapter is to show you some of the general effects that computers have had on organizations.

The administrative activities of planning, organizing, staffing, and controlling must be performed in any organization if the organization's goals are to be achieved. Therefore, you will find a brief discussion of these activities in the first section of the chapter. In a later section, you will see how computer usage can have an impact on the performance of these planning, organizing, staffing, and controlling functions.

In the second section of the chapter, the types of organizations affected by computers are classified into economic and public categories. Economic organizations are typically engaged in the producing, financing, and marketing activities that involve private decision making, while public organizations are engaged in the governmental, health care, and educational activities that involve public policy decisions. A number of ways in which computer usage can affect each of these types of organizations are discussed.

A consideration of the ways in which computers, terminals, and communications equipment will be utilized to handle many of the office functions performed in organizations of all kinds is presented in the next section. Recent developments in word processing and electronic mail/message systems receive particular attention.

Finally, after the implications of computer usage on the performance of administrative functions are discussed, the last section considers the standardization pressures that are being felt by many computer-using organizations.

Thus, after studying this chapter, you should be able to:

- Identify and explain the basic administrative activities performed by decision makers in organizations.

- Discuss and give examples of how economic and private organizations may be affected by computer usage.

- Explain why changes may be expected in the office environments of many organizations, and why developments in word processing and electronic mail/message systems are receiving attention.

- Outline some of the implications of computer usage on the functions of planning, organizing, staffing, and controlling.

- Explain how computer usage may lead to standardization pressures.

- Understand and use the key terms listed at the end of the chapter.

An *organization* is a changing and ongoing system in which people and resources interact in a rational and orderly manner to accomplish common goals. Government agencies, hospitals, schools, churches, businesses, military units, Boy and Girl Scout groups, Rotary clubs—all these entities are organizations. Computer systems, by manipulating data and solving problems, may produce qualitative changes in an organization's information system. Since information is the cement that holds any organization together, the computer has had the effect of changing the structure and policies of many organizations.

The purpose of this chapter is to look at (1) the *administrative activities* which must be performed in an organization, (2) the *types of organizations affected by computers,* (3) the *introduction of computer technology into an office environment,* (4) the *organizational implications of computer usage,*[1] and (5) the *standardization pressures that computers have created in organizations.* In the following chapters we will look at the effect of computers on *individuals.*

ADMINISTRATIVE ACTIVITIES

As we saw in Chapter 1, *planning, organizing, staffing,* and *controlling* are important activities in any organization because the successful achievement of organizational goals depends on how well they are performed. In a later section of this chapter we shall examine some of the computer's implications for each of these activities. Now, however, let us summarize these administrative functions briefly.

Planning

The *planning* function looks to the future; to plan is to decide in advance a future course of action. Thus, planning involves making decisions with regard to (1) the selection of both short- and long-run strategies and goals, (2) the development of policies and procedures that will help accomplish objectives or counter threats, (3) the establishment of operating standards that serve as the basis for control, and (4) the revision of earlier plans in the light of changing conditions. The steps followed in *planning*

---

[1] The computer, of course, is only one of the technological developments currently affecting organizations and individuals (other developments include rapid transportation systems and new innovations in communications). It is not possible to isolate completely the computer effects from those which may be due to other technological advances. For example, the level of *productivity* in an organization—i.e., the amount of goods or services possessing economic value that individuals and machines can produce in a given time period—is likely to be affected by computer usage, but productivity may also be affected by a multitude of other factors.

and in arriving at rational decisions are about the same as those followed in conducting a systems study—i.e., the steps are: (1) *identifying the problem or opportunity,* (2) *gathering and analyzing relevant facts,* (3) *determining suitable alternatives,* (4) *evaluating and selecting the most appropriate alternative,* and (5) *following up on the decision(s).* Of course, administrative skill and quality information are needed during each of these planning activities.

Organizing

The *organizing* activity involves the grouping of work teams into logical and efficient units in order to carry out plans and achieve goals. Organizational units, for example, may be formally grouped according to (1) *type of work* performed, (2) *geographic area,* and/or (3) *type of physical good produced, handled, or distributed.* Administrators at each organizational level receive formal authority to assign goal-directed tasks; they then must motivate and coordinate team efforts if goals are to be achieved. The formal organizational (or authority) structure clarifies for employees the place in the organization of each job, the formal lines of authority and reporting relationships among positions, and the assigned role of a work unit in the total structure. Of course, an organizational structure must be flexible because of constantly changing technological, social, and economic factors.

Staffing

Although one aspect of the *staffing* function consists of selecting people to fill the positions that exist in the organizational structure, the staffing activity also includes (1) training employees to meet initial or changing job requirements, (2) preparing employees for changing conditions, and (3) reassigning or removing employees if such action is required.

Controlling

Unlike planning, which looks to the future, the *control* function looks at the past and the present. It is a follow-up to planning; it is the check on past and current performance to see if planned goals are being achieved. *The steps in the control function are*

1 *Setting standards.* Proper control requires that predetermined goals be established by planners. These standards may be expressed in *physical terms* (e.g., units produced, quantities tested, or machined tolerances permitted) or in *monetary terms* (e.g., operating-cost budgets). The setting of realistic standards requires quality information.
2 *Measuring actual performance.* Timely and accurate performance information is essential to control.

3 *Comparing actual performance with standards.* **Comparison** informa-tion is action-oriented. Computers can provide this information to managers on an *exception basis only* when performance variations are outside certain specified limits.

4 *Taking appropriate control action.* If performance is *under control,* the administrator's decision may be to do nothing. However, if actual per-formance is not up to the standard, it may be because the standard is unrealistic. Therefore, replanning may be necessary to revise the stan-dard. Unfavorable performance may have to be corrected by reorga-nizing work groups or adding more personnel. Thus, the control actions taken may require further planning, organizing, and staffing activities. If outstanding performance is noted, the appropriate action may be to reward the individuals or groups responsible.

The *order* of the administrative activities presented here is a logical one, and we shall use this order to present material in a following section. In practice, however, administrators carry out these activities simulta-neously, and it is not practical to insist on a particular sequence in all situa-tions.

TYPES OF ORGANIZATIONS AFFECTED BY COMPUTERS

Organizations using computers are likely to be engaged in processing operations that have one or more of the following characteristics: (1) a large volume of input data, (2) repetitive processing tasks, (3) the need for speed in processing and retrieval, (4) the need for a high degree of accuracy, and (5) processing complexities that require or encourage computer usage.

The types of organizations affected by computers may be classified into *economic* and *public* categories. Economic organizations include those engaged in financing, marketing, producing, and servicing activities that involve private decision making. Public organizations, on the other hand, include those engaged in government, law enforcement, public health, education, and other social activities that involve public policy de-cisions. In the following sections let us briefly examine some of the effects of computers on these types of organizations.

Economic Organizations

Economic organizations that have large volumes of data to process in re-petitive fashion include financial institutions such as banks and insurance companies, marketing organizations such as retail department store chains, and extractive enterprises such as oil companies that may pro-duce in one country and sell on credit to customers in other countries. Quick-responding and accurate information systems are needed by such economic organizations as airlines and other transportation and travel-oriented concerns, and private research laboratories must often deal with complexities that require computer usage.

Computers are used in economic organizations to improve the quality of, and accelerate the flow of, information, to thus speed up and improve the performance of planning, decision-making, and control activities, and to thereby improve efficiency and raise the level of productivity in the organization. Since, during the last decade, the overall increases in productivity in United States industries have trailed those of many other industrial nations, the need for greater computer usage is recognized by many decision makers in economic organizations.

Certain economic organizations may also be affected by computer usage in the following ways:

1 *Through the organization's use of electronic funds transfer systems (EFTS).* Originally labeled the "cashless society" and then the "less-check society," the EFTS concept is dependent on computers and permits (1) the electronic transfer of money among financial institutions and economic organizations on a national scale, (2) the use of automated clearing houses that electronically handle the settlement of transactions among banks and the Federal Reserve System, (3) the electronic transfer of *preauthorized* payroll and bill payments by organizations and individuals, (4) the electronic authorization for immediate cash and credit transactions—e.g., between a bank customer drawing on funds in a checking or savings account and a merchant at

FIGURE 9-1
This customer-activated financial transaction facility displays instructions and interacts with customers to guide them through the steps necessary to complete a financial transaction.
(Burroughs Corp.)

a point-of-sale location, and (5) the installation at convenient locations in banks and remote sites of electronic terminals (see Figure 9-1) that enable customers to withdraw and deposit cash, open new accounts, and receive other financial services. Although at this writing some legal and regulatory confusion exists and the future scope of EFTS cannot be fully determined, it is obvious that (a) *commercial banks* are interested in EFTS as a means of improving the efficiency of their operations and preserving their dominant position in the payments system, (b) *other thrift institutions* (credit unions, savings banks, etc.) view EFTS both as a commercial banking competitive threat and as an opportunity to play a larger future role in the nation's payment system, (c) *small retailers* see EFTS as a means of reducing bad check losses and safely increasing credit sales, (d) *large retailers may view* EFTS as a threat to their own private credit card business, and (e) *national credit card organizations* see themselves as a vital part of any system issuing national *debit* cards (a debit card allows holders to make purchases or obtain cash electronically from their funds on deposit). In short, organizations and individuals all have a vital stake in the ways that computers can influence how "money" is transmitted and accounted for. We will consider possible EFTS implications again in later chapters.

2 *Through the organization's use of point-of-sale (POS) terminal systems.* You have seen in Chapter 4 that the grocery industry has selected a Universal Product Code (UPC) to represent the types of products sold in supermarkets. An automated check stand may scan the UPC symbol and transmit the data to a computer that looks up the price, possibly updates inventory and sales records, and forwards price and description information back to the check stand. Such a POS terminal system can increase efficiency and provide customers with faster and more accurate service. You have also seen in Chapter 4 how other retail organizations use POS terminals equipped, perhaps, with handheld wands to process sales transactions quickly and accurately. Of course, the data that are captured during the transaction become the input for reports that managers can use to make decisions about sales planning and inventory control.

3 *Through the organization's ability to change the employment situation.* The use of computers has created hundreds of thousands of new jobs in economic organizations, and many employees are currently working in challenging and satisfying positions. However, the use of computers has also eliminated the need for certain jobs or has modified the content of the jobs that remain. For example, very reliable low-cost microcomputer control devices are currently being substituted in cars and elsewhere for the now-obsolete mechanical, electrical, and pneumatic control units that were produced in the past by thousands of workers. In manufacturing operations, programmable "manipulators," or *robots,* are being installed in ever-increasing numbers to improve efficiency and productivity. (We will have more to say about

robots in later chapters.) In some cases displaced individuals have found it difficult to find suitable new employment, and in other cases the remaining jobs have become less fulfilling.

4 *Through the threat to the organization's security.* There are organizations whose very existence has been threatened by computer-system control problems. They have failed to design adequate controls to prevent theft, fraud, espionage, sabotage, accidental erasure of vital records, and/or physical destruction (e.g., through fire or flood) of important files. In one reported case, for example, an organization received a long-distance call from a computer operator who had failed to report for work. The operator was calling from a European city with disturbing news: He claimed to have the only tape of a vital master file and announced that he would return it only when the organization had deposited a large amount in a numbered Swiss bank account. His claim was quickly checked and found to be correct, and the ransom was reluctantly paid. Other organizations have been equally vulnerable. The subject of security will be considered again in later chapters.

5 *Through the organization's ability to compete.* Many small hardware- and software-producing organizations have gone bankrupt trying to compete in the computer industry itself; larger organizations such as RCA, General Electric, and Xerox have lost hundreds of millions of dollars in futile competitive efforts; and IBM, the industry giant, is currently defending itself against antitrust suits. Also, organizations with limited computing capabilities may be less able to compete against organizations which have greater resources, with the result being that computers may contribute to a greater concentration of economic and social power. In manufacturing, for example, larger organizations with the necessary resources to acquire expensive computer-controlled robots to handle certain assembly operations may achieve economic gains at the expense of smaller organizations. In the service sector, larger law or public accounting firms with terminals connected to expensive data retrieval services may provide services to their large and powerful corporate clients that are not available to the less-affluent clients of smaller firms.

6 *Through the organization's use of computers across national boundaries.* International airlines have reservation systems that cross many national boundaries; international news agencies have worldwide information and retrieval networks; stock quotation services have expanded to provide their customers with up-to-the-minute quotations from the major securities exchanges in the free world; and engineering, extracting, and manufacturing organizations link multinational facilities by computer-communications networks for planning and control purposes. Such broad networks may be expected to improve decision making and efficiency for the multinational organizations, but they may also increase the tension among nations and the companies that operate within their boundaries. Nations claim sovereignty over the types of changes that occur within their borders, but

rapid cultural, social, and economic changes may result from the operations within their jurisdiction of powerful multinational corporations using global technology. Organizations may thus find that computer usage has brought them into greater conflict with national governments. In the mid-1970s, for example, *The Reader's Digest* was denied permission by the Swedish government to process a large file containing information on Swedish households at a data center located in another country. Invoking their Data Act of 1973, which restricts the creation and use of data files on their citizens, the Swedes reasoned that permitting *The Reader's Digest* to export a large amount of information about Swedish citizens might invade their personal privacy and might also compromise Swedish national security. At this writing, "transborder data flow" is a hot issue in Europe. Germany, Norway, and France[2] have followed the Swedish example by passing their own data protection laws, and most other European countries are working on similar legislation. Many multinational organizations and many organizations in the United States feel that these barriers to international data transmission are a form of trade restriction and an obstacle to the free exchange of scientific and cultural information.[3]

7 *Through the organization's need to protect individual privacy.* Existing and proposed laws require that some organizations handle and use computerized information about people in ways that will not invade their privacy. These laws may differ in every state (and in every country) in which an organization operates, and complying with them may be expensive. The subject of privacy will be considered again in later chapters.

8 *Through other organizational uses.* Additional ways in which organizations may be affected by computer usage are discussed in the chapters in Part 5 that deal with "Selected Computer Uses in Society."

Public Organizations

Many of the public concerns of modern nations have become so intertwined with computer technology that they are virtually inseparable. For example, government agencies such as the Internal Revenue Service and the Social Security Administration have such large volumes of data to process in repetitive fashion that they *must* use computers; law enforcement agencies, public hospitals, and government space and missile laboratories need the quick-responding and accurate information systems made possible by computers; and the large size of many public organiza-

---

[2] French officials were once upset by the fact that an American economic modeling firm appeared to have more economic data on France than was available in any French data bank.

[3] For more information on this transborder data-flow issue, see John Eger, "Transborder Data Flow," *Datamation*, pp. 50ff, November 15, 1978; and "National Barriers to Data Flow," *Dun's Review*, pp. 93ff, July 1978.

tions encourages computer usage as a means of dealing with complexities brought about by size.

In the past, some socially beneficial organizations such as hospitals, law enforcement agencies, schools, and welfare offices were not as successful as larger economic and public enterprises in using computers because (1) they were often rather small in size and lacked the necessary personnel and financial resources, and (2) they were often governed by regulations which specified what data were to be gathered and processed and what interaction with other similar organizations was to be allowed.

Today such constraints are less restrictive. Many social service organizations have grown in size to meet increasing demands for their services, and this growth has made it possible to justify computer usage as a means of reducing costs and/or improving services. Also, of course, the cost of computing power has been significantly reduced in recent years. (The greater availability of computing power may, in fact, have been a major *contributing force* leading to the development of new programs and the growth of many existing services provided by public organizations.) Finally, increased cooperation between some governmental agencies and other social service organizations is resulting in the development of standardized data-base information systems that can be used jointly by similar organizations in a county or state or nationwide. In later chapters, cooperative applications of computers in government, health, and education organizations will be discussed.

In addition to the above developments, *computers may affect certain public organizations in the following selected ways:*

1   *Through their support of scientific decision-making techniques.* In a historical sense, a number of scientific agencies such as the National Aeronautics and Space Administration and the Atomic Energy Commission have been added in government; professional scientists have been included in some public policy decisions and have been consulted by government officials in the policy-making process; and computerized information systems and data banks for gathering, analyzing, storing, and retrieving information have been implemented in public organizations. One result of these trends is that the computer-based decision-making tools used to tackle scientific and industrial management problems have been applied in the attempt to solve public problems at the federal, state, and local levels. The state of California, for example, has called on aerospace firms to conduct systems studies on problems such as police protection and waste management. It should be noted, however, that the decision-making techniques developed for military, space, and industrial applications have not always been appropriate for the social problems to which they have been applied. In some cases, precise computer-generated analyses of the behavior of complex humanistic systems have simply not

been relevant to the real-world social, political, and economic problems that face individuals and groups.[4]

2 *Through their use in the election process.* Computers may be used in the election process in several ways, and they may thus have a direct impact on the composition of government bodies. *Prior to election day,* a state has to define the boundaries of its congressional districts according to the latest census. The political party in power in a state is essentially free to draw up district boundaries in *any way* so long as each district contains about the same population. For decades, state political leaders have used this opportunity to arrange new boundaries to benefit their own candidates and parties at the expense of their opponents. Thus, this process—called *gerrymandering*—isn't new, but the computer has greatly increased the potential for such finagling. In addition to population data, the computer can also store and process data on registered voters and party strength. Thus, the use of the computer permits the party in power to process more data than was previously possible in order to create more sophisticated gerrymanders. In Indiana, for example, one district that had been L-shaped with only 8 corners became, with the computer's help, a district with 24 corners; furthermore, a black community that usually votes Democratic was removed from this district and added to an ultrasafe Republican sector in order to deny these votes to the Democratic incumbent. (Needless to say, in Indiana the Republicans were defining the boundaries; in some other states the Democrats have had the advantage.) The point is, however, that skillful gerrymandering with the help of a computer "can easily convert one party's majority at the polls into the other party's majority in a legislative or congressional delegation."[5] Also prior to the election, a candidate's staff may compile data on voters, including such variables as age, sex, party affiliation, economic status, issues of interest, ethnic background, etc. These data may then be processed by computers programmed to prepare lists of probable supporters for voter registration and fundraising drives and to compose "individualized" letters appealing to the particular interests of the voter. This "marketing" of the candidate like a bar of soap is not necessarily undesirable if the information gathered about the views of the voters on important issues helps the candidate do a better job of explaining his or her position to them. The net result may be better communication between the candidate and the electorate. However, if individualized letters are used to promise one thing to one type of voter and another (perhaps contradictory) thing to voters from different economic and ethnic backgrounds, then

[4] For more information on the limitations of using scientific tools to solve social problems, see Ida R. Hoos, "Can Systems Analysis Solve Social Problems?" *Datamation,* pp. 82–83ff, June 1974; and C. C. Gotlieb and A. Borodin, *Social Issues in Computing,* Academic Press, New York, 1973, pp. 126–137.

[5] Robert W. Dietsch, "The Remarkable Resurgence of Gerry's Gambit," *Saturday Review,* p. 42, June 3, 1972.

politicians have used the computer to deceive and manipulate the voters. Computers are also used *on election day* to predict the outcome of contests on the basis of early returns from key districts, and they are used *after the polls close* to count the votes. As we will see in later chapters, present computer systems cannot be considered totally secure. Thus, computerized vote counts, like manual tabulations, could conceivably be altered either accidentally or deliberately. In a primary election not too long ago in Washington, D.C., for example, it was finally discovered that a test tape used earlier in a system shakedown had been accidentally included with the live voting results, had been counted without incident, and had become part of the vote tally!

3   *Through their impact on government operations.* Computers are being used in government in planning, decision-making, and controlling applications at the federal, state, and local levels. In some cases, those government agencies with well-organized and sophisticated computer resources have gained power at the expense of other government organizations. If there is a disparity, for example, between the use of computers by a legislative branch and an executive department, and if, as is likely, the department has a data processing advantage, the legislators may be required to use either less timely and incomplete data or interpreted and filtered information obtained from the department itself in order to pass judgment on a departmental proposal or budget. In Chapter 13, we will consider some specific applications of computers in government and law.

4   *Through their impact on health care services.* Computers are being applied to help solve some of the existing problems in health care systems. Certain tests and tasks that highly trained and expensive personnel have traditionally performed have been turned over to computers in an attempt to control costs, and certain procedures for collecting and analyzing large amounts of complex data have been followed by computer programs in order to obtain accurate diagnoses and improve the effectiveness and quality of health care. In Chapter 14, we will look at some secific ways in which computers are being used for health care planning, decision making, and controlling.

5   *Through their impact on educational programs.* Computers may be used in educational programs by teachers to plan for individualized instruction, and by students to obtain immediate feedback of successes and failures in achieving learning objectives. In Chapter 15, we will consider further the subject of computers in education.

COMPUTERS IN THE OFFICE

The "office of the future" (the "automated office") in which computers, terminals, and communications equipment will be utilized to perform many office functions has been predicted for at least the last 10 years, but progress has generally not lived up to these predictions. However, much

"WP at Manufacturers Hanover"

According to Edith Handeler, assistant vice president of Manufacturers Hanover Trust's Operations/Records Management Division, word processing and records management go hand in hand.

The two fields are closely related, Handeler says, because both word processing and records management are concerned with documents from their creation, through storage, to ultimate destruction. Reflecting this philosophy is Handeler's job, which puts the areas of records management and word processing under her supervision.

The operators in the word processing area are involved with providing services for the bank's executives. The input ranges from correspondence, through manuals, to computer analyses. Letters to be processed are sent to the operators by the executives in hard copy, computer printout, or dictated form. They utilize floppy disks, which can hold a maximum of 60 letters.

In the records management area, Handeler's supervision mandates that all letters, at their time of creation, receive two carbon copies. The original is mailed, the writer receives a carbon, and a copy is sent to the central file room.

All materials are coded with an identifying number, and are in a color-coded mobile file system, filed by subject matter. The diskettes, kept in the word processing room, are filed under the writer's name.

Handeler and her staff have sent directives on word processing and records management to the executives who use her department. They are currently preparing forms for the users to complete when sending materials to word processing. The data includes—author's name, type of document, subject matter, and code. This, Handeler maintains, will promote sound records management practices.

The Services Management Department, which runs Handeler's division, also controls mail and phone operations, as well as delivery systems.

It is evident that the expertise records management brings to document storage and retrieval is being utilized to its fullest with word processing and other record output at Manufacturers Hanover Trust, New York.

Source: "Word Processing at Manufacturers Hanover," *Information and Records Managemen* p. 13, May 1979. Reprinted with permission.

of the necessary technology is now either in place or expected soon; there is a recognition on the part of organizational leaders that productivity gains in offices have lagged far behind the gains achieved in other organizational units; and the costs of electronic office equipment are falling while the costs of office labor are rising.[6] These and other factors are likely to lead to a number of evolutionary changes in the office environments of many organizations in the next few years.[7]

Office Functions and Problems

The functions performed in offices consist of the data processing activities described in Chapter 1. In a traditionally organized office, data are typically written or typed on source documents, and these documents are read, classified, and sorted. Calculations may be performed on the data, and the facts may be summarized. Written communications between offices within an organization and between offices of independent organizations are usually transmitted by mail and may take the form of letters, bills, purchase orders, and other documents that must be dealt with in an orderly way. Once the data and records have been manipulated and communicated, they must be stored in a safe place, and must be available for retrieval and reproduction when needed. Office workers typically use typewriters, desk calculators, file cabinets, and copying machines in their work.

Although the necessary data processing work is usually accomplished in offices that follow these traditional methods, problems are likely to develop. *A few of these problems are:* (1) Monotonous job specialization can lead to boredom, frequent errors, high personnel turnover, and high training costs, (2) people may be unable to locate records in large files because the records may have been stored under a number of different classification schemes, and (3) costs associated with storing and duplicating documents within an organization, as well as the costs of preparing and mailing documents, are often very high. (An IBM estimate is that a typical one-page letter that has been dictated, typed, and corrected will cost a corporation over $6.)

How Can Computers Help in the Office?

Since a computer is a fast electronic symbol-manipulating device, and since office work basically involves symbol manipulation, it is only natural that organizations would turn to computers for help. Developments in *word processing* and *electronic mail/message systems* have received particular attention.

---

[6] In the past decade, American farmers have invested about $35,000 per worker in equipment to increase productivity about 185 percent. American industrial workers, aided by an investment of $25,000 per worker, have boosted productivity about 90 percent. In the office during the same period, however, workers have been supported by equipment worth less than $2,000 on the average, and their productivity has increased by only 4 percent! It is not surprising, then, that with office labor costs rising 6 to 8 percent annually, and with electronic equipment costs falling 30 percent per year, organizational leaders are now receptive to the idea of investing in new office technology in order to reduce rising labor costs and improve productivity.

[7] Some large offices now have robotic carts that automatically travel along designated routes to pick up and deliver mail. A press release describing these carts noted that they could be called "Robby" or (you may not be ready for this) "Norman the Mailer."

VON NEUMANN AND THE STORED PROGRAM

FIGURE 9-2
John von Neumann. (*UPI.*)

John von Neumann was born in Hungary and studied chemistry and mathematics at the universities of Berlin and Budapest and at the Technische Hochschule in Zurich. After coming to the United States in 1930, he taught at Princeton University, and he became a member of the Institute for Advanced Study in 1933.

Von Neumann joined Goldstine, Eckert, and Mauchly to fulfill the Army's request for a computer more powerful than ENIAC. The Electronic Discrete Variable Automatic Computer (EDVAC) was developed between 1946 and 1952. Von Neumann suggested that instructions for the computer as well as data be stored in the electronic memory of the computer. Up to this point, instructions had been entered by punched cards, punched paper tape, or wired boards. Von Neumann's concept of the stored program, now a basic part of all computer design, allowed the computer to execute instructions at its internal rate of speed rather than the much slower methods previously used.

Word processing   As used here, the term word processing describes the use of electronic equipment to create, view, edit, manipulate, transmit, store, retrieve, and print text material. The widespread use of word processing devices began in 1964 when IBM announced the Magnetic Tape Selectric Typewriter (MTST). Frequently used form letters and paragraphs were typed once, and the words were recorded on tape. The MTST was then used to automatically prepare repetitive prerecorded letters or to compose letters and reports consisting of selected prerecorded paragraphs.

After the introduction of MTST, IBM and many other manufacturers brought out other devices that used magnetic cards, cassettes, and internal belts as the recording media. In recent years, *stand-alone* and *multiple-station* word processing systems with keyboards for text input, visual display screens for text viewing and editing, floppy disks for text storage, and various kinds of printers and data transmission attachments for text output have been produced by dozens of vendors (Figures 9-3 and 9-4). If you think this description of a word processing system sounds very much like the micro- and minicomputer systems discussed in Chapter 6, you are right. Some dedicated word processing devices—i.e., devices that are used exclusively for word processing—are basically spin-offs of small computers and intelligent terminals that have received hardware modifications and/or specialized software. Although they are not dedicated exclusively to the task, most micro- and mini-sized computers (as well as larger processors) can be used as word processors simply by loading an appropriate word processing program into the system.[8]

A modern word processing system is an amazingly flexible tool. As text is keyed into the system, it is displayed on the screen and automatically recorded on a storage medium such as a floppy disk. Carriage returns are automatic, corrections are made easily, and sentences and para-

[8] For example, Michael Shrayer's Electric Pencil is a popular microcomputer word processing software package that can be purchased in the form of a tape cassette or floppy disk. Once the Electric Pencil program is loaded into a personal computer, the computer effectively becomes a word processor.

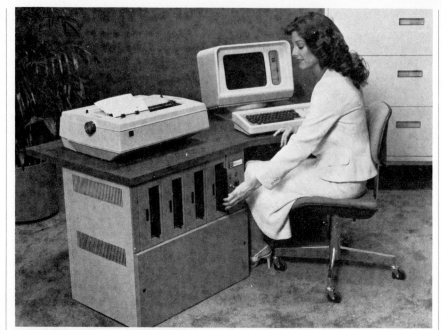

FIGURE 9-3
This *stand-alone* word processing system has a keyboard, visual display screen, four diskette drives, and a 55-character-per-second printer. (*3M Co.*)

FIGURE 9-4
This *multiple-station* word processing system is capable of supporting 14 stations. Up to 8,000 pages of text can be stored on magnetic disks for retrieval as needed. (*Wang Laboratories, Inc.*)

graphs can be added, deleted, or moved around in the document or report being prepared. When the displayed text is correct, instructions about output format can be added. For example, the system can be instructed to automatically put headings and numbers on each page of a report, center headings on the page, and produce specified top, bottom, left, and right margins. Finally, the document or report can be printed at the local station, or it can be transmitted electronically to a word processor located at a distant point via data communications channels. Thus, letters and reports need not be mailed but can be printed for the first time on the receiving equipment.[9] A printed copy may not be needed at the sending station since the text is available in an electronic file medium.

In addition, as we have seen, several prerecorded paragraphs can be called up from the dozens that are in storage and can then be assembled to prepare a quick response to a communication. An entire stored report can also be searched for specified words or phrases, and these characters can be deleted or replaced with other words or phrases. This global search feature can be used, for example, to substitute names in contracts, correct a word that has been misused or misspelled several times in a report, or substitute an abbreviation or acronym for a longer phrase.

Electronic mail/message systems   An electronic mail/message system (EMMS) in offices can deliver, by electronic means, messages that would otherwise probably be forwarded through the postal system or sent verbally via the telephone. As you know, the postal service is relatively slow and messages are sometimes lost. Telephone communication requires that (1) the message recipient can be found, and (2) the recipient is willing to be interrupted to take the call. Surprisingly enough, studies have shown that only about one in four calls made to people in organizations goes through on the first try. Thus, EMMSs have been developed in response to these deficiencies in the alternative message delivery systems. An EMMS can perform the following functions:

1   *Provide message distribution services.* A message may be sent (via satellite in many cases) on the first try, and at any time, to a *specified individual* who has a storage "mailbox" in the message system. It is not necessary to locate the recipient or interrupt him or her at an inopportune time. Rather, the recipient can periodically review messages at a visual display terminal, fire off responses and other messages, and, *if necessary,* make a printed copy of a communication. Alternatively, it is just as easy for the sender to transmit a message to an identified *group of people* as it is to send it to a single individual. Users with portable terminals can access the message network from any phone to enter or receive messages. Individuals and groups using the message system may be members of a single organization or may belong to many different organizations.

---

[9] Continental Illinois National Bank of Chicago has offices in Europe and New York. A proposal to a customer in Belgium can be prepared on the Brussels word processing equipment and relayed to New York, where it is printed and studied. Changes may be made to the proposal in New York before it is sent to Chicago, and additional changes may be made in Chicago. Finally, the proposal can be forwarded back to Brussels, where it is printed and delivered to the customer. All this can be done in a single day. See Richard G. Canning, "Computer Support for Managers," *EDP Analyzer,* p. 3, May 1979.

2 *Provide transmission of copies of documents and pictures.* An original document is placed in a sending *facsimile,* or *fax,* machine, and a communications link-up is made with a receiving fax device at another location. As the sending machine scans the document, the receiving device reproduces the scanned image. Thus, when the transmission is completed, the receiving device has produced a duplicate, or "facsimile," of the original (Figure 9-5). The use of fax machines is not new, but a great deal of emphasis is currently being placed on improving fax systems.

3 *Provide computerized conferences.* A computer-based EMMS permits "conferences" to be held at the convenience of the participants. Since the conference dialog may be stored, it is not necessary for all participants to be online at their terminals at the same time; of course, it is not necessary that they be physically present at the same place. Rather, a person may sit down at a terminal at a convenient time, call up any conversations he or she has not seen, make additional comments, respond to questions, etc., and then sign off. Interruptions of other important work may thus be avoided, and a permanent history of all conference discussions may be recorded.[10]

4 *Provide message reception services.* Once the message has been delivered, the message system may provide additional services to help the recipient take appropriate action. For example, the recipient may (*a*) forward the message to others with or without further comments, (*b*) store the message in a "personal attention needed" electronic file, or (*c*) store the message in a subordinate's electronic file with instructions for the subordinate to take the necessary action.

SOME BROADER ORGANIZATIONAL IMPLICATIONS OF COMPUTERS

In the preceding pages, we have only outlined a few examples of how certain types of economic and public organizations have been (or may be) affected by computer usage in offices and in other areas. But if instead of reading a few abbreviated examples, you studied several thousand computer-based information systems in detail, you would probably arrive at some *general* conclusions about the effects that computers have had on activities such as planning, organizing, staffing, and controlling in organizations of *all* types. What's that you just said? "If that clown thinks I am going to spend all that time. . . ." Oh very well then. . . .

[10] For more information on this subject, see Richard G. Canning, "Computer Message Systems," *EDP Analyzer,* pp. 1–13, April 1977; Murray Turoff, "Computerized Conferencing: Present and Future," *Creative Computing,* pp. 54–57, September/October 1977; Ronald P. Uhlig, "Human Factors in Computer Message Systems," *Datamation,* pp. 120ff, May 1977; and Jacques Vallee, Robert Johansen, and Kathleen Spangler, "The Computer Conference: An Altered State of Communication?" *Creative Computing,* pp. 58–59, September/October 1977.

FIGURE 9-5
(*Top left*) In a Gulf Oil Corporation dispatching system, customers phone orders into a central location. (*Top center*) Delivery dispatch forms are then prepared in an efficient delivery sequence. (*Top right*) Copies of these forms are first transmitted by fax machines to a distribution terminal in a few seconds. (*Right*) Forms are then used for driver and truck delivery assignments. After delivery, terminal personnel use the fax equipment to transmit data on the delivery back to the central location. (*3M Co.*)

319

Planning and Decision-Making Implications

We can look at this broad topic from at least two viewpoints. *First,* we can examine the implications of *planning with computers; second,* we can consider some computer-oriented *decision-making techniques* that are now being used.

Planning with computers Generally speaking, the use of *computers can have an impact on the planning function by:*

1 *Causing faster awareness of problems and opportunities.* Computers can quickly signal out-of-control conditions requiring corrective action when actual performance deviates from what was planned. Masses of current and historical internal and external data can be analyzed by the use of statistical methods, including trend analyses and correlation techniques, in order to detect opportunities and challenges. Timely information can be forwarded quickly to a decision maker by a computer-based EMMS. Planning data stored online may permit administrators to probe files and receive quick replies to their questions (see Figure 9-6).

2 *Permitting administrators to give timely consideration to more complex relationships.* The computer gives the manager the ability to evaluate *more* possible alternatives (and to consider *more of the internal and external variables* that may have a bearing on the outcome of these alternatives). It makes it possible for managers to do a better job of identifying and assessing the probable economic and social effects of different courses of action. The awareness of such effects, of course, influences the ultimate decision. In the past, oversimplified assumptions would have to be made if resulting decisions were to be timely. More complex relationships can now be considered and scheduled.

3 *Assisting in decision implementation.* When decisions have been made, the computer can help transmit the decision over an EMMS, and it can assist in the development of subordinate plans that will be needed to implement these decisions. (Computerized conferences can be of value at this point.) Computer-based techniques to schedule project activities have been developed and are now widely used. Through the use of such techniques, resources can be utilized and controlled effectively.

Decision-making techniques A number of quantitative aids have been introduced, which utilize computers to provide the framework for decision-producing analyses. These techniques (which are often classified under the headings of *operations research* or *management science*) can be used to (1) speed up problem or opportunity awareness, (2) permit more timely consideration of increasingly complex relationships, and (3) assist in decision implementation. In particular, the computer-based techniques of *network analysis, linear programming, and simulation* have organizational implications.

FIGURE 9-6
Managers can query files and
receive quick replies
from data stored online.
(*Burroughs Corp.*)

Network analysis Both PERT (Program Evaluation and Review Technique) and CPM (Critical Path Method) are network models which are used to plan, schedule, and control complex projects. The basic concepts of PERT and CPM are similar. The following procedure is used to set up a network model:

1   *All the individual activities* to be performed in the project must be identified.
2   The *sequence of each activity* must be determined; i.e., it must be known what elements have to be completed prior to the start of a particular activity and what tasks cannot commence until after its completion.
3   The *time interval* required to complete each activity must be estimated.
4   The *longest sequence* of events in the project must be identified. The sum of the individual activity times in this sequence becomes the total project time, and this sequence of activities is known as the *critical path*.

The use of such a model in a construction project, for example, improves the *planning* function because it forces managers to identify *all the project activities that must be performed. Control* is also improved because attention can be focused on the sequence of activities in the critical path. Managers quickly become aware of potential problems. If a critical activity begins to slip behind schedule, steps can be taken quickly to correct the situation. By trading project cost against project time, several alternative paths can be computed initially to help in planning. By a greater commitment of resources, managers can often reduce the time required to complete certain activities in the critical path (and thus reduce total project time). The effect of a greater resource commitment, however, is often higher project cost (see Figure 9-7). Network models can simulate the effects on time and cost of a varying resource mix. Computations for small networks can be produced manually, but a computer is needed with networks of any significant size.

FIGURE 9-7
Reducing of project time may
be possible if greater costs
are acceptable.

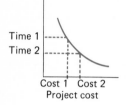

Linear programming Linear programming models are used to find the *best combination* of limited resources to achieve a specified objective (which is, typically, to maximize economic results or minimize costs). One important class of linear programming applications is in blending operations, where the objective is often to minimize the cost involved in the production of a given amount of blended product. For example, cattle feed may be a mixture of minerals, grains, and fish and meat products. The prices of these ingredients are subject to change, and so the least expensive blend required to achieve specified nutritional requirements is subject to variation. Linear programming can help managers determine quickly the correct blend to use to minimize cost while meeting product specifications.

In addition to blending, linear programming is being used for such diverse purposes as preparing work schedules, selecting media for advertising purposes, determining minimum transportation costs from given supply points to specified points of delivery, and determining the most profitable product mix that may be manufactured in a given plant with given equipment. Practically all linear programming applications require the use of a computer (Figure 9-8). As a powerful *planning* tool, linear programming enables managers to select the most appropriate alternative from a large number of options. It is also a technique that may aid managers in carrying out their other functions. Its use in preparing work schedules, for example, has definite staffing implications.

Simulation In the physical sciences, experiments may be performed in a laboratory by using small models of a process or an operation. Many complex variations may be possible in these tests, and the results show the scientists what happens under certain controlled conditions. Simulation is similar to scientific experimentation. Perhaps Figure 9-9 will clarify the meaning of simulation. At its base, Figure 9-9 rests on reality or fact. In complex situations, few people (if any) fully understand all aspects of the situation; therefore, theories are developed which may focus attention on only part of the complex whole. In some situations models may be built or conceived in order to test or represent a theory. Finally, *simulation* is the use of a model in the attempt to identify and/or reflect the behavior of a real person, process, or system.

In organizations, administrators may evaluate proposed projects or strategies by constructing theoretical models. They can then determine

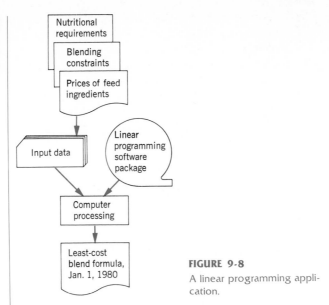

FIGURE 9-8

A linear programming application.

what happens to these models when certain conditions are given or when certain assumptions are tested. Simulation is thus a trial-and-error problem-solving *approach;* it is also a *planning aid* that may be of considerable value to organizations.

Simulation models have helped top business executives decide, for example, whether to expand operations by acquiring a new plant. Among the dozens of complicating variables that would have to be incorporated into such models are facts and assumptions about (1) present and potential size of the total market, (2) present and potential company share of this total market, (3) product selling prices, and (4) investment required to achieve various production levels. Thus, simulation has helped top executives in their planning and decision-making activities.

Simulation has also been useful in (1) establishing design parameters for aircraft and space vehicles, (2) refining medical treatment techniques, (3) teaching students, (4) planning urban improvements, and (5) planning transportation systems where variables such as expected road usage, effects of highway construction on traffic load, use of one-way streets, etc., are considered. In later chapters, several simulation applications will be studied in greater detail.

Organizing Implications

The fact that new information systems have been (and are being) designed and implemented was noted in Chapter 2; some ways in which computer elements are being introduced into an office environment were mentioned a few pages earlier. What was not given adequate attention in these earlier discussions, however, is the fact that changes in information

FIGURE 9-9

A simulation model.

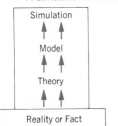

systems and office environments have often led to significant organizational changes as well. As computer-based systems are designed and implemented, there is often a need to reconsider the answers to several important and interrelated organizing questions. Included in these questions are: (1) *Where will decision making occur?* (2) *Where will data be processed?* and (3) *Where will data be stored?*

Where will decision making occur? The concept of *centralization of authority*[11] refers to a concentration of the important decision-making powers in the hands of a relatively few top executives. *Decentralization of authority,* on the other hand, refers to the extent to which significant decisions are made at lower levels. In very small organizations, *all* decision-making power is likely to be centralized in the hands of the owner or manager; in larger groups, the question of centralization or decentralization *is a matter of degree*—i.e., it is a question of how much authority is held at different levels. The extent to which authority is delegated to lower levels depends, in part, on such factors as (1) the managerial philosophy of top executives, (2) the availability of qualified subordinates, and (3) the availability of good operating controls. Since all these factors may change, it is apparent that the degree of centralization of authority is subject to revision.

When a computer is used, a greater degree of centralized control *can* be supported in an organization because top administrators can be furnished with information from dispersed departments in time to decide on appropriate action. Without computers, such action must often be determined by a lower-level manager because of time, distance, and familiarity factors. But although greater centralized control *can be supported* with a computer, it is *not necessarily a requirement.* The degree of centralized authority and control that *should* exist in the new system is determined by managerial philosophy and judgment, not by computer usage. The impact of the path chosen on future organizational structure, basic philosophy and policies, and managerial authority of managers below the top echelons will be great.

Where will data be processed? Prior to the introduction of computers, data processing activities were generally handled by departments on a separate and thus decentralized basis. When computers first appeared, however, the tendency was to maximize the use of the expensive hardware by establishing one or more central processing centers to serve the organization's needs. Today, the rapid reduction in hardware costs and the development of distributed processing systems have made it feasible for organizations to use either a centralized or a decentralized approach to *data processing.* Thus, many organizations must now decide to what extent (if any) they will centralize their data processing operations. Should

---

[11] *Authority* is defined here as the right to give orders and the power to see that they are carried out.

small computers be used by individual organization units, or should these units furnish input to (and receive output from) one or more central computer centers which can process data originating at many points? (See Figure 9-10.)

The possible considerations in favor of the centralized approach are:

1 *It may permit economies of scale.* With adequate processing volume, the use of larger and more powerful computing equipment may result in reduced operating costs.

2 *It may facilitate systems integration.* For example, achieving statewide agreement on welfare recipient identification numbers may be a necessary step in integrating the procedures required to process and analyze welfare records. Such agreement, through the development of standardized files, is more likely to occur for efficiency reasons when processing is handled at a central point.

3 *It has certain personnel advantages.* It may be possible to concentrate fewer skilled programmers at a centralized site and thus make more effective use of their talents.

4 *It may permit better utilization of processing capability.* With a centralized operation, organizationwide priorities can be assigned to processing tasks. Those jobs which are of greatest importance are, of course, completed first.

Included among the possible advantages of decentralization are the following:

1 *Greater interest and motivation at division levels.* Division managers in control of their own computers may be more likely to (a) maintain the

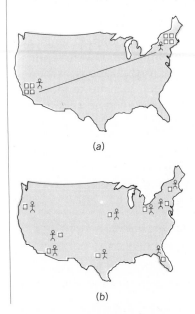

(a)

(b)

FIGURE 9-10
(A) Centralization and (B) decentralization of data processing activities.

accuracy of input data and (*b*) use the equipment in ways that best meet their particular operating needs.

2 *Better response to user needs.* The systems standardization typically required for centralized processing may not be equally suitable for all divisions. With decentralization, special programs can be prepared to meet exact divisional needs. In addition, although a smaller machine will probably be slower than the centralized equipment, it should be remembered that central machine time must be allocated to several users. Information considered important to one division may be delayed because higher priority is given to other processing tasks. Thus, the fact that a smaller machine allows for prompt attention to a given job may lead to faster processing at the division level.

3 *Reduced downtime risks.* A breakdown in the centralized equipment or the communications links may leave the entire system inoperative. A similar breakdown in one division, however, does not affect other decentralized operations.

There is no general answer to the question of where data *should* be processed. Some small organizations have opted for central computers because their departments often lack sufficient volume to justify separate machines. Some large organizations have achieved a greater degree of centralization by establishing several regional data centers. Other organizations have followed a *distributed processing compromise approach* to the centralization-decentralization issue by combining larger central computers (and centralized data files) with small processors, minicomputers, and intelligent terminals at operating levels. The central processor(s) serves the local processors by managing large data bases and by executing those jobs which require extensive computations (see Figure 9-11).

Where will data be stored?   Before computers came along, data were typically stored at the using departments, although some summary facts needed to prepare organizationwide reports were maintained at centralized sites in large organizations. When computers first appeared, however, we have seen that the tendency was to maximize the use of expensive hardware by setting up centralized computer centers. Not sur-

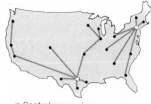

□ Central processing
complex

• Intelligent terminal/satellite
minicomputer

FIGURE 9-11
Distributed processing compromise approach.

prisingly, the tendency was also to establish and store large centralized data bases at these central sites on such media as magnetic tape and disks.

In most cases, data with organizationwide significance will continue to be stored at a central site. But with the reduction in hardware costs, the increase in data communications facilities, and the development of distributed computing networks, there is no technical reason why applications-oriented files with local significance cannot be returned to the outlying user departments for storage and maintenance. Thus, many organizations are now in the process of deciding to what extent (if any) they will relocate the storage of previously centralized computer-based data to using departments.[12]

Regardless of how organizations answer the question of where to locate decision making, data processing, and data storage, it is likely that some work groups may be realigned, some tasks may be consolidated or eliminated, and some departments may be expanded while others are eliminated or curtailed. A probable result of these organizational shifts is the resistance of individuals to such changes.

Staffing Implications

Since, as we have just seen, computer information systems may contribute to organizational stress, they are also likely to bring about a need for personnel adjustments. Among the staffing implications of computer usage are the need to (1) recruit, select, and train personnel for new jobs, (2) deal with those whose jobs have been eliminated or reduced in content or appeal, and (3) cope with resistance to change in a computer environment. We shall briefly consider the selection and training of computer personnel here; in Chapter 11 we shall consider the other staffing topics.

Selecting employees for computer-related jobs Some of the positions created by computer usage can be classified into the following categories: (1) *systems analysis and design,* (2) *program preparation,* and (3) *computer operation.*

Although there are often several grades of *systems analyst* (senior, junior, etc.), the job basically consists of (1) examining the basic methods

---

[12] There are *possible advantages to the centralized storage approach* in situations where (1) unified control and strict adherence to standards are desired, (2) the partitioning or replication of files adds system security problems, (3) file sizes are large and many transactions do not originate at local levels, and (4) the application is too critical to run the risk of having data updated at one location and not at another. On the other hand, there are also *possible advantages to a distributed data storage approach* in situations where (1) data communication costs between central and local sites can be substantially reduced by moving frequently accessed records to the user's location, (2) the performance of data communications facilities and/or the central computing center presents problems of system reliability for users, (3) user interest and motivation is improved through faster access to, and better control over, records that are locally stored, and (4) the redundancy found in replicated files can add storage backup and a degree of added data security to the system.

and procedures of current information systems and (2) modifying, redesigning, and integrating these existing procedures into new systems specifications as required to provide the needed information. Typically, the analysts must know a great deal about the particular organization as well as the uses and limitations of computers.

The job of the applications *programmer* is to take the systems designs of the analyst and transform these specifications into machine instructions or programs. In most cases the programmer will work very closely with the analyst during the systems-design phase. In smaller organizations, the systems-analysis and program preparation functions are often combined.

The duties of the *computer operator* include setting up the processor and related equipment, starting the program run, checking to ensure proper operation, and unloading equipment at the end of a run. Some knowledge of programming is needed.

To fill the jobs described above, it is necessary to *recruit* potential candidates and then *select* from among those candidates the right people for the jobs. Figure 9-12 summarizes the general recruitment and selection process. The chosen candidates may then need to be trained to prepare them for their new duties.

Training computer personnel Extensive training must be given to those selected to be systems analysts and programmers. In addition to having a *knowledge of the organization and its environment,* the systems analyst must also understand the *techniques of systems analysis and design.* There is lack of uniformity at the present time in the methods used to train (*educate* is probably a better word) analysts to meet the latter requirement, although the Association for Computing Machinery (ACM) has recommended college undergraduate and graduate curricula for programs in systems analysis and design. Consulting firms, private institutes, and other educational organizations conduct systems-analysis seminars on a limited basis. An in-house systems training program utilizing senior analysts as instructors has proved effective.

A third requirement of analysts is that they possess a *general understanding of computer hardware and software.* The formal training given to analysts in this area may parallel or be identical with the formal training received by programmers.

Programmer training is a continual, lengthy, and expensive process. To the surprise (and dismay) of many administrators, it has been found that *at least six months* is generally required before programmers attain a *minimum* level of proficiency. Training costs per programmer may run into the thousands of dollars. In addition to the training available from vendors and through in-house activities, programming skills are also taught by consultants, professional organizations, colleges and universities, and vocational schools.

Equipment manufacturers and vocational schools also offer brief courses to train equipment operators. On-the-job training is often the only preparation required.

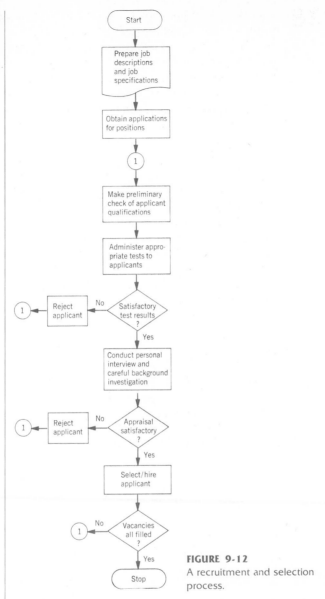

FIGURE 9-12
A recruitment and selection
process.

Controlling Implications

You will recall that the general control procedure consists of several steps: (1) the establishment of predetermined goals or standards, (2) the measurement of performance, (3) the comparison of actual performance with the standards, and (4) the making of appropriate control decisions.

The information output of the computer can help the administrator in many ways to carry out this procedure. First of all, better information can lead to better planning and the creation of *more realistic standards.* Computer simulation can assist managers in setting goals by showing them the effects of various alternative decisions when certain conditions are assumed, and computer-based network models such as PERT and CPM can improve planning (and therefore control) by forcing managers to identify all project activities that must be performed.

Computer data and word processing systems can also help administrators control by gathering, classifying, calculating, summarizing, and communicating *actual performance data* promptly and accurately. Once performance data are read into the computer, it is possible for the machine to *compare* the actual performance with the established standards. Periodic reports showing this comparison can be prepared; in some systems triggered reports, based on the *principle of exception,*[13] may be furnished to the manager only when variations are outside certain specified limits.

It is also possible to program the computer so that it signals when *predetermined decisions* should be carried out. For example, a program may specify that when the inventory of a certain basic part falls below a given level, an output message signals the need to reorder and indicates the reorder quantity. By thus relieving people of many of the routine operational control tasks, the computer frees them to devote more time to (1) planning future moves and (2) leading the all-important human resources of the organization. Such a human-machine relationship, in other words, makes it possible for people to concentrate more of their attention on the heuristic area of intellectual work—an area in which they are far superior to the machine—while the machine is permitted to take over the well-structured control tasks. Figure 9-13 is a generalized illustration showing the place of a computer system in the overall control process of an organization.

Economic Implications

From an economic standpoint, the acquisition and use of all but the smallest computers cannot be taken lightly. An investment involving thousands of dollars (or a few million dollars) may be needed. We know from Chapter 1 that a computer *can* improve the economic position of an organization, but there is no guarantee that economic benefits *will* be obtained merely because a computer is installed. On the contrary, many organizations have invested large sums in computers and have received benefits of *less* than a dollar for each dollar spent. One large bank, for example, decided to implement a total information-processing concept consisting of six large information systems. Unfortunately for the bank, however, only one system was eventually completed, and the loss sus-

---

[13] In Chapter 18 of Exodus, Jethro gives good advice when he tells Moses to delegate some of his routine leadership duties to subordinates and concentrate his attention on the more important exceptions, which the subordinates are unable to handle. This idea is called *the principle of exception* in management literature.

tained in the futile attempt to develop the other five is estimated at $12 million. A report of the General Accounting Office of the federal government noted that after nine years and $7.7 million, the Federal Aviation Aministration was still trying to develop several information systems (poor systems studies accounted for this lack of success).

The computer feasibility studies conducted in the early and mid-1960s were usually made to determine whether money could be saved (i.e., the decision to acquire a computer was often based on estimates of cost displacement). But the economic picture of an organization may also be enhanced if information is provided that will enable administrators to make better decisions and give better service to patients, clients, customers, etc. Unfortunately, it is difficult (perhaps even impossible) to assign a precise dollar value to such benefits.

Yet it is the opinion of several authorities that the information systems that designers are now working on are often more than merely data and/or word processing systems and thus should not be justified solely on the basis of earlier tangible cost-displacement criteria. Rather, it is argued, the value of information should be determined by what administrators can do with it instead of what it costs to produce. In short, many of the important benefits of these new systems will be intangible, and although by definition intangible benefits are not subject to precise quantitative measurement, designers and managers are still faced with the problem of assigning approximate values to them. But in quantifying intan-

FIGURE 9-13
Organizational control and
the computer.

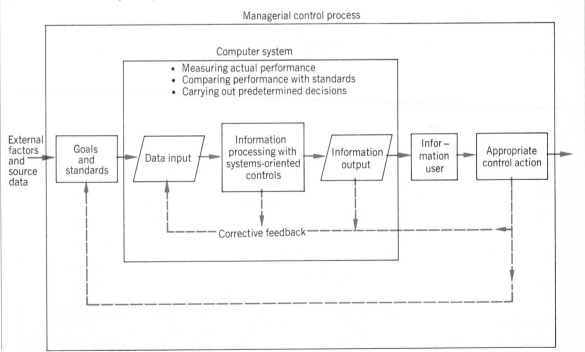

gibles, there is always the danger that errors in assumptions and judgment will lead to economically unsound systems decisions.

To summarize, then, computer acquisition and use may require administrators to make decisions involving large sums of money; the investment of this money may lead to economic benefits, but this end is by no means assured; and greater consideration may have to be given to qualitative or intangible factors (with the risks involved) in future decisions about computer systems. In educational institutions, for example, economic factors cannot be ignored (school boards do not have unlimited resources). But many school systems have considered computers as instructional tools and have acquired them for instructional purposes. Although it may be impossible to assign quantitative values to the insights gained by students interacting with computers in computer-assisted instructional programs, few are likely to argue that such uses do not provide intangible (and valuable) benefits. Of course, in a profit-seeking organization, a top executive might be tempted to have nothing to do with computers because of the possible economic consequences of unwise decisions. But this course of nonaction might be the most hazardous of all because the executive must also consider the possible economic implications of *not keeping pace with competitors* in the development and use of new information systems.

STANDARDIZATION PRESSURES

A *standard* defines or completely specifies something so that people and machines that must use it, know about it, and/or produce it do so in a common and uniform way. Of course, simple information systems with few if any standards can be designed. But as broader and more integrated systems are developed within organizations, and as the interaction of these systems with other complex external systems becomes more extensive, standards are needed to reduce systems-design time and facilitate training of systems users. We have seen that in a data-base system, input data must be commonly defined and consistently organized and presented throughout the organization. Such a requirement, in turn, calls for strict input discipline and a thinking through of processing procedures to a degree not required when clerks are available to handle irregularities; it also means that someone in the organization must be given the overall authority to *standardize* (and approve any necessary changes to) data, files, and programs which have organizationwide usefulness so that inconsistencies are not introduced into the system.

However, standardization of input data definitions, files, and software is expensive and involves problems such as proper timing, flexibility, and the danger of smothering innovation, as well as the difficulty of purging faulty data and defining software standards. Although complex and standardized systems tend to be economical (since they may eliminate duplication of effort) and quite efficient in file organizing and processing, they

"Technology Set to Revolutionize Business"

While most corporations and government agencies valiantly strive to throttle rising data processing and communications costs, they unwittingly allow the far larger costs of office administration and clerical information handling to go relatively unchecked. So says Harvey Poppel, senior vice president of the management consulting firm of Booz, Allen, Hamilton. Speaking at a recent meeting of the Computer and Communications Industry Association in Palm Beach, FL, Poppel noted that US businesses spend more on secretaries, typists and mail services than they do on computers and communications services. "And the average productivity gains of white collar workers have lagged far behind the gains of blue collar workers or the productivity improvements of any of the capital asset utilization categories," he added.

For the business world to survive, Poppel warned, the application of information technology must catch up with the dazzling advances made in other areas of human endeavor. "And catch up it will," he predicted.

Over the next decade, Poppel envisions a revolutionary role for business information systems, manifested principally by:

- More powerful aids to decision making in the form of computerized market and financial models and integrated, readily accessible data banks of customer, competition, design and costing information;

- Greater personnel efficiency and job fulfillment from the use of terminal-assisted work stations that enable individuals to perform multiple functions, often handling a transaction from start to finish. Also, the use of audio, video and computer conferencing will reduce undesirable travel and eventually make business communications capabilities available for occasional work at home;

- Higher managerial and organizational productivity resulting from the use of ubiquitous desk terminals that will handle correspondence needs electronically, schedule, record and expedite activities, and report vital internal and external news. These terminals will be tied together within each organization through integrated voice, data and image networks.

As we move into the era of the electronic office, the major bridge that has to be crossed is to understand the various individuals that make up an office and to view them as "human work stations in support of some subset of the organization's objectives," says Poppel.

"We're no longer dealing as we have in the DP past with only a limited segment of an individual's activities—for example, the few minutes a manager might take each week to read a report or to provide forecast input to a computer system. Rather, we're dealing with the totality of the time which our office people spend doing their work. Which means we have to understand what makes office people productive and how we can boost their productivity."

Source: Morris Edwards, "Technology Set to Revolutionize Business," *Infosystems*, p. 45, January 1979. Reprinted with permission of the publisher.

also tend to be quite formal, proceduralized, and rigid; as a result they tend to have difficulty in dealing with input errors or with legitimate but rare exceptions to standard procedures.

Pressure to standardize information systems (and the format of input data and output reports) that interact with external institutions is being felt by organizations in many fields of activity. Law enforcement agencies, social welfare offices, health departments, educational systems—these and other types of organizations are developing standards in order to cooperate more effectively in sharing information about individuals. This increased efficiency in gathering, processing, and retrieving information is probably a need of modern society. But, of course, standardization may also lead to unwanted conformity[14] and to the realization that one is increasingly being considered as a code number rather than an individual. As we will see in Chapter 11, the creation of standardized data banks has already led to a legitimate concern about the invasion of an individual's right to privacy. The problem facing society is to determine how to obtain the maximum benefits from modern information technology without being dominated by its use.

LOOKING BACK

The following points have been emphasized in this chapter:

1 Computer-using organizations have experienced various changes that may be directly traceable to the computer. These changes have occurred in the administrative activities of planning, organizing, staffing, and controlling.
2 The steps followed in planning are to (a) identify the problem or opportunity, (b) gather and analyze relevant facts, (c) determine suitable alternatives, (d) select the most appropriate alternative, and (e) fol-

---

[14] As an example, considerable effort is required to match a longhand letter of complaint about a magazine subscription with the computer subscription record. "So magazine publishers may eventually strengthen their current polite request that the customer send back a copy of the mailing label, and say, in effect, 'If you don't provide us with your name and address in our machine-readable format, we probably can't respond to you at all.'" See Victor A Vyssotsky, "Computer Systems in Business: More Evolution than Revolution," *Management Review*, p. 21, February 1979.

low-up on the decision(s) and plans. The *organizing* activity involves the grouping of work teams into logical and efficient units in order to carry out plans and achieve goals. The *staffing* function consists not only of selecting and training people for positions but also preparing people for changing conditions. Finally, the *control* function involves (*a*) setting standards, (*b*) measuring actual performance, (*c*) comparing actual performance with standards, and (*d*) taking appropriate control action.

3   Organizations making extensive use of computers are likely to be engaged in processing operations that have one or more of the following characteristics: (*a*) a large volume of input data, (*b*) repetitive processing tasks, (*c*) the need for speed in processing and retrieval, (*d*) the need for a high degree of accuracy, and (*e*) processing complexities that require or encourage computer usage. Selected ways in which certain economic and public organizations may be affected by computer usage have been presented in this chapter.

4   A number of evolutionary changes are likely to occur in the office environments of many organizations in the next few years. As noted in the chapter, word processing and electronic mail/message systems are being introduced to boost office productivity and to help overcome some of the problems encountered when traditional office methods are used.

5   The decision to introduce and use a computer in an organization has implications that go far beyond the mere acquisition of a piece of technical equipment. Information vital to the support of planning and control decisions is affected by the computer system that develops; the entire organizational structure may undergo stress and alteration; the nature and number of jobs are affected; the economic consequences are often hard to predict; and the decision-making techniques that have been used by managers in the past may have to be changed.

6   A current trend in organizations is to develop broader information systems and standardized data banks. A desire for greater economy and efficiency is behind the standardization pressure, but standardization may also lead to systems rigidity, unwanted conformity, and the possibility of invasion of privacy.

▶ KEY TERMS

After reading Chapter 9, you should be able to define and use the following terms:

planning	computerized conferencing
organizing	PERT and CPM
staffing	critical path
controlling	linear programming

gerrymandering
word processing
global search
electronic mail/message system
facsimile machine

simulation
centralization of authority
principle of exception
standard
standardization pressures

▶ REVIEW AND DISCUSSION QUESTIONS

1 What activities or functions must be performed by administrators?
2 (a) What is involved in the planning function? (b) What steps must be followed in planning?
3 Explain what is involved in (a) the organizing function and (b) the staffing function.
4 Identify and discuss the steps in controlling.
5 (a) What types of organizations are affected by computers? (b) Give some examples of how economic organizations may be affected by computer usage. (c) How may computers affect public organizations?
6 How may computers affect (a) an organization's handling of money? (b) the employment situation in an organization? (c) the security of an organization? (d) an organization's ability to compete both domestically and across national borders? (e) the decision-making techniques used in an organization? (f) the election process and other government operations? (g) health care and educational organizations?
7 (a) What are the organizational implications of planning with computers? (b) What are some uses of network analysis, linear programming, and simulation?
8 (a) Discuss the possible organizing implications of computer usage. (b) What are the staffing implications?
9 (a) What are the possible control implications of computer usage? (b) The economic implications?
10 "Pressure to standardize information systems is being felt by organizations in many fields of activity." Explain why this statement is true and discuss the possible advantages and disadvantages of this trend.
11 "Although the necessary data processing work is usually accomplished in offices that follow traditional methods, there are also likely to be problems." (a) What are some of these problems? (b) How can computers help in the office?
12 "A modern word processing system is an amazingly flexible tool." Discuss this statement and give examples of some word processing features.
13 Identify and discuss the functions that may be performed by an electronic mail/message system.

SELECTED REFERENCES

In addition to the references suggested in the chapter footnotes, you might wish to examine the following sources:

Ashner, Katherine: "Evaluating Word Processing Systems," *Government Data Systems,* pp. 26ff, July/August 1979.

Burstyn, H. Paris: "Electronic Fund Transfers: A Promise or a Threat?" *Personal Computing,* pp. 58ff, May 1978.

Connell, John J.: "The Office of the Future," *Journal of Systems Management,* pp. 6–10, February 1979.

Diebold, John: "Information Resource Management—The New Challenge," *Infosystems,* pp. 50–51ff, June 1979.

Hallam, Stephen F., Donald D. Scriven, Mark R. Bomball, and James A. Hallam: "Basic Steps in Developing Simulation Models," *Data Management,* pp. 26–29, April 1975.

Hansen, John R.: "Retail Terminals Mind the Store," *Infosystems,* pp. 54ff, March 1979.

Holmes, Fenwicke W.: "IRM: Organizing for the Office of the Future," *Journal of Systems Management,* pp. 24–31, January 1979.

Miller, Frederick W.: "Checkless Society Gets Closer," *Infosystems,* pp. 48ff, March 1979.

"New Growth Industries—And Some Dropouts," *Business Week,* pp. 188–189ff, September 3, 1979.

Rhodes, Wayne L., Jr.: "Facsimile—New Life for an Old idea," *Infosystems,* pp. 42ff, September 1979.

Sirbu, Marvin A., Jr.: "Automating Office Communications: The Policy Dilemmas," *Technology Review,* pp. 50–57, October 1978.

Stewart, Jon: "Computer Shock; The Inhuman Office of the Future," *Saturday Review,* pp. 14–17, June 23, 1979.

Van Rensselaer, Cort: "Centralize? Decentralize? Distribute?" *Datamation,* pp. 86ff, April 1979.

Chapter 10

INDIVIDUALS AND COMPUTERS: SOME POSITIVE VIEWS

We assert that knowledge is power. But the basis of knowledge is structured and accessible data. Computers provide the structure to data and communications provide the access to data. Thus, in a society where people have possession of their own computers and the freedom to communicate (i.e., the ability to structure and access data), the people hold the knowledge and, therefore, the ultimate power.
—Edwin J. Istvan

Individuals are affected by computer usage both in their dealings with organizations and in their private lives. The purpose of this chapter is to outline just a few of the ways in which computers are helping people.

In the first section of the chapter, you will find a brief discussion of how people in their roles as administrators or employees benefit from their organizations' use of computers. Later chapters will also present examples of ways in which employees gain from computer usage.

The second section of the chapter examines some of the areas in which our private lives are improved and/or enriched by (1) the ways that economic and public organizations use computers, and (2) the ways that we can utilize personal computers.

Finally, in the last section, a summary is given of the views of those who are optimistic about the future effects of computer usage on society.

Thus, after studying this chapter, you should be able to:

- Explain how administrators and employees may benefit from their organizations' use of computers.
- Identify and discuss a number of the possible benefits that private individuals may receive from their dealings with computer-using economic organizations. (Nine benefit categories are mentioned in the chapter.)
- Identify and discuss some of the possible benefits that private individuals may receive from computer-using public organizations. (Three broad benefit categories are mentioned in the chapter.)
- Outline several ways (four categories are included in the chapter) that individuals may benefit from personal computing.
- Summarize the views of those who are optimistic about the future effects on society of computer usage.
- Understand and use the key terms listed at the end of the chapter.

You saw in the last chapter that computers are applied in countless organizational settings where data are processed on a regular basis and/or where problem complexities leave no other alternative. And you saw in Chapter 6 that hundreds of thousands of microcomputer systems have been acquired by individuals for entertainment and other personal applications. Thus, the changes brought about by computer usage are bound to affect individuals both in their dealings with organizations and in their private lives. There are possibly only a few hermits who do not participate in one or more computer-using organizations in some capacity, or who are not served or affected by one or more of these organizations. In the future, the lives of an increasing number of us will be affected by our use of personal computers.

The nature of this computer influence will depend on decisions consciously made by people and on the indirect and perhaps unintentional effects of the application of the computing tools which people use. There are two schools of thought in contemporary literature about the ultimate influence of computers on individuals. The *optimistic school* believes that freedom and individuality—their presence and their potential—are encouraged by the use of computers. The *pessimistic school* holds an opposite view—that computer usage represents a threat to human freedom and individuality.

Examples of the present and potential benefits associated with computer use are often the focus of newspaper headlines and the subject of magazine articles. There can be no doubt that computer usage has already had a very strong positive influence on (and will continue to offer substantial benefits to) large segments of society in general and many individuals in particular. The purpose of this chapter is to outline just a few of the ways in which computers are helping people. (Dozens of other ways will be discussed in the chapters in Part 5.) Thus, in the following pages of this chapter we will examine some of the (1) *benefits to individuals in organizations* (i.e., on the job), (2) *benefits to people in their private lives,* and (3) *optimistic views* associated with computer usage. However, we should not lose sight of the fact that since the computer is one of the most powerful technological forces in society today, its use can also create potential dangers and problems.[1] These dangers and problems are the subject of the next chapter.

BENEFITS TO INDIVIDUALS IN ORGANIZATIONS

Both *administrators* and *employees* are the beneficiaries of their organizations' use of computers.

Administrators

High-level executives have, in some cases, been able to use better and more timely information in order to reassume some of the decision-making powers previously delegated to subordinates. In other cases, executives have, with a greater feeling of confidence in their ability to monitor performance through computer-produced reports, delegated additional authority to subordinates. However, the primary role of top executives

---

[1] Do you remember the section entitled "Technological Change and Social Change" in Chapter 2? As we saw then, the use of the automobile has had both positive and negative social effects.

lies in formulating objectives and policies and planning and guiding over-all organizational strategy. Computer-based systems should, through the use of improved simulation techniques, help remove some of the uncertainties from the usually unique and ill-structured problems that top administrators face. And top executives, like lower-level managers, may use electronic mail/message systems to reduce telephone interruptions, improve the dissemination of messages to subordinates, and reduce the time required for scheduled meetings through the use of computerized conferencing techniques. But substantial changes in the role of the top executive have not occurred, and are not expected in the near future, because people, not computers, make the hard decisions.

A most important role of *lower-level supervisors* is to provide face-to-face communication, direction, and leadership to operating employees. But these administrators have, in the past, been caught in a squeeze between rising costs for personnel and materials on the one hand and the need to maintain cost controls and remain within budget limits on the other. Computer usage has benefited administrators in business and government, as well as in school systems, hospitals, and other social service organizations, by permitting them to (1) schedule operations more efficiently, (2) maintain better control over economic resources, and (3) cope with a generally increasing level of paperwork. By relieving supervisors of many of their clerical duties, computers have made it possible for them to give more attention to the important personnel administration aspects of their work.

Administrators occupying *middle-level positions* in an organization,[2] like all managers, must perform the activities of planning, organizing, staffing, and controlling. As a result of computer information systems, some middle managers no longer need to spend as much time in controlling because the computer can be programmed to take over many of the clerical control activities—e.g., it can signal with a triggered report whenever actual performance varies from what was planned. Time saved in controlling has enabled some middle-level administrators to devote more attention to planning and directing the work of subordinates. More accurate and timely organizationwide information supplied by the computer has given some administrators the opportunity to spend more time identifying problems, recognizing opportunities, and planning alternate courses of action. In this respect, then, their jobs have become more challenging and more nearly resemble those of chief executives. With administrators having more time to devote to departmental employee matters, improved morale may be expected; furthermore, the more timely information that is now available to some middle managers puts them in a position to be able to react more rapidly to external changes.

---

[2] *Middle managers* may be defined as those who are above the lowest level of supervision and below the highest level of a self-contained operating organization. Thus, the term *middle manager* is rather nebulous and is applied to a number of levels in many organizations. The difficulties of generalizing about such a wide range of positions should be recognized.

Employees

Programmers, systems analysts, and *computer operations* personnel whose jobs depend on the use of computers; *operations researchers* using the techniques of linear programming, simulation, etc.; *scientists* conducting research into complex problem areas that could not be considered without computers; *design engineers* and *architects* using computers to simplify design work and increase the alternatives that can be considered; *structural engineers* using computer models to predict the effect of stresses on different structural configurations; *lawyers* using legal data banks to locate precedent cases in order to serve clients better; *sales personnel* who receive more timely information about customers and product inventories and who are able to promise more efficient handling of sales orders in order to serve their customers better and thus improve their sales performance; *teachers* who have been able to devote more time to giving students individual attention because record-keeping and grading chores have been reduced and because computer-assisted instruction techniques have reduced the time-consuming routine drill work; *clerical employees* whose job duties have changed from routine, repetitive operations to more varied and appealing tasks—all these individuals are among the beneficiaries of the use of computers in organizations.[3] Computer information systems have furnished them with well-paying jobs, and/or the systems have replaced routine procedures with more challenging and rewarding opportunities to use their creative abilities. Since the six chapters in Part 5 deal with selected uses of computers in society, and since *these chapters will give more specific information on ways in which employees gain from computer usage,* we will not pursue the subject any further at this time.

BENEFITS TO INDIVIDUALS IN PRIVATE LIFE

Private individuals—all of us—receive benefits from the ways in which both *economic* and *public* organizations use computers. We can also be entertained and served through our individual use of *personal computers.*

Benefits from Economic Organizations

We all know that the federal government provides certain services to individuals that require the use of computers. Without computers, for example, the Social Security Administration could not keep up with the payment of benefits to widows, orphans, and retired persons, and the Federal Aviation Administration could not effectively control the aircraft traffic in congested areas. But we sometimes fail to realize the extent to which we benefit from the use of computers by economic organizations.

---

[3] Congratulations! You have just completed the longest sentence in this book.

Some (but certainly not all) of the possible benefits that private individuals may receive from their dealings with computer-using economic organizations are:

1   *Benefits of greater efficiency.* Most of us have probably been disturbed by the way prices have increased for many of the goods and services we buy. However, what we may perhaps fail to realize is that to the extent that businesses have avoided waste and improved efficiency and productivity through the use of computers, the *prices we now pay may be less than they would otherwise have been.* Edmund Berkeley, editor of *Computers and People,* has estimated that "the use of computers on a large scale has made prices lower by 10 to 30 percent and often much more, than they would be without computers."[4] For example, about one-third of all the dairy cows in the nation are now bred, fed, milked, and monitored for productivity with the help of computers. The average "computerized" cow will produce 30 percent more milk than a typical cow that is not subject to computer analysis. By applying the latest knowledge and techniques, the dairy industry today can produce all the milk that was supplied 15 years ago with only half as many cows. To the extent that computer applications significantly improve *productivity*—i.e., the amount of goods or services possessing economic value that individuals and machines can produce in a given time period—these productivity gains can lead to (*a*) a stronger competitive position in the world for the United States, and (*b*) higher levels of real income for an increased number of individuals.

2   *Benefits of higher-quality products.* In addition to possibly having an impact on the prices we pay *to* economic organizations, computers may also play a role in improving the quality of the products we receive *from* them. For example, you saw in Chapter 6 that microcomputers are now installed in cars to provide a more efficient means of controlling the engine's fuel mixture, ignition timing, and exhaust emissions. If you are late for an appointment and low on gas, and if there is a deserted stretch of highway ahead, an on-board micro will monitor the gas consumption, rate of speed, and miles to destination to tell you if you should take the time to look for an open service station. The microcomputer will also perform engine diagnostic functions and pinpoint problems. In other areas, computer-controlled tools can produce machined parts with closer tolerances than were feasible with previously used equipment, computer-controlled manipulators or robots can be used to assemble products or components in a precise way, and process-control computers can be used to carefully monitor the flow of chemical raw materials into a blending tank so that the finished product is of a more uniform quality.

3   *Benefits of better service.* Economic organizations also use computers

---

[4] Edmund C. Berkeley, "How Do Computers Affect People?" *Computers and People,* p. 6, April 1975.

to improve the services they provide to customers, clients, patients, etc. Computer processing techniques, for example, make possible (*a*) shorter waiting lines at airline ticket offices and at the reservation desks of hotels, motels, and car-rental agencies, (*b*) faster and more accurate answers to the inquiries of people served by the organization, (*c*) better matching of the needs of home buyers to the available listings of homes for sale, (*d*) more convenient handling of purchase transactions through the use of credit cards, and (*e*) more efficient control of inventory in retail outlets so that popular items are reordered in time to avoid frustrating out-of-stock situations.

4   *Possible benefits of EFTS.* You saw in the last chapter that financial and retailing institutions are very interested in the use of electronic funds transfer systems (EFTS). How can these systems benefit individuals? Although EFTS are still in the formative stages and the fully developed version(s) will be shaped by intense competition and government regulation, their general shape is clear enough for us to identify certain advantages for individuals. In a *checkless payment system,* for example, authorized credits to specified individuals from an employer, pension fund, etc., are recorded on magnetic tape along with the name of the recipient's bank and his or her bank account number. The tape is delivered to the paying organization's bank. This bank sorts out its own customers, deposits the payment amounts to their accounts, and then transfers the remaining names to an *automated clearing house* (ACH) facility. An ACH computer sorts the remaining names according to their banks and then notifies these banks of the amounts to be deposited in the specified accounts. A benefit of this EFTS approach is that it eliminates the fear of theft of checks. Millions of people are now receiving direct-deposit social security payments in lieu of mailed checks. As one recipient living on Chicago's South Side has noted, "It's better for [the check] to be in the bank than to take the chance of having it in your mailbox."[5] Another way in which EFTS may benefit individuals involves the use of terminals conveniently located anywhere that substantial numbers of nontrivial financial transactions occur. EFTS terminals owned by financial institutions and connected to their computers may be located in such public places as shopping centers and supermarkets. As we saw in Chapter 4, an individual can insert his or her "debit" (or "money") card[6] into an *automated teller machine* (Figure 10-1), key in appropriate data in response to instructions given on a terminal display, and make deposits or withdraw cash. Other EFTS terminals connected to the computers of financial institutions may be located at the *point-of-sale* (POS) counters of retail outlets and may be used in conjunction with store-owned POS sta-

---

[5] *Wall Street Journal,* p. 15, November 18, 1975.

[6] A *debit* card is similar in appearance to a credit card. Unlike a credit card, which is used to charge purchases that will be paid for at some future date, a debit card causes funds to be withdrawn at once (and automatically) from the card user's checking or savings account.

FIGURE 10-1
A self-service automated teller
machine that may be placed
in a public location to serve
individuals. (*NCR Corp.*)

tions. After an individual has supplied a debit card, these EFTS stations (which may also be located at hotels, hospitals, sports centers, etc.) can be used to (*a*) identify the individual, authorize credit, and/or authorize debit card cash advances, (*b*) guarantee the availability of funds to cover the individual's checks (Figure 10-2), and/or (*c*) transfer funds between accounts, e.g., from the individual's account to the merchant's account. The systems to handle this last application are not widely used at this time.[7] When they are more fully developed, the individual might make a request at a store's terminal for an electronic transfer of funds to pay for a purchase. The terminal would then send a message to the person's bank asking for approval of the transfer. If the account had the necessary funds (or if the person was eligible for sufficient credit), the bank's computer would (*a*) send a message approving the transaction to the merchant's terminal, and (*b*) see to the transfer of the payment funds to the merchant's account. This EFTS approach would give individuals the benefits associated with completing transactions for cash (speed, lack of "red tape," etc.) without the possible dangers associated with carrying large amounts of cash. Of course, the two parties to the transaction might use different banks, and so one or more ACH facilities would be used in the transaction to

[7] Hollywood Federal Savings and Loan in Hollywood, Florida, has had such a system in operation since 1977. Individuals can use their debit cards at over 700 POS locations to instantly transfer money from their accounts to the merchants' accounts. The merchants are charged 2 percent of the value of each transaction, and this amount is credited to the buyer's account. Thus, the merchant gets instant payment, and the buyer gets a 2 percent "cash" discount.

Depository

Cash
dispenser

Bank
card
slot

Display
screen

Transaction
keyboard

FIGURE 10-2
EFTS station at a retail outlet.
(IBM Corp.)

switch and process messages. Fully developed *cash transfer systems* will depend on a strong national network of ACHs; at this writing, a nationwide net of ACHs in over 30 major cities from coast to coast is in full operation (Figure 10-3). In addition to receiving funds directly into their accounts, using an automated teller machine in a convenient public place to handle their banking business, and having their checks automatically approved at a POS location, individuals may also be able to use EFTS to *automatically pay their bills*[8] from a home terminal, generally a telephone. Individuals with dial phones can call a bank operator seated in front of a visual display terminal to handle the transaction; people with Touch-Tone phones can communicate directly with the computer at the financial institution. Finally, another development made possible by the electronic transfer of money is a relatively new bank plan to cut down on the flow of paper through the use of *check truncation.* Truncation is simply a fancy word used by the banking industry to refer to a system where cancelled checks would not be returned to the check writers. As soon as a check was deposited in a bank, the bank would convert the data on the check into electronic impulses, which would then be transferred to the check writer's bank. Instead of receiving the cancelled checks at the end of the month, the writer would get a descriptive statement. The actual checks would be kept for a few months, placed on microfilm, and then destroyed. A writer would be able to get a copy of a check if it was needed. Financial institutions will save postage and handling costs through the use of truncation, and individuals may share the benefits of these cost savings by not having to pay as much for banking services.

5   *Possible benefits of UPC.* Merchants selling products coded with the Universal Product Code (UPC) symbols discussed in Chapter 4 expect

---

[8] According to the consulting firm of Frost & Sullivan, the implementation of bill payments via home terminals will become the fastest-growing EFTS service during the 1980s.

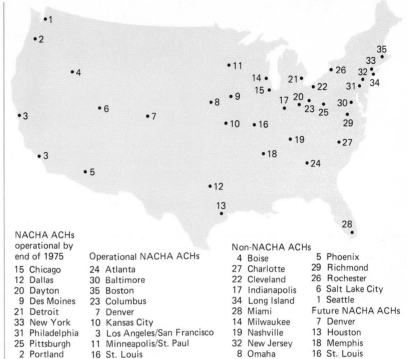

FIGURE 10-3
The nationwide network of
automated clearing houses.
Many of these ACHs
belong to the National
Automated Clearing House
Association. (*NACHA.*)

NACHA ACHs operational by end of 1975	Operational NACHA ACHs	Non-NACHA ACHs	
15 Chicago	24 Atlanta	4 Boise	5 Phoenix
12 Dallas	30 Baltimore	27 Charlotte	29 Richmond
20 Dayton	35 Boston	22 Cleveland	26 Rochester
9 Des Moines	23 Columbus	17 Indianapolis	6 Salt Lake City
21 Detroit	7 Denver	34 Long Island	1 Seattle
33 New York	10 Kansas City	28 Miami	Future NACHA ACHs
31 Philadelphia	3 Los Angeles/San Francisco	14 Milwaukee	7 Denver
25 Pittsburgh	11 Minneapolis/St. Paul	19 Nashville	13 Houston
2 Portland	16 St. Louis	32 New Jersey	18 Memphis
		8 Omaha	16 St. Louis

to receive the benefits of greater efficiency and reduced costs. But their customers may also find that a UPC system (*a*) reduces their waiting time and gives them faster service at checkout counters, (*b*) reduces the chances for human error at checkouts, and (*c*) provides them with an *itemized* sales receipt rather than just a tape with a column of numbers.

6   *Possible recreational benefits.* Some organizations are using computers for the sole purpose of amusing and entertaining individuals. For example, the computer of Recreational Computer Systems, Inc., Atlanta, Georgia, is used for just this purpose. In one application, image enhancement technology developed for the Mariner spacecraft project has been used to convert a small customer photograph into a 12- by 12- inch mosaic of computer printer characters (Figure 10-4).[9] In addition to image enhancement, *computer photography* (also developed for the space program) is now being used to entertain people. A TV camera captures the desired image (from a photograph or a live subject). The image is frozen and is then transferred by computer to a T-shirt, handbag, posterboard, etc. *Computer animation* is being used to give the illusion of movement to inanimate objects by

[9] The original 12- by 12-inch mosaic in Figure 10-4 obviously had to be reduced to fit on the page. Unfortunately, the computer could do nothing to enhance the features of the subject of the photograph.

FIGURE 10-4
Computer-produced mosaic
from customer photograph.
(*Recreational Computer
Systems, Inc.*)

electronic means. The results of computer animation are now seen in movies and on TV. For example, a briefing-room scene in the movie *Star Wars* that showed how a rebel pilot could maneuver down a trench on the surface of the battle station "Death Star" was accomplished by means of computer animation. And entertaining games containing microcomputers are being built by dozens of economic organizations.

7 *Possible aid to the handicapped.* Kurzweil Computer Products is an organization that builds the Kurzweil Reading Machine—a desk-top device that accepts written material printed in most common styles and sizes of type and converts the print into a synthetic voice output. Printed material is placed face down on a glass plate, where it is scanned by an electronic camera. The camera transmits its image to a minicomputer which is programmed to separate the image into character forms, recognize the letters, group the letters into words, compute the pronunciation of words, and produce the necessary speech sounds. This amazing machine sells for less than $20,000 and operates at normal speech rates, i.e., about 150 words per minute.[10] An-

[10] Raymond Kurzweil, the developer, received the ACM's Grace Murray Hopper Award in December 1978. This award is given annually in recognition of a major contribution to the computer industry by a person below the age of 30.

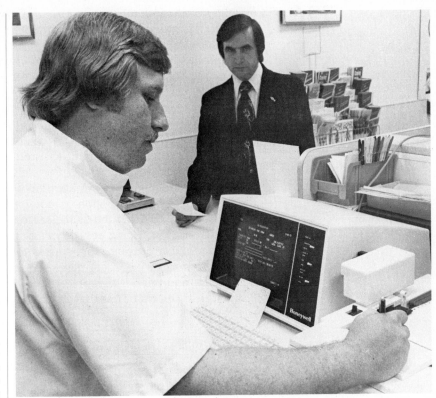

FIGURE 10-5
A pharmacist uses a minicomputer system to check a patient's medical profile against possible allergies to any ingredients in a new prescription. (*Honeywell, Inc.*)

other organization (ARTS Associates, Inc.) has produced programs that permit a computer to communicate with the blind by producing braille printouts. We saw in Chapter 6 that a microcomputer could be used to control a device that would permit severely handicapped persons to feed themselves even though they have no upper limb responses. And computer-based man-machine analyses are making it possible to develop more effective artificial limbs for amputees.

8 *Benefits of improved safety.* Computer usage can contribute to an individual's personal safety in a number of ways. Computer-controlled braking systems in aircraft and in future cars may help prevent dangerous skids and produce the optimum stopping distance in all weather conditions. Minicomputer systems in pharmacies can be used to check a patient's medical profile against possible reactions to any ingredients in a new prescription or to determine the possibility of dangerous interactions between the ingredients in old prescriptions and those in the new prescription (Figure 10-5). And computers permit gas utility companies to do a better job of managing and controlling the pipeline leaks that can seriously jeopardize public safety. Dispatchers can provide work crews with complete information on outstanding leaks in an area, including work-history details and prior gas leaks. New leaks can be identified and old leaks analyzed through on-line terminals.

9 *Benefits of better information retrieval.* A New York surgeon contacted a medical library when a near-term pregnant woman lapsed into a hepatic coma. He needed immediate information on exchange blood transfusions for the woman. Using a computer terminal and an IBM information retrieval program, the librarian was able to search more than a half-million medical documents in a few minutes to get the information needed by the surgeon to perform an emergency blood transfusion. The patient recovered fully from the hepatitis. Although most information retrieval projects obviously do not involve life-or-death situations, quick computer-assisted retrieval can save time and aggravation for many individuals. People whose interests range from the hobbyist looking for information on a particular stamp or coin to the citizen seeking information on congressional hearings can locate sources quickly by using the online search services offered by several organizations. The *Dialog* service of Lockheed Information Systems, for example, can provide rapid access to over 20 million document references in over 100 data bases. System Development Corporation's *Orbit* and the Bibliographic Retrieval Services (BRS) system are both large suppliers of online data-base information.

Benefits from Public Organizations

We all receive benefits from the ways in which public organizations use computers. Some (but again certainly not all) of these possible benefits which private individuals may receive from their dealings with computer-using public organizations are:

1 *Benefits from computers in government and law enforcement.* There are so many applications of computers in government and law enforcement that all of Chapter 13 is devoted to this topic. Therefore, we need introduce only a few examples at this time. One obvious benefit of government computer usage is that to the extent that this usage results in *greater efficiency,* the taxes we now pay (high as they are) may be less than they would otherwise have been. Los Angeles County, for example, expects to save $10 million annually through the use of its Welfare Case Management Information System; New York City is saving over $150,000 per year just by employing a new method of printing food stamp authorizations; and Philadelphia is saving $350,000 annually merely by using optical character recognition technology to capture payment data from a variety of tax revenue documents. Another benefit is that individuals may now receive *better service* from government agencies. The Los Angeles County welfare system mentioned above can process new applicants quickly and keep records updated on a daily basis so that recipients can receive their checks on time and at the right address. In contrast to the bureaucratic runaround that often accompanies a call to city hall, a Long Beach, California, system enables citizens calling city hall with an in-

FIGURE 10-6
This installation in Maywood, Illinois, is one of three VA network centers in the nation. (The other two are in Los Angeles and Philadelphia.) Computers at the three regional centers are linked to distributed minicomputers located at 59 VA offices in the United States and Puerto Rico. (*Honeywell, Inc.*)

quiry or complaint to dial a single number, get the right department, and be guaranteed a response (the computer creates a record of each call, prints a letter to the caller, and sends a copy to the appropriate city council representative). If a final disposition on a call is not received within a given period of time, a follow-up procedure is initiated. State and local governments are also using computers to (a) match people looking for work with available jobs, (b) gather data for the purpose of controlling air and water pollution, (c) design safer roads, (d) study the incidence of fires and crimes in various locations in order to improve public safety, (e) coordinate traffic signals to improve traffic flow, reduce transportation delays and costs, and allow emergency vehicles such as ambulances to have priority at an intersection, (f) locate and recover stolen cars (and apprehend those who may be driving them), and (g) store the names and addresses of invalids online so that when a fire alarm is received, a dispatcher can determine whether an invalid lives at the address and then notify fire fighters of the invalid's location in order to avoid the loss of precious time. All these applications have obvious benefits for individuals. And the federal government—the world's largest user—is employing computers in thousands of ways ranging from (a) processing satellite data in order to prepare more accurate weather forecasts, to (b) developing wheelchairs that respond to voice directions so that quadriplegics will enjoy greater mobility and freedom, to (c) installing systems that enable any of the nearly 40 million Americans eligible for veterans' benefits to walk into any Veterans Administration (VA) office in the country and within seconds begin the filing process for VA compensation, pension, and education benefits. (The records of all living veterans are available online at a center such as the one shown in Figure 10-6).

"Computerized System Aids Energy Conservation in Municipal Buildings"

When city officials in Vineland, New Jersey, opened the doors of their new City Hall in October, 1971, energy conservation was not an immediate concern.

"But with a national energy crisis upon us, and with annual energy bills of over $200,000, we thought we should take a closer look at our own energy consumption," commented Raymond Smith, director of electrical utilities for Vineland.

In the fall of 1975 a group of Vineland city officials began an investigation into the cost effectiveness of a centralized energy management system. Smith formed a committee, including the business manager, purchasing agent and comptroller, to review a series of presentations, comparisons and demonstrations of energy conservation systems.

After analyzing the data, Smith proposed to the City Council that a computerized energy management system be installed.

Specifications were written for the proposed system, and the city put the bid out early in 1977 to several suppliers. After consideration, they chose a Delta 1000 energy management system from Honeywell.

Installed in September, 1977, the system controls all environmental factors within the City Hall, plus a police building which is tied to the system via leased telephone lines. By controlling inside temperatures, turning back thermostats when areas are unoccupied and monitoring equipment, maximum energy efficiency can be achieved.

Although the equipment in both buildings is still being fine-tuned, according to the manufacturer, when fully operational this Delta 1000 system should realize a cost avoidance of approximately $40,000-50,000 during the first year.

Furthering their committment to energy conservation, these city officials are now considering tying additional city buildings to the system, including schools and libraries within the city.

Although the system is now leased, plans call for the purchase of equipment as a permanent management tool for energy conservation.

Source: "Computerized System Aids Energy Conservation in Municipal Buildings," *Government Data Systems,* p. 36, September–October 1978. Reprinted by permission.

2 *Benefits from computers in health care.* An entire chapter—Chapter 14—is also devoted to this topic, and so only a few examples need be mentioned here. One interesting application is the use of computer-generated maps of a geographic area to predict and depict the possible diffusion of an epidemic as well as to search for possible cor-

FIGURE 10-7
These oystermen in Alabama's Mobile Bay benefit from a computer model that shows how to keep the bay's ship channels clear without endangering their oyster beds. (*IBM Corp.*)

relations between environmental factors in the area and the area's incidence of cancer. Other applications use computers to provide (a) faster and more thorough approaches to the preparation and analysis of medical histories, (b) faster and more thorough testing to detect and identify disease, (c) more accurate methods of physiological monitoring, (d) better control of lab test results, and (e) better control of pharmacy services at public hospitals. Still other computers are used to train doctors and other health care personnel by simulating a patient with an emergency condition. The student is given the symptoms and is challenged to save the patient before time runs out by using a logical progression of diagnostic tests and treatments. Student errors are pointed out immediately by the computer.

3 *Benefits from computers in education.* You guessed it: Chapter 15 deals exclusively with this topic, and so only a few examples are given here. At the University of Notre Dame, botanists are using computers to identify endangered species of plants so that they may not become extinct. (Since many important medicines come from plants, potentially valuable chemicals may be lost when a species becomes extinct.) At San Antonio College in Texas, students with writing handicaps gain needed skills in a remedial English laboratory by practicing the basic concepts of sentence structure and usage at a computer terminal. At Louisiana State University, a chemical engineering professor has constructed a computer simulation model that helps explain how solid particles move in fluids. For those who like oysters, one benefit of this model is that ship channels can be dredged periodically, and the sediments can be deposited elsewhere, without endangering the oyster beds or the livelihood of those who work them (Figure 10-7). Re-

searchers at the University of Wisconsin are working on a tiny computer that can be carried around by heart patients to continuously monitor the heart's rhythm and sound a warning in case of trouble.

Benefits from Personal Computing

You saw in Chapter 6 that personal microcomputers could be used in the home for entertainment and other personal computing applications. Since the applications of personal computers in the home can be as numerous and varied as human ingenuity and imagination will permit, the benefits of personal computing are also limited only by human ingenuity and imagination. The following examples indicate merely a few of the possibilities.

1   *Entertainment and hobby benefits.* Unlike dedicated chess computers and other specialized electronic games, a personal computer is a general-purpose game-playing machine that may be programmed to play chess one minute and football or "Star Trek" the next. In fact, a personal computer can entertain you with hundreds of challenging games. The game-playing programs are packaged on tape cassettes or floppy disks and are available from computer stores and other retail and mail-order outlets. Program authors, like songwriters, receive royalties on the sale of their works. *CLOAD* magazine is "printed" monthly on a tape cassette and sent to subscribers. Each cassette contains "programs of the month" ranging from games to programs of a practical nature. Of course, only a computer can read this "magazine." Another storehouse of information for the personal computer owner is available from a data bank called, appropriately enough, The Source. To tap the data base and the more than 2,000 programs in The Source, the user pays a hookup fee, dials a toll-free number, and then pays an hourly service charge. In return, The Source allows the user access to the latest news, energy-saving suggestions and automotive news, the data banks of *The New York Times* and United Press International, theater and sports attractions, daily horoscopes and biorhythm reports, foreign-language tutorials and physics lessons, recipes and personal finance information, backgammon and Monopoly games—the list goes on and on! Finally, in addition to being a hobby in itself, the personal computer can help coin and stamp collectors maintain (a) the content of their inventories, and (b) data on the cost, present value, and profit (or loss) of their holdings.

2   *Educational benefits.* Games can be educational as well as entertaining. For example, children can learn to identify the letters of the alphabet and match these letters to the appropriate keys on the keyboard by "shooting" letters as they bounce around on the screen. The key corresponding to the target letter is "fired"; if the ricochet angle and lead time are correct, the target letter will be hit. As The Source example above indicates, personal computers can be used to learn a new subject. Educators agree that the home computer can be a powerful

FIGURE 10-8
Preparing a budget using a
personal computer. (*Radio
Shack Div., Tandy Corp.*)

motivating and learning tool. When children (and adults) use personal computers, they have some real control over what they learn, how they learn, and how fast they learn. Making a sophisticated machine do one's bidding is fun for many people, and writing a computer program requires a person to analyze and understand the subject being studied. In addition, using word processing software with a personal computer encourages people to polish their writing skills because changes and corrections are made easily.

3   *Personal finance benefits.* A personal computer could help you (a) prepare your budget (Figure 10-8) and balance your checkbook, (b) control your installment purchases, (c) control your home's energy usage, and (d) analyze your investments and prepare your tax returns. If you wanted information on current stock prices, you could call the toll-free number of one service, obtain access to the data base of Dow-Jones & Company, and use the service's programs to obtain quotes and other information on any stock listed on any of the six major exchanges in the United States. If you were trying to decide whether to buy a home or a piece of rental property, you could load an available program into your computer, supply the necessary input data (e.g., purchase price, down payment, loan term, taxes, closing costs, utility costs, mortgage interest rate, insurance cost, etc.), and find out exactly what the costs and financial benefits are.[11]

[11] For such a program, see Larry L. Seversen, "Viewing Real Estate Investments," *Personal Computing*, pp. 22–25, October 1979.

4 *Benefits of greater personal efficiency.* We have seen that handicapped persons can use microcomputers to control devices that make them more efficient and give them a new degree of independence. Other people can also use personal computers to save time and/or use time more efficiently. For example, WHATSIT is a personal information retrieval program that enables a user to store up to 25,000 entries on a single online disk. The data are loaded onto the disk according to the subject keys that the user selects. Additional entries can be entered and indexed in any appropriate sequence at any time, and old entries can be deleted at any time. Instead of spending a lot of time looking in a desk, bookcase, or file cabinet for information such as names, telephone numbers, addresses, birthdays, recipes, warranty expiration dates, hobby inventory items, and countless other things worthy of retrieval, the user can simply enter the appropriate subject key or keys at the terminal, and the information is retrieved in a second or two.

THE OPTIMISTIC OUTLOOK

One hundred years from now, historians will consider the development of computer technology to be a major (if not *the* major) contribution of our time. But they may also conclude in future decades that computers were machines that we had not yet learned how to use. Oh, these later historians may admit that we had developed some effective data processing, but if today's optimists are correct, historians may also write that we had only begun to realize the computer's potential in more important areas— i.e., in those areas which improve the quality of life and the well-being of people themselves. Optimistic forecasters believe that *greater freedom and individuality,* and a *more human and personalized society,* will result from future computer applications.

Greater Freedom and Individuality

The optimistic view of the future is that greater freedom and individuality are encouraged by the use of computers. Optimists note the individual benefits, such as those mentioned in preceding sections, and they expand and project those benefits into the future. They foresee no insurmountable problems in society's adapting to the changes brought about by increased computer utilization. The greater productivity that results from computer usage, they contend, will lead to an increased standard of living, a shorter work week, and increased leisure time. Although it will be a challenge for human beings to put aside age-old attitudes toward work and learn to use creatively the free time they will have in the future, the optimists believe that people can learn to use their leisure in ways that are contemplative and self-fulfilling.

Also, it is argued, people will be freed from the basic struggle to maintain their existence and will have the time and resources to pursue

FIGURE 10-9
Left to right: William Shockley,
Walter H. Brattain, and
John Bardeen. (*The Bettmann
Archive.*)

THE TRANSISTOR REVOLUTION BEGINS

Until 1955 to 1960, computers were constructed of vacuum tubes which made them very large. In addition, they generated so much heat that they had to be kept in air-conditioned rooms. With the advent of transistors, which were about one two-hundredth the size of vacuum tubes, computers could be made much smaller. They generated less heat, were more reliable, and were less expensive.

The replacement of vacuum tubes by transistors developed from the work of Walter Brattain, John Bardeen, and William Shockley at Bell Telephone Laboratories. In 1956 they received the Nobel Prize in Physics "for their research on semiconductors and the discovery of the transistor effect."

According to Brattain's original notes, "on December 23, 1947, two gold contacts less than two-thousandths of an inch apart were made to the same piece of germanium; and the first transistor was made. This was an eventful day. . . ."

the activities of their choice. (Since individuality has been defined as the "freedom to exercise choice according to one's own scale of preference,"[12] it will thus be enhanced.) Aristotle's prophecy that "When looms weave by themselves, man's slavery will end" is cited by the optimists. Nonhuman slaves (computers and automated tools controlled by computers) will liberate many people from the unpleasant working conditions that have evolved from Charles Dickens' England of the 1800s and Upton Sinclair's United States of the early 1900s. No longer will people have to spend long hours at an assembly line, for example, tightening a few bolts on the monotonous widgets passing by, when a computer-directed and uncomplaining robot can do the work accurately and inexpensively.

More Human and Personalized Society

Optimists also believe that the sophisticated computer systems of the future will permit a more human and personalized society that will further reduce the need for individual conformity. They argue that the complexity of our present society, the millions of people crowded into it, and the inadequacy of our present information systems act to encourage conformity and thus to restrict personalization and human freedom of choice. However, when sophisticated information systems are developed and widely used to handle routine transactions, it will be possible to focus greater personal attention on exceptional transactions. Therefore, more humanistic attitudes will emerge.

In short, optimists note that the following examples are merely the early tip of a future iceberg:

1 Automated health testing provides more information on each patient and greater personalization in patient care. Instead of using broad general standards or norms to evaluate a patient, a physician can obtain from the computer more specific norms for each patient, depending on the patient's age, sex, height, weight, etc.
2 After waiting hours to see a young and inexperienced intern or a harried and resentful senior-staff physician, a welfare patient at a clinic is often subjected to rushed, impolite, and haphazard medical care. When compared with this type of care, a polite and thorough computer program to determine a patient's medical history and current symptoms may be the more humane and personalized alternative.
3 Computer-assisted instruction techniques can give terminal-using students personalized lessons selected on the basis of the student's level of knowledge and past performance.

[12] Robert M. Gordon, "Computers and Freedom, Individuality and Automation: Challenge and Opportunity," *Computer,* p. 30, September/October 1971.

"On-Line to City Hall"

Tired of getting the bureaucratic runaround when you call city hall? In Long Beach, Calif., a computer helps citizens avoid this frustration.

In many cities, when a citizen calls city hall with an inquiry or a complaint, he might be transferred to three or four departments before reaching the right one. And even then he has no assurance that his problem would be solved.

In Long Beach, the city's System/370 Model 158 has been programmed to enable residents to call a single number, get the right department and be guaranteed a response. The program is called the Citizen Service and Information System.

The city also benefits from the system—it helps determine citizens' concerns, pinpoints responsibilities within city hall and compiles statistics that may reveal undetected problems.

"We instituted the system recently to get in closer contact with the citizens," says City Manager John Dever. "We wanted to find out what was on their minds—what they really want and need.

"So far," he says, "the response has been fantastic. We had 700 calls the first two days and about 100 a day since then."

Instead of guessing which department might handle his inquiry, a Long Beach resident now has to dial only a single number. A clerk seated at a display terminal takes the name, address and phone number and the inquiry.

Then the clerk searches a list of information areas displayed on the terminal screen to see who would handle the question.

Information areas range from animal regulation, bicycle routes and consumer protection to refuse collection, senior citizen services and sidewalk repair. Each area lists various kinds of problems and where to turn. For instance, under sidewalk repair, sidewalks damaged by tree roots are the responsibility of the Street Tree Division. Other types of sidewalk damage are referred to the Public Works Department.

The caller is then put through to the proper agency, or the information is referred for him.

The computer also automatically prints a letter to the caller. The hand-signed letter thanks him for his request, tells him which department is handling it and gives him an inquiry number to refer to in case he wants to call or write back.

A copy of the inquiry also is forwarded to the appropriate city council representative so that he is aware of problems in his district.

A record is created on each call and stored in the computer. It shows the caller, the inquiry, the date received, the department referred to and the final disposition of the case.

"If we don't get a final disposition on a call within a predetermined period of time, the department is called to see what's going on," Mr. Dever says.

"We want to be sure to take care of all requests, one way or the other. Otherwise, citizens will feel we're just taking their calls and not doing anything about them."

Statistical analyses compiled from the inquiries help point out potential problem areas and guide the city in formulating new policies and procedures, Mr. Dever says. For example, a series of complaints about broken sidewalks in the same area may indicate that trees in the parkways need replacing. Reports also show which departments are responding the fastest.

The system also can be updated instantly. For example, if responsibilities change or a new ordinance enacted, that information can be put into the program and become immediately available to the clerks who operate the terminals.

"Citizens who have used the system and told us about it think it's great," Mr. Dever says. "They say it's something we've needed for a long time."

Source: "On-Line to City Hall," *Data Processor,* p. 9, January 1978. Courtesy of IBM.

4   Reservation systems at airlines and hotels permit clerks to store more personalized information about customers than would otherwise be possible. If a customer needs unusual services, these can be entered into the system and provided at the proper time.

5   A computerized community "bulletin board" that stores offers by individuals to buy and sell items, indicates commonly needed services that are available in the community, and contains public service announcements can be established to draw a community closer together. In fact, Community Memory is just such a project of Resource One, a nonprofit group of San Francisco computer professionals.

6   Computer conferencing is enabling an elderly crippled woman in a New Jersey nursing home to communicate daily with a child suffering from cerebral palsy. Although the two have never met, "Grandma" and the child share a companionship that is close to loving. Each is eager to "listen" to the other, and each gives the other an emotional uplift. Future applications such as this can bring a new meaning to the lives of thousands of people.

The following points have been emphasized in this chapter:

1 Computer usage is bound to affect individuals both in their dealings with organizations and in their private lives. The purpose of this chapter was to outline just a few of the ways in which computers are helping people.

2 Some administrators and employees in organizations have found their jobs more challenging and rewarding because of computer systems, and individuals in private life have received benefits from the ways in which both economic and public organizations use computers. For example, the prices we now pay to economic organizations for some goods and services may be less because of computer usage than they would otherwise have been, and the quality of these goods and services has often been improved through computer usage.

3 Without computers, the possible benefits of EFTS and UPC would not be feasible, handicapped persons would be denied tools that give them greater independence and make their lives more meaningful, and retrieving needed information would be a much more tedious task.

4 Greater efficiency and better service are also benefits that individuals receive from the use of computers by federal, state, and local governments. Many beneficial applications of computers exist in the areas of public health care and education.

5 Personal computers can be used by individuals for entertainment, educational purposes, personal finance applications, and applications that save time and result in greater personal efficiency.

6 Optimistic forecasters note the current benefits being received from computers, and they anticipate that computer applications in the future will lead to greater freedom and individuality on the one hand, and a more human and personalized society on the other. Unfortunately, some other forecasters are not so confident, as we will see in the next few chapters.

▶ | KEY TERMS

After reading Chapter 10, you should be able to define and use the following terms:

productivity	check truncation
checkless payment system	computer animation
automated clearing house	computer photography

REVIEW AND DISCUSSION QUESTIONS

1 (a) How have top-level administrators benefited from computer usage? (b) How have middle-level administrators benefited? (c) Lower-level supervisors?
2 Identify employees of organizations who have benefited from computer usage and explain how they have been helped.
3 Discuss how the following individuals in organizations may benefit from computer usage: (a) law enforcement officers, (b) members of Congress, (c) school teachers, (d) nurses, (e) district office managers.
4 Identify and discuss two ways (not mentioned in the chapter) in which individuals in private life may benefit from computer usage (a) by economic organizations, and (b) by public organizations.
5 Identify and discuss two ways (not mentioned in the chapter) in which individuals may benefit from personal computing.
   Note: For the preceding two questions, you may wish to refer to such periodicals as Byte, Computer, Computers and People, Creative Computing, Datamation, Infosystems, Interface Age, onComputing, and Personal Computing.
6 Discuss the optimistic view of the future use of computer systems.
7 (a) How may EFTS benefit individuals? (b) What are some possible benefits of UPC?
8 (a) How may computers aid the handicapped? (b) How may they contribute to greater personal safety?

SELECTED REFERENCES

Bell, Fred: "Classroom Computers: Beyond the 3 R's," Creative Computing, pp. 68–70, September 1979.

Dutton, Geoffrey H., and William G. Nisen: "The Expanding Realm of Computer Cartography," Datamation, pp. 134–137ff, June 1979.

Kiester, Sally Valente: "It's Student and Computer, One on One," Personal Computing, pp. 67–69, March 1978.

Mann, Robert W.: "Technology for Human Rehabilitation," Technology Review, pp. 44–52, November 1978.

Meyers, Edith: "EFT: Momentum Gathers," Datamation, pp. 53–55, October 1978.

Miller, Frederick W.: "Checkless Society Gets Closer," Infosystems, pp. 48ff, March 1979.

Splittgerber, Fred L.: "Computer-based Instruction: A Revolution in the Making?" Educational Technology, pp. 20–25, January 1979.

Teicholz, Eric: "Processing Satellite Data," Datamation, pp. 117–121ff. June 1978.

Chapter 11

INDIVIDUALS AND COMPUTERS: SOME NEGATIVE VIEWS

Although computer systems can help people in countless ways, it is also possible for them to have a negative impact on some individuals. The purpose of this chapter is to outline some of the adverse effects that computer usage may produce. As you read this chapter, however, you should keep two important thoughts clearly in mind. *First,* some of the potential adverse effects such as the dehumanizing of society and the loss of individual privacy that are often attributed to computer systems may often be the subtle consequences of complex and interrelated technological forces operating in a society with a growing population density. And *second,* computers, being inanimate objects, do no wrong—but the people who use them sometimes do. Computer application decisions should be made after the positive and negative consequences of the application have been carefully studied. Unfortunately, the fallible humans who design computer-based systems have sometimes overlooked the negative elements and the computer—rather than the poorly-designed system—has received the blame.

In the first section of the chapter, you will see how administrators and employees in organizations may lose their jobs or suffer a loss of status and prestige because computers have been introduced into processing systems or have taken over the control of other machines. The individual resistance that frequently accompanies the change to computer usage in organizations is also discussed in this section.

The second section examines how people in private life may be harassed, inconvenienced, depersonalized, and victimized in other ways by computer-based systems that employ questionable data processing practices.

The question of the security of an individual's private records that are stored in computer systems is the subject of the third section. Records that are not secured against theft, fraud, or accidental or malicious scrutiny and manipulation can obviously harm individuals. Unless records are accurate and secure, an individual's right to privacy is likely to suffer. This important privacy issue is the topic of the fourth section of the chapter.

Finally, in the last section, a summary is given of the views of those who are pessimistic about the future effects of computer usage on society.

Thus, after studying this chapter, you should be able to:

- Describe how different categories of administrators and employees may be harmed by their organizations' use of computers.

- Explain why resistance to change may be expected when computers are introduced into an organization.

- Discuss how questionable data processing practices have had adverse effects on the private lives and records of individuals.

- Outline how a lack of data security and physical security can lead to undesirable consequences for individuals

- Explain how an individual's legitimate right to privacy may be adversely affected by the use of computers.

- Summarize the views of those who are pessimistic about the future effects of computer usage on society.

- Understand and use the key terms listed at the end of the chapter.

When machines are in league with men, the soul of the alliance must be human, lest its ends become less than human.
—John Diebold

As you saw in the last chapter, the computer—one of the most powerful technological forces in society today—is having a very strong positive influence on organizations in general and on many individuals in particular. But as you also saw in Chapter 2, an attitude of wariness and skepticism has replaced the feeling that technological possibilities are inevitably desirable in the minds of many citizens. In some cases this attitude may have been produced by an awareness of how certain types of technology have polluted the environment; in other cases this attitude may have been created as a result of the breakdown of intricate systems in a complex society.

In the past, some *individuals in organizations* have received a reduction in status or have been displaced; at the present time, some are being threatened with obsolescence and displacement because of information-systems changes. The negative impact is not limited to individuals on the job. Many *individuals in private life* have also had relationships with computerized data processing systems that have not been favorable. (It is entirely possible, of course, that people can be victimized both on the job and in connection with their private affairs.) Thus, in the following pages of this chapter we will examine the *negative impact* of computer systems on (1) *employment and organizational stress,* i.e., on the individual's job, (2) *data processing practices* that affect an individual's private records, (3) the *security of those records,* and (4) the *privacy of individuals.* Finally, we will look at *how pessimists view the future impact of computer usage on individuals.*

COMPUTERS, EMPLOYMENT, AND ORGANIZATIONAL STRESS

The victims of computer systems in some organizations have included *administrators* at all levels and *employees* in many occupations.

Administrative Victims

Top-level administrators are the ones who approve the installation of computer systems. In giving their approval, they obviously do not expect to be victimized. And yet, in a sense, a number of top administrators have been computer victims. As we saw in Chapter 9, many have been disappointed in the economic effects of their installations; some have discovered too late that poor security provisions in the computer center have left their organizations *more* vulnerable to theft, espionage, and sabotage; and more than a few have been disappointed because their new information systems have not given them the service and support for decision making they were led to believe would be provided.

Some *administrators below the top levels* whose decisions were highly structured and repetitive have found that those decisions were programmable on a computer. The information systems have therefore taken over those duties, and the need for as many administrators to perform the remainder of the job duties has been reduced.[1] In some organizations, those who were not displaced found their jobs less challenging because, although they retained the duties that required less judgment and skill, their other tasks that required the skilled interpretation of systems information were moved upward in the organization or were taken over by the information-systems staff. As noted in Chapter 9, centralization of information-processing activities is occurring in some organizations today. In some cases, administrators are finding that they have little voice in determining the information they will receive or in the design of the new systems which will be used to monitor their performance.

Many *lower-level supervisors* have suffered because their departments have been eliminated, merged with others, or reduced in scope and status as a result of the installation of computer information systems. When computers displace employees, the supervisor of those employees is no longer needed.

Displaced Employees

Clerical employees   Clerical employees have often been displaced by computers. It should be noted, however, that displacement and unemployment are not the same. *Unemployment* refers to the total number of people involuntarily out of work. *Displacement* occurs when the jobs of individual workers are eliminated as a result of technological change. *If* these displaced workers cannot find similar jobs elsewhere and *if* they cannot find work in other occupations, then there is, indeed, an increase

When more and more people are thrown out of work, unemployment results.
—Calvin Coolidge

---

[1] For example, New York's Citibank, the nation's second largest bank, is now installing distributed data and word processors and electronic mail/message systems in its offices around the world. According to a Citibank vice president, "about 10 percent of middle-management personnel could be cut. 'The salaries of 700 are saved,' he said, 'and the remaining 7,300 can use the technological advances to manage more efficiently.'" See Jon Stewart, "Computer Shock: The Inhuman Office of the Future," *Saturday Review,* p. 17, June 23, 1979.

in the unemployment figures. Optimists and pessimists disagree on the ultimate effects of computers and automated tools on total employment. Both schools of thought would agree, however, that to the employee being displaced, the future consequences are of secondary importance. The displaced victim is likely to be in sympathy with the famous economist who noted wryly that "in the long run we are all dead."

Studies have shown that computer usage can displace large numbers of people.[2] The extent to which displacement actually occurs and the significance of the problem in particular cases may depend in large measure on the following factors:

1   *The rate of growth of the organization and the economy.* If the organization is growing rapidly so that more work must be done to handle the expanding volume, there may be little or no effect on the number of workers employed. Reassignment of surplus workers to different departments may, of course, be required.

2   *The objectives sought.* Is the organization introducing a computer system for processing purposes that could not otherwise be considered? Or is it to save money by eliminating existing jobs? Objectives obviously play a part in determining the degree of displacement.

3   *The care in planning and preparation.* Administrators should give careful thought to the displacement problems that they are likely to encounter. If displacement is not expected, employees should be so informed; if jobs are to be eliminated, plans should be made to protect present employees as much as possible.

4   *The types of occupations threatened.* In the past, few clerical workers were laid off in larger organizations when job reductions occurred.[3] This was possible because workers in affected departments who quit during the many months between the time the computer order was placed and the time the conversion was completed were simply not replaced. Thus, a potentially serious layoff problem often has not developed.

Production employees   When the affected jobs are *not* of the clerical type, the displacement problem may be more severe. The affected workers may be older employees or lower-level managers whose skills are no longer needed. They are not as likely to quit, and so attrition may not be of much help; they may also find it more difficult to retrain for different jobs at an appropriate level.

---

[2] For example, you may remember that in the last chapter it was pointed out that Los Angeles County expects to save $10 million annually through the use of a Welfare Case Management Information System. Much of the savings would come from an initial reduction of 500 employees. A total of 900 jobs will be eliminated over a three-year period. See "New Computerized Welfare System: Big Savings Predicted," *Government Data Systems*, pp. 6–7, May/June 1978.

[3] Small organizations have not been as successful in preventing layoffs, possibly because there may not have been other departments to which surplus workers could be reassigned.

Displacement is occurring in some *skilled production-oriented occupations,* such as those which involve the operation of certain metalworking tools and typesetting devices, as a result of the installation of computer-controlled machines. Although such employees may be protected to some extent by union contract agreements, the demand for their skills is declining.[4]

A more serious displacement problem, however, is likely to result from the increased use of computer-controlled *robots*[5] in *assembly operations.* The automobile industry is a leading user of robots that for several years have performed such automotive production tasks as stamping, heat-treating, welding, and spray painting. Of course, robots will perform these dreary, dirty, and/or dangerous tasks without complaint, and the "first-generation" robots have usually been applied in such areas of worker discontent. But production techniques are now changing rapidly in the automobile industry. In the $80 billion retooling program required to build smaller cars that will meet the 1985 mileage and emission standards, auto manufacturers are replacing old machines with a new generation of robots. According to the Society of Manufacturing Engineers, "20% of the direct labor in automobile final assembly will be replaced by programmable automation by 1985 and 50% by 1995. By 1988, half of the direct labor in small component assembly will be replaced. Inspection work will be even more automated."[6] And according to Robert Lund, a researcher at the Massachusetts Institute of Technology Center for Policy Alternatives, the result of this creation of computerized and robotized plants will be a substantial permanent sector of unemployment. The forthcoming changes, Lund believes, will "divide workers into very highly skilled and very low-skilled categories, wiping out the intermediate skill range vital for a sense of upward mobility."[7]

Professional employees   Nor are employees in the *professions* immune from the effects of computer usage. The advancement in scientific and engineering knowledge (which may be attributed in part to the expanding use of computers) makes it increasingly difficult for *scientists and engineers* to keep abreast of their fields.[8] They must have the ability and will-

---

[4] In West Germany, union members have recently gone on strike in printing and metalworking organizations to protest the introduction of computer-controlled equipment and the resultant downgrading of the skill needed to operate the new equipment.

[5] The word *robot*—based on the Czech word *robota,* which means "forced labor"—entered the English language in 1922 when a new play written by a Czechoslovakian dramatist named Karel Capek opened in New York. In the play, entitled *R.U.R.,* the firm of Rossum's Universal Robots developed a line of artificial humans. As these labor-saving robots increased in sophistication, they developed a lust for power, turned on their creators, and ultimately destroyed humanity.

[6] "UAW Fears Automation Again," *Business Week,* p. 95, March 26, 1979.

[7] Ibid., p. 95.

[8] The President of the American Association for the Advancement of Science has concluded that scientists must constantly review, extend, and reorganize their knowledge or accept the fact that in about eight years they will be beyond hope as teachers or practitioners.

ingness to learn about computers, adopt new theories and techniques, and, perhaps, go through several "retreading" periods in their careers simply to retain marketable skills. Otherwise, as Paul Armer has observed, they may "become, over time, uneducated and therefore incompetent at a level at which they once performed quite adequately."[9] The possible suffering and anxiety associated with the conviction that technical obsolescence is likely in a relatively short time is thus something that some professionals may have to learn to live with.

Some *physicians* may, for example, find it difficult to accept the use of computers in medicine because of the conviction that the machines may reduce their intellectual contributions to health care and help paramedical personnel "usurp" their duties. Since computers are already moving into roles traditionally played by physicians at dozens of automated clinical laboratories and electronic screening centers across the nation, it is not suprising that some physicians have joined some other professionals in the belief that they are likely to become future computer victims.

Individual Resistance to Change

In view of the ways in which computer usage has damaged some individuals in organizations, it is also not surprising that resistance to systems change is the rule rather than the exception.

Forms of resistance   Resistance may appear in many forms. At one extreme, individuals may temporarily feel threatened by a change, but after a brief adjustment period they resume their previous behavior. At the other extreme, reaction may be evidenced by open opposition and even destruction. Between these extremes may be found a number of other symptoms, including (1) withholding data and information, (2) providing inaccurate information, (3) distrusting computer output, and (4) showing lowered morale.

Reasons for resistance   Although some are motivated to seek changes by a dissatisfaction with the status quo or by the desire to be a leader in the use of new technology, these changes may appear to others to be a *threat*—a threat that prevents them from satisfying certain basic needs or that decreases the level of their need satisfaction. The fact that a proposed change *does not* actually affect an employee's need satisfaction may be irrelevant from a resistance standpoint. *What is relevant* in this situation is that if employees *believe* that they are threatened by the proposed change *does not* actually affect an employee's need satisfaction

---

[9] Paul Armer, "The Individual: His Privacy, Self Image, and Obsolescence," *Computers and People,* p. 21, June 1975. Armer has named this thought the "Paul Principle" because it goes hand in hand with the "Peter Principle," which states that individuals will rise in an organization until they reach their level of incompetence.

that the change will not affect them adversely, or when they adjust to a change that does in fact have undesirable implications, will equilibrium return and resistance tend to disappear.

Some of the *reasons why people may resist computer systems changes are:*

1 *The threat to security.* Computers have a reputation for replacing people; therefore, there is the understandable fear of loss of employment and/or reduction in salary.
2 *The reduction in social satisfaction.* The introduction of a new system often calls for a reorganization of departments and work groups. When change causes a breaking up of compatible human relationships, resistance may be anticipated.
3 *The reduction in self-esteem and reputation.* Individuals need to feel self-confident, but self-confidence may be shaken by lack of knowledge about and experience with the new system. The equipment is strange to them, and they may fear that they will be unable to acquire the new skills necessary to work with it. In short, their self-esteem may suffer as a result of the change; therefore, the change may be resisted. Egoistic needs relating to the reputation of the individual are also threatened by change. Fear of loss of status and/or prestige is an important reason for resistance by both managers and employees.[10]

Individuals who resist It is generally conceded that nonsupervisory employees may resist change because of the reasons just listed. A greater obstacle to successful computer operations, however, may be *managerial* resistance to change. Although administrators may suffer economic losses because of the change to computer processing, the more usual motivating force behind their resistance is the threat of a reduction in ego-need satisfaction. Many managers feel that their positions are being threatened (and indeed this is sometimes the case). In a very real sense, those who may be most affected by the change are being asked to help plan and implement it.

Suggestions for reducing resistance Unfortunately, there is no simple formula that prevents resistance and ensures successful computer usage. But there are some guidelines and suggestions—developed as a result of practical experience and social research—which may, when used with care, help reduce the level of organizational stress. Included in these suggestions are steps to:

---

[10] For example, if the change threatens to reduce the number of employees in, and the importance of, a department, the department manager may oppose the change because to admit that the change is needed is to admit that he or she has tolerated inefficiency—an admission that can hardly be expected to enhance the manager's reputation. Employees who have the respect of fellow workers because of their knowledge of the old system may also suffer a loss of prestige. When new procedures are installed, these employees are no longer looked to for information because their knowledge of the new procedures may not be any greater than that of other workers.

1 *Keep individuals informed.* Information relating to the effects of any change on their jobs should be periodically presented to personnel at all levels. Topics discussed should include loss of jobs, transfers, the extent of necessary retraining, the reasons for (and the benefits of) the change, the effect on various departments, and what is being done to alleviate employee hardships.

2 *Seek individual participation.* Individuals are more likely to support and accept changes that they have a hand in creating. Psychologists tell us that participation has three beneficial effects. First, it helps the employee satisfy ego and self-fulfillment needs. Second, it gives the employee some degree of control over the change and thus contributes to a greater feeling of security. Third, the fear of the unknown is removed.

3 *Consider the timing of the change.* Unreasonable conversion deadlines should be avoided. Employees need time to get used to one major change before another is initiated.

DISPUTABLE DATA PROCESSING PRACTICES

It should be apparent by now that computer systems have taken on increasingly responsible tasks in many organizations and are now performing vital functions in our society. Since, for example, airplanes are prevented from colliding over congested airports by computerized air traffic control systems, and since an individual's personal assets may be dependent on the security and accuracy of an ACH computer system, it is essential that in the data processing steps performed by computers *vital and relevant data are not lost or stolen, errors are not introduced into the data, and data are not stored, retrieved, modified, or communicated without proper authorization.*

If the data processing carried out by computer systems always measured up to the criteria emphasized in the preceding sentence, we could probably dispense with most of the materials found in the remainder of this chapter and in Chapter 12. Unfortunately, questionable data processing practices have had adverse effects on the private lives and records of individuals.

Review of Data Processing Steps

Data processing, you will recall, consists of one or more of the following steps: (1) originating and recording, (2) classifying, (3) sorting, (4) calculating, (5) summarizing, (6) storing, (7) retrieving, (8) reproducing, and (9) communicating. In the remainder of this chapter we will examine some of the possible ways in which the performance of these data processing steps may lead to undesirable results for individuals.

Data Originating and Recording: A Lack of Control?

According to the Organization for Economic Cooperation and Development (OECD), in 1985–1987, 6 or 7 times the present volume of new information will be produced. The OECD also foresees that by 1987 "the degree of automation of information will approach a hundred times that of today." In other words, computers will have to do more of the processing work if we are to cope with this avalanche of information. This thought probably does not upset most individuals.

What is upsetting to many people, however, is the staggering volume of *information of a highly personal nature* that has been (and is being) collected by governmental agencies and private organizations. In the *government sector,* for example, a study conducted a few years ago by the Senate Subcommittee on Constitutional Rights found that 858 data banks in 54 federal agencies contained a total of more than 1.25 *billion* records and dossiers on individuals.[11] These hundreds of federal data banks, when combined with more than 600 others operated by the states and more than 1,700 others operated by cities and counties, provide governmental entities with specific public and private information on virtually every citizen. Figure 11-1 indicates just a few of the uses of some of these data banks. In addition, of course, there are hundreds of *private organizations* —e.g., *credit bureaus*—that engage in investigative reporting for a fee.

Since a Senate study has concluded that 17 percent of the federal data banks have absolutely no statutory authority and 84 percent are not *explicitly* authorized by law, and since the nation's most secret intelligence operation, the National Security Agency (NSA), "possesses the computerized equipment to monitor nearly all overseas telephone calls and most domestic and international printed messages—and . . . has made heavy use of its Orwellian technology,"[12] individuals may not be suffering from paranoia if they conclude that there soon may be "no place to hide" from legal/illegal information systems that have an almost limitless capacity to record, store, and retrieve information about their thoughts and activities. The NSA, for example, has devices that

> monitor thousands of telephone circuits, cable lines and the microwave transmissions that carry an increasing share of both spoken and written communications. Computers are programmed to watch for "trigger" words or phrases indicating that a message might interest intelligence analysts. When the trigger is pulled, entire messages are tape recorded or printed out. . . . The prime targets of the monitoring are Soviet-bloc diplomats, military officers and espionage agents in the U.S. But . . . the agency also played a role in Operation Chaos, the surveillance of antiwar activists between 1967 and

The meek shall inherit the earth, but not its mineral rights.
—J. Paul Getty·

---

[11] These figures *understated* the actual situation at the time because several agencies failed to cooperate fully in the study. Furthermore, it was reported that in trying to get an accurate picture, the subcommittee encountered "disdain," "evasion," "delay," "inadequate and cavalier responses," "arrogance," etc., from various agencies.

[12] "No Place to Hide," *Newsweek,* p. 19, September 8, 1975.

Many state motor vehicle agencies are selling registration lists to anyone.

The Internal Revenue Service supplies tax information on individuals to state treasury agencies, to other federal departments, and to congressional committees.

The Family Assistance Act of 1970 permits exchange of information within the federal government of data from the Social Security Administration (with 25 million files) and the Department of Labor (with 10 million files).

Federal investigators have access to: (1) 14 million life histories from the Department of Defense; (2) 8 million dossiers from the Civil Service Commission; (3) a blacklist of business people considered poor business risks from the General Services Administration; (4) 264 million police records, 323 million medical histories, and 279 million psychiatric records; (5) 194 million sets of fingerprints, and rosters of individuals considered to be antisocial and anti-American from the FBI; (6) 100,000 names of persons considered dangerous to top government officials from the Secret Service; (7) records of people who have been married more than twice (from the Passport Office); and (8) reports on the marital stability of couples (from the Federal Housing Administration).

FIGURE 11-1
Uses of data banks.

1974. . . . So far, Federal law does not specifically prohibit the NSA's brand of surveillance. Direct tampering with "wire, cable, or the like connection" is illegal. But no one at the NSA has to shinny up a telephone pole and clamp alligator clips onto a terminal box. Instead, the agency plucks electronic pulses out of thin air, and current laws make no mention of the "carrier frequencies" employed by microwave.[13]

Existing technology and the availability of mounds of computer-accessible data on individuals could lead to future temptations to misuse the data in ways not originally intended. Facts about age, sex, income, marital status, spending habits, etc., could be analyzed in a trial-and-error fashion just to see what might happen. If not properly controlled, computer technology could conceivably lead to the type of surveillance system illustrated in Figure 11-2. Frank T. Cary, chairman of the board of IBM, sums up the situation very well with these words:

In the past you had to be famous or infamous to have a dossier. Today there can be a dossier on anyone. Information systems, with a seemingly limitless capacity for storing and sorting information, have made it practical to record and transfer a wealth of data on just about anyone. The result is that we now retain too much information. The ambiguous and unverified are retained along with legitimate data. . . . One way of preventing misuse of personal information is to discourage its collection in the first place.[14]

The preceding paragraphs have indicated some of the general con-

---

[13] Ibid., pp. 19–20.

[14] Quoted by Hanna Shields and Mae Churchill in "The Fraudulent War on Crime," *The Nation*, p. 655, December 21, 1974.

DAILY SURVEILLANCE SHEET, 1987, FROM A NATIONWIDE DATA BANK

Dennie Van Tassel
Head Programmer
San Jose State College
125 S. 7th St.
San Jose, Calif. 95114

The "Daily Surveillance Sheet" below is offered as some food for thought to anyone concerned with the establishment of the proposed "National Data Bank". Hopefully, it will help illustrate that *everyone* should be concerned.

```
               NATIONAL DATA BANK
             DAILY SURVEILLANCE SHEET
                  CONFIDENTIAL
                  JULY 11, 1987


SUBJECT.   DENNIE VAN TASSEL
           SAN JOSE STATE COLLEGE
           MALE
           AGE 38
           MARRIED
           PROGRAMMER

PURCHASES.
           WALL STREET JOURNAL                     .10
           BREAKFAST                              1.65
           GASOLINE                               3.00
           PHONE (328-1826)                        .10
           PHONE (308-7928)                        .10
           PHONE (421-1931)                        .10
           BANK (CASH WITHDRAWL)              (120.00)
           LUNCH                                  2.00
           COCKTAIL                               1.00
           LINGERIE                              21.85
           PHONE (369-2436)                        .35
           BOURBON                                8.27
           NEWSPAPER                               .20


               ** COMPUTER ANALYSIS **

OWNS STOCK (90 PER CENT PROBABILITY)

HEAVY STARCH BREAKFAST.  PROBABLY OVERWEIGHT.

BOUGHT 3.00 DOLLARS GASOLINE.  OWNS VW.  SO FAR THIS WEEK HE HAS BOUGHT 12.00
DOLLARS WORTH OF GAS.  OBVIOUSLY DOING SOMETHING ELSE BESIDES JUST DRIVING THE
9 MILES TO WORK.

BOUGHT GASOLINE AT 7.57.  SAFE TO ASSUME HE WAS LATE TO WORK.

PHONE NO. 328-1826 BELONGS TO SHADY LANE - SHADY WAS ARRESTED FOR BOOKMAKING IN
1972.

PHONE NO. 308-7928.  EXPENSIVE MEN.S BARBER - SPECIALIZES IN BALD MEN OR HAIR
STYLING.

PHONE NO. 421-1931.  RESERVATIONS FOR LAS VEGAS (WITHOUT WIFE).  THIRD TRIP
THIS YEAR TO LAS VEGAS (WITHOUT WIFE).  WILL SCAN FILE TO SEE IF ANYONE ELSE
HAS GONE TO LAS VEGAS AT THE SAME TIME AND COMPARE TO HIS PHONE CALL NUMBERS.

WITHDREW 120.00 DOLLARS CASH.  VERY UNUSUAL SINCE ALL LEGAL PURCHASES CAN BE
MADE USING THE NATIONAL SOCIAL SECURITY CREDIT CARD.  CASH USUALLY ONLY USED
FOR ILLEGAL PURCHASES.  IT WAS PREVIOUSLY RECOMMENDED THAT ALL CASH BE OUTLAWED
AS SOON AS IT BECOMES POLITICALLY POSSIBLE.

DRINKS DURING HIS LUNCH.

BOUGHT VERY EXPENSIVE LINGERIE.  NOT HIS WIFE.S SIZE.

PHONE NO. 369-2436.  MISS SWEET LOCKS.


PURCHASED EXPENSIVE BOTTLE OF BOURBON.  HE HAS PURCHASED 5 BOTTLES OF BOURBON
IN THE LAST 30 DAYS.  EITHER HEAVY DRINKER OR MUCH ENTERTAINING.


              *** OVERALL ANALYSIS ***

LEFT WORK AT 4.00, SINCE HE PURCHASED THE BOURBON 1 MILE FROM HIS JOB AT 4.10.
(OPPOSITE DIRECTION FROM HIS HOUSE.)

BOUGHT NEWSPAPER AT 6.30 NEAR HIS HOUSE.  UNACCOUNTABLE 2 1/2 HOURS.  MADE 3
PURCHASES TODAY FROM YOUNG BLONDES.  (STATISTICAL 1 CHANCE IN 78.)  THEREFORE
PROBABLY HAS WEAKNESS FOR YOUNG BLONDES.
```

FIGURE 11-2
Monitoring of an individual by a computer surveillance system. (Reprinted with permission from *Computers and People,* August 1975. Copyright by and published by Berkeley Enterprises, Inc., 815 Washington St., Newtonville, MA 02160.)

cerns associated with the data processing step of originating and recording. Some more specific problems associated with this step are:

1   *Gathering data without a valid need to know.* Dozens of examples of questionable data-gathering activities by government and private agencies could be cited. The examples illustrated here merely serve to outline the problem. For a number of years, the Justice Department maintained a computer-based Inter-Divisional Information System (IDIS) to gather data about, and keep track of, the "agitational activities" of political dissidents. In the early 1970s, at Senate hearings on federal data banks, former Assistant Attorney General Robert Mardian (later convicted of Watergate-related activities) defended the IDIS and gave assurances that it was used only on a "need to know" basis. However, Senate investigators later discovered IDIS printouts being used by the Central Intelligence Agency; after examining the IDIS files, they concluded that "massive amounts of irrelevant information had been compiled on innocent individuals."[15] In spite of these revelations, the Justice Department later attempted to upgrade the IDIS. This effort was blocked by congressional opposition, and IDIS computer tapes were subsequently placed in locked files so as to be inaccessible for operational use. (Of course, civil libertarians and legal scholars may wonder why the files were not destroyed rather than merely locked up.) The second example of questionable data-gathering activities involves the private organizations that collect personal information about individuals for insurance companies, employers, and credit grantors. It is common practice for insurance companies to ask a private consumer reporting agency to investigate a policy applicant's background to help determine the sort of underwriting risk he or she would be. This is understandable since certain personal habits —e.g., heavy drinking or participation in a hazardous sport—may involve obvious health risks. The problem is that the data gathered generally go beyond those which have provable risk value to an insurance company. These data are frequently gathered by an interviewer from two or three of the applicant's neighbors or acquaintances. In about 20 minutes, the interviewer will ask a respondent questions "about the applicant's use of alcohol or narcotics (how much? how often? what kind? when? where?), whom he's living with if not his wife, whether there is 'anything adverse about his reputation, lifestyle, and home environment,' and if there is any news of domestic troubles or reports of dubious business practices."[16] Questions calling for such detailed and impressionistic responses in such a short period of time are an open invitation to gossip, hearsay, half-truths, and faulty moral assessments and innuendos. Furthermore, some of these questions may have little bearing on the insurability of an applicant. (In California, a state law

---

[15] Linda Flato, "Washington Datalink," *Computer Decisions*, p. 11, May 1975.
[16] See James Traub, "The Privacy Snatchers," *Saturday Review*, p. 17, July 21, 1979.

prohibits an insurance company from denying coverage on the grounds of marital status or sexual orientation.) But this is the data-gathering method used by Equifax, Inc., the nation's largest consumer reporting service. The applicant's file is added to the millions of other similar files in the Equifax computer data bank. Once stored, the contents of the file are then available to others, such as credit grantors and potential employers, for a small fee.

2 *Gathering inaccurate and incomplete data.* We have just seen that the data-gathering methods used by Equifax can easily permit inaccuracies to be introduced into a computer data bank. (Each year about 200,000 people lodge complaints against the firm.) More "computer errors" may be attributed to inaccurate and incomplete data input than to either hardware failure or incorrect software. *Unintentional mistakes* in filling out input forms, keying records, coding accounts, etc., are common enough in any record-keeping system. But the consequences may be more serious in a computer-based system because there may be fewer individuals to catch errors and because the speed with which inaccurate information is made available to system users may be much faster than the speed with which errors are detected and corrected. For example, in converting data on a questionnaire into machine-readable form, a keypunch operator may hit the 1 key instead of the 2 key (where the 1 is the code for "yes" and the 2 is the code for "no") on a question concerning a felony conviction, a prior bankruptcy, or a history of mental disorder or venereal disease. You can appreciate the possible consequences of this simple unintentional mistake! In one actual case, a keypunching mistake resulted in an electric bill (and subsequent warnings about nonpayment) being sent to the wrong address. You have probably already guessed the outcome: One cold night the electricity was cut off as a result of a computer-prepared disconnect message, and the household was without power until the error could be corrected. Additional problems can result from cases of *mistaken identity.* Good, bad, and indifferent input data prepared by grantors of credit usually find their way into credit bureau data banks. If your name is not keyed correctly, if your address has changed, if you have a common name, or if you are not consistent in the way you use your first name and initials, you may be confused with some other individual (and with your luck it would be a "deadbeat" rather than a millionaire). Thus, as Robert L. Patrick has observed:

> Despite all the programming done by all the clearing-houses to date, these mistaken identities do occur, they are troublesome, and they are one of the primary reasons why credit reporting agencies treat individuals unfairly.[17]

Unfortunately, in addition to the unintentional mistakes that occur in

---

[17] Robert L. Patrick, "Privacy, People, and Credit Services," *Datamation,* p. 49, January 1974.

the input data gathered by consumer reporting firms, *deliberate errors* have also been introduced into these data banks which are so important to individuals. For example, a former Equifax interviewer "told the Senate Banking Committee that he had completely invented 25 percent of his reports, and that he was far from alone in doing so. An underwriter generally sympathetic to Equifax recalls several 'skywritten' reports, in which the inspector gave a clean bill of health to an applicant who turned out to be dead."[18] Finally, in addition to errors of commission, input data are also subject to serious *errors of omission*. If, for example, an individual is arrested and accused of, say, auto theft, this fact will probably be entered into several law enforcement data banks. But if the individual is found to be innocent of the charges, this very important fact that is needed to complete the record may *not* be entered into the data banks.

> It is estimated . . . that of the arrest records held by the FBI's National Crime Information Center (a data bank in which states voluntarily participate), 70 percent contain no information on the final disposition of the cases. The spread of automation has allowed for easy and indiscriminate circulation of arrest records (whether or not followed by conviction) and unverified data. What's more, prospective employers, credit agencies, and other non-law-enforcement bodies are given access to individual criminal records.[19]

3 *Problems of confusion and bewilderment associated with data gathering.* There have been several verified cases of frustrated individuals actually firing bullets into computers. And the number of such incidents would probably be much larger if individuals confused and bewildered by computer data-input procedures had followed their initial impulses. A significant cause of this confusion, of course, is that people affected by an information system are often not informed of what the system does or how it works. The result of this confusion may be the belief on the part of individuals that they have been tricked or deceived by the system. For example, in signing an application form for an insurance policy, an individual may not know that the fine-print statement at the bottom of the form authorizes a firm representing the insurance company to quiz neighbors and acquaintances for "any and all information" about the applicant. Individuals also may not realize that the supplied data may be entered into third-party data banks and used in rather secretive ways. Individuals may also find it confusing to operate the computer input devices that are replacing more familiar forms and procedures. Automated voting systems, for example, have confused voters and have produced questionable

[18] James Traub, "The Privacy Snatchers," *Saturday Review,* p. 17, July 21, 1979.

[19] Constance Holden, "Privacy: Congressional Efforts Are Coming to Fruition," *Science,* p. 715, May 16, 1975.

tallys. Finally, people have been bewildered by the use of the deposit slips with magnetically encoded account numbers that banks supply to customers. It is reported that in at least one case a man distributed his encoded deposit slips about the lobby of a bank, where they were used by bewildered depositors who wrote their names and account numbers on the slips. Since the names and handwritten numbers were ignored by the bank's MICR equipment, however, the deposits were credited to the account number encoded on the slips. The following morning our resourceful swindler closed out his $67,000 account and proceeded on his way.

Classification and Sorting, Standardization, and Depersonalization

We saw in Chapter 1 that the *classifying* step in data processing involved identifying and arranging items with like characteristics into groups or classes. Classifying is generally accomplished through the use of predetermined codes. Although numeric, alphabetic, and alphanumeric codes may all be used, code *numbers* are more efficiently dealt with by computer systems than are alphabetical names. Thus, individuals are commonly identified by numbers—e.g., as social security, student, time-card, alien-status, naturalization, credit account, license and permit, military service, and selective service numbers—in computer data banks. After the data are classified, they are then usually *sorted* in a predetermined sequence to facilitate processing.

Classifying and sorting input data according to some commonly defined and consistently organized coding scheme can lead to more *standardized* information systems. As we saw in Chapter 9, the standardization now taking place in organizations may result in economies and increased efficiency. It was also noted, however, that standardization could lead to unwanted depersonalization. As an individual comes in contact with an increasing number of computer systems, the use of numerical codes for identification purposes may also be expected to increase. Although individuals may understand that their being treated as numbers can lead to standardized and efficient computer usage by organizations, they may wish that it were not so. Instead of being numerically coded and molded to meet the computer's needs, they might prefer that the computer systems be designed so that they would be treated as persons rather than numbers. *This is not likely to happen.* Of course, as standardization spreads, individuals may need to remember fewer code numbers —e.g., their social security numbers may be substituted for several different codes. In fact, the social security number is now being used as the personal identifier in a growing number of large data systems. The Internal Revenue Service, The U.S. Army, colleges and universities, state driver's license departments, insurance companies, banks, credit bureaus

"Donald Duck Skirts Federal Pay Audit Safeguards. . . ."

Government DP managers are still reeling following revelations of computer payroll payments to Donald Duck, Mickey Mouse and other cartoon characters. The bizarre incident, dubbed the "Walt Disney affair," has investigators examining auditing and check-writing safeguards at federal agencies.

The situation came to light during hearings by a House Civil Service subcommittee on payroll abuse or possible fraud in government pay procedures. In the course of checking auditing safeguards at various agencies, investigators fed the names of 30 cartoon characters into the IBM 7074 at the Department of Housing and Urban Development (HUD). The computer promptly approved salary payments to the fictitious employees. Included was a check for $99,900 to Donald Duck, which should have been rejected on its face value because the maximum federal annual pay level is $47,500. General Accounting Office investigators checking audit procedures explained that many safeguards originally written into the HUD system were dropped when computer operators faced a core storage capacity shortage.

. . . . And Prompts Unit on Agency Computer Loopholes

Concern prompted by incidents like the "Walt Disney affair" has led to establishment of a new watchdog unit to pinpoint weaknesses in government payment programs and computer controls. Comptroller General Elmer Staats created the unit following revelations of fraud and lack of controls in federal payroll, vendor payment and other cash disbursement programs.

The Special Task Force for Prevention of Fraud will pay special attention to controls over payrolls, based on the conclusion that if not properly implemented they offer many possibilities for fraud or error. Staats points out that where systems and controls are properly planned and operated, the possibility of error and fraud is reduced. But where systems do not exist or are improperly used, he adds, chances for mistakes or theft "increase dramatically."

Source: "Donald Duck Skirts Federal Pay Audit Safeguards," *Infosystems,* p. 30, January 1979. Reprinted by permission of the publisher.

—these and many other organizations may know you as 353-27-4765. The threat of an eventual "universal identifier," of course, is that the separate data records you have established for particular purposes can easily be consolidated through the use of the common number, and the combined data can be merged into a large personal dossier.

In addition to treating individuals as numbers, standardized procedures, once established, tend to become inflexible[20] Thus, if an individual's needs do not conform to the "norms" of the system, there may be difficulty in getting the system to deal properly with the exception. This tendency to try to force everyone into the same mold may naturally give the individual a feeling of helplessness in trying to cope with a cold, impersonal, and remote organization. A Mr. D'Unger, for example, wrote several organizations asking them to spell his name correctly. He received several replies, all telling him that it was impossible because of the equipment employed by the systems. A computer expert then looked into the matter and found that the line printers involved had the apostrophe available, but the systems did not bother to use it.

System Miscalculations

The data processing step of calculating involves the arithmetic manipulation of the data. Miscalculations are primarily due to human errors in preparing input data, designing and preparing programs, and operating the hardware. Thus, when the computer itself is blamed for some foul-up, it is frequently being used as a convenient "scapegoat" to cover up human error, carelessness, or indifference. Or, perhaps, it is being used to add credibility to false claims. For example, the Allen Piano and Organ Company of Phoenix, Arizona, advertised on a radio broadcast that its computer had made a mistake and as a result the firm was overstocked with furniture which it was now offering at bargain prices. When a local computer professional, on behalf of the Association for Computing Machinery, contacted the firm and offered to repair any malfunctioning computer hardware free of charge, it transpired that the company did not have a computer and did not use any computing service!

Of course, the unfortunate fact remains that people may believe such false advertising because they are aware of computer-system miscalculations that actually *have occurred*. We can conclude this section with a few pitiful examples of computer-system "atrocities" that have had a negative impact on individuals.

1 Some voters in areas using computerized vote-counting systems may have been disenfranchised. For example, the validity of the count of the computer-processed ballots in Washington, D.C., and Austin, Texas, in past elections is subject to question.[21]

2 A New York City employee failed to get his check for three pay periods after a computer payroll system was installed. Finally, after the

---

[20] This tendency toward inflexibility is *not* an inherent flaw of computer usage. Actually, computerized systems can make individual treatment possible and can cater to individuality for less cost than manual systems. But uniform and rigid treatment costs even less to provide and is thus the approach too often used by systems designers.

[21] For more details on these elections, see James Farmer, "Computerized Voting: Many Happy Returns?," *Computer Decisions*, pp. 20–23, November 1974; and Linda Flato and Hesh Wiener, "Washington Slept Here," *Computer Decisions*, pp. 28ff, November 1974.

employee had initiated legal action against the city, a program bug was discovered and removed, and Mr. Void was at last paid.

3   Individuals have been arrested for "stealing" their own cars. The sequence of events goes something like this: The car is stolen, the theft is reported to a law enforcement data bank, the car is recovered (perhaps in another jurisdiction) and returned to its owner, the recovery is *not* entered into the data bank, and the owner is then picked up while driving his or her recovered property. Since the arrest may also be entered into the data bank, but the final disposition may not be, the owner may wind up with an arrest record for "grand theft-auto." If you do not think this can be serious, you should consider the plight of the ex-Marine from Illinois who has been jailed several times for desertion because of incorrect information stored in the FBI's computerized National Crime Information Center.

THE SYSTEMS SECURITY ISSUE

If the data processing steps discussed in the last section could always be carried out in such a way that vital and relevant input data are accurate and complete when they *enter* the computer information system; are *classified, sorted,* and updated properly when necessary; do not become inaccurate through subsequent errors of omission, commission, or *calculation;* and are not distorted or lost through system malfunctions or operating mistakes, we could be confident about the *integrity* of the data and we could be assured that many of the unfavorable individual experiences discussed in the previous section would not occur in the future.

Even if we were successful in establishing procedures to ensure data integrity, this would not be enough to eliminate the adverse effects that computer systems may have on the private lives of individuals. The other data processing steps of summarizing, storing, retrieving, reproducing, and communicating must also be adequately controlled. It does not help much for an individual to know that the information relevant to him or her that has been summarized and stored in a data bank is accurate and complete if he or she also knows that the information is *not secured* and protected against theft, fraud, or accidental or malicious scrutiny and manipulation.

Both information integrity and security are needed to protect an individual's *right to privacy*—i.e., to protect the legitimate right of an individual to limit access to personal and often sensitive information to persons authorized to use it in the individual's best interest. If a lack of integrity in a law enforcement data bank permits the arrest of an individual for driving his or her own car and then results in the creation of an arrest record that may not be purged from the system, and if a lack of systems security subsequently permits the indiscriminate circulation of this arrest record to prospective employers and credit agencies, these deficiencies have certainly contributed to an invasion of the individual's privacy. In short, data

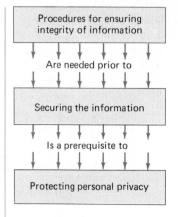

Procedures for ensuring
integrity of information

Are needed prior to

Securing the information

Is a prerequisite to

Protecting personal privacy

FIGURE 11-3
The relationship between
data integrity, systems security, and personal privacy.

integrity, information security, and personal privacy are interrelated, as
shown in Figure 11-3.

For our purposes, *systems security* involves (1) the protection of summarized and stored *data* against accidental or malicious disclosure
(through unauthorized retrieval, reproduction, and communication),
modification, restriction, or destruction, and (2) the *physical* protection of
hardware and software against damage or destruction from such hazards
as fire, flood, and sabotage. Thus, from the individual's point of view, confidential records should be preserved and used only by authorized persons for approved purposes, and the equipment and programs that are
needed to store and retrieve them should be protected against damage
or penetration.

Problems with the security of information systems existed before and
during the time that computers first began to replace file cabinets. But the
vulnerability of computer systems has increased substantially in recent
years, and so the security issue has become much more important. Early
computers were generally located in self-contained installations, were accessible to a relatively small number of specialists, and were employed to
process batches of data in a single stream. As computer systems increased in number and became more sophisticated, however, many
more individuals had access to information systems, the use of shared resources and jointly used data became common, and direct interaction
with a computer became a routine operation for even casual users. Such
an environment has obviously increased the difficulty of maintaining security. In addition to the security difficulties caused by easy systems access
by many people, the vulnerability of systems has also increased because
(1) the information to be found in a relatively complete and up-to-date
data bank may be of sufficient value to provide the incentive for outsiders
to seek access to it, and (2) an increased number of individuals have now
been trained in computer science and in the skills required to program,
penetrate, and manipulate computer systems.

Lack of Control Over Security

Since the security of computer systems has been recognized as a significant problem only in recent years, the computer *hardware* in general use today was not designed with security provisions in mind. Even the existing computer systems being used for military purposes cannot be considered secure. Thus, the security provisions that do exist are found in the software and in the organizational policies, administrative procedures, and data processing controls that may exist in the particular system.

When it comes to security, existing *software* is indeed soft. Clever individuals have had no difficulty in breaking through the security provisions of those computer operating-system programs that they have sought to penetrate.[22] In fact, a favorite activity of some bright students on college campuses has been to successfully infiltrate the college computer system. As an example, two students—one a theology major!—at little Southern Missionary College in Collegedale, Tennessee, "broke through" the file-security system used in the Hewlett-Packard 2000 series time-shared computers and devised programs that decoded protected files.[23]

Whether the invader be a theology major who doth covet a neighbor's files for the challenge presented, or whether he or she be a thief, a criminal manipulator, a saboteur, or a spy, the invader has found that the computer center of an organization may be its nerve center, that it usually contains sensitive information, and that it is often vulnerable to attack. Without adequate computer security provisions, (1) an individual, as we have seen, may suffer a loss of privacy, and (2) an organization may be

When two people meet to decide how to spend a third person's money, fraud will result.
—Herman Gross

[22] One authority sums up the present situation with these words: "Because computer operating systems are not completely predictable, we have no analytical method for proving that an OS is *not* performing unauthorized acts; thus there is no systematic defense against any of several known techniques by which a programmer could corrupt a system for illicit gain." See Vin McLellan, "A Question of Vulnerability," *Datamation*, p. 71, September 1979. Echoing these thoughts, George Davida, Professor of Computer Science at the University of Wisconsin at Milwaukee and chairman of the Institute of Electrical and Electronic Engineers' Committee on Security and Privacy, has noted that it is virtually impossible to achieve complete data-base security. "Data base security should be called data base *insecurity*," says Davida. "If asked at this time whether we can protect privacy, the answer is *no*." See Victor Block, "Washington Info," *Infosystems*, p. 18, September 1979.

[23] The challenging (and disturbing) "game" of outsmarting computer systems has reached epidemic proportions in some places. For example, it is reported that computer science students at one university reached a skill level that allowed them to write programs whose sole purpose was to "crash" the operating system of the school's computer. "There was keen competition among the best students to crash it elegantly, irreparably, frequently, and undetectably. . . . The computer, of course, spent most of its time being crashed or initialized. . . . The solution was a purely political one: every Thursday morning was set aside as 'crash time' and students could run their programs from the operator's console and reinitialize the system themselves." (See Peter G. W. Keen and E. M. Gerson, "The Politics of Software System Design," *Datamation*, p. 84, November 1977.) And a computer hobbyist from Florida claims to be able to get into anybody's system with a few telephone calls. He has obtained over $100,000 from a Canadian department store, has managed to acquire credit cards against which nothing is ever billed, and has received credit from airlines for tickets he did not buy. (See *Creative Computing*, p. 128, July/August 1977.)

exposed to danger through theft of money or goods, careless handling of computerized records, espionage, and/or sabotage.

Some specific examples of the results of inadequate control over information-systems security are presented briefly in the following paragraphs. The implications of these breaches of security for individuals are then examined.

Inadequate control over data security Failure to protect data and records that have been stored in a computer system can have several results:

1 *Theft of money and goods.* An employee or an outsider can steal data and/or programs and sell them. He or she can acquire and use them intact to support an ongoing fraud or embezzlement; can add, subtract, or substitute transactions in the data for fraud or embezzlement purposes; and can do these things at the computer site or at a remote terminal hundreds of miles away. In fact, given the numerous reports of computer crimes involving the theft of money, programs, or other goods that have appeared in print in recent years, it almost seems as though G. K. Chesterton was thinking about computer manipulators when he wrote: "Thieves respect property. They merely wish the property to become their property that they may more perfectly respect it." It is not surprising, of course, that embezzlers and other thieves would become more interested in computerized financial records. After all, the job of accounting for the assets of many organizations has now been entrusted to computer systems, and the moves by the banking industry in the direction of EFTS will simply hasten this trend. In the past, paper money was introduced and thieves used presses; now, plastic money (credit cards) and magnetic money (money cards with magnetic strips, computer tapes, and disks) are used and thieves are using embossers and computers. And they are making big "hauls." According to the Federal Bureau of Investigation (FBI), the average *reported* computer crime loss suffered by organizations is about $500,000, compared to an average bank robbery loss of $3,200 and an average noncomputer embezzlement loss of $23,500. The FBI also estimates that only *1* percent of computer crimes are detected; of those which are discovered, only about one in eight is reported to law enforcement officers![24] Given these statistics, it is little wonder that some computer security experts are fearful that the movement toward electronic transfer of funds systems will

---

[24] Computer crimes are hard to detect because they are usually committed by bright individuals inside an organization who know (1) where the assets are, (2) how to bypass the software security provisions designed to protect the assets, and (3) how to cover their tracks to avoid discovery. If, through some slip-up, an individual joins the tiny percentage who are caught, there is a good chance that he or she will not be prosecuted because (1) victims of computer crimes—large organizations for the most part—are embarrassed by their misfortune and do not want the adverse publicity that comes from publicly admitting that their systems were insecure, and (2) there is at this writing no specific federal statute (and only a few state laws) that makes computer crime a crime. (However, legislation sponsored by Senator Abraham Ribicoff of Connecticut may be passed to close this loophole.)

bring on computer attacks by organized crime. (Computer personnel at Chicago banks have already been caught dipping into bank computer accounts to pay off loan shark and gambling debts.) A widely discussed example of a "computer crime" is the case involving the chief teller at a Union Dime Savings Bank branch in New York City, who was charged with stealing about $1.5 million from the bank's accounts. Hundreds of legitimate accounts were manipulated; money was transferred to fraudulent accounts and then withdrawn; and false information was fed into the bank's computer so that when quarterly interest payments were due, the legitimate accounts appeared intact. All this was done by a person who did not have direct access to the computer. Other techniques used by computer-wise thieves include (a) deducting a few cents in excess service charges, interest, taxes, or dividends from thousands of accounts and writing themselves a check for the total amount of the excess deductions and (b) reporting inventory items as broken or lost and then transferring the items to accomplices.[25] In short, it has been estimated that losses suffered by organizations as a result of fraud and embezzlement now exceed those caused by robbery, loss, and shoplifting—and the computer is playing an active part in an increasing number of theft cases.

2 *Misrepresentation of facts.* Major stockholders, for example, could distort the financial facts produced by computer systems in order to obtain illegal gain. Overvalued assets, understated liabilities, and other false representations could be used in criminal manipulations.

3 *System penetration and espionage.* As Figure 11-4 indicates, a modern computer system is vulnerable to attack and penetration at many points and from many people both inside and outside the organization. The motivation for such penetration may range from simple curiosity and the challenge of solving a puzzle or playing a joke on the one hand,[26] to stealing the secrets and confidential records of an indi-

---

[25] For additional techniques and examples, see Brandt Allen, "The Biggest Computer Frauds: Lessons for CPAs," *The Journal of Accountancy,* pp. 52–62, May 1977; Brandt Allen, "Embezzler's Guide to the Computer," *Harvard Business Review,* pp. 79–89, July/August 1975; Richard G. Canning, "The Importance of EDP Audit and Control," *EDP Analyzer,* pp. 1–13, June 1977; Hal Lancaster, "Rise of Minicomputers, Ease of Running Them Facilitates New Frauds," *Wall Street Journal,* pp. 1ff, October 15, 1977; Laton McCortney, "Is Paper Products Case Tip of the Iceberg?" *Datamation,* pp. 148–149, March 1977; Donn B. Parker, *Crime by Computer,* Charles Scribner's Sons, New York, 1976; Marshall Romney, "Detection and Deterrence: A Double Barreled Attack on Computer Fraud," *Financial Executive,* pp. 36–41, July 1977; K. S. Shankar, "The Total Computer Security Problem: An Overview," *Computer,* pp. 50–61, June 1977.

[26] As noted earlier, college students have often successfully penetrated the security provisions of computer systems for this reason. Even high school students are now enjoying the "game." In London, for example, a 15-year-old schoolboy, with no special knowledge of computers and with no equipment other than a remote terminal located in his school, was able, over a four-month period of "browsing" at the terminal, to (1) penetrate the security system of a major timesharing service, (2) gain access to the secret files stored by other users so that he could easily read and change them without being detected, and (3) completely take over the system, cut off other users, change their system passwords, and even alter the amount of their computing service bills. In this case, the boy never did anything with the secret information he obtained, and he wrote the timesharing service telling them what he had done. In other instances, however, the system (and its legitimate users) has not been so fortunate.

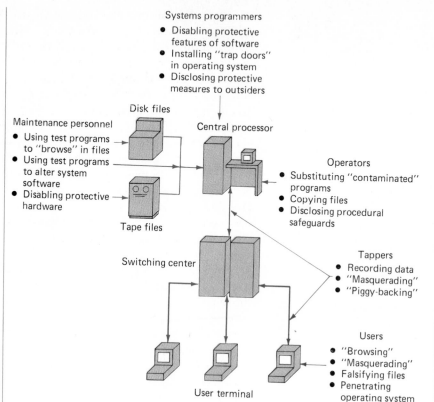

Systems programmers
- Disabling protective features of software
- Installing "trap doors" in operating system
- Disclosing protective measures to outsiders

Disk files

Central processor

Maintenance personnel
- Using test programs to "browse" in files
- Using test programs to alter system software
- Disabling protective hardware

Operators
- Substituting "contaminated" programs
- Copying files
- Disclosing procedural safeguards

Tape files

Switching center

Tappers
- Recording data
- "Masquerading"
- "Piggy-backing"

Users
- "Browsing"
- "Masquerading"
- Falsifying files
- Penetrating operating system

User terminal

FIGURE 11-4
System penetration and espionage. (Source: Tom Alexander, "Waiting for the Great Computer Rip-off," *Fortune,* p. 144, July 1974.)

vidual or a competitor or causing the competitor's system to "crash"—i.e., become inoperable—on the other. As shown in Figure 11-4, programmers, operators, and maintenance personnel usually have the opportunity to penetrate systems security, and they may do so for personal grudges or for personal gain, e.g., for a bribe from an outsider. Operators, for example, can make duplicate copies of master tapes for outsiders in a few minutes, and programmers can insert code into an operating system in such a way that it provides a "trap door" for penetration at any convenient time in the future.[27] But even without help from within an organization, unscrupulous outsiders may gain access to the secrets and confidential records stored in an organization's computer system. (Of course, sensitive information about patients, clients, students, present and potential customers, secret processes, research in progress, simulation programs used in decision making, etc., could be of considerable value to blackmailers, spies, and unethical competitors.) Among the techniques employed against online systems are "masquerading" and "piggybacking." Penetrators obtain the passwords of legitimate users by wiretapping or other

---

[27] For further information on this penetration technique, see Vin McLellan, "Of Trojan Horses and Trap Doors," *Datamation,* pp. 71–72, September 1979.

means and then use these passwords to masquerade as authorized users in order to get access to the system and to other people's files. In one case, a minicomputer was hooked to a wiretapped line and was used to impersonate a timesharing host computer. The mini intercepted user calls to the legitimate processor, obtained a record of user identification numbers and passwords, and then informed users that the system was overloaded and requested that they call back in an hour. The identification of many users was thus obtained. The piggybacking approach is similar in that a small computer or "bootleg" terminal is attached to a tapped communications line where it may intercept and modify legitimate messages. A bank-to-bank transmission could be intercepted, for example, and additional credits to the tapper's accounts could be added to the message. It should be pointed out here that the penetrator or spy does not have to resort to wiretapping. Electronic devices are available that will pick up electromagnetic radiations given off by computing equipment and convert these radiations into humanly readable form (in one demonstration, receiving devices coupled to a printer were placed in a truck, the truck was parked next to an unshielded computer center, and the output being produced by the computer's printer was received and copied in the truck). Also, obtaining carelessly discarded carbon paper, output listings, and other documents is an important source of information. In short, those with motivation, financial resources, and access to computer skills may find that, as one authority has stated, penetrating today's computer system is about as difficult as solving the crossword puzzle in a Sunday paper.

Inadequate control over physical security Security-conscious designers of computer centers would probably be in favor of placing the hardware in a separate building protected by a high fence and isolated from other structures. "A major computer service center did just that—and a few months later, a light aircraft crashed into the roof and destroyed the building, the computers, and all on-site records."[28] In addition to falling aircraft, the computer site may be damaged or destroyed because of the following hazards:

1 *Fire* In the mid-1970s, thousands of military records were destroyed when the Army Records Center in St. Louis experienced a very large fire. Perhaps to avoid such a catastrophe, an East Coast chemical company "secured" its computer in a room with an advanced chemical fire-suppression system and with a two-hour fire-rated facility to house the library of tapes, disks, and paper documents. Additional backup tapes and documents were stored two blocks away. Unfortunately, a raging fire swept through the entire plant, destroyed a nine-block area, and wiped out the computer center and the backup materials.

[28] "Computer Security: The Imperative Nuisance," *Infosystems,* p. 25, February 1974.

2 *Flood.* Water can be particularly damaging to electronic components, wires, and cables. In fact, in the fire at the Army Records Center, the damage caused by water was more severe than the damage caused by the fire itself. It has been estimated that hundreds of computer centers were flooded in the mid-Atlantic states by the rains that accompanied tropical storm Agnes, and various hurricanes have produced serious damage. Even computer centers located several floors above ground level have been flooded by faulty fire sprinkler systems, broken water pipes, and the efforts of fire fighters working on still-higher floors.

3 *Sabotage.* Improper handling of input media can cause damage with a resulting loss of data, and entire files stored on magnetizable media can be erased accidentally. In addition to these hazards, important files are also vulnerable to deliberate damage and destruction. Cases of disgruntled employees changing programs to sabotage data and using magnets to ruin tapes containing data and programs have been reported. Several computer centers have been destroyed by bombs. And it is not uncommon for programmers who work for timesharing organizations to buy time on their competitor's system, get on a terminal, and then make every effort to test, penetrate, and then crash the competitor's system.[29]

Impact on Individuals

The lack of control over computer systems security has resulted in undesirable consequences for individuals. Economic loss, inconvenience, dehumanization, loss of vote, loss of privacy—these are just a few of the aggravations suffered by individuals because computer systems were not secure.

Individuals as well as organizations *lose money* to the computer thief. In one instance, a computer was used to send out phony invoices to individuals. The thief knew that some people pay authentic-looking bills automatically, without questioning their validity. When a phony bill was questioned, however, the thief would merely send back a form letter saying, "Sorry. Our computer made an error." A person's finances could also become fouled up as a result of the penetration of an EFTS by an enemy or an unethical competitor.[30] Invalid charges from organizations selected by

---

[29] For example, Proprietary Computer Systems, Inc., of Los Angeles, a computer timesharing service, noticed that unauthorized accesses were being made to their system and notified the FBI. The investigation resulted in a July 1979 federal grand jury indictment against a vice president of Browne Information Systems, a New York competitor. The indictment charged that the vice president had obtained confidential information from the Los Angeles system 196 times, and had deleted codes to keep customers from accessing the Los Angeles system. See Edith Myers, "This Crime Was Reported," *Datamation*, p. 101, September 1979.

[30] Here's another true example: A Chicago woman was mailed a bank debit card and a personal identification number without having requested them. Both were intercepted by a thief and used to empty a $600 account of hers and run up an additional overdraft of $1,200. The bank then froze the woman's other account because she was overdrawn. It took an attorney and two months of wrangling with the bank to get her money released.

the penetrator—e.g., insurance companies, utilities, or department stores—could be entered against the individual's accounts. At best, the resulting mess would probably involve long delays and great *inconvenience* to straighten out; at worst, it could result in financial ruin.

A lack of control in handling input media can also result in inconvenience. Suppose a shift supervisor at a computer center servicing dozens of banks processes a tape containing a day's checks and deposits but fails to properly record this processing run. The next shift supervisor may then rerun the tape with the result being that double deposits and double withdrawals may appear in customer accounts. (You, of course, are delighted with your double credit, but I am really chapped by my double withdrawal. And we are both inconvenienced by the later attempts to straighten out this fiasco.)

Finally, as we have seen in earlier pages, a lack of control over systems security can lead to the invasion of an individual's legitimate *right to privacy.* Since this is the subject of the next section, we will not dwell on it here. It should be pointed out here, however, that the majority of computer systems installed in the nation today are *not* secure enough to meet the personal data confidentiality conditions required by existing laws; nor are they secure enough to protect the privacy rights which existing laws give to individuals.

THE PRIVACY ISSUE

We know that for years private and public organizations have been building separate files containing "threads" of information about those with whom they come in contact. And we know that the use of these files has led to past abuses of individuals' legitimate right to keep to themselves (or to have kept on a confidential basis) those facts, beliefs, thoughts, and feelings which they do not wish to divulge publicly. But many of these older files are incomplete and poorly maintained. Thus, the value of their contents may be such that unauthorized persons have little incentive to snoop. *The development of computer data banks, however, has changed the situation.*

Dossiers and the Invasion of Privacy

Unlike the information stored in older systems, files maintained in large, integrated computer data banks may be more complete, less subject to deterioration, and therefore more worthy targets for unscrupulous persons bent on ferreting out information of a private and confidential nature. Seemingly innocent data recorded and stored at one time may be retrieved and correlated quickly and inexpensively by the computer (perhaps through the use of social security numbers) with other data collected from different sources and at different times to reveal potentially damaging information about individuals. It might then be possible to bring pressure to bear on the individuals to make them do things they

As every man goes through life, he fills in a number of forms for the record, each containing a number of questions. There are thus hundreds of little threads radiating from each man, millions of threads in all. If these threads were suddenly to become visible, people would lose all ability to move.
—Alexander Solzhenitsyn

Strive at all times to bend, fold, spindle and mutilate. Know yourself; if you need help, call the FBI. Exercise caution in your daily affairs, expecially with those persons closest to you. That lemon on your left, for instance. . . .
—Anonymous in *Deteriorata*

might otherwise not have done. In short, computers can facilitate the performance of the data processing steps of *storing, retrieving, reproducing,* and *communicating* in ways that can negatively affect an individual's privacy and reputation. The indiscriminate retrieval and dissemination of questionable arrest records and the impressionistic data gathered on insurance applicants referred to earlier are examples of this fact.

Thoughtful opponents of consolidated data banks acknowledge that such banks *can* help public and private organizations provide individuals with some of the benefits discussed in the last chapter—e.g., better and more efficient service and greater safety. They agree, for example, that the problems brought about by mobile criminals and the lack of communication between fixed law enforcement jurisdictions can be reduced through the use of consolidated police information systems. Despite the merits that such broad systems may have, their opponents are concerned about the threat they might eventually present to an individual. This concern is perhaps best summarized in a *Saturday Review* cartoon which shows a distressed executive listening to a telephone message. The message is: "This is the Computer Data Bank. Leave $100,000 in small bills in Locker 287 at the Port Authority Bus Terminal or I'll print out your complete dossier and send it to your wife." Among the more specific objections which have been voiced in these pages and elsewhere against large data banks are: (1) *Information may be obtained* from confidential sources *without the knowledge or consent* of the individual, (2) there may be *no easy means of verifying the accuracy, completeness, or subjective quality of the dossier*—factual errors or misleading information may seriously damage an individual's reputation, (3) there is *lack of security*—sensitive and confidential personal information may be obtained and used by unauthorized and unscrupulous people who will find ways to penetrate the safeguards of a computer system, and (4) there may be *eventual loss of personal freedom*—the creation of superbanks with complete computer-based dossiers on individuals would give considerable power to those in charge of the banks, and this development might be the beginning of a drift toward the "Big Brother" state created by George Orwell in his book *1984*.

Impact on Individuals

Several negative effects of computer usage that are linked to the subject of individual privacy have already been presented in earlier pages of this chapter. Therefore, a few additional examples and speculations here should be sufficient to demonstrate how a computer system or network may be used for *surveillance*, for the creation of a *climate that restricts individual freedom,* and for *other abuses.*

EFTS surveillance possibilities Although the electronic funds transfer systems being designed and implemented by banks and other financial institutions are not intended for *surveillance,* they may be easily adapted to this purpose in the future, as we saw in Figure 11-2. The use of *cash* in a transaction reveals little or no information about the parties to the transaction; when a *check* is written, a record is created of the payer, the payee, and the transaction amount; and when a *debit card* is used, all this information, along with the transaction time, location, and nature of the transaction, is recorded. Thus, if all your nontrivial financial transactions were normally to be processed through EFTS computers, a *daily record* of much of *what* you do and *where* you do it could be prepared. Thus, the situation illustrated in a *New Yorker* magazine cartoon of a husband and wife trying to decide what movie to see and the wife asking her husband "What would look good on our dossier?" could become less amusing and more possible in the future. Furthermore, if you were to decide to use cash for a transaction that you wished to keep private, the cash acquisition might be quite conspicuous (and suspicious?). A few years ago, a group of computer, communication, and surveillance experts was gathered and given the following hypothetical problem: As advisers to the head of the KGB (the Russian secret police), they were to design an *unobtrusive* surveillance system to monitor the activities of all citizens and visitors inside the U.S.S.R. As Paul Armer testified in Congressional hearings:

> That exercise . . . was only a two-day effort. I am sure we could add some bells and whistles to increase its effectiveness somewhat. But the fact remains that this group decided that if you wanted to build an unobtrusive system for surveillance, you couldn't do much better than an EFTS.[31]

Of course, EFTS proponents in the financial community maintain that adequate laws can be passed to prevent surveillance abuse. But critics are not so sure. They point out that existing check authorization systems, and systems such as VISA, MasterCard, and American Express, can "flag" individual accounts so that if a "flagged" individual tries to cash a check or make a purchase someone (police perhaps?) can be notified of the individual's exact location. They are fearful that future operators of EFTS networks would be unable to resist the pressures from government organizations to allow the EFTS to be used for surveillance purposes.

List-compiling abuses   Mailing lists giving details about individuals are regularly compiled and sold by both private and public organizations. State auto licensing agencies, for example, sell lists to auto equipment suppliers. There is probably not much harm in this if it results only in your receiving literature that tries to persuade you to buy seat covers a few weeks after you have registered your new car. But what about the case of the computer dating service that sold its list of female clients to a publishing organization that printed and sold through local newsstands lists of "Girls Who Want Dates"? Try to tell one of those girls that her privacy hasn't been invaded!

[31] See Paul Armer, "Computer Technology and Surveillance," *Computers and People,* p. 11, September 1975. For additional information on EFTS surveillance, see H. Paris Burstyn, "Electronic Fund Transfers: A Promise or a Threat?," *Personal Computing,* pp. 58ff, May 1978.

Freedom restrictions Consider the following facts:

1 Computerized records have been used by the Department of Health, Education, and Welfare to track down fathers who have deserted children on welfare. This operation, officially called the Parent Locator Service (and unofficially referred to as "Dadnet"), legally accessed the "confidential" master files of the IRS, the Social Security Administration, the Pentagon, and the Veterans Administration.

2 Thousands of law enforcement officers and bank, employment agency, and credit company clerks have easy access to networks containing information on millions of people. Many of these officers and clerks without any real "need to know" may while away the time browsing through the records of friends and acquaintances just to see what they can uncover.[32]

3 In at least one state, the name, social security number, and diagnosis of patients hospitalized for psychiatric treatment were reported to the Department of Mental Health—and were then made available to insurance companies, chiefs of police, the motor vehicle department, and all other licensing agencies.[33]

4 Most categories of personal information gathered for legitimate research purposes by reputable social, political, and behavioral scientists do not enjoy any statutory protection. Thus, sensitive personal information gathered by well-intentioned researchers may be obtained through a subpoena issued by a court, legislative committee, or other government body and put into data banks for future use. If the researchers, who may have assured the respondents that their replies would be kept in strictest confidence, refuse to honor the subpoena and turn over the data, they may be cited for contempt and be made to suffer the consequences. Given that alternative, they generally surrender the data.

The awareness of such facts and such uses of large computerized data banks tends to have a sobering effect on individuals—it tends to restrict their freedom, and it tends to have a chilling effect on their actions

[32] A bored deputy sheriff in Massachusetts spent one night running his family through the FBI's National Crime Information Center. The results: "His mother was listed because, when she was 18, neighbors complained of a noisy sorority party (no arrests). His stepfather, a respected businessman, was listed because he complained to the police that he had *received* a bad check." In all, 10 out of 11 of the deputy's family were listed. See Francis W. Sargent, "The National Crime Information Center and Massachusetts," *Computers and Automation,* p. 8, December 1973.

[33] In recent testimony before the House Subcommittee on Government Information and Individual Rights, Dr. Alfred Freedman, president of the National Commission on Confidentiality of Health Records, commented that "patients and practitioners legitimately complain that insurers often ask for much more information—photocopied hospital records, for example, and highly detailed psychiatric reports—than they really need. In addition, once information is collected by an insurance company or investigative agency, it is widely traded within the entire industry. . . ." Thus, says Freedman, "many individuals will not use their psychiatric coverage for fear of repercussions at work." See Victor Block, "Privacy Impacts DP World," *Infosystems,* p. 94, June 1979.

FIGURE 11-5
Grace Hopper. (*Wide World
Photos.*)

HOPPER IS PIONEER IN FIELD OF COMPUTER LANGUAGES

After her graduation from Vassar, Grace Hopper received a Ph.D. from Yale in 1934.
Hopper was an officer in the Naval Reserve, and during World War II she was assigned to the Naval Ordnance Computation Project at Harvard. At the war's end, she
became a Harvard Research Fellow. She developed the operating programs of the
Mark I while at Harvard.

Hopper later joined the Eckert-Mauchly Computer Corporation, where she
worked with the UNIVAC as a senior mathematician. Grace Hopper is a pioneer in
the field of computer languages and she played an important role in the development of COBOL (COmmon Business Oriented Language).

even when the data are accurate, the use of the data is authorized by law, and controls on the use of the data are imposed. You may agree that runaway fathers should help support their children if possible, but you may also begin to wonder whether a future system might not be designed to "track" you down; you may be in favor of the use of computers to curtail crime, but you may also resent being listed with felons in an unsecured data bank; you may be in favor of mental health departments keeping records on psychiatric patients, but you may also have your doubts about the wisdom of recommending to disturbed friends that they seek professional help; and you may believe that a university professor should conduct a study that requires the gathering and analyzing of personal data, but you may not feel free to personally participate in that study. In short, you may now tend to behave differently (and less freely) than you once would have because of your increasing awareness that what you say and do may become part of some computer record.

The optimist says: "This is the best of all possible worlds." The pessimist says, "That's right."
—Joseph Weisenbaum

THE PESSIMISTIC OUTLOOK

The pessimistic view of the future is that the effects of computer usage will *not* lead to greater freedom and individuality. On the contrary, pessimists note how computers have been used to damage individuals, and they foresee increasingly harmful trends. Computers (and the technological advances that they spawn), some argue, will tend to dominate our lives as a society and as individuals. We shall be swept along in a technological tide over which we shall have little control—the harassed victims of a depersonalized and dehumanized process that places greater value on efficiency than on the more noble qualities of life.

Critics of the effects of computer usage have evidence to show that questionable practices in originating and recording data are common; that dossiers containing incorrect, ambiguous, and unverified data on individuals are produced; that correct personal data are misused; that systems miscalculations are frequent; that stored sensitive personal data are often not secured and protected against theft, manipulation, and malicious scrutiny; and that those facts, beliefs, thoughts, and feelings which people want to keep to themselves (or have kept on a confidential basis) are repeatedly revealed and disseminated. The net effect, pessimists contend, is that individual freedom will be severely threatened by computer-usage pressures leading to greater regimentation and conformity.

On the economic front, the pessimists argue, more people will be displaced and then unemployed as the advances in technology are accelerated. As jobs are eliminated by machines, purchasing power is certain to decline. A monumental economic depression may result from the overproduction of machines and the decline in demand, and this could lead to a severe political upheaval and a change in our form of government. The future appears bleak to the pessimists; the visible increase in

"Attorney Ponders Legal Questions of Crimes Involving Data Communications"

Attorney Susan Hubbell Nycum pauses in mid-sentence, caught in a thought, and peers out the window of her office. Below, downtown traffic winds between San Francisco's gray buildings, which are set against bay water glinting with late afternoon sun.

"Our challenge is to determine exactly where computers fit into the old categories of law, and, where we have to, create new categories," she says, waving her hand toward a wall of books that are stacked from floor to ceiling. "Right now there is no one-to-one analog between law and technology."

Concerned

The blonde-haired, blue-eyed Nycum has a special concern: the problems brought by the "democratization" of the computer out of its traditional headquarters cubbyhole and into field uses that are linked back to the central office along communications lines. That has "more than logarithmically increased the potential for legal problems," she says. "You can now rob a bank from the comfort of your own living room, wearing a T-shirt and having a cold beer."

As chairperson of the American Bar Association's prestigious Science and Technology Section, Nycum hopes to bring up such questions as the security and, perhaps more importantly, the liability posed by the proliferation of data communications. She is uniquely qualified to raise these issues, for although she considers herself one of the top three legal experts on computers in the nation, her colleagues place her at the head of the list.

And although she considers herself to be "dull," Nycum's life is by no means languid. She sings in the church choir, likes opera, and is a student of Greek mythology and the Greek language. Moreover, Nycum also has a career that has been, and still is, just as active as the game of tennis that she plays. She was a "law and computers" fellow at Stanford University, got hands-on experience as the assistant director of multimillion-dollar computer centers at Carnegie Mellon University, and for the last eight years has been a co-investigator at SRI International, Menlo Park, Calif., in a National Science Foundation study that has produced the clearest description of the potential for computer abuse. She has even fought and won some of the antitrust battles against IBM.

Liability

But problems of computer security—"that stuff on Hawaii Five-O"—isn't her main concern. Another legal problem looms on the horizon: product liability.

"Sometimes when I tell a company what could happen, their response is, 'You're just saying that to scare us,'" she says.

Nycum asks companies to think, for example, about a software "glitch" that gives an air traffic controller wrong information, causing an air disaster; a node in a data communications network that fails at a critical moment and causes the loss of important sales; and a memory storage device that "crashes" in a hospital, resulting in misplaced medical records.

At the heart of those problems are legal questions, such as What is information? Is it a "thing" that can be covered by the strict liability laws that dictate who can sue and for how much when an axle breaks on a truck and a bystander is killed? Or is it a service such as that rendered by an accountant who has limited liability for the effects of his mistakes?

Legalities

It makes a difference. An insurance company that issues inadequate coverage in its policies because of faulty information generated by data communications hardware and software can be sued for millions of dollars. But can the injured party sue the vendor of the electronics data processing system? Yes, if information is a product; probably no, if it is a service, she explains. If one company taps another's information base, via communications links, and steals trade secrets, can it be prosecuted? Two judges have said the culprit can't be charged with receipt of stolen property—the standard legal approach—because millions of blips of electricity don't count as property under present legal definitions, Nycum says.

Another unresolved legal problem is equally basic to the growth of data communications: What is a person? "Only people and corporations can be considered persons," says Nycum. And "there's a strong suspicion in the business community" that foreign countries that want to hassle a multinational corporation can find an unusually effective tool in unnecessary regulations on the company's data transmissions, usually written in the name of protecting privacy.

Conflicts

Nycum feels that the future headlines about spectacular computer robberies will have to share the page with equally spectacular headlines about computer and communications liability. Computer makers, software writers, systems designers, network users, and information customers will be the defendants and plaintiffs of a new generation of legal battles as the human conflict moves from the arena of paper interaction to electronic interaction.

Source: "Attorney Ponders Legal Questions Involving Data Communications," *Data Communications,* pp. 47–48, May 1979. Reprinted by permission.

human anxiety, the alienation of certain groups in our society, the erosion of confidence in our ability to survive difficult national periods, and the lack of trust in the large bureaucratic organizations that are monitoring and regulating the affairs of individuals seem to them to be omens of things to come as technological change is accelerated.

The fears expressed in the above summary of the pessimistic view are not all new, nor are they all related solely to the future impact on individuals of computers alone. For at least 100 years people have feared that automatic machines might develop consciousness and turn on their creators. In 1872, for example, a science fiction work entitled *Erewhon* was published by Samuel Butler. Residents of Erewhon, fearing that people would some day stand in the same relation to machines as "the beasts of the field" now stand to people, attacked and destroyed nearly all the machines in Erewhon.

► LOOKING BACK

The following points have been emphasized in this chapter:

1 Although some administrators and employees have benefited by the use of computers on the job, others have not been so fortunate. Some have lost their jobs or have suffered a loss of status and prestige when computer systems were installed, and others have suffered anxiety at being forced to give up familiar surroundings and procedures and to learn new techniques. Clerical employees, for example, have often been displaced by computers, and production employees are being threatened (and sometimes displaced) by the rapidly increasing use of computer-controlled robots.

2 Individual resistance frequently accompanies such changes and may take many forms; it may also come from all levels in an organization. By knowing and following certain guidelines and suggestions with care, the changers may be able to reduce the level of opposition.

3 In private life some people (who may have been helped on the job by computers) have been inconvenienced, harassed, confused, and bewildered by computer information systems employing disputable data processing practices. In many systems there seems to be a lack of control over the data originating and recording step. Data are sometimes gathered without a valid reason; when a valid reason does exist, gathered facts are sometimes used in ways that were not originally intended.

4 A distressing number of individuals have also been the casualties of systems errors of commission and omission and/or the relatively helpless victims of a cold, impersonal, and remote computer system that classifies, sorts, and treats them as depersonalized numbers. Systems miscalculations have also victimized individuals.

5 Information integrity and security are needed to protect an individual's legitimate right to privacy. Systems security involves the protection of both the data and the hardware and software used to process the data. Computer security difficulties are caused by the fact that many skilled people may have access to the system and by the fact that the value of the stored data may warrant the attempt to penetrate and/or manipulate the system. Although there are hardware and software security provisions in a typical system, these provisions are seldom capable of blocking the attempts of a skilled penetrator. Some examples of the results of the failure to control data security and the security of the hardware and software were presented in this chapter. The lack of control over computer systems security has resulted in economic loss, inconvenience, dehumanization, and a loss of privacy for individuals.

6 Computers can facilitate the data processing steps of storing, retrieving, reproducing, and communicating in ways that can negatively affect an individual's privacy and reputation. Although there are benefits to be obtained from the creation of broad private and government data banks, there is also a real concern about the threat these data banks might present to an individual. Ways in which computers are used (or could be used) for surveillance, for the creation of a climate that restricts individual freedom, and for other abuses were presented in the chapter. Seeing such effects as these, pessimists paint a bleak picture of the future.

▶ KEY TERMS

After reading Chapter 11, you should be able to define and use the following terms:

displacement	right to privacy
unemployment	system penetration
robot	data security
resistance to change	physical security
data integrity	EFTS surveillance possibilities
systems security	

▶ REVIEW AND DISCUSSION QUESTIONS

1 (a) How have administrators been the victims of computer usage? (b) How have employees been victimized?
2 What is the distinction between displacement and unemployment?
3 What factors influence the significance of the displacement problem when computers are introduced into organizations?

4 "Employees in the professions may be subject to adverse effects as a result of computer usage." Discuss this statement.

5 (a) Why do administrators resist change? (b) Why do employees resist?

6 How may resistance to change be reduced?

7 "Questionable data processing practices have had adverse effects on the private lives and records of individuals." Discuss this comment.

8 How may a lack of control over data originating and recording lead to undesirable results for individuals?

9 How may computer-system classification and sorting practices lead to undesirable results for individuals?

10 Westinghouse Electric Corporation has a grant from the National Science Foundation to experiment with the use of robots to replace people in low-volume or batch-manufacturing operations—the types of operations that account for about 75 percent of all United States manufacturing. According to a Westinghouse spokesperson, "complex assembly tasks will continue to be performed by people, but many repetitive, boring tasks, and those performed in an unpleasant environment can and should be automated." Discuss this statement.

11 "Data integrity, information security, and personal privacy are interrelated." Define these terms and discuss this statement.

12 Explain how a lack of data security and physical security can lead to undesirable consequences for individuals.

13 Why has the vulnerability of many computer systems increased in recent years?

14 (a) How may a lack of control over data security result in the theft of money and goods? (b) How may lack of control result in system penetration and espionage?

15 What are the hazards that can damage or destroy a computer site?

16 "The lack of control over computer systems security has resulted in undesirable consequences for individuals." Discuss this statement.

17 (a) What benefits have been cited to justify the establishment of broad consolidated data banks? (b) What problems might such data banks pose for individuals?

18 (a) Discuss the EFTS surveillance possibilities. (b) How may questionable activities by government organizations create a climate that restricts individual freedom?

19 According to pessimists, what is likely to be the future result of computer usage?

20 (a) Are you an optimist or a pessimist about the future impact of computer systems on individuals? (b) Why?

21 In George Orwell's *1984,* Big Brother controls individuals through sensors housed in the two-way (send-receive) television screens located in all homes, government offices, and public squares. The sensors tune in on individuals and monitor their heartbeats. Recently, a

young physiologist, seeking to measure the physiological activities of salamanders, created a delicate instrument that can detect and record from a distance an animal's heartbeat, respiration, and muscle tension. In all, Orwell described 137 "futuristic" devices in *1984* (which was published about 30 years ago). About 100 of these devices are now practical. Do you think that a democratic society has anything to fear from such technology?

▶ SELECTED REFERENCES

In addition to the numerous references suggested in the chapter footnotes, you might be interested in the following sources:

Bell, Daniel: "Communications Technology—For Better or for Worse," *Harvard Business Review,* pp. 20–22ff, May/June 1979.

Dorn, Philip H.: "The Automated Office: The Road to Disaster?" *Datamation,* pp. 154ff, November 15, 1978. (A rebuttal to this article is found in Petersohn, Henry H.: "Automation: The Road to Survival," *Datamation,* pp. 211ff, July 1979.

Haskell, Bruce V.: "Robots in Fiction," *Creative Computing,* pp. 118–119, January 1979.

Hentoff, Nat: "Privacy and the Press: Is Nothing Sacred?" *Saturday Review,* pp. 22–23, July 21, 1979.

Remick, Carl: "Robots: New Faces on the Production Line," *Management Review,* pp. 25–28ff, May 1979.

Rosenfeld, Albert: "How Anxious Should Science Make Us?" *Saturday Review,* pp. 16–21, June 9, 1979.

Welton, Jon R.: "Freedom and the Computer," *Creative Computing,* pp. 108–110, September/October 1978.

Chapter 12
CONTROLLING THE NEGATIVE IMPACT

In the last chapter, you saw how computer usage could have a negative impact on some individuals. Concerned and responsible citizens in the computer industry, government, and other areas of society are, of course, aware of these negative possibilities. Thus, a considerable amount of thought has gone into devising ways to counter the potentially adverse effects of computer usage. The purpose of this chapter is to briefly survey a few of the controls that have been developed to counter the negative impact. (Much additional information may be found in the entire books that have been written on this subject.)

In the first section of the chapter, you will be introduced to a few of the input, processing, output, and retention control techniques that can be used to maintain data integrity.

The second section discusses some of the system security controls that may be used. Separation of duties within the computer department and the use of auditors are among the controls discussed in this section. A number of computer-operation controls are also considered.

Finally, in the last section, some of the legal and social controls used to help maintain an individual's right to privacy are discussed.

Thus, after studying this chapter, you should be able to:

- Give examples of some input, processing, output, and retention controls that may be used to maintain data integrity.

- Explain how organizational separation of duties and the use of auditing techniques can help maintain system security.

- Identify some of the system-design, programming, and computer-operation controls that may be used to maintain system security.

- Discuss how legal and social controls have been used to restore some balance in favor of personal privacy rights.

- Understand and use the key terms listed at the end of the chapter.

We have now seen that computer usage can (1) produce records on individuals that may be inaccurate, incomplete, and lacking in integrity in other ways, (2) contribute to systems security problems, and (3) result in an invasion of an individual's right to privacy. Thus, in this chapter we need to examine some of the *integrity, security,* and *privacy controls* that have been devised in an attempt to counter the negative effects of computer usage.

INTEGRITY CONTROLS[1]

Computer information systems should undergo periodic examinations or *audits* by skilled *auditors* so that errors and irregularities may be detected and corrected, and so that system integrity may be established and maintained. To be assured that a system will provide accurate, complete, and reliable information, the auditor should check to see that (1) all *input* data are correctly recorded, (2) the *processing* of all authorized transactions is accomplished without additions or omissions, (3) the processing steps such as classifying, sorting, calculating, summarizing, etc., are performed accurately, and (4) the *output* of the system is distributed on a timely basis and only to those who are authorized to receive it. Furthermore, the safety and integrity of the data *retained* by the organization should be checked.

Input Controls

The purpose of input controls is to make sure that (1) *all* authorized input transactions are identified, (2) these transactions are *accurately recorded* in a machine-usable form at the *right time,* and (3) *all* these transactions are then sent to the processing station. Among the control techniques that may be adopted are:

1 *The use of prenumbered forms.* Whenever possible, a simple and effective control is to use serially numbered forms so that documents may be accounted for. A missing number in the sequence signals a missing document.

2 *The use of control totals.* When batch processing is used, certain totals can be computed for each batch of source documents. For example, the total dollar-sales figure may be computed on a batch of sales invoices prior to, perhaps, keypunching. The same calculation can be made after keypunching to see whether the figures compare. Control totals do not have to be expressed in dollars. They can be the totals obtained from adding figures in a data field that is included in all source documents being considered. A simple count of documents, cards, and other records is an effective control total. For example, the number of cards processed in the computer-operating department can be compared with the count of the number of cards that are delivered for processing. Similar comparisons between records read on magnetic tape and the number of input source documents may be

[1] A wealth of additional information on this topic may be found in Richard G. Canning, "The Importance of EDP Audit and Control," *EDP Analyzer,* pp. 1–13, June 1977; "Data Processing Control Practices Report," *Systems Auditability and Control Study,* The Institute of Internal Auditors, Inc., Altamonte Springs, Fla., 1977; William C. Mair, Donald R. Wood, and Keagle W. Davis, *Computer Control and Audit,* 2d ed., The Institute of Internal Auditors, Inc., Altamonte Springs, Fla., 1976; D. E. Morgan and D. J. Taylor, "A Survey of Methods of Achieving Reliable Software," *Computer,* pp. 44–51, February 1977; and Robert L. Patrick, "Sixty Ingredients for Better Systems," *Datamation,* pp. 171ff, December 1977.

possible. Of course, with control totals as with other data controls, the volume of transactions and the importance of the data should determine the degree of control and the amount of money spent to maintain that control.

3   *The use of transcription methods.* One means of controlling data transcription is to have knowledgeable clerks conduct a preaudit of source documents prior to recording the transactions in a machine-usable form. If input is by means of punched cards, the card verifier can be used. Transaction recording devices are available that can reduce errors caused by recopying, keypunching, illegible records, and loss of documents.

4   *The use of programmed checks on input.* Program instructions can be written to check on the reasonableness and propriety of data as they enter the processing operation. For example, program checks can be written to determine whether (*a*) certain specified limits are exceeded, (*b*) the input is complete, and (*c*) a transaction code or identification number is active and reasonable. When online processing is used, lockwords or passwords may be required from remote stations before certain files can be made accessible.

Processing Controls

Processing controls are established to (1) determine when data are lost or not processed and (2) check on the accuracy of arithmetic calculations. These controls may be classified into *hardware* and *software* categories. Important hardware controls include parity checks (i.e., checks that test whether the number of digits in an array is odd or even) and the use of dual reading and writing heads in input/output equipment. Although not a built-in hardware control, a definite program of *preventive maintenance* can pay big dividends by reducing the number of machine malfunctions.

Software or programmed controls include the input checks mentioned above. The number of possible programmed controls that may be used is limited only by the programmer's imagination. Some of the possibilities are included in Figure 12-1*a*.

Output Controls

Output controls are established as final checks on the accuracy and propriety of the processed information. Among the output control methods that may be employed are those presented in Figure 12-1*b*.

Retention Controls

Data controls do not end with the preparation of accurate and proper output information. Rather, further controls must be established in order to retain some records in machine-readable form for an extended period of time. Why is long-term retention necessary? *One* reason is to satisfy an

1 *The use of record count.* As a check against a predetermined total, the computer can be instructed to count the number of records that it handles in a program run.

2 *The use of tape labels.* The *external* labeling of magnetic tapes should be carefully controlled. These outside labels may give those interested such information as the tape contents, program identification number, and length of time the contents should be retained. *Internal* header and trailer control labels may also be recorded on the tapes themselves. The first (or *header*) record written on the tape gives the program identification number and other information. Before actual processing begins, then, a programmed comparison check may be made to make sure that the correct tape reel is being used. The last (or *trailer*) record contains a count of the number of other records on the tape.

3 *The use of sequence check.* In batch processing, the records are in some kind of sequence, e.g., by employee number or stock number. Programmed checks to detect out-of-sequence and missing cards and records prevent a file from being processed in an incorrect order.

4 *The use of structural check.* A test of the transactions to be processed can be made to determine whether the debits and credits called for represent acceptable combinations. Transactions with unacceptable debit and credit combinations are rejected.

(*a*)

1 *The use of control totals.* How do the control totals of processed information compare with the input control totals? For example, is there agreement between the number of records that were delivered for processing and the number of records that were actually processed? A basic output control technique is to obtain satisfactory answers to such questions.

2 *The review of interested parties.* Feedback on a regular basis from input-initiating and output-using departments points out errors that slip through in spite of all precautions. Follow-up action must be taken to correct any file inaccuracies that may be revealed.

3 *The use of systematic sampling.* Auditors can check on output by tracing randomly selected transactions from source documents through the processing system to the output destination. This should be done on a regular and systematic basis.

4 *The use of prenumbered forms.* Certain output forms should be prenumbered and accounted for in the same manner as input documents. Blank payroll-check forms, for example, should be closely guarded.

(*b*)

FIGURE 12-1
(*a*) Possible processing controls. (*b*) Possible output controls.

IRS ruling that *requires* the preservation of certain machine-readable records by many computer-using organizations for tax audit purposes. A *second* reason (although given the "persuasiveness" of the first reason, a second is not required) is that management decision making may be aided by having historical data readily available and easily incorporated into simulation models that might uncover possible trends and relationships.

Although punched paper media, microfilm, and magnetic disk packs may be used for long-term data storage, magnetic tape is by far the most popular retention medium. Thus, controls in most cases must be designed to protect archival magnetic tapes against dust, improper temperature and humidity fluctuations, and electromagnetic radiation.

SYSTEM SECURITY CONTROLS[2]

Since easy access to the computer by people with the skills needed to manipulate the system is a primary reason for the difficulty in maintaining security, an important step in achieving a more secure system is to separate the activities of those working *within* the computer department.

Organization and Internal Control

There should be an organizational separation between those knowledgeable employees who design and prepare the new systems and those who prepare the input data and operate the equipment. In other words, analysts and programmers should design, maintain, and make necessary changes (according to specified procedures) on programs, but they *should not* be involved with day-to-day production runs; equipment operators, on the other hand, should not have unrestricted access to completed computer programs, nor should they be involved with making changes in data or programs. Whenever feasible, completed programs and their supporting documents should be kept and controlled by a librarian who is not engaged either in planning or maintaining programs or in operating processing equipment. These programs and documents should be issued to interested parties only upon proper authorization.

Auditing and Security Control

Although no exact audit procedure is used, auditors seek to determine by observation, inquiry, and review of charts and manuals (1) whether a proper organizational separation of duties has been made, (2) whether

---

[2] A number of the sources cited in the preceding footnote also provide information on system security. Additional references on this subject are: Richard G. Canning, "Integrity and Security of Personal Data," *EDP Analyzer*, pp. 1–14, April 1976; "Comprehensive EDP Security Guidelines," *The Australian Computer Journal*, pp. 25–37, March 1976; Lance J. Hoffman, *Modern Methods for Computer Security and Privacy*, Prentice-Hall, Inc., Englewood Cliffs, N.J., 1977; Jerome Lobel, "Planning a Secure System," *Journal of Systems Management*, pp. 14–19, July 1976; K. S. Shankar, "The Total Computer Security Problem: An Overview," *Computer*, pp. 50–61, June 1977; August W. Smith, "Data Processing Security: A Common Sense Approach," *Data Management*, pp. 7–8ff, May 1977; and Stuart E. Madnick, "Management Policies and Procedures Needed for Effective Computer Security," *Sloan Management Review*, pp. 61–74, Fall 1978.

adequate controls have been created not only to maintain integrity but also to safeguard assets against fraud and other irregularities, and (3) whether existing security policies and procedures are being complied with.

During the course of the auditor's examination, attention is turned to the *audit trail* to monitor systems activity and to determine whether security (and integrity) controls are effective. The audit trail begins with the recording of all transactions, winds through the processing steps and through any intermediate records which may exist and be affected, and ends with the production of output reports and records. By selecting a representative sample of previously processed source documents and following the audit trail, the auditor can trace these documents through the data processing systems to their final report or record destinations as a means of testing the adequacy of systems procedures and controls.

In a manual system, a visible and readily traceable paper trail is created from the time source documents are prepared until output reports are produced. With the introduction of computer systems, however, the form of the trail has changed. Of course, *it cannot be eliminated* because of the desire for good internal control and because of tax and legal requirements. The Internal Revenue Service (IRS), in a report on the use of EDP equipment, has said that the audit trail, or the ability of a system to trace a transaction from summary totals back to its source, must not be eliminated. Nevertheless, intermediate steps in the information systems that were previously visible have *seemed to vanish* into magnetizable and erasable media.

Nor will the audit trail become more visible in the future. The increased use of online direct-access storage devices to hold intermediate data and the substitution of online processing techniques for batch processing will result in an even greater decrease in the visible portion of the trail. For example, source documents may be replaced by machine-language recordings made with transaction recording equipment; input data will originate from widely dispersed locations through the use of remote terminals (again, no paper documents need be involved); and a reorder message for a basic part may be transmitted by the computer to the supplier through the use of data communications facilities, with no paper documents being prepared. In examining such systems, the auditor must be satisfied that adequate controls are incorporated to prevent unintentional or deliberate damage to "invisible" files and records stored in an erasable medium. To comply with IRS requirements, for example, source data originating from online terminals may have to be "logged," or collected, in a separate operation by the system as they are processed. At prescribed intervals, the collected input data may then be sorted, listed, and stored in a suitable form so that the audit trail is preserved (see Figure 12-2).

Test data may be used in the examination by the auditor regardless of the type of system being studied. Just as the programmer uses simulated

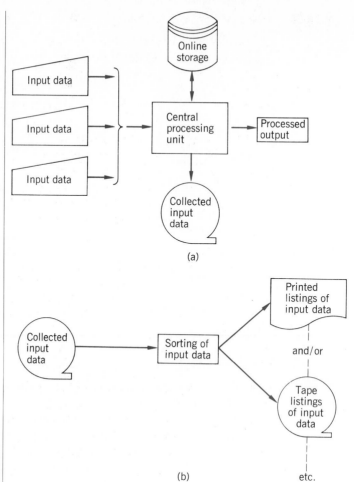

FIGURE 12-2
Preserving an audit trail in online processing environment. (*a*) Collection of source data originating at online terminals. (*b*) Periodic sorting, listing, and storing of collected source data.

input data to check programs during the debugging and testing stage, so too may an auditor use test decks to check on program integrity and security controls. Both valid and invalid transactions are included in the test data. The auditor will probably prepare erroneous input data that violate control provisions. The invalid input should test specific system controls so that the auditor may be assured of the reliability of the information system being checked. Of course, the fact that a program passes the auditor's test does not mean that the tested program always receives accurate input data or is always the one that is used during processing. Reasonable but incorrect input data may be supplied, and a fraudulent patch may be inserted into the program during subsequent processing runs. Thus, integrity controls and the following *systems-design, programming,* and *computer-operation controls* must also be studied by the auditor.

Systems-Design Controls

We have seen in earlier chapters that systems and program *documentation* is needed to provide a means of recording, analyzing, and communicating information. Good documentation promotes operating efficiency; it also *provides the basis for the evaluation and control of new and existing computer systems.* New system specifications should be designed (and documented) with audit and control considerations in mind. (It is expensive to ignore control aspects and then have to revise and rework a designed system. The participation of a knowledgeable auditor in the design phase so that proper controls may be built in and so that the audit trail does not vanish in fact as well as in appearance is thus a wise precaution.) Without good supporting documents and flowcharts on existing systems, managers and auditors will probably not know if and when systems changes have been made. In short, poor documentation represents a basic internal control weakness. Therefore, one of the most important controls that can be exercised over systems design is to assign authority to one or more individuals to make sure that systems and program flowcharts, decision tables, manuals, etc., are correctly prepared *and maintained.* Specifically written control procedures should be established for this purpose.

Programming Controls

A detailed explanation of the purpose of each program together with copies of all related documents should be kept in a *program file.* A manual containing *standard programming procedures* should also be prepared and kept up to date. The operating policies and approaches that are to be followed should be specified. Among the topics to be covered are program documentation methods and standards, program testing and modification procedures, magnetic tape labeling and retention policies, and the use of standardized symbolic names to describe data.

A definite procedure should be formulated to handle *program changes.* Changes should be made only after written approval is given by someone in a position of authority, e.g., the manager of the affected department. It is sometimes a good policy to postpone making a number of minor changes until the end of an accounting cycle so that data handling remains consistent throughout the accounting period. Changes in programs should be made by authorized programmers, not by computer-operating personnel. All changes should be charted and explained in writing; when completed, they should be reviewed and cleared by someone other than a maintenance programmer. All documents related to the change should be made a part of the permanent program file.

Computer-Operation Controls

Computer-operation controls may be maintained in the following ways:

1 *By the use of appropriate manuals.* A standard *operating manual* should include an explanation of the procedures established to deal with such things as the issuance and return of program and data tapes and cards and the means of scheduling and keeping records of equipment operating time. A manual of *program operating instructions* should be available to tell the operator how each program should be run. These instructions can specify the peripheral equipment to use, the console-switch settings to make, the action to take on all program halts, the exceptions to standard procedures and routines that may be needed, the input data to use, and the disposition of the output information obtained.

2 *By the creation of a physical security program.* Definite controls should be established to safeguard programs and data from fire and water damage or destruction. Duplicate program and master file tapes may have to be kept at a location away from the computer site. A fireproof storage vault at the computer site is a wise precaution. The importance of proper identification of and control over library tapes, cards, disks, and blank forms cannot be overemphasized. Adequate insurance protection should be provided. A waste-disposal procedure to destroy carbon papers and other media containing sensitive information should be followed.[3] And proper shielding of equipment to reduce electromagnetic radiation is necessary in some situations.

3 *By control over console intervention.* It is possible for computer operators to bypass program controls. They have the ability to interrupt a program run and introduce data manually into the processor through the console keyboard. With organizational separation of program preparation and computer operation, and with operators having access to object programs and not source programs, it is unlikely that an operator will have enough knowledge of the program details to manipulate them successfully for improper purposes. However, the possibility of unauthorized intervention should be reduced in a number of ways. Since, for example, the console typewriter may be used to print out a manual intervention, the paper sheets in the typewriter can be prenumbered and periodically checked. Other approaches using locked recording devices may be employed. For example, a microcomputer could be used to record and analyze the processing actions performed by the host computer as well as any interventions in the host's operation; that is, the micro could be used like a flight recorder in an airplane. The recorder monitors the performance of the plane

[3] Almost $1 million in telephone equipment was stolen from Pacific Telephone & Telegraph Company by a clever thief who, at the age of 16, found in the telephone company trash cans information on Bell System operating procedures, manuals on system instructions, and a guide book called *Ordering Material and Supplies.* Catalogs and authority code numbers were also acquired from trash cans! The thief obtained a special input device and then accessed the Bell System computer to input coded order and authority numbers. The ordered equipment was then picked up by the thief at a company warehouse (he had also bought a used telephone company van for the purpose). After being caught and paying his debt to society, the thief started a consulting service called EDP Security, Inc.

Security
key lock

FIGURE 12-3

Authorized users are given a
key to unlock the terminal
keyboard. (*INCOTERM Corp.*)

and its crew, but it is not accessible to the crew. Additional control techniques include rotating the duties of computer operators (or others in sensitive positions)[4] and having them account for computer operating time (manual intervention is slow, and manipulation can thus result in processing times that are longer than necessary for affected runs).

4   *By controlling the use of online terminals.* Control procedures to identify authorized users of the system should obviously be given special attention. Such identification is typically based on something that users *know* (e.g., a password), something they *have* (e.g., a card with a magnetically coded identification number, a badge, or a key such as the one used in Figure 12-3 to unlock the terminal keyboard), some *personal quality* they possess (e.g., fingerprint or "voice print" characteristics that can be stored by the computer system and used for identification purposes), or some combination of these elements. Passwords are most commonly used, but when used frequently (and carelessly) these words lose their security value. A better approach, perhaps, would be to have the computer provide the user, each day, with a different word or code that the user could then modify by following a secret procedure in order to gain access to the system. For example, the computer could send the user a 6-digit password. The user could then add the day's date to it and send back the second and fourth digits of the sum. Once an authorized user has been identified and has gained access to the system, various techniques employing

---

[4] Managers should be alert to the risk inherent in having employees who never take vacations, who refuse promotion or rotation, who have access to the premises when no one else is present, and who are always around when the books are closed at the end of an accounting period.

cryptography — that is, "hidden writing"—are available to thwart those who would intercept the messages traveling between the computer and the remote terminal. For example, data encryption techniques for coding and decoding messages can be implemented on silicon chips located in the terminals and host computers. If an authorized user wants to access or send sensitive data, the host computer may generate a random *session key* — a key to be used only for that exchange. This session key is sent to the terminal encrypt/decrypt circuitry and a copy is retained at the host. Any data passing from a host program to the terminal are automatically encrypted by the host, transmitted, and then decrypted by the terminal. (Of course, the reverse occurs when the message originates at the terminal.) This coding/decoding process is invisible to the user. At the end of the session, the session key disappears. The data that have been transmitted would be unintelligible to anyone without the one-time session key.[5]

5   *By controlling access to the computer site.* Only authorized personnel should be allowed access to equipment, data files, and programs. The techniques used to identify authorized terminal users that have just been mentioned can also be used to control site access. For example, at the entrance to the computer room at the First National Bank of Chicago, a person seeking entry must first type an identification number. The computer then asks that certain words which it has selected at random be spoken into a microphone by that person. If the voice characteristics of the person at the microphone match those of an admissible employee, the person is admitted. Such precautions may be necessary because easy access invites fraud and/or damage. To illustrate, one visitor to an insurance company computer center (a member of a touring garden club) was so impressed by the blinking lights and spinning tapes that she decided to take home a souvenir. "She later said, 'I hope I didn't do anything wrong. There were all those boxes of cards on the table, and I just reached into the middle of a box and took one.' "[6] A good rule, in summary, is that *"nobody* and *nothing* should be permitted into the computer room unless they or it *needs* to be there *then."*[7]

PRIVACY CONTROLS

An individual's "right" to privacy has been discussed at various times in this book, but the word *privacy* does not appear anywhere in the Constitution. What, then, is the legal status of privacy? An early consideration of

---

[5] For an interesting account of cryptography techniques, see Lawrence Sandek, "Privacy, Security, and Ciphers," *Data Processor,* pp. 2–6, January 1978; and Richard A. Shaffer, "Companies Use Codes to Ward Off Thieves and Safeguard Secrets," *The Wall Street Journal,* pp. 1ff, June 16, 1978.

[6] Brandt Allen, "Danger Ahead! Safeguard Your Computer," *Harvard Business Review,* p. 100, November/December 1968.

[7] Harold Weiss, "Computer Security: An Overview," *Datamation,* p. 45, January 1974.

"Privacy Goals, Company Policies Seen at Odds"

The former chairman of the Privacy Protection Study Commission charges that privacy policies of many major US firms conflict with wishes of the general public. The greatest progress toward privacy protection, according to David Linowes, has been made by two industries that face the most stringent government regulatory restraints—insurance and credit card companies.

Linowes, a professor of political economy and public policy at the University of Illinois, made his remarks in an interview previewing release of a survey of privacy policies followed by a number of the nation's largest companies. The gist of the study, conducted by the university, is that the majority of firms does little on its own. This inactivity, Linowes noted, contrasts with results of another poll by Louis Harris & Associates indicating that most Americans are concerned with confidentiality practices in private industry.

For example, while about 83 percent of respondents to the Harris poll said employers should notify employees before releasing personal information from their files, the University of Illinois survey indicates that about 40 percent of large corporations have no policy to govern release of personnel data.

Source: "Privacy Goals, Company Policies Seen at Odds," *Infosystems*, p. 18, August 1979. Reprinted with permission of the publisher.

privacy as a legal concept was presented in 1890 by Louis Brandeis and Samuel Warren in an article entitled "The Right to Privacy." In 1928, after being appointed to the Supreme Court, Justice Brandeis again took up the concept when he wrote in a minority opinion: "The right to be let alone is the most comprehensive of rights and the right most valued by civilized men."[8]

Of course, what one person may consider to be a privacy right may be judged by others to be an item of genuine public concern. For example, if a newspaper reporter unearths the fact that a congressman has put a number of relatives on the government payroll for no good purpose, and if the reporter then reveals this fact and prints the names and salaries of the relatives, she has undoubtedly infringed on their privacy. But she has also used rights guaranteed to her in the Bill of Rights (the First Amendment's freedom of speech and freedom of the press) to perform a public service. Thus, there may be legitimate rights operating against privacy in some situations. In short, since privacy is not one of the specific

---

[8] The Supreme Court has since held that the right of privacy is implied in the rights spelled out by the First, Third, Fourth, and Fifth Amendments to the Constitution.

constitutional rights, and since a balance has to be struck between the need for privacy on the one hand and society's need for legitimate information on the other, *the extent to which individuals are given privacy protection must depend on judicial and legislative decisions.* That is, the *continuous* task of balancing human rights against basic freedoms in order to establish privacy controls is the responsibility of the judicial and legislative branches of government.

Legal Controls

Recognizing that rapid advances in computer technology have given users of that technology the ability to gather and store information that (1) goes beyond the legitimate information needs of society and (2) can lead to excessive and unnecessary intrusions into an individual's personal privacy, lawmakers have been busy in recent years in an effort to restore some balance in favor of privacy. The result has been that numerous federal statutes and about 150 state bills have been passed over a brief time span to control the invasion of privacy.[9]

Some *examples of existing privacy laws* are:

1 *Fair Credit Reporting Act of 1970.* This federal law gives individuals the right to know what information is kept on them by credit bureaus and other credit investigation agencies. Individuals also have the right to challenge information they consider to be inaccurate and to insert brief explanatory statements into the records in disputed cases. Certain items of adverse information may not be included in a report on an individual after the items have reached specified ages.
2 *State "Fair Information Practice" Laws.* The California Fair Information Practice Act of 1974 spells out the rights of individuals when dealing with state government data banks. Individuals have the right to (*a*) know what information is kept on them in the various state computer data banks, (*b*) contest the "accuracy, completeness, pertinence, and timeliness" of the stored data, (*c*) force a reinvestigation of the current status of personal data, and (*d*) resolve disputes in ways spelled out by the law. The Minnesota Privacy Act (and acts passed by other states) contains similar provisions.
3 *Privacy Act of 1974.* This important privacy legislation was passed by Congress late in 1974 and signed into law by President Ford on January 1, 1975. It became effective late in September 1975. The act is aimed at some of the uses and abuses of *federal government* data banks. Some of the provisions of this law are: (*a*) With the exception of classified files, civil service records, and law enforcement agency investigative files, individuals have the right to see their records in fed-

---

[9] During the Ninety-fifth Congress (1977–1978), nearly 200 bills were introduced that addressed some aspect of privacy. And the Ninety-sixth Congress was referred to in some sources as the "privacy Congress" for its interest in this topic.

eral data banks, (b) they may point out errors in their records, and if these errors are not removed, they may ask a federal judge to order the correction, (c) federal agencies must periodically publish in the *Federal Register* a listing of their files along with the categories of individuals whose records are listed in the files, (d) when federal agencies request personal information, they must tell individuals whether their cooperation in supplying the information is required by law, (e) unless specifically authorized by law, federal agencies cannot sell or rent personal data bank information, nor can they monitor an individual's religious or political activities, and (f) no federal, state, or local government agency can design a *new* information system based upon the use of the social security number. A Privacy Protection Study Commission was also established to monitor enforcement of the law and to study issues that will have to be resolved in the future. For example, the Commission is specifically given authority in the act to examine personal information activities in the medical, insurance, education, employment, credit and banking, credit reporting, cable television, telecommunications and other media, travel and hotel reservations, and EFTS areas. After a two-year study, the Commission issued a final published report in July 1977.[10] At this writing, it appears that additional laws will eventually be passed to incorporate the Commission's recommendations and to expand the scope of the Privacy Act to include the data banks maintained by federal, state, and local law enforcement agencies, state and local governments, and businesses.

Social Controls

In addition to the establishment of legal controls, an aroused public concern for the right of privacy is needed to produce the climate necessary to ensure compliance with privacy laws. But social restraint is also needed to resist further lawful abuses of personal privacy rights. If the potential privacy implications are considered prior to the design of any new systems, if systems designers are motivated to create new procedures that are more private and personalized, and if employees and supervisors who handle personal information will protect that information and treat it with the respect it deserves, there will be fewer legal violations of the privacy rights of individuals.

A group of California computer professionals and civil liberties advocates recently showed the kind of positive control that can be exerted when they joined forces to kill a Juvenile Information System in the Santa Clara Probation Department just two days before it was to be implemented. The system would have centralized scattered files on juveniles so that police and probation officers would have immediate access to them. In addition to juvenile delinquents, the system would also have in-

---

[10] The title of this report is *Personal Privacy in an Information Society,* U.S. Government Printing Office, Publication 052-003-00395-3, July 1977.

"To Preserve Privacy Take Care What You Tell and to Whom . . ."

Americans equate the right to privacy with the right to "life, liberty and the pursuit of happiness," and many are concerned with invasion of their privacy.

A national poll recently conducted for Sentry Insurance by Louis Harris & Associates, Inc., showed that 64 percent of the American public is concerned over threats to personal privacy. In particular, only 27 percent believe there are adequate safeguards to protect personal information stored in computers.

President Carter has proposed legislation to reduce the masses of information collected by federal, state and local governments and protect that already stored.

But private credit agencies, banks and the like have dossiers on millions of Americans and horror stories of misuse and abuse of this information can be found.

"There are several reasons you should take steps to protect your privacy," says Richard Kovacevich, senior vice president of Citibank, which has just published a booklet, "Strictly Confidential," about the steps the bank takes to protect information it collects.

"If some outside party had access to all your financial transactions, for example, they could know everything about you, your political beliefs, your religion, how you spend your money—they would have everything but an oil portrait," Kovacevich said in an interview.

Even though people will try to outdo each other in "telling all"—their occult religious and radical political beliefs, their unconventional lifestyles—they will be shocked if asked about their financial affairs and rightly so, Kovacevich said.

"The sanctity of individual privacy is a very important part of our constitution—it's important that there isn't a Big Brother out there who can draw on personal information at will," he said.

Even though much of the information collected by government probably is not necessary, in the banking and business sectors there's what Kovacevich calls a "privacy tradeoff." For example, a bank rightly demands enough information about a potential borrower to have reasonable assurance that the loan will be repaid. It releases just enough information to assure a merchant, for instance, that a specific check won't bounce.

To keep the dissemination of private information to a minimum, Kovacevich said, "You must treat private items in a responsible way. There's a lot of sloppiness in handling personal finances.

"Most Americans carry things in their wallet or purse that they don't need and that can be abused in the hands of the wrong person," he said.

Also, the fewer organizations one deals with the less information is spread around.

"Many people deal with three or four banks, 25 department stores and 10 gas companies," Kovacevich said. "They have given private information to all of these concerns and they carry credit cards to prove it."

Whenever you give private information to anyone, you have a right to ask why they need the information and what they intend to do with it, Kovacevich said.

"Obviously, you can't design a system that can't be broken if someone is determined," Kovacevich said.

"But if the individual is concerned enough to know what laws are and are not on the books to protect them, and business takes adequate precautions, invasion of privacy could be made tremendously difficult and expensive."

"Consumers should demand this protection," he said.

Source: "To Preserve Privacy Take Care What You Tell and To Whom," Nacodoches, Texas *Sentinel,* p. A4, July 15, 1979. Reprinted by permission of United Press International.

cluded the names of so-called predelinquents who have never committed a crime or been accused of one. Rather, the youths might have been truants or runaways, or they might have been abused or neglected and had thus been referred to the police. The objections of the concerned group to the creation of police system records on such children, however, was enough to halt the program.

A number of private organizations have responded to the Privacy Protection Study Commission's call for voluntary restraints to protect the privacy rights of their employees and customers.[11] For example, large insurance companies such as Aetna Life & Casualty Company, Equitable Life Assurance Society, and Mutual of Omaha have voluntarily placed substantial restrictions on their use of the consumer reporting agencies discussed in the last chapter.

[11] For more information on this subject, see John Perham, "New Push for Employee Privacy," *Dun's Review,* pp. 112–114, March 1979.

FIGURE 12-4
John Kemeny. (*Wide World Photos.*)

KEMENY ANTICIPATES COMPUTER'S IMPACT

John Kemeny, the president of Dartmouth College, was aware of the impact that computers would have on our society. He was equally aware that few students were prepared to deal with the computers that would one day become part of their lives. Kemeny wanted students to take at least one computer course while they were in college.

Because existing computer languages were too complicated for students to master in a short time, Kemeny and Thomas Kurtz developed the BASIC language in 1963-1964. BASIC (Beginners All-purpose Symbolic Instruction Code) is an easy-to-learn language for inexperienced programmers.

Kemeny estimated that one student sharing the computer's time with 30 others could complete in one afternoon the calculations that took one year of around-the-clock work at the Los Alamos atomic laboratories in 1945.

BASIC is now used by students on a regular basis and is offered by virtually all computer manufacturers.

The following points have been emphasized in this chapter:

1   Computer usage can produce records on individuals that lack integrity, may not be secure, and may result in a loss of privacy; therefore, controls on integrity, security, and privacy are needed to counter the negative effects of computer usage. Input, processing, and output controls should be examined by auditors to detect and correct errors and irregularities so that system integrity may be established and maintained. Several integrity control methods have been presented in the chapter.

2   Separation of duties within the computer department is an organizational technique that can help maintain the security of an information system. Auditors should also check on the adequacy of the security control arrangements that have been made. During their examinations, auditors trace transactions through the audit trail to determine whether security controls are effective. Systems-design, programming, and computer-operation controls should also be tested for weaknesses. Several security control suggestions are presented in the chapter.

3   The extent to which individuals are given privacy protection must depend on judicial and legislative decisions. Federal statutes and dozens of state bills have been passed to control the invasion of privacy. Several existing privacy laws are summarized briefly in the chapter. In addition to legal controls, however, concerned individuals in society can join together to resist further lawful abuses of personal privacy rights.

▶ │ KEY TERMS

After reading Chapter 12, you should be able to define and use the following terms:

integrity controls	system security controls
audit	audit trail
auditors	cryptography
control total	Fair Credit Reporting Act
programmed input checks	Privacy Act of 1974

▶ │ REVIEW AND DISCUSSION QUESTIONS

1   (a) Into what categories may integrity controls be classified? (b) Give some examples of integrity controls.

2 Of what significance is organizational structure in maintaining security control?

3 (a) What is the audit trail? (b) Why is it needed? (c) Can it be eliminated?

4 Larger computer systems may now use CRT terminals rather than console typewriters. Although this tends to speed up the operation of the console, it may also have security control implications. How might control over console intervention be affected in this situation? (*Hint:* See Figure 12-2.)

5 (a) Into what categories may security controls be classified? (b) Give some examples of security controls.

6 "What one person may consider to be a privacy right may be judged by others to be an item of genuine public concern." Discuss this statement.

7 Discuss some of the legal controls that are available to restore some balance in favor of privacy.

8 What can concerned individuals do to resist abuses of personal privacy rights?

9 (a) Do you believe that adequate safeguards can be devised to protect individuals from the negative impacts of computer usage? (b) Defend your answer.

SELECTED REFERENCES

In addition to the references suggested in the chapter footnotes, you might wish to examine the following sources:

Block, Victor: "Privacy Impacts DP World," *Infosystems,* pp. 94ff, June 1979.

Hentoff, Nat: "Privacy and the Press: Is Nothing Sacred?" *Saturday Review,* pp. 22–23, July 21, 1979.

Hirsch, Phil: "Europe's Privacy Laws—Fear of Inconsistency," *Datamation,* pp. 85–88, February 1979.

Madnick, Stuart E.: "Management Policies and Procedures Needed for Effective Computer Security," *Sloan Management Review,* pp. 61–74, Fall 1978.

Sykes, D. J.: "Positive Personal Identification," *Datamation,* pp. 179–180ff, November 1, 1978.

Part Five

(Herb Levart, Photo Researchers.)

Part Five
SELECTED COMPUTER USES IN SOCIETY

(Christa Armstrong, Photo Researchers.)

(Bruce Roberts, Photo Researchers.)

In Part 4, we saw some of the social implications of computers for organizations and individuals. Another objective of this book is to describe some of the uses of computers in a number of social environments. Thus, in Part 5, we shall examine computer applications affecting such areas as government and law, health, education, the humanities, science and engineering, and business. Since computers are often used for planning, decision-making, and control purposes, applications in the six chapters of Part 5 are often organized into these major categories. Of course, other means of classifying computer usage are also employed.

The chapters included in Part 5 are:

Chapter 13
COMPUTERS IN GOVERNMENT AND LAW

The purpose of this chapter is to outline selected computer applications in federal, state, and local governments. Some implications and uses of computers in the legal profession and in the courts are also considered.

In the first section of the chapter, you will see a few of the ways in which the federal government is making use of computer systems. The applications discussed are classified under (1) planning and decision-making, (2) control, and (3) law enforcement categories.

The second section will give you an idea of some of the ways that state and local governments have found to use computers. The applications discussed in this section are classified under the same categories used in the section dealing with the federal government.

Finally, in the last section, you will see how computer usage has had an impact on lawyers and on the techniques used by lawyers to prepare their cases. This section also briefly examines the use of computers in court administration.

Thus, after studying this chapter, you should be able to:

- Give a number of examples of how computers are used in the federal government for (1) planning and decision-making, (2) control, and (3) law enforcement purposes.

- Give a number of examples of how computers are used in state and local governments for (1) planning and decision-making, (2) control, and (3) law enforcement purposes.

- Explain why lawyers should have a knowledge of computers.

- Outline some ways in which computers are used in the courts.

- Understand and use the key terms listed at the end of the chapter.

Several goals of this book were mentioned in Chapter 1, and most of them have now been considered. However, a remaining objective is to examine *some*[1] of the ways in which computers are being applied in various social enviroments. The purpose of this chapter, therefore, is to look at some of the uses of computers in governmental and legal environments. To be more specific, the purpose of this chapter is to outline selected computer applications in (1) *the federal government,* (2) *state and local governments,* and (3) *the legal profession and legal procedures.*

It is perhaps appropriate at this point to mention a classification

---

[1] There are thousands of different applications being processed with computers. Obviously, only a brief overview of a few uses can be treated in this chapter and in each of the chapters that follow.

theme that is repeated in most of the remaining chapters. We have seen that computers are often used for planning, decision-making, and control purposes. Thus, in this chapter (and in the ones to follow), applications are often classified into (1) planning and decision-making and (2) control categories. Of course, other means of classifying computer usage are also employed.

COMPUTERS IN THE FEDERAL GOVERNMENT

Existing broad social and political problems such as creeping urban decay, air and water pollution, energy-related issues and traffic congestion have been mentioned earlier. In addition to attacking these problems, governmental agencies must give greater attention in the future to such social needs as more comprehensive health care, better transportation planning, and improved public safety. Governmental agencies at all levels in our society are involved. But because of the interrelated (and interstate) nature of many of the existing social needs and because of the magnitude of the economic resources which must be made available to deal with many of the problems, citizens expect the federal government to provide direction and resources to effect many of the necessary improvements. In seeking solutions to difficult social problems, federal government administrators need timely, accurate, and relevant information.

Computers are used in the federal government for (1) *planning and decision-making,* (2) *control,* and (3) *law enforcement purposes.* Let us look at applications in each of these usage categories.

Planning and Decision Making in the Federal Government

Governmental planners and decision makers have a mandate to effectively use public funds and resources in ways that best serve the needs of society. Unfortunately, government policy makers have often been required to function in settings where the data available for public policy making are inadequate and/or inaccurate. Although the federal government has amassed and stored a vast body of statistical data, it is not yet able to measure satisfactorily "the human toll of illness, the pollution of the environment, the quality of our education, and the nature of the alienation expressed in burning and looting in the ghetto . . . and crime in the city streets."[2]

Since effective planning begins with an understanding of the existing situation, and since information detailing social conditions as they actually exist is not always available, it is not surprising that public planning in the past has failed to remedy many types of problems. With the development

[2] Abe Gottlieb, "The Computer and the Job Undone," *Computers and Automation,* p. 19, November 1970.

of new information systems, however, the hope of government planners is that they will have higher-quality information with which to (1) make better plans and decisions, (2) improve operating efficiency, and (3) better serve society. Some *examples of how computers are now being used for planning and decision-making purposes at the federal government level* are discussed below.

Environmental planning *Technology assessment* is a phrase used in the federal government to refer to the evaluation of the consequences of technological change beyond short-term economic costs and benefits. Because many of the problems of environmental quality are the result of changes in technology, use of the technology-assessment concept has become increasingly important in environmental planning and in the protection of our natural resources. The National Environmental Policy Act requires federal agencies to include a detailed statement in every proposal for legislation (or other major federal action) that significantly affects the quality of the environment. The detailed statement should outline such points as (1) the environmental impact of the proposed action, (2) any adverse environmental effects that cannot be avoided, and (3) any irreversible and irretrievable commitments of resources that would be required in the proposed action. As a result of this act, greater emphasis has been given to the use of computers for ecological and environmental research and planning.

Some *specific examples of computer usage in environmental planning are:*

1   The Department of Health, Education, and Welfare has sponsored the development and use of a highly sophisticated computer simulation to predict the life-sustaining ability of rivers. The simulation model consists of interrelated equations that represent oxygen supply and biochemical oxygen demand in a river. Up to 450 simultaneous first-order differential equations (and a 450 × 450 matrix) are required by the model. In addition to analyzing existing river conditions, the model can also be used by planners to gain insights into the cause-and-effect relationships of water pollution so that preventive action can be taken to protect a river or so that corrective measures can be initiated to restore a polluted stream to a satisfactory condition.

2   A nationwide system of computers is helping the planners of the United States Geological Survey (an agency of the Department of the Interior) find answers to problems of water supply. What will be the result, for example, of major alterations of a river's flow pattern by an electric power company for generating purposes? What will be the effect on sewage and waste assimilation, on aquatic life, and on other current uses of the water? Computer simulation models are helping planners arrive at answers to such questions.

3   The Soil Conservation Service of the Department of Agriculture uses radio signals reflected from ionized meteor trails in the earth's atmo-

sphere to relay data on snowfall and rainfall from sensors located at 160 remote stations in 10 Western states to central data-collection sites in Boise, Idaho, and Ogden, Utah. The data are processed by minicomputers at these sites, forwarded to the Conservation Service's Portland, Oregon, Technical Service Center, and then distributed to farmers, ranchers, and government irrigation agencies in the 10-state area. The data on the amount of snowfall in the mountains are particularly important to these agricultural planners because about 85 percent of the annual water supply in the 10-state area comes from melting snow. A similar system is used by six government agencies in Alaska.

4   Researchers at the Idaho National Engineering Laboratory are using a number of minicomputers in their efforts to develop a method for reprocessing the radioactive wastes produced by nuclear power plants. Burial is a current method of waste disposal, but this technique poses a potential hazard to the environment. Burial is also inefficient because much of the original uranium—and the energy it represents—is not consumed during power plant operation. Thus, the search for a method of recycling radioactive wastes is important from the standpoints of both safety and economy.

Weather forecasting   A mathematical model has been in existence for years with equations that describe how changes in such atmospheric variables as air pressure, temperature, humidity, and velocity of the air occur over time. Thomas Crowley has succinctly summarized the use of computers in weather forecasting:

> At least as long ago as 1911, it was pointed out that the weather could be predicted by solving these equations. If the pressure, temperature, humidity, and velocity of the air are known for the same instant of time at many points around the world, the solution of the equations is mathematically quite straight-forward and accurately predicts what these quantities will be 1 hour, 1 day, or 1 week later. A network of weather stations around the world can make the measurements necessary to provide the initial conditions for these calculations, but it happens that a tremendous number of numerical calculations are required. Without a computer these computations required months of work, and there was obviously no point to predicting the weather if the weather was already over! . . .

> Immediately after it became clear that digital computers would vastly speed up such calculations, mathematicians and meteorologists intensified study of this method of prediction. Although the first results were crude, by 1962 a useful system was in routine operation.[3]

This early system used about 2,000 measurement reports to establish the initial conditions, and then a large computer of that day required one hour to make a one-day prediction.

[3] Thomas H. Crowley, *Understanding Computers*, McGraw-Hill Book Company, New York, 1967, pp. 105–106.

FIGURE 13-1 " — and you predicted POSITIVELY no chance of precipitation for today!"

As you saw in Chapter 6, supercomputers are now being used in weather forecasting. The current forecast programs are more sophisticated and more accurate than the early ones, but there is still room for considerable improvement. In fact, the current programs that tax the capabilities of the world's largest computers are crude models of what meteorologists would use if only more powerful computers were available. Our supercomputers apparently are not super enough.[4]

Weather data are collected by the federal government several times each day from thousands of input points scattered around the world. The data come from aircraft, Coast Guard ships, ocean buoys maintained by the Coast Guard, ground stations, and space satellites. These data are processed at the Suitland, Maryland, computer center operated by the National Oceanic and Atmospheric Administration (NOAA), a division of the Department of Commerce. Processed forecast information is distributed by NOAA's National Weather Service branch and generally reaches the public by radio and television broadcasts and newspaper accounts.

[4] For additional information on weather forecasting, see Francis J. Balint, "Modeling the Weather," *Datamation*, pp. 131–133ff, May 1978. For an interesting account of weather research conducted by the National Severe Storms Laboratory, see Carl A. Posey, "Open Sesame!," *NOAA Magazine*, pp. 20–23, April 1979.

Military planning Computers are being used increasingly by military planners and decision makers. A multibillion-dollar World Wide Military Command and Control System has been developed for use by military commanders from the President on down. This system was developed in the mid-1970s and consists of 35 large computers at 26 command posts around the world.[5] It is not difficult to envision, in the years to come,[6] a system which could receive and integrate information from battlefield computers, intelligence agents, spy satellites, and other military and political sources to form an overall picture for top-level planners such as the President and the Joint Chiefs of Staff. Because of technology, military decisions formerly made in the field may increasingly involve decision makers at much higher levels. The United States military today has well over 20 telecommunication satellites positioned to transmit data to and from all points in the world.[7] Thus, the data transmission capability needed by future military systems should be available when needed.

At the present time, computers are being used by military planners to *simulate wars*—i.e., to sharpen analytical skills and gain experience in decision making through the use of "war games." In fact, Dr. Ruth Davis, former Director of the National Bureau of Standards' Institute for Computer Sciences and Technology, is of the opinion that the first battles of World War III may already have been fought with computers rather than cannons. In an address to an international meeting of computer professionals in Stockholm, Sweden, Dr. Davis said:

> World War I was fought with chemistry. World War II was fought with physics. World War III is being fought with computer science. The first battles of World War III may well have occurred when mathematical formulations of strategies and counter-strategies of realistic proportions were able to be tried out as war games on computers. With realistic wars fought in 20 minutes or 20 hours on computers, decisions to engage in such encounters [between large computer using nations] have been nil.[8]

Computers are also used by military leaders for planning and controlling logistics—i.e., for managing the procurement, storage, and transportation of needed supplies and equipment. During the tragic Vietnam period, computers were used to evaluate information supplied by battlefield sensors. The possible use of sensors requires a brief explanation. Seismic, magnetic, odor, visual, and microphone sensors can be dropped on suspected enemy positions by aircraft. These sensors may be disguised as

---

[5] Some of the problems associated with the development and use of this complex system are discussed in James North, "Hello Central, Get Me NATO: The Computer that Can't," *The Washington Monthly*, pp. 48–52, July/August 1979.

[6] Alas, the assumption here is that people will continue to behave in the future as they have in the past.

[7] The number of communications satellites available to the world's civilian users is only about one-sixth of the number employed by the United States military.

[8] "Newsdata," *Computer Decisions*, p. 8, October 1974.

FIGURE 13-2

(*Above*) Traffic control center for the Welland Canal section of the St. Lawrence Seaway. Ships are under constant surveillance by a computerized system. (*Paolo Koch, Photo Researchers.*) (*Right*) Scientists at the U.S. Geological Survey Water Resources Team at Phoenix, Arizona, wiring sections of a watertable computer. Data on past and present wells, streams, rivers, rainfall, pumping volumes, and population projections are fed into wall-sized computerized electronic maps to provide complex data for future water use. (*Joe Munroe, Photo Researchers.*)

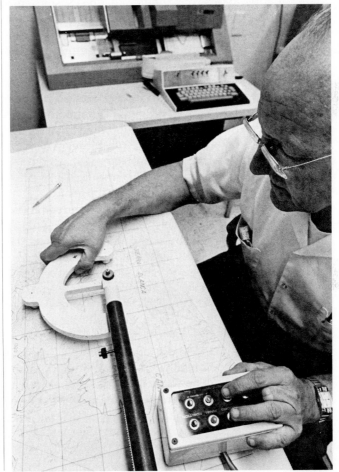

(*Above*) NORAD headquarters inside Cheyenne Mountain, Colorado Springs, Colorado. (*Myron Wood, Photo Researchers.*) (*Right*) Computer-controlled map making. Here, a drafting machine applies contour elevations on a newly developed state of Arizona map. (*Herb Levart, Photo Researchers.*)

twigs or animal droppings and may hang in trees or fall to the ground. Some may explode when touched. Messages from the sensors may be transmitted to human-operated aircraft or pilotless drone planes. A computer monitors the information received from the sensors and evaluates what caused the sensor to transmit. Experimental computer systems have been developed that, in response to a sensor "beep," will select the proper ordance delivery equipment (say artillery pieces), order the proper fuses for the shells, aim the weapons, and fire them. A less sophisticated "automated battlefield" approach was used in Vietnam. Computers in Vietnam and Thailand monitored sensor data and projected them on CRT screens or printed them. Computer controllers then dispatched the destruction to the targets reported by the sensors. (One more tragedy of that era is that a number of innocent people—and their livestock—may have been killed or injured by this approach.)

Planning research examples   Computers are used by the federal government for research purposes in many agencies and for many types of applications. The Federal Reserve System, the nation's central banker, is one arm of the government that has often used computers for planning and decision making. A member of the Federal Reserve Board of Governors, for example, may use a computer in researching the trade-offs between inflation and unemployment at given times prior to making monetary policy judgments. Or the governor may use the computer to research the concentration of banks in a particular market area prior to making a decision on a merger application. Federal Reserve economists are currently developing and refining a large-scale research model of the United States economy. This model may help planners gain new insights into the economy's structure; it may also prove valuable in predicting (through simulation) what the possible effects of alternative monetary policies may be.

Another arm of the federal government that uses computers for planning research is the Census Bureau—one of the first organizations to use computers. By classifying, sorting, and manipulating census data, the Bureau can assist planners in weighing the needs and problems of whole groups or any segment of the population. For example, information about families living in poverty areas can be analyzed. Also, the computers can pigeonhole the massive national census data by state, county, congressional district, city, or even city block if research and planning needs are served by such information.

The Department of Agriculture, in a joint effort with NOAA and the National Aeronautics and Space Administration (NASA), is using the *Landsat* earth-orbiting satellite to view the croplands planted in wheat and other grains in such important growing regions as the United States, the Soviet Union, Canada, Australia, and India. The satellite photos allow planners to estimate the acreage under cultivation, and the worldwide weather data supplied by NOAA during the growing season permit them to develop computer-based crop yield models and make harvest predictions. A better foreign crop assessment capability, of course, is of considerable importance to those who must make decisions about domestic agricultural policy.

Congressional data systems   Members of Congress are expected to perform in at least three capacities: as *lawmakers* deciding on important legislation, as *responsible representatives* of their states or districts, and as *public servants* who will try to assist their constituents on both important and trivial matters. To perform these roles, they need accurate, complete, and timely information. Even though much substantive work is performed by the several working committees, each member of Congress must still do research, form opinions, and make decisions on dozens of bills each session. And, of course, the number of bills to be considered is increasing each year. It is not surprising, then, that representatives have voted on bills in the past without understanding all the implications of the legislation. In fact, it is a difficult task for members of Congress and their staff aides to maintain even the most rudimentary knowledge of the content and status of "major" legislation.

During the Ninety-first Congress, subcommittees were established by both the House and the Senate to study the use of computers in legislative operations. Subsequently, and not surprisingly, one of the first congressional computer applications tackled by the staff assembled for the purpose was the creation of a bill status system. This system, called LEGIS, which became operational early in 1973, records, stores, and provides prompt computer response to inquiries about the current status of all bills and resolutions before Congress. A computer-controlled electronic voting system was also implemented in 1973 in the House.[9] Visual display consoles are installed at the majority and minority tables and are capable of displaying in-progress vote information organized by whip zone and by members. Congressional data systems now process questionnaires, schedule activities, and perform data analysis services for committees. A SOPAD system provides members with an up-to-the-minute "summary of procedings and debates" taking place on the floors of the House and Senate, and FAPRS (Federal Assistance Program Retrieval System) helps members determine what federal loans and grants can be used by their constituents.

Political campaigns   The use of computers has increased significantly in the last decade in federal and state election campaigns. Political canidates (employing direct-mail advertising techniques) have used computers to

---

[9] As you might expect, some representatives have not felt comfortable with such "gadgetry." One Kentucky Democrat who has been in the House for 25 years doesn't trust this electronic voting system. "It's a marvelous sight," says a younger member. "He punches his card into one machine, then he walks across the floor and punches in at another machine, just to make certain it's OK." See James M. Perry, "Congressmen Discover Computer and Use It to Keep Voters in Tow," *The Wall Street Journal*, p. 14, March 15, 1978.

(1) maintain mailing lists of voters, (2) prepare labels to mail campaign literature, (3) print form letters containing such "personalized" information as the voter's name, address, birthday, etc., (4) select voters with certain characteristics for a specific campaign message, and (5) maintain lists of campaign contributors. In addition to these rather routine applications, computer usage has expanded into the political planning and decision-making area. Computers have been used to plan and schedule a candidate's campaign activities so that the best use is made of available time and resources. Campaign trips have been planned using the mathematical programming concepts developed by transportation organizations in order to eliminate unnecessary travel and ensure that key geographical regions are given the most effective coverage. Electronic mail/message systems utilizing timeshared computers and remote terminals have been used by presidential and vice-presidential candidates traveling their separate ways to make sure that there is no conflict in their public statements. The results of frequent random samples of the voting public may be transmitted to a central computer by dispersed campaign workers in order to quickly detect shifts in voter opinion and to gauge the effects of an opponent's campaign. This information would obviously be of value in planning and decision making.

Control in the Federal Government

Obviously, computers are used by many federal government agencies for control purposes. The Internal Revenue Service, for example, uses multiple computers to monitor the returns of individual and corporate taxpayers. Filed reports of interest paid to individuals by organizations may be compared against interest income reported by the taxpayer. Without computers, such comparisons would probably not be possible. Computers may also be used by the IRS in randomly selecting and making preliminary audits of tax returns.

A *military application* of the use of computers for control and monitoring purposes is found in the air defense system for North America. Over a dozen computers at the nerve center of the North American Air Defense Command (located inside Cheyenne Mountain near Colorado Springs, Colorado) accept, store, and constantly update masses of data from worldwide radar installations, weather stations, and other intelligence sources. Every object produced by human beings that is in earth orbit is tracked. Radar sets scanning the Eurasian land mass feed data into the computer. If a rocket is launched, the computers are able to calculate its trajectory quickly. If an all-out nuclear strike were aimed at North America from Soviet rocket sites, the warning time would be 15 to 25 minutes. (Time enough for the President to trigger a United States nuclear retaliation; but by the time United States rockets took off, few of us would be around to cheer or bewail this grim spectacle.)

Computers are also used for *environmental control* purposes. Agencies processing environmental data with the help of computers include the Air Pollution Control Office and the Water Quality Office of the Environmental Protection Agency, the National Center for Health Statistics, the U.S. Geological Survey, and the Department of Agriculture. Setting environmental quality standards is a function of several federal agencies. For example, the Federal Water Quality Act of 1965 requires the states to set acceptable quality standards on interstate streams or submit to federal agency guidelines. The Air Pollution Control Office has issued Air Quality Criteria documents. Monitoring of environmental quality is, of course, necessary to determine appropriate standards and/or to check on whether established standards are being met. Staffed or unstaffed monitoring stations may be used to send data to centrally located computer systems. One monitoring example is the work being done by the Division of Motor Vehicle Pollution Control of the Air Pollution Control Office. Basic applications being handled by timeshared computers include calibration of emission-testing equipment, processing and storing emission data after testing, and analysis and interpretation of data for future testing and development purposes.

Computers in Federal Law Enforcement

The Federal Bureau of Investigation makes extensive use of computers. The FBI's computerized National Crime Information Center (NCIC) is an automated nationwide police information network. Online terminals installed at local police stations are connected to central police computers in the states and to the NCIC computers in Washington (the central state computers are, of course, also connected to the NCIC network). Electronic direct access to the arrest records of individual citizens is thus possible in a short period of time. Obtaining such information can help federal, state, and local law enforcement officers make decisions about arresting, searching, detaining, interrogating, and investigating those suspected of having committed crimes. The NCIC computers also store information on stolen property and wanted persons. More than 260,000 transactions involving fugitives, stolen property, and criminal history records are handled daily, and an average of over 1,000 positive responses ("hits") involving wanted persons and stolen property are produced daily. (One unfortunate driver was arrested in Pineville, Kentucky, after stopping to use the restroom at a state police post. A routine check to the NCIC quickly revealed that the driver was violating parole in Lansing, Michigan.)

In 1968, Congress passed the Omnibus Crime Control and Safe Streets Act that established the Law Enforcement Assistance Administration (LEAA) as an agency of the Department of Justice. This agency administers federal grants to state and local law enforcement organzations. Some of the LEAA grants have been used for acquisition of computers by local and state police forces.

In spite of the fact that the FBI's data bank and the state data-base systems help law enforcement agencies with fixed geographical jurisdictions cope with the activities of increasingly mobile criminals, we have already seen that many concerned citizens question whether the issues of *individual freedom* and the *right to privacy* are being given proper consideration. As was pointed out in the last chapter, bills have been introduced in Congress to expand the scope of the Privacy Act of 1974 to include the data banks maintained by federal, state, and local law enforcement agencies. Until such bills are passed, however, the question will remain largely unanswered.

When he was an assistant attorney general, Supreme Court Justice William Rehnquist contended that "self discipline [by] the executive branch will answer virtually all of the legitimate complaints. . . ." He further added that the Justice Department would " 'vigorously oppose any legislation which . . . would effectively impair' the current surveillance and information-gathering activities of law enforcement agencies supported by federal funds."[10] Civil libertarians may dispute Rehnquist's position. Instead, they are apt to echo Juvenal's question: "But who guards the guardians?"

COMPUTERS IN STATE AND LOCAL GOVERNMENTS

The 50 states, 3,000 counties, and 18,000 cities and towns in the United States all require processed data. Obviously, not all these governmental entities use computers. But in attempting to acquire better information in order to cope with growing urbanization, an increasing crime rate, larger populations, inadequate social welfare programs, etc., many state and local government units have turned to computer processing in recent years. In fact, state and local governments represent one of the fastest-growing markets for computer hardware and software.

State and local governments, like the federal government, use computers for (1) *planning and decision-making* (2) *control,* and (3) *law enforcement purposes.* Let us look at applications in each of these usage categories.

Planning and Decision Making in State and Local Governments

The preliminary statements made earlier on planning and decision making at the federal level apply here: state, county, and city planners have often been required to function in settings where the data available for public policy making are inadequate and/or inaccurate. The hope of these administrators, however, is that new computer-based systems will provide them with higher-quality information with which to make better plans and decisions and improve operating efficiency. In the mid-1970s, most states were implementing or planning for information systems that would permit the interchange of information among agencies. Such state

---

[10] Phil Hirsch, "LEAA: Who Guards the Guardians?" *Datamation,* p. 31, June 15, 1971. Law enforcement officials are opposed to expanding the scope of the Privacy Act of 1974 to include their operations.

efforts are continuing at the present time. And many neighboring counties and cities are also pooling resources to jointly acquire hardware and software for mutually beneficial planning and decision-making purposes. A few examples of how computers are now being used for these purposes at the state and local government levels are presented below:

Legislative data systems A number of state legislatures—New York, Washington, Florida, Pennsylvania, Hawaii, and North Carolina, to name just a few—make effective use of computers to index, store, process, and retrieve statutory material; draft bills; prepare roll-call vote reports; provide census population data for planning purposes; address mailing labels; monitor fiscal data; and provide other information and services to lawmakers and their staffs.[11] As long ago as 1965, for example, a computerized Legislative Index made it possible for Florida legislators to quickly determine the status of any piece of pending legislation in order to (1) answer an inquiry from a constituent, (2) follow the progress of their own bills and other bills that were of particular interest to them, (3) determine the actions (if any) taken by colleagues in supporting or opposing a particular bill, and (4) evaluate possible alternative plans, strategies, and decisions. The Florida Legislative Index has also proved helpful to news reporters covering legislative activities.

Social welfare planning In social welfare agencies, as in other organizations, computer usage can be of value in administrative planning and decision making. For example, in the administration of one social welfare agency—Family Service of Metropolitan Detroit—computer-processed data have speeded up administrative analysis and improved program planning. Caseloads of social workers, median income of the families served, size and composition of families (presence of young children, aged dependents, etc.), family stress caused by such factors as separations, divorces, and unemployment—all this information is used by Detroit administrators to analyze the effects of possible changes in agency policies and services. Better internal information on existing welfare cases and caseloads combined with external information on population growth and migration can be used to plan future agency needs far enough in advance to prevent unexpected crises from developing.

Social welfare *simulations* have been designed for planning purposes. At New York University, for example, Dr. Isidor Chein has built a model to estimate the effects of housing developments and social welfare efforts on juvenile delinquency. The model incorporates 45 social economic factors such as income, educational background, and the quality of the living units in about 2,000 neighborhoods. The incidence of delinquency in a neighborhood is compared with the number and type of public housing units and with existing social programs. The model can thus

[11] An excellent source of information on the use of computers by state legislatures is Robert L. Chartrand and Jane Bortnick, *State Legislature Use of Information Technology,* Greenwood Press, Westport, Conn., 1978.

give social welfare planners an idea of what may happen to the delinquency rate if more public housing is built or if a mix of social programs is implemented.

Other computer applications with social planning implications are (1) the Social Service Index of Alameda County, California, which contains the names of over 600,000 people and is used by those working in health, welfare, and probation agencies, (2) the East Bay (California) Regional Park District's system (Figure 13-3) that handles public reservations to the 21 park and recreation areas in operation, and (3) the COMPASS II project of Prince Georges County, Maryland, that will identify senior citizens, expedite processing of applications for assistance from elderly residents, permit case workers to function more effectively by reducing their paperwork load, and determine whether new programs are required to meet the needs of the aging.

Urban planning It is no secret that many urban planners are currently facing an explosion of problems. Traffic congestion; pollution of air and water; tensions within and between racial, ethnic, and economic groups; deteriorating public housing, services, and facilities—all these problems (and others) are facing many areas. Those planners who would try to alleviate such problems need improved information systems that will give them accurate, timely, and relevant information.

FIGURE 13-3
California's East Bay Regional Park District's computer system handles park and recreation-area reservations. (*IBM Corp.*)

Attempts have been made to develop more comprehensive urban information systems that would provide planners with this quality information. For example, *traffic congestion* problems have been tackled by planners using computers to simulate traffic flow patterns. Variables such as the expected distribution of trips, the type of travel modes used, and the routes traveled are used to estimate the flow of persons and vehicles on transit facilities and roads. (The travel mode used and the route selected by the simulated traveler may, in turn, depend on such variables as travel time, cost, convenience, etc.) Simulation is used to plan proposed roads and to use existing roads in the most efficient way. Various alternative transportation systems can be evaluated through computer simulation. In evaluating alternative traffic systems, however, the planner must take into consideration the interactions which exist between transportation systems and other aspects of urban life. All too often in the past, traffic planners have begun road construction without considering recreational, housing, and other alternative land-use needs.

The need to consider alternative uses of land as a vital input of detailed traffic models has, in fact, resulted in the development of local and regional *land-use models.* Included in land-use simulation equations are future expectations as to population, employment, number of households, income, and distribution of available land for commercial and residential purposes. Given alternative zoning and economic development plans and different assumed growth rates, the land-use model may provide planners with data about expected income, employment, and population distributions. These data, in turn, can be used as input into traffic planning simulations. In the Washington metropolitan area, a computer land-use data system is used for planning purposes. This system receives data from continuously updated files and is of value to satellite governments as well as Washington planners.

Also in the Washington area, the council members of Montgomery County, Maryland, were recently faced with the need to consider future county growth levels and patterns in order to respond to the pressures being exerted by developers, environmentalists, and taxpayer associations. A computerized impact evaluation system was utilized to analyze the overall effects on the county of different rates of growth and different patterns of population distribution. The findings of a *fiscal impact analysis* provided the basis for plans involving taxation, county services, and the issuance of bonds.

Control in State and Local Governments

From monitoring a city's power generating station to controlling a county sewage treatment plant, and from controlling traffic signals[12] to monitoring statewide water projects, computers are being used to supervise

---

[12] For an interesting account of how engineers are using computers to control traffic, see "Take Guesswork Out of Traffic Control," *The American City & County,* pp. 31–32ff, January 1979

"Automation Strengthens Sheriff's Office"

One of the important functions of the Sheriff's Department in Ocean County, New Jersey, is the responsibility for maintaining custody of the criminal history records for the County. Rising population and seasonal peaks associated with any resort area have severely strained the capability to serve the courts and other agencies, both public and private, with required information on file.

Under the direction of Sheriff James N. Rutter, a study team headed by Lieutenant John Sadowski was formed to evaluate methods of improving the department's efficiency and at the same time, develop meaningful investigative and identification techniques based on the mass of data accumulated. The system selected was the Ragen Information Management System 90, a totally integrated process for automated records management.

The current operation has effectively eliminated the maintenance of subsidiary index files (name to number, etc.). Records are duplicated on 16mm microfilm and simultaneously cross-referenced in a multiple of ways. The acquired indices update an on-line electronic memory, providing automated retrieval of documents in seconds. In addition, the system provides an expanded search and statistical tool of great value in the Department's effort to increase the County resources for the detection and apprehension of criminals.

A few of the outstanding benefits and new opportunities resulting from the System are:

- All of the varied records (criminal histories, fingerprnts, mug shots, etc.) are now centrally located where they are required for demand access. They are completely secure in the System 90 terminal, which does not require human intervention in the selection of cartridges or the microfilm images within them.

- The collection of a variety of identifiers pertinent to the acquired records for the System allows the detectives to search its electronic memory, with only partial data in hand. The ability to peruse data in file, matching known physical characteristics, criminal methods and fingerprint codes, represents a heretofore impossible task with limited skilled personnel.

- The collected data associated with document entry into the System is utilized in a number of important ways. Lists are generated, permitting analysis of varied crime incidents geographically and chronologically. Municipalities within the County can now be alerted to program effective control programs and efficient manpower allocation routines.

Although space savings, file integrity and efficiency were important, the overall impact of implementing computer-assisted micrographics in the Department added new dimensions to its service capability. Assurance of privacy rights, via totally secure document storage capability and effective utilization of compiled data and associated documentation for law enforcement, all lead to better serving the citizens of Ocean County.

Source: "Automation Strengthens Sheriff's Office," *Information and Records Management,* p. 28ff., May 1979. Reprinted with permission.

countless activities at the state, county, and local levels. Such applications as tax collection and revenue control and control of inventories of government-owned property are quite common. Fire fighters can often maintain better control over dangerous situations because dispatchers at city fire departments are able to enter the address of a fire into an online system and get an instant and early read-out of any special problems or hazards that may exist on or near the fire location. But perhaps some of the most interesting applications are those found in the areas of *conservation* and *environmental control.*

California's multimillion-dollar State Water Project, for example, is designed to *conserve* water by moving it from surplus areas in northern California to needy areas in the south and west. Water is moved hundreds of miles through a network of canals, tunnels, gates, pipelines, pumping stations, and power plants. All these facilities are monitored and controlled by computers located at five remote control centers. In the event of emergency, a control center will quickly shut down the affected part of the system—e.g., should a canal be broken by an earthquake, check gates in the affected section would be closed immediately to prevent serious loss of water.

Other conservation applications of computers are:

1   A computerized street-lighting design concept has been tested in Philadelphia by the Franklin Institute Research Laboratories. One of the findings was that cities can achieve energy savings ranging up to 60 percent with no loss in visibility by replacing 400-watt mercury vapor street lamps with 150-watt high-pressure sodium lights.[13]
2   South Carolina has used a computer to identify, track, and help conserve rare or irreplaceable natural and humanmade resources in more than 400 areas across the state. These areas range from the breeding ground of the rare loggerhead sea turtle near the Atlantic coast to stands of virgin timber.

[13] See Gary M. Chamberlain, "Visibility Index Brightens Street Light Design Picture," *The American City & County,* pp. 41–44, April 1979.

3 The Ontario, Canada, Ministry of Natural Resources uses a computer system to predict the location and time of forest fires. A network of lightning sensors throughout the province records the number of lightning discharges within a 20-mile radius. With a formula that considers fuel and weather conditions, it is then possible to predict the number and location of expected fires. Early detection is, of course, important in controlling damage from forest fires.

States and cities are also using computers to monitor, evaluate, and control the levels of *water and air pollution.* The Empire State System of New York collects water and air data from water and air monitoring stations located at critical sites around the state. Data from the stations are automatically forwarded to a central computer (each air monitoring station reports every 15 minutes, and each water station transmits once every hour). Upon receiving transmitted data, the computer edits the message, sends any necessary operating instructions to the station, compares edited information to acceptable environmental standards, and, if standards are not met, sends an appropriate alarm message to either the Air Resources or Pure Waters Division of the Department of Environmental Conservation. Corrective action may then be taken. Once each day a complete system report is prepared.

Other computerized pollution control systems are:

1 The system of the Ohio River Valley Water Sanitation Commission (composed of members from eight states and the federal government) feeds hourly data into a central computer from electronic monitors spotted along the Ohio River and its tributaries. The stations measure such variables as temperature, dissolved oxygen, chloride content, and oxidation-reduction potential (a measure of water's propensity to chemically act as an oxidizing or reducing agent). Daily reports on water-quality conditions along the river are prepared by the computer.

2 The computer system of the Miami Conservancy District monitors the water-quality conditions along the Great Miami River in Ohio. The cost of the system is distributed among the 15 cities and towns, 5 counties, 5 power plants, and 35 industries that hold permits from the Ohio Water Pollution Board to discharge their treated waste water into the river. Each of the 60 users of the river must make periodic reports on stream loading. In addition, portable monitoring stations mounted on trailers continously record various parameters of water quality for input into the central computer.

3 A computer-controlled air pollution monitoring system is being operated by the city of Philadelphia. Several automatic sensing stations, online to a computer, measure wind speed and direction, particulate matter, oxidants, sulfur dioxide content, and carbon monoxide content. This information may be transmitted instantly to a city

computer, where it may be further processed. Uses of the system include predicting and issuing warnings of potentially dangerous air pollution conditions and quickly detecting sources of pollution so that inspectors can gather additional evidence for legal action. A similar system is being operated by air pollution control agencies in Santa Barbara County and San Luis Obispo County in California.

4   The level of noise pollution of aircraft leaving Honolulu International Airport is being monitored by a network of outdoor microphones connected to a computer inside the airport control tower. Airport officials need to regulate flight patterns to control noise because the mild climate allows people to keep their windows open throughout the year, leaving Hawaiian citizens more vulnerable to aircraft noise.

Computers in State and Local Law Enforcement

As we saw earlier, many state, county, and municipal law enforcement agencies are connected to the FBI's NCIC data bank. However, there are also numerous law enforcement computer systems below the federal level (Figure 13-4).[14] The following examples are representative:

[14] A study of the use of computers by police departments is found in Kent W. Colton, "The Impact and Use of Computer Technology by the Police," *Communications of the ACM,* pp. 10–20, January 1979.

FIGURE 13-4
Law enforcement terminal in use in Lane County, Oregon.
(IBM Corp.)

1 Los Angeles County's Automated Justice Information System keeps track of an average of 11,000 inmates in several jails and other institutions. Booking information on arrested persons is entered into direct-access storage devices from a number of online terminals. New information is added to a person's record as it is received. Information such as jail location, bail amount, dates of scheduled court appearances, etc., is available on demand. Los Angeles County also has an Automated Want and Warrant System that keeps track of those wanted by the police. In one case, a University of Southern California student was stopped for making an illegal left turn. Upon inquiry, the police officer found that 48 traffic violations covering a three-year period were charged against the student and fines totaling $555 were unpaid. In addition, a system combining television and computer technologies to automatically retrieve law enforcement records was installed a few years ago (see Figure 13-5).

2 The Law Enforcement Information Network (LEIN) at Michigan State Police headquarters in East Lansing contains online information about wanted persons, stolen cars and other property, and revoked or suspended drivers' licenses. A patrol officer can radio the license number

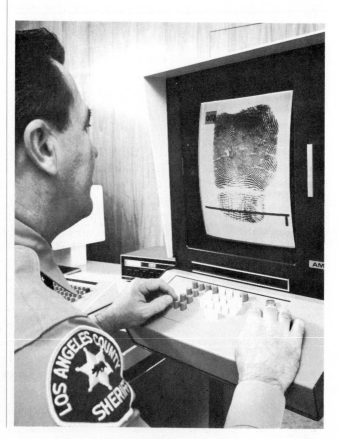

FIGURE 13-5
Information retrieval system for law enforcement. (*Ampex Corp.*)

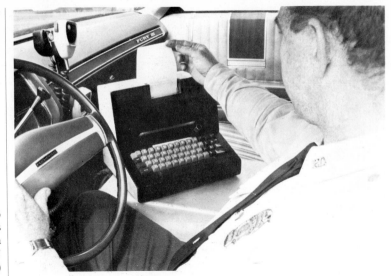

FIGURE 13-6
Police officers in squad cars
now have direct access to a
central computer file. (*IBM
Corp.*)

of a car he or she has stopped or is chasing and can be warned to exercise extra caution if the car is stolen or if the occupant is believed to be dangerous. Police in Michigan cities are using terminals connected to the state system to see whether arrested individuals are also wanted elsewhere. In one 24-hour period, Detroit police found that 17 persons they were holding were wanted in other jurisdictions. Of course, LEIN is also tied into NCIC.

3   The Kansas City, Missouri, Police Department's system gives police officers in squad cars direct fingertip access to distant computer files (Figure 13-6). The mobile terminal system enables officers to type inquiries on the terminal's keyboard and receive printed responses from a computer.

4   The District of Columbia Department of Corrections uses an inmate accounting system that helps the department plan more meaningful rehabilitation programs while, at the same time, it keeps track of the 400 inmate transfers that take place daily between the district's 22 correctional units (Figure 13-7).

5   The New York Statewide Police Information Network (NYSPIN) has a central computer complex in Albany that serves hundreds of online terminals located in state and municipal agencies, criminal justice departments, the FBI, the National Auto Theft Bureau, and the Federal Bureaus of Narcotics and Customs. The NYSPIN system is also interfaced with a number of other computers including those at the NCIC, the National Law Enforcement Telecommunications System in Phoenix, Arizona, and the Department of Motor Vehicles in Albany. Most of the functions performed in all the systems described above are available with NYSPIN.

FIGURE 13-7
Correction personnel use computer to keep track of the transfer of inmates.

6   The CLEAR (County Law Enforcement Applied Regionally) system of Cincinnati and Hamilton County, Ohio, is a network with over 80 terminals in the city and county. Extensive files on stolen property, wanted persons, outstanding traffic citations and warrants, arrest and conviction records of individuals, etc., are maintained. In addition, CLEAR is also linked to the Ohio state system, to the LEIN network in Michigan, and to the NCIC; it has been copied by San Francisco, West Palm Beach, Fort Lauderdale, and the state of South Carolina. A group of CLEAR users has formed an organization to exchange ideas and programs.

COMPUTERS, LAWYERS, AND THE COURTS

In this section we will first consider the impact of computer usage on lawyers and on the techniques used by lawyers in preparing their cases. We will then briefly examine the possible influence of computers on court administration.

Computers and Lawyers

Although some law firms and lawyers have not yet shown much interest in computers, this neglect is diminishing. *One reason* is that others are using computers more, and laywers are therefore encountering more legal problems that are influenced by the use of computers. Clients and opponents are using computers to process records, and these records may be entered as evidence in court cases. How reliable are they? Could they have been manipulated by a program patch to present an incorrect procedure? In some cases, lawyers have to call computer experts to testify to the validity of computer-produced evidence just as they have to use expert testimony from medical doctors and engineers in other situations. Lawyers thus need to learn enough about computers to communicate with the experts testifying for or against their clients. In short, lawyers have had to heed the advice given by a law professor over a decade ago:

> The expert on computer-controlled production comes in, and you ask him, 'How did the program and the machine work to produce this result?' If all he will say is 'This program califlams the whingdrop and reticulates the residual glob,' it is perfectly clear that you are going to have to study up somewhat, in order to make up your mind about what went on.[15]

Another reason why lawyers are showing greater interest in computers is that more electronic systems are being developed for use inside the legal profession. Keeping track of a lawyer's time for billing purposes; maintaining the accounting records of a law firm; performing estate planning computations; searching for, retrieving, and displaying information on legal precedents from legal data banks—applications such as these can all be performed in a law office at a timesharing terminal or on a small computer.

There are several organizations that offer a *legal information retrieval service* for subscribers. Mead Data Central, Inc., of Dayton, Ohio, for example, has a LEXIS retrieval system that contains millions of case law citations. The system supplies document, page, and line numbers in response to key words entered by users. Users are charged for connect time and also pay a search surcharge. Mead also offers NAARS, an accounting research and retrieval system that contains financial statements from about 4,000 companies. The NAARS service is a valuable tool of corporate lawyers as well as accountants. Another legal research and retrieval system is WESTLAW, a service of West Publishing Company of St. Paul, Minnesota. Summaries of hundreds of thousands of cases reported in state and federal courts over the past two decades are available to WESTLAW users. Inquiries are entered through visual display terminals, summaries are displayed on the screen in seconds, and printouts of case summaries can be obtained at the press of a buttom.

Before concluding this section, mention should also be made of the use of computers by the Senate committee lawyers who investigated the Watergate crimes in the early 1970s. An online computer was used to allow investigators to make immediate comparisons of the often-conflicting testimony given by different witnesses.

Computers and the Courts

Computers can be very useful in court administration. The current backlog of pending cases in many of the nation's courts is thwarting justice and is,

---

[15] Vaughn C. Ball, "The Impact of Data-processing Technology on the Legal Profession," *Computers and Automation*, p. 44, April 1968.

"Computers Go to Court"

Prosecution of criminal cases involves costly and time-consuming procedures for local governments. But in Contra Costa County, California, where court activity has increased 40 percent in the last year, a computerized court management system has stabilized costs and made more information available more quickly to court officials.

According to Tom Falce, County Director of the Law and Justice Systems Development Project, the county has taken its first step in the development of a distributed data processing network of computers to manage the entire criminal justice system.

Minicomputer systems in each of the county's four lower courts are processing the collection of parking citation fines and preparing schedules of court resources and activities.

Contra Costa County incorporates 13 cities and is California's eighth largest county, with a population of 600,000. The area endures a heavy volume of traffic; and in recent years the rising incidence of illegal parking has been one of the local government's major concerns. In the city of Walnut Creek, for example, 50,000 parking tickets were issued last year.

The county's lower courts are responsible for collecting parking and other traffic violation fines as well as arbitrating these infractions, if challenged; mediating misdemeanors like petty theft or drunk driving; and conducting preliminary hearings for felonies like rape, murder and armed robbery.

Each of the county's lower courts employs a staff to process the collection of fines and to schedule court activities. Prior to computerization, these tasks were performed manually; but employees had trouble keeping up with an increasing workload.

To expedite the flow of information among the county's criminal justice departments, the county formed the Justice Automation Advisory Committee to investigate automation as an alternative method to manual operations.

The committee concluded that automation was the most efficient and economical solution to the problem.

An IBM 370/158 mainframe computer in the county's central data processing facility in Martinez was performing a number of county functions like processing the payroll, maintaining welfare records, and calculating property taxes. But this computer was operating in a batch mode, which produced delays between data entry and processing. The county needed a different kind of computer system—one that could capture data at the source, could be operated easily, and could provide ready answers to questions.

The staff selected Data General computer systems with 32K core memory, 10 megabyte disks, three Dasher display terminals and medium-speed printers, which were all installed in the first of the four lower courts in November 1977. Application software was written in Interactive COBOL.

The systems were operational in the pilot court in the spring of 1978 and system implementation in the other courts began.

"The computers are managing the whole parking system here," Falce said, "which is really a high-volume, accounts receivable type of application." Administrative personnel at each court enter citation data into the computer, which determines if the violation is legitimate, calculates the bail or fine and later records payment and subsequent court actions.

The computer also records nonstandard or exceptional violations—those committed by persons with out-of-state registrations, multiple violations, and so forth.

The criminal calendar application schedules the activities in the courtrooms as well as the resources available and reports the action taken by the court on the cases scheduled. This function essentially designates the who, what when, where and why of a particular case and prepares an agenda. What, when, where and why are easily determined; but any number of individuals, in addition to attorneys, may be asked to attend a hearing, such as the probation officer or law enforcement officer.

These case details are input to the systems, the agenda is compiled and reports are generated on the system printers and distributed to the parties involved. Case data from individual courts is also examined at this time to determine if a defendant has any other offenses pending in another court in the county. "The criminal calendar is very important," Falce said. "because it is absolutely critical that all agencies are aware of the court agenda." Each of these agencies schedules its activity and resources around this agenda, so coordination and accuracy are essential.

Source: "Computers Go To Court," adapted from Data General press release, July 3, 1979. Reprinted by permission of Data General.

in fact, creating injustices. (A guilty person may remain unpunished because witnesses have forgotten details, moved away, or even died during the long delay period, and an innocent person accused of a crime who does not have the ability to raise bail may be kept in jail for many months before trial.)

In Philadelphia, where the case load has nearly doubled in the last eight years, a computer system is being used for court administration. Since it went into operation, the system has helped to significantly reduce the backlog of criminal and civil cases. Reports generated by the computer on a daily or weekly basis include trial calendars, defendant and witness subpoenas, notices to the prisoner facility 23 miles away to bring defendants to court, and details of courtroom availability. In civil cases, when "certificates of readiness" (stating that the case is ready for trial) are filed by both parties, the information is stored in the system. A daily trial listing is prepared and published in a Philadelphia legal newspaper each morning. Lawyers for the top 20 cases on the daily list must appear in a court call room. Delays due to attorney conflicts have been significantly reduced. Courts in Jackson County (Kansas City), Missouri, Los Angeles County and Contra Costa County, California, Milwaukee County, Wisconsin, and the state of Washington are among those which use computers for similar administrative purposes.

Another way that computers can increase court efficiency is by helping to improve *jury selection* procedures. Once a month in the District of Columbia, approximately 10,000 residents are qualified for jury duty by a computer. These citizens then become anonymous 6-digit numbers stored in the computer at Superior Court. The tasks of selecting jurors, preparing summonses, and producing the related reports required by the courts are performed by the computer. From the time one is qualified for jury duty until one's name is printed on a summons, one remains a number in storage. About 1,000 of the 10,000 qualified citizens will be selected as jurors to try the monthly civil and criminal cases that come before the Washington courts. Courts in Marion County, Indiana, and St. Louis County, Missouri, also use computers for jury selection procedures.

▶ LOOKING BACK

The following points have been emphasized in this chapter:

1 The purpose of this chapter has been to outline selected computer applications in federal, state, and local governments. We have also considered some of the factors and applications affecting the legal profession and the courts.
2 Government planners at all levels have a mandate to efficiently use public funds and resources in ways that best serve the needs of society. High-quality information is needed by planners to achieve their objectives, and hundreds of computer applications have been developed to supply planners with better information. Federal government decision makers are actively using computers in such areas as environmental planning, weather forecasting, and military planning; state and municipal decision makers are concerned with such areas as social welfare planning and urban planning. Members of Congress and legislators are finding legislative data banks to be of value and are exploring the use of computers in political campaigns.
3 The control function is being performed at all levels of government by computer systems. Conservation and environmental control applications by federal, state, and municipal agencies are rapidly increasing as the dangers of pollution become more obvious.

4   Millions of dollars has been channeled into the development and use of law enforcement computer systems. Many of these systems are tied together at the state levels, and the state systems are, in turn, linked to the FBI's NCIC system. Thus, a nationwide network of police data banks is now operational. Such a network helps law enforcement agencies with fixed geographical jurisdictions cope with the activities of increasingly mobile criminals, but there are many concerned citizens who believe that the issues of individual freedom and the right to privacy have not been given proper consideration as these interlocking data banks have been developed.

5   Lawyers are now using computers in their law practices for billing purposes and for the retrieval of legal precedents. And courts are finding that computers can be very helpful in court administration activities and jury selection procedures.

▶ KEY TERMS

After reading Chapter 13, you should be able to define and use the following terms:

technology assessment	"Hit"
war games	legislative data systems
battlefield sensors	social welfare simulation
LEGIS	land-use model
SOPAD	LEXIS
NCIC	WESTLAW

▶ REVIEW AND DISCUSSION QUESTIONS

1   Discuss and give examples of how computers have been used for planning and decision making at the federal government level.

2   (a) How can computers be used in environmental planning? (b) How can computers be used in forecasting the weather?

3   "Computers are increasingly being used by military planners." Discuss this statement.

4   (a)What is a legislative data bank? (b) For what purposes is such a data bank used?

5   How may computers be used in political campaigns?

6   (a) Give examples of ways in which computers are used by the federal government to perform the control function. (b) Give examples of state and local government control activities.

7   (a) What is the NCIC? (b) What functions does it perform? (c) Identify two other systems that are tied into NCIC.

8 Discuss and give examples of how computers have been used for planning and decision making at state and local government levels.

9 (a) How may computers be used for social welfare planning? (b) For urban planning?

10 How are computers being used by state and local governments for law enforcement purposes?

11 (a) How may computers affect the legal profession? (b) The courts?

12 Consider the following case: A Decision Information Distribution System (DIDS)—a low-frequency radio network to warn people quickly of impending attack—has been under development in the Pentagon. If this system materializes, all citizens would be expected to buy a specially designed unit capable of receiving DIDS warning broadcasts. The DIDS system would also warn listeners of impending floods, hurricanes, and similar emergencies, and would provide other services which the Pentagon is still studying. Because of the warning functions of DIDS, the receiving units in the homes of citizens could be turned on *automatically* by the message-sending agency (the circuitry to do this has already been developed). Under questioning by a congressional subcommittee member, a Pentagon delegate admitted that the DIDS receiver could also be converted into a *transmitter*. A subcommittee staff member has commented: "They'll ultimately decide to go ahead with DIDS because they'll be evaluating only its *technical* performance, not its *political* possibilities." Plans have been made to seek funds to install DIDS units on new radio and TV sets. A coast-to-coast network could be in operation in a few years. *Question:* On balance, is DIDS a good idea?

SELECTED REFERENCES

In addition to the references suggested in the chapter footnotes, you might wish to examine the following sources:

"Computers Go to Court," *Personal Computing,* pp. 13–14, October 1979.

Cranford, Gerald, and Warren Glimpse: "Geocoding the 1980 Census: Improving Data Access and Use," *Government Data Systems,* pp. 12–13ff, July/August 1979.

Daniel, Royal, and Alan Paller: "Data Processing's Role in Complex Litigation," *Datamation,* pp. 206–208ff, May 1978.

Jost, Steve: "The Automated Congressional Office," *Data Management,* pp. 46–47ff, May 1979.

Mahan, Sheila, Gary Spivac, and Robert Swank: "Plotting Land Use in Oregon," *Datamation,* pp. 155–159ff, November 1, 1978.

Milway, William B.: "Minicomputers Get Wide Usage by the Army," *Creative Computing,* pp. 101–103, May 1979.

Nathanson, R.: "The Police Information Network of New York State," *Computers and People,* pp. 14–16, March 1978.

Newkirk, Glenn: "Information Technology and State Legislatures," *State Legislatures,* pp. 13–15, January 1979.

Chapter 14
COMPUTERS AND HEALTH

◆ LOOKING AHEAD

The purpose of this chapter is to outline a few of the uses of computers in health fields.

In the first section of the chapter, you will see how computers are being utilized in *medical planning and decision-making* applications. For example, some computer-assisted diagnosis and research techniques and some physiological simulation procedures are discussed.

The second section deals with the use of computers for the control of such things as the physiological status of patients, laboratory tests, and the dispensing of drugs.

A third section discusses the subject of *information retrieval* in a health care context, and the final section introduces you to some of the elements that may be found in a *hospital information system.*

Thus, after studying this chapter, you should be able to:

- Give a number of examples of how computers are used for purposes of diagnosis and medical research.

- Explain how computers may be used in the preparation and retrieval of medical records.

- Outline how physiological simulations may be used in the training of health care professionals.

- Give a number of examples of how computers are applied for medical control purposes.

- Discuss a system for retrieving information from the thousands of health-related periodicals being published each month.

- Identify some of the elements that have been included in the computer-based information systems of hospitals.

- Understand and use the key terms listed at the end of the chapter.

When first introduced into hospitals several years ago, computers were used primarily for accounting and record-keeping purposes. Administrative applications, of course, still account for a substantial amount of computing time, but the medical profession has utilized the computer in scores of new ways to improve health care in recent years. From helping to diagnose the cause of illness to controlling laboratory tests, and from aiding in the research on drug addiction to the continuous monitoring of a patient's condition, computers are proving their value to patients, doctors, and hospitals.

One need not look far to discover *reasons for the accelerating use of computers in health fields:*

1 There is a serious shortage of doctors, nurses, and medical technicians. By relieving scarce personnel of routine tasks, computers can help increase their effectiveness.

2 Computers may make it possible for physicians and health scientists to conduct research that will extend the frontiers of medical knowledge. Without computers, some promising types of research could not be explored.

3 Computers can help improve the quality of a physician's diagnoses on the one hand, and can help improve the control of important medical processes on the other. Physicians, patients, and hospital administrators will thus benefit.

4 Medical knowledge is advancing rapidly. The ability to acquire and quickly apply new information may mean the difference between life and death. Computers are needed to retrieve relevant information rapidly.

5 There is still considerable room for improvement in the administrative systems of many hospitals—improvements that may be made through the use of computers.

Many of the general topics mentioned above will be considered in more detail in this chapter. In the pages that follow we will consider (1) *planning and decision-making applications,* (2) *control applications,* (3) *information retrieval systems,* and (4) *hospital information systems.*

COMPUTERS IN MEDICAL PLANNING AND DECISION MAKING

Applications of computers which have medical planning and decision-making implications include (1) *computer-assisted diagnosis and research,* (2) *medical history preparation and retrieval,* (3) *study of drug side effects,* (4) *physiological simulations,* and (5) *menu planning.*

Computer-Assisted Diagnosis and Research

Some physicians are now using the computer as a *diagnostic tool* in hospitals and clinics. At a number of "multiphasic" screening centers around the country, for example, patients are given physical examinations consisting of a series of basic tests. An electrocardiogram, chest x-ray, and urine test, along with measurements of blood pressure, lung function, vision, hearing, intraocular pressure (a test for glaucoma), height, and weight, are among the items included in the examination. Data from the tests may be fed into the computer in a separate operation (Figure 14-1), or the testing equipment may be linked directly to the computer for an automatic transfer of results. Once the data are received, the computer can compare test measurements against the standards established in the

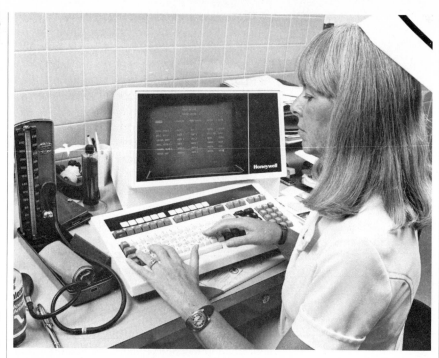

FIGURE 14-1
Computer-assisted physical examinations. (*Honeywell, Inc.*)

program. Within a few minutes after the examination procedures are completed, the computer output is ready. The test results are reported, and if they fall outside prescribed limits, procedures that should be repeated and/or additional tests that should be conducted may be indicated. The computer may also be programmed to suggest tentative diagnoses to explain abnormal test results. The patient's physician, of course, is responsible for the final diagnosis.

One advantage of *computer-assisted physical examinations* is that they free doctors from routine testing procedures, conserve their time, and enable them to give more attention to patient diagnosis and treatment. Physicians in northern Florida are using a health center computer at the University of Florida for patient testing; the Kaiser Foundation Hospital in Oakland, California, is processing about 4,000 people per month through its 19-step physical examination; and Good Samaritan Hospital in Cincinnati has a successful multiphasic testing program.

Statistical techniques can also be used for diagnostic purposes. Upon receiving a listing of symptoms and findings from a doctor, the computer can check and compare these symptoms against a description of diseases that are known to cause them. The computer may be programmed to supply the doctor with a listing of the known diseases, the statistical probability of each disease being the cause of the reported symptoms, a listing of medical references to check, and other possible variables to look for before arriving at a diagnosis. By correlating symptoms against diseases, a computer might also be able to produce statistics that would reveal previously unsuspected relationships. For example, at the University of Pittsburgh, Drs. Jack Myers and Harry Pople have developed a diagnostic system they call INTERNIST. The system includes about 350 diseases and 2,800 disease manifestations. There is a listing of the associated manifestations that are known to occur with each disease, along with a statistical estimate of the frequency of occurrence. Using INTERNIST, a physician can sit at a terminal and provide information on a patient. After considering the initial data, the program begins asking questions about the patient. During this questioning, INTERNIST tells the physician what diagnoses it is considering and what data it is temporarily disregarding. The program may provide its diagnosis for the doctor in a few minutes. In order to save the patient money by avoiding unnecessary lab tests, INTERNIST is programmed to deal with the least costly diseases first.

Another diagnostic approach involves the use of the *clinical algorithm*. The clinical algorithm, or *protocol*, is a step-by-step set of instructions to guide paramedical workers in the management of common complaints. Computers are not necessarily required to process the instructions, but they can be used to (1) analyze symptoms, (2) branch to various parts of the algorithm when certain symptoms or data items are present or absent, and (3) determine whether specific therapy should be employed, whether additional information should be collected, or whether the case should be referred to an M.D. Of course, as we saw in Chapter 11, some doctors may not be happy about the fact that computers are being programmed and protocols are being used in ways that permit trained paramedical personnel to perform some of the diagnostic tasks and make some of the therapeutic decisions that were once handled exclusively by physicians. They may feel that "Little by little, the specialness of the doctor is stripped away: his interviewing technique can be replaced by a branching electronic sequence, his diagnostic acumen is nothing more than a collection of thresholds and logic trees, his therapeutic decisions simply programmed probabilities."[1]

Computers are also being used for such diagnostic purposes as (1) displaying heart function on a CRT from motion-picture x-rays and calculating the volume and width of the patient's left ventricle—the heart's pump, (2) analyzing the measurement of radioactive isotopes in any given portion of the body in order to detect the possible presence of a malignant growth (most malignant nodules in the thyroid gland, for example, do not absorb the radioactive iodine given to the patient, and so the absence of radioactive material would be considered suspicious), and (3) determining by means of a computer-aided tomography (CAT) scanner—a device that x-rays tiny slices of body structures and then combines the thousands of shots into a single picture—the area in the brain that has been damaged by a stroke so that the proper medication can be given right away.

[1] Jerry Avorn, M.D., "The Future of Doctoring," *Atlantic,* p. 77, November 1974.

Computer-assisted *research* is providing insights into:

1 *Causes and prevention of stroke.* A stroke usually occurs suddenly and is due to a disruption in the normal flow of blood in the brain. Statistical research to correlate many of the factors suspected of causing stroke is being conducted by the Iowa Heart Association. By isolating the most important causes of stroke, the researchers could then educate the public on possible preventive measures and contribute information of value in stroke diagnosis and treatment.

2 *Subtle differences in the ways drugs affect people.* Dr. Peter Witt, Director of Research for North Carolina's Department of Mental Health, has conducted studies to determine how such drugs as LSD, mescaline, etc., affect the web-weaving ability of spiders. A computer compared the webs produced by drugged spiders against the characteristics of a normal web. Results of the comparisons were used to gain insight into the possible effects of drugs on the human brain and body.

3 *Ways in which the brain stores and retrieves information.* At UCLA's Brain Research Institute, computer analysis of brain waves has improved the understanding of brain function and has made it possible to analyze subtle patterns that indicate information transfer.

4 *Patterns of drug addiction.* There is currently no agreement among highly respected specialists on the causes of drug addiction, nor is there any consensus among experts on what constitutes a cure. However, the National Institute of Mental Health has a research program under way at 16 treatment agencies that will, it is hoped, shed new light on the causes of addiction and its treatment. Each of the 16 agencies assesses the effectiveness of its own efforts, and each agency supplies information to the data bank established at the Institute of Behavioral Research at Texas Christian University. Data on addicts are obtained when they are initially admitted for treatment and at two-month intervals thereafter. Computer analyses of the data gathered on several thousand addicts and their responses to different treatment approaches may lead to future agreement on the causes and cures of addiction.

5 *Possibility of bringing sight to the blind.* University of Utah scientists are working on an electronic vision system that, it is hoped, will enable blind people to "see" well enough to move about safely and read ordinary printed material. Images from a semiconductor camera in an artificial eye would be scanned by a microprocessor (located in the frame of the user's glasses) that then computes a pattern and sends the data to an array of electrodes implanted in the blind person's brain to re-create the image.

6 *Study of the defects of the inner ear.* A series of mathematical equations has been developed by IBM scientists and researchers at the Ear Research Institute of Los Angeles to learn more about hearing defects that originate in the nearly inaccessible cochlea, or inner ear. A computer model uses the equations to simulate experiments that could not be performed on the cochlea itself.

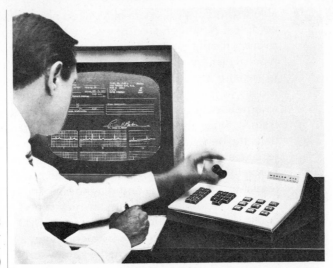

FIGURE 14-2
Information retrieval of medical records. (*Mosler Information Services Division.*)

Medical History Preparation and Retrieval

In developing a record of a patient's medical history, a usual practice is for the doctor (or nurse) to ask the patient a series of questions about past illnesses or health problems. In areas where heredity may be a factor, the patient is also asked questions about the health of blood relatives. This history taking is a time-consuming aspect of the patient-physician relationship. Computers can be used to reduce the time involved and to tailor the questions to the patient's situation.

At the Mayo Clinic in Minnesota, Dr. John Mayne has developed a system that displays medical history questions and multiple-response choices on the screen of a CRT terminal. The patient answers the questions by pointing to the appropriate response with a light pen—a device attached to the terminal that permits the computer to detect the response selected. Medidata Sciences, Inc., in Massachusetts also uses an online visual display device to project questions for patient response. The patient answers by pressing one of the five buttons opposite the most appropriate answer to the question. The computer is programmed to follow certain question paths depending on the answers received. For example, if the question is "Do you smoke?" and the answer is yes, several additional questions will be asked; if the answer is no, these questions will be omitted. After the patient has answered all relevant questions, the medical history can be printed out for the doctor's use, or it may be stored on magnetizable or microfilm media.

Once the patient's history and medical records are available in machine-accessible form, they may be retrieved by the physician as necessary for review and updating (Figure 14-2). Although the medical records of most people are currently kept and manually maintained in file cabinets in a doctor's office, it is possible that in the future this record-keeping function will increasingly be handled by a computer data bank. With available technology, this data bank need not be located in a large computer complex. Any interested physician can enter patient data into an office microcomputer system for rapid online retrieval. These data could include type of ailment, level of severity, date of most recent procedure, type of treatment, results of most recent examination, etc.[2] When a patient moves (or changes doctors), personal health records may be transferred to a new data bank, alleviating the need for completing a new medical history. Since the patient is often a poor transmitter of personal health data, the new doctor would probably have a more complete and accurate record available through a terminal than would otherwise be possible. Better information about patients should prove valuable in preventing potential health problems and diagnosing illnesses.

One example of a computer-maintained medical data bank is found in New York City. Records of about 20,000 children from low-income families are kept up to date by a computer at New York University. Data pertaining to the children can be retrieved by physicians using terminals located at Bellevue Hospital.

Study of Drug Side Effects

Even though a drug may be tested extensively prior to being placed on the market, it is possible that undetected side effects can occur. Combining the new drug with other medications and administering the drug to patients with illnesses or in conditions not encountered during the testing period can result in the appearance of side effects that were previously unsuspected. A computer system can be used to gather data on the experiences of many physicians with a particular drug over time. Shared drug experiences should give faster indications of the efficacy of a particular product and the possibility that the product was responsible for unfortunate results. Computer analyses could be made to reveal a relationship between the use of a drug and reported undesirable consequences. Knowledge of such a relationship would certainly be valuable to doctors in their planning and decision making. Perhaps the magnitude of a tragedy, such as that which occurred a few years ago when a number of babies were born deformed because their mothers were given thalidomide during pregnancy, could be reduced by the use of a data bank of shared drug experiences.

Physiological Simulations

Imagine a patient who suffers nausea, blockage of the bronchial tubes, and heart attacks several times daily. Such a "patient" is Sim One, a lifelike

---

[2] For an account of how a physician is using an office micro for patient information retrieval purposes, see Lee Felsenstein, "Microurologistically, Of Course," *Creative Computing,* pp. 130–131, November/December 1978. See also William S. Walker, "Filing Medical Records," *Personal Computing,* p. 28, July 1979.

"Computer Locates Compatible Donor Kidneys"

When a donor kidney becomes available for transplanting, a compatible recipient must be located in the fastest possible time since the kidney transplant must be completed within 24 hours (and ideally inside 20 hours) to be successful. In France, this problem has been solved through a real-time computer program known as RITRAN, which rapidly selects those persons with the most compatible medical characteristics from a list averaging about 1800 possible recipients. The computer picks out a number of names, but the physician in charge of the transplant operation makes the final selection of the recipient.

The list of possible recipients and their medical data is kept on magnetic tape in a direct access file of a UNIVAC 1108 computer system owned by Air France and sited at the airline's computer center at Valbonne, southern France. This file can be accessed by physicians on a round-the-clock basis.

The computerized transplant service is managed by Association France-Transplant, headquartered at the Saint-Louis Hospital, Paris. Air France provides its computer services to the Association.

Twenty-six medical/surgical teams throughout France and in Switzerland, Holland and Spain use teletypewriter terminals to communicate directly with the 1108 system in Valbonne and with each other.

Upon receiving the characteristics of the donor kidney, the computer searches its file and responds with a list of coded information giving data on persons with the same or very similar compatibility features.

The information lists the person's name, his country, city, sex, date of birth and transplantation team. The essential medical data includes blood group, graft urgency, Human Leucocyte Antigens (HLA, individual identifying cell markers used as compatibility identifiers), the existence of preformed antibodies, dialysis schedule, any temporary incompatibilities and emergency data. Another consideration is the priority factor—how long has the person been on the waiting list for a kidney transplant? The minimum risk is entailed in the transplant operation when both the donor and recipient's HLA is identical.

The list of recipients is updated daily through the teletypewriter network using a program known as RITREC. Currently, about 500 kidney transplants are performed yearly in France, with most of the recipients selected through the Association. On an average day the UNIVAC 1108 computer processes from two to four inquiries concerning recipients. The success rate on renal transplants in France is currently running about 60%.

Association France-Transplant was created in 1969 to coordinate the work of the various medical/surgical teams performing kidney transplant work in France, as well as with other European organizations engaged in similar activities. Other European groups include UK Transplant (in the United Kingdom), Eurotransplant (in Belgium, Holland and Luxembourg) and Scanditransplant (the Scandinavian countries—Sweden, Norway, Denmark and Finland).

Another version of the RITRAN program keeps on file a choice of blood donors compatible for persons who may need transfusions of special types of blood cells, such as leucocytes, which help maintain immunity to infections, and platelets, which function during blood clotting.

Source: Courtesy of Sperry Univac Division of Sperry Corporation, Blue Hill, Pa.

computer-controlled mannequin used by resident doctors at the University of Southern California to develop their skills in anesthesiology. Sim One has a heartbeat, pulse, blood pressure, and a breathing action; its eyes open and close, and the pupils dilate and constrict; its jaw opens and closes; and its muscles twitch and flutter. These computer-controlled human reactions are used to simulate various conditions and emergencies that the student doctors may expect to encounter with real patients. An incorrect decision during a simulation can lead to the death of poor Sim One. If a student makes a mistake, the computer may flash a warning light. At the end of a training session, the computer prepares a printed critique of the student's efforts. The value of computer simulation in sharpening the skills and decision-making abilities of doctors has been demonstrated at USC.

Other physiological simulation systems include the MUMPS system at Massachusetts General Hospital and the system at the Royal College of Physicians and Surgeons of Canada. Each of these systems supplies student doctors with the symptoms of patients admitted to a hypothetical emergency ward. The student must make quick decisions; the computer responds as the patient would, and/or it reports the results of lab tests ordered by the student. Finally, a CASE (Computer-Aided Simulation of the clinical Encounter) system is used by the American Board of Internal Medicine to assess the clinical competence of practicing Board-certified internists. An internist takes three CASEs involving representative patients, and these CASEs are used in evaluating the internist's skills, knowledge, and clinical judgment.[3]

Menu Planning

Hospital dietitians are using computers to plan patient meals. At Georgia's Central State Hospital, for example, a computer-assisted menu-

---

[3] For more information on this and other simulation systems, see Robert G. Votaw and Barbara B. Farquhar, "Current Trends in Computer-based Education in Medicine," *Educational Technology*, pp. 54–56, April 1978.

planning system is in operation. Menu items are now repeated less often, thereby giving patients greater variety in the foods they receive. The computer analyzes nutrient values of foods, prepares menus for 90-day time periods, and supplies day-by-day food requirements to purchasers in advance of needs (thus permitting the more efficient shopping that has helped cut food costs by 5 percent). Dietitians are able to modify the 90-day menu plan to take advantage of favorable food-buying opportunities. A nutritional analysis is run at the end of a 90-day period to verify that all meals met nutritional specifications and to provide information that could lead to better future planning. At University Hospitals of Cleveland, where 150 recipes are used to cook 7,500 meals per day, a computer prepares printouts that are needed by cooks, controls inventories of ingredients, and saves the hospital an estimated $325,000 for food and $500,000 for labor.[4]

HEALTH CONTROL

Control of (1) *the physiological status of patients,* (2) *blood bank inventories,* (3) *the dispensing of drugs in hospitals,* and (4) *laboratory tests* are among the many applications of computers in medicine.

Physiological Monitoring

Several real time computer systems are being used for patient monitoring. For example, patients who are critically ill, those who have just had major surgery, and those who have recently suffered heart attacks can be connected to computer-monitored sensing devices capable of immediately detecting dangerously abnormal conditions. If necessary, the system would, of course, flash a warning signal to doctors and nurses. Such body functions as heartbeat, blood pressure, respiratory rate, and temperature may be monitored. At the Pacific Medical Center in San Francisco, the body functions of patients in the cardiopulmonary intensive care unit are *continuously* checked; at Los Angeles County Hospital, patients suffering from circulatory shock are monitored about once every five minutes.

Blood Bank Inventory Control

A blood bank must meet the requests made upon it for blood, while at the same time it must minimize waste of this very important medical resource. Demands for whole blood are unpredictable, but it cannot be stockpiled in large quantities because of a 21-day shelf life. Supplies of

---

[4] See "What's for Supper Tonight? Ask the Computer," *Data Processor,* p. 24, February 1979. For a description of a menu-planning system, see Nan Unklesbay and Kenneth Unklesbay, "An Automated System for Planning Menus for the Elderly in Title VII Nutrition Programs," *Food Technology,* pp. 80–83, August 1978.

FIGURE 14-3
(*Right*) Computerized diagnosis of heart disease at Tokyo University. (*P. Koch, Photo Researchers.*) (*Below*) Most hospitals now have computerized filing systems. (*Jan Lucas, Photo Researchers.*) (*Opposite above*) Medical secretary uses computer to update patient's records. (*Guy Gillette, Photo Researchers.*) (*Opposite below*) Nuclear medicine technologists use computerized equipment to scan bones and organs without x-ray. (*Bruce Roberts, Photo Researchers.*)

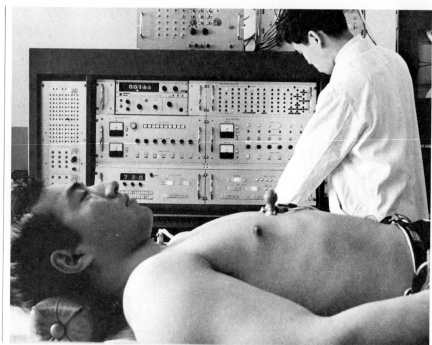

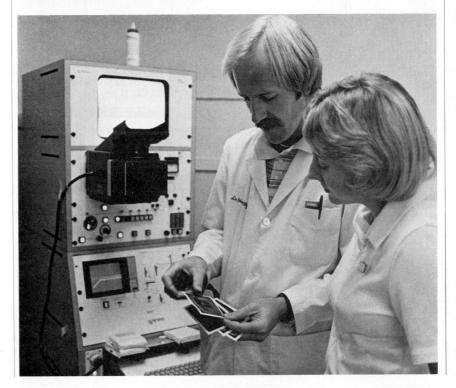

blood received from donors are also unpredictable. The blood type demanded by patients and supplied by donors is subject to variation. Determining proper inventories of blood to maintain at the bank and at hospitals is difficult, as is determining the needed ratio of whole blood to blood components. At the Milwaukee Blood Center, an average of 175 units per day is collected, a daily inventory of 1,500 units of whole blood and blood components is maintained, and about 1,000 clerical transactions are performed at the bank each day—e.g., adding to and subtracting from the inventory, shipping blood to hospitals, converting whole blood into blood components, etc. A computer system may be used to (1) handle these transactions, (2) help control blood management, and (3) speed the right blood to the right person at the right time.

In addition to helping control inventories of whole blood, computer technology is also being applied in continuous-flow devices (Figure 14-4) that remove blood from a donor's arm, separate out the needed constituents, and return the remaining blood components to the donor's other arm. Only a small amount of blood is outside the donor's body at any time, and the donor's body regenerates the extracted components in a very short period.

Hospital Drug Control

Since the creation (in 1971) of the Federal Bureau of Narcotics and Dangerous Drugs, hospitals have been required to maintain records on more than 300 drugs in order to comply with tougher federal drug-control laws. (This control requirement tripled the number of drugs on which records had to be kept.) Because hospital personnel may dispense thousands of doses of medication to patients each day, the task of maintaining pharmacy records is substantial. Furthermore, time spent by nurses in filling out forms is time taken away from that which they can spend treating patients. Seven hospitals of the Franciscan Sisters of the Poor located in Ohio, Kentucky, and Kansas have joined together to develop a drug-reporting system to provide better control over the narcotic items dispensed. Each hospital has a data station linked directly to the central computer in Cincinnati. All information about patient medication is relayed to the computer for processing. Summary reports, including those required to comply with narcotic-control laws, are prepared by the computer and sent back to the participating hospital. This system has reduced the paperwork load on nurses and has given better control information to local pharmacies. Other hospitals—e.g., Cleveland Metropolitan General Hospital and the Jackson-Madison County Hospital in Jackson, Tennessee—make use of computer programs that can signal to pharmacists whether newly prescribed drugs will be likely to react adversely with other medications the patient may be receiving, or whether the new drugs are likely to cause an allergic reaction. If not challenged by the system, the prescription is filled and the computer prints out the label to be affixed to it.

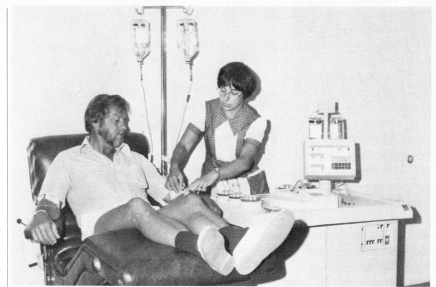

FIGURE 14-4
A blood cell separator used to remove needed blood constituents from a donor's blood. (*IBM Corp.*)

Control of Laboratory Tests

Some of the more successful applications of computers in hospitals are found in the laboratory. Computer processing of data related to test ordering, specimen identification, and test result reporting is now common. (As we saw earlier in the chapter, multiphasic screening centers employ computers to control test procedures and report results.) From the doctor's initial request for a test to the printing of test results, a computer may be used to monitor each step in the process (Figure 14-5). Automated testing may lead to greater accuracy and faster reporting of findings. Also, the information reported may be in a more useful format—e.g., abnormal results may be emphasized for special attention and compared with normally expected readings for those in the patient's age and sex category.

One example of a computer-controlled laboratory program is IBM's Clinical Laboratory Data Acquisition System, which enables hospitals to link dozens of lab instruments directly to a computer for automatic monitoring and reporting of test results. The system may, for example, collect, analyze, and verify data extracted from blood specimens by an automatic blood-testing device. At the same time, it can monitor the operation of the device to make sure that it is calibrated correctly and working properly. At the end of each test run, the computer prints the results for the patient's physician, for lab records, for administrative reports, and for patient-billing purposes. In addition to providing information that is accurate and more timely, the system also reduces the time that technicians must spend on paperwork and instrument checking. Other organizations such as Digital Equipment Corporation and Honeywell Information Systems have similar laboratory programs available.

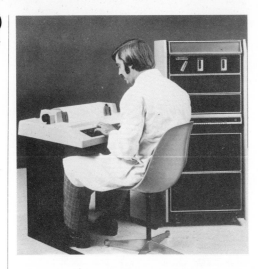

FIGURE 14-5
Programmable data logger
that collects, records, and
processes data from laboratory instruments. (*Digital
Equipment Corp.*)

INFORMATION RETRIEVAL SYSTEMS

The subject of information retrieval for health purposes may be considered from at least two viewpoints. *First,* there is the need for retrieval of
information about patients; *second,* there is the doctor's need to have
quick access to those portions of the rapidly expanding store of medical
information which are needed.

A few pages earlier we briefly considered the subject of retrieval of
patient information, and so we need not spend much time here on the
subject. It should be noted, however, that efforts are being made by a
number of hospitals to prepare and maintain patient records in a direct-
access retrieval system from the moment the patient is admitted. A hospital retrieval system might operate in the following way: (1) A doctor,
nurse, or other authorized user who wishes to make an inquiry about a
patient may activate the system through an online terminal (Figure 14-6),
(2) a CRT or typewriter terminal may be used at the station to display or
print one or more indexes of the types of information available, and the
user selects the appropriate type—e.g., test results, medication administered, etc.—through the use of a keyboard or light pen, and (3) assuming
that the history of "medication administered" is the information being
sought, the user may type in the patient's name or medical record number, and the medication history will then be displayed. Of course, users
can also update patient records from the inquiry stations. And when patients are being discharged, their complete records will be available for
billing purposes.

There are over 5,000 medical and health-related periodicals being
published each month. Physicians cannot be expected to regularly read
more than a few of these journals, but in ignoring the others they are undoubtedly missing information that would be of value to them in their

practice and/or their research. To help alert doctors to articles that would be of interest to them the National Library of Medicine in Washington has developed MEDLARS (Medical Literature Analysis and Retrieval System). References to over 1 million articles are stored in MEDLARS; input comes from about 2,500 periodicals, including 1,000 non-English journals; and the average article is cross-classified (or indexed) in nearly a dozen standardized ways according to its content. In addition to producing *Index Medicus,* a monthly report that includes references on newly indexed articles, MEDLARS also provides a search service to authorized users. A search request may be phoned to one of the 12 MEDLARS regional centers. A MEDLARS computer center (there is more than one) then processes the request. An online retrieval service has also been developed to improve responsiveness. MEDLARS is now online in medical centers around the country.

HOSPITAL INFORMATION SYSTEMS

What is a hospital information system (HIS)? There seems to be no single definition that authorities in medicine, hospital administration, and information processing can agree upon. To some the words imply a *total information system* encompassing the entire informational needs of all hospital personnel; to others, they refer only to computer-based billing and accounting operations associated with hospital administration; and to still others, a HIS is defined to be merely all the applications that are being processed on the computer at their particular hospital. For our purposes, a *HIS* may be defined as the processing procedures developed in a hospital and integrated as necessary for the purpose of providing physicians and hospital personnel with timely and effective information.

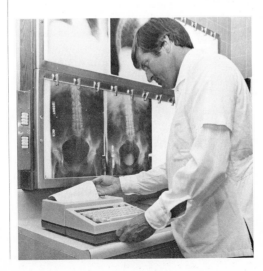

FIGURE 14-6
Patient data provided to on-line terminal user. (*NCR Corp.*)

FIGURE 14-7
Small hospital computer
system. (*IBM Corp.*)

The extent to which systems integration is needed varies, of course, from one hospital to another. Some of the elements that have been included in the computer-based information systems of hospitals are listed below. (Few hospitals have extensive applications in *all* these areas.)

1 *Clerical and accounting elements.* As noted at the beginning of the chapter, computers were first introduced into hospitals to perform accounting and record-keeping operations. Accumulating patient charges, keeping track of health insurance coverages, ordering and then controlling supplies and medicines, preparing patient bills, accounting and paying for services and supplies purchased, preparing personnel payrolls—these are but a few of the business-type applications that a hospital must process. And equipment is now available to support comprehensive financial management systems for smaller hospitals (Figure 14-7).

2 *Information retrieval elements.* Discussions of some information retrieval applications have been presented in earlier pages.

3 *Scheduling elements.* Computers are being used to schedule (a) appointments of patients in outpatient clinics, (b) the performance of tasks by service departments, and (c) the use of specialized hospital facilities and equipment.

4 *Medical planning, research, and control elements.* Many of these computer applications have been described in earlier pages. Control of laboratory tests represents the most popular current type of computer application in the planning, research, and control category.

5 *Peer review elements.* Federal government regulations that went into effect early in 1975 created Professional Standards Review organizations (PSROs) at the local levels to conduct peer reviews—i.e., to review such things as admissions (is the patient in the right place to re-

"Blind Benefit from Reading Machine"

"The Kurzweil Reading Machine is the greatest breakthrough for the blind since Braille was developed," Harold Snyder, president of ACCESS for the Handicapped, Inc., said. Introduced in 1975, the Kurzweil Reading Machine (KRM) and the new desk top KRM model are able to convert books, magazines, reports and letters into spoken English in a matter of seconds and currently are being used in both educational and office settings. The reading machine greatly increases the employability of blind and visually-impaired adults and gives them immediate access to most types of printed material.

Snyder received his KRM on loan from Kurzweil Computer Products, Inc. while he was coordinator for handicapped programs at the Smithsonian National Air and Space Museum in Washington, D.C. When he left NASM in November, 1978, the museum had no use for the KRM, and Synder brought it to his non-profit company.

At ACCESS, he uses his KRM to demonstrate the machine's capabilities to his clients, who are interested in hiring more blind or visually-impaired people. Snyder himself reads about 80 percent of his documents and 90 percent of his correspondence with the KRM and uses the device to teach blind children from the D.C. schools.

The reading machine should be viewed as only one of many reading tools that blind people must know, however, he stressed. "They still must be able to read and write Braille effectively. Simply listening to the KRM is only a passive activity," Snyder said. "The blind must learn to use the readers effectively to scan reading materials, for instance, to pick out lead sentences of paragraphs or to read chapter summaries." The KRM cannot read newsprint, carbon copies or photocopies nor can it interpret graphic diagrams and charts.

Another user, Kay Chase, works in the Department of Health, Education and Welfare's Office of Education as an educational programs specialist and projects officer and said she would have to hire a full-time reader to help her read all the grants and other materials in her job if she didn't have a KRM.

"I used to use an optacon which only reads 100-110 words per minute compared to the KRM which can read 150 words and the desk top model which can read 250-300 words per minute," Chase stated. "The greatest advantage of the KRM is its convenience—I can read almost anything I want as fast as I can."

Snyder believes private industry will be encouraged to purchase KRM for their offices through the available tax incentives for reasonable research and development of the KRM, and several government agencies besides HEW have KRMs in their offices, including the Veteran's Administration, the

Justice Department and the Rehabilitation Services Administration, Chase said.

The KRM consists of a custom-designed computer, an optical character recognition system (OCR), a natural voice synthesizer, a "talking" keyboard and a speaker to amplify the spoken messages. An updated desk top model has additional features, according to the manufacturer. These features include a more compact size; a speech rate faster than human speech; a hand tracking option that enables the user to scan a page and read the material more selectively; improved human speech quality; a "talking" calculator that can perform trigonometric, logarithmic and exponential functions; and special interfaces that allow the KRM to convert English text from a computer or CRT terminal into speech.

A hardware-software attachment is currently being developed under contract with the Library of Congress which will automatically translate printed material into Braille, Kurzweil said.

After a few hours of training, a blind person can read almost any type of printed material. The user places the material to be read face down on the glass surface of the scanner, the company explained. The OCR system then scans the printed page and transmits the image in electronic form to an image enhancement system. This system increases the contrast of the printed material and brings out particular features that improve the recognition process.

A contrast circuit allows the desk top KRM to read a wider variety of combinations of paper and ink, Kurzweil said.

Once the enhanced image is in digital form, the computer in the reading device is programmed to separate the image into character forms, recognize the letters on the page, group the letters into words, and compute the pronunciation of each word.

The computer's memory stores over a thousand linguistic rules plus 1,500 exceptions to those rules and then correctly pronounces each word. In addition, the system can compute and deliver appropriate inflections in pronunciation, the firm said.

Users have a variety of controls on the accompanying "talking" keyboard that permit them to determine how the material should be read. They can speed up or slow down the rate of reading, adjust the tone of the voice from high to low, and change the volume.

Other controls enable users to instruct the machine to repeal the previous few lines, spell out words, enunciate punctuation, indicate capitalization, and mark certain words or phrases for later reference.

The development of the omni-font OCR system provided the major breakthrough in reading machines in late 1974. Previously only limited-font OCR machines existed and these devices would only recognize as few as one or

as many as 20 styles of type. They were also restricted to materials of high printing quality, a spokesman for Kurzweil said. The omni-font OCR system is able to read the approximately 300 type fonts in common use, and also handle such print aberrations as broken type, connected letters or smudges on the page.

Source: Lillian M. O'Connell, "Blind Benefit from Reading Machine," *Information World*, p. 5, May 1979. Reprinted by permission.

ceive the needed care?), bed utilization (did the patient spend an appropriate time in the hospital?), and care (did the patient get tests that were not needed, or was there a failure to administer needed tests?). The creation of PSROs has forced hospitals to use computers to provide the peer review data just as the passage of Medicare legislation forced most hospitals to use computers or computer services for financial management processing.

▶ LOOKING BACK

The following points have been emphasized in this chapter:

1   The purpose of this chapter has been to outline a few of the rapidly increasing uses of computers in health fields. In the area of medical planning and decision making, for example, computers are now being used to assist doctors in diagnosing illnesses, and computer-assisted research is providing new insights into the way the body functions and into the causes and cures of disease.

2   By placing the medical history of a patient in a data bank, one or more doctors can retrieve and update it as needed. Better information about a patient's medical background should enable doctors to do a more effective job of preventing potential health problems and detecting illnesses.

3   Studies of drug addiction and drug side effects are being facilitated through computer usage, computer simulation is sharpening the skills and decision-making abilities of student (and practicing) doctors, and hospital menus are being planned with the help of machines.

4   Control of (1) the physiological status of patients, (2) blood bank inventories, (3) hospital narcotic dispensing, and (4) laboratory tests are also important medical applications of computers.

5   To help alert doctors and other health care professionals to documents that may be of interest to them, the National Library of Medicine has developed the MEDLARS retrieval system.

6   New hospital information systems that are quicker responding and broader in scope are being developed by hospitals around the nation.

After reading Chapter 14, you should be able to define and use the following terms:

multiphasic screening center	patient medical history
INTERNIST	CASE
clinical algorithm (protocol)	Sim One
CAT scanner	MEDLARS
computer-assisted diagnostic	HIS
techniques	PSRO
physiological simulation	

◆ REVIEW AND DISCUSSION QUESTIONS

1   Why is there an accelerating use of computers in health fields?
2   "Some physicians are now using the computer as a diagnostic tool in hospitals and clinics." Discuss this statement.
3   How can a computer be of value in physical examinations?
4   What benefits are being derived from computer-assisted research in medicine?
5   (a) How can a computer be used to take a medical history? (b) Would there be any advantages to a medical record data bank? (c) Would there be any possible disadvantages to such a data bank?
6   How can a computer assist in the study of drug side effects?
7   (a) What is Sim One? (b) What is Sim One used for?
8   (a) How can a computer be used for physiological monitoring? (b) For blood bank inventory control?
9   Discuss the use of computers in controlling laboratory tests.
10   "The subject of information retrieval for health purposes may be considered from at least two viewpoints." Identify and discuss these two viewpoints.
11   What types of applications may be included in a HIS?
12   In the 1970s, physicians found that the radiation therapy used to treat certain thyroid diseases in the 1950s actually caused thyroid tumors to occur at a later time in a patient's life. Similarly, high doses of Diethylstilbesterol were later found to produce uterine tumors. (a) How could a computerized medical record retrieval system be of help in these cases? (b) Do the possible advantages of such a retrieval system outweigh the potential dangers?

◆ SELECTED REFERENCES

In addition to the references suggested in the chapter footnotes, you might wish to examine the following sources:

Groner, G. F., et al.: *Applications of Computers in Health Care Delivery: An Overview and Research Agenda,* The Rand Corporation, Santa Monica, Calif., 1974.

Hansen, James V.: "Progress in Health Care Systems," *Journal of Systems Management,* pp. 14–21, April 1975.

Lublin, Joann S.: "Controlling a Killer: Solid Gains Are Shown in Preventing Strokes and Treating Victims," *The Wall Street Journal,* pp. 1ff, July 18, 1979.

Shapiro, Howard M.: "Computers in Medicine: Chaos ex Machina?" *Computer Decisions,* pp. 23ff, July 1977.

Chapter 15
COMPUTERS IN EDUCATION

The purpose of this chapter is to outline a few of the ways in which computers can be used as tools in the educational process.

In the first section of the chapter, you will see how computers are being utilized in *educational planning and decision making.* For example, ways in which computers can be used to manage individualized instruction programs are discussed.

The second section of the chapter deals with the ways computers are being used to *control* educational applications such as testing and error analysis. In the third section you will be introduced to the approaches used in *computer-assisted instruction* (CAI). Some CAI applications as well as a listing of the advantages and problems of CAI are considered.

Finally, a section on the use of *simulation* as a teaching aid is presented.

Thus, after studying this chapter, you should be able to:

- Give a few examples of how computers are used in educational planning and decision making.

- Explain how computers are used in planning for individual instruction.

- Discuss how computers may be used for student testing purposes and for the analysis of student responses to test questions.

- Identify the approaches used in CAI, give a few examples of CAI applications, and outline some of the advantages and problems associated with this educational technique.

- Describe how simulation may be used as a teaching aid.

- Understand and use the key terms listed at the end of the chapter.

I t is possible to consider the subject of computers in education in at least two ways. *First,* computer hardware and software can be considered as *subjects for study.* Most colleges now offer courses in computer programming, and a number of institutions of higher education offer undergraduate and graduate degrees in computer science. Also, vocational training in computer programming and computer operation is being offered by some of the nation's high schools. Since we have already studied computer hardware and software topics in Chapters 3 through 8, we will not concern ourselves here with these subjects. Rather, *our objective in this chapter* is to view the computer in a *second way*—i.e., as a *tool to be used in the educational process.*

Computers can bring to the educational process such attributes as untiring patience, around-the-clock availability, and individualized and student-paced instruction programs. Thus, the future of computers in the educational process is assured. However, progress to date in applying computers in the instructional process has been relatively slow. Such factors as (1) the lack of knowledge about the learning process, (2) the inadequacy (and/or the cost) of past hardware/software educational packages, and (3) the resistance to change in many school systems have accounted for the comparatively slow development of instructional applications. But the hardware/software and resistance constraints may become much less severe in the near future as low-cost microcomputer systems developed specifically for educational use gain wider acceptance, and as innovative teachers and administrators overcome resistance.

A primary purpose of using computers as an instructional tool in the classroom should be to *provide insight* and not merely compute numbers or process documents. In other words, "An ounce of insight remains worth a ton of processing. That we can type faster than he could pen, offers no assurance that we will write better plays than Shakespeare."[1] And, it might be paraphrased, the fact that a high school student with a computer can solve equations faster today than Einstein could earlier in this century certainly does not mean that the student could formulate the theory of relativity. Fortunately, computer usage in the classroom *can* lead to improved student performance in thinking logically, formulating problem solution procedures, and understanding relationships. As you know from your own program preparation experiences, a thorough understanding of a problem is needed before a program can be written for a computer solution. By having to approach problems in a logical and systematic way (and by being motivated to do this by the chance to use a computer), a student is likely to receive valuable learning experiences.

Computers may be used in education for (1) *planning and decision making,* (2) *control,* (3) *computer-assisted instruction,* and (4) *simulation.* Let us look at applications in each of these categories.

PLANNING AND DECISION MAKING IN EDUCATION

Curriculum Planning

Research is being conducted into ways of using computers for curriculum planning. It is reasoned that if college students, for example, are given aptitude, interest, and achievement tests when they enter a school, it should then be possible to use this information to develop two- to four-year plans for the courses and number of sections needed to satisfy student goals. (Such plans, of course, would have a direct bearing on staffing needs and on the physical facilities required.) Researchers would, in effect, produce a plan that would be based on explicitly set and objectively

---

[1] Murray Laver, "User Influence on Computer Systems Design," *Datamation,* p. 116, October 1969.

measured educational goals of students. A thorough analysis of the concepts and tasks that would have to be measured in order to satisfy those goals would be required, and students would be expected to follow a specified educational path.

Although impressive efforts have been made by researchers in the area of curriculum planning, their progress thus far has not been great. It is not surprising that this is the case. After all, some fields of study may not lend themselves to neatly programmed paths leading to clearly specified goals; some students may stray from the "ideal" path as they realize that their interests have changed; and a great deal more must be discovered about learning processes before effective predetermined curriculum plans and controls will be accepted by most educators.

Planning for Individual Instruction

Operating on the reasonable assumptions that (1) individual differences exist between students (interests, goals, learning abilities, etc.) and (2) programs tailored to the needs of individuals are educationally more effective than those aimed at "average" groups of students, some educational institutions are seeking to plan and implement more individualized programs of instruction. Up to now, individualized instruction programs have been used primarily with gifted or handicapped students, and separate facilities and special teachers have often been employed. But similar programs for students who do not fall into these categories are not yet widely used. As one educational researcher wrote a few years ago:

> Attempts at individualization in conventional classroom environments by the most imaginative of teachers is likely to lead to at best modest success and at worst nervous frustration. The major difficulty in such an undertaking . . . is the management of instruction for large numbers of students with widely varying competencies and needs.[2]

But the computer is a tool that may now permit teachers in conventional classroom settings to manage individual instruction programs. *Computer-managed instruction* (CMI) is a name sometimes given to this use of the machines. A properly programmed computer may help teachers to (1) manage a student's schedule of activities as the student progresses through a program of instruction, (2) periodically test the student's mastery of the material presented, and (3) determine an appropriate tutoring plan for students who are having difficulty with some phase of the program.[3] Educational research centers at such schools as the University of Pittsburgh and Florida State University are working on

[2] Richard L. Ferguson, "Computer Assistance for Individualizing Instruction," *Computers and Automation,* p. 27, March 1970.

[3] Remedial tutoring is one use for computer-assisted instruction. We will discuss other uses in a later section.

FIGURE 15-1
(*Right*) Science students use computer to analyze experimental data. (*George Whiteley, Photo Researchers.*) (*Below*) Data Processing Center at the University of Florida is used by various departments for processing research. (*Van Bucher, Photo Researchers.*) (*Opposite above*) Stanford University graduate students conducting experiments in the behavioral neurophysiology lab. (*Van Bucher, Photo Researchers.*) (*Opposite below*) Sociologist uses computer to analyze data from a research project. (*Ray Ellis, Photo Researchers.*)

FIGURE 15-2
A sales training encounter with the PLATO system. (*Control Data Corp.*)

CMI projects.[4] At one elementary school participating in a University of Pittsburgh project, a computer is being used to make required day-to-day instructional plans and decisions. In the science curriculum, for example, a student may specify a particular subject he or she wishes to study. The computer may then be used to evaluate the student's background in order to determine any needed prerequisite lessons prior to beginning the study of the specified topic. Control Data Corporation's PLATO system has extensive capabilities for implementing CMI in an industrial training setting as well as in public and private academic institutions. Sales training courses, for example, are given to salespersons in this country (Figure 15-2), and businesses in South Africa are using PLATO computer-based education programs to provide needed in-house training for their employees (Figure 15-3).

There have been some charges that using computers in the educational process will "dehumanize" instruction and make robots of students. There might be some validity to these charges if all students were required to spend the day in front of a computer terminal going through the same exercises and if the only or main source of curriculum content consisted of what a few educational programmers selected to put into the machines. Advocates of CMI maintain, however, that the computer is simply a supporting tool that relieves teachers of unnecessary tasks and

[4] For more information on CMI, and for additional application examples, see the following sources: Kenneth L. Bowles, "Microcomputer-based Mass Education," *Journal of Personalized Instruction,* pp. 151–156, Fall 1978; Philip R. Christensen, "Computer-assisted Test Construction for Individualized Instruction," *Educational Technology,* pp. 45–49, March 1979; Sally Valente Kiester, "It's Student and Computer, One on One," *Personal Computing,* pp. 67ff, March 1978; H. S. Pennypacker, "The Computer as a Management Tool in Systems of Personalized Instruction," *Journal of Personalized Instruction,* pp. 147–150, Fall 1978; and Fred L. Splittgerber, "Computer-based Instruction: A Revolution in the Making?" *Educational Technology,* pp. 20–25, January 1979.

helps them individualize instruction. They point out that students can progress through the curriculum materials at their own pace and can skip certain elements if their educational backgrounds make this possible. How, they argue, can a more flexible curriculum be objectionable? Besides, they contend, most students would prefer attention from a machine to neglect from an overworked teacher. And how many times, they ask, have you, as a student, really been helped in a remedial or tutorial way by overworked teachers? Skeptics about the use of computers in the classroom maintain, however, that the high cost of preparing computer-based instructional programs is bound to result in the use of prepared materials for much longer periods of time and at numerous schools. Thus, they maintain, materials are more likely to become obsolete, curriculum standardization is probably inevitable, and the autonomy of local schools will suffer. These arguments serve at least to illustrate one noncontroversial point: In education, as in other fields, computer usage may threaten to sweep aside current practices, may introduce new problems, and may create resistance to change.

Before concluding this section, one other noncontroversial topic should be mentioned—the use of computers to aid educationally handicapped children. Children of migrant farm workers, for example, are constantly being shifted from one school to another. By the time a child's records find their way to one school, the child may have moved to another. To make it possible for teachers to better understand the needs of these students and plan programs that meet student needs, the National Migrant Student Record Transfer System, a data bank run by the Arkansas Department of Education, can be used for rapid storage and retrieval of the records of over 1 million students. (A student's record can be retrieved and forwarded quickly to any of the more than 16,000 schools in 47 states and Puerto Rico that are linked with the computer at Little Rock.) Also, computers are being used in Atlanta to convert standard

FIGURE 15-3
A PLATO training session for employees in South Africa.
(*Control Data Corp.*)

FIGURE 15-4
Computers convert printed
materials into braille for use
by blind students. (*IBM Corp.*)

printed materials into braille copies for use by blind students (Figure 15-4).

Class Scheduling

Computers are speeding up the scheduling of classes every term in hundreds of schools. Improved class scheduling procedures may make it possible for school administrators to make better plans and decisions about the use of such resources as teachers, textbooks, and classroom space. Purdue University was one of the first institutions to experiment with using computers to fit thousands of students into hundreds of classes. The Purdue system now handles the scheduling of over 20,000 students with a few hours of computer time, and it produces an assortment of class lists, enrollment reports, and other byproducts. Many other universities (such as Rhode Island, Massachusetts, MIT, Illinois, and Notre Dame) and public school systems (such as the Palo Alto, California, unified school district) also have computerized class scheduling.

Athletic Planning

Borrowing from the techniques employed by professional football teams, some colleges are now using computers to analyze the teams of rival schools. By determining an opponent's offensive and defensive tendencies, a coach can prepare a "game plan" in the hope that it will contain the opposition and permit his own offense to exploit defensive weaknesses. To illustrate, the Kent State University team receives a computer analysis (Figure 15-5) that lists all the formations previously used by an opponent, the total attempts of each formation, the percentage of time a formation has been used, the number of running and passing plays attempted, and the types of runs and passes. The computer also gives an analysis of an opponent's tendencies in certain down and distance situations. Computers are also being used to (1) schedule, score, and administer rodeo events sponsored by the Western colleges that belong to the National Intercollegiate Rodeo Association,[5] and (2) profile the strengths and weaknesses of United States Olympic athletes so that coaches can plan ways to improve their performance.

CONTROL IN EDUCATION

Two control applications of computers in education are found in the areas of *testing* and *error analysis*.

[5] See Joel Shechter, "Computers on the College Rodeo Circuit," *Computer,* pp. 58–59ff, February 1978.

FIGURE 15-5
Colleges use computers to analyze the teams of rival schools. (*Burroughs Corp.*)

Probably the most common *testing* application is the use of computers to score objective tests that students have answered on sheets which they mark with a special pencil. Computed measures such as arithmetic means and standard deviations can be used by teachers to compare class performance against norms or standards—a necessary step in educational control. In another area of testing—interactive computer-assisted testing—student progress can be determined quickly, students can get immediate feedback of their successes and mistakes, instructors can be relieved from having to grade the tests, and control information can be supplied to teachers, indicating activities where student performance is not up to expectations. To illustrate, at Dartmouth College randomized vocabulary tests in Latin may be taken by students. Sitting at an online terminal, students select the Latin lesson or lessons they wish to be checked on. The computer program may randomly select Latin words from the indicated lesson, and the students must then respond with the English meanings. If the students miss on the first try, they are given one more chance before the correct response is supplied; if they have no idea what the correct response should be, they can type a question mark and the proper word will be presented. Of course, the computer is keeping track of the students' success (or lack of success) during the exercise. Because the Latin words are selected randomly from a lesson, it is not likely that students would ever get the same list of words twice. (You will remember that a similar interactive computer-assisted program for testing multiplication skills was written by Maude Crabbie back in Chapter 8.)

The stored results of computer-assisted testing may also be used for *error-analysis purposes*. The types of errors being made by students during testing can be analyzed, and suggestions for eliminating detected deficiencies may be supplied to the student and/or the teacher at the end of the session. Error analysis by computer can also be accomplished without the use of online interaction. For example, at the University of Minnesota in Duluth, medical students answer test questions by making marks on an answer sheet. The answer sheets are then fed into the compact test-scoring device shown in the foreground of Figure 15-6a. The scanned student answer data are then transmitted via telephone lines to a university computer. Within an hour or so after taking an exam, students know how they scored on the test, which questions they missed and why they missed them, and how they compared with other students taking the test. At the same time, the instructor receives a complete analysis of the test (Figure 15-6b) that helps spot strengths and weaknesses in student performance and in the individual questions constituting the exam. This feedback, of course, helps the faculty improve test strategy and methodology. Additional error-analysis procedures can be performed at a terminal located near the test scorer (Figure 15-6c).

COMPUTER-ASSISTED INSTRUCTION

What is *computer-assisted instruction* (CAI)? As is so often the case when coming to grips with computer-related terminology, one can find different definitions advanced by different authorities. In some definitions, the distinction between computer-managed instruction and CAI becomes blurred. In this text we refer to the former (CMI) as primarily an exchange of information between *teachers* and computers, while the latter phrase (CAI) is used to refer to situations where *students* and computers interact and where instruction takes place. As we saw earlier in the chapter, a CMI program may indicate to a teacher that a child needs remedial tutoring, and this makeup work may be completed using CAI, but the two phrases should not be confused. In short, then, we are using *CAI* to refer to a learning situation in which the student interacts with (and is guided by) a computer through a course of study aimed at achieving certain instructional goals.

In a typical CAI setting, the student sits at an online device (usually either a typewriter terminal or a visual display) and communicates with the program in the CPU (Figure 15-7). Interaction may take place in the following way: (1) The computer presents instructional information and questions, (2) the student studies the information or instructions presented, answers the questions, and, perhaps, asks questions of his or her own, and (3) the computer then accepts, analyzes, and provides immediate feedback to the student's responses, and it maintains records of the student's performance for evaluation purposes. (In short, the interaction is likely to include the elements found in the program Maude Crabbie wrote in Chapter 8.)

FIGURE 15-6
Error-analysis system at the University of Minnesota at Duluth. (*3M Co.*) (*Right*) The answer sheets held by the instructor are read by the text scorer in the foreground, and the data are transmitted to a university computer.

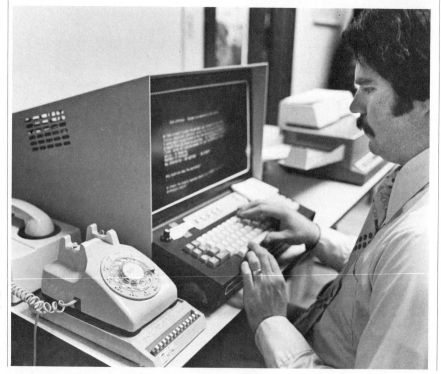

FIGURE 15-6 (Continued)
(*Above*) The computer then supplies the instructor with a detailed statistical analysis of a test and an item analysis of each question. (*Right*) A remote terminal can be used to perform sophisticated test-analysis procedures.

Thus far, most CAI development efforts[6] have been concentrated in three areas—the *drill-and-practice, tutorial,* and *dialogue* areas.

CAI Approaches

The simplest and most used form of CAI is the *drill-and-practice* approach that is designed to complement instruction received from teachers, printed materials, and other noncomputer sources. Student responses are given to factual questions presented by the computer. Learning is facilitated because the computer can quickly supply correct answers as feedback to student mistakes; however, new material is generally not introduced, and the student-computer interaction is highly structured so that little or no deviation from a programmed sequence of steps is allowed. The drill-and-practice approach has been found useful in learning areas such as mathematics, statistics, languages, reading, spelling, etc., where substantial memory work is required.

A second and more complex level of interaction between a student

[6] For a good history of the development of CAI, see Patrick Suppes and Elizabeth Macken, "The Historical Path from Research and Development to Operational Use of CAI," *Educational Technology,* pp. 9–11, April 1978.

FIGURE 15-7
Students at a Huntington Beach, California, high school interacting with a CAI program. (*IBM Corp.*)

"Naval Academy Cited as Academic Computing Model"

Following a National Science Foundation survey of some 7,000 agencies and institutions, the Naval Academy has been selected as an "exemplary" facility in the use of computers and listed among only 21 in the nation to serve as "case studies for academic computing."

The Naval Academy was selected for excellence in such areas as student and faculty use of computers, the variety of computer applications and the volume of available data.

Since 1969, all midshipmen have been required to take courses in the use of computers and in the present school year 100 percent of the midshipmen and about 65 percent of the faculty are involved in computer-related instruction.

A total of 157 courses, about half the total at the Naval Academy, require midshipmen to complete at least one project on a computer. In many others, computers are available as educational tools.

In addition to their educational use, computers are being utilized more and more in administrative areas at the Naval Academy. Student registration is traditionally a hectic time at any college or university. At the Academy this process used to involve over 75 faculty and staff members. In 1972, a mathematics professor worked up a fully-automated student registration system. Since 1975, midshipmen have punched in their own registration twice each school year in a 10-minute process which involves only four staff members.

The Human Resources Research Organization survey was stimulated by a growing national interest among educators in utilization of the computer in academic institutions. The "exemplar" facilities, including the Naval Academy, were selected to help administrators and faculty at other institutions determine the nature and scope of computer facilities that might be best for their use. Additionally, the data is designed to assist federal, state and local planners in deciding whether and what computer use might be "productive for particular educational settings and goals."

Source: "Naval Academy Cited as Academic Computing Model," *Government Data Systems*, p. 6, January–February 1979. Reprinted by permission.

and a CAI computer program is found in the *tutorial* approach. With this approach, the program assists in presenting new material to the student. The intent of the tutorial approach, of course, is to have the computer program approximate the actions of a private (and very patient) tutor working with an individual student. Numerous branching opportunities in the CAI program permit a choice of materials to be presented, depending on how a student responded to the previous question. However, the student-computer interaction is still structured; the sequence in which information is presented is prescribed,[7] and the expected student responses must all be anticipated by the program author. Tutorial CAI programs have been developed by Stanford University researchers for reading and elementary mathematics courses.

At the *dialogue* level of CAI interaction, new material would be presented to the student, and the student would be free to ask questions, request data, and give responses in a relatively unstructured way. The interaction would thus resemble the dialogue occurring between a student and a human tutor. Formidable problems remain to be solved before this type of "ideal" system becomes operational, but researchers are currently working on the problems.

CAI Applications

In addition to those mentioned above, a few other interesting applications of the CAI concept are:

1   The use, at P.S. 106 in New York City, of Leachim, a computer-controlled teaching robot that is programmed to talk directly and personally to fourth-grade pupils. When the teacher suggests that a child work with the robot, a key is turned on, and the child dons a headset and begins taking verbal instructions from the machine. Leachim knows the name, family background, hobbies, and interests of each student; furthermore, depending on the student's responses (which are given by punching buttons corresponding to the alternatives in a multiple-choice question), the robot may compliment and encourage the student or scold him or her for being inattentive. During the course of the student-robot "conversation," maps, diagrams, etc., may be flashed on a nearby screen.[8]

2   Rochester Institute of Technology's use of CAI to help deaf students prepare for technical studies at the college level. The CAI programs are in such areas as mathematics, thermodynamics, biochemistry, and electronics.

3   Pennsylvania State University's use of CAI in its music education program. A display station and audio play-record unit are used. Such aspects of music theory as recognition and classification of intervals and scales, melodic and harmonic dictation, and detection of auralvisual discrepancies in reading scores have been found to be appropriate applications of CAI.

4   Ohio State University's use of CAI to teach an entire course in medical terminology. The instructor functions simply as an educational consul-

[7] Students may follow any one of a number of anticipated paths in the program to a terminal point, but each of these paths has been programmed, and the overall sequence of presentation of material is fixed. Any unexpected (and therefore unprogrammed) answer, of course, cannot be accepted by the computer.

[8] For more information, see Marvin Grosswirth, "Leachim the Teaching Robot," *Datamation,* pp. 64–67, August 1974.

tant and is now able to supervise over 400 students per quarter in the course rather than the previous limit of 60.

5   The University of Illinois's use of the PLATO system at its Champaign-Urbana campus to help teach 150 subjects ranging from physics to Swahili. The PLATO system was developed at Illinois with the help of Control Data Corporation, and it is now being marketed by Control Data Education Corporation. PLATO delivers instructional materials in the form of text, drawings, and animated graphics. Users communicate with the lesson materials through the keyboard or by touching the screen. PLATO terminals are available on a number of other campuses.

6   The University of California at Irvine's Physics Computer Development Project, which enables students to control the timing of their progress through the introductory physics course. Different CAI modes are selected by students, and a management system keeps a record of student progress.

Advantages and Problems of CAI

Some of the *advantages* of CAI are: (1) Individual help is available to a student who might otherwise be ignored in a classroom, (2) by being able to privately move at their own pace, gifted children are not bound, slower students are not rushed, and shy students are not embarrassed by incorrect answers given in public, (3) the computer is impartial, patient, and objective, (4) the teacher is relieved of routine drill-and-practice work and can devote more time to giving students individual attention, and (5) the student gets immediate feedback to answers given, and the teacher gets a report of errors made so that corrective action can be planned.

Despite the actual and potential advantages of CAI, some *problems* remain to be overcome before its promise can be fully realized. Included among these problems are: (1) The cost of hardware—even though it is dropping rapidly—and the cost of acquiring or developing CAI software may exceed the available funds in many school districts, (2) the incentive and personnel to develop appropriate CAI computer programs may not be present in many school systems, (3) the technical difficulties encountered by students—e.g., waiting to access an overloaded system, system "crashes" in the middle of a lesson, communication line problems, etc.—can still occur often enough to cause frustration, and (4) the resistance to change of a large number of educators is caused, in part, by the fact that CAI is relatively new and the extent of its effectiveness has not yet been demonstrated to them.

SIMULATION AS A TEACHING AID

You have already been introduced to the concept of simulation in Chapter 9. Also, you have already seen one example of how computer simulation may be used as a teaching aid. From the last chapter you will recall that a plastic-skinned mannequin (Sim One) is being used to train student doctors in anesthesiology techniques. But teaching simulations do not require physical models. Although it is beyond the scope of this section to attempt a detailed listing of all the ways computer simulations are being used for teaching purposes, a few interesting simulation examples may be described briefly.[9]

1 High school physics students in Lexington, Massachusetts, have written a program that simulates an Apollo moon landing. The object of the program is to have a physics student land the spacecraft safely —an operation requiring the student to apply information that she or he has learned about gravitational effects and Newton's laws of motion. The simulation begins with the spacecraft traveling at a velocity of 3,600 miles per hour and at an altitude of 120 miles above the moon. Every 10 seconds a "radar" check is made and measurements are taken of velocity and remaining fuel. At this time, the student must tell the computer the amount of fuel to use during each of the following 10 seconds. A safe landing requires a touchdown at a speed of a tenth of a mile per hour or less, with an exhausted fuel supply. Most students "crash" on their first landing attempt and must then go back and make calculations to support the decisions they will make on the next attempt. These calculations, of course, reinforce the physics concepts being taught. Similar lunar lander simulation programs are now available for microcomputers at most computer retail stores. In addi-

[9] In these examples, students learn by being placed in a situation where they are expected to make decisions in order to achieve certain goals. They are not lectured to; rather, they gain insights by (1) exploring and manipulating variables in a setting that simulates real-life situations, and (2) assessing the consequences of their own decisions. The computer program may also include a critical analysis of the students' performance during the simulation.

FIGURE 15-8
(Reprinted from *Educational Technology*, September 1973. Reprinted by permission of *Educational Technology*, Englewood Cliffs, N.J.)

"Now, do your best on this lesson, Roland, because the machine is programmed to deal quite severely with wrong answers."

"Computer Days"

Marie K. Stavrides, a third-grade teacher at Branch Brook Elementary School in Smithtown, New York, won the 1978 CIBA-GEIGY Award for Exemplary Elementary Science Teaching, cosponsored by NSTA and CESI. CIBA-GEIGY Corporation, in Ardsley, New York, is an international pharmaceutical firm. Annually, CIBA-GEIGY expresses its interest in education at the elementary school level by sponsoring a $1000 award and an all-expense-paid trip to the NSTA national convention for the winner. Mrs. Stavrides developed "computer literacy" among her students with a project reported below.

I believe the future computerized society so frequently talked about is here now. It's no longer somewhere in the future. Today's use or misuse of the computer will affect the future. Elementary school teachers, children, and parents must be shown that these electronic machines are tools invented by people to aid learning and creation. Teachers have a responsibility to familiarize their students with this technology, making children understand that this complex machine is a useful tool.

A computer has been part of Branch Brook and our mathematics program for two years. It is a Hewlett Packard 2000 and has a teletype terminal; its language is BASIC.

The staff does not do research; rather, the computer is used as a learning aid. There are 156 children, kindergarteners through fifth graders, for instance, who are on the Computer Assisted Instruction program, using the Hewlett Packard Math Drill and Practice Program. The children love working with the computer and are thrilled when they are correct. The computer "knows" each child by ID numbers. Each classroom has an assigned time slot for the week. Children are on all ability levels. They rarely miss their turns. Some children move to math levels two or three years above grade level, which thrills their teachers!

Other children are instructed in computer literacy. Still others play games on the computer, which acquaints them with the machine. The computer then becomes a "friend" rather than something to fear. Children whose classrooms are near the computer room watch to see when it is not being used so they can go in, if only for a short time. Children are taught computer programming. Sequential ordering skills and logical thinking are emphasized; for example, constructing flow charts. Our ultimate goal is to design ways to integrate the computer throughout the curriculum, making it a part of Branch Brook's educational program. We're succeeding—it seems now as though our computer has always been there.

Sessions before and after school are another aspect of our computer program. Any third through fifth grader can attend the after-school sessions. A student receives weekly usage time on a rotating basis. The after-school sessions continue throughout the school year. In the spring second graders join the sessions. High school student computer volunteers help run the after-school sessions. Our students learn how to turn the terminal on, how to log in and off, and how to get programs from the computer library. Children are encouraged to read about computers and watch for computers being used in the community. Twice weekly, older children who know how to use the computer bring in their younger sisters and brothers, introducing them to the computer. The older children love showing off their computer and the younger children are fascinated.

Teachers, Parents, and Computers

Several teachers reviewed logic skills so they could hold logic tutorials with gifted students. Periodically, there is a time before school in the morning for Branch Brook's teachers to use the computer. They try the drills their students take. University courses are available to the staff through SUNY at Stony Brook.

An assistant and I run four training sessions a year for parents. After training, parents sign up for sessions in the computer rooms. Several older children are also trained as assistants.

"Computer Week," in the spring, provides an opportunity for every child in the school to use the terminal. A special program is written for the computer. Children experienced in computer use are aides and helpers during the two week period. Some escort children to the computer room while others are computer instructors. Teachers receive dittos before "Computer Week" which introduce children to our computer.

Elementary school children should be growing up using and learning about the computer. They should have happy moments realizing that the computer is an invention of people, that it is under the control of people, that it is programmed by people, and that it must be used only to serve people.

Source: Marie K. Stavrides, "Computer Days," *Science and Children,* p. 18, September 1978. Reprinted with permission of Science and Children September 1978. Copyright 1978 by the National Science Teachers Association, 1742 Connecticut Ave., NW, Washington, DC 20009.

tion to its ASTRO lunar lander simulation, the Talcott Mountain Science Center in Connecticut has programs named POLLUTE (a water pollution simulation) and WEATHERWISE (a simulation to help students learn how to interpret weather data so that they can pilot a ship safely across the Atlantic Ocean from New York to Iceland).

2 History students may be paired up (one representing the North, the other the South) to make decisions about tactics, troops, supplies, etc., prior to the beginning of a specific Civil War battle. The object of the simulation, of course, is to win the battle. Since the simulation program is based on actual Civil War conflicts, the history student is moti-

vated to learn about the clashes because he or she will be "participating" in them. (It is possible for an informed "Southern general" to defeat an uninformed Northern opponent at the Battle of Gettysburg.) Elementary students in Yorktown Heights, New York, are also encouraged to take a greater interest in history by being placed in the role of the king of ancient Sumer. The "king" makes decisions about ruling the kingdom, and the computer acts as the king's prime minister and chief adviser.

3 The School of Forestry at the University of Georgia uses a program to simulate a forest and the effects on the forest of various cutting practices. Students make decisions about tree harvesting and are thus able to test and put into practice concepts in forestry management that they have been taught.

4 Computer-controlled cockpit simulators are used to train airline pilots in nighttime takeoffs and landings. During a landing, the student pilot "sees" the airport as projected on the screens of two CRTs and reflected through a series of mirrors to the forward-facing windows of the "aircraft." Of course, pilots can be trained in various emergency procedures in safety. In a similar application, high school students are "driving" simulators that have dashboard instruments, steering wheels, gear selectors, etc. Students practice by using a realistic motion-picture roadway projected on a screen. A computer monitors their progress and displays the results on the instructor's console.

▶ LOOKING BACK

The following points have been emphasized in this chapter:

1 The purpose of this chapter has been to outline a few of the ways in which computers can be used as educational tools. Computers can bring to the educational process such attributes as patience, around-the-clock availability, and individualized and student-paced instruction programs. Thus, although progress to date in applying computers in the instructional process has been relatively slow, the future of the machines in education is assured. A primary purpose of using computers as an instructional tool should be to provide insight and not merely to compute numbers or process documents.

2 In educational planning and decision making, computers are being applied in the areas of curriculum planning and planning for individual instruction. *Computer-managed instruction* is the name given to the use of computers to assist teachers in the administration of individual instruction programs; *computer-assisted instruction* refers to situations where students themselves interact with computers and where instruction is presented or reinforced. Charges have been made that using computers in the educational process will "dehumanize" in-

struction and make robots of students. Perhaps these fears are exaggerated, but in education as in other fields, computer usage may sweep aside some current practices and introduce new problems. Such changes are likely to be resisted by some educators.

3 Control applications of computers in education are found in the areas of testing and error analysis. In some subjects, CAI methods are well suited for testing student progress. The simplest and most used form of CAI is the drill-and-practice approach; other forms are the tutorial and dialogue approaches. The advantages and problems of CAI are discussed in this chapter.

4 Computer simulations may be used as teaching aids. Students learn by making decisions and by learning of the consequences of those decisions. Theories can be put into practice, and valuable experience can be gained in a safe and inexpensive way.

KEY TERMS

After reading Chapter 15, you should be able to define and use the following terms:

computer-managed instruction (CMI)
PLATO
computer testing in education
computer error analysis in education

computer-assisted instruction (CAI)
drill-and-practice CAI approach
tutorial CAI approach
simulation in education

REVIEW AND DISCUSSION QUESTIONS

1 What attributes can computers bring to the process of education?
2 What factors account for the slow progress to date in applying computers in the instructional process?
3 "A primary purpose of using computers in education should be to provide insight." Discuss this statement.
4 (a) How can computers be used in curriculum planning? (b) In planning for individual instruction?
5 (a) What is meant by computer-managed instruction? (b) What is meant by computer-assisted instruction?
6 "Using computers in education will dehumanize instruction and make robots of students." Evaluate this statement.
7 (a) How can computers be used in class scheduling? (b) In athletic planning?
8 Discuss two control applications of computers in education.

9 Identify and discuss the three CAI approaches.
10 (a) What are the advantages of CAI? (b) What are the problems to be solved before CAI achieves its potential?
11 Discuss ways in which computer simulation can be used for instructional purposes.

▶ SELECTED REFERENCES

In addition to the references suggested in the chapter footnotes, you might wish to examine the following sources:

Atkinson, Richard C.: "Futures: Where Will Computer-assisted Instruction (CAI) Be in 1990?" *Educational Technology,* pp. 60ff, April 1978.
Barstow, Daniel: "Computers and Education: Some Questions of Values," *Creative Computing,* pp. 116–119, February 1979.
———: "The Talcott Mountain Science Center," *onComputing,* pp. 34ff, Winter 1979.
Brown, Dean, and A. El-Ghannam: "Computers for Teaching," *Computer,* pp. 16–22, January 1973.
Byerly, Gayle A.: "CAI in College English," *Computers and the Humanities,* vol. 12, pp. 281–285, 1978.
Cavin, Claudia S., E. D. Cavin, and J. J. Lagowski: "The Use of Computer-assisted Instruction to Provide Optional Assistance to Students," *Educational Technology,* pp. 42–45, June 1979.
Garrett, Herbert E.: "The Minicomputer as a Tool for Learning," *The Matyc Journal,* pp. 26–30, Winter 1979.
Magidson, Errol M.: "Student Assessment of PLATO: What Students Like and Dislike about CAI," *Educational Technology,* pp. 15–19, August 1978.
Mowrer, Donald E.: "The Computer vs. the Professor," *Creative Computing,* pp. 78ff, September 1979.

Chapter 16
COMPUTERS AND THE HUMANITIES

The purpose of this chapter is to outline a few of the ways in which computers can be used in the humanities.

In the first section of the chapter, you will see how computers are being used to *help decision makers* form judgments about the authenticity of art objects and the authorship and analysis of literary works.

The second section points out the problems associated with using computers for *language translation,* and the third section discusses the preparation of *concordances* that are of value to literary scholars.

A fourth section presents a few examples of how computers can be used to *help create* meaningful *art* in the areas of graphics, music, and sculpture.

Finally, sections are devoted to the uses of computers in *museums, historical research,* and *archaeological studies.*

Thus, after studying this chapter, you should be able to:

- Give a few examples of how computers may be used for decision making in a humanistic environment.

- Explain why machine techniques for natural-language translation have failed to live up to earlier optimistic predictions.

- Define the term *concordance* and give some examples of existing concordances.

- Discuss a few examples of computer usage in the creation of graphic art, music, and sculpture.

- Identify four ways in which museum personnel use computers, and give examples of such usage.

- Present some examples of computer usage in historical research and archaeological studies.

- Understand and use the key terms listed at the end of the chapter.

If a group of individuals were asked to select a field of study that would probably remain unaffected by the computer, many would probably select one of the humanistic disciplines. After all, the humanities are concerned with qualitative considerations and with the expressive, moral, and contemplative aspects of life, while computers deal with quantitative matters and with relatively depersonalized data. It is true that computers may have less of an impact in the humanities than they are having in the other areas described in Chapters 13 through 18. But we will see in this chapter that *it is not true* that the humanities will remain unaffected by computer usage. On the contrary, computers *are* currently having the following impact on the humanities: (1) Research time and effort are being saved, (2) researchers are attempting studies that would otherwise be impractical, and (3) research is sometimes leading to unanticipated results that provide investigators with new discoveries and new insights.

Should computers be used in humanistic research? Apparently many researchers think so, or they would not be using them. There is, however, a vocal group of humanists who argue that computer usage degrades humanistic research by placing an exaggerated emphasis on quantifiable factors. If this charge is true, the computer is not to blame, for scholars have, for example, been *manually* dissecting poetry and novels and using quantitative image-analysis methods for a number of years. As Jacques Barzun, a critic of the use of computers in humanistic research, has observed:

> Now it has been shown again and again by good critics that counting images of running water or the frequency with which a particular image or metaphor occurs in Shakespeare proves absolutely nothing except the industry of the indexer. . . . Now the computer will do only one thing. It will multiply, speed up, and extend this particular fallacy of analysis.[1]

In short, the critics believe that the research being done with computers is usually not worth doing.

Thus, the question "Should computers be used in humanistic research?" involves judgments about the value of the results produced. But, of course, in *any* type of computer application the results may be very valuable, totally worthless, or somewhere in between, depending on the skill of the researcher in programming the computer to supply worthwhile output. In the pages that follow, you will be introduced to some of the applications of computers in the humanities. More specifically, applications in (1) *decision making,* (2) *language translation,* (3) *concordance preparation,* (4) *the fine arts,* (5) *museums,* (6) *historical research,* and (7) *archaeology* will be described. Perhaps at the end of the chapter you will be able to form your own judgment about the utility of an analytical engine in a humanistic environment.

DECISION-MAKING APPLICATIONS

Computers have been used to aid experts in making judgments about (1) *the authenticity of art objects,* (2) *the authorship of literary works,* and (3) *the analysis of literary works.*

Art Authenticity

At New York's Metropolitan Museum of Art, Carl Dauterman has used a computer to study the sets of coded marks found on Sèvres porcelain—an eighteenth-century French porcelain that is commonly forged. Pieces

---

[1] Jacques Barzun, *Computers for the Humanities?* Yale University Press, New Haven, Conn., 1965, p. 149.

of genuine porcelain have coded sets of painted and incised marks that identify individual workers, dates, types of paste, etc. There can be 10 different painted and incised marks on a single piece of porcelain. The computer can compare and cross-correlate the combinations of painted and incised marks found on genuine articles. Thus, the computer correlations can serve as a warning flag against forged pieces by revealing how normal patterns of agreement among various markings are violated. One print-out, for example, revealed 13 pieces of procelain with suspicious markings.

Authorship Identification

The *Federalist Papers* consist of 77 essays written to persuade New York citizens to ratify the United States Constitution. Although they were published anonymously, it is generally agreed that John Jay wrote 5 of the essays, Alexander Hamilton wrote 43, James Madison wrote 14, and Hamilton and Madison collaborated on 3. A quick tally (without a computer) tells us that the authorship of 12 essays has not been accounted for. There is no dispute that the author of each of the remaining essays was either Madison or Hamilton. In spite of the fact that after Hamilton's death Madison claimed to have written the 12 papers, scholars have been debating the validity of this claim for years. Since the writing styles of Hamilton and Madison were quite similar, it appeared that the issue would remain unresolved. However, Frederick Mosteller of Harvard and David Wallace of the University of Chicago have used a computer to determine that Madison was probably, as he claimed, the author of all 12 disputed essays. How was this done? Thank you for asking. The papers known to be written by Madison and Hamilton were first analyzed for stylistic differences. Statistical concepts were then employed to produce a test that would discriminate correctly between the writings of the two authors in all cases. (The test resulted in positive values being computed when Madison was known to be the author, while negative values resulted when Hamilton's papers were analyzed.) Since counts and calculations involving 100,000 words were involved, the study would have been virtually impossible without the use of a computer.

Computers have also been used in studies attempting to identify the authors of portions of the Old Testament of the Bible. The authorship of the Book of Isaiah, for example, has vexed scholars for centuries. The first 12 chapters are generally attributed to Isaiah; the authorship of the remaining 54 chapters is disputed. On the one hand, there are scholars who believe that Isaiah wrote the entire work; on the other hand, there are many more who contend that after the first 12 chapters the book was written by a varying number (from two to four) of the other anonymous prophets. In an attempt to shed some light on this emotionally charged controversy (disputants have long ago ceased to be on speaking terms), Y. T. Radday, Lecturer in charge of Hebrew Studies at the Israel Institute of Technology, has employed a computer in his authorship study. Although

Radday was convinced at the beginning of his analysis that Isaiah had written the entire book, his final conclusion was that multiple authors were involved. The probability that the author of Chapters 1 to 35 wrote Chapters 40 to 66 was computed to be only 1 in 100,000.[2]

Similar studies of disputed authorship have been made in the New Testament. Reverend Andrew Q. Morton and James McLeman have published a controversial analysis showing that the 14 Epistles of the Apostle Paul were written by Paul and several others. Authorship studies of Plato's Seventh Letter and the works of Homer have also been conducted. In summary, computers can be quite helpful in authorship identification, assuming that meaningful and quantifiable stylistic patterns can be correctly detected for a known or unknown author. Of course, most humanists would agree that much work remains to be done in developing generally acceptable techniques for stylistic comparison.

Literary Analysis

In addition to possibly identifying the author(s) of controversial literary works, computers may also be used for other language and literary analysis purposes. For example, there is sometimes a dispute over *when* a known author wrote a particular work. In one such case, Ernest Hemingway wrote to a journalist in 1951 that he was working on the story that was subsequently published in 1952 as *The Old Man and the Sea*. But Darrell Mansell, a Dartmouth English professor, was "convinced that Hemingway wrote the novel much earlier, in 1935 or 1936, put it away, then dusted it off in 1951 and claimed to be in the process of writing it."[3] To test his hypothesis, Mansell used statistical techniques to compare passages from *The Old Man and the Sea* against four other Hemingway works whose dates of composition are fairly certain. The conclusion of this study supported the hypothesis: The resemblance between *The Old Man and the Sea* and the work that was written in 1936 was much greater than the resemblance between other works written at other times.

Another use of computers in literary analysis is in matching existing medieval manuscripts against the records of such manuscripts that were created by medieval libraries. This kind of matching makes it possible to determine information about the origin of the manuscript such as the scribe's name, date of copying, etc. Before 1450, medieval libraries had to protect themselves against having a borrower return an inferior substitute manuscript in place of the more expensive work that had been lent out. (The printing press had not yet been invented, and every copy of a text was handwritten and was an edition in itself.) A protective technique —the *dictio probatoria*—was originated in the thirteenth century at the

---

[2] For further information on this interesting study, see Yehuda T. Radday, "Isaiah and the Computer: A Preliminary Report," *Computers and the Humanities,* vol. 5, pp. 64–73, 1970.

[3] Darrell Mansell, "*The Old Man and the Sea* and the Computer," *Computers and the Humanities,* vol. 8, p. 195, 1974.

College de Sorbonne in Paris and was later used all over Europe. The technique consisted of having a library clerk record in a register (1) the title and value of a work being checked out, and (2) the exact text found at the beginning of a later page or folio in the manuscript. (This technique was sound because it was very unlikely that any two scribes would write the same quantity of text in the preceding folio(s).) Since such *probatoria* records exist to "fingerprint" at least 10,000 manuscripts, computers can now be used to match the medieval records with existing manuscript collections.[4]

LANGUAGE TRANSLATION

A robot with lofty inflection
read Stein in the poetry section,
but read it, "Arose is arose is arose,"
and thought it concerned resurrection.
—Gloria Maxson

In 1954, a computer with a stored vocabulary totaling 250 words and six rules for determining word relationships in sentences was programmed to translate a few Russian sentences into English. This small demonstration program was widely publicized, and it was then commonly predicted that computers would be used extensively in the future to translate documents from one natural language into another. The reasoning was that since computers could hold a large number of, say, Russian-English synonyms in storage, and since grammar rules for the two languages could probably be programmed, there should be a substantial amount of machine translation in the future.

Relative to 1954, it is now "the future." Are computers being extensively used for language translation today? The answer is no. After about 25 years of effort, researchers have found the task much more formidable than was originally expected. There are at least two reasons for this. *First,* grammarians have not been very successful in determining all the appropriate rules of grammar for any specific natural language. *Second,* a good translation requires that the meanings of words (*semantics*) in a particular context be taken into consideration in making translation decisions. This is not as easy as you might think. For example, the sentence "Time flies like an arrow" may seem clear to you, but it is subject to several machine interpretations. One incorrect translation, for example, might be: "Time the speed of flies as quickly as you can." ("Time" is considered a verb.) Another false interpretation might be: "Certain flies enjoy an arrow." ("Time" is now considered an adjective, and "like" is interpreted as a verb.) Of course, a programmer could easily write rules to ensure a correct interpretation in this particular case. But then how would the machine interpret the sentence "Fruit flies like a banana"? With the word "flies" treated as a verb in this sentence, the translation in another language would obviously be ridiculous.

---

[4] For more information on this subject, see Daniel Williman and Margarita Dziedzic, "*Dictio Probatoria* as Fingerprint: Computer Discovery of Manuscript Provenances," *Computers and the Humanities,* vol. 12, pp. 89–92, 1978.

"Computer Speaks Chinese"

Two Cambridge University linguists have made it possible for a Chinese-speaking computer operator to communicate directly with a computer in Chinese. Robert Sloss and Peter Nancarrow devised the system as a do-it-yourself project in order to speed their work on a new Chinese-English dictionary.

"I don't think we could have done it if we'd had a lot of money," said Mr. Nancarrow. "Without money, you have to think harder. You have to solve the problem with your brain instead of buying a lot of equipment." The two men built their first working model in three days on Mr. Sloss's kitchen table, using a child's Meccano set (similar to an Erector set), bits of plastic, some string, and a cardboard tube.

Telegraphic communications and data storage in Chinese have previously been accomplished by translating each of the 4,500 characters into numbers. "The error rate was absolutely prodigious," said Mr. Nancarrow.

The number of characters was a problem for the two linguists until they discovered the joys of the square root. A grid of 66 centimeters, or 26 inches, square would give them 4,356 boxes, each one centimeter, or one-third of an inch, square. Then they wrapped the grid around a drum. The position of any character on the grid could be stated in two numbers: 22 across, 43 down.

Teaching a computer to "write" Chinese was easy. Mr. Sloss and Mr. Nancarrow fed the coordinates for each character into the computer memory with instructions for drawing the ideographs. Cambridge technicians then built a prototype production model for about $2000.

Cable and Wireless, a British communications organization, has bought the rights to the invention. A Chinese trade delegation has visited Cambridge to see the machine work. "They reacted as if they had seen an electronic dog talking," Mr. Sloss said.

Source: *Creative Computing,* p. 162, May 1979. Used by permission of *Creative Computing,* P.O. Box 789-M, Morristown, N.J. 07960.

Despite the problems, some progress *is* being made on the language-translating front. For example, Professor Allen Tucker and others at Georgetown University in Washington, D.C., have developed a Spanish-to-English computer translation system for the Pan American Health Organization that is producing about 5,000 words of translations per day. In addition, English-to-Spanish and Portuguese-to-English translating programs are in experimental use.

CONCORDANCE PREPARATION

A *concordance* is an alphabetical listing of the principal words in one or more literary works with references to the passages in which they occur. Computers have been used widely in the preparation of concordances and indexes. Concordance preparation, in fact, represents the greatest single use of computers in the field of literary scholarship.

There is, of course, nothing new about the preparation of concordances. Alexander Cruden, an Englishman, produced a concordance to the Bible in 1737 (after which he was confined in a madhouse for 10 weeks before he escaped); F. S. Ellis published a concordance to the poems of Shelley in 1892 after six years of work; and Lane Cooper, a Cornell University professor, published a concordance to the works of Wordsworth in 1911.

> By lashing on squadrons of graduate students and discontented Ithaca housewives and junior colleagues (incidentally, three of these people died during the operation), Professor Cooper accomplished the immense labor of cutting and pasting, stamping and alphabetizing, hundreds of thousands of slips of paper in less than a year. It was a labor that might have taken one man twenty years.[5]

A good concordance can be quite valuable to a literary scholar, but the above paragraph indicates that a great deal of endurance is required of those who would manually prepare such a work. (Father Robert Busa, the director of a 60-person project in Italy to index Greek and Latin texts, has described the endeavor as a "marvelous way of expiating sin"[6]—and Father Busa was utilizing computer techniques!) It is little wonder, then, that computers were quickly pressed into literary service to take over much of the tedious work involved. Several concordance-generating programs are now available, and numerous concordances have been prepared in classical and biblical literature, in languages other than English, and in English and American literature.[7] A computer-prepared concordance of the transcripts of the tape recordings that were released by the Nixon administration during the Watergate episode has also been prepared by Cornell University's Stephen Parrish.[8]

COMPUTERS IN THE FINE ARTS

The following eloquent comment on the importance of art is found in a computer publication:

[5] Stephen M. Parrish, in *Computers for the Humanities?* Yale University Press, New Haven, Conn., 1964, p. 57.

[6] Ibid., p. 58.

[7] For an interesting and witty account of the problems associated with work of this type, see Benn Ross Schneider, Jr., *Travels in Computerland,* Addison-Wesley Publishing Company, Inc., Reading, Mass., 1974.

[8] An analysis of this concordance may be found in Geoffrey Stokes, "The Story of P," *Harpers,* pp. 6–9ff, October 1974.

When human beings approach the meaning of art, when they attempt to define it in words, they must come near to the meaning of life and pull at the strings of philosophy. . . . Art is important to society because man's life should have meaning, not to someone else, but to himself. Individual men without meaning in their lives cannot produce a society or a civilization with meaning. Art is . . . important to man . . . because without art he cannot survive as a human being. Art is man's outward expression and impression and integration of himself with his universe.[9]

How, then, in a field that appeals to individual imagination and personal feelings, can there be a place for an "unfeeling" computer? To one group of artists, the answer is that there can be *no* place for an analytical machine in the realm of art; to another group, the answer is that computers can be used to *analyze existing art;* and to a third group, computers can be used to *help create meaningful new art.*[10] Let us look briefly in this section at a few computer applications in *graphics, music,* and *sculpture.*[11]

Michael Noll has programmed a computer to generate *drawings* in the style of the Dutch painter Piet Mondrian. Mondrian's 1917 painting entitled "Composition with Lines" consists of a large number of vertical and horizontal bars of varying length arranged in a more or less orderly manner. Noll's computer-produced drawing arranged similar bars in a random fashon. When 100 people were asked to compare copies of the Mondrian and the computer pictures and decide (1) which was artistically better and (2) which was produced by a machine, the results were interesting. Only 28 percent were able to identify the Mondrian picture correctly, and 59 percent preferred the computer picture. Noll's use of computers has gone beyond imitation. Interesting works have been produced by specifying some form of order in the program and by then allowing the

[9] C. B. S. Grant, "Computers Put Traditional Creative Arts Education on Verge of Collapse," *Data Processing Magazine,* pp. 60–61, October 1969.

[10] The third group would not necessarily disagree with the second. As might be expected, however, there is disagreement among artists about the computer's role in art. At an American Musicological Society national meeting, for example, there was a stormy session resulting in a widening gulf between scholars in the noncomputer group and those who have adopted the computer as a tool.

[11] For a wealth of additional information on computer art, and for additional examples of applications not covered in this section, you may wish to consider the following sources: Sydney Alonso, Jon H. Appleton, and Cameron Jones, "A Special Purpose Digital System for Musical Instruction, Composition, and Performance," *Computers and the Humanities,* vol. 10, pp. 209–215 1976; Nancy Altmayer, "Music Composition: A Different Approach," *Creative Computing,* pp. 74–76ff, April 1979; Deborah Blakely, "New Tool for the Sculptor; Computerized 'Clay,'" *Creative Computing,* pp. 46–47, June 1979; John Craig, "The Music Men and Their Incredible Printing Machine," *Creative Computing,* pp. 48–49, June 1979; Linda Hirschmann, "Computers and Dance," *Creative Computing,* pp. 42–45, August 1979; Hubert S. Howe, Jr., "Creativity in Computer Music," *Byte,* pp. 158ff, July 1979; Ruth Leavitt (ed.), *Artist and Computer,* Creative Computing Press, Morristown, N.J., 1976; Robert E. Mueller, "Idols of Computer Art," *Creative Computing,* pp. 100–106, May/June 1978; Robert A. Parker, "The Aesthetic World of the Computer," *Personal Computing,* pp. 57–59, January 1978; Neesa Sweet and Vicky O'Hara, "Technology and the Times: Computer Graphics," *Personal Computing,* pp. 48–53, February 1978; Russ Walter, "Creating Computer Art," *Creative Computing,* pp. 84–86, May/June 1978; and Gary Wittlich, Donald Byrd, and Rosalee Nerheim, "A System for Interactive Encoding of Music scores under Computer Control," *Computers and the Humanities,* vol. 12, pp. 309–319, 1978.

computer to incorporate random patterns. Thus, the computer "creates" pictures which may amaze the artist programmer. Art students at the University of New Mexico are encouraged to take programming and computer graphics courses. Professor Charles Mattox believes that preparing a program helps students understand some of the factors involved in artistic creation because they must concentrate on the form and other characteristics of the work, rather than on how well the work is drawn.

Some particularly interesting examples of computer graphic art have been created by Thomas J. Huston and Katy Owens. Figure 16-1 is entitled "FLORES EN FORTRANES," and in the original, Thomas Huston has used red, blue, and green colors to produce a striking 16- by 25-inch work. Figure 16-2 is Katy Owens's "Dawn of Creative Computing"; in the

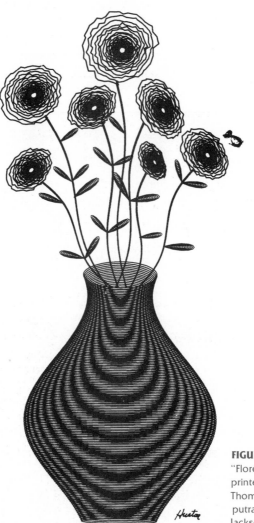

FIGURE 16-1

"Flores En Fortranes." (Reprinted by permission of Thomas J. Huston and Computra, Inc., Suite 2, 3306 W. Jackson, Muncie, IN 47304.)

FIGURE 16-2
Katy Owens's "Dawn of
Creative Computing." (Re-
printed by permission of
Computra, Inc., Suite 2, 3306
W. Jackson, Muncie, IN
47304. Copyright by Katy
Owens.)

original 12- by 16-inch picture, red, green, brown, and blue colors are applied on a yellow background to create an exciting effect.[12]

In addition to producing visual art, a computer may also be programmed to produce (or "synthesize") *sound*. More than a decade ago
on a Decca record ("Music from Mathematics"), a computer played—
and "sang"!—"A Bicycle Built for Two." Another Decca record ("Voice of
the Computer") released in the early 1970s contains a variety of short
pieces and samples of digital sound synthesis. Computer scientists and
musicians at MIT, Illinois, Michigan State, Iowa State, Princeton, Oberlin,
and other locations are currently experimenting with the use of computers in music *composition*. One early composition was entitled "Pushbutton Bertha" and was played over the ABC network; another early composition was the "ILLIAC Suite for the String Quartet." Yale's J. C. Tenney
uses a computer to compose and then play music. He provides certain
constraints in his program. The computer is then permitted to select
notes at random and play the resulting composition. The results can surprise the artist. Computers have also been used creatively in the field of
choreography. In addition to these creative applications, however, it
should be noted that computers are also being used in musicology for
computer-assisted instruction (discussed in the last chapter) and for the
analysis of existing works. One researcher at Berkeley, California, for example, is studying folk songs. Such elements of folk tunes as range, number of phrases, pattern of refrains, final cadences, etc., are being coded so
that they can be compared and analyzed. And at Princeton, the music of
Josquin Desprès has been coded for study and analysis.

In Boston's Government Center is a spheroid *sculpture* 7 feet in diameter. It is made of Cor-ten steel, a product that rusts in a controlled
way to produce a permanent and attractive deep red color. The spheroid
was designed by sculptor Alfred Duca; it was created with the help of a

---

[12] These examples of computer art are copyrighted by the artists and are presented here
with their permission.

flame cutting machine controlled by a computer-produced punched paper tape. Sculptor Duca used a computer because the complex three-dimensional form he visualized would have been difficult, perhaps even impossible, to complete without machine assistance. In short, the computer permitted the vision to become a reality.

COMPUTERS AND MUSEUMS

Museum personnel have been interested in using computers for *four principal purposes:* (1) to maintain regional or national data banks for storing and retrieving information of interest to participants, (2) to catalog and control the inventory of items in the collection of a large museum, (3) to provide public access to computing facilities, and (4) to support their own particular research projects whenever appropriate. (We have already seen an example of this fourth purpose—the study of Sèvres porcelain— so we will not discuss this purpose further in the following paragraphs.) The first two purposes, of course, are closely related in that both are concerned with automated retrieval of information about museum holdings.

To achieve the *first* purpose listed above, several museum information systems have been developed. Over 20 art museums in New York, Washington, D.C., and other cities, for example, have joined together to form an information retrieval system known as the Museum Computer Network. At the University of Oklahoma, a system has information stored on the holdings of over 30 museums in Oklahoma and Missouri. To avoid a proliferation of small museum networks, each of which would probably be unable to conveniently exchange data-bank information with the others, the Smithsonian Institution sponsored a meeting in 1972 to discuss the requirements and capabilities of the retrieval systems in existence at that time. This meeting led to the formation of the Museum Data Bank Coordinating Committee (MDBCC)—an organization that gives advice and information on the use of computers for museum data storage and retrieval. Similarly, in England, an information retrieval group of the British Museums Association is working on the development of an integrated museum cataloging system—one that would meet the needs of that nation's science, history, and art institutions. Other computer data banks are serving museums in France and Germany.

Museum personnel at the Smithsonian Institution are interested in computers for the *second purpose* mentioned above. The Smithsonian's Museum of Natural History has over 50 million specimens of fossils, flowers, fish, birds, etc. A million new specimens are being added each year. In one section alone, crustacean specimens in 500,000 bottles occupy more than 10 miles of shelves. Detailed information about the museum's holdings is of interest to researchers in colleges, hospitals, and other museums. To enable scientists to locate specimens (and information about

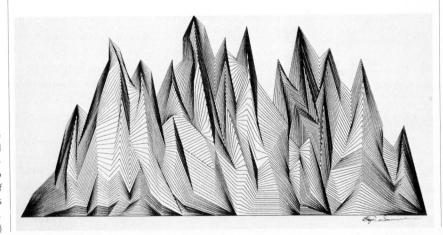

FIGURE 16-3
Computer-designed
drawings, such as those illustrated here, force the artist to
concentrate on the form of
the piece rather than its
execution. (*Margot Granitsas,
Photo Researchers.*)

the specimens) more quickly, the museum has developed an electronic data bank. Other large museums with vast holdings that are planning similar computer catalogs are the National Museum of Natural Sciences in Canada and the National Museum of Anthropology in Mexico.

Finally, personnel in several innovative museums around the nation are interested in computers for the *third* purpose mentioned above—to provide public access to computing facilities. At the California Museum of Science and industry in Los Angeles and at the Franklin Institute in Philadelphia, group demonstrations of computer usage are given to the public. In the visitors' center at the Children's Museum in Boston, several CRT terminals are connected to a minicomputer. Visitors are free to use the terminals at their own pace and on their own initiative. Each year the Community Research Center of the Oregon Museum of Science and Industry in Portland gives dozens of students the opportunity to carry out independent research projects using the museum's minicomputer. The Lawrence Hall of Science, a science museum on the Berkeley campus of the University of California, has two computer rooms with multiple terminals where organized workshops are offered to schoolchildren and others. In addition, Lawrence Hall also has terminals located in its exhibition area for public use any time the exhibits are open.[13] Furthermore, each morning Lawrence Hall personnel load a "Science Shuttle" van with a dozen microcomputers and set up a temporary computer laboratory at a school somewhere in the San Francisco Bay area. "During the day up to 120 students will experience the joy and excitement of learning and creating programs using interactive computers. For some students this might be a one-time introductory workshop, while for others it will be one in a series of programming and problem-solving classes."[14]

COMPUTERS AND HISTORICAL RESEARCH[15]

A growing number of historians are using computers and statistical techniques to aid them in their research efforts. Quantitative historians typically gather and analyze masses of data found in such public documents as state, county, and city records, voting records of public officials, federal government census reports, etc. Studies dealing with economic history sometimes incorporate data from nongovernmental sources.

Some *examples of computerized historical research* are described below.

[13] For more details, see Robert A. Kahn, "Public Access to Personal Computing: A New Role for Science Museums," *Computer,* pp. 56–65, April 1977.

[14] Joyce Hakansson and Leslie Roach, "A Dozen Apples for the Classroom," *Creative Computing,* pp. 52–54, September 1979.

[15] For further information on this subject, see Harry S. Stout, "Quantitative Studies and the American Revolution," *Computers and the Humanities,* vol. 10, pp. 257–264, 1976; Charles Tilly, "Computers in Historical Analysis," *Computers and the Humanities,* vol. 7, pp. 323–335, 1973; and Philip R. Vandermeer, "The New Political History: Progress and Prospects," *Computers and the Humanities,* vol. 11, pp. 265–278, 1978.

1 William Aydelotte has correlated biographical data with the voting records of over 800 members of the British Parliament of 1841–47. His findings "disproved several pet theories concerning English reformism in the 1840s, notably those of economic determinism, Tory paternalism, and aristocratic benevolence."[16] Thomas Alexander has, with the help of a computer, studied the roll-call voting patterns of members of Congress between 1836 and 1860. And Allan Bogues's analysis of roll-call voting in the Civil War congresses showed that party loyalty served to control the strife between radical Republicans and New England moderates. Other analyses of voting records have been (and are being) conducted.

2 Theodore Rabb has made a study of English overseas investments between 1575 and 1630. A computer was used to process data on 5,000 individual investors and 3,000 members of Parliament.

3 Western historians have assumed that young single men were responsible for opening up the frontier between 1840 and 1860. Jack Eblen used census data from an 88-county sample to show that "frontier-opening" had been a family undertaking, although the men were somewhat younger than the national average age at the time.

4 Stephen Thernstrom has used census data, tax lists, marriage licenses, birth records, etc., to study social mobility patterns. A sample of 8,000 Boston residents was selected from the 1880 census, the 1910 marriage license records, and the 1930 birth records. By tracing these individuals through later public records, Thernstrom was able to generalize about social mobility among various ethnic and religious groups over a long time span.

5 John Schutz has spent five years in New England sifting through dusty family Bibles, yellowed letters, and colonial newspapers to compile a massive amount of data on 2,700 legislators in more than 150 districts over a period of 100 years. A computer was then used to process these facts. His conclusion: The American Revolution was brought about by a group of free-wheeling, amateur legislators who were not lawyers, who generally served only a few years, and who didn't want the British telling them how to run their lives.

COMPUTERS AND ARCHAEOLOGY

A number of statistical techniques and simulation methods have been developed by computer-using archaeologists and statisticians to analyze and classify archaeological data, and several computer data banks have been created for the storage and retrieval of archaeological information. Some *examples of computer usage in archaeology* are described below:

1 George Cowgill of Brandeis University has studied the origin and

[16] Robert P. Swierenga, "Clio and Computers: A Survey of Computerized Research in History," *Computers and the Humanities,* p. 7, September 1970.

"New Tool for the Sculptor— Computerized 'Clay'"

In most computer art, the artist uses the computer to create an actual work of art. But Ray Jacobson, a sculptor at Carleton College in Northfield, Minnesota, has put the computer to a different use. Jacobson used the computer as a tool to produce the raw material to create ten large two-dimensional "sculptures."

His work also differs in another way from most computer art. Instead of starting with a computer program as most computer artists do, Jacobson started with six miniature sculptures he cast in bronze, and then used the computer to extend them on a flat surface so that he could look at sculpture in a two-dimensional rather than a three-dimensional plane.

Sound impossible? Not according to the complex method Jacobson developed to "translate" his three-dimensional bronzes onto paper and canvas.

"You can look at sculpture from many different angles," he explains. Jacobson teaches studio art courses in sculpture at Carleton College, where he is chairman of the art department. "I used the computer as an aid to more perceptibly read sculpture in the traditional manner, namely as a multi-silhouette phenomena, and then convert that reading to a two-dimensional surface."

Jacobson's objective was to explore form and shape in sculpture in a new way, in an attempt to expand his sculpture vocabulary. His sculpture images are a direct expression of that quest, and they are derived directly from the original bronze sculptures, via the computer. It was a process involving many steps.

After Jacobson made the small bronze sculptures he had them photographed from several different angles. He then made simplified drawings from the photographs, recording the contours as well as the dark and light areas of the photographs.

With the help of two students from Carleton College, he then transferred these simplified drawings onto a specially-made grid and coded the shapes according to their gray, black and white values (1 = white, 2 = gray, 3 = black).

The next step involved writing a computer program whereby Jacobson's shapes could be stretched, shrunk, expanded, juxtaposed, etc., on a computer screen. David Neiman of Newington, Connecticut (a Carleton student), wrote the computer program, using Tektronix plotting images and a Tektronix 4006 terminal connected to a DEC PDP-11-70 RSTS/E computer system.

Working closely with Jacobson, Andy Luebker of Stillwater, Minnesota, a Carleton sophomore, projected images on the computer screen based on information from the coded grid. They started out with simpler black and white shapes and then moved on to more complicated shapes with more complex tonal ranges, shrinking, expanding, juxtaposing and combining the images on varying backgrounds. Jacobson spent many hours with Luebker at the computer terminal, providing the artistic direction while Luebker handled the technical manipulation of the computer. They made 100 workable, unique images reflecting the characteristics of the three-dimensional bronzes on a flat surface.

Jacobson then selected five of these images printed by the computer and had them photographically enlarged. The result was five large and graphic two-dimensional "sculptures." These large sculptures dramatize the computer language itself and the shape qualities derived from the small scale bronzes. Jacobson then went a step further. Still using the computer generated images as his raw material, he painted five large acrylics on canvas which he also calls two-dimensional sculpture.

Both the large computer images and the acrylics are tinged with technology, Jacobson says, "another worldly creation in which the human hand has had only indirect influence." In fact, none of these pieces were shaped exclusively by the human hand. Throughout the project, Jacobson allowed chance and randomness to contribute to the development of his sculptures. When creating the bronzes, for example, Jacobson allowed his carved wax molds to "erode" in a molten wax solution before he cast them. Also, the computer was programmed to provide random and chance elements to emerge while the artist plotted designs on the screen.

"There was an erosion effect going on," Jacobson explains. "Just as natural forces wash and shape a rock with water, sand or wind, and give shape to the world around us, I was nursing these forms, orchestrating the shape of the computer images. These works represent a combination of natural forces and technology."

Jacobson's artistic effort culminated in an exhibit that included not only the six bronzes and ten two-dimensional "sculptures," but also a printout of the computer program, samples of the photographs of the bronzes from different angles, the contour drawings and coded grid of these photographs, and 60 of the 8" × 10" computer images.

From bronze, to computer image to acrylic, the exhibit is a testimony to the compatibility of art and technology, and to the computer's capability to be a useful tool to the artist.

Ray Jacobson has taught at Carleton College since 1955. His works have been exhibited extensively in public and in private galleries and have won many awards. He has executed numerous sculpture commissions, most recently a sculpture/fountain for the Minnesota Valley County Library in Mankato, Minnesota.

Source: *Creative Computing*, p. 46, June 1979. Used by permission of *Creative Computing*, P.O. Box 789-M, Morristown, N.J. 07960.

growth of the pre-Aztec city of Teotihuacan in central Mexico. Using a computer programmed to sketch a map of the city on the basis of the site information presented, Cowgill has been able to show the types of neighborhoods that existed in a city that covered an area 8 or 9 miles square. For example, an *almena* is a ceramic roof decoration that was found in the upper-class neighborhoods. Since the computer can produce a map showing the number of *almenas* discovered on every site, it is thus possible to see that an elite neighborhood was located near the "main street." The computer mapping for various time periods shows that building density was high and that there was a high degree of planning.

2   Luraine Tansey of San Jose City College uses information contained in a computer data bank to classify and data pre-Columbian art found in Mexico and Central America.

3   Ray Winfield Smith has used a computer to solve the puzzle of 35,000 decorated blocks of stone found in Egypt. The blocks were originally thought to be the remains of a single temple, but after classifying the blocks the computer showed that there had been a large complex of temples and buildings stretching across the desert for over a mile.

4   James Strange of the University of South Florida is restoring an ancient synagogue in the village of Khirbet Shema that was destroyed around A.D. 417. The site is located 90 miles north of Jerusalem. When most of the dimensions of the building site were known, the computer was used to make engineering calculations to determine the missing structural parameters. The computer was also used to make drawings of what the building probably looked like.

▶   LOOKING BACK

The following points have been emphasized in this chapter:

1   The purpose of this chapter has been to outline a few of the ways in which computers can be used in a humanistic environment. Although there are scholars who argue that computers have no place in the humanities, the fact is that a small but growing number of humanists are finding the computer to be a useful tool in their work.

2   Computers have been used to aid experts in making judgments about the authenticity of art objects and the authorship of literary works. They have also been used in analyzing literary works to determine when a known author wrote a work, and when and where existing medieval manuscripts were originated.

3   Although machine-language translation techniques have failed to live up to earlier optimistic predictions, some progress is now being made in this field.

4   A concordance is an alphabetical listing of the principal words in one

or more literary works with references to the passages in which they occur. Computers have been used widely in the preparation of concordances and indexes that are of value to literary scholars.

5 Computer programs have been used to create new art and to analyze existing art. Examples of applications in graphics, music, and sculpture were included in the chapter.

6 There is an unquestioned future for computers in museum information retrieval systems, and they permit historians and archaeologists to manipulate masses of data to arrive at relationships and insights that might otherwise remain undetected.

KEY TERMS

After reading Chapter 16, you should be able to define and use the following terms:

authorship identification studies
literary analysis studies
language translation
concordance
fine arts computer applications
historical research with computers

museum information retrieval systems
museum inventory control systems
archaeological studies

REVIEW AND DISCUSSION QUESTIONS

1 What impact are computers having on the humanities?
2 (a) Should computers be used in humanistic research? (b) Support your answer.
3 Give examples of how computers have been used for authorship identification.
4 (a) Are computers being extensively used for language translation today? (b) Why?
5 (a) What is a concordance? (b) How can a computer be of assistance in concordance preparation?
6 Discuss computer applications in the fine arts.
7 "Museum personnel have been interested in using computers for four principal purposes." Identify and discuss these purposes.
8 Discuss ways in which computers have been applied in historical research.
9 How have computers been applied in archaeological research?

SELECTED REFERENCES

In addition to the sources suggested in the chapter footnotes, you might also be interested in the following references:

Cassidy, Frederic G.: "Computer-aided Usage 'Labeling' in a Dictionary," *Computers and the Humanities,* vol. 11, pp. 89–99, 1977.

Computers and People. Each year, the August issue of this periodical presents numerous examples of computer art.

Computers and the Humanities. This quarterly publication is an excellent source of information on the topics presented in this chapter.

Computer Studies in the Humanities and Verbal Behavior. A quarterly publication with articles of interest to humanists.

Ernst, David: *The Evolution of Electronic Music,* G. Schirmer, Inc., New York, 1977.

Gilmore-Bryson, Anne: "Reconstruction of Illegible Portions of a Damaged Manuscript with the Help of the Computer," *Computers and the Humanities,* vol. 11, pp. 157–162, 1977.

Hertlein, Grace C.: "Computer Art: Review, 1968; Survey, 1978; Predictions, 1988," *Computers and People,* p. 8, August/September 1978.

Imhof, Arthur E.: "The Computer in Social History: Historical Demography in Germany," *Computers and the Humanities,* vol. 12, pp. 227–236, 1978.

Phelan, Walter S.: "The Study of Chaucer's Vocabulary," *Computers and the Humanities,* vol. 12, pp. 61–69, 1978.

Scollar, Irwin: "Image Processing via Computer in Aerial Archaeology," *Computers and the Humanities,* vol. 11, pp. 347–351, 1977.

Tucker, Allen B., Jr., Giuliano Gnugnoli, Long Vo Nguyen, and Bedrich Chaloupka: "Implementation Considerations for Machine Translation," *Proceedings of the ACM National Conference,* vol. II, pp. 884–890, 1978.

Chapter 17
COMPUTERS IN SCIENCE AND ENGINEERING

The purpose of this chapter is to outline a few of the ways in which computers can be used in the fields of science and engineering.

In the first section of the chapter, you will see how scientists and engineers are using computers for *planning and decision-making* purposes. The examples selected for discussion deal with (1) aerospace topics, (2) computer-aided design, (3) production planning, (4) simulation, and (5) scientific information retrieval.

In the second section of the chapter, computer concepts and applications dealing with operational and transportation *control* are presented. The operational control material is discussed from the standpoints of (1) process control, (2) production control, and (3) inventory and storage control.

Thus, after studying this chapter, you should be able to:

- Give examples of how computers may be used in aerospace applications.

- Discuss how computer-aided design (CAD) can increase productivity, and how CAD may be used in the design of such things as electronic circuits, ships, airplanes, staellites, highways, buildings, and cars.

- Explain how computers may be used to plan and schedule production on assembly lines and in job shops.

- Give examples of how computers can be applied for scientific simulation and information retrieval.

- Differentiate between open- and closed-loop process-control operations and give examples of computer usage in process control.

- Point out ways that computers may be utilized to control (1) production on an assembly line or in a job shop, (2) quantity and location of parts in an inventory, and (3) transportation on land and sea and in the air.

- Understand and use the key terms listed at the end of the chapter.

In Chapter 3 we examined some of the characteristics of *scientific* and *file processing* applications—the two types of applications into which most of the current computer tasks can be classified.[1] It is fortunate that Part 5 of this book (which also includes this chapter and the succeeding one on computers in business) is entitled "Selected Computer Uses in Society," for obviously only a few selected applications can be chosen from the

---

[1] A brief review of scientific and file processing characteristics might be in order at this point.

thousands that exist in *both* the scientific/engineering and file processing (business) categories. In the online library of applications programs maintained by General Electric for its timesharing customers alone, for example, are over 500 programs of general interest to scientific and business users. Of course, many hundreds of other more specialized applications have been programmed for computers by scientists, engineers, and business data processors.

Because this must be a chapter and not an encyclopedia, we shall limit our discussion of computer uses in science and engineering to a few selected applications in the important areas of (1) *planning and decision making* and (2) *control.* Sources of additional information on scientific computing are listed in the "Selected References" section at the end of the chapter.

PLANNING AND DECISION MAKING

From the hundreds of interesting applications that could have been included in this section, we have selected examples dealing with (1) *aerospace topics,* (2) *computer-aided design,* (3) *job planning,* (4) *simulation,* and (5) *scientific information retrieval.* Of course, in Chapters 13 and 14 we have already discussed other examples of the planning and decision-making uses of computers for scientific purposes. In Chapter 13, for example, we saw how physical and social scientists were using the machines for government-sponsored environmental planning, weather forecasting, social welfare planning, and urban planning. And in Chapter 14, we saw how computers were being used in medical science for diagnostic and research purposes.

Aerospace Applications

Okay, Houston, we've got a problem here.

Say it again, please.

Houston, we've had a problem. We've had a main bus undervolt. . . . It looks to me, looking out the hatch, like we're venting something into space.

It was 10:08 P.M. on the evening of April 13, 1970. The communications were between Astronaut James Lovell in the Apollo 13 spacecraft and the Mission Control Center of NASA at Houston. An oxygen tank had exploded and had made the service module useless. The lunar module, designed for a quick dash to the lunar surface, had become a lifeboat. As everyone knows, the crew returned safely to earth four days later. Without computers they would never have made it. (Of course, without computers they would never have been thousands of miles out in space to begin with.) Vital data from the crippled spacecraft had to be analyzed;

FIGURE 17-1
Relay station between the
Mission Control Center at
Houston and the Apollo
spacecraft. (*UNIVAC Div.,
Sperry Rand.*)

emergency courses of action had to be evaluated; unplanned course corrections had to be computed; different reentry plans had to be formulated; and all plans and decisions had to be made in a very brief time span. In short, an entirely new type of mission had to be planned in real time—i.e., while three astronauts were moving through space at thousands of miles per hour. This dramatic episode vividly showed the world the role computers have played in the space program. The installation shown in Figure 17-1 relayed data between the Apollo spacecraft and Houston.

In nonemergency situations, the computer was also used to simulate and plan each phase of an Apollo mission. For example, astronauts spent many hours "flying" the lunar module to and from the moon's surface in a computer-controlled model on Long Island, New York. Every likely maneuver was practiced over and over again. (We saw in Chapter 15 that physics students are routinely using a computer for a similar—but simplified—purpose today.)

Although the Apollo program in the late 1960s and early 1970s understandably received a great deal of publicity, *other important aerospace projects* are providing valuable information:

1 At NASA's Goddard Space Flight Center at Greenbelt, Maryland, the Telemetry Data Processing Facility (Figure 17-2) reduces telemetry data from over a dozen orbiting scientific satellites into proper form for study and analysis by scientists. Instruments in satellites such as the orbiting Geophysical Observatory and the Interplanetary Monitoring Platform have performed experiments and transmitted results to

earth. The data received from worldwide tracking stations are processed, and the information is forwarded to scientists located throughout the United States, Canada, and Europe. This information, in turn, adds to the storehouse of scientific knowledge, leads to plans for additional space experiments, and serves to reinforce or change existing scientific theories.[2]

2   At the University of Toledo, information from NASA's Orbiting Astronomical Observatory has enabled researchers to "see" more stars than can be observed from earth. Material floating in space between stars has been studied to determine the possibility of the existence of life elsewhere in the universe. Also, studies have been conducted to determine the nature of stars and their locations in space. Complex computer simulation models of the universe can be built to predict the lives of stars. Rapid advances have been made in the field of astronomy in the past two decades, and much of the work currently being done in the field could not be attempted without computers. At the University of Toledo, for example, one job contained 7.2 billion calculations that would have taken 250 operators at desk calculators 30 years to complete (working eight-hour days). A computer did the job in 10 hours.

3   Scientists at the Laboratory for Applications of Remote Sensing at Purdue University have used a computer to analyze the multispectral scanner data obtained by NASA's *Landsat* satellites while passing over the Great Lakes region of the United States and Canada. Maps produced as a result of the analysis pinpoint industrial and agricultural

[2] A series of High-Energy Astronomy Observatory satellites have also been launched by NASA. For more information on these devices, see Nicholas Panagakos and Don Worrell, "High-energy Astronomical Observatory Satellite," *Computers and People*, p. 26, March/April 1979.

FIGURE 17-2
Telemetry data processing.
(*UNIVAC Div., Sperry Rand.*)

areas that may be dumping pollutants into the lakes. Of course, once pollution sources are identified, plans can be made to minimize further environmental damage.[3]

Computer-Aided Design

Economists tell us that the amount of goods or services possessing economic value that individuals can produce in a given time period—i.e., their *productivity*—is dependent on such factors as (1) the attitudes, health, and training of individuals, (2) the abundance of natural resources, and (3) the amount of capital equipment available and the technological sophistication of this equipment. Computers, as we have seen, are sophisticated tools that can significantly improve productivity; productivity gains, in turn, can lead to a stronger competitive position in the world; and improved productivity can also lead to higher levels of real income for an increased number of individuals. Thus, computers may be incorporated into the design and production process to improve productivity and thereby to benefit many individuals.

Certain steps are generally required in the development of a wide range of items such as electronic circuits, ships, highways, or buildings. These steps are (1) preliminary design, (2) advanced design, (3) model development, (4) model testing, (5) final design, and (6) production and construction. All these steps are being facilitated by the use of computers. Steps 1 and 2 often involve computer simulation to eliminate from consideration possible designs that are not suitable. (We shall have more to say about simulation in a following section.)

In the past, preliminary sketches, design drawings, and engineering drawings were usually prepared very early in the design and development of new products and projects. When designers or engineers had a new thought, they would make some preliminary sketches to get the idea down on paper so that it could be analyzed more thoroughly. As the design was modified, additional drawings would be required; when the design was finally approved, further detailed production drawings were prepared. Thus, the preparation of drawings could occupy a substantial portion of the designers' time. And time spent at the drafting board was time that could not be devoted to considering other (perhaps better) alternative designs.

As we saw in Chapter 4, special electronic pens and CRT graphical display devices now make it possible for the computer to receive human sketching directly. Changes and modifications in the sketches of an engineer can be made quickly. Once the initial drawings are finished and displayed on the CRT to the engineer's satisfaction, the computer may then

---

[3] Other interesting uses of *Landsat* satellites are described in Charles Croteau, "Remote Sensing," *Water Spectrum*, pp. 47–53, Summer 1979; Norman Sperling "Examining Planet Earth," *Sky and Telescope*, pp. 126–131, February 1979; and Eric Teicholz, "Processing Satellite Data," *Datamation*, pp. 117–121ff, June 1978.

be instructed to analyze the displayed design and report on certain characteristics. Interactive communication between designer and computer may continue until a design with a desirable set of characteristics is produced. Such interaction between designer and machine is now relatively common. In addition, it may be common in the future to have the computer prepare (1) detailed engineering blueprints from the stored design, and (2) numerical control tapes that program automatic machine tools to precisely produce component parts of new products according to the blueprint specifications. Thus, it may be common in the future for the computer to interact with the engineer from the time the initial idea was conceived until the final production step is completed.

In the remainder of this section, let us look briefly at some of the *applications of computer-aided design.*[4]

1   *In electronic circuit design.* Computers are now being used to assist engineers in designing circuits for *other computers* (Figure 4-30, page 143). Several hundred programs are available to help electronic engineers in their circuit design work. An engineer may define the circuit requirements, and then the computer develops, analyzes, and evaluates trial designs that may meet the requirements. A trial design may be modified by the engineer as required. The computer then analyzes and evaluates the modification. Computer-aided design is also used to plan (*a*) the layout of integrated circuits, (*b*) the location of circuit boards in the computer, and (*c*) the ways in which these boards will be interconnected. An example of a state-of-the-art computer-aided design system is SCALD (Structural Computer-Aided Logic Design), which was developed as part of a U.S. Navy effort at Lawrence Livermore Laboratory in California. The goal of the Navy team is to put the supercomputers of today on one to four chips within the next four to six years! While conventional large-scale computer design efforts (also using computers) may now take 100 person-years to complete, a large Navy processor—the S-1—was completed using SCALD with only two person-years of design effort.[5]

2   *In ship design.* Computers may do much of the detailed design work such as determining the positioning of hull reinforcing members, determining welding requirements, and generating numerical control programs to control the flame cutting machines that are used to shape steel plates.

3   *In aircraft design.* Aircraft designers working at a CRT display can draw the shape of a fuselage and have the computer analyze the physical characteristics of the shape; they can also vary the position, angle, and

[4] For a discussion of *computer-aided design* (CAD) and *computer-aided manufacturing* (CAM), see Donald E. Hegland, "The Many Faces of CAD/CAM," *Production Engineering,* pp. 56–60ff, June 1979.

[5] For further details on this exciting design and development project, see Vin McLellan, "Massive Tasks for Chips," *Datamation,* pp. 90ff, September 1979.

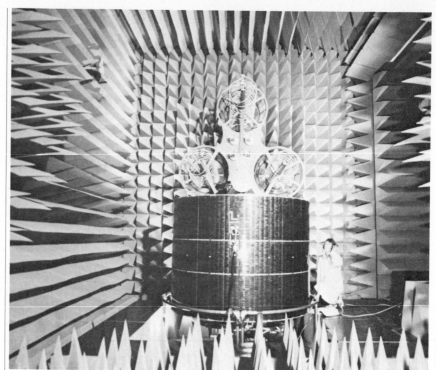

FIGURE 17-3
A *Marisat* satellite undergoing a test in an anechoic chamber before being launched. The anechoic chamber screens out environmental electromagnetic and sound energy so that engineers can ensure that the circuits packed into the satellite do not interfere with each other.
(*IBM Corp.*)

length of the wings and have the computer report on structural strength and life characteristics.

4 *In satellite design.* In addition to receiving data from orbiting satellites, computers are used to design the satellites themselves. The *Marisat* communications satellite (shown undergoing tests in Figure 17-3) is used by the U.S. Navy and international commercial maritime operators to provide an instant link between ship and shore. A computer at Hughes Aircraft Company was used for structural analysis, thermal analysis, and simulation tests of this satellite. For example, the computer helped determine how structurally sound each design was during the planning stages, and what sort of temperature ranges the *Marisat* could handle.

5 *In highway design.* The Ohio Highway Department has a computer system that enables design engineers to quickly determine the social and economic impact of proposed road construction. The system permits engineers to consider factors such as alternate routes, amount of earth to be moved or added, number of citizens that will be forced to relocate, and construction costs of alternate routes. Aerial photographs are converted by computer into three-dimensional topographical maps. Proposed routes are then plotted on these maps, and a computer is used to evaluate the alternatives.

6 *In architectural design.* New building designs can be analyzed and evaluated by computer. Space planning—i.e., the process of locating rooms and/or work stations in a structure—is facilitated by the computer testing of different approaches to determine the optimum locations for various users of the building. Physical characteristics of planned buildings can also be evaluated. For example, the computer might be asked to work out the acoustical characteristics of a theater that the designer has sketched. The sketch may then be modified by the architect on the basis of the computer analysis, or the machine may be instructed to display a theater with more desirable acoustics.

7 *In automobile design.* Automobile manufacturers are using computers to evaluate the structural characteristics of alternative designs. Engineers can "assemble" models of the components in a car and then "road test" the proposed car design on a simulated drive route. A chassis cross-member, for example, can be redesigned to reduce weight, and the effects of the change can be determined by a computer program. This design approach significantly reduces the costly and time-consuming process of making and testing a series of prototype parts until the desired results are obtained.[6]

Production Planning and Scheduling

Industrial engineers are using computers extensively for production planning and scheduling purposes. The amount of planning and scheduling required varies from one production process to another. An assembly line which produces a standard item with little or no variation requires less in the way of planning and scheduling than does the operation of a machine shop where nonstandard items are produced every day and where different jobs require different raw materials and different machine operations.

This does not mean, of course, that assembly-line operations are simple to plan and schedule. On a farm-tractor assembly line, for example, thousands of component parts must come together at the right time, at the right place, and in the right sequence. Manually planning and scheduling such an assembly process can take weeks; the use of computers can slash the time dramatically, and the computer can print out the parts requirements and schedules for use by assembly personnel. When automobiles rather than tractors are being assembled, the job naturally becomes more complex because of the numerous color combinations that must be matched correctly and the modifications that must be made whenever certain options are installed (e.g., whenever air-conditioning is installed on a car at the factory, that car is usually equipped with a heavier-duty cooling and electrical system).

Unlike an assembly line, however, a *job shop* does *not* produce the same general product every day. Rather, a wide variety of products are

---

[6] For further information on this topic, see Robert W. Decker, "Computer Aided Design and Manufacturing at GM," *Datamation*, pp. 159–161ff, May 1978.

produced, and the shop is typically organized by types of machines used (i.e., lathes may be at one location, stamping machines at another, etc.). Also unlike an assembly line, the *sequence* of operations *varies* in a job shop from one product to another. Not surprisingly, the planning and scheduling is more difficult because each job may require completely different raw materials and a completely different production sequence. In one job, for example, drill presses may be required near the end of the project, and in another job the same machinery may be needed at an early stage. Engineers must attempt to plan and schedule operations to minimize bottlenecks at one location and slack periods at another. In short, planners must seek to minimize waiting times for raw materials, maximize the use of expensive machinery, and complete the jobs on the dates promised the customers. Computers are used in this complex environment to help planners obtain maximum total performance at the lowest possible cost.

Simulation

The topic of simulation was discussed in Chapter 9, and we have seen numerous examples in earlier chapters of the use of computers for scientific simulation purposes. In Chapter 13, for example, we saw that simulation was being used by government scientists and planners to (1) predict the life-sustaining ability of rivers, (2) predict, from a model of the United States economy, the possible effects of government policies on inflation and unemployment, (3) predict the effect of government policies in the social welfare area, and (4) plan proposed roads and use existing roads in the most efficient manner. Also, sections in Chapters 14 ("Physiological Simulations") and 15 ("Simulation as a Teaching Aid") described some scientific uses of computers. Thus, we need not spend much more time here discussing simulation applications.

What must be emphasized, however, is the importance of using the computer as an actor—i.e., using it to act out a vast number of roles dealing with both immediately *practical* problems and *theoretical* scientific concepts. Instead of building an expensive physical model of a prototype product or processing plant for experimentation and testing, a mathematical model can be substituted and a computer can be used for evaluation purposes. Time and money are saved, and better results are frequently obtained.

As we saw earlier in this chapter, preliminary and advanced design work is often facilitated by computer simulation. In addition, the computer has been programmed to play such diverse *pragmatic* roles as (1) a coal mine to enable engineers to develop and pretest a new coal-ripping machine, (2) a new computer to permit engineers to determine potential performance and check circuit designs, (3) a rocket to help test the performance of various mixtures of rocket fuels, (4) a bay that is being polluted to help authorities develop pollution-control plans, (5) a bankrupt

531

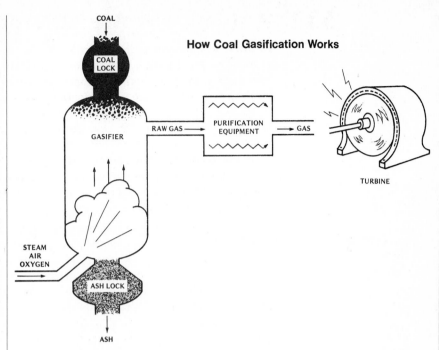

How Coal Gasification Works

COAL

COAL LOCK

GASIFIER

RAW GAS

PURIFICATION EQUIPMENT

GAS

TURBINE

STEAM
AIR
OXYGEN

ASH LOCK

ASH

FIGURE 17-4
IBM scientists in Palo Alto are trying to help determine whether the coal-gasification process can be a viable alternative energy source. The process calls for raw coal to be released through a coal lock into the gasifier, where it is blasted by a combination of steam, air, and oxygen. Ash is filtered out, and the raw gas produced is purified before being used in gas turbines or to create steam for steam turbines. IBM researchers are using a computer to help determine the most efficient process.
(*IBM Corp.*)

railroad that needs to be reorganized so that it can return to profitability, and (6) a coal-gasification plant to enable scientists to study the effects of changing certain operating conditions within the gasifier, thus helping design better processes and operate them more efficiently. (Figure 17-4 gives further details on this last role.)

Computers are also being used in science as active participants in the formulation of new *theoretical* concepts. Theories dealing with the creation of the universe, the lives of stars, etc., may be evaluated by simulations. New information gathered by space probes and satellites can be used to further test the validity of existing theories. The greatest impact of computers on science may come from this partnership between theoreticians and machines.

Scientific Information Retrieval

The Smithsonian Science Information Exchange (SSIE) is helping ensure that unnecessary duplication of research effort (with the resulting waste of human and financial resources) does not happen too frequently. The SSIE, a division of the Smithsonian Institution, is also helping manage a large part of the billions of dollars spent on basic research each year by the government. Information on research in progress, including about 90 percent of the nonclassified federally funded projects as well as thousands of projects supported by private sources, is reported to the SSIE by scientists. Project descriptions are analyzed and indexed, and a 200-word

"Automatons Are All Around"

The future of industrial robots looks black—in terms of ink, that is. It took the robot business years to pass from prototype to profit, but the industrial robot's ability to, quite literally, lend a hand around the shop is gaining recognition. Here are just a few specific applications robots have received:

- International Harvester/Canada has applied robots to a heat-treating and forming line used in producing harrow disks. The robots have resulted in improved quality, increased production volume, and better production control. And the workers who were replaced are delighted, having been reassigned to work that is not so hot and heavy.

- Xerox uses robots in manufacturing a family of duplicator parts. Robots were chosen over single-purpose hard automation because their flexibility can accommodate the model changes and variable demand of this operation. The robots' manufacturer also notes that this soft automation "resulted in a high degree of unit machine independence, minimized control system complexity, and included the ability to support and maintain the equipment by plant maintenance personnel."

- Robot welding systems at several Chrysler assembly plants have reduced the time and cost required by model changeovers. "This, along with the flexibility of the system during operation, is important to us because we operate with fewer assembly lines than most of our competitors," said Richard A. Vining, vice-president of Chrysler's Stamping and Assembly Division, where the first system was planned. "When you've got fewer lines, you need more flexibility to handle your product mix."

- Labor costs are rising, but small-batch manufacturers may find hard automation too expensive for their low-volume needs. Do-ALL Co., a leading supplier of machine tools, cutting tools, and precision measuring equipment, increased productivity by incorporating robots in a small-batch system using conventional and NC equipment. The robot operation combines the programming convenience of computer numerically controlled equipment (CNC) with a simplified approach to parts classification, thus boosting efficiency without the expense of group technology using computer-aided design/computer aided manufacturing (CAD/CAM) techniques.

Source: Carl Remick, "Robots: New Faces on the Production Line," *Management Review*, p. 29, May 1979 (New York: AMACOM, a division of American Management Associations, 1979).

abstract is then stored in the SSIE data base. Requests for stored information are received from research scientists and others with an interest in a subject. (The SSIE data base may be accessed through Lockheed's *Dialog* online retrieval service or through System Development Corporation's

Orbit service.) A cancer researcher, for example, could get (1) a summary of all cancer research in progress, (2) a more detailed listing of research in specific areas such as cancer virology or cancer chemotheraphy, and (3) a listing of scientists and agencies currently working in specific research areas. When research in progress is completed, the project information may be removed from the computer files and stored on a medium such as microfilm where it may be retrieved when needed. This historical file at SSIE goes back 25 years. Information on about 100,000 projects is now stored in the computer each year. Having access to information about ongoing scientific projects is of obvious value to other scientists for planning and decision-making purposes.

In addition to the SSIE, the National Technical Information Service of the Department of Commerce has a data bank that stores detailed information on federal government research. Weekly computer-produced newsletters inform interested parties of the latest research results in their fields. One such newsletter, for example, is titled *Computers, Control & Information Theory*. Online retrieval services such as *Dialog* and *Orbit* can now supply the researcher with references to most of the scientific and technical articles published today. *Dialog* alone has over 100 data bases and more than 22 million document references.

CONTROL

*Robots in a factory uprising
considered of no compro-
mising,
and loudly kept stating
to those arbitrating
that dull work was deme-
chanizing.*
—Gloria Maxson

The points made in the introduction to the section on planning and decision making just concluded are equally valid for this section. Since there are hundreds of interesting uses of computers in the area of scientific and engineering control, we can consider only a few applications here; however, we have already discussed other scientific control applications in Chapters 13 (e.g., pollution and environmental control) and 14 (e.g., physological monitoring and control of laboratory tests). In this section, concepts and applications dealing with *operational control* and *transportation control* are presented.

Operational Control

Operational control may be classified into at least three categories: *process control, production control,* and *inventory and storage control*. Let us look briefly at each of these categories.

Process control Computerized process-control systems are being used to monitor *continuously operating* facilities such as oil refineries, chemical plants, steel mills, electric power generating stations, and paper mills. These processes are similar in that they convert input materials and energy into output materials, products, converted energy, and waste. During the process, instruments measure variables such as pressure, tem-

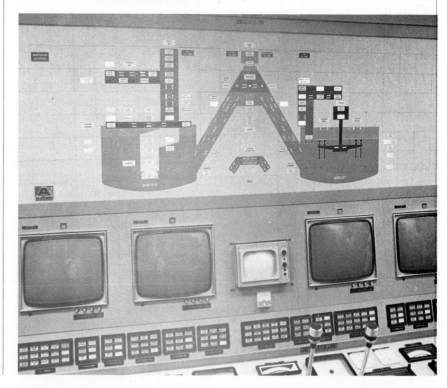

FIGURE 17-5
(*Above*) Main control room for Bay Area Rapid Transit, Oakland, California. (*Tom McHugh, Photo Researchers.*) (*Right*) Control room of the Phenix, the first nuclear reactor of the breeder type to be built in France. (*F. Bibal, Photo Researchers.*) (*Opposite above*) Computer center of the W. A. C. Bennett Dam, which crosses the Peace River in British Columbia, Canada. (*Nancy Simmerman, Photo Researchers.*) (*Opposite below*) Telephone company engineers have developed this "three-way" dialing computer control center which allows callers to dial a third party. (*Paul Sequeira, Photo Researchers.*)

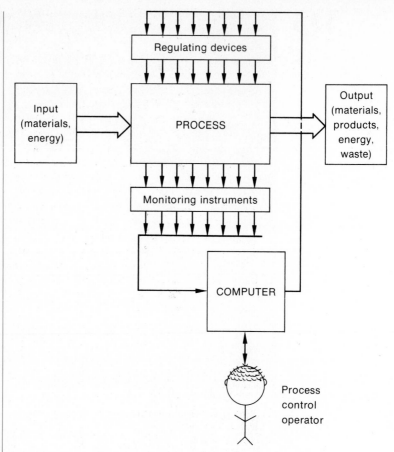

FIGURE 17-6
A computerized process-
control system.

perature, flow, and so on. If the process is deviating from an acceptable standard, regulating devices are adjusted to bring the process back into control. In an *open-loop* operation, the computer records instrument readings, compares the readings against standards, and notifies process-control personnel of needed manual adjustments in regulating devices; in a more complex *closed-loop* operation (Figure 17-6), the computer receives measurements, makes comparisons, and, *in addition,* sends signals to the regulatory devices to make the necessary changes. Of course, human operators may monitor the overall process and instruct the computer to make occasional changes in control parameters in particular situations, but the control operation is essentially automatic. Use of the computer in this way permits quicker-responding and more accurate control than would otherwise be possible. The use of minicomputers for process-control applications is expanding rapidly. Minis are also being used in labs to check on the quality of the output of the process (Figure 17-7).

To get some idea of the value of process-control computing, let us consider the following hypothetical narrative. (The facts *are* true; only the names have been changed to protect the innocent.)

It was Tuesday, September 22, 1970. It was hot in Philadelphia. I was working the day watch in the control room of PJM—the Pennsylvania–New Jersey–Maryland Interconnection—an electric power pool that coordinates power distribution to 20 million people from the 500 generating units belonging to PJM's 12 participating companies. My partners' names are Wednesday and Saturday. My name is Thursday. Every two seconds our computer monitors generation and transmission-line power flow. If deviations from preselected standards are detected on the nearly 4,000 miles of transmission lines, the computer runs a check to give me details on system conditions. In addition, every five minutes the computer simulates the effect of unexpected breakdowns in selected generators and transmission lines. In spite of the heat wave and the peak use of electricity for air-conditioning, it looked like it would be a routine day at the control room. Then, at 8 A.M., the Oyster Creek Number One generator in New Jersey went out of service. Quick computations showed that PJM would not have enough generating capacity in the afternoon unless output levels were increased. I tried to buy power from neigh-

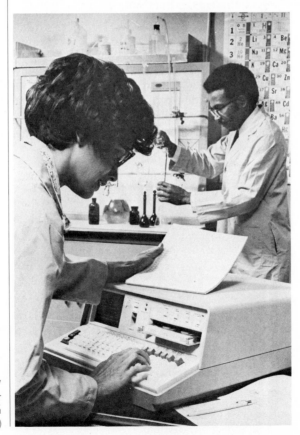

FIGURE 17-7
Minicomputer is used for quality control in research laboratory. (*IBM Corp.*)

boring power networks but none was available (one smart aleck offered to sell me a D-cell battery). Anyway, by increasing output, PJM was meeting the demand. But then, at 2:29 P.M., the Number Two generator at the Keystone complex in western Pennsylvania overheated, tripped its circuit breaker, took 750 megawatts of power out of the network—and ruined my coffee break. Fortunately, the computer had already simulated the loss of Keystone Number Two. To relieve overloaded lines, generation had to be shifted throughout the network. Generators serving overloaded lines had to be curtailed; those serving safe lines had to be speeded up. The computer evaluated alternative ways of meeting needs and we were somehow able to prevent a major power failure by optimizing the use of the network.

Another monitoring system used by *consumers* of large amounts of electricity is designed to control and reduce energy consumption. A computer-controlled power demand system (Figure 17-8) may be linked to electric metering equipment. The consumer develops priorities for electrical equipment that is not critical to the operation of the facility— e.g., outdoor lighting, air-conditioning, water heaters, etc. By automatically cutting off noncritical electrical loads at certain times, the system can reduce power demand peaks and power consumption at factories, building complexes, hotels, and shopping centers.

Production control In an earlier section, we discussed production planning and scheduling. The production-control function, of course, is a follow-up to this planning and scheduling. During the actual production on an assembly line or in a job shop, data entry stations (Figure 17-9) may be used to transmit such facts as the time spent on an operation, the status of a machine tool, the size of a queue requiring work, or the need for machine setup or repair. The computer may then be used to compare the

FIGURE 17-8
Power demand system.
(*Digital Equipment Corp.*)

actual conditions against the production plan in order to determine whether appropriate control action is required.

In addition to controlling the *overall production process,* computers may also be used to *control individual production tools* such as shapers, milling machines, and drill presses (see Figure 1-17, page 35). Numerically controlled machine tools, directed by computer-produced tapes, can be used to automatically produce precision parts meeting blueprint specifications.[7] An early use of *numerical control* (NC) machines was in the aircraft industry to cut airplane sections from solid metal. But NC machines are now employed for such dissimilar tasks as constructing prefabricated house walls and producing hydraulic presses. Rapid operation and low scrap losses are two advantages of these automatic machines.

Finally, as we have seen in earlier chapters, programmable *robots* are machines controlled by *built-in computers* that can sense the need for, and then take the actions necessary to perform, various assembly tasks. The use of robots rather than humans may result in improved quality control. A human welder on an automobile assembly line may leave out a couple of welds so that a consumer gets a car with rattles; a robot programmed to do the same welding operation may produce more consistent quality.

Inventory and storage control Transaction recorders such as the one shown in Figure 17-10 are often used to keep control of the *inventory* of parts and materials used in production. Let us assume, for example, that an employee needs a dozen hinges to complete a job. The employee

---

[7] A popular programming language used to produce computer output to guide numerical control machines is called APT (*Automatically programmed tooling*).

FIGURE 17-9
Online terminal used to improve production data gathering and control.
(*IBM Corp.*)

FIGURE 17-10
Transaction recording station. *(IBM Corp.)*

gets the hinges and an identification card from a supply station. The card identifies the hinges by part number and contains any other *fixed* information (such as unit price) that is necessary. The worker inserts the card into a transaction recorder and then keys or moves levers to indicate the *variable* part of the transaction—the number of hinges taken, the job number, etc. The worker then pushes a TRANSMIT button to send the data to the computer, where they are checked for accuracy and then accepted to update the proper record in the inventory file. If an error is detected, a signal may be relayed back to the recording station.

Computers may also be used for materials *storage* control. The Aircraft Division of Rohr Corporation resembles a large job shop. In order to better control the flow of shop orders between production operations, an "automatic warehouse" system has been developed. When jobs are not being worked on in a production department, they are stored somewhere in the nearly 17,000 cubicles in the warehouse. Prior to being stored, however, a parts pallet is given an identification number by a clerk. This number is keyed into Rohr's main computer, which assigns the pallet to an available storage space. The main computer then sends the assigned location to a warehouse computer which, in turn, activates automatic cranes and conveyor systems to store the pallet in the designated space. When the parts pallet must be retrieved, the warehouse computer reverses the process: the pallet location is identified, and cranes and conveyors are activated for retrieval purposes.

Transportation Control

Microcomputers have been installed by the thousands in systems designed to control *automobile traffic* lights. Although the constant goal of such systems is to regulate vehicle and pedestrian flow, the control requirements are subject to considerable variation depending on such factors as the type of intersection, the traffic patterns, and the time of day. However, standardized microcomputer controllers can be programmed to adjust to the differing traffic environments.

Transportation control is also needed at *sea,* where in spite of sophisticated radar systems, hundreds of large ships are involved in collisions each year. The problem is that radar does not differentiate obstacles in a ship's path. To overcome this problem of possibly mistaking an oil tanker for a buoy, computers with collision assessment programs have been installed on the bridges of ships. The assignment program can automatically differentiate between ships, debris, and land masses. In addition, the bridge computer can plan the ship's route to conserve fuel. Once the ship is in port (Figure 17-11), computers can help in controlling the warehousing, inventory, and distribution services offered to shippers.

A computer-aided control system is helping the *air traffic* controllers at Chicago's O'Hare International Airport. Since they are responsible for 30 million passengers and 600,000 flights each year, the controllers need

FIGURE 17-11
A computer continuously
tracks the location of items
being shipped or received
at this port in Portland,
Oregon. (*IBM Corp.*)

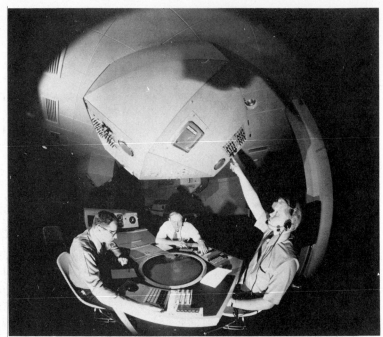

FIGURE 17-12
Computer-aided air traffic
control. (*UNIVAC Div.,
Sperry Rand.*)

all the help they can get. The control system sends out special "beacon" signals to aircraft within a 50-mile radius of O'Hare. Answering signals from aircraft give the plane's identity, altitude, and speed. This returned information is processed by a computer and is instantly displayed on a controller's radar screen next to the "blip" of light that represents the plane (Figure 17-12). Over 100 aircraft can be tracked and controlled simultaneously by the system. By not having to ask pilots by radio for a plane's identity and altitude and by not having to trust this information to memory or notes, the controller can have more time to do a better job of directing and controlling aircraft. More efficient traffic control, of course, should result in increased safety.

"Taking the Measure of Space"

Before the era of the man-made satellite, scientific measurement was essentially earthbound. For two decades now, with scientific experiments carried onboard satellites, the scientist has been reaching out for knowledge in the vacuum of space. As he has intensified his extraterrestrial pursuits, he has added a new dimension to the scope and complexity of scientific investigation.

Earthbound scientific inquiry—astronomy with its huge telescopes, the particle accelerators of high energy physics—was the exclusive domain of the scientist and his technicians. This is no longer true. The fundamental principle of all measurement—the measurement isn't complete until the data is in the hands of the experimenter in a form he can use—has required the use of large-scale digital communications networks and information storage and retrieval systems. In April 1978, a telemetry on-line processing system (TELOPS), developed by IBM's Federal System Division for NASA's Goddard Space Flight Center in Greenbelt, Maryland, became part of some of mankind's most intricate, far-reaching scientific investigations.

The first U.S. satellite, Explorer 1, launched on January 31, 1958, weighed 30 pounds. Over half of this weight was made up of scientific instruments to detect radiation and micrometeorites. These first measurements from space confirmed a prediction made years earlier by the head of the physics department at the University of Iowa; that there existed regions of intense radiation surrounding our planet, traped there by the earth's magnetic field.

These regions, known as the Van Allen radiation belts, were the first discoveries made with scientific satellites; the growing list now includes the solar wind, the quasi-stellar objects at the edge of our universe called quasars, and the magnetosphere—the magnetic envelope around the earth that wards off most of the deadly streams of atomic nuclei from deep space known as cosmic rays.

New Technologies; More Questions

With new, lighter materials and ultralightweight low-powered solid-state electronics, the intensity and variety of investigation has increased. One satellite may now house 30 or more different experiments with instruments measuring such phenomena as X-rays and ultraviolet light from solar flares, gamma rays from far beyond our galaxy, and radio waves from the planet Jupiter.

Scientists have been searching for answers to add to the list of discoveries: Do flares and other solar activity follow classical sunspot cycles? Are high energy radiations from deep space the echoes of the "big bang" from which the universe might have been created 10–15 billion years ago? Are the periodic bursts of radio waves from the planet Jupiter related to the orbit of its mysterious satellite Io?

Improvements in technology increased the number and complexity of the questions; and harder questions meant harder problems in getting the data back down to earth and in the hands of the scientists.

The solution was a new system in which the principal role would be played by TELOPS (a telecommunications on-line processing system). It was designed by NASA's Goddard Space Flight Center (GSFC) and IBM, and features a mass storage system that combines the data capacity of a large tape library with the access speed of on-line disk storage, and includes a communications input unit that accepts input rates up to 2.688 million bps with simultaneous outputs to the remote stations for retransmission requests at up to 1.344 million bps.

Source: *Datamation*, pp. 127–129, September 1979. Reprinted with permission of *Datamation*® magazine, © Copyright by Technical Publishing Company, A Division of Dun-Donnelley Publishing Corporation, A Dun & Bradstreet Company, 1979—all rights reserved.

The following points have been emphasized in this chapter:

1 The purpose of this chapter has been to outline a few of the ways in which computers can be used in science and engineering. There are, of course, thousands of computer applications in these fields.

2 Computers are routinely used for planning and decision-making purposes in a number of areas discussed in the chapter. In space flight (with or without astronauts), for example, computers are indispensable.

3 In computer-aided design work, computers may interact with engineers to analyze displayed sketches. For example, computers are currently aiding in the design of electronic circuits, ships, cars, airplanes, satellites, highways, and buildings.

4 Industrial engineers are using computers extensively for the planning, scheduling, and controlling of production on assembly lines and in job shops. And scientist and engineers are using computers as actors—i.e., using them to act out a multitude of roles dealing with both immediately practical problems and theoretical scientific concepts.

5 To avoid duplication of scientific research effort, computers are also being used to store and retrieve descriptions of research in progress.

6 In the area of control, computers are used to monitor process-control systems. Either an open-loop or a closed-loop approach may be used. Production and inventory and storage control are also common engineering applications of computers. New and improved transportation-control systems use computers to increase safety on land, at sea, and in the air.

▶ KEY TERMS

After reading Chapter 17, you should be able to define and use the following terms:

Goddard Space Flight Center
Landsat
productivity
computer-aided design
SCALD
Marisat
production planning
assembly line
job shop

scientific simulation
SSIE
Dialog
Orbit
open-loop process control
closed-loop process control
numerical control machines
robot

REVIEW AND DISCUSSION QUESTIONS

1   What role did computers play in the Apollo 13 emergency?
2   "Although the Apollo program has received much publicity, other aerospace projects are providing valuable information." Identify other projects and discuss the role of computers in those projects.
3   (a) How can computers aid a designer? (b) Discuss five applications in computer-aided design.
4   (a) What is a job shop? (b) How does a job shop differ from an assembly line? (c) How can computers be used in production planning and scheduling?
5   "Computers can be used to simulate models dealing with both practical problems and theoretical concepts." Discuss this statement and give examples of both types of simulations.
6   (a) What is the Smithsonian Science Information Exchange? (b) For what is it used?
7   (a) What are the characteristics of an open-loop process-control operation? (b) Distinguish between an open-loop and a closed-loop process-control system.
8   (a) What are numerical control machines? (b) How are they controlled?
9   How can the use of computers improve transportation safety?

SELECTED REFERENCES

A large numer of publications contain references about the use of computers in science and engineering. A few of the periodicals to consider are: (1) *Communications of the ACM*, (2) *Computer*, (3) *Control Engineering*, (4) *Datamation*, (5) *Industrial Engineering*, (6) *Infosystems*, (7) *Production Engineering*, (8) *Science*, and (9) *Scientific American*. You will not find a dearth of material!

In addition to the sources suggested in the chapter footnotes, you might also wish to examine the following references:

"Balancing Workloads and Resources," *Data Processor*, pp. 12–14, September 1979.
"A Computer Model with a Track Record," *Infosystems*, pp. 20–21, January 1979.
"Data Acquisition System Automatically Monitors Steel Rolling Mill," *Computer Design*, pp. 62–63ff, June 1977.
Dorr, Fred W.: "The Cray-1 at Los Alamos," *Datamation*, pp. 113–118ff, October 1978.
Hart, Donald E.: "Second Generation Robots Have Eye for Industry," *Data Management*, pp. 13–14ff, June 1979.

Lusa, John M., and Steven Stibbens: "Manufacturing Opts for Productivity," *Infosystems,* pp. 57ff, May 1979.

Panagakos, Nicholas, and Arnold Heller: "Computer Models and Displays the Evolution and Interaction of Galaxies," *Computers and People,* pp. 24–25, May/June 1979.

Tekulsky, Mathew: "The Human-Dolphin Interface," *Interface Age,* pp. 93–94, July 1979.

Tobias, William: "Source Data Collection," *Production Engineering,* pp. 55–57, February 1979.

Chapter 18
COMPUTERS IN BUSINESS

The purpose of this chapter is to outline a few of the ways in which computers can be used in business.

In the first section of the chapter, you will see how business-persons are using computers for *planning and decision-making* purposes. The examples selected for discussion deal with (1) market forecasting and planning, (2) financial planning, (3) business simulation models, and (4) operational planning.

In the second section of the chapter, examples of computer-based *business control* applications are presented.

Thus, after studying this chapter, you should be able to:

• Outline a planning and decision process followed by many high-level business executives.

• Give examples of how computers may be used in market forecasting and planning and in financial planning.

• Explain how computer-based business simulation models may be used in planning and decision making, and give examples of such usage.

• Discuss ways in which computers may be employed in operational planning.

• Present examples of computer usage for business control purposes.

• Understand and use the key terms listed at the end of the chapter.

As noted in the introductory paragraph of Chapter 17, scientific and file processing applications account for the bulk of all computer usage. Most business applications fit into the file processing category. Of course, file processing is not limited to business organizations: (1) Government agencies process files containing the records of taxpayers and welfare recipients in collecting taxes and paying benefits, (2) hospitals process files of patient records to prepare bills, (3) school systems process grade records of students to prepare report cards, (4) religious organizations process membership donations and other records (in the "automated abbey" shown in Figure 18-1, inventory control and other tasks associated with running a 600-acre dairy farm are being processed), and (5) all these organizations process files containing employee data to prepare payrolls and other personnel reports. Such applications as these, however, are closely related to similar "bread-and-butter" applications in the accounting and personnel areas of a business. For example, there are obvious similarities between a hospital's billing of its patients and the billing

FIGURE 18-1
"Automated abbey."
(*Burroughs Corp.*)

operation associated with the credit card purchases of an oil company's products. Each billing operation has input data transactions and produces an output statement.

In this chapter, as in the other chapters of Part 5, we cannot hope to do more than consider a few selected business applications. As in Chapter 17, we will limit our discussion to the important areas of (1) *planning and decision making* and (2) *control.* Sources of additional information on business uses of computers will be indicated in footnotes and listed in the "Selected References" section at the end of the chapter.

PLANNING AND DECISION MAKING

The expansion in the scope of scientific inquiry, and the acceleration in the *speed* or *rate* with which new knowledge is put to use, is having a significant impact on business planning and decision making. The Department of Commerce estimates that prior to World War I there was an average wait of 33 years between an invention and its application; by World War II the lag time had dropped to 10 years; and now the delay has been reduced further. For example, the laser was invented in 1958 and was being applied seven years later for manufacturing and surgical purposes. And several computer generations have been introduced since 1950. The implications of an accelerating rate of change are obvious to business managers: A major change which might have required five years to implement a decade ago must now be completed in a shorter period if the firm is to remain competitive. On the one hand, management reaction time is constantly shrinking, while, on the other hand, each decision made involves more risk and is valid for a shorter time span. Furthermore, as reac-

FIGURE 18-2
(*Right*) The computerized board of the New York Stock Exchange. (*P. Koch, Photo Researchers.*) (*Below*) Businesses use computer systems to control inventory, accounts payable, accounts receivable, and payroll, and to project future sales. (*UNIVAC Div., Sperry Rand.*) (*Opposite above*) Checks are printed to allow the account number and amount to be read by a magnetic character readers. (*IBM Corp.*) (*Opposite below*) Status of a customer's account is indicated on a terminal that is tied directly to a central computer. (*Burroughs Corp.*)

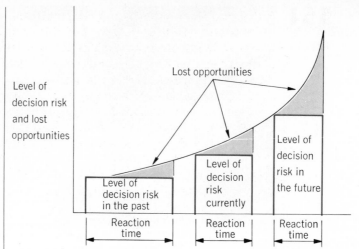

FIGURE 18-3
Implications of an accelerating rate of change.

tion time diminishes, opportunities for profitable action are lost because preoccupied managers fail to reach out and grasp them (see Figure 18-3).

The planning and decision process followed by many high-level business executives may resemble the one shown in Figure 18-4: The business strategies, long-term goals, product and economic assumptions, etc., of these executives serve as the basis for market forecasts; this expectation of *how many* items can be sold then becomes the basis for determining (1) how and when to acquire materials and make the items (the production plans), (2) how and when to have the money on hand to pay

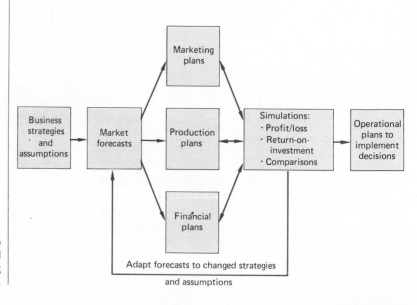

FIGURE 18-4
A business planning and decision-making environment.

for the acquired materials and produced items (the financial plans), and (3) how and when to promote and distribute the items (the marketing plans); and these plans are then used in simulations to estimate such variables as profit and return on investment. Of course, the results of these simulations may bring about changes in established plans, and/or the results may cause changes in strategies and assumptions. Once initial simulations have been concluded and high-level plans have been made, operational plans at lower levels are often needed to implement the decisions.

A few examples of computer usage in (1) *market forecasting and planning,* (2) *financial planning,* (3) *business simulation,* and (4) *operational planning* are given in this section. Production planning and scheduling was discussed in the last chapter, and so we need not consider it here.

Market Forecasting and Planning

Business managers must plan and make decisions about marketing new and existing products (and/or services), changing existing products, and promoting new and existing products. In making their market plans and decisions, managers are increasingly relying on the results of market research efforts. The American Marketing Association defines *market research* as "a systematic gathering, recording, and analyzing of data about problems relating to the marketing of goods and services." Since we know that a computer is especially suited for recording and analyzing data, it stands to reason that computers can make a valuable contribution in market research and thus in market forecasting and planning.

Market researchers gather statistical data on consumer preferences from consumer surveys and from the results of market testing in limited geographic areas. Past sales data on similar products in an industry may be obtained from the company's own past sales records and through the facilities provided by online information retrieval services. For example, the Cybernet Division of Control Data Corporation has combined resources with Economic Information Systems, Inc., to produce an online retrieval system that offers market researchers share-of-market data for all major firms in all the geographic, industrial, and business markets of the United States.[1] Other online retrieval services—e.g., Lockheed's *Dialog*— supply market research users with a wealth of population and economic data. The data gathered from these sources may be processed by a computer to produce summary statistical measures (market percentages, arithmetic means, product rankings, etc.). These summary measures may then be analyzed by managers or by computer programs. These analyses, in turn, can be used as input to computerized statistical forecasting procedures that may be used to project sales volume into the future, given assumptions about pricing, economic trends, promotional effort, com-

---

[1] For further details, see Jay M. Gould, "Share of Market Data," *Online,* pp. 22–25, January 1979.

"Computer Games That Planners Play"

The hottest planning tool around today is computer modeling, in which planners construct sophisticated business models to test hypotheses on a wide range of decisions at much lower cost and at greater speed than ever before. Programmed into a computer, typically, are the historical data on a business—the "what happened and how" information of the past—along with specific assumptions for the future. Against those data, planners can play "what if" games covering nearly any contingency. Complex software is now available for the basic modeling job, as well as programs that pinpoint the issues that ought to be addressed for each industry. The goal is to be able to measure in advance the effect on the business of any decision and to react rapidly in a changing environment.

"The computer allows managers to play games with their businesses without taking any of the risks," says Joe R. Micheletto, vice-president at Ralston Purina Co. But experts warn that strategic modeling is only as good as the information on which it is based. To prevent poor models, planners are turning to planning consultants who offer software models and to outside data bases for such diverse information as econometric forecasts and weather predictions. The information contained in such data bases is generally broader-based than companies with limited research capabilities can develop themselves.

Rolled Together

Of course, companies also compile their own data bases. At R. J. Reynolds Industries Inc., for example, the main strategic plan is compiled from information from each of the corporation's six operating units. In that way, the company can project its cash flow at any given point and can predict shortfalls in any division and the impact that they would have on the main corporate growth goals. "When you take all these companies with different dynamics and roll them together, you can come up with patterns that aren't immediately apparent when you look at them separately," says Douglas A. Graham, director of corporate planning systems. The model, he explains, can pinpoint cash flow from one area of the company that can be invested immediately in another.

Reaction Time

At Public Service Electric & Gas Co., the total corporate plan is run once a day, on average, to test the impact on the New Jersey utility's costs, its equipment use, and the financial impact of such business decisions as a cutback in fuel purchases during an unexpectedly warm winter week. Equally important is the speed with which the computer generates a bottom-line picture. "If an oil embargo were announced tomorrow," asserts William E. Scott, executive vice-president, "within 24 hours we would be able to know the major impact of it and could begin reacting."

The Right Questions

Problems can arise with computer-based planning if executives do not have a clear idea of the kind of information they want to get out of the computer. In the early 1970s, Potlatch Corp. was burned when it tried to simulate too many variables. "You don't start out by trying to make a model of the world," says Charles L. Neuner, vice-president for planning. Neuner simplified Potlatch's planning model, because the company did not really need to make precise long-range plans. "Trees take 80 years to grow," he explains. "We could plant trees against a certain end use, but who wants to count housing starts in the year 2030?"

But while computer modeling may call attention to problems, it cannot solve them. "A computer has no perspective and no qualitative judgment," says Fletcher H. Hyler, product manager at Digital Equipment Corp. "While it helps to find answers to questions, it cannot tell executives which questions to ask."

Source: "Computer Games That Planners Play." Reprinted from the December 18, 1978 issue of *Business Week* by special permission, © 1978 by McGraw-Hill, Inc., New York, N.Y. 10020. All rights reserved.

petitive reactions, and so on. Armed with this information, managers may be able to do a better job of planning marketing strategies. In many companies, market plans become the basis for inventory acquisition plans and production plans.

Of course, the use of computers in market planning is not limited to larger businesses. Over 20,000 farmers in Texas and Oklahoma, for example, are using a computer to determine when to deliver more than 1 million bales of cotton to market each year. The computer in the Telcot network developed by the Plains Cotton Cooperative Association links 150 cotton gins in the two states to buyers' offices in Dallas and Lubbock, Texas, and Memphis, Tennessee. Farmers can go to any of the gin offices and tell at a glance how many bales have sold, as well as the price and quality of each bale (Figure 18-5). When a farmer decides to sell, the sales offer is entered into the computer. The farmer can ask for a fixed price and either sell for that amount, accept a counteroffer, adjust the price, or remove the fixed price and offer the cotton to all buyers on a bid basis.

Financial Planning

Provisions must be made in a business to have adequate financial resources available to carry out marketing and production plans. The costs and revenues associated with alternative estimates of promotion plans and prices, and sales and production volumes must be analyzed to determine the financial implications (Figure 18-6). To evaluate these implications (and to determine the expected profitability of various alternatives), financial managers frequently use computer programs to make cash flow

FIGURE 18-5
Farmers keeping track of
activity in the cotton
market. (IBM Corp.)

FIGURE 18-6
Analyzing financial resources.
(IBM Corp.)

analyses, time-series financial forecasts, and loan and interest rate projections. Decisions about the advisability of making investments in new plants and equipment are often made with the help of a computer.

Computers may also be used by finance managers to analyze a customer's financial standing in order to make decisions about credit terms. Current financial statements from customers may be analyzed by a computer to provide answers to such questions as the following: (1) Based on past performance, will the firm have sufficient cash for future operations, or will additional financing be needed? (2) Has the firm been depending on creditors for operating capital? (3) If creditors are supplying the operating capital, how much cash would the firm have to raise if suppliers demanded payment? Answers to these questions are of importance to a credit manager faced with the decision of whether to extend credit. If a potential customer is judged to be in a marginal financial position, the credit manager can use this information to plan the best financial strategy to employ.

In another application, the director of research at Akron National Bank and Trust Company uses a computer to prepare a weekly report for use by top bank executives. This report is used to support plans and decisions regarding overall management of assets. Included in the report are comparisons of performance between Akron National and other banks in the Akron, Ohio, area and in the Fourth Federal Reserve District. (Weekly input data from the Federal Reserve Board are incorporated into the planning reports.) Also, comparisons of year-to-date financial ratios against the previous year's performance are presented. In addition to weekly planning reports, the research director is also using the computer to forecast deposit and loan flows and to estimate bank profitability.

Business Simulation Models

As we have seen in Chapter 9, simulation is a planning aid that may be of considerable value to *top-level executives.* A simulation model may, for example, help a company president decide whether to expand operations by acquiring new production facilities. Among the dozens of complicating variables that would have to be included in such a model would be facts and assumptions about (1) present and potential market size, (2) present and potential share of the market, (3) selling prices at different production volumes, and (4) capital investment required to achieve different production levels. Thus, a good model can help an executive in strategic planning and decision-making activities.

Simulation may also be helpful to *middle-level business managers* in planning and decision making. For example, simulation models are used to improve inventory management. The problem of managing inventories is complicated because there are conflicting desires among organizational units, and what is best for one department may not be best for the entire firm. To illustrate, the purchasing department may prefer to buy large quantities of supplies and raw materials in order to get lower prices;

the production department also likes to have large inventories on hand to eliminate shortages and make possible long—and efficient—production runs; and the sales department prefers large finished-goods inventories so that sales will not be lost because of out-of-stock conditions. The finance department, on the other hand, views with concern large inventory levels since storage expense is increased, risk of spoilage and deterioration is increased, and funds are tied up for longer periods of time. Through the use of simulated inventory amounts and simulated assumptions about such factors as reorder lead times and the cost of being out of stock, managers can experiment with various approaches to arrive at more profitable inventory levels.

A practical application of the use of simulation might be in order at this point. Potlatch Forests, Inc., a producer of lumber and wood pulp products, has a corporate planning staff that has developed an overall corporate financial model. Given assumptions from top executives about economic conditions, capital expenditures, etc., for a five-year future period, simulation runs produce estimated financial statements for each of the five years. Executives then analyze the simulated financial statements. If results are judged to be disappointing, executives may change variables in the model that are under their control—e.g., future capital expenditures—and the simulations are repeated. When acceptable financial results are obtained, they become the targets for planning at lower levels in the company. When feasible, lower-level plans are formulated (again, simulation models are used), and they are assembled into an overall corporate plan.

Of course, the output of simulation models is only as good as the facts and assumptions that go into the computer.[2] National economic data and assumptions about the national economy are usually an integral part of a corporate simulation model. Several organizations such as Lionel D. Edie, Data Resources, Inc., Dun & Bradstreet, Chase Econometric Associates, and the National Bureau of Economic Research provide extensive *national economic data bases* that are available to subscribers to their services. Additional data bases of value to builders of business models are supplied by online retrieval services such as *Dialog* (Lockheed), *Orbit* (System Development Corporation), and BRS (Bibliographic Retrieval Services). Also, General Electric's MAP system was originally developed for internal use by that organization but is now available to timesharing customers. When combined with a firm's internal information, the national economic data provided by these services may enable managers to more accurately model a firm's future.[3]

---

[2] The U.S. Geological Survey uses a complex computer-based model to come up with estimates of the oil and gas reserves that might be found in the government's offshore tracts that oil companies bid on. In one area 50 miles off New Jersey's shore, the model "estimates that reserves in the area range from 400 million to 1.4 billion barrels of crude oil and from 2.6 trillion to 9.4 trillion cubic feet of natural gas. But oilmen in Houston irreverently call this computerized approach SWAG—for 'Scientific Wild-Ass Guess.'" See *Business Week,* p. 116, September 20, 1976.

[3] For an excellent discussion of business planning techniques and the use of simulation models, see "The New Planning," *Business Week,* pp. 62–66ff, December 18, 1978.

From this brief discussion, we can see that *business simulation models may offer such advantages as* (1) controlled experimentation involving alternative policies and the consideration of many variables, (2) the ability to enhance operational understanding, and (3) the means of providing effective managerial training in decision making. However, *simulation disadvantages may include* (1) the time and cost required to develop the model, (2) the use of oversimplified or incorrect assumptions hidden in the model, and (3) the possible lack of enthusiastic support for the model from managers who may be expected to use it.

Operational Planning

Lower-level operational plans generally cover a shorter time span and are based on overall strategies, assumptions, and goals. Such plans, in other words, are designed to achieve efficiency of performance in the short term once market forecasts, sales quotas, advertising programs, production schedules, and financial and personnel resources are known. (Of course, as we saw in the Potlatch example described above, computer simulation models may also be used in this phase of business planning.)

In their operational planning activities, trucking companies use computers to plan daily pickup and delivery routes. Among the complicating factors that must be considered are (1) the large number of pickup and delivery points, (2) warehouse locations, (3) frequency of daily pickups and deliveries, and (4) types of trucks available. In addition to planning and scheduling truck movements to give good service and maximize the consolidation of freight hauled by each unit, trucking firms have also used simulation techniques to evaluate the effects of changes in routes, demand for services, number and/or locations of warehouses, and changes in equipment.

Airlines, like trucking firms, also use computers to plan routes—in this case to select flight plans. Given data on wind velocity and air turbulence from scores of geographical locations, a computer program can consider these factors in arriving at an optimum flight plan. For example, when a flight plan is needed, the computer is given the final destination, locations of any intermediate stops, expected payload, type of aircraft, and published schedule times. One or more plans are then computed, taking wind and turbulence factors, along with these other variables, into account. The pilot then chooses from among the alternatives prepared. Generally, the preferred plan is the one which gets the plane to its destination(s) on time and with minimum fuel consumption. However, another alternative is likely to be selected if turbulence conditions on the "least-cost" route would result in passenger discomfort.

A professional football team is another type of business that uses computers in operational planning. A few organizations scout college players and gather statistical data about them for the pro draft each year (Figure 18-7). One organization is QUADRA (serving the Dallas Cowboys, Los Angeles Rams, San Francisco 49ers, and San Diego Chargers); another is BLESTO (originally the Bears, Lions, Eagles, Steelers Talent Orga-

FIGURE 18-7
Pro football team's link to computer during pro draft. (*UNIVAC Div., Sperry Rand.*)

nization, but later including the Bills, Chiefs, Colts, Dolphins, and Vikings). A scouting organization may gather 40,000 scouting reports in a year, and computer processing is needed to handle the data volume. Tex Schramm, Dallas Cowboy president, and Art Rooney, Jr., owner of the Pittsburgh Steelers, were among the first executives to bring computer analysis into pro football. In addition to planning and decision-making uses for player acquisition, computers are also used by many pro football teams for play-analysis purposes. We have already discussed this type of application in Chapter 15, however, and so we need not spend more time here on the subject.

CONTROL

Computers are effectively used in the few representative business control applications presented below:

1   *In financial institutions.* Many savings institutions make use of online transaction recording devices to communicate directly with their central processor. When a customer wishes to make a deposit, he or she presents a savings book and the amount of the deposit to the teller, who inserts the book into a recorder and keys in the transaction data. The data are then sent to the computer, which adjusts the customer's savings balance. The updated information is relayed back to the remote station, where it is entered in the customer's savings book. Only

a few seconds is required to complete the transaction. In addition to providing better customer service, such a system may also provide better control. Managers of a savings bank may have quick access (through monitoring stations) to up-to-the-minute deposit and withdrawal information because totals may be adjusted after each transaction. Such information may be compared with expected deposit and withdrawal levels in order to make decisions about cash needs and short-run investment proposals. Peak activity periods can also be computed for each remote station to aid managers in effectively controlling the use of personnel. Furthermore, as we have seen, financial institutions can install transaction control terminals (Figure 18-8) at department stores, supermarkets, and other retail outlets to control (1) the electronic transfer of funds between accounts and (2) the authorization of credit and the verification of checks.

2 *In inventory control.* A large percentage of a firm's assets may be tied up in raw material, work in process, and finished-goods inventories. As we saw a few pages earlier, computer simulation models can be used to plan and control inventory levels in different departments. Of course, if increased effectiveness in inventory control serves to reduce necessary inventory levels, a significant amount of investment capital may be released for other productive purposes. Computers may be programmed to provide effective control of inventory items by (a) predicting production and/or sales trends on the basis of past records, (b) keeping track of warehouse stock (remember the Rohr Aircraft warehouse system in the last chapter?), and (c) keeping track of sales at different locations. If stock of a fast-moving sales item or production part drops below a predetermined level, the computer may be programmed to automatically reorder the item or part in economical

FIGURE 18-8
EFTS transaction control
terminal. (*Burroughs Corp.*)

quantities; if sales of an item in one location are brisk while at another point the item is a slow mover, the computer may be programmed to shift inventory to where it is needed most. One organization using a computerized inventory-control system is Martin-Brower Corporation, a Chicago-based distributor of paper products, nonperishable food products, and service supplies to drive-in restaurants specializing in fast service. Martin-Brower has 10 warehouses and a 5,000-item inventory to control. The system estimates future demand by computing current market trends and seasonal fluctuations for items like bags and cups. A forecast is prepared for each warehouse. The system also reports two or three times a week on the demand rate for each item in the inventory. Items that appear to be in short supply are flagged by the system, and recommended reorder quantities are computed. Managers then make the reorder decision based on their knowledge of the situation. Another computerized inventory-control system found in the fast-food restaurant business is operated by the Carl's Junior fast-food chain in California. When a customer places an order at the counter, a cashier touches the appropriate boxes on a terminal keyboard containing all the menu items (Figure 18-9). Each time a cashier enters a sale, the data are fed automatically into a mini-computer system. By using beginning inventory and sales data, the system can determine the inventory items that must be reordered. Finally, other organizations using computerized inventory-control systems include Ford and General Motors automobile dealers. Terminals in thousands of independently owned dealerships (Figure 18-10) are connected to Ford and GM computers located at parts distribution

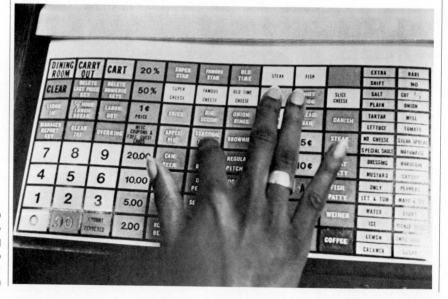

FIGURE 18-9
Online terminal used by fast-food chain to control food inventory and speed up order handling. (*Pertec Computer Co.*)

FIGURE 18-10
Dealer's terminals are connected to parts distribution centers. (*Texas Instruments.*)

centers around the country. These terminals are used for the ordering and control of parts inventories.

3 *In combating credit card fraud.* National Data Corporation (NDC) of Atlanta is using computers to control the illegal use of credit cards. In the NDC computers are daily updated lists of stolen credit cards issued by most of the nation's oil companies and by members of the Interbank Card Association. Oil company service-station managers may make a toll-free call to NDC if they suspect that a card may be stolen or if the amount of the purchase exceeds a specified amount. The manager gives the name of the card-issuing company, the card number, and the purchase amount. If the card number matches the number of a card reported stolen, lost, or cancelled, the station manager is notified quickly; if not, the computer registers an approval and a code number to the manager, who is then protected against any financial loss. (Should the manager accept a charge over the specified amount and the card turn out to be a stolen one, the station is liable for the loss.) Over a million calls a month are received by NDC.

4 *In controlling tire recalls.* In the early 1970s, a new-tire recall regulation of the National Highway Traffic Safety Administration took effect. Tire suppliers are required to maintain, for at least three years, records of those who purchased new tires. Tires are identified by a serial number that includes the manufacturer's code number, the size of the tire, and the week it was produced. Should a tire be found defective, all other tires produced by the manufacturer during that week may have to be recalled. With annual sales of 300 million tires, the task of keeping buyer records is obviously a formidable one. Axicom Systems, Inc., of Paramus, New Jersey, has established a Tire Safety Registry system to handle the entire record-keeping problem. Tire dealers, at the time of purchase, fill out forms giving the necessary information (buyer's

"Meeting User Needs Key to Info Future"

Looking at the information processing industry's future at a recent management meeting, Sperry Univac President Richard L. Gehring said: "Now, more important than ever, is the need to fully integrate the data processing function into the overall business operations. It cannot stand alone, isolated, and survive in the future."

As keynote speaker at a recent Society of Management Information Systems meeting in Chicago, Gehring continued: "It's obvious your systems must be designed to accommodate information growth requirements. You have all the tools at your disposal to make the system fit their (users') needs. The reverse is a luxury we can no longer afford."

"The greater the squeeze on your spendable corporate dollars, the greater the need for the mind-amplifying power of the computer," he said. "With that goes the need to expand its usage—to exploit its potential." And he noted that "our systems today are being used in only about 10 percent of the potential uses.

"I believe we are moving from an era of 'use-ability' to one of 'user ability'," he added. "As manufacturers and information managers, it's our collective job to show that computing processes can be understood and fully controlled by the ultimate user. The opportunity to do just that is continually increasing.

"Hardware and software technologies are putting us closer to the real users —wherever they are. But we have to make certain our advancing technology serves them, not ourselves," Gehring said.

"As manufacturers, we'll continue to be your first line of support. Our responsibilities are increasing right along with yours," he told the MIS managers about future years. "We have to make sure you have all the choices you need to best serve your users."

Source: "Meeting User Needs Key to Info Future," *Infosystems*, p. 22, September 1979. Reprinted by permission of the publisher.

name, address, tire numbers, etc.). These forms are then sent to Paramus, where the information is kept in online storage devices. If a recall is necessary, the computer retrieves from a batch in question the names and addresses of all purchasers of tires. Buyers are then notified by certified mail of the recall and are instructed to return the tires to a dealer for replacement.

5 *In controlling merger operations.* Computers and the critical-path method of scheduling activities were used several years ago to control the merger of General Electric's computer operations into Honeywell. Stanley M. Seeds, the merger coordinator, established a

"merger war room" to effect the changeover. Since moves were being made in 18 countries, a smooth work flow and tight control were required.

LOOKING BACK

The following points have been emphasized in this chapter:

1 The purpose of this chapter has been to discuss briefly a few of the ways in which computers can be used in business in the areas of (*a*) planning and decision making, and (*b*) control.
2 Computers can make a valuable contribution in market research and thus in market planning. Statistical market analyses, for example, can be used as input to computerized statistical forecasting procedures that may be used to project sales volume into the future. Financial planning is another area where computers have been used to good advantage. Programs to calculate important financial ratios, analyze cash flow, and assist in capital investment planning are available. Computer usage in planning business operations can also contribute to improved efficiency and better utilization of a firm's resources.
3 Simulation is a planning aid that may be of considerable value to business managers at all levels. Of course, the output of simulation models is only as good as the facts and assumptions that go into the computer.
4 A few representative uses of computers for business control purposes were outlined in the chapter. Procedures for financial and inventory control were discussed, and techniques used to combat credit card fraud and control tire recalls were considered.

KEY TERMS

After reading Chapter 18, you should be able to define and use the following terms:

market research	national economic data bases
market forecasting	inventory control
Telcot network	credit card fraud control
financial planning	BLESTO
business simulation models	QUADRA

REVIEW AND DISCUSSION QUESTIONS

1 "File processing is not limited to business organizations." Discuss this statement.

2 How may computers be used in market planning?
3 How may computers be used for financial planning purposes?
4 "Computer usage in business operations can contribute to improved efficiency and better utilization of a firm's resources." Give examples to support this statement.
5 (a) How may simulation models aid business executives in planning? (b) "The output of simulation models is only as good as the facts and assumptions that go into the computer." Discuss this statement.
6 (a) How can a computer be used for inventory-control purposes? (b) For combating credit card fraud?

◆ SELECTED REFERENCES

Among the periodicals that commonly report on business uses of computers are *Administrative Management, Banking, Business Horizons, Business Week, California Management Review, Computers and People, Computer Decisions, Datamation, Data Management, EDP Analyzer, Financial Executive, Harvard Business Review, Infosystems, Journal of Systems Management, Management Review, Office, Personal Computing,* and *The Wall Street Journal.*

In addition to these periodicals, you may find the following sources to be of interest:

Andres, William A.: "The Business of Retailing, and Management Information Systems," *Computers and People,* pp. 7–10, March/April 1979.
"Cotton's Electronic Market," *Data Processor,* pp. 8–11, June 1979.
Hertzberg, Daniel: "Managing the Money for Big Firm Requires Many Quick Decisions," *The Wall Street Journal,* pp. 1ff, August 13, 1979.
Kronholz, June: "Computer Replaces Rawhide in Running Modern Beef Operation," *The Wall Street Journal,* pp. 1ff, September 1, 1978.
Parker, Robert: "A Computer at the NFL Draft," *Tempo* (Touche Ross & Company), vol 24, pp. 32–36, 1978.
Wysocki, Bernard, Jr.: "Executives Discover Computers Can Help Them in Daily Routine," *The Wall Street Journal,* pp. 1ff, July 6, 1979.

Part Six

Part Six
COMPUTERS AND SOCIETY BEYOND 1984

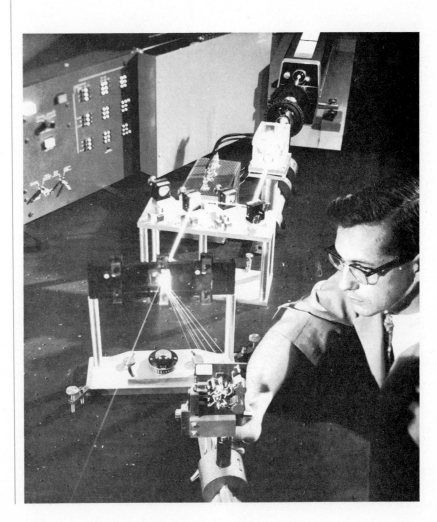

(IBM.)

In 1949, when people first read George Orwell's *1984,* with its eerie visions of a society controlled by "Big Brother," they probably took some comfort in the fact that 1984 was a distant 35 years in the future. But those 35 years have slipped away. The fictional version of 1984 was frightening; now, as we move into—and then beyond—1984, what is likely to be the reality? In this final part of the book, we will briefly try to anticipate some of the answers to this question.

The chapter included in Part 6 is:

19 *Tomorrow's Outlook*

Chapter 19
TOMORROW'S OUTLOOK

The purpose of this chapter is to briefly speculate on some of the computer—and computer-driven—developments that may be possible through the 1980s.

The *technological outlook* for computer *hardware* and *software* is considered in the first section of the chapter. The consideration of possible hardware developments is discussed from the standpoint of *I/O devices* and *central processors.*

As we move from an industrial society that emphasizes standardized mass production to a new information/communications society that will produce customized and individualized configurations of products and services, it will be necessary to develop future information systems that are *quicker-responding* and *broader in scope.* The *outlook for such information systems* is the subject of the second section of the chapter.

Finally, in the last section, the future *outlook for individuals* is considered.

Thus, after studying this chapter, you should be able to:

- Discuss some of the possible developments in hardware, software, and information systems that you expect in the 1980s.
- Present the optimistic and pessimistic views about the future impact of computer systems on individuals.
- Form some opinions of your own on the future impact that computer systems are likely to have on society.
- Understand and use the key terms listed at the end of the chapter.

I n spite of the profound warning contained in an old proverb ("Prediction is difficult, particularly when it pertains to the future"), in this final chapter we shall attempt to summarize briefly some of the computer—and computer-related—developments that may be expected in the next few years. The topics to be considered can be classified as (1) the *technological outlook,* (2) the *information-systems outlook,* and (3) the *outlook for individuals.*

THE TECHNOLOGICAL OUTLOOK

Although the explosion in electronics technology is having a profound effect on such things as the way time and other variables are measured (with digital display devices), food is cooked (with microwave devices), and people are entertained (with home videotape recorders and video-disk players), we shall limit our discussion in this section to the outlook for computer *hardware* and *software*.

Computer Hardware

Numerous changes may be expected in the next few years in *I/O devices* and *central processors*.

I/O equipment In the *data entry* field, there will probably be little change in the performance of *punched card* equipment in the next several years. Although punched cards are still an important I/O medium, their use peaked in 1969, and the total demand for punched card equipment will continue to decline in the future. By the late 1980s, many existing keypunches and stand-alone data entry systems will have been replaced by *multifunction online terminals* that capture data at the point of transaction. (Many of these terminals will perform *both* word processing and data processing functions.) Of course, many organizations cannot convert overnight to the use of online terminals to capture data (and words) at the point of transaction. Thus, *optical character recognition* (OCR) equipment (which is dropping significantly in price) will often be used to avoid the need to rekey data captured by nonelectronic data entry devices such as typewriters. The use of offline multistation *keyboard-to-disk* storage devices for data entry purposes is therefore likely to decline gradually over the next decade. *Speech recognition* will become the preferred means of supplying input data to future computers in a growing number of applications.

Impact printers will not change significantly in speed in the next few years. A booming market for the low-speed line and character impact printers used with micro- and minicomputers is likely; improvements in dot-matrix character printers may result in output that is of full-strike typewriter quality; and prices of these low-speed printers are likely to drop substantially. New *nonimpact printers* in the 1,000-line-per-minute speed range will appear to challenge the chain- and drum-type impact machines. Since these new printers will be much less expensive, they will succeed in replacing many of the older "workhorses." New systems requiring a great deal of archival storage will bypass printing altogether and make much greater use of lower-cost *computer-output-to-microfilm* (COM) equipment. There should also be some cost reduction in *magnetic tape drives* in the next few years, and there should be a doubling in transfer speeds as the amount of data packed in an inch of tape doubles. Overall, however, the life cycle of magnetic tape may have reached its peak.

Direct-access storage devices will continue to be a hotbed of research activity for years to come. Such devices will be developed to provide virtually unlimited online secondary storage at a very modest cost. *Storage hierarchies* will continue—i.e., the fastest auxiliary storage utilizing the latest technology will be more expensive and may have less storage capacity than slower and less expensive alternatives. Mass storage approaches (in various stages of research and development) that are being considered by equipment designers include:

1 *Higher-density direct-access systems.* Recording techniques using magnetic disk surfaces that will significantly increase the density of data storage on a given surface are expected to be developed in the near future. It will not be long before the contents of over 600 books of this size can be stored in a disk device occupying the space of two small present-day floppy-disk drives. About 10 million bits of data are currently being stored on a square inch of disk surface; in the next six or seven years, there will be a tenfold improvement—to 100 million bits or more.[1] The costs of disk storage will also drop dramatically. (A 20 million-character disk drive for personal microcomputers will soon be available for less than $1,000.)

2 *More efficient and reliable magnetic bubble systems.* Free of the mechanical motion required with disks and drums, bubble devices are expected to evolve rapidly; they will become more reliable and much lower in cost. Storage density will be very high (well over 1 million characters will be stored on a single bubble chip). Future storage devices—"flubbles?"—may combine the best features of floppy disks and bubble chips in small and medium-sized systems.

3 *Optical direct-access systems.* Information may be stored on a special light-sensitive plate by modulating electric pulses onto a *laser* light beam that is directed to a given area on the plate surface. A negative image of the varying light pattern—called a *hologram*—is etched on the plate surface, and storage is thus accomplished. To retrieve information (without erasing it), a less intense laser beam is directed to the appropriate hologram to project the image onto sensors that will convert the light into electrical representations of the stored information. A single beam of light, can cause the immediate transfer of a "page" of data. Theoretically, storage density and I/O speed are very high. Also, reliability is enhanced because of the absence of moving parts.

The *dollar amount* of sales of *online terminals* is expected to increase by about 50 percent in the decade prior to 1988 (see Figure 19-1). In terms of the *number of terminals sold each year,* the market is likely to double in size in this same period. Much of this growth is expected to be in the categories of *typewriterlike terminals* (or *teleprinters*), *intelligent visual display terminals,* and *specialty terminals.*

Many of the typewriterlike terminals of 1988, however, will have undergone considerable change. They will be "intelligent" devices contain-

[1] See A. S. Hoagland, "Storage Technology: Capabilities and Limitations," *Computer,* pp. 12–18, May 1979; and Edward K. Yasaki, "Signals of a Real Explosion," *Datamation,* pp. 52–53, August 1979.

575

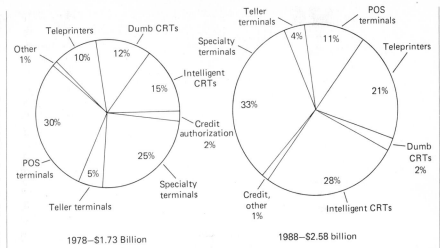

FIGURE 19-1
Expected changes in the
market for terminals between
1978 and 1988. As you
can see, sales are expected
to increase by almost
50 percent—from $1.73
billion to $2.58 billion.
(Source: Stephen A. Caswell,
"Computer Peripherals: A
Revolution Is Coming,"
Datamation, p. 85, May 25,
1979.)

1978—$1.73 Billion

1988—$2.58 billion

ing microprocessors and bubble or semiconductor memory chips, and they will be used in organizations to meet both word and data processing needs. As data entry stations, they will be used to capture and relay facts to a distributed or host computer; as *communicating word processors,* they will be used to distribute (and receive) electronic mail and messages; and they will also be used by participants in the computerized conferences described in Chapter 9.

Intelligent visual display terminals will also be used for word processing and data entry applications. Sales of such specialized multiunit data stations as *POS terminals* and *teller terminals* will grow rapidly in the early 1980s, but by 1988 market saturation may cause a tapering off of sales to replacement levels. However, other specialized terminals such as those used in (1) security systems to read industrial and office badges, (2) manufacturing data entry systems, and (3) brokerage houses are poised for rapid growth. Hand-held portable terminals that will be linked to a computer by radio transmission will also probably experience enormous growth.

The proliferation in the number of intelligent terminals installed during the 1980s will, of course, be accompanied by the creation of new *distributed processing networks* in many more organizations. These organizations will be (1) using the intelligent terminals to carry out autonomous word and data processing operations, and (2) utilizing a host and/or node computer(s) to serve the terminals by managing data bases and by executing those jobs which require extensive computations.

Central processors There will continue to be substantial reductions in the *size* of electronic circuits. The average number of components (transistors, resistors, etc.) packed on advanced integrated circuit chips has about doubled every year since 1965, and this trend is likely to continue through the 1980s. By the end of the 1980s, tiny memory chips capable of storing 64K bits will give way to chips of about the same size that may have up to 200 times the storage capacity. We have already seen that processors with more computing power than large machines of just a few years ago are already dwarfed by their peripherals. Long before the end of the 1980s, 32-bit *microcomputers* with 1 million bits of RAM storage will be fabricated on a single chip. These single-chip microcomputers will (1) employ the same instruction sets as present-day mainframe models, (2) execute up to 1 million instructions per second, and (3) accept without modification the large libraries of software written for such mainframe families as the IBM System/370. By way of comparison, the largest present-day System/370 model (the 3033) occupies several cubic yards of space and can execute 5 million instructions per second. (Of course, by the end of the 1980s, a mainframe model may execute 70 million instructions per second and have 16 million bytes of primary storage and a large cache memory section. Such a model could be packaged in a 6-inch cube!)[2]

As the above paragraph indicates, *greater speed* will accompany further size reductions. Future supercomputers will be able to execute thousands of millions of instructions per second by harnessing many powerful micro-sized computers in a parallel assembly. *Superconductive cryogenic circuits* employing the *Josephson junction*—named for British Nobel Prize winner Brian Josephson—will be in use by the end of the 1980s. These circuits operate in a liquid helium bath at close to absolute zero temperature (more than 400 degrees below zero on the Fahrenheit scale). At that temperature, barriers that would ordinarily restrain the flow of electricity lose their resistive ability. The switching speeds of the Josephson junction circuit are up to 100 times faster than those of the circuits used in large present-day mainframes.

What about the *cost* of future central processors? You already know the answer to this question: For a given level of computing power, cost will continue to drop like a brick. The cost of primary storage in a CPU represents a significant part of the total cost. Table 19-1 shows the cost trends for 1 million bytes (a *megabyte*) of primary storage. As you can see, the retail price per megabyte was about $95,000 in 1975, but it is expected to be $80 by 1991! Other components in the CPU are likely to experience similar trends.

We saw in Chapter 5 that *microprograms* stored in *read-only memory* (ROM) devices may be used to interpret the problem-solving instructions written by a programmer and to translate these instructions into steps that the hardware can accept. For years, microprograms have also been used to permit one computer to interpret and execute instructions written for a different machine. In other words, the microprograms (also called *stored logic* and *firmware*) would analyze and decode foreign in-

---

[2] See David L. Stein, "Price/Performance, Semiconductors, and the Future," *Datamation*, pp. 14–16ff, November 25, 1979.

Year	Bits/Chip*	Component Cost/MB†	Chips/MB	PCB + Labor‡	Total Cost to Manufacture/MB	Retail Price/MB§
1975	1K	$19,294	8,192	$4,588.	$23,882.	$95,528.
1977	4K	8,152	2,048	1,147.	9,299.	37,196.
1979	16K	3,444	512	287.	3,731.	14,924.
1981	64K	1,455	128	72.	1,527.	6,108.
1983	256K	615	32	18.	633.	2,532.
1985	1M	260	8	4.5	264.5	1,058.
1987	4M	110	2	1.1	111.1	444.4
1989	16M	46	½	0.28	46.28	185.12
1991	64M	20	⅛	0.07	20.07	80.28

* RAM chip density (bits/chip) is expected to quadruple every two years for the next 10 years. (Robert N. Noyce, "Microelectronics," *Scientific American,* September 1977.)

† In 1975 RAM cost was 0.23¢/bit. RAM cost has decreased 35%/year since 1970, and this trend is expected to continue. (Robert N. Noyce, op. cit.)

‡ Printed circuit boards, miscellaneous components, and labor cost are related directly to component count. It was figured here at $0.56/RAM chip, the actual figure for 16K RAM boards in 1978.

§ Retail price is figured at four times the cost to manufacture. This allows 100% markup (doubling the price) by both the manufacturer and the retailer, the actual practice in today's personal computing industry.

Source: Portia Isaacson, "1984's Information Appliances," *Datamation,* February 1979, p. 216.

structions into the elementary operations that the particular CPU was designed to execute (Figure 19-2).

In addition to permitting one computer to *emulate* another, it is also feasible to use various combinations of plug-in microprograms with *generalized* central processors to create custom-built systems for specific users. This "computer within a computer" approach can facilitate standardized CPU manufacturing and maintenance operations; it also makes it possible to convert critical, difficult, or lengthy software routines into microprograms that can be executed in a fraction of the time previously required. Furthermore, it is possible for vendors and users to *permanently* fuse their most important microprograms into ROM chips and thus, in effect, convert important software into hardware.[3] Figure 19-3 illustrates how a computer manufacturer or user can create a customized computer system. Unlike the special-purpose computers of earlier years, however, the same processor can now be adapted to different functions by a simple change of microprograms. As Figure 19-3 indicates, if nonpermanent microprograms are desired, they may be loaded into a writable storage device that can be plugged into the CPU, and if permanent firmware is needed, it may be fused onto ROM chips by a special writing device.

[3] Persons subscribing to *CLOAD* magazine can now get a tape cassette each month that is filled with game and educational programs for their personal computers. It is likely that "ROM of the Month" clubs will also spring up in the 1980s to send subscribers new applications programs written in ROM chips that can be plugged into personal micros.

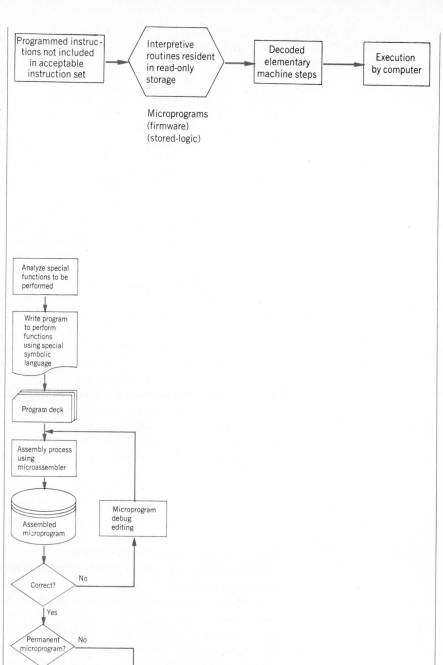

FIGURE 19-2
A use of microprograms, or firmware (which is software substituted for hardware and stored in read-only memory).

FIGURE 19-3
Procedure for customizing a computer with microprograms.

Computer technology will probably make much greater use of firmware in the future. By converting functions currently being performed with software into circuit elements (which are becoming less expensive), the need for some of the detailed (and very expensive) programming currently being done may be reduced. For example, in performing its functions of scheduling, control, etc., the operating system (OS) software discussed in Chapter 2 uses storage space in, and the time of, the CPU—space and time resources that might otherwise have been used for mathematical or data processing tasks. To reduce this OS overhead, resident microprograms operating at hardware speeds may be substituted for some of the tasks currently being accomplished at relatively slow speeds with a series of OS program instructions. Also, specialized microprocessors and microprograms are likely to be used frequently in the future in place of software for language translation, data security, and data manipulation and control. We saw in Chapter 4 how "front-end" processors are used to relieve the host CPU of data communications functions. In the future, "back-end" processors may also be commonly used to handle data-base management functions and to control the movement of data between various storage elements in a storage hierarchy. Thus, the traditional and still very popular *uniprocessor* computer system that features single control, storage, and arithmetic-logic units will give way in the future to *multiprocessor* systems in all but the smallest installations. Of course, the component micro- and mini-sized processors dedicated to performing the specialized functions such as data-base management and security are likely to be smaller than those reserved to process user jobs in multiple and simultaneous streams. But future users—connected to such a multiprocessor system, perhaps, by intelligent terminals that further distribute and decentralize the computing power of the network—may expect faster, more reliable, and more secure service.

Computer Software

There are numerous technical articles being published that predict with confidence the course of hardware development over the next decade. But this confidence is not found in the few articles dealing with the future of software development. Perhaps this is due to the fact that the development of software will continue to be slower, much more expensive, and more painful than hardware development because the functions performed by software are now (and will continue to be) more complex than the operations performed by hardware. Of course, as we saw in the preceding section, many of the functions now being performed by OS and system software may be taken over by future hardware elements. And the future use of multiprocessor systems may *reduce* the need for complex *multiprogramming* software that permits instructions from several programs to be interleaved and executed on a single processor. In short, the total-cost trends for information systems discussed in Chapter 2 (and

"Living: Pushbutton Power"

*The Computer Revolution May Make Us Wiser,
Healthier and Even Happier*

*It is 7:30 a.m. As the alarm clock burrs, the bedroom curtains swing silently apart, the Venetian blinds snap up and the thermostat boosts the heat to a cozy 70°. The percolator in the kitchen starts burbling; the back door opens to let out the dog. The TV set blinks on with the day's first newscast: not your **Today** show humph-humph, but a selective rundown (ordered up the night before) of all the latest worldwide events affecting the economy—legislative, political, monetary. After the news on TV comes the morning mail, from correspondents who have dictated their messages into the computer network. The latter-day Aladdin, still snugly abed, then presses a button on a bedside box and issues a string of business and personal memos, which appear instantly on the genie screen. After his shower, which has turned itself on at exactly the right temperature at the right minute, Mr. A. is alerted by a buzzer and a blue light on the screen. His boss, the company president, is on his way to the office. A. dresses and saunters out to the car. The engine, of course, is running . . .*

*After her husband has kissed her goodbye, Alice A. concentrates on the screen for a read-out of comparative prices at the local merchants, and markets. Following eyeball-to-eyeball consultations with the butcher and the baker and the grocer on the tube, she hits a button to commandeer supplies for tonight's dinner party. Pressing a couple of keys on the kitchen terminal, she orders from the memory bank her favorite recipes for oysters Rockefeller, **boeuf à la bourguignonne** and chocolate **soufflé,** tells the machine to compute the ingredients for six servings, and directs the ovens to reach the correct temperature for each dish according to the recipe, starting at 7:15 p.m. Alice then joins a televised discussion of Byzantine art (which she has studied by computer). Later she wanders into the computer room where Al ("Laddy") Jr. has just learned from his headset that his drill in Latin verb conjugation was "groovy."*

Wellsian fantasy? Verne-Vonnegut put-on? Maybe. But while this matutinal scenario may still be years away, the basic technology is in existence. Such painless, productive awakenings will in time be as familiar as Dagwood Bumstead's pajamaed panics. And, barring headaches, tummy aches and heartaches, the American day should proceed as smoothly as it begins. All thanks to the miracle of the microcomputer, the supercheap chip that can electronically shoulder a vast array of boring, time-consuming tasks.

The microelectronic revolution promises to ease, enhance and simplify life in ways undreamed of even by the utopians. At home or office, routine chores will be performed with astonishing efficiency and speed. Leisure time, greatly increased, will be greatly enriched. Public education, so often a dreary and capricious process in the U.S., may be invested with the inspiriting quality of an Oxford tutorial—from preschool on. Medical care will be delivered with greater precision.

Letters will not so easily go astray. It will be safer to walk the streets because people will not need to carry large amounts of cash; virtually all financial transactions will be conducted by computer. In the microelectronic global village, the home will again be the center of society, as it was before the Industrial Revolution.

Source: "Living: Pushbutton Power," *Time,* p. 46, February 20, 1978. Reprinted by permission from *Time,* The Weekly Newsmagazine; Copyright Time Inc. 1978.

shown in Figure 2-11, page 59) will encourage the replacement of expensive software with cheap hardware whenever possible.

The comments just made in the preceding paragraph should not, however, be interpreted to mean that there will be no progress in software development. On the contrary, existing *languages* such as BASIC, COBOL, FORTRAN, etc., will be enhanced and improved to accommodate the *structured programming* approach discussed in Chapter 7. Furthermore, new very high level languages will be developed to solve particular types of problems so that nonprogrammer users can conveniently make use of computing capabilities. From the users' standpoint, such languages will be more like their native English (or German, French, Spanish, etc.), and they will be *conversational* — i.e., the computer itself will keep track of the acceptable vocabulary of the language, and it may display permissible alternate terms and statements to users in a "question and answer" format until the problem is satisfactorily formulated. The machine will then compute the answer to the problem. Thus, the users' major skill will be in their ability to state problems, and they will be assisted by a "dialogue" with the computer as it seeks to find out what they want to say.

Conversational programming is likely to be a feature of the *data-base management software* described in Chapter 2 (and in Figure 2-21, page 72). In 1974, there were only about 1,500 true data-base management systems in worldwide use. By 1988, however, there will be tens of thousands of these software systems in operation; they will be more comprehensive, they will be large and may require up to a million characters of storage to operate effectively, and they will enable the end-user of the information to frequently bypass the services of applications programmers. Additional provisions to ensure the *integrity* and *security* of stored information will be incorporated into future data-base software as well as future hardware.

Finally, *program development aids* such as structured programming will result in higher programmer productivity, shorter program development times, and more understandable and error-free program modules. And the trend toward the geater use of packaged programs will accelerate rapidly.

THE INFORMATION-SYSTEMS OUTLOOK

We are now in a period of transition between an old industrial society that emphasizes standardized mass production and distribution and a new information/communications society that will carefully fit standard components together to produce highly customized and individualized configurations of products and services.[4] The traditional batch-processing computer installations used to good advantage in a standardized setting are economical, are well suited to many types of routine applications, and are going to continue to be used to process large volumes of information. But the trend toward a customized and individualized society will require future systems that will be *quicker responding* and *broader in scope* than these traditional installations.

Quick-Response Systems

As we have seen, emphasis is currently being given to the development of (1) distributed computer systems with logic and storage capability moved to the point of origin of transactions, (2) user-oriented interactive programming languages designed to enable operating personnel to get information quickly without having to wait for the help of an applications programmer, and (3) direct-access storage devices, online terminals, and multiprocessor computer configurations. These developments, in turn, signal a definite trend in the direction of quick-response systems that will give remote users immediate access to very powerful computing facilities. *Real time processing* will become increasingly common in those applications where immediate updating of records is justifiable. When the time limitations are not so severe, *online processing,* with periodic updating of those records which affect other users of a distributed network, will often replace traditional batch-processing methods. Source data will frequently be keyed directly into the computer system, thus eliminating the need for cards and/or tapes in many applications. As we have seen, the same terminals used to enter data will also be used as communicating word processors to distribute (and receive) electronic mail and messages.

With increased emphasis being placed on quick-response systems, there will obviously be greater use of *data communications* facilities. In fact, the transmission of data is expected to continue to increase by at least 35 percent *each year* between now and the late 1980s. New data communications services will be established, and the current services offered by data carrier organizations will be expanded to meet this demand. Satellites will be used more extensively in space, and the *fiber optic* and *laser* technology discussed in Chapter 4 will be used in land-based trans-

---

[4] See "The End of the Industrial Society," *Business Week,* pp. 2–4, September 3, 1979.

BUY BACK POLICY

SELL YOUR TEXT BOOKS FOR CASH

at the Bookstore during finals week of each quarter.

YOUR TEXTS MAY BE WORTH UP TO 50% OF THE PRICE YOU PAID <u>IF:</u>

1) The text is being used at De Anza the following quarter
2) The Bookstore is not overstocked on that title

Current editions NOT USED OR NEEDED the following quarter at De Anza will be worth only the WHOLESALE MARKET VALUE.

OUTDATED EDITIONS WILL NOT BE ACCEPTED

RECEIPTS NOT NEEDED

The Bookstore cannot guarantee the buyback of any book at any time

De Anza College Bookstore - (408) 996-4455

A $6.00 service charge will be assessed on returned checks

PROTECT YOUR INVESTMENT
SAVE THIS RECEIPT

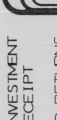

NO RECEIPT - NO RETURNS

Beginning of the quarter returns policy

A full refund will be given on new or used books IF.....

1) YOU PRESENT YOUR CASH REGISTER RECEIPT

2) You do not marr or write in your books - Return new books in Publisher Condition

3) Wrapped or boxed merchandise must not be unwrapped or opened

4) You may return books for fall, winter, or spring by the END OF THE SECOND WEEK from the START of that respective QUARTER

5) The Manager or Assistant Manager reserves the right to make the decision on the RESALEABLE CONDITION of the text

***** STANDARD RETURN POLICY OF OTHER THAN TEXTS *****
Two Working Days from the date on receipt

---

4   11   3
3.05 TX   B
1.50 TX
24.55 TL
25.00 CA
.45 CH
04   1836

mission channels. Data transmission line costs will be reduced by up to 50 percent by the mid-1980s; when the use of fiber optic/laser channels becomes widespread, this technology will reduce enormously the cost of communications. At that point, an individual will be able to utilize transmission resources that only the largest organizations can now afford.

Broader Systems

Many of the quick-response systems that will be developed in the next few years will take a broader data-base approach to the needs of the organization. (Given the rapid growth expected in data-base management software, this is not a surprising prediction.) The data-base approach can be flexible; that is, it may be used by organizations combining large centralized computers (and a centralized data base) with nonintelligent terminals located at the operating level, it may be used by organizations with a smaller central processor to maintain a centralized data base for a network of distributed minicomputers and outlying intelligent terminals, or it may be used by organizations adopting some other alternative.

Regardless of the technical approach used, the trend in many organizations will be to define, classify, and store certain types of basic data commonly so that better integration will be possible. The development efforts to produce data banks that will replace a multitude of the independent files maintained at the present time will probably continue at a more rapid pace in spite of the potential dangers to individual privacy. Why will this happen? It will probably happen because managers will have to respond to future changes that may occur at a much faster rate than in the past. Therefore, decision makers forced to make quicker choices involving greater risks will press for relatively complete information rather than settle for information in bits and pieces located in scattered files.

Possible Future Applications of Computer Systems and Technology

There'll be computers of size, and some they will miniaturize to do the small tasks that everyone asks, from scratching, to knotting of ties.
—Gloria Maxson

The following applications seem to be *technically* possible during the 1980s; whether they are all *socially desirable,* however, is another matter. Most of the applications that have been included in speculations in earlier chapters are not repeated here.[5] Applications that are considered here have been arbitrarily classified into those which may affect individuals in *private life* and those which may have an impact on individuals in *organizations.* Of course, the development, for the home, of new computer-controlled products that would affect the private lives of some people would also have an impact on individuals in the organizations that developed the products.

---

[5] Speculations about EFTS systems, for example, have been treated earlier and are therefore not included here.

Applications affecting private individuals Some of the computer-related applications that could affect the lives of people at home and at play in the 1980s are:

1 *Home and hobby applications.* There will be a flood of microprocessors on small chips into the home in the 1980s. They will be used to control most home appliances; television sets will use them to perform automatic fine tuning and color-regulating operations; and typewriters will become similar to some of today's stand-alone word processors by incorporating them for control, storage, and duplication purposes. Of course, inexpensive personal computers with considerable power will be much more widely used for home recreation and education purposes. *Videodisk players* attached to television sets currently use metallic "records" to provide viewers with up to an hour's worth of television programming for approximately the price of a phonograph record. A videodisk can also store immense quantities of data. Future home systems may merge videodisk players and personal computers into a combination that can either include a television screen or be attached to a TV set. Videodisks for this "visual computer" could be sold in stores and may contain complete *interactive* entertainment, hobby, and educational sequences including computer programs, audio segments, and video materials. In short, an exciting environment designed to simultaneously stimulate the user's senses could be created. Home-delivered videodisks could someday supplement or replace newspapers and magazines with a more versatile product.[6] A more immediate impact on the print media, however, may come from the home systems (patterned along the lines of the *Viewdata* system[7] developed in the United Kingdom) that will begin to emerge in the 1980s. Massive data bases including the latest news and weather information, airline schedules, tax information, want ads, public welfare information, retail store sales information, etc., will be stored in a central computer system. A page of this information will be requested from a home microcomputer connected to a telephone or cable television line, and the requested page will be returned over the line to a receiving screen. If the viewer wants a permanent copy, the page can be printed by the home computer system. In short, users can browse through the electronic newspaper/magazine/encyclopedia, select the sections that interest them, and thus tailor the information to their individual needs.[8]

2 *Opinion polling in the home.* Subscribers to the QUBE cable television system in Columbus, Ohio, are permitted to choose incoming pro-

---

[6] See Joseph P. Martino, "The Future of Telecommunications," *Current*, p. 28, June 1979.

[7] This system is now called *Prestel* in the United Kingdom.

[8] See Anthony Smith, "All the News That Fits in the Databank," *Saturday Review*, pp. 18–19, June 23, 1979.

grams from 30 channels. But the cable can also be used to communicate *outgoing* messages; in other words, subscribers can talk back to the tube. By pressing a button, a viewer can respond to a politician, evaluate the features in a local newspaper, and give an opinion on a contestant in a talent program (an electronic "gonging"?). Responses can be recorded and tabulated by a computer. As similar systems spread throughout the nation, national "town meetings" could be called to provide political leaders with the instant electronic "votes" of citizens on important issues.

3   *Telemedicine applications.* Satellite communications between ill or injured persons in remote areas and specialists in urban areas should be in widespread use in the late 1980s. Medical aides in remote areas can administer the emergency treatment recommended by a specialist backed up by diagnostic computing resources. Instrumented hospital beds in remote clinics may regularly be linked with computers and/or intensive-care monitors at an urban hospital.

Applications affecting organizations   A few of the computer-related applications that may have an impact on organizations in the 1980s are:

1   *Computer-assisted manufacturing.* As we have seen in earlier chapters, micro- and mini-sized computers are now routinely used to control individual production tools such as milling machines and shapers. As we have also seen, computer-controlled robots are being developed rapidly, and tens of thousands of them will be installed in assembly operations during the 1980s. Automobile workers will soon be working alongside robots capable of assembling components such as carburetors and alternators. In fact, in studies conducted jointly by the University of Michigan and the Society of Manufacturing Engineers, it is predicted that by 1988 (1) half the direct labor in such small-component assembly will be replaced, (2) the production control function will be automated to the point that 80 percent of all in-process technology will be computer-controlled, and (3) 50 percent of the work force remaining on the production floor will be highly skilled and trained engineers and technicians needed to keep the automated plants operating.[9] Since many of the robots installed during the 1980s can be switched from the production of one item to another simply by changing the program, it will be feasible to keep equipment busy by having it produce small quantities of a number of different customized and individualized items. Thus, small-lot manufacturing may become nearly as economical as mass production is today. In fact, computers and robots may reduce overall costs in small-lot manufacturing by more than 50 percent during the 1980s. Since the machines that will

[9] See Dan Appleton, "A Manufacturing Systems Cookbook, Part 1," *Datamation*, pp. 179ff, May 1979.

be used in future mass production operations will themselves be produced in small lots, the net effect is that they will be relatively less expensive, and so may be the prices of the items they produce.

2   *Automatic meter reading.* At this writing, many telephone companies have installed computer-controlled testing equipment to check on the condition of telephone lines. In the 1980s, gas, electric, and water meters may be connected to these telephone lines so that as the system automatically tests line condition, it will also read the meters for the utility companies.

3   *Attending meetings electronically.* We saw in Chapter 9 that an *electronic mail/message system* (EMMS) can now be used to permit "conferences" to be held at the convenience of the participants. Telephone and/or cable TV lines may be combined with computers in a future extension of this EMMS concept to provide an integrated voice-data-picture communication system for some organizations. By the late 1980s, it may be possible for some employees such as managers, teachers, engineers, typists, etc., to perform some of their job duties in offices located in the home. Typists, for example, could receive dictation by phone and handwritten drafts by facsimile, and they could return finished copy via communicating word processors. Thus, the transmission of information may be substituted for the transportation and concentration of humans. Technology can be substituted for energy; to some extent communications can replace commuting. Organizations may find it less costly to furnish certain employees with the necessary terminals and communications lines so that they can work at home much of the time, rather than establishing offices for them in expensive buildings. Witnesses could testify at government hearings without leaving their hometowns. They could go to a local courthouse and be sworn in, and their testimony could be recorded and transmitted to the hearings room at the state or national capital. The need to crowd together into cities may be reduced; communities of interest and interaction may be linked electronically rather than by geographic boundaries.

4   *Educational applications.* The same low-cost computer/television systems that will entertain and educate in the home in the 1980s will also be used in schools. More importantly, perhaps, these low-cost systems will lead to the development of innovative and much-needed educational software. Bright students will learn the subject matter and will help teach other students by writing educational programs at home and at school; hobbyists (including teachers) with home computers will write programs with high educational value for their own children and will then share these programs with others; and clubs of computer hobbyists may make the preparation of good educational programs a club project. Future homework may consist of a student taking a computer tape cassette or videodisk home and playing it on the family system. Table 19-2 gives some predictions for CAI.

TABLE 19-2
Predictions for computer-assisted instruction by 1990

	Home Preschool	Secondary Schools	Higher Education	Industry	Community Institutions
1977 Acceptance	Zero	Widely dispersed emerging	Widespread	High level limited implementation	On the horizon
1977 Utilization	None	Basic skills (heavy)	Skill and survey type instruction (moderate)	Testing and training drills (light)	Vocabulary and procedural info. in health areas Basic skills and conditioning programs (light)
1990 Acceptance	Widespread	Widespread	Universal	Heavy	Broad by social and health instit.
1990 Utilization	Heavy use in concept development	Universal for skill development and high level concept development	Extensive for entry level courses and high level professional development and continuing education	Heavy in specific training skills and management development	Heavy use by health industry for upgrading diagnostic skill Heavy use for rehabilitation and deterrent programs in criminal justice

Source: John J. Hirschbuhl, "Futures: Where Will Computer-assisted Instruction (CAI) Be in 1990?" *Educational Technology,* p. 63, April 1978.

THE OUTLOOK FOR INDIVIDUALS

The Optimistic View

We saw in Chapter 10 that optimistic forecasters believe that computer usage will result in greater freedom and individuality and a more human and personalized society. They point to the computer applications described in Chapter 10, in Chapters 13 through 18, and in parts of the preceding section to prove their contention that the benefits to be obtained far outweigh any temporary difficulties and inconveniences.

For example, the computer-assisted manufacturing trends described in this chapter and elsewhere, and the resulting outlook for productivity gains, they are convinced, will lead to an increased standard of living, a shorter work week, and increased leisure time. And home computers may be used to stimulate the analytical and intellectual abilities of individuals and add to their enjoyment of this increased leisure time. Furthermore, optimists foresee a time when opinion polling in the home will bring about a higher level of democracy because citizens will take a greater interest in important local and national issues when their opinions are sought on a frequent and regular basis. Of course, as we know, these optimistic views do not go unchallenged.

The Pessimistic View

The pessimistic view of the future, as we saw in Chapter 11 and in sections of other chapters, is that the effects of computer usage will *not* lead to greater freedom and individuality. On the contrary, pessimists can examine many of the same applications as optimists and come to the opposite conclusion that computer usage will (1) dominate our lives as a society and as individuals and (2) sweep us along in a tide over which we—the harassed and exposed victims of a depersonalized and dehumanized process that places greater value on efficiency than on the more noble qualities of life—shall have little control.

Pessimists do agree with optimists, however, that computer-assisted manufacturing techniques will result in enormous gains in productivity. But the pessimists argue that when humans must compete with robots, the humans will lose—they will lose their jobs, they will lose their security, and they will lose their personal dignity. The pessimists look at the possibility of opinion polling in the home with alarm. What is to prevent the system from monitoring the individual? How do individuals know that the information they reveal about themselves in responding to questions is kept private? Furthermore, is it really a good idea, the pessimists ask, to have instant polls of public opinion on controversial issues? Many times in our past history, they point out, sober minority opinion has been found to be preferable to the "lynch mob" mentality of the majority. Finally, pessimists can also see dangers in educational applications. For example, research has been conducted on the feasibility of installing voice-print ana-lyzers into future computerized teaching systems. These analyzers would be able to determine the student's identity and also his or her mental sta-bility and emotional state. Optimists say that this voice analysis will enable the system to determine whether a student is unhappy, angry, nervous, or cheerful so that a teaching program may be selected automatically to re-spond in a more personal way to the student's mood. But pessimists are convinced that such monitoring of individuals, with the concomitant dan-ger to privacy, is truly an Orwellian prophecy come true.

A Final Note

Is it possible in this last section to draw any conclusions from the dozens of different viewpoints that have so often been presented in the pages of this book? Perhaps. We can conclude, for example, that there are at least three different contemporary views of computers and technological change:

1   *Computers and technology are an unblemished blessing.* This uncritical optimistic view holds that technology is the source of all progress for the individual and society, that social problems will inevitably be solved through the application of technology, and that every new technological possibility will automatically be beneficial.
2   *Computers and technology are an unbridled curse.* This pessimistic view holds that technology increases unemployment, leads to deper-sonalization and bewilderment, threatens an individual's right to dig-nity and privacy, and threatens to pollute and/or blow up the world.
3   *Computers and technology are undeserving of special attention.* This un-concerned view is that technology has been with us for decades, and we are now better educated and more able than ever before to adapt to the new ideas and changes which it has brought (and will bring).

Each of these views is deficient, although each probably contains an element of truth. The optimists are correct when they conclude that new technology often creates new opportunities for society; the pessimists are correct when they conclude that new problems are often created by new tools; and the unconcerned are correct when they conclude that so-cial institutions (e.g., schools) can, and often do, play an important role in tempering the effects of technology.

No one is sure about the future effects on employment of technolog-ical advances. Computers have caused displacement. But has the devel-opment of the computer caused a larger number of people to be unem-ployed than would otherwise have been the case? In other words, have computers reduced the total number of jobs available in the total labor market? Professor Yale Brozen, University of Chicago economist, ex-pressed the views of many authorities a few years ago when he wrote:

The reigning economic myth is that automation causes unemployment. It has only a slight element of truth—just enough to make the proposition plausible. Automation does cause displacement. A few become unemployed because of it. However, it does not create unemployment in the sense that a larger number are unemployed than would have been if no automation had occurred. . . . Many persons point to specific persons unemployed as a result of [automation]. What they fail to do is point to the unemployed who found jobs because of automation or to those who would have joined the jobless if new technology had not appeared.[10]

A majority of current economists are probably of the belief that (1) displacement must not be prevented and (2) unemployment is best avoided by high levels of capital investment, unhampered mobility of capital and labor, and a continuing high level of technological progress. Since other nations are strongly committed to the concept of factory automation and the goal of higher productivity, our alternative to technological progress is apt to be economic stagnation and a declining standard of living.

Pessimists have definitely pointed out influences and possibilities that the concerned citizen should keep in mind. Many pessimists do *not* disagree with the optimistic position that computer technology *could* increase freedom, individuality, social justice, and well-being. But the pessimists doubt that the effort to increase social awareness and give adequate attention to necessary safeguards will be made.

The predictions of optimists or pessimists will become facts or fables if people make them so. We cannot know what people *will* do in the future. They *could* achieve the optimistic vision. But if in using computers they choose procedures that are impersonal and coldly efficient, they should not be surprised if the results are inhumane and inflexible. Thus, in the years ahead it will be up to concerned and informed citizens who have an awareness of the potential dangers to see that the optimistic view prevails. Of course, developing such citizens has been a primary purpose of this book.

[10] Yale Brozen, "Putting Economics and Automation in Perspective," *Automation,* vol. 11, p. 30, April 1964.

"More Leisure in an Increasingly Electronic Society"

Americans in the year 2029 may very well feel that they are living in the best of times. There will be an abundance of all things needed for the good life: food, energy, clean air, and water. Electronic wizardry will make it possible to attend a business meeting in Phoenix, shop for a dress in New York, vote in a Presidential election, and gamble in Las Vegas—all without leaving the home. Medical technology will conquer the major killers, cancer and stroke, so that Americans will be healthier than ever.

The U.S. will not become a land of plenty overnight, though. Until 2000, people will have to sacrifice to survive shortages of energy and other resources. But that process may well serve as a catharsis for society, stimulating Americans to continue to redefine "progress." Consumers will seek out products that are smaller, more efficient, nonpolluting, and reusable. American inventiveness will see to it that these needs are met.

This will happen because the resource shortages of the next two decades will have made a great impression upon older Americans. Just as those who lived through the Depression remembered what it meant to be unemployed, those who live through shortages will remember what it means to run out. They will want to conserve, never quite believing that resources are limitless. Younger people, never having learned wasteful habits, will conserve from the start. Even today, the trend is evident among young people, who are the customers most eager to buy small cars.

The American urge to consume will still be satisfied, but with goods and services that are resource-efficient. Theodore J. Gordon, president of The Futures Group, calls this trend "conspicuous conservation" and predicts that "we'll compare our solar heaters and electric cars at cocktail parties." So by the time that the U.S. has achieved energy independence, conservation will have permeated every facet of life.

While overcoming the resource crunch is crucial, society will be left with other knotty problems. Many will result from advanced technology. Increasingly, assembly-line jobs—in which people deal primarily with machines—are being automated, and many experts believe that this process will accelerate as new, more capable robots take over basic manufacturing tasks. At the same time the service industries, which necessitate human contact between workers and clients, have mushroomed. "It is more stressful to deal with humans eight hours a day than with a machine," notes one psychologist.

In addition, technology will speed job obsolescence, and much of the population will have to seek new careers. Many will have to go back to school to learn new skills. Others will be less adaptable and will find the transition difficult, if not impossible. "Many people will fall through the cracks," predicts Edith Weiner, executive vice-president of Weiner, Edrich, Brown, a management consulting firm.

Ironically, in the U.S. of 2029, there will be few, if any, limits to what a person can do or become. Education will be available to everyone. Equal employment will be a reality for women and minorities. People who are used to living within prescribed boundaries, with their role determined by society, may be overwhelmed by this freedom. "How do people achieve an identity when all things are possible?" asks Martin L. Ernst, vice-president for management sciences for Arthur D. Little Inc.

Some fear that one response may be more religious cults, headed by strong, charismatic leaders, such as the late Reverend Jim Jones, where members take their place in a structured societal system and have their roles determined by someone else. Others predict that the government may have to establish a federal career-planning program to restrict the options offered to each individual. One positive result could be increased interest in the arts. "We can expect some kind of artistic renaissance," predicts Arnold Mitchell, director of the values and lifestyles program at SRI International. A person forced to work as a salesman, for example, might seek job satisfaction through weaving blankets or making pottery.

While some will struggle to adjust to society's new freedoms, others will thrive. When a job ceases to be fun, an individual will simply switch to something else. "We used to say that the average person changed jobs three to five times in a lifetime," says Frederic R. Brodzinski, an educator who is vice-president of the New York chapter of the World Future Society. "Now we'll be able to say that he'll change his career at least three times."

Technology will effect enormous changes in the job and in the workplace. A home-based computer, hooked to a television set to provide video display, will make it possible for a person to work from home—an option that more and more people are likely to choose as transportation costs continue to rise. In many respects, working at home will be a step back to the 1800s, when mother, father, and children lived and worked together. Herbert Gerjuoy, senior staff scientist for The Futures Group, believes that returning to the "little house on the prairie" setup will have many positive influences on society. "It will strengthen the family, strengthen the relationship between husband and wife, and return us to the pattern of children going into their parents' occupations," he says.

Others, though, do not expect the work-at-home trend to go so far. "There's nothing in the world that requires so much discipline and is as lonesome as sitting home and working," says Lillian W. Deitch, one of Gerjuoy's colleagues with The Futures Group, for which she is manager of socioeconomic studies. Those who think like Deitch believe that nothing, not even electronics, can substitute for being at the center of the action. "We communicate on a different level when we're within a few feet of each other," says J. Kenneth Craver, recently retired as futures research manager at Monsanto Co.

Even if the home does not become everyone's workplace, the home computer will drastically affect the way Americans live. From the comfort of the living room, they will vote, do library research, or call up a consultant's tax expertise. And almost certainly, the information-processing industry and the retailing industry will collaborate to change consumers' buying habits. Instead of driving to several stores to look at sofas, a shopper could view them on the TV screen and order by punching a button.

The computer will be a big time-saver, and many people will enjoy more leisure. Passive entertainment will become more important, and it will be centered on the TV screen. But the traditional fare of scheduled programs will not survive. Instead, a consumer will summon from his vast entertainment library movies, books, and news from any era. Or he will be able to call up an environment designed to stimulate all the senses simultaneously.

Not all entertainment will be passive. As occupations become safer and, in many cases, even more routine, there will be a demand for activities that offer—or appear to offer—an element of physical risk. For those who can afford it, there will be vacations on the moon. "The American fascination with space will resurface," predicts one futurist.

Spurring the growth of leisure activities will be the improved health and the longer lifetimes made possible by medical advances. By 2000, artificial limbs will be perfected and the bionic man will be a reality. As scientists unlock more secrets of the cell, doctors will be able to interfere with the biological processes that now cause cancer, diabetes, heart trouble, genetic diseases, and aging.

With better health and longer productive lifetimes, some feel, the people of the 21st century will lavish more attention on their bodies. One beauty expert predicts that "people will go to a salon to be totally pampered, and it will be bigger and more comprehensive than anything we know today." And visits to the plastic surgeon will be as commonplace as visits to the dentist. Eager to show off their bodies, both men and women will favor minimal, stretchy, close-fitting synthetic clothing—carefully designed to hold in body heat in the winter and to allow the body to breathe in the summer.

Although beef will remain a major source of protein, U.S. consumers will supplement diets with such cheaper proteins as soybeans, synthetic proteins, and plankton from the sea. And as one aspect of the efficient use of resources, consumers will be food producers, too. Greenhouses on rooftops and in backyards, trapping solar energy and mitigating the waste of the food-distribution chain, will allow people to grow fruits and vege-tables at home.

There will be continuing effort by industry, prodded by government, to undo the damage it has done to the nation's waterways. It will be a costly, painstaking venture; many believe that some bodies of water—such as the James River in Virginia and the Hudson River in New York—are fouled beyond hope. But in 25 years there will be a noticeable improvement.

As for cleaning the air, solving the energy problem will remove a large barrier. But the gains that will be made will be made at society's in-sistence. Once technology demonstrates that the U.S. can have both a clean environment and unlimited supplies of energy, environmentalism will return in force.

Although resolving the energy-vs.-environment conflict will remove one issue that divides society, others will remain. Women will continue to make gains, and by 2029 most women will expect to have both a career and a family. But the inability to resolve many of the career conflicts that will occur between husband and wife will dramatically increase the divorce rate.

Increasingly, the corporation will take over the role of the mother, supplying day-care facilities where children can be tended around the clock. But the emotional toll on children will be high. Experts believe that the early years are the most important in a child's development, and they predict that the lack of contact with a parent during this time will create a feeling of alienation that will harm the individual's human relationships later on.

Other conflicts may erupt between the older and younger generations. Around the year 2010, the baby-boom children of the 1940s will reach retirement age. But because of medical advances, many may choose to work longer, thus making it difficult for younger employees within corporations to move up. Some experts believe that this factor alone could lead to serious generational conflicts.

The U.S. will be less of a melting pot in the future. In the past, ethnics such as the Italians, Jews, Poles, and Scandinavians have learned English to become part of the mainstream of American life. The more recent immigrants—most notably the Spanish-speaking—have demonstrated an unwillingness to follow that lead. As a result, the U.S. has begun to accommodate the needs of such minority groups. In many major cities, advertisements, school curricula, newspapers, radio stations, and television programs are no longer exclusively English. The situation is bound to intensify. The native-born U.S. population will level between now and 1990. In the Latin American countries, though, "we're going to see a tidal wave of people," notes Daniel Bell, the Harvard sociologist; already, 48% of the Mexican population is under 17 years old because of a significant decrease in infant mortality. Some of that immense population growth to the south is certain to spill over the U.S. borders.

The result will be increased societal tensions among the various ethnic groups. And some worry about the ability of the social fabric to withstand such tensions. "A key issue is whether we in the U.S. will be able to govern ourselves in a way that allows us to reach consensus on the big issues," worries Roy C. Amara, president of the Institute for the Future.

Thus, despite the real material progress that will occur over the next 50 years, some futurists doubt whether a "happiness index" would reveal the average citizen in 2029 to be happier than his counterpart in 1979, or even 1929. But Edward L. Flom, manager of industry analysis for Standard Oil Co. (Indiana), epitomizes the underlying optimism of many Americans—perhaps a majority—when he guesses that "basically, it will be the same story as in the past: Your children will be better off than you are, and their children will be better off than *they* are."

Source: "More Leisure in an Increasingly Electronic Society." Reprinted from the September 3, 1979 issue of *Business Week* by special permission, © 1979 McGraw-Hill, Inc., New York, N.Y. 10020. All rights reserved.

The following points have been emphasized in this chapter:

1   Dramatic developments are expected in the next few years in computer hardware. Some of the likely changes have been outlined in this chapter. For example, it is expected that central processors will become much smaller, faster, and cheaper; the number of online terminals sold each year will have doubled by 1988; and microprograms will be used extensively to permit the substitution of hardware for expensive software.

2   Distributed processing networks using intelligent terminals and other small processors will gain rapidly in popularity.

3   In the software area, new conversational languages and data-base management software will receive greater emphasis. Much of the new software will be developed using structured programming concepts.

4   Future information systems will be quicker responding and broader in scope than the average installation in operation today. Data communications services will have to be expanded to handle the rapid increase in data transmission. A network of distributed processors and a broader data-base approach will be frequently used to respond to the needs of organizations and decision makers.

5   The future uses of computers are viewed by some people with optimism, while others believe that computers and technology are likely to be the curse of humanity. Which view—optimism or pessimism —will prevail? No one knows. Predictions of each group will become facts or fables only if people make them so. An enlightened citizenry, aware of the dangers, can help bring about the optimistic version.

▶ | KEY TERMS

After reading Chapter 19, you should be able to define and use the technical terms reintroduced from earlier chapters as well as the following terms:

teleprinter	conversational languages
specialty terminal	videodisk
Josephson junction	*Viewdata* system
firmware	QUBE system
back-end processor	electronic "town meetings"

▶ | REVIEW AND DISCUSSION QUESTIONS

1   Discuss the changes that may be expected in the next decade in I/O equipment.

2 What changes may be expected in future central processors?
3 How will future hardware developments support (a) distributed processing networks? (b) quick-response systems? and (c) data-base systems?
4 Discuss how microprograms (firmware) may be used in the future.
5 What changes may be expected in software in the next decade?
6 "We are now in a transition between an old industrial society and a new information/communications society." Discuss this statement.
7 (a) Are you an optimist or a pessimist about the future impact of computer systems on individuals? (b) Defend your answer.

▶ SELECTED REFERENCES

In addition to the sources suggested in the chapter footnotes, you might also be interested in the following references:

Bell, Daniel: "Communications Technology—For Better or for Worse," *Harvard Business Review*, pp. 20–22ff, May/June 1979.

"Beyond DP: The Social Implications," *Datamation*, pp. 98–100ff, July 1979.

Boraiko, Allan A.: "Harnessing Light by a Thread," *National Geographic*, pp. 516–534, October 1979.

Branscomb, Lewis M.: "Information: The Ultimate Frontier," *Science*, pp. 143–147, January 1979.

Business Week, September 3, 1979. This fiftieth anniversary issue has many articles on the future.

Datamation, November 25, 1979. This special edition is entitled "Entering the '80s: A Decade of Growth."

Collins, Glenn: "The Good News About 1984," *Psychology Today*, pp. 34–35ff, January 1979.

Ferkiss, Victor: "Technology Assessment and Appropriate Technology," *National Forum* (Phi Kappa Phi Journal), pp. 3–7, Fall 1978.

Istvan, Edwin J.: "New Issues Confronting the Information Systems Planner," *Infosystems*, pp. 54ff, June 1979.

McCracken, Daniel D.: "The Changing Face of Applications Programming," *Datamation*, pp. 25–27ff, November 15, 1978.

Miller, William C.: "What Will the Future Bring for Education," *Phi Delta Kappan*, pp. 287–289, December 1978.

Moore, Gordon: "VLSI: Some Fundamental Challenges," *IEEE Spectrum*, pp. 32–37, April 1979.

Myers, Ware: "The Need for Software Engineering," *Computer*, pp. 12–24, February 1978.

Osborne, Adam: *Running Wild—The Next Industrial Revolution*, Osborne/McGraw-Hill, Inc., Berkeley, Calif., 1979.

Rosenfeld, Albert: "How Anxious Should Science Make Us?" *Saturday Review*, pp. 16ff, June 9, 1979.

Appendix A
CARD PUNCH OPERATION

The purpose of this supplement is to acquaint you with some of the fundamentals of keypunch operation so that you may prepare the necessary cards to run short programs or make changes in existing program or data cards. The purpose is *not* to make you a highly skilled keypunch operator. Thus, only the most basic uses of the card punch are discussed here.

A card punch commonly encountered is the IBM model 29 (Fig. A-1). The keyboard and functional control switches for this machine are shown in Fig. A-2.

The *shaded* keys on the keyboard are used to control certain machine operations; the *unshaded* keys are used to punch the indicated characters. Depressing the NUMERIC shift key causes the character indicated on the upper portion of the key to be punched. As you will note, the alphabetic keys are located just where they would be on a typewriter.

TYPICAL OPERATION TO PREPARE SHORT PROGRAMS

The operating steps in punching a typical student program may be outlined as follows:

1 Turn on the *main line switch,* shown in Fig. A-1.
2 Load blank cards into the *card hopper* face forward with the 9-edge down.

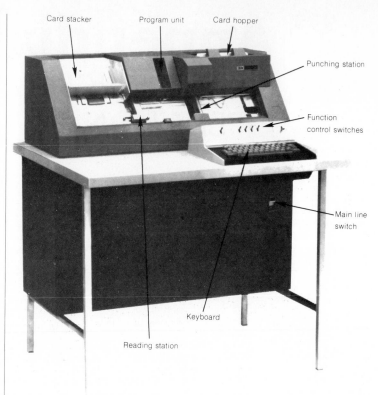

Card stacker   Program unit   Card hopper

Punching station

Function control switches

Main line switch

Keyboard

Reading station

FIGURE A-1
Model 29 Card punch.
(IBM Corp.)

3 Turn on the AUTO FEED and PRINT functional control switches, shown in Fig. A-2, and switch the *program control lever* (located right below the program unit shown in Fig. A-1) to the right.

4 By depressing the FEED key, you will move a card from the hopper to the entrance to the *punching station.* Pressing the FEED button a second time will drop a second card and properly align the first card at the punching station.

5 Punch the necessary data into the card.

6 If the last column punched is column 80, the completed card will be automatically advanced to the *reading station,* and a new blank card will be positioned at the punching station. If the last column punched is *not* column 80, the card may be advanced by pressing the REL key.

7 The punched card advanced to the reading station and the following card positioned at the punching station move together—i.e., as columns 1, 2, 3, etc., of the completed card pass under the reading station, the *same columns* of the following card are being positioned under the punching station. This synchronization feature permits data to be duplicated in the second card. If the DUP key is depressed, data sensed in the completed card will be automatically reproduced in the same columns of the following card.

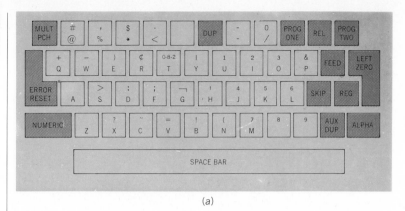

(a)

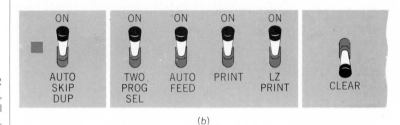

(b)

FIGURE A-2
(*A*) Card punch keyboard,
(*B*) functional control
switches.

8   When the last card has been punched, the CLEAR function switch on the model 29 may be used to move it to the *card stacker*.
9   Turn off the main line switch.

SINGLE-CARD PREPARATION

It is often necessary to add one or two cards to a deck or to replace an existing card with a corrected or undamaged one. The operating steps to follow in these situations are:

1   Turn on the main line switch.
2   Turn off the AUTO FEED switch, turn on the PRINT switch, and switch the program control lever to the right to disengage the program unit.
3   Put a blank card into the *card hopper* and press the FEED key to move the card to the *punching station*. Then press the REG key to align the card under the punches.
4   Punch the card as required and then press the REL key to release it from the punching station.
5   The card can be cleared to the stacker by depressing the CLEAR switch.
6   Turn off the main line switch.

Appendix B
AN OVERVIEW OF FORTRAN

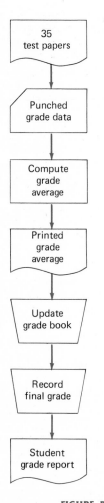

FIGURE B-1
Grade preparation system.

The purpose of this appendix is to present an overview of the FORTRAN programming language. FORTRAN is used here to code a simple program. Since entire books are available on this language, only a brief outline is given. Nevertheless, the material presented here will acquaint you with (1) the general structure and (2) some of the characteristics of FORTRAN. Before beginning the language discussion, however, it might be appropriate to pause here long enough to review the problem to be coded.

THE PROBLEM

A simple problem has been selected so that problem details will not confuse the issue while introductory language and coding concepts are presented. The problem is that Professor Hal I. Tosis wishes to compute an average (arithmetic mean) grade for a student based on the 35 tests he has given during the semester. (Professor Tosis teaches a rigorous course!) In the *system* flowchart in Figure B-1 we see that the system followed by Hal Tosis is one in which the grade data for the student are punched into cards that are then fed into a computer for processing. The computed average is printed, and Professor Tosis manually updates his grade book and then prepares his final grade report on the student. (We shall be concerned with only one student, but, of course, any number of student grade averages could easily be automatically processed by the computer.)

In Hal's grade preparation diagram, a single processing box is labeled "compute grade average." Unfortunately, such an instruction is not sufficient for the computer. Thus, as a part of the programming process, the programmer must specify each step needed to compute the average grade. In short, the *single* processing box labeled "compute grade average" becomes the basis for the detailed *program* flowchart shown in Figure B-2.

At the end of the current term, the sole survivor in Professor Tosis's course is Mr. A. Valiant Student. Each of the 35 grades recorded for Mr. Student represents a single record. The processing operation involves adding together the individual grade scores. After each grade record is processed, it is then written on an output report. When all records are processed, the machine then computes and prints a summary measure—the average score—which becomes the basis for Val's course grade. The

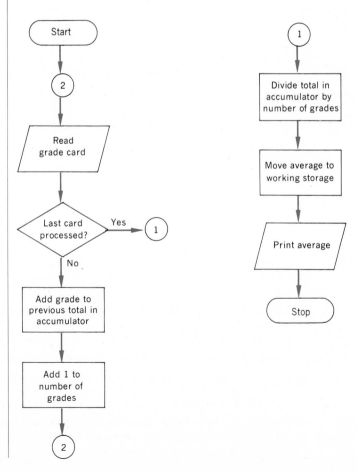

FIGURE B-2
Program flowchart to
average grades.

output report will have the appearance of Figure B-3. The 35 input grade scores, of course, are also indicated in Figure B-3.

In the remaining pages of this appendix we shall look at the way a program written in the FORTRAN language uses this input data to produce the output information.

FORTRAN CODING

FORTRAN was developed primarily for scientific and engineering purposes, but it is also used in nonscientific applications where extensive files are not being manipulated. Figure B-4 shows the coding for Hal Tosis's average grade problem.

Program Statements

The FORTRAN source program shown in Figure B-4 is composed of several types of *statements,* which may be classified into the following categories: (1) *input/output,* (2) *arithmetic assignment and computation,* and (3) *program control.* Those statements that are referred to in other parts of the program are assigned arbitrary numbers on the left side of the coding sheet by the programmer. Each statement is punched on one or more cards. The numbers below the "FORTRAN STATEMENT" heading on the coding sheet refer to columns of a punched card. Thus, the first statement in Figure B-4 would be punched in columns 7 to 32 of the first card in the source program deck. A *comment* card may be included in a program to provide an explanatory note by punching a C in column 1 and then by punching the message in the remaining columns. Such a card would not be processed during compilation. When a statement will not fit on a single card (or line), it may be continued on a following card through the use of a character, e.g., 1 to 9, in column 6 of the continuation card.

Input/Output Statements

Input data may, of course, be in alphabetical or numerical form. In FORTRAN, numerical data are commonly classified into *integer* and *real* numbers. An integer number is a decimal value *without a decimal point;* for example, 35,262 and 75 are integer numbers. A real number is simply a decimal value that *does have a decimal point;* for example, 6.25, 0.325, and −0.987 are real numbers. A real number may also be presented in an exponential, *scientific notation,* or *floating-point notation* form. How? I'm glad you asked. It may be done by simply expressing the number as a value between 1 and 10 multiplied by an exponent (E) or power of 10. For example, the floating decimal expression 3.68E + 02 means 3.68×10^2, which is 368 in fixed decimal notation.[1] And 1.26E − 02 means

NAME   A.V. STUDENT

TEST RESULTS
75
50
55
0
100
100
75
100
100
50
0
75
100
67
63
97
63
93
57
67
83
0
100
100
72
75
63
87
93
75
100
100
100
100
90

2,625

AVERAGE   75

---

[1] Alternatively, the value could be expressed as a decimal fraction between 0.1 and 1.0 multiplied by a power of 10. Thus, the *normal form* floating-point numeral .368E + 03 means 0.368×10^3, which is also 368 in fixed decimal notation.

X28-7327-6 U/M050
Printed in U.S.A.

PROGRAM	AVERAGE OF TEST SCORES			PAGE 1 OF 1
PROGRAMMER	JOHN Q. PROGRAMMER	DATE 1/26/7—	PUNCHING INSTRUCTIONS / GRAPHIC / PUNCH	CARD ELECTRO NUMBER*

```
      READ (1,10)N,ANAME1,ANAME2
10    FORMAT(I2,2X,2A10)
      IF(N)100,100,20
20    ITOTAL=0
      WRITE (3,30)ANAME1,ANAME2
30    FORMAT(10X,4HNAME,2X,2A10/)
      WRITE (3,40)
40    FORMAT(21X,12HTEST RESULTS)
      DO 70 I=1,N,1
      READ (1,50)ISCORE
50    FORMAT(I3)
      WRITE (3,60)ISCORE
60    FORMAT(23X,I4)
      ITOTAL=ITOTAL+ISCORE
70    CONTINUE
      IAVE=(ITOTAL+(N+1)/2)/N
      WRITE (3,80)ITOTAL
80    FORMAT(12X,I5/)
      WRITE (3,90)IAVE
90    FORMAT(5X,7HAVERAGE,11X,I4)
100   STOP
      END
```

FIGURE B-4

$1.26 \times 1/10^2$ or .0126 in customary form. Also, the decimal values 123000 and −.0000123 may become $1.23E + 05$ and $−1.23E − 05$ in floating-point notation. Floating-point notation is conveniently used to express very large or very small quantities.

The first line of code in Figure B-4 is a READ statement, which is used to read input data from an input device (generally a card reader) into primary storage. The fifth line of code is a WRITE statement, which is used to write output information from primary storage to an output device (generally a printer). The form of READ and WRITE statements is

$$\boxed{\text{READ } (i,n) \text{ list} \qquad \text{WRITE } (i,n) \text{ list}}$$

where i refers to the input or output device that will be used in the operation; n indicates the statement number of an appropriate FORMAT[2] statement; and "list" refers to the variable names that are to be read or written. Thus, in the first statement of Figure B-4, the programmer is indicating that a card reader (1) is to be used to input the *variable names* N, ANAME1, and ANAME2 according to the format specified in statement number 10. And in the WRITE statement in the fifth line of Figure B-4, the programmer is specifying that a printer (3) is to be used to print ANAME1 and ANAME2 in accordance with FORMAT statement number 30.

---

[2] Because the letters O, I, and Z resemble the digits 0, 1, and 2, they are often written Ø, I̲, and Z̶ on coding sheets to reduce keypunching errors.

The variable names are symbols invented by the programmer to represent quantities that may have different values. Certain rules must be followed in assigning variable names. The variable name N, for example, is an integer quantity that represents the number of test grades being averaged. The letter G, however, could not have been used for this purpose because variable names that represent integer values must begin with the letters I, J, K, L, M, and N. Names beginning with other letters represent real numbers. When the first READ statement is executed, specific values from the data card will be assigned to the three variable names listed; i.e., N will be assigned a 2-digit integer number while ANAME1 and ANAME2 (the variable tags used to identify the name of the student in storage) may each accommodate 10 alphanumeric characters. How does the computer know this? Because this information is contained in FORMAT statement number 10. The I2 in this statement refers to a two-digit integer value (for the storage location to be labeled N); the 2X specifies two blank spaces; and the 2A10 specification means that the two storage locations labeled ANAME1 and ANAME2 may each accommodate 10 alphanumeric characters.

The general form of the FORMAT statement is

$$n \; (\text{FORMAT} \; (s_1, s_2, \ldots , s_m)$$

where n is a statement number and s represents a specification that describes the type and arrangement of an item in the order in which it appears on the input or output record. Some commonly encountered data specifications are presented in Figure B-5.

FIGURE B-5
FORMAT statement specifications

Specification	Description	Examples
Iw	An integer value which is w characters in width.	I4 might refer to 2625. I2 might refer to 35.
Fw.d	A real number having w characters, with d digits to the right of the decimal point.	F8.2 might refer to 12345.25 (where the decimal point is counted as a character).
Ew.d	A real number written in floating-point notation having w characters, with d digits to the right of the decimal point.	E8.2 might refer to a value of 1.67E + 06 (counting the decimal point as a character), which is 1.67×10^6 or 1670000. in customary notation.
wX	Skip over w characters.	10X means to skip 10 characters.
nAw	Alphanumeric data having w characters may be read or written into each of n fields.	2A10 means two fields may each accommodate up to 10 alphanumeric characters.
wH	Print exactly as written the next w characters in the FORMAT statement.	12HTEST RESULTS means to print TEST RESULTS on the output document.

Arithmetic Assignment and Computation Statements

The form of the *arithmetic assignment* statement resembles a mathematical formula. The statement ITOTAL = 0 means that zero is assigned to the variable name ITOTAL (which must represent an integer quantity because the first letter is I). In FORTRAN the "equals" sign *does not* necessarily mean equality; rather, it means that the value of the expression to the right of the sign is assigned to the storage location having the name of the variable to the left of the sign. Thus, as we see in Figure B-2 in the line below statement number 60, ITOTAL = ITOTAL + ISCORE obviously is not a mathematical equation. What this line does mean is that the values stored in ITOTAL and ISCORE will be added and the result will be assigned to the ITOTAL location (thus erasing the previous ITOTAL contents).

The five basic arithmetic operations performed in FORTRAN are:

Operation	FORTRAN symbol
Addition	+
Subtraction	−
Multiplication	*
Division	/
Exponentiation	**

The *order* of computations performed in an arithmetic operation follows specific rules. Parentheses are often used to designate the order of operations. Moving from left to right in an arithmetic expression without parentheses, one has to observe the following:

1 All exponentiation (raising to a power) is performed first.
2 All multiplication and division operations are then completed.
3 Finally, all addition and subtraction take place.

If parentheses are used, the computations within the parentheses are handled first, using the above order rules. If several sets of parentheses are nested within one another, the operations in the innermost group are performed first. To illustrate, let us consider the following statement found in Figure B-4, which computes Val Student's average grade for the 35 test scores:

$$\text{IAVE} = (\text{ITOTAL} + (N + 1)/2)/N$$

The first part of the expression evaluated would be $(N + 1)$ in the innermost set of parentheses. The result in our problem would be:

$$\text{IAVE} = (\text{ITOTAL} + 36/2)/N$$

Within the remaining set of parentheses, the division operation would be performed first, and the resulting value of 18 would be added to the contents of the storage location labeled ITOTAL.[3] This total would then be divided by the number of test scores (35).

Program Control Statements

FORTRAN statements are executed sequentially until the sequence is altered by an unconditional or conditional branch instruction. An example of an acceptable FORTRAN *unconditional* branching statement is GO TO 100, where 100 refers to a statement number. An example of a *conditional* branch statement is IF (N) 100,100,20, which is on the third line of Figure B-4. The general form of the IF statement is

$$\text{IF } (a)n_1, n_2, n_3$$

where a refers to an arithmetic computation to be performed or a variable name. *If* the value of a turns out to be *negative,* program control will be transferred to statement number n_1; *if* a is zero, control moves to a statement number n_2; and *if* a is a *positive* value, control transfers to n_3. In our example in Figure B-4, control will branch to statement number 100 (STOP) in the event that N is mistakenly entered as a negative value or as zero. Normally, of course, statement number 20 will be executed in sequence.

An additional program control statement is illustrated in Figure B-4. The line that reads

$$\text{DO 70 I } = 1,\text{N},1$$

controls a program *loop*. The general form of such a DO statement is

$$\text{DO n i} = m_1, m_2, m_3$$

where the DO n portion of the statement indicates the instructions included in the DO loop; i.e., all statements down to and including the last one numbered n constitute the DO loop. Thus, in our program example, the *range* of the loop goes from the DO statement down to and including statement number 70 (CONTINUE). In this loop the program will:

1 Read a test score data card from the card reader and store the value in a storage location named ISCORE, which can accept a 3-digit integer number. Or

$$\text{READ } (1,50) \text{ ISCORE}$$
$$50 \text{ FORMAT } (\text{I3})$$

---

[3] Since integer values are used in this averaging program, the purpose of $(N + 1)/2$ is to round off computations of the average grade to the nearest integer value.

2   Print the score value in a column that is 23 spaces to the right of the left margin of the output document (see Figure B-3). Or

```
WRITE (3,60) ISCORE
60 FORMAT (23X I4)
```

3   Add the test score (ISCORE) to the value stored in ITOTAL and return the accumulated total to ITOTAL. Or

```
ITOTAL = ITOTAL + ISCORE
```

4   Return to the beginning of the loop or branch away, depending on the number of iterations that have been made.

How does the computer know when to stop the loop? This is determined by the remainder of the DO statement. The i portion sets up an integer variable name, which acts as an *index.* The value of m_1 is the *initial value* given to the index; the value of m_2 is the value of the index when the looping should be *completed;* and the value of m_3 is the amount by which the index should be increased after each iteration through the loop (if this value is 1, it may be omitted). In our example, the index (1) is initially set at 1 (m_1). After each pass through the loop, the index is tested to see if m_2 (in this case 35) has been reached. If it has not been reached, the index is increased by 1 (m_3) and another iteration occurs; if it has, program control moves to the statement *following* the one specified in the DO instruction. In our example, the average grade would be computed following the termination of the DO loop.

As a result of our studying FORTRAN language characteristics, we have just about completed the description of the grade averaging program. Let us summarize this program by referring to Figure B-6, a flowchart that graphically presents the program logic using the terminology of the statements coded in Figure B-4. The numbers in parentheses in Figure B-6 refer to the lines of code in Figure B-4.

The first two lines of code—a READ statement and an associated FORMAT statement—provide the processor with data about the number of grades and name of the student. Following a test for reasonableness of input data (line 3), a variable name (ITOTAL) is identified and given a temporary integer value of zero (line 4). The first two printed lines on the output report (see Figure B-3, page 602) are prepared using the WRITE and FORMAT statements coded in lines 5 to 8 of Figure B-4 (the slash character at the end of FORMAT statement number 30 caused the printer to space between the first and second print lines). The DO loop just discussed is found in lines 9 to 15 of the coding sheet. At the termination of the looping, ITOTAL contains the accumulated test score points. The average grade is computed to the nearest integer value in line 16. This grade is 75. The last two printed lines on the output report are prepared

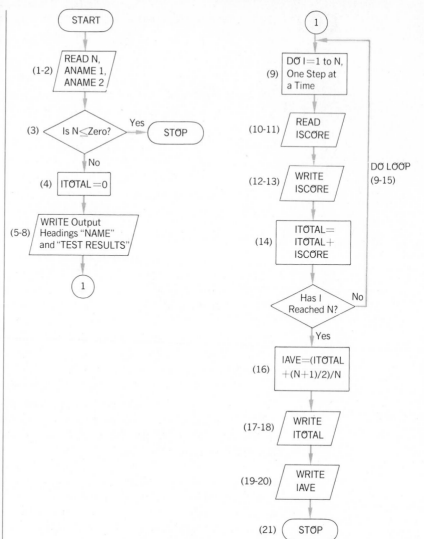

FIGURE B-6
Grade averaging (FORTRAN)
flowchart. (Numbers in
parentheses refer to the
lines of code in Figure B-4.)

using the program statements on lines 17 to 20. STOP and END statements are used to conclude FORTRAN programs.

This completes our brief introduction to FORTRAN, a language that is relatively easy to learn and widely accepted. Although not well suited for processing large files, it is often used for analysis purposes by government, health, education, and business organizations.

GLOSSARY

The communication of facts and ideas in any field is dependent on a mutual understanding of the words used. The purpose of this appendix, then, is to present definitions for some of the terms that are often used in the field of information processing.

Absolute address A machine-language address assigned to a specific location in storage.

Access See *direct-access, random-access, remote-access, serial-access.*

Access time The elapsed time between the instant when data are called for from a storage device and the instant when the delivery operation begins.

Accumulator A register or storage location that forms the result of an arithmetic or logic operation.

Address An identification (e.g., a label, name, or number) that designates a particular location in storage or any other data destination or source. Also, a part of an instruction that specifies the location of an operand for the instruction.

ADP Automatic Data Processing.

ALGOL (ALGOrithmic Language) An algebraic, procedure-oriented language similar to FORTRAN that is widely used in Europe.

Algorithm A set of well-defined rules for solving a problem in a finite number of operations.

Alphanumeric   Pertaining to a character set that includes letters, digits, and, usually, other special punctuation character marks.

Analog computer   A device that operates on data in the form of continuously variable physical quantities.

ANSI (American National Standards Institute)   Formerly ASA and USASI.

APL (A Programming Language)   A mathematically-oriented language frequently used in timesharing.

Arithmetic unit   The part of a computing system containing the circuitry that does the adding, subtracting, multiplying, dividing, and comparing.

Assembly program   A computer program that takes nonmachine-language instructions prepared by a programmer and converts them into a form that may be used by the computer.

Auxiliary storage   A storage that supplements the primary internal storage of a computer.

Background processing   The execution of lower-priority computer programs during periods when the system resources are not required to process higher-priority programs.

BASIC (Beginners All-Purpose Symbolic Instruction Code)   A terminal-oriented programming language frequently used in timesharing.

Batch processing   A technique in which a number of similar items or transactions to be processed are grouped (batched) for sequential processing during a machine run.

BCD (Binary-Coded Decimal)   A method of representing the decimal digits zero through nine by a pattern of binary ones and zeros (e.g., the decimal number 23 is represented by 0010 0101 in 8-4-2-1 BCD notation).

Binary digit   Either of the characters 0 or 1. Abbreviated "bit."

Binary number system   A number system with a base or radix of two.

Bit   See *binary digit.*

Block   Related records, characters, or digits that are grouped and handled as a unit during input and output.

Branch   An instruction that transfers program control to one or more possible paths.

Buffer   A storage device used to compensate for the difference in rates of flow of data from one device to another—e.g., from an IO device to the CPU.

Byte   A group of adjacent bits operated upon as a unit.

Call   A transfer of program control to a subroutine.

Cathode ray tube (CRT)   An electronic tube with a screen upon which information may be displayed.

Central processing unit (CPU)   The component of a computer system with the circuitry to control the interpretation and execution of instructions. Also called the *main frame.*

Channel   (1) A path for carrying signals between a source and a destination. (2) A track on a magnetic tape or a band on a magnetic drum.

COBOL (COmmon Business-Oriented Language) A high-level language developed for business data processing applications.

Code A set of rules outlining the way in which data may be represented; also, rules used to convert data from one representation to another. To write a program or routine.

Collate To combine items from two or more sequenced files into a single sequenced file.

COM Computer-Output Microfilm.

Compiler A computer program that produces a machine-language program from a source program that is usually written in a high-level language by a programmer. The compiler is capable of replacing single source program statements with a series of machine language instructions or with a subroutine.

Computer network A processing complex consisting of two or more interconnected computers.

Conditional transfer An instruction that may cause a departure from the sequence of instructions being followed, depending upon the result of an operation, the contents of a register, or the setting of an indicator.

Console The part of a computer system that enables human operators to communicate with the computer.

Counter A device (e.g., a register) used to represent the number of occurrences of an event.

CPU See *central processing unit.*

CRT See *cathode ray tube.*

Cybernetics The branch of learning which seeks to integrate the theories and studies of communication and control in machines and living organisms.

DASD Direct-Access Storage Device.

Data administrator The one responsible for defining, updating, and controlling access to a data base.

Data bank See *data base.*

Data base A stored collection of the libraries of data that are needed by an organization to meet its information processing and retrieval requirements.

Data-base management system The comprehensive software system that builds, maintains, and provides access to a data base.

Data processing One or more operations performed on data to achieve a desired objective.

Debug To detect, locate, and remove errors in programs and/or malfunctions in equipment.

Decision table A table giving all the conditions to be considered in the description of a problem, together with the actions to be taken.

Density The number of characters that can be stored in a given physical space—e.g., an inch of magnetic tape.

Digital computer A device that manipulates discrete data and performs arithmetic and logic operations on these data. Contrast with *analog computer.*

Direct-access Pertaining to storage devices where the time required to retrieve data is independent of the physical location of the data.

Documentation The preparation of documents, during system analysis and subsequent programming, that describe such things as the system, the programs prepared, and the changes made at later dates.

Downtime The length of time a computer system is inoperative due to a malfunction.

EBCDIC An 8-bit code used to represent data in modern computers.

Edit To correct, rearrange, and validate input data. To modify the form of output information by inserting blank spaces, special characters where needed, etc.

EDP Electronic Data Processing.

Emulator A stored logic device or program that permits one computer to execute the machine-language instructions of another computer of different design.

Executive routine A master program that controls the execution of other programs. Often used synonymously with *executive, monitor,* and *supervisory routines.*

Field A group of related characters treated as a unit—e.g., a group of adjacent card columns used to represent an hourly wage rate. An item in a record.

File A collection of related records treated as a unit.

Flowchart A diagram that uses symbols and interconecting lines to show (1) a system of processing to achieve objectives (system flowchart) or (2) the logic and sequence of specific program operations (program flowchart).

FORTRAN (FORmula TRANslator) A high-level language used to perform mathematical computations.

Generator A computer program that constructs other programs to perform a particular type of operation—e.g., a report program generator.

Hardware Physical equipment such as electronic, magnetic, and mechanical devices. Contrast with *software.*

Heuristic A problem-solving method in which solutions are discovered by evaluating the progress made toward the end result. A directed trial-and-error approach. Contrast with *algorithm.*

Hollerith code A particular type of code used to represent alphanumeric data on punched cards.

Hybrid computer A data processing device using both analog and discrete data representation.

Information Meaning assigned to data by humans.

Information retrieval The methods used to recover specific information from stored data.

Input/output (I/O) Pertaining to the techniques, media, and devices used to achieve human/machine communication.

Instruction A set of characters used to direct a data processing system in the performance of an operation—i.e., an operation is signaled and the values or locations of the instruction operands are specified.

Interface A shared boundary—e.g., the boundary between two systems or devices.

Internal storage The addressable storage in a digital computer directly under the control of the central processing unit.

Interpreter A computer program that translates each source language statement into a sequence of machine instructions and then executes these machine instructions before translating the next source language statement. A device that prints on a punched card the data already punched in the card.

I/O See *input/output.*

Item A group of related characters treated as a unit. (A record is a group of related items, and a file is a group of related records.)

Job A collection of specified tasks constituting a unit of work for a computer.

Jump A departure from sequence in executing instructions in a computer. See *conditional transfer.*

K An abbreviation for kilo or approximately 1,000 in decimal notation. (To be more accurate, K is equal to 2^{10} or 1,024.)

Key An item that is used to identify a record.

Label One or more characters used to identify a program statement or a data item.

Language A set of rules and conventions used to convey information.

Library routine A tested routine maintained in a library of programs.

Loop A sequence of instructions in a program that can be executed repetitively until certain specified conditions are satisfied.

Machine language A language used directly by a computer.

Macro instruction A source language instruction that is equivalent to a specified number of machine language instructions.

Magnetic ink character recognition (MICR) The recognition of characters printed with a special magnetic ink by machines.

Magnetic storage Utilizing the magnetic properties of materials to store data on such devices and media as disks, drums, cards, cores, tapes, and films.

Management information system An information system designed to supply organizational managers with the necessary information needed to plan, organize, staff, direct, and control the operations of the organization.

Memory Same as *storage.*

MICR See *magnetic ink character recognition.*

Microcomputer The smallest category of computer, consisting of a microprocessor and associated storage and input/output elements.

Microprocessor The basic arithmetic, logic, and storage elements required for processing (generally on one or a few integrated circuit chips).

Microprogram A sequence of elementary instructions that is translated by a micrologic subsystem residing in the CPU.

Microsecond One-millionth of a second.

Millisecond   One-thousandth of a second.

Minicomputer   A relatively fast but small and inexpensive computer with somewhat limited input and output capabilities.

MIS   See *management information system.*

Mnemonic   Pertaining to a technique used to aid human memory.

Monitor routine   See *executive routine.*

Multiplex   To simultaneously transmit messages over a single channel or other communications facility.

Multiprocessing   The simultaneous execution of two or more sequences of instructions by a single computer network.

Multiprocessor   A computer network consisting of two or more central processors under a common control.

Multiprogramming   The simultaneous handling of multiple independent programs by interleaving or overlapping their execution.

Nanosecond   One-billionth of a second.

Natural language   A human language such as English, French, German, etc.

Object language   The output of a translation process. Contrast with *source language.* Synonymous with *target language.*

Object program   A fully compiled or assembled program that is ready to be loaded into the computer. Contrast with *source program.*

OCR (Optical Character Recognition)   The recognition of printed characters through the use of light-sensitive optical machines.

Offline   A term describing persons, equipment, or devices not in direct communication with the central processing unit of a computer.

Online   A term describing persons, equipment, or devices that are in direct communication with the central processing unit of a computer.

Operand   The data unit or equipment item that is operated upon. An operand is usually identified by an address in an instruction.

Operating system   An organized collection of software that controls the overall operations of a computer.

Operation code   The instruction code used to specify the operations a computer is to perform.

Patch   The modification of a routine in an expedient way.

Peripheral equipment   The input/output devices and auxiliary storage units of a computer system.

Picosecond   One-thousandth of a nanosecond.

PL/I (Programming Language I)   A high-level language designed to process both scientific and file-manipulating applications.

Pointer   A data item in one record that contains the location address of another logically related record.

Procedure-oriented language   A programming language designed to conveniently express procedures used to solve a particular class of problems.

Program   (1) A plan to achieve a problem solution; (2) to design, write, and test one or more routines; (3) a set of sequenced instructions to cause a computer to perform particular operations.

Program flowchart See *flowchart*.

Program library A collection of programs and routines.

Programmer One who designs, writes, tests, and maintains computer programs.

Programming language A language used to express programs.

Radix The base number in a number system—e.g., the radix in the decimal system is 10. Synonymous with *base*.

Random-access Descriptive storage devices where the time required to retrieve data is not significantly affected by the physical location of the data.

Real time Descriptive of online computer processing systems which recieve and process data quickly enough to produce output to control, direct, or affect the outcome of an ongoing activity or process.

Record A collection of related items of data treated as a unit. See *item*.

Register A device capable of storing a specific amount of data.

Remote access Relating to the communication with a computer facility by a station (or stations) that is distant from the computer.

Report program generator (RPG) Software designed to construct programs that perform predictable report-writing operations.

Routine An ordered set of general-use instructions. See *program*.

Secondary storage See *auxiliary storage*.

Serial access Descriptive of a storage device or medium where there is a sequential relationship between access time and data location in storage—i.e., the access time is dependent upon the location of the data. Contrast with *direct access* and *random access*.

Simulation To represent and analyze properties or behavior of a physical or hypothetical system by the behavior of a system model. (This model is often manipulated by means of computer operations.)

Software A set of programs, documents, procedures, and routines associated with the operation of a computer system. Contrast with *hardware*.

Solid state Descriptive of electronic components whose operation depends on the control of electric or magnetic phenomena in solids, such as transistors and diodes.

Source language The language that is an input for statement translation.

Source program A computer program written in a source language such as FORTRAN, BASIC, COBOL, etc.

Statement In programming, an expression or generalized instruction in a source language.

Storage Descriptive of a device or medium that can accept data, hold them, and deliver them on demand at a later time. Synonymous with *memory*.

Structured programming An approach or discipline used in the design and coding of computer programs. The approach generally assumes the disciplined use of a few basic coding structures and the use of top-down concepts to decompose main functions into lower-level components for modular coding purposes.

Subroutine   A routine that can be a part of another routine or program.

Supervisory routine   See *executive routine*.

System   (1) A grouping of integrated methods and procedures united to form an organized entity; (2) an organized grouping of people, methods, machines, and materials collected together to accomplish a set of specific objectives.

System flowchart   See *flowchart*.

System analyst   One who studies the activities, methods, procedures, and techniques of organizational systems in order to determine what actions need to be taken and how these actions can best be accomplished.

Throughput   The total amount of useful work performed by a computer system during a given time period.

Timesharing   The use of specific hardware by a number of other devices, programs, or people simultaneously in such a way as to provide quick response to each of the users. The interleaved use of the time of a device.

Top-down methodology   A disciplined approach to organizing complexity by identifying the top-level functions in a system and then decomposing these functions into a hierarchy of understandable lower-level modules.

Unconditional transfer   An instruction that always causes a branch in program control away from the normal sequence of executing instructions.

Utility routine   Software used to perform some frequently required process in the operation of a computer system—e.g., sorting, merging, etc.

Virtual storage   Descriptive of the capability to use online secondary storage devices and specialized software to divide programs into smaller segments for transmission to and from internal storage in order to significantly increase the effective size of the available internal storage.

Word   A group of bits or characters considered as an entity and capable of being stored in one storage location.

Word length   The number of characters or bits in a word.

INDEX